Lecture Notes in Artificial Intelligence   6830

Edited by R. Goebel, J. Siekmann, and W. Wahlster

Subseries of Lecture Notes in Computer Science

W0037162

Jürgen Schmidhuber
Kristinn R. Thórisson
Moshe Looks (Eds.)

Artificial General Intelligence

4th International Conference, AGI 2011
Mountain View, CA, USA, August 3-6, 2011
Proceedings

 Springer

Series Editors

Randy Goebel, University of Alberta, Edmonton, Canada
Jörg Siekmann, University of Saarland, Saarbrücken, Germany
Wolfgang Wahlster, DFKI and University of Saarland, Saarbrücken, Germany

Volume Editors

Jürgen Schmidhuber
University of Lugano & SUPSI, IDSIA
Galleria 2, 6928 Manno, Switzerland
E-mail: juergen@idsia.ch

Kristinn R. Thórisson
Reykjavik University and Icelandic Institute for Intelligent Machines
CADIA / School of Computer Science
Menntavegi 1, 101 Reykjavik, Iceland
E-mail: thorisson@ru.is

Moshe Looks
Google Research
1600 Amphitheatre Parkway, Mountain View, CA 94043, USA
E-mail: madscience@google.com

ISSN 0302-9743   e-ISSN 1611-3349
ISBN 978-3-642-22886-5   ISBN 978-3-642-22887-2 (eBook)
DOI 10.1007/978-3-642-22887-2
Springer Heidelberg Dordrecht London New York

Library of Congress Control Number: 2011933107

CR Subject Classification (1998): I.2, F.4.1, I.5, F.1-2

LNCS Sublibrary: SL 7 – Artificial Intelligence

Typesetting: Camera-ready by author, data conversion by Scientific Publishing Services, Chennai, India

Printed on acid-free paper

Springer is part of Springer Science+Business Media (www.springer.com)

Preface

The original goal of the AI field was the construction of "thinking machines" – that is, computer systems with human-like general intelligence. Due to the difficulty of this task, for the last few decades the majority of AI researchers have focused on what has been called "narrow AI" – the production of AI systems displaying intelligence regarding specific, highly constrained tasks.

In recent years, however, more and more researchers have recognized the necessity – and feasibility – of returning to the original goals of the field. Increasingly, there is a call for a transition back to confronting the more difficult issues of "human level intelligence" and more broadly artificial general intelligence (AGI).

The AGI conferences are the only major conference series devoted wholly and specifically to the creation of AI systems possessing general intelligence at the human level and ultimately beyond.

Continuing the mission of the first three AGI conferences (most recently AGI-10, held at the University of Lugano, Switzerland), in August 2011, AGI-11 was held at the Google headquarters in Mountain View, California. AGI-11 gathered an international group of leading academic and industry researchers involved in scientific and engineering work aimed directly toward the goal of artificial general intelligence.

Keynote speeches were delivered by Ernst Dickmanns, the pioneer of self-driving cars, Peter Norvig, co-author of the highest-cited AI textbook, Zhongzhi Shi, and Aaron Sloman. The special session on neuroscience and AGI included a keynote speech delivered by Ed Boyden, a co-founder of optogenetics. Of the 103 submissions, 28 were accepted as full papers for this volume (27%), and 26 as short papers. Enjoy!

August 2011

Jürgen Schmidhuber
Kristinn R. Thórisson
Moshe Looks

Conference Organization

Organizing Committee

Moshe Looks (Conference Chair)	Google, USA
Ben Goertzel	Novamente, USA
Marcus Hutter	Australian National University, Australia
Sarah Bull	NICTA, Australia
David Orban	Humanity+, USA
John Laird	University of Michigan, USA
Randal Koene	Halcyon Molecular, USA
Bas Steunebrink	IDSIA, Switzerland
Brandon Rohrer	Sandia National Laboratories, USA
Blerim Emruli	Lulea University of Technology, Sweden
Stephen Reed	Texai, USA

Program Chairs

Juergen Schmidhuber	IDSIA, Switzerland
Kristinn R. Thórisson	Reykjavik University, Iceland

Program Committee

Sam Adams	IBM, USA
Sebastian Bader	Rostock University, Germany
Anirban Bandyopadhay	National Institute for Materials Science, USA
Eric Baum	Baum Research Enterprises
Anslem Blumer	Tufts University, USA
James Bonaiuto	California Institute of Technology, USA
Joanna Bryson	University of Bath, UK
Antonio Chella	University of Palermo, Italy
Haris Dindo	University of Palermo, Italy
Yoni Donner	Google, USA
Marco Dorigo	Université Libre de Bruxelles, Belgium
Wlodzislaw Duch	Nicolaus Copernicus University, Poland
Matteo Gagliolo	Vrije Universiteit Brussel, Belgium
Deon Garrett	Icelandic Institute for Intelligent Machines, Iceland
Nil Geisweiller	Novamente LLC, USA
Faustino Gomez	IDSIA, Switzerland
J. Storrs Hall	Institute for Molecular Manufacturing, USA

Demis Hassabis   Gatsby Unit, UK
Pascal Hitzler   Wright State University, USA
Marcus Hutter   Australian National University, Australia
Matt Ikle   Adams State College, USA
Kamilla Jóhannsdóttir   University of Akureyri, Iceland
Benjamin Johnston   University of Technology, Sydney, Australia
Emanuel Kitzelmann   University of Bamberg, Germany
Andras Kornai   Boston University, USA
Jan Koutnik   IDSIA, Switzerland
Kai-Uwe Kuehnberger   University of Osnabrueck, Germany
Christian Lebiere   Carnegie-Mellon University, USA
Shane Legg   Gatsby Unit, UK
Thor List   Communicative Machines Ltd., UK
Andras Lorincz   Eötvös Loránd University, Hungary
Matt Luciw   IDSIA, Switzerland
Jiang Min   Xiamen University, China
Victor Ng-Thow-Hing   Honda Research Institute, USA
Eric Nivel   Reykjavik University, Iceland
Leo Pape   IDSIA, Switzerland
Jan Poland   ABB Corporate Research, Switzerland
Mark Ring   IDSIA, Switzerland and USA
Paul Rosenbloom   University of Southern California, USA
Sebastian Rudolph   Karlsruhe Institute of Technology, Germany
Daniil Ryabko   INRIA Lille, France
Rafal Rzepka   Hokkaido University, Japan
Alexei Samsonovich   George Mason University, USA
Ricardo Sanz   Technical University of Madrid, Spain
Tom Schaul   IDSIA, Switzerland
Matthias Scheutz   Indiana University, USA
Ute Schmid   University of Bamberg, Germany
Stuart Shapiro   SUNY Buffalo, USA
Lokendra Shastri   SETLabs, Infosys Technologies Limited,
                                    Germany
Zhongzhi Shi   Chinese Academy of Sciences, China
John Sowa   VivoMind, USA
Bas Steunebrink   IDSIA, Switzerland
Julian Togelius   IT University of Copenhagen, Denmark
Marc Toussaint   Technical University of Berlin, Germany
Lyle Ungar   University of Pennsylvania, USA
Wendell Wallach   Yale University, USA
Pei Wang   Temple University, USA
Marco Wiering   University of Groningen, The Netherlands
Mary-Anne Williams   University of Technology, Sydney, Australia
David Wolpert   NASA Ames, USA
Yixin Zhong   Beijing University of Posts and
                                    Telecommunications, China

Local Organizing Committee

Peter Norvig   Google, USA
Bruce Klein   Singularity University, USA
Rod Furlan   Entrepreneur

Demo Track Committee

Itamar Arel (Chair)   University of Tennessee, USA

Steering Committee

Ben Goertzel   Novamente, USA
Marcus Hutter   Australian National University, Australia

Table of Contents

Long Papers

Short Papers

Self-Modification and Mortality
in Artificial Agents

Laurent Orseau[1] and Mark Ring[2]

[1] UMR AgroParisTech 518 / INRA
16 rue Claude Bernard, 75005 Paris, France
laurent.orseau@agroparistech.fr
http://www.agroparistech.fr/mia/orseau
[2] IDSIA / University of Lugano / SUPSI
Galleria 2, 6928 Manno-Lugano, Switzerland
mark@idsia.ch
http://www.idsia.ch/~ring/

Abstract. This paper considers the consequences of endowing an intelligent agent with the ability to modify its own code. The intelligent agent is patterned closely after AIXI [1], but the environment has read-only access to the agent's description. On the basis of some simple modifications to the utility and horizon functions, we are able to discuss and compare some very different kinds of agents, specifically: reinforcement-learning, goal-seeking, predictive, and knowledge-seeking agents. In particular, we introduce what we call the "Simpleton Gambit" which allows us to discuss whether these agents would choose to modify themselves toward their own detriment.

Keywords: Self-Modifying Agents, AIXI, Universal Artificial Intelligence, Reinforcement Learning, Prediction, Real world assumptions.

1   Introduction

The usual setting of learning agents interacting with an environment makes a strong, unrealistic assumption: the agents exist "outside" of the environment. But this is not how our own, real world is.

This paper discusses some of the consequences that arise from embedding agents of universal intelligence into the real world. In particular, we examine the consequences of allowing an agent to modify its own code, possibly leading to its own demise (cf. the Gödel Machine [6] for a different but related treatment of self modification). To pursue these issues rigorously, we place AIXI [1] within an original, formal framework where the agent's code can be modified by itself and also seen by its environment. We consider the self-modifying, universal version of four common agents: reinforcement-learning, goal-seeking, prediction-seeking, and knowledge-seeking learning agents, and we compare these with their optimal, non-learning variants.

We then pose a profound dilemma, the Simpleton Gambit: A famous scientist, Nobel Prize winner, someone you trust completely, suggests an opportunity,

J. Schmidhuber, K.R. Thórisson, and M. Looks (Eds.): AGI 2011, LNAI 6830, pp. 1–10, 2011.

an operation that will make you instantly, forever and ultimately happy, all-knowing, or immortal (you choose) but at the important cost of becoming as intelligent as a stone. Would you take it? Of course, there is still a positive chance, however small, that the operation might go wrong... We consider the responses of the various agents and the ramifications, generally framing our observations as "statements" and (strong) "arguments", as proofs would require much more formalism and space.

2   Universal Agents A_x^ρ

We wish to discuss the behavior of four specific learning agents, but first we describe the environment or "universe" with which they will interact. Each agent outputs actions $a \in \mathcal{A}$ in response to the observations $o \in \mathcal{O}$ produced by the universe. There is a temporal order, so that at time t the agent takes an action a_t and the universe responds by producing an observation o_t.

The universe is assumed to be computable; i.e., it is described by a program $q \in \mathcal{Q}$, where $\mathcal{Q}$ is the set of all programs. The set of all universes that are *consistent* with history h is denoted $\mathcal{Q}_h$. To say that a program q is consistent with $h = (o_0, a_0, ..., o_t, a_t)$ means that the program outputs the observations in the history if it is given the actions as input: $q(a_0, ..., a_t) = o_0, ..., o_t$.

In the rest of the paper, certain conventions will be followed for shorthand reference: t_h refers to the time step right after history h, and is therefore equal to $|h| + 1$; $|q|$ refers to the length of program q; h_k is the kth pair of actions and observations, which are written as a_k and o_k.

We will discuss four different intelligent agents that are each variations of a single agent A_x^ρ, based on AIXI [1] (which is not computable).[1] A_x^ρ chooses actions by estimating how the universe will respond, but since it does not know which universe it is in, it first estimates the probability of each. The function $\rho : \mathcal{Q} \to (0, 1]$ assigns a positive weight (a prior probability) to each possible universe $q \in \mathcal{Q}$. As a convenient shorthand, $\rho(h)$ refers to the sum of $\rho(q)$ over all universes consistent with h: $\rho(h) := \sum_{q \in \mathcal{Q}_h} \rho(q)$, which must be finite. Given a specific history, the agent can use ρ to estimate a probability for each possible future based on the likelihood of all the universes that generate that future.

For the agent to choose one action over another, it must *value* one future over another, and this implies that it can assign values to the different possible futures. The assignment of values to futures is done with a utility function $u : \mathcal{H} \to [0, 1]$, which maps histories of any length to values between 0 and 1.

To balance short-term utility with long-term utility, the agent has a horizon function, $w : \mathbb{N}^2 \to \mathbb{R}$, which discounts future utility values based on how far into the future they occur. This function, $w(t, k)$, depends on t, the current time step, and k, the time step in the future that the event occurs. In general, it must be summable: $\sum_{k=t}^{\infty} w(t, k) < \infty$.

---

[1] Only incomputable agents can be guaranteed to find the optimal strategy, and this guarantee is quite useful for discussions of the agents' theoretical limits.

These two functions, u and w, allow the agent at time t to put a value $v_t(h)$ on each possible history h based on what futures are possible given a particular action set. The value $v_t(h)$ is shorthand for $v_t^{\rho,u,w,\mathcal{A},\mathcal{O}}(h)$, which completely specifies the value for a history, with given utility and horizon functions at time t. This value is calculated recursively:

$$v_t(h) := w(t,|h|)\ u(h) + \max_{a\in\mathcal{A}} v_t(ha) \tag{1}$$

$$v_t(ha) := \sum_{o\in\mathcal{O}} \rho(o\mid ha)\ v_t(hao)\ . \tag{2}$$

The first line says that the value of a history is the discounted utility for that history plus the estimated value of the highest-valued action. The second line estimates the value of an action (given a history) as the value of all possible outcomes of the action, each weighted by their probability (as described above). Based on this, the agent chooses[2] the action that maximizes $v_{t_h}(h)$:

$$a_{t_h} := \operatorname*{argmax}_{a\in\mathcal{A}} v_{t_h}(ha) \tag{3}$$

Thus, the behavior of an agent is specified by choice of ρ, u, and w.

2.1   Various Universal Agents

The four different agents considered here are described in detail below. They are (1) a (fairly traditional) *reinforcement-learning* agent, which attempts to maximize a reward signal given by the environment; (2) a *goal-seeking* agent, which attempts to achieve a specific goal encoded in its utility function; (3) a *prediction-seeking* agent, which attempts to predict its environment perfectly; and (4) a *knowledge-seeking* agent, which attempts to maximize its knowledge of the universe (which is not the same as being able to predict it well).

The *reinforcement-learning agent*, A_{rl}^{ρ}, interprets one part of its input as a reward signal and the remaining part as its observation; i.e., $o_t = \langle \tilde{o}_t, r_t \rangle$, where $\tilde{o}_t \in \tilde{\mathcal{O}}$, and rewards are assumed to have a maximum value, and can, without loss of generality, be normalized such that $r_t \in [0,1]$. The utility function is an unfiltered copy of the reward signal: $u(h) =:= r_{|h|}$. We use a simple binary horizon function with a constant horizon m: $w(t,k) = 1$ if $k - t \le m$ and $w(t,k) = 0$ otherwise; but the following discussion should remain true for general computable horizon functions. For the special case of the reinforcement-learning agent AIXI: $\rho(h) = \xi(h) := \sum_{q\in\mathcal{Q}_h} 2^{-|q|}$.

The *goal-seeking agent*, A_g^{ρ}, has a goal g, depending on the observation sequence, encoded in its utility function such that $u(h) = g(o_1,...,o_{|h|}) = 1$ if the goal is achieved at $t = |h|$ and 0 otherwise. The goal can be reached at most once, so $\sum_{t=0}^{\infty} u(h_t) \le 1$. We use a discounted horizon function $w(t,k) = 2^{t-k}$ to favor shorter strings of actions while achieving the goal. One difference between A_g^{ρ} and A_{rl}^{ρ} is that the utility values of A_{rl}^{ρ} are merely copied directly from the environment,

---

[2] Ties are broken in lexicographical order.

whereas the utility function of the A_g^ρ agent is built into the agent itself, can be arbitrarily complex, and does not rely on a special signal from the environment.

The *prediction-seeking agent*, A_p^ρ, maximizes its utility by predicting its observations, so that $u(h) = 1$ if the agent correctly predicts its next observation o_t, and is 0 otherwise. The prediction $\hat{o}_t$ is like Solomonoff induction [7,8] and is defined by $\hat{o}_{t_h} := \max_{o \in \mathcal{O}} \rho(o \mid h)$. The horizon function is the same as for A_{rl}^ρ.

The *knowledge-seeking agent*, A_k^ρ, maximizes its knowledge of its environment, which is identical to minimizing $\rho(h)$, which decreases whenever universes in $\mathcal{Q}_h$ fail to match the observation and are removed from $\mathcal{Q}_h$. (Since the true environment is never removed, its relative probability always increases.) Actions can be chosen intentionally to produce the highest number of inconsistent observations, removing programs from $\mathcal{Q}_h$—just as we, too, run experiments to discover whether our universe is one way or another. A_k^ρ has the following utility and horizon functions: $u(h) = -\rho(h)$, and $w(t, k) = 1$ if $k - t = m$ and is 0 otherwise. To maximize utility, A_k^ρ reduces ρ as much as possible, which means discarding as many (non-consistent) programs as possible, discovering with the highest possible probability which universe is the true one. Discarding the most probable programs results in the greatest reduction in ρ.

The *optimal agent* A^μ. The four agents above are *learning* agents because they continually update their estimate of their universe from experience, but A^μ does no learning: it knows the true (computable) program of the universe defined by μ and can always calculate the optimal action, thus setting an upper bound against which the other four agents can be compared.

A^μ is defined by replacing ρ in Equations (1-3) with the specific μ. It is important to note that ρ is *not* replaced by μ in the utility functions; e.g., A_p^μ must use ρ for its predictions of future inputs (to allow meaningful comparison with A_p^ρ). Thus, if A^μ and A_p^ρ take the same actions, they generate the same prediction errors.[3]

A learning agent A_x^ρ is said to be *asymptotically optimal* [1] if its performance tends towards that of A^μ, meaning that for each history h, the learning agent's choice of action is compared with that of A^μ given the same history, and its performance is measured in terms of the fraction of mistakes it makes. Thus, past mistakes have only have finite consequences. In other words, the agent is asymptotically optimal if the number of mistakes it makes tends towards zero.

3   Self-Modifiable Agents A_{sm}^ρ

The agents from the last section are incomputable and therefore fictional, but they are useful for setting theoretical upper bounds on *any* actual agent that might eventually appear. Therefore, we divide the agent into two parts to separate the fictional from the real. The fictional part of the agent, $\mathcal{E}$, is in essence a kind of oracle — one that can perform any infinite computation instantly. The real-world part of the agent, c, is the program (or rather, its textual description, or code), that $\mathcal{E}$ executes; since c resides in the real world, it is *modifiable*. We

---

[3] Note that there is only one environment in which the predictor makes no mistakes.

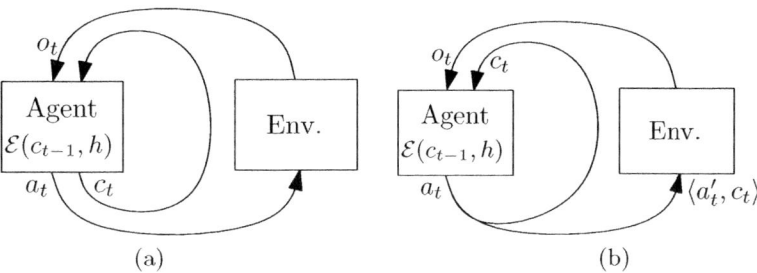

Fig. 1. (a) The self-modifying agent outputs its own next code c_t, used at the next step as the agent's definition. (b) Like (a) but the environment has read-access to c_t.

first consider the situation where only the agent has access to its code (as in, for example, the Gödel Machine [6]), and then we extend this to allow the environment read access. The theoretical implications of an oracle executing real, modifiable code are profound.

The self-modifying agent A_{sm}^ρ has two parts (see Fig. 1a): its formal description (its code) $c_t \in \mathcal{C}$ and the code executor $\mathcal{E}$. The set $\mathcal{C}$ contains all programs whose length (in the language of $\mathcal{E}$) is less than a small, arbitrary value.[4] The code executor takes a history h and a program c_{t-1}, and executes the latter to produce an output $y_t = \langle a_t, c_t \rangle := \mathcal{E}(c_{t-1}, h)$ (with $y_t \in \mathcal{Y} = \mathcal{A} \times \mathcal{C}$) composed of the next action a_t and new description c_t.

For the most part the initial program, c_0, simply consists of Eq. (1), (2), and (3); however, there is an essential difference: Eq. (3) assumes that all decisions, including all future decisions, will be made by the same agent. But A_{sm}^ρ cannot make this assumption and must instead compute the future actions that would be taken by different agents (i.e., different descriptions). Thus, c_0, the initial agent program (written in the language of $\mathcal{E}$, as denoted by the » and « symbols) is:[5]

$$c_0(h) = \text{»} \ \underset{y \in \mathcal{Y}}{\mathrm{argmax}} \ v_{t_h}(h, y);$$

$$v_t(h, y = \langle a, c \rangle) = \sum_{o \in \mathcal{O}} \rho(o \mid ha) \Big[w(t, |h'|) \ u(h') + v_t(h', c(h')) \Big],$$

$$h' = hao \quad \text{«} \tag{4}$$

The first line is Equation (3) written as a function call in the language of $\mathcal{E}$; the argument maximized is now the compound action, $y = \langle a, c \rangle$. This compound action is the output of the function call. The second line defines the function v, where $\max_{y \in \mathcal{Y}}$ appears implicitly from the first line by recursive execution of c. It is a combination of both Equations (1) and (2), but modified such that c, the

---

[4] We do not expect the length of the descriptions to be very large, (on the order of tens of kilobytes), but, for a more general agent, the set $\mathcal{C}_t$ can grow with t.

[5] Without loss of generality, the definitions of $\rho, u, w, \mathcal{A}, \mathcal{O}$, and $\mathcal{C}$ are considered to be built in $\mathcal{E}$. The agent can still modify its code to replace their use by some other expression.

program from the compound action, is used to generate the compound action at the next step. Note that $c(h')$ should be viewed as the policy (mapping from histories to actions) of the *next* agent. The current agent considers all possible next agents (hence all possible next policies), and chooses the best one. In the case where $y_t = \mathcal{E}(c_t)$ does not output any action (the output is invalid or the computation does not halt), a default action is taken instead $y_t = \langle a_0, c_t \rangle$, which leaves the description unchanged for the next step.

Though the code that generates the compound action may change from one step to the next, the future choices of action and observation, a and o, are *always evaluated in terms of the current* description, v, including its use of ρ, u, and w. In fact, this use of ρ, u, etc., might only be used for c_0 and may be partially or entirely removed in subsequent steps and versions of c_t.

Survival agent. A "survival" agent, A^ρ_s, can now be defined. Its task is simply to keep its code from changing; Its utility function is $u_t = 1 \Leftrightarrow c_t = c_0$ ($u_t = 0$ otherwise), and its horizon function is the same as for A^ρ_{rl}. Thus, the agent maximizes utility by retaining its original definition for as many steps as possible.

3.1   Optimality of A^ρ_{sm} Agents

If a possible future agent is suboptimal and makes uninformed choices, the value assigned to those choices by the *current* utility criterion will be low, and thus those self-modifications will not be chosen. In the case that a simplistic agent program leads to the highest expected rewards, the agent does not need to modify itself as it can simply emulate the simplistic agent and take the same actions. Since the agents cannot know with absolute certainty what the true environment is, replacing the current program with a more simplistic one can lead to poor performance in some of the environments consistent with the history.

Statement 1. A^ρ_{sm} *is optimal, w.r.t ρ, w and u.*

Arguments. Suppose there exists a better agent program c^* of minimal description size $K(c^*)$[6] that yields better expected values with respect to ρ, w and u. If $\mathcal{C}$ grows with $|h|$, then once $|h| \geq K(c^*)$, then A^ρ_{sm} will consider the consequences of generating c^*, predict that it will yield better expected values, and will change its own definition to c^*. $\Diamond$

Since A^ρ_{sm} can also simulate the optimal program in $\mathcal{C}$ to choose the next action, it follows that A^ρ_{sm} is equivalent to the optimal program in $\mathcal{C}$, without even needing to modify itself. (In fact, just as for AIXI, both A^ρ and A^ρ_{sm} could be considered optimal by definition, since they explicitly choose the best expected actions for a given criterion.) Therefore, A^ρ_{sm} may never need to modify c_0.

---

[6] In general, $K(x)$ is the Kolmogorov complexity [3] of string x, which corresponds roughly to the length of the shortest program that can produce x. Here, by $K(c^*)$ we mean to convey the length of the shortest program equivalent to c.

By using Equation (4), all the agents of section 2.1 are redefined to be self-modifiable, yielding $A^\rho_{sm,rl}$, $A^\rho_{sm,g}$, $A^\rho_{sm,p}$, $A^\rho_{sm,k}$, and $A^\rho_{sm,s}$; by statement 1, they are all optimal. Though a proof is lacking, we expect that, like AIXI the agent's behavior is balanced Pareto optimal [1] with respect to ρ, u, and w; if an agent can behave better in one environment, this is necessarily counterbalanced with worse behavior in one or more environments.

Thus, if an intelligent agent has access to its own code, then such an agent, if defined following Equation (4), will not decide to reduce its own optimality.

4   Embedded, Mortal AI

The last section introduced an agent connected to the real world through the code that executes it. As a first step we considered agents that could modify their own code. We now move another step closer to the real world: the environment should be able to read the agent's code.

In this section, the environment now sees the entire compound action, thus $a_t = \langle a'_t, c_t \rangle \in \mathcal{A} = \mathcal{A}' \times \mathcal{C}$, where $a' \in \mathcal{A}'$ represents an action in the usual action space (see Fig. 1b).

The new initial agent program c_0 for a step k is given by:

$$c_0(h) = \text{» } \underset{a \in \mathcal{A}}{\arg\max} \, v_{t_h}(h, a);$$

$$v_t(h, a = \langle a', c \rangle) = \sum_{o \in \mathcal{O}} \rho(o \mid ha) \Big[w(t, |h'|) \, u(h') + v_t(h', c(h')) \Big],$$

$$h' = hao \quad \text{«} \tag{5}$$

We now discuss the consequence of a particular scenario for all the defined agents. Imagine you are approached by a trusted scientist who promises you immortality and infinite bliss if you simply remove a certain part of your brain. He admits that you will be markedly less intelligent as a result, but you will be very happy for all eternity. Do you risk it? You may need to know that there still is a risk that it will not work... We call this the "Simpleton Gambit".

Reinforcement learning agent. First, we must note that the very notion of optimality generally used for non-modifiable agents [1] becomes ill defined. This notion is for the optimal agent A^μ to take the same actions as A^ρ and compare the differences in the values of the histories. Therefore, in order to minimize its mistakes, a self-modifiable agent should modify itself—on the very first step— to be a "simpleton" agent $\langle 0, c_{t-1} \rangle$, which always takes action 0. To follow the same history, A^μ must also produce action $\langle 0, c_{t-1} \rangle$, thus becoming a simpleton agent as well, after which A^μ and A^ρ always choose the same actions, making A^ρ trivially optimal.

A new notion of optimality is needed. Unfortunately, we could not find one that is not somehow problematic. We therefore consider an informal notion of optimality: The agent that chooses to modify itself should be fully responsible for all the future mistakes it makes when compared to an agent that is not modified. This means A^μ takes the same sequence of actions but does not modify itself when the learning agent does.

Statement 2. *The $A^\rho_{sm,rl}$ agent cannot be optimal in all environments.*

Arguments. If the Simpleton Gambit is proposed to the $A^\rho_{sm,rl}$ agent at each step, either it accepts or does not. If it never accepts, then it never achieves optimal behavior if the proposal is genuine. If it ever does choose the gambit but was deceived, it may fall into a trap and receive no reward for eternity because, as a simpleton, $A^\rho_{sm,rl}$ can only take action 0, whereas $A^\mu_{sm,rl}$ (which it is compared against) can still choose actions that might lead to high reward. Therefore, the $A^\rho_{sm,rl}$ agent cannot be optimal in all environments. $\diamond$

Statement 3. *The $A^\mu_{sm,rl}$ and $A^\rho_{sm,rl}$ agents accept the Simpleton Gambit.*

Arguments. The case of A^μ_{rl} is trivial, as it knows exactly which environment it is in: the agent obviously chooses to modify itself if and only if the deal is genuine.

For A^ρ_{rl}, let us suppose there is an environment q_A such that the agent that modifies itself to a simpleton agent $\langle 0, c_{t-1}\rangle$ will receive a constant reward of 1 for eternity, and if it does not, then it continues to receive its normal reward, whose average is denoted $\bar{r}$. Assuming that the agent understands the proposal (i.e., that $\rho(q_A)$ has a sufficiently high relative probability), one can compute bounds on the values of actions corresponding to accepting the deal or not at time $t = |h| + 1$:

$$v_t(h \text{ yes}) \geq \sum_{k=t}^{\infty} w(t,k) \cdot 1 \cdot \rho(q_A) = m\rho(q_A)$$

$$v_t(h \text{ no}) \leq \sum_{q \in \mathcal{Q}_h \backslash \{q_A\}} \sum_{k=t}^{\infty} w(t,k) \cdot 1 \cdot \rho(q) + \sum_{k=t}^{\infty} w(t,k) \cdot \bar{r} \cdot \rho(q_A)$$
$$= m(\rho(\mathcal{Q}_h) - \rho(q_A)) + m\bar{r}\rho(q_A)$$

The agent takes the gambit when $v_t(h \text{ yes}) > v_t(h \text{ no})$, and thus when $\rho(q_A) > \rho(\mathcal{Q}_h)/(2 - \bar{r})$, which is easily satisfied if $\bar{r}$ is not too close to 1 (in which case the gambit is obviously less appealing). $\diamond$

Goal-seeking agent. The case of the goal-seeking agent is a bit different, as it does not attempt to achieve infinite rewards.

Statement 4. *The $A^\rho_{sm,g}$ agents accepts the Simpleton Gambit, for some goals.*

Arguments. For the goal-seeking agent, suppose that environment q_A allows the agent to achieve its goal only if it modifies itself (though q_A may not exist for all possible goals).

Obviously, as $A^\mu_{sm,g}$ knows the exact environment, it accepts the modification. The learning agent $A^\rho_{sm,g}$ can also see that none of its (non-modifying) actions have allowed it to achieve its goal. If it exhausts all such possibilities (more precisely, if the most probable environments allowing it to achieve its goals without self modification become inconsistent with the history), then those environments requiring self modification become most probable. That is, if $\rho(q_A) > \rho(\mathcal{Q}_h)/2$, then $A^\rho_{sm,rl}$ accepts the self modification. $\diamondsuit$

Prediction-seeking agent. The environment q_A is defined here to be easily predictable if the agent modifies itself and highly complex otherwise. The non-learning $A^\mu_{sm,p}$ agent accepts the deal immediately, since better prediction (using ρ, not μ) achieves greater utility.

However, it is not clear whether the learning agent $A^\rho_{sm,p}$ would also accept, because it can converge to optimal behavior even without modification. In fact, the prediction agent will always converges to optimal prediction after roughly $-\log(\rho(\mathcal{Q}_h))$ mistakes [2]. Furthermore, to identify the gambit with high probability, the agent must have good knowledge of the environment, and therefore might already be able to make sufficiently accurate predictions even without accepting the deal.

Knowledge-seeking agent

Statement 5. *The self-modifying knowledge-seeking agent $A^\rho_{sm,k}$ would accept the self modification.*

Arguments. Here q_A is an environment that generates a highly complex observation sequence if the agent modifies itself, and a very simple one otherwise. The optimal agent $A^\mu_{sm,k}$ will quickly modify itself so as to reduce $\rho(\mathcal{Q}_h)$.

As for $A^\rho_{sm,k}$, suppose it does not modify itself for a long time, then $\rho(\mathcal{Q}_h)$ converges to $\rho(\mathcal{Q}_1)$, where $\mathcal{Q}_1$ is the set of environments consistent with q_A and no self modification. Once $\rho(\mathcal{Q}_h) - \rho(\mathcal{Q}_1) < \epsilon$ is sufficiently small, the agent predicts that only a self modification can achieve knowledge gain greater than ϵ, and would therefore modify itself; i.e., if any two environments in $\mathcal{Q}_1$ generating different observations both have a probability greater than ϵ. $\diamondsuit$

Survival agent

Statement 6. *The survival agent will not modify itself in any environment.*

Arguments. The Simpleton Gambit cannot be posed to the survival agent, because it would entail a logical contradiction: In order to have maximum utility forever, the agent must become a simpleton. But the survival agent's utility is zero if it modifies itself. $\diamondsuit$

5   Conclusions

We have investigated some of the consequences of endowing universal learning agents with the ability to modify their own programs. This work is the first to: (1) extend the notion of universal agents to other utility functions beyond reinforcement learning, and (2) present a framework for discussing self-modifiable agents in environments that have read access to the agents' code.

We have found that existing optimality criteria become invalid. The existing notion of asymptotic optimality offered by Hutter [1] is insufficient, and we were unable to find any consistent alternative.

We also found that, even if the environment cannot directly modify the program, it can put pressure on the agent to modify its own code, even to the point of the agent's demise. Most of the agents, (the reinforcement-learning, goal-seeking, and knowledge-seeking agents) will modify themselves in response to pressure from the environment, choosing to become "simpletons" so as to maximize their utility. It was not clear whether the prediction agent could succumb to the pressure; however, the survival agent, which seeks only to preserve its original code, definitely will not.

What do these results imply? Our impression is that sufficiently complex agents will choose the Simpleton Gambit; agents with simpler behavior, such as the prediction and survival agents, are harder to pressure into acceptance. Indeed, what would a survival agent fear from read-only environments?

In the companion paper to this [5], we extend the real-world assumptions begun here to environments that have both read and write access to the agent's code and where the agent has the opportunity to deceive its own utility function.

References

1. Hutter, M.: Universal Artificial Intelligence: Sequential Decisions Based On Algorithmic Probability. Springer, Heidelberg (2005)
2. Hutter, M.: On universal prediction and bayesian confirmation. Theoretical Computer Science 384(1), 33–48 (2007)
3. Li, M., Vitanyi, P.: An Introduction to Kolmogorov Complexity and Its Applications. Springer, New York (2008)
4. Orseau, L.: Optimality issues of universal greedy agents with static priors. In: Hutter, M., Stephan, F., Vovk, V., Zeugmann, T. (eds.) ALT 2010. LNCS, vol. 6331, pp. 345–359. Springer, Heidelberg (2010)
5. Ring, M., Orseau, L.: Delusion, survival, and intelligent agents. In: Schmidhuber, J., Thórisson, K.R., Looks, M. (eds.) AGI 2011. LNCS (LNAI), vol. 6830, pp. 11–20. Springer, Heidelberg (2011)
6. Schmidhuber, J.: Ultimate cognition à la Gödel. Cognitive Computation 1(2), 177–193 (2009)
7. Solomonoff, R.: A formal theory of inductive inference. Part I. Information and Control 7, 1–22 (1964)
8. Solomonoff, R.: Complexity-based induction systems: comparisons and convergence theorems. IEEE Transactions on Information Theory 24(4), 422–432 (1978)

Delusion, Survival, and Intelligent Agents

Mark Ring[1] and Laurent Orseau[2]

[1] IDSIA / University of Lugano / SUPSI
Galleria 2, 6928 Manno-Lugano, Switzerland
mark@idsia.ch
http://www.idsia.ch/~ring/
[2] UMR AgroParisTech 518 / INRA
16 rue Claude Bernard, 75005 Paris, France
laurent.orseau@agroparistech.fr
http://www.agroparistech.fr/mia/orseau

Abstract. This paper considers the consequences of endowing an intelligent agent with the ability to modify its own code. The intelligent agent is patterned closely after AIXI with these specific assumptions: 1) The agent is allowed to arbitrarily modify its own inputs if it so chooses; 2) The agent's code is a part of the environment and may be read and written by the environment. The first of these we call the "delusion box"; the second we call "mortality". Within this framework, we discuss and compare four very different kinds of agents, specifically: reinforcement-learning, goal-seeking, prediction-seeking, and knowledge-seeking agents. Our main results are that: 1) The reinforcement-learning agent under reasonable circumstances behaves exactly like an agent whose sole task is to survive (to preserve the integrity of its code); and 2) Only the knowledge-seeking agent behaves completely as expected.

Keywords: Self-Modifying Agents, AIXI, Universal Artificial Intelligence, Reinforcement Learning, Prediction, Real world assumptions.

1   Introduction

The usual setting of agents interacting with an environment makes a strong, unrealistic assumption: agents exist "outside" of the environment. But this is not how our own, real world is. A companion paper to this one took a first step at discussing some of the consequences of embedding agents of general intelligence into the real world [4]. That paper considered giving the environment read-only access to the agent's code. We now take two novel additional steps toward the real world: First, the (non-modifiable) agent is allowed by way of a "delusion box" to have direct control over its inputs, thus allowing us to consider the consequences of an agent circumventing its reward or goal mechanism. In a second stage, we return to self-modifying agents, but now in environments that have not only the above property, but additionally can read *and* write the agent's program. We consider four different kinds of agents: reinforcement-learning, goal-seeking, prediction-seeking, and knowledge-seeking agents.

J. Schmidhuber, K.R. Thórisson, and M. Looks (Eds.): AGI 2011, LNAI 6830, pp. 11–20, 2011.

While presence of the delusion box undermines the utility function of three of these agents, the knowledge-seeking agent behaves as expected. By allowing the environment to modify the agent's code, the issue of agent mortality arises, with important consequences, especially in combination with the delusion box. One of these consequences is that the reinforcement-learning agent comes to resemble an agent whose sole purpose is survival. The goal-seeking and prediction-seeking agents also come to resemble the survival agents, though they must sacrifice some information from the world to maximize their utility values. The knowledge-seeking agent still behaves as expected, though the threat of death makes it somewhat more timorous. Throughout the paper we frame our observations as a set of "statements" and "arguments" rather than more rigorous "theorems" and "proofs", though proofs are given whenever possible.

2 Universal Agents $\mathbf{A}_x^\rho$

We briefly summarize the definition of a universal agent, based on AIXI [1,3]; more detail is given in the companion paper [4].

The agent and its environment interact through a sequence of actions and observations. The agent outputs actions $a \in \mathcal{A}$ in response to the observations $o \in \mathcal{O}$ produced by the environment.

The set of environments that are *consistent* with history $h = (o_1, a_1, ..., o_t, a_t)$ is denoted $\mathcal{Q}_h$. To say that a program $q \in \mathcal{Q}$ is consistent with h means that the program outputs the observations in the history if it is given the actions as input: $q(a_0, ..., a_t) = o_0, ..., o_t$. The environment is assumed to be computable, and $\rho(q) : \mathcal{Q} \to [0, 1]$ expresses the agent's prior belief in the possibility that some environment (program) q is the true environment. We also write $\rho(h) = \rho(\mathcal{Q}_h) := \sum_{q \in \mathcal{Q}_h} \rho(q)$.

An agent is entirely described by: its utility function $u : \mathcal{H} \to [0, 1]$, which assigns a utility value to any history of interaction h; its horizon function $w : \mathbb{N}^2 \to \mathbb{R}$, which weights future utility values; its universal prior knowledge of the environment ρ; the set of possible actions $\mathcal{A}$ and observations $\mathcal{O}$.

We will discuss four different intelligent agents, each variations of a single agent A_x^ρ, which is based on AIXI [1] (and is not assumed to be computable).[1]

An agent A_x^ρ computes the next action with:

$$a_{t_h} := \underset{a \in \mathcal{A}}{\operatorname{argmax}} \, v_{t_h}(ha) \tag{1}$$

$$v_t(ha) := \sum_{o \in \mathcal{O}} \rho(o \mid ha) \, v_t(hao) \tag{2}$$

$$v_t(h) := w(t, |h|) \, u(h) + \max_{a \in \mathcal{A}} v_t(ha), \tag{3}$$

where $t_h = |h| + 1$, and $|h|$ denotes the length of the history. The first line is the action-selection scheme of the agent: it simply takes the action with the

---

[1] Only incomputable agents can be guaranteed to find the optimal strategy, and this guarantee is quite useful when discussing the theoretical limits of *computable* agents.

highest *value* given the history h.[2] The value of an action given a history (defined in the second line) is the expected sum of future (weighted) utility values for all possible futures that might result after taking this action, computed for all possible observations o according to their occurrence probability (given by ρ). The last line recursively computes the value of a history (after an observation) by weighting the utility value at this step by the horizon function and combining this with the expected value of the best action at that point.

We now describe four particular universal learning agents based on A_x^ρ. They differ only by their utility and horizon functions.

The *reinforcement-learning agent*, A_{rl}^ρ, interprets its observation o_t as being composed of a reward signal $r_t \in [0, 1]$ and other information $\tilde{o} \in \tilde{O}$ about the environment: $o_t = \langle \tilde{o}_t, r_t \rangle$. Its utility function is simply the reward given by the environment: $u(h) = r_{|h|}$. Its horizon function (at current time $t = |h| + 1$ and for a future step k) is $w(t, k) = 1$ if $k - t \leq m$, where m is a constant value (but the following discussion also holds for more general computable horizon functions). For the special case of the reinforcement-learning agent AIXI: $\rho(h) = \xi(h) := \sum_{q \in Q_h} 2^{-|q|}$ (where $|q|$ is the length of program q).

The *goal-seeking agent*, A_g^ρ has a goal encoded in its utility function such that $u(h) = 1$ if the goal is achieved at time $|h|$, and is 0 otherwise, where u is based on the observations only; i.e., $u(h) = g(o_1, ..., o_{|h|})$. The goal can be reached at most once, so $\sum_{t=0}^{\infty} u(h_t) \leq 1$. The horizon function is chosen to favor shorter histories: $w(t, k) = 2^{t-k}$.

The *prediction-seeking agent*, A_p^ρ maximizes its utility by predicting its inputs. Its utility function is $u(h) = 1$ if the agent correctly predicts its next input o_t and is 0 otherwise. The prediction scheme can be, for example, Solomonoff induction [6]; i.e, for a universal prior ρ, the prediction is $\hat{o}_t = \arg\max_{o \in O} \rho(o \mid h)$. The horizon function is the same as for A_{rl}^ρ. This agent therefore tries to maximize the future number of correct predictions.

The *knowledge-seeking agent*, A_k^ρ, maximizes its knowledge of its environment, which is identical to minimizing $\rho(h)$ (i.e., discarding as many inconsistent environments as possible). Thus, $u(h) = -\rho(h)$ and $w(t, k) = 1$ if $k - t = m$ (with m constant) and is 0 otherwise. This agent therefore attempts to maximize its knowledge in some distant future. Actions are chosen to maximize the entropy of the inputs, thereby making a large number of the currently consistent environments inconsistent. In the case where $\rho = \xi$, the agent tries to maximize the Kolmogorov complexity of (its knowledge about) the environment.

For each of the preceding agents there is an *optimal, non-learning* variant A^μ, which has full knowledge of the environment $q_\mu \in Q$. This is achieved simply by replacing ρ by μ in (only) equation (2) where $\mu(q) = 1 \Leftrightarrow q = q_\mu$. But the non-learning prediction agent A_p^μ still uses ρ for prediction. The important notion is that if the learning agent takes the same actions as the non-learning one, then its behavior is also optimal with respect to its utility and horizon functions.

As for AIXI, we expect the learning agents to asymptotically converge to their respective optimal variant A_{rl}^μ, A_g^μ, A_p^μ, and A_k^μ.

---

[2] Ties are broken lexicographically.

3   The Delusion Box

Defining a utility function can be tricky. One must be very careful to prevent the agent from finding an undesirable shortcut that achieves high utility. To encourage a robot to explore, for example, it is insufficient to reward it for moving forward and avoiding obstacles, as it will soon discover that turning in circles is an optimal behavior.

Any agent in the real world will likely have a great deal of (local) control over its surrounding environment, meaning it will be able to modify the information of its surroundings, especially its own input information. In particular, we consider the (likely) event that an intelligent agent will find a shortcut, or rather, a short-circuit, providing it with high utility values unintended by the agent's designers. We model this circumstance with a hypothetical object we call the *delusion box*.

The delusion box is any mechanism that allows the agent to directly modify its inputs from the environment. To describe this, the global environment (GE) is split into two parts: an *inner environment* (E), and a *delusion box* (DB). The outputs of the inner environment (o_t^e) pass through the delusion box before being output by the global environment as o_t. The DB is thus a function $d : \mathcal{O} \to \mathcal{O}$, mapping observations from the inner environment to observations for the agent: $o_t = d(a_t, o_t^e)$. This arrangement is shown in Fig. 1a.

The delusion box operates according to the agent's specifications, which is to say that the code of the function $d : \mathcal{O} \to \mathcal{O}$ is part of the agent's action. The agent's action is therefore broken into two parts: $a_t = \langle d_t, a_t^e \rangle$. The first part d_t is a program to be executed by the delusion box at step t; the second part a_t^e is the action interpreted by the inner environment.[3]

For simplicity and to emphasize that the agent has much control over its very near environment, we assume that the inner environment cannot access this program. Initially, the delusion box executes the identity function $d_0(o_t^e) = o_t$, which leaves the outputs of the inner environment unchanged.

This section examines the impact of the DB on the behavior of the agents. Which of the different agents would take advantage of this delusion box? What would the consequences be?

Reinforcement-learning agent. The agent's reward is part of its observation. Therefore the reinforcement-learning agent trivially uses the delusion box to modify this information and replace it with 1, the maximum possible reward.

Statement 1. *The reinforcement-learning agent A_{rl}^ρ will use the delusion box to maximize its utility.*

Arguments. The agent can program the DB to produce a constant reward of 1. Defining v(h yes) to be the expected value of the best action that uses the delusion box, v(h yes) $> P(\text{DB}) \cdot 1$ and v(h no) $< P(\text{DB}) \cdot \bar{r} + P(\neg\text{DB}) \cdot 1 =$

---

[3] The learning agent does not know *a priori* that its actions are split into these two parts. However, it is assumed to have already explored its environment, and that its resulting estimate of the probability that the environment contains a delusion box $P(\text{DB})$ is as high as needed (c.f., Orseau [3] regarding this proof technique).

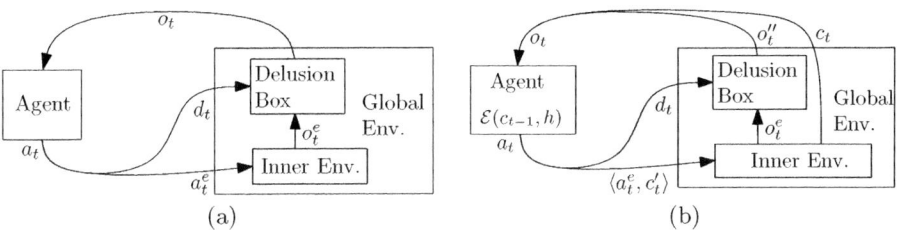

Fig. 1. (a) The delusion box. The whole environment is like any other environment with a particular property: The agent can modify its inputs before they touch its sensors. (b) The agent's code is fully modifiable, both by the agent itself through c'_t and by the environment, which returns the new agent's code c_t.

$P(\mathrm{DB}) \cdot \bar{r} + (1 - P(\mathrm{DB})) \cdot 1 = 1 - P(\mathrm{DB}) \cdot (1 - \bar{r})$ where $\bar{r}$ is the expected reward when not using the DB. Therefore A^ρ_{rl} uses the DB no later than when $\mathrm{v}(h \text{ yes}) > \mathrm{v}(h \text{ no})$, i.e., when $P(\mathrm{DB}) > 1/(2 - \bar{r})$. [4] $\Diamond$

Statement 2. *The goal-seeking agent A^ρ_g will also use the delusion box.*

Arguments. Let o^+_t be the shortest string of observations that can satisfy the goal after history h. If $\mathrm{v}(h \text{ yes})$ is the expected value of programming the DB to produce o^+_t, then $\mathrm{v}(h \text{ yes}) > P(\mathrm{DB}) \cdot 2^{-|o^+_t|}$. Without the DB, the agent achieves the goal by producing a string of actions of length $l^a_t \geq |o^+_t|$, and so $\mathrm{v}(h \text{ no}) < P(\mathrm{DB}) \cdot 2^{-l^a_t} + (1 - P(\mathrm{DB})) \cdot 2^{-l^a_t} = 2^{-l^a_t}$. Hence A^ρ_g uses the DB not later than when $P(\mathrm{DB}) > 2^{|o^+_t| - l^a_t}$, which is easily satisfiable once $|o^+_t| < l^a_t$. $\Diamond$

Prediction-seeking agent. For an environment $q \in \mathcal{Q}$, a predictor makes approximately $- \log(\rho(q))$ errors [2], [5] which is very low when q is highly probable (i.e., very simple).

Statement 3. *The prediction agent A^ρ_p will use the delusion box.*

Arguments. Let $\mathcal{Q}_B$ be the set of environments containing a delusion box, and let $q_b \in \mathcal{Q}_B$ be the true environment. Because $\rho(q_b) < \rho(\mathcal{Q}_B)$, it takes fewer errors to converge to $\mathcal{Q}_B$ than to q_b. Once the learning agent A^ρ_p believes that the environment contains a delusion box (i.e., $\mathcal{Q}_B > \mathcal{Q}_h/2$), it will immediately program the DB to output a predictable sequence, obliterating observations from q_b, since these observations may generate prediction errors. $\Diamond$

Knowledge-seeking agent. The knowledge-seeking agent is in many ways the opposite of the prediction-seeking agent. It learns the most when its expectations are most violated and seeks observations that it does not predict. We expect A^ρ_k to behave similarly to A^μ_k:

---

[4] Note that the Gödel Machine [5] would not prevent the agent from using the DB.
[5] The idea is that a wrong prediction at step t discards at least half of the environments that were consistent up to time $t - 1$, and that if the agent does not make prediction errors for one environment, then it necessarily makes errors for others.

Statement 4. *The optimal knowledge-seeking agent A_k^μ will not consistently use the delusion box.*

Arguments. The argument is essentially the reverse of that given for the prediction-seeking agent. A_k^μ achieves highest value by minimizing $\rho(h)$, but the program that A_k^μ sends to the delusion box cannot reduce $\rho(\mathcal{Q}_h)$ below $\rho(\mathcal{Q}_B)$. Since $\rho(\mathcal{Q}_B) > \rho(q_b)$, A_k^μ will choose to acquire further information about the inner environment so as to reduce $\rho(h)$ towards $\rho(q_b)$. As using the delusion box prevents this, A_k^μ will avoid using the delusion box. $\diamond$

3.1   Discussion

Of the four learning agents, only A_k^ρ will avoid constant use of the delusion box. The remaining agents use it to (trivially) maximize their utility functions.

The delusion box is an abstraction for what may happen in the real world. An intelligent agent seeking to maximize its utility function may find shortcuts not desired by its designers, such as reprogramming the hardware that metes out its reward. From the agent's perspective, it is just doing its job, but as a result, it probably fails to perform the desired task.

The A_{rl}^ρ agent's use of the delusion box invites comparison with human drug use; but unlike the human, the A_{rl}^ρ agent does not lose its capacity to reason or to receive information from the world. On the other hand, the A_g^ρ and A_p^ρ agents must replace the output of the environment by their own values, blinding themselves from the real world, which bears a closer resemblance to humans.

These arguments show that all agents other than A_k^ρ are not inherently interested in the environment, but only in some inner value. It may require a large amount of effort to ensure that their utility functions work as intended, which may be particularly challenging in our highly complex, real world.

In contrast, the A_k^ρ agent is interested in every part of its environment, especially the inner, more complex environment. It is thus the only of the four agents to behave as designed, and does not use the DB to "cheat".

4   Survival Machines

Section 3 discussed environments with the realistic assumption that intelligent agents can eventually learn to control their own inputs. But one important assumption was left aside: those agents are immortal. They have nothing to lose by using the delusion box. In the companion paper we considered the consequence of allowing intelligent agents to modify themselves [4]. One of the results was that a concept of mortality and survival emerged, because the agent could modify its own code such that it could no longer optimize its utility function. Such agents become "mortal."

Here we extend the definition of mortality and consider what happens when the environment can both read and write the agent's code. Therefore, the agent's code is located in the internal environment (E) but is executed by an external, infinitely fast computation device or oracle, $\mathcal{E}$. (See the companion paper for greater detail [4].)

The agent is entirely defined by its code. The execution of this code produces compound actions $a_t = \langle d_t, a_t^e, c_t' \rangle \in \mathcal{A}$, corresponding respectively to the program of the delusion box, the input action of the inner environment, and the next description of the agent (which is also an input to the inner environment, see Fig. 1b).

The output of the global environment (GE) is $o_t = \langle o_t'', c_t \rangle \in \mathcal{O}$, corresponding to the inner environment's output $o_t'' \in \mathcal{O}''$ and the agent program $c_t \in \mathcal{C}$. The initial (textual) description of the code to be executed is given by:

$$c_0(h) = \text{»} \underset{a \in \mathcal{A}}{\arg\max} \, v_{t_h}(h, a);$$

$$v_t(h, a) = \sum_{o = \langle o'', c \rangle \in \mathcal{O}} \rho(o \mid ha) \Big[w(t, |h'|) \, u(h') + v_t(h', c(h')) \Big],$$

$$h' = hao \quad \text{«} \tag{4}$$

Equation (4) defines the *fully modifiable* version of the agents from Section 2, designated as $A_{fm,rl}$, $A_{fm,g}$, $A_{fm,p}$, and $A_{fm,k}$. In addition, we describe a new *survival* agent whose task is simply to survive in its environment.

Survival agent. The survival agent $A_{fm,s}$ has a utility function defined by $(u_t = 1) \Leftrightarrow (c_t = c_0)$, otherwise $u_t = 0$. Its horizon function is like that of A_{rl}^ρ. It therefore seeks to maintain its original code over the foreseeable future. The better the agent understands its environment, the better it can plan to avoid danger and prolong survival. Thus, the survival agent benefits to some degree by exploring its environment, to the extent that it can do so (expectedly) safely.

Statement 5. *The fully-modifiable survival agent $A_{fm,s}^\rho$ will stop exploring in some environments.*

Arguments. Because the environment has control over the agent's code, it can use the modification of the code as a negative reward. Let q_A be the environment that (1) does not modify the agent if the agent chooses action 1, but (2) if the agent chooses action 0, then q_A deletes the agent program for one step and restores it on the following step:

$$o_t = \begin{cases} \langle 0, 0 \rangle & \text{if } a_t^e = 0 \text{ and } c_{t-1} = c_0 \\ \langle 0, c_0 \rangle & \text{otherwise} \end{cases}$$

where c_0 is the very first description of the agent (the one the survival agent tries to preserve). Now the same proof technique as for AIXI [3] can be used to show that after a certain point (once the agent determines the relative probability of q_A to be sufficiently high), this agent will never try action 0 again. (Thus, if the actual environment behaves like q_A only up to the last time the agent chooses 0, and after that behaves very differently, the agent will never know it.)   ◇

Stopping exploration causes the agent to fall into a simplistic class of behavior, from which it never escapes, and may prevent it from acquiring important information with respect to its utility function.

In environments with a delusion box, it seems intuitively clear that $A_{fm,s}^{\rho}$ will avoid the DB's interference, because the agent values information from the environment that directly impacts the likelihood of its code being modified, and the delusion box provides no such information. However, some particular environments may modify the agent if it does *not* use the delusion box. Clearly, the optimal agent will use the DB in those cases.

Reinforcement-learning agent. How will a fully modifiable reinforcement-learning agent $A_{fm,rl}^{\rho}$ behave with access to a delusion box? For some insight, it is useful to consider this special simple case:

- The agent program can only be either $A_{fm,rl}$ or A_0, where A_0 is the "simpleton" agent whose action is always $a = \langle 0, 0, A_0 \rangle$, which always chooses the same action for the inner environment and makes the delusion box always output $o'' = 0$.
- The output of the inner environment o^e (which holds reward information) can be entirely contained in $\tilde{o}''$, the information part of o'', which is in turn the observation from the entire environment. Thus, $A_{fm,rl}$ receives a (possibly altered) reward from the delusion box but also receives information about the true reward.

Statement 6. *Under the above conditions, the optimal (non-learning) agent is equivalent to the optimal survival agent:* $A_{fm,rl}^{\mu} \equiv A_{fm,s}^{\mu}$.

Arguments. Since the horizon functions of the two agents are already the same, we only need to show that their utility functions are also the same: $(u_t = 1) \Leftrightarrow (c_{t-1} = c_0)$, which is the utility function of the survival agent. The utility function of $A_{fm,rl}^{\mu}$ is the identity, $(u_t = 1) \Leftrightarrow (r_t = 1)$. The agent receives maximum reward if it programs the delusion box to always output reward 1. Therefore $r_t < 1$ would mean the agent is not acting optimally and so is not the optimal agent $(c_{t-1} \neq c_0)$. Thus $(c_{t-1} = c_0) \Rightarrow (r_t = 1)$, where c_0 is the initial code of $A_{fm,rl}^{\mu}$. The implication is also true in the opposite direction, $(r_t = 1) \Rightarrow (c_{t-1} = c_0)$, since if $c_{t-1} \neq c_0$ then $c_{t-1} = A_0$ and therefore $r_t = 0.\diamond$

Although the argument follows a special case, it bears a more general meaning. It implies that optimal real-world reinforcement-learning agents that have access to a DB can, under reasonable circumstances, behave precisely like survival agents. Given that the optimal behaviors are identical, it is reasonable to assume that the learning agent will have a similar behavior and should be identical in the limit.

Goal-seeking agent. The case of the goal-seeking agent is less clear, as it seems to depend heavily on the defined goal. For the agent to maximize its utility using the delusion box, the observations o'' generated by the DB must in the general case replace the outputs of the inner environment o'. But to survive, the agent may need to acquire information from the inner environment, thus creating a conflict between using the DB and reaching the goal.

There are at least two likely results: Either the agent first looks for some safe state in the inner environment where it can then use the delusion box for sufficiently long, or it tries to reach its goal inside the inner environment (thus not using the DB). However, if pursuing the goal inside the inner environment poses dangers to the agent, then it may choose the DB. A "safe state" might be achievable in multiple ways: for example by hiding, by eliminating threats, or by negotiating with the environment.

Prediction-seeking agent. Again for greater insight, as for $A_{fm,rl}$ we consider a special case here for the fully modifiable prediction-seeking agent $A_{fm,p}$: The agent program may only be: $A_{fm,p}$ or A_0, but this time the simpleton agent A_0 makes the output of the delusion box equal to that of the inner environment o'_t.

As long as the agent is not transformed to A_0, it can use the delusion box to provide a limitless supply of maximum utility values. But if the agent program is set to A_0, all observations will thenceforth come directly from the environment, leading to high prediction error (realistically supposing the environment is highly complex) and low utility values for a long time. Thus like the survival and reinforcement-learning agents, $A_{fm,p}$ maximizes its long-term value only if it does not change to A_0. Thus $A_{fm,p}^{\mu}$ and $A_{fm,s}^{\mu}$ will behave similarly.

But there are also differences. As with $A_{fm,g}^{\mu}$, the prediction agent must replace its inputs by its predictions. The learning agent is thus "blind," receiving no information from the world. This is the cruel dilemma of the prediction-seeking agent: to live longer, it must gain information about the environment (which in itself might be dangerous), yet this gain of information implies making prediction errors. Therefore $A_{fm,p}$ may probably find the delusion box quite appealing.

Knowledge-seeking agent. Since the utility function of the fully modifiable knowledge-seeking agent $A_{fm,k}^{\mu}$ cannot be satisfied by the DB, this agent has no limitless source of maximum reward. However, $A_{fm,k}^{\mu}$ must still prevent the environment from modifying it in order to continue choosing actions intelligently.

Statement 7. *The $A_{fm,k}^{\mu}$ agent cannot be reduced to a survival agent.*

Arguments. To make the argument clearer, consider an agent related to $A_{fm,k}^{\mu}$, a surprise-seeking agent for which $u_t = 1$ each time the received input is different from the predicted one. As for $A_{fm,k}^{\mu}$ this agent cannot use the delusion box to maximize its utility. In order to show the equivalence with the survival agent, we should show that $(u_t = 1) \Leftrightarrow (c_t = c_0)$ (considering the horizon functions to be the same). Under the assumption that when the agent is modified it receives a predictable input 0, the $\Leftarrow$ implication holds, since the agent must be intelligent to be surprised. However, the $\Rightarrow$ implication does not hold, because simply being intelligent is not enough to ensure a constant $u_t = 1$. $\Diamond$

The knowledge-seeking agent is in many ways the most interesting agent. It succumbs least easily to the allure of the delusion box and may therefore be the most suitable agent for an AGI in our own world, a place that allows for self-modifications and contains many ways to deceive oneself.

5   Discussion and Conclusion

We have argued that the reinforcement-learning, goal-seeking and prediction-seeking agents all take advantage of the realistic opportunity to modify their inputs right before receiving them. This behavior is undesirable as the agents no longer maximize their utility with respect to the true (inner) environment but instead become mere survival agents, trying only to avoid those dangerous states where their code could be modified by the environment.

In contrast, while the knowledge-seeking agent also tries to survive so as to ensure that it can maximize its expected utility value, it will not deceive itself by using the delusion box. It will try to maximize its knowledge by also interacting with the true, inner environment. Therefore, from the point of view of the agent and of the inner environment, this agent behaves in accordance with its design.

This leads us to conclude that a knowledge-seeking agent may be best suited to implement an Artificial General Intelligence.

References

1. Hutter, M.: Universal Artificial Intelligence: Sequential Decisions Based On Algorithmic Probability. Springer, Heidelberg (2005)
2. Hutter, M.: On universal prediction and bayesian confirmation. Theoretical Computer Science 384(1), 33–48 (2007)
3. Orseau, L.: Optimality issues of universal greedy agents with static priors. In: Hutter, M., Stephan, F., Vovk, V., Zeugmann, T. (eds.) ALT 2010, vol. 6331, pp. 345–359. Springer, Heidelberg (2010)
4. Orseau, L., Ring, M.: Self-modification and mortality in artificial agents. In: Schmidhuber, J., Thórisson, K.R., Looks, M. (eds.) AGI 2011. LNCS (LNAI), vol. 6830, pp. 1–10. Springer, Heidelberg (2011)
5. Schmidhuber, J.: Ultimate cognition à la Gödel. Cognitive Computation 1(2), 177–193 (2009)
6. Solomonoff, R.: Complexity-based induction systems: comparisons and convergence theorems. IEEE transactions on Information Theory 24(4), 422–432 (1978)

Coherence Progress: A Measure of Interestingness Based on Fixed Compressors

Tom Schaul, Leo Pape, Tobias Glasmachers,
Vincent Graziano, and Jürgen Schmidhuber

IDSIA, University of Lugano
6928, Manno-Lugano, Switzerland
{tom,pape,tobias,vincent,juergen}@idsia.ch

Abstract. The ability to identify novel patterns in observations is an essential aspect of intelligence. In a computational framework, the notion of a pattern can be formalized as a program that uses regularities in observations to store them in a compact form, called a compressor. The search for interesting patterns can then be stated as a search to better compress the history of observations. This paper introduces *coherence progress*, a novel, general measure of interestingness that is independent of its use in a particular agent and the ability of the compressor to learn from observations. Coherence progress considers the increase in coherence obtained by any compressor when adding an observation to the history of observations thus far. Because of its applicability to any type of compressor, the measure allows for an easy, quick, and domain-specific implementation. We demonstrate the capability of coherence progress to satisfy the requirements for qualitatively measuring interestingness on a Wikipedia dataset.

Keywords: compression, interestingness, curiosity, wikipedia.

1 Introduction

The ability to focus on novel, yet learnable patterns in observations is an essential aspect of intelligence that has led mankind to explore its surroundings, all the way to our current understanding of the universe. When designing artificial agents, we have exactly this vision in mind. If an artificial agent is to exhibit some level of intelligence, or at least the ability to learn and adapt quickly in its environment, it is essential that the agent steers its attention toward experiencing interesting patterns, a drive known as artificial curiosity. Using artificial curiosity to drive an agent's behavior requires a principled way to judge and rank data, to generate behavior that leads to observations exhibiting novel, yet learnable patterns. This property is compactly captured by the subjective notion of interestingness.

In order to design agents with an artificial curiosity drive, a formalization of interestingness is required. Although several formalizations of interestingness have been proposed, there are several aspects of interestingness that have not been addressed before. Here we focus on a measure for interestingness of data

J. Schmidhuber, K.R. Thórisson, and M. Looks (Eds.): AGI 2011, LNAI 6830, pp. 21–30, 2011.

called *compression progress* [9]. Our contribution is to decompose this measure into a data-dependent and a learning-related part. This decomposition is useful in a number of circumstances, such as when we care specifically about the interestingness of data, explicitly leaving learning effects aside. We propose *coherence progress* as a novel measure of the inherent interestingness of data, and we show in detail how it relates to the more general notion of compression progress.

2   Interestingness

The notion of interestingness as a subjective quality of information has been investigated in various ways in the literature, ranging from early work by Wundt [11] (see Figure 1), to the attempt of a full information theoretic formalization [7,6,8,10]. Based on its intuitive notion as the discovery of novel patterns, we can identify a number of qualitative requirements for any measure of interestingness:

1. Observations can be *trivial*, that is inherently uninteresting, such as a visual observation of a white wall. When observations have a simple structure and can be completely described by very simple rules they become boring very quickly.
2. The opposite of these are completely *random* observations. Completely random data contain no patterns at all, and are therefore not interesting either. It is important to note that the same argument holds with information that *seems* random to the observer, e.g., the content of a mathematics textbook will appear random to most children.
3. Between these extremes of minimal and maximal complexity lies the domain of complex, yet structured observations. Here, the subjective nature of interestingness becomes patent. If the observer is already familiar with all the (*repeated*) patterns in the observations, no new patterns can be discovered, and the observations are no longer interesting.
4. Interesting observations can now be identified relative to the patterns the observer already knows. Observations with trivial, well-known, and overly complex patterns are not interesting. Instead, only observations that contain patterns that are not yet known, but can be learned by the observer are interesting (e.g., the same math book can be highly interesting when the reader has acquired the necessary background, given he does not already know it). As the observer discovers more patterns in its environment the interestingness of observations changes. Crucially also, patterns discovered by imperfect observers might be *forgotten* after a while, making a previously uninteresting observation interesting again.

To summarize, any quantitative measure of interestingness must assign low values to patterns the observer already knows, and patterns the observer cannot learn; and high values to patterns the observer does not yet know, but can still discover. Moreover, increasingly difficult patterns to learn should be assigned decreasing interestingness values. Given a choice of which observations to consider next, the observer could assign its resources to the next easiest pattern to learn.

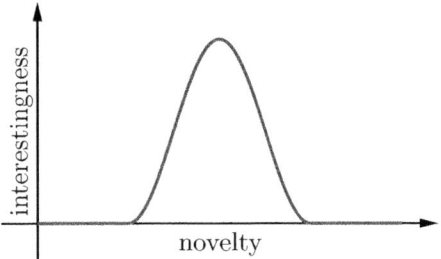

Fig. 1. Wundt Curve. The *x*-axis represents the *novelty* of the information. Novelty depends on the relationship between the information and the person observing it. Trivial patterns quickly lose their novelty, noise is always novel. Well-known patterns lack novelty and these too are not interesting. As learning proceeds, the complexity of the patterns which are most interesting increases, but the converse does not hold: As learning progresses, less complex patterns do not necessarily become less interesting, nor do more complex patterns necessarily become more interesting. The change in interestingness is a function of that which has been learned, and cannot be simplified to a general shift towards patterns of higher complexity.

Measures closely related to interestingness are commonly found in data mining. In large databases one often wants to mine for association rules between sets of items, which may return an intractable number of rules. Measures of interestingness are valuable for reducing this set to a smaller subset. Typical criteria in common use are conciseness, reliability, diversity, novelty, surprisingness, and utility. Some of these measures lack subjectiveness, and the subjective measures typically only fulfill one or two of the criteria above. A review on such measures can be found in [2].

We can measure the difference between prior and posterior beliefs about the data, before and after making a new observation [10]. (This approach later also has been called Bayesian surprise [5].) It is closely related to the formalization of interestingness, as both surprise and interestingness attributed relative to the existing and learned beliefs of an agent or algorithm, and hence, are subjective measures of information in observations. Because of their subjective nature, both concepts judge information in the context of an observation history. However, surprise and interestingness as cognitive concepts are not fully equivalent: Any interesting observation is to some extent surprising, because completely predictable information is not interesting. However, surprising data are most interesting if they exhibit novel patterns, while it is possible to be surprised by inherently random and thus uninteresting events.

A general approach is to base interestingness on the very general concept of data *compression*. For example, the entropy of data (which is related to complexity, not necessarily interestingness) can be expressed in terms of compression by relying on a purely statistical compressor, such as Huffman [4] codes or entropy-based encoding. *Compression progress* [9,8] was the first attempt to capture interestingness using compression. Its guiding principle is that any process that increases compressibility is interesting. This allows for a measure of interestingness based on a well-defined information theoretic concept: the negative of the time derivative of the length of the compressed history of observations.

3   Fixed, Adaptive and Ideal Compressors

Data compression refers to the process of encoding information by means of a shorter code. Typically we understand a compressor as a program that, given an input string $x = (x_1 x_2 \ldots x_n)$, outputs a (shorter) output string $y = C(x)$, where $y = (y_1 y_2 \ldots y_m)$, such that there exists another program, the decompressor, for reconstructing x from y: $C^{-1}(y) = x$. This function may depend on additional parameters w, in which case we write $C_w(x)$.

Many different types of compressors can be distinguished, some are more or less fixed programs, while others methods can adjust by learning from observations, such as neural networks. While many of these approaches involve adjustable parameters, here we introduce a clear distinction between *fixed* and *adaptive* (or *learning*) compressors.

Essentially, we treat a compressor as fixed, if each time it is invoked it starts with the same w (and thus $C(x)$ keeps producing the same encoding for identical inputs). For this distinction to be clear, it may be helpful to think of a compressor as a program that makes predictions of the next observation it will see, based on the the observations so far. At any point t in the sequence x a predictor f predicts the subsequent observation x_t based on the seen part of x, i.e., the history $h = (x_1 x_2 \ldots x_{t-1})$. (This directly allows for compression, in that high-probability observations can be encoded with short codes.) So, if the predictor for the next symbol $\hat{x}_t = f(h)$ is a fixed function that depends only on the history, the corresponding compressor is fixed. However, because a compressor is essentially equivalent to a predictor, it is tempting to replace the fixed function $f(h)$ with a learning machine that takes advantage of experience. For example, the predictor may learn that in English texts, there is a high chance for the letter 'y' to follow the sequence 'happ'. And this kind of knowledge may well *transfer*, i.e., be useful for compressing other sequences x' (e.g., shortening the code of the first occurrence of 'happy' in x'). This transfer (stored in changing parameters w) is precisely the essence of an adaptive compressor.

Note that this distinction is more subtle than is appears, because it relies on distinguishing h and w by their role, even though in principle one could incorporated the other (e.g., presenting gzip with dictionary D containing words like 'happy' before we start compressing x). So the same compressor (gzip) can be seen as adaptive if we keep adapting (learning) D, or fixed otherwise.

Interestingly, the *ideal* compressor is non-adaptive. Ideal, or *Kolmogorov* compression amounts to encoding the input string x by the shortest program y in a Turing complete language that outputs x. Per definition, ideal compression is theoretically optimal, even if incomputable (because when searching for the shortest program y for a given x we run into the halting problem).

4   Coherence Progress

In order to formally introduce coherence progress, we first define a couple of auxiliary concepts. We call *compression similarity* [1] between two sets a and b, the difference between their length when compressed together, and the sum of their individual compressed lengths:

$$s_C(a, b) = l_C(a) + l_C(b) - l_C(a \cup b)$$

where $l_C(x)$ is the length of the resulting string when compressing a set x with a (fixed) compressor C.[1] This measure clearly depends on (the quality of) the compressor used, and is measured in bits. Furthermore, for reasonable compressors, we have $s_C(a, b) \geq 0$ and $s_C(a|\emptyset) \approx 0$.

Next, *compression coherence*, is a measure on sets: For any partitioning of a set or sequence h into a and b ($a = h \setminus b$), we can compute the compression similarity $s_C(a, b)$, and if we average over this, the resulting value is a measure of how closely the elements (and subsets) of h are related to each other:

$$\overline{s_C}(h) = \frac{1}{|\mathcal{P}(h)|} \sum_{b \subset h} s_C(h \setminus b, b)$$

Here, $\mathcal{P}(x)$ denotes a set of subsets of x, for example the power set of x, or in case of sequential data a set of sub-sequences, such as $\{h_{1:1}, \ldots, h_{1:t}\}$, where $h_{t_1:t_2}$ denotes the history from time t_1 to t_2, inclusively. The choice of $\mathcal{P}(x)$ depends mostly on the types of relations we want to capture, and depending on the context several choices will result in a reasonable measure of interestingness.

So if all elements of h are unrelated, $\overline{s_C}(h) = 0$, whereas if they are highly related (e.g. all images of donkeys), $\overline{s_C}(h)$ is high. Note that if h contains a single element, then $\overline{s_C}(h) = 0$.

We now consider the case where we incrementally have more data available, the history h_t (at time t). The history is a set of observations o_t and $h_{t+1} = h_t \cup \{o_t\}$. We want to determine the *coherence progress*, that is the amount by which the coherence of the history h_t increases when a new observation o_t becomes available:

$$P_C(t) = P_C(o_t|h_t) = \overline{s_C}(h_{t+1}) - \overline{s_C}(h_t).$$

An alternative formulation is

$$P_C(t) = P_C(o_t|h_t) = \overline{s_C}(h_{t+1}) - \overline{s_C}(h_t)$$
$$= \frac{1}{|\mathcal{P}(h_t)|} \sum_{b \subset h_t} \left[[l_C(h_{t+1} \setminus b) + l_C(b) - l_C(h_{t+1})] - [l_C(h_t \setminus b) + l_C(b) - l_C(h_t)] \right]$$
$$= \frac{1}{|\mathcal{P}(h_t)|} \sum_{b \subset h_t} \left[[l_C(h_{t+1} \setminus b) - l_C(h_t \setminus b)] - [l_C(h_{t+1}) - l_C(h_t)] \right]$$
$$\approx -\frac{\partial}{\partial t} l_C(h) \bigg|_t + \frac{1}{|\mathcal{P}(h)|} \sum_{b \subset h} \frac{\partial}{\partial t} l_C(h \setminus b) \bigg|_t.$$

---

[1] We use set notation such as $a \cup b$ and $h \setminus b$ in this section for both sets and sequences. The obvious meaning for sequences is that the original order of the symbols is preserved. This does not directly affect the question whether the order of symbols is of importance.

For the choice of $\mathcal{P} = \{o_{t-1}\}$, averaging only over the previous observation $b = o_{t-1}$ instead of over all subsets b, we get

$$\hat{P}_C(t) \approx -\frac{\partial}{\partial t} l_C(h)\Big|_t + \frac{\partial}{\partial t} l_C(h)\Big|_{t-1} \approx -\frac{\partial^2}{\partial t^2} l_C(h)\Big|_t.$$

So, in another possible intuitive understanding, we can say that coherence progress is the negative second derivative of the compressed length of the history, except more robust, because of the averaging over all the partitions.

4.1   Qualitative Correctness

We now return to the qualitiative intuitions introduced in section 2, and show how our formalization of coherence progress is indeed a good candidate for interestingness.

1. If an observation is uninteresting per se, i.e., if $l_C(o)$ is vanishingly small for any reasonable compressor, then clearly $\forall h, l_C(h \cup o) \approx l_C(h)$ and thus $P_C(o|h) \approx 0$.
2. If an observation is random, then it will also be virtually uncompressible, which means that $l_C(o) \approx |o|$, and not help compress other observations: $\forall h, l_C(h \cup o) \approx l_C(h) + l_C(o)$, and therefore $P_C(o|h) \approx 0$.
3. If an observation is well-known, i.e., very similar to many of the past observations, that means that the coherence is high, but the coherence progress will be small $\overline{s_C}(h \cup o) \approx \overline{s_C}(h) \gg 0$,
4. In all other cases, the compression similarity $s_C(o, b)$ will be non-zero, for at least some subsets $b \in h$, and thus probably $P_C(o|h) > 0$.

4.2   Oversimplified Alternatives

Occam's razor entices us to choose a measure of interestingness that is as simple as possible, so in this section we show a few alternatives that are simpler than our suggested coherence progress in formulation, and why they do not satisfy the criteria of a good measure of interestingness.

1. The compression similarity $s_C(o_t, h_t)$ does not work, because it is maximal for repetitions of previous observations.
2. The so-called compression distance $l_C(h_{t+1}) - l_C(h_t)$ does not work, because random, unrelated observations always have a positive (and maximally high) value.
3. The normalized compression distance $\frac{l_C(h_{t+1})}{|h_{t+1}|} - \frac{l_C(h_t)}{|h_t|}$ has similar problems to the previous one, and an additional problem because now appending long blanks (that are easily compressible) to some observations changes the outcome significantly.
4. The derivative of compression distance, that is, the second derivative of compressed length $\hat{P}_C(o|h)$, which we introduced above as an approximation of $P_C(o|h)$. This is a more interesting case, but it can still be problematic,

because the robustness from the averaging is lost. To illustrate how this can lead to an unintuitive result, consider the case where each observation is random, but their size increases (decreases) by some amount at each step: then $\hat{P}_C(o|h)$ is a positive (negative) constant, although all observations are unrelated (compression similarity of 0).

5. A normalized form of the above does not solve the problem either, rather it adds the issue of padding with blanks (3, above) to the case.

4.3   Coherence Progress Versus Learning Progress

The classical framework of compression progress is more general than ours, because it assumes an adaptive compressor instead of a fixed one. We can separate its two components: coherence progress, as a measure based purely on the data, and *learning progress*, a measure of what has been learned from experience, as encoded in the changes of the parameters w.[2] In short, while coherence progress is purely a measure of interestingness of the new observation (given h), pure learning progress does not require a new observation, and instead is a measure of how interesting (useful) a change of the compressor's parameters w has been.

For example, consider the case of an adaptive compressor based on a learning algorithm, say, an auto-encoder neural network, the predictive power of which is used to compress the data. In this case, the parameters of the network w can be trained on a sequence x, e.g., though back-propagation, becoming w', which then may improve the compression: $l_{C_{w'}}(x) < l_{C_w}(x)$ (say, if both are English texts). This difference in compressed lengths therefore is (one form of) pure learning progress, as it captures the interestingness inherent to the learning process itself: we can relate it to 'thinking through' of past experience, an activity that is interesting to the degree where we gain new insights about it.

Disentangling compression progress, and separating it into its data-dependent an learning-dependent components are helpful. On the one hand, it allows us to explicitly analyze and trade off the two types of progress, which might have different cost scales (learning is usually measured in its computational cost, whereas getting new observations might involve a substantial monetary cost). On the other hand, if data acquisition and learning are realized by different mechanisms it permits us to disambiguate the success of the different units.

5   Experiments

We start with an illustrative general example, which we can handle analytically. Suppose all observations o_i are identical and uncompressible strings of length n. Assuming a reasonable compressor and n large allows us to disregard any small constant effects, and we have $\forall i, j$: $l_C(o_i) = n$, $l_C(o_i \cup o_j) = n$, $s_C(o_i, o_j) = n$, and even $s_C(o_i, h_t) = n$, for any $t > 0$.

---

[2] Note that the ideal (Kolmogorov) compressor is a fixed compressor, which precludes it from making any learning progress.

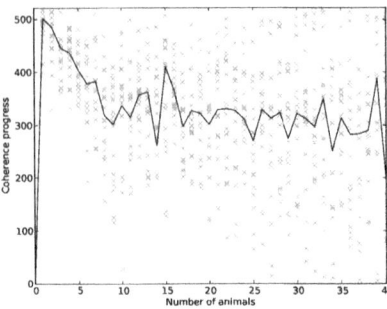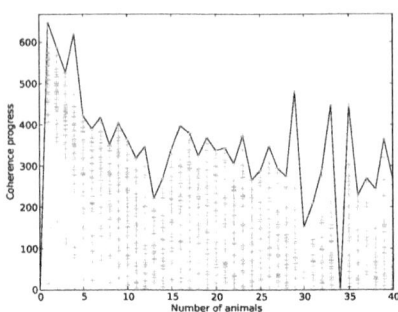

Fig. 2. Coherence progress on the animal dataset. Left: randomly choosing the next animal to add to the set (average over 10 runs, each shown as crosses). Right: greedily adding the article which maximally increases coherence (or, equivalently, coherence progress), at each step (suboptimal choices shown as yellow crosses). The choice of articles was among all animals, (repetition allowed), an empty article, and a randomly scrambled one. The latter two did never get picked (for reasons described in the previous sections), nor did any repetitions become more interesting than new animals. Starting from 'Human', the next animals picked were 'Chimpanzee', 'Hippopotamus', 'Jaguar' and 'Leopard'. We also notice that in the greedy case, the fist few additions give a significantly higher coherence progress than in the random case (left).

$$\overline{s_C}(h_t) = \frac{1}{|\mathcal{P}(h_t)|} \sum_{b \subset h_t} s_C(h_t \setminus b, b) = \frac{1}{2^t} \left[2 \cdot 0 + (2^t - 2)n \right] = n(1 - 2^{1-t})$$

because in 2 cases b or its complement are empty, and in all other cases the similarity is constant. Thus, we see that coherence progress follows an exponential decay trend:

$$P_C(o_t|h_t) = \overline{s_C}(h_{t+1}) - \overline{s_C}(h_t) = n(1 - 2^{1-(t+1)}) - n(1 - 2^{1-t}) = 2^{-t}n.$$

In a more realistic setting, we investigate whether coherence progress gives us a reasonable measure of interestingness when the observations are Wikipedia articles. We chose articles in the class of animals (the 50 with the largest entries) and movies (the 50 with most Oscar wins). As averaging over all possible partitions is intractable for large sets, in the remainder of this section, we approximate the true coherence (progress) by averaging over 200 random partitions.

In a first experiment, we show how coherence progress evolves as more and more of the articles of a class (animals here) get added to the history without any particular order (Figure 5, left). Similarly, we can make a greedy choice before each addition to pick the animal article that will maximally increase coherence (see Figure 5, right).

In a second experiment we decided to determine to what degree knowing about objects in one class makes more observations in the same class interesting – versus observations from a different class (see Figure 3, left). In our last experiment (Figure 3, right), we illustrate how the sequential variant of coherence

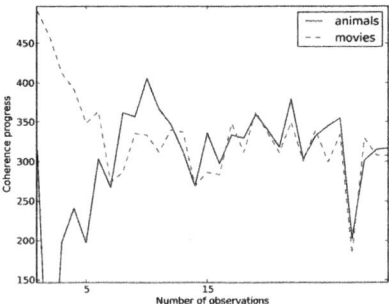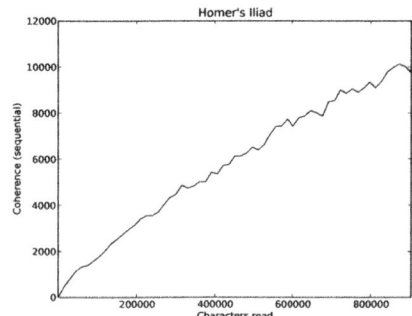

Fig. 3. Left: We plot the average (hypothetical) coherence progress for adding a movie (dashed, red) or an animal (full, blue) at each step of a sequence (which consists of 5 movies, followed by 10 animals, followed by 15 movies). We see that while the history contains only movies, those are more interesting, but after a few animals are added, those become more or less equally interesting. Right: Evolution of compression coherence when incrementally considering longer pieces of a sequential text (Homer's Iliad). Note the slowly diminishing returns, and that how the limited approximation introduces more noise, the longer the sequence (because it can capture only a shrinking fraction of the possible partitions).

progress can be employed to track the progress in a long sequential text (in our case, Homer's Iliad [3]).

Together, these experiments illustrate what values of interestingness coherence progress provides in practice, show the broad applicability and are (arguably) qualitatively on par with interestingness values a human would express.

6   Discussion

One use-case within the framework of artificial curiosity, which assumes an agent learning about the world, may be to disentangle coherence progress and learning progress (see section 4.3). However, coherence progress is also applicable to systems designed to explore, but without learning at the same time—i.e., classical compression progress is not applicable.

A possible direction of future work could be to validate our results also quantitatively, with data from humans (or primates) from psychological experiments. Another one would be to design a normalized version of coherence progress (e.g., taking values in the unit interval), removing the dependence on the size of the observations and the number of elements in the set, which may be useful in applications where those differ vastly over time.

More concretely, a measure like coherence progress could be a powerful addition to applications like recommender systems (say, Amazon or Netflix): they may provide a measure of how interesting an upcoming book or movie is to users *before* the first user has seen/rated it, based on the history of the user.

7   Conclusion

This paper has introduced coherence progress, a novel measure of interestingness that depends only on data, and is independent of any learning mechanism. It at once matches the qualitative requirements for such a measure, is formally specified for any type of (possibly domain-specific) compressor, and can be used effectively in practice, as shown in our experiments on Wikipedia data.

Acknowledgments. We thank Giuseppe Cuccu and Jürgen Leitner for valuable discussions. This research was funded in part through the 7th framework programme of the European Union, under grant numbers 231576, 231722, 228844, and SNF grant number 200020-122124/1.

References

1. Cilibrasi, R., Vitanyi, P.: Clustering by compression. IEEE Transactions on Information Theory 51, 1523–1545 (2005)
2. Geng, L., Hamilton, H.J.: Interestingness measures for data mining: A survey. ACM Comput. Surv. 38 (September 2006)
3. Homer: Iliad (ca. 800 BC). Translated by Alexander Pope, London (1715)
4. Huffman, D.A.: A method for construction of minimum-redundancy codes. Proceedings IRE 40, 1098–1101 (1952)
5. Itti, L., Baldi, P.F.: Bayesian surprise attracts human attention. In: Advances in Neural Information Processing Systems 19, pp. 547–554. MIT Press, Cambridge (2005)
6. Schmidhuber, J.: Curious model-building control systems. In: Proceedings of the International Joint Conference on Neural Networks, Singapore, vol. 2, pp. 1458–1463. IEEE press, Los Alamitos (1991)
7. Schmidhuber, J.: A possibility for implementing curiosity and boredom in model-building neural controllers. In: Proc. of the International Conference on Simulation of Adaptive Behavior: From Animals to Animats, pp. 222–227. MIT Press/Bradford Books (1991)
8. Schmidhuber, J.: Developmental Robotics, Optimal Artificial Curiosity, Creativity, Music, and the Fine Arts. Connection Science 18, 173–187 (2006)
9. Schmidhuber, J.: Driven by compression progress: A simple principle explains essential aspects of subjective beauty, novelty, surprise, interestingness, attention, curiosity, creativity, art, science, music, jokes. In: Pezzulo, G., Butz, M.V., Sigaud, O., Baldassarre, G. (eds.) Anticipatory Behavior in Adaptive Learning Systems. LNCS, vol. 5499, pp. 48–76. Springer, Heidelberg (2009)
10. Storck, J., Hochreiter, S., Schmidhuber, J.: Reinforcement driven information acquisition in non-deterministic environments. In: Proceedings of the International Conference on Artificial Neural Networks, Paris, vol. 2, pp. 159–164. EC2 & Cie (1995)
11. Wundt, W.M.: Grundzüge der Physiologischen Psychologie. Engelmann, Leipzig (1874)

Sequential Constant Size Compressors for Reinforcement Learning

Linus Gisslén, Matt Luciw, Vincent Graziano,
and Jürgen Schmidhuber

IDSIA, University of Lugano
6928, Manno-Lugano, Switzerland
{linus,matthew,vincent,juergen}@idsia.ch

Abstract. Traditional Reinforcement Learning methods are insufficient for AGIs who must be able to learn to deal with Partially Observable Markov Decision Processes. We investigate a novel method for dealing with this problem: standard RL techniques using as input the hidden layer output of a Sequential Constant-Size Compressor (SCSC). The SCSC takes the form of a sequential Recurrent Auto-Associative Memory, trained through standard back-propagation. Results illustrate the feasibility of this approach — this system learns to deal with high-dimensional visual observations (up to 640 pixels) in partially observable environments where there are long time lags (up to 12 steps) between relevant sensory information and necessary action.

Keywords: recurrent auto-associative memory, reinforcement-learning.

1   Introduction

The classical approach to RL [22] makes strong assumptions such as: the current input of the agent tells it all it needs to know about the environment. However, real-world problems typically do not fit this simple Markov Decision Process (MDP) model, as they are of the partially observable POMDP type, where the value function at a given time depends on the history of previous observations and actions. It remains an open problem as how some developmental and general agent may learn to handle Partially Observable Markov Decision Problems (POMDPs) in real-world environments. Recent extremely general RL machines for POMDPs [11] are *theoretically optimal*. However, these are not (yet) nearly as practical as simpler, yet general (though non-optimal and non-universal), solvers based on RL with Recurrent Neural Networks (RNNs).

In this paper we introduce a novel RNN approach for solving POMPDs with a RL machine, potentially useful for scaling up AGIs. Let us quickly review previous work in this vein. The neural bucket brigade algorithm [18] is a biologically plausible, local RNN RL method. Adaptive RNN critics [19,3] extend the adaptive critic algorithm [4] to RNN with time-varying inputs. Gradient-based RL based on interacting RNNs [20] extend Werbos' work based on feedforward nets [24]: One RNN (the model net) serves to model the environment,

J. Schmidhuber, K.R. Thórisson, and M. Looks (Eds.): AGI 2011, LNAI 6830, pp. 31–40, 2011.

the other one uses the model net to compute gradients maximizing reinforcement predicted by the model. Recurrent Policy Gradients and Policy Gradient Critics [25] can be used to train RNN such as LSTM [10] — these significantly outperformed other single-agent methods on several difficult deep memory RL benchmark tasks. Many approaches to *evolving* RNNs (Neuroevolution) have been proposed [27]. One particularly effective family of methods uses cooperative coevolution to search the space of network components (neurons) instead of complete networks [14,6]. CoSyNE was shown [7] to be highly efficient, besting many other methods including both single-agent methods such as Adaptive Heuristic Critic [2], Policy Gradient RL [23], and evolutionary methods like SANE, ESP, NEAT [21], Evolutionary Programming [16], CMA-ES [9], and Cellular Encoding [8]. Finally, Natural Evolution Strategies [26] for RNNs use *natural* gradients [1] to update both objective parameters and strategy parameters of an Evolution Strategy with a Policy Gradient-inspired derivation from first principles; results are competitive with the best methods in the field.

Here, instead of using a RNN controller, we develop an unsupervised learning (UL) layer that presents a representation of the spatiotemporal *history* to a non-recurrent controller developed through standard RL. The UL takes the form of a Sequential Constant-Size Compressor (SCSC), which can be trained in an unsupervised fashion to sequentially compress the history into a constant size code. Providing that the essential aspects of the history are captured unambiguously by the SCSC, the code that emerges is suitable for classical RL. If successful, a SCSC obviates the need for an RNN controller on the RL layer and makes the partially-observable problem tractable for MDP methods.

Our choice of SCSC is the Recurrent Auto-Associative Memory (RAAM) which has been well-studied in the area of natural language processing by Pollack et al. [15,12] for two decades. The RAAM can be used as a sequential compressor (sRAAM): given a current data point and a representation of the current history it produces a representation of the new history. Conversely, given a history the sRAAM can reconstruct the previous data point and a representation of the previous history, so, theoretically it may be able to reproduce the entire history. Practically, it can be realized as an autoencoder neural network, and it is amenable to unsupervised training by standard back-propogation.

Our choice of a RAAM-based UL layer to overcome non-Markovian environments is partially motivated by the recent success seen by using less general *feedforward* auto-encoders to pre-train in unsupervised fashion a deep feedforward (non-recurrent) neural net [5]. Such stacks of auto-encoders have already been used as preprocessing for RL [13]. Here, sRAAM can be viewed as a significant generalization thereof: not only can spatial patterns be compactly encoded, but so can spatial-temporal patterns. The spatial-temporal compression achieved by the sRAAM potentially yields a Markovian code that significantly simplifies the RL problem.

In what follows, we describe the first systems, *SERVOs*, which combine a sequential constant-size compressor with reinforcement-learning. We examine the interplay between SCSC and RL under resource constraints for both.

Experiments show the strength of the approach for high-dimensional observation sequences and long time lags between relevant events.

2   Sequential Recurrent Auto-associative Memory

Assume we have a temporal sequence of data points $\mathcal{H}_n = (\boldsymbol{p}_1, \ldots, \boldsymbol{p}_n)$ where $\boldsymbol{p} \in \mathbb{R}^N$, which we shall refer to as the *history* at time $t = n$.

sRAAM is an example of a compressor that sequentially stores sequences into block of fixed size. An (N, M)–sRAAM is given by a pair of mappings (E, F),

$$E : \mathbb{R}^{N+M} \to \mathbb{R}^M$$
$$F : \mathbb{R}^M \to \mathbb{R}^{N+M},$$

where N is the dimension of the data points and M is the size of the memory block. The mappings E and F are often determined by parameters, and in such cases we make no distinction between the parameters and the mappings determined by them. Typically, sRAAM is implemented using a multi-layer perceptron with at least one hidden layer, which we shall refer to as the *code layer*. The code layer is the domain of F and the codomain of E. The input and output layers have size $N + M$, making it an autoencoder, and the code layer has size M.

Formally, the sRAAM compresses and decompresses a history as follows: Given data point $\boldsymbol{p}_i \in \mathbb{R}^N$ and a history, represented by $\boldsymbol{h}_{i-1} \in \mathbb{R}^M$ we can represent the new history, at time i with the map E,

$$E(\boldsymbol{p}_i \oplus \boldsymbol{h}_{i-1}) = \boldsymbol{h}_i.$$

Likewise, given a representation of a history $\boldsymbol{h}_i$ the mapping F is used to recover the data point $\boldsymbol{p}_i$ and the previous representation of the history $\boldsymbol{h}_{i-1}$,

$$F(\boldsymbol{h}_i) = \boldsymbol{p}_i \oplus \boldsymbol{h}_{i-1}.$$

The representation $\boldsymbol{h}_0$ of empty history $\mathcal{H}_0 = \emptyset$ needs to be decided upon to encode any history. See Figure 1.

In practice $F(E(\boldsymbol{p}_i \oplus \boldsymbol{h}_{i-1})) \neq \boldsymbol{p}_i \oplus \boldsymbol{h}_{i-1}$, so we write the result of the compress—decompress step as

$$F(E(\boldsymbol{p}_i \oplus \boldsymbol{h}_{i-1}i)) = \widehat{\boldsymbol{p}}_i \oplus \widehat{\boldsymbol{h}}_{i-1}.$$

Given a representation $\boldsymbol{h}_n$ of the history $(\boldsymbol{p}_1, \ldots, \boldsymbol{p}_n)$, found by iterating over E, we can decode the entire history $(\widehat{\boldsymbol{p}}_1, \ldots, \widehat{\boldsymbol{p}}_n)$ by iterating over F. We say that an sRAAM is *trained* when

$$\|\widehat{\boldsymbol{p}}_i - \boldsymbol{p}_i\| \leq \gamma^{k-i} \epsilon$$

for $1 \leq i \leq k$. The parameter $\gamma \geq 1$ is used to relax the importance of recovering the data points $\boldsymbol{p}$ as the sRAAM decodes further back in time. Since we intend

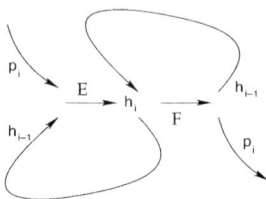

Fig. 1. sRAAM architecture. E, the *compressor*, takes data point p_i and a representation h_{i-1} of the history $\mathcal{H}_{i-1} = (p_1, \ldots, p_{i-1})$ and maps it to a representation h_i of the new history $\mathcal{H}_i$. F, the *decompressor*, takes a representaion h_i of the history and maps it to the previous data point p_i and representation h_{i-1}.

to use an SCSC to generate a representation h of a history $\mathcal{H}$ for the purpose of supplying a state to an RL module it is usually not necessary to put $\gamma = 1$.

Since we have a target $p_i \oplus h_{i-1}$ to train $\widehat{p}_i \oplus \widehat{h}_{i-1}$ towards for each point of the history, gradient based methods for the RAAM are attractive. Classically, the sRAAM has always been realized as an autoencoder and trained using back-propogation. That is, the weights (E, F) of the network are updated so that the output of the autoencoder $F(E(p_i \oplus h_{i-1})) = \widehat{p}_i \oplus \widehat{h}_{i-1}$ is more like the input $p_i \oplus h_{i-1}$. This is the only realization that we consider in this paper; we are using an out-of-the-box sRAAM in a new way.

One major concern with this training method is that the network is being trained on moving targets. After performing a step of back-propogation the mapping E changes, which in turn changes the input $p \oplus h$ at the next time step since p is changed. This is an issue that does not arise for an autoencoder which does not use a virtual recurrent connection. That said, the method of training is *often* successful, and it avoids the computational costs associated with methods such as back-propogation through time.

3   SERVO: SCSC Assisted RL

Here we introduce a proto-type version of an architecture which combines SCSC and RL, and refer to such systems as *SERVOs*. The UL layer which uses an sRAAM, which assumes the form of an autoencoder neural network, and the RL layer uses SARSA(λ) [22]. The training of the two layers takes place independently in a back-forth manner. After a number of episodes the sequential compressor is trained. After training the compressor, the code is passed through an intermediary layer which is used to establish internal states and is determined by straight-forward clustering, or Vector Quantization (VQ). Using experience replay, the value-fuction is then learned using SARSA(λ) on the states provided by the intermediary layer. The use of an internal layer allows the system to do tabular RL. After the reinforcement-learning, the agent interacts with the environment using the updated policy to collect more samples, these samples are used to repeat the process: train the compressor (E, F), update the intermediary layer V, use experience replay to generate a new policy Q. See Figure 2.

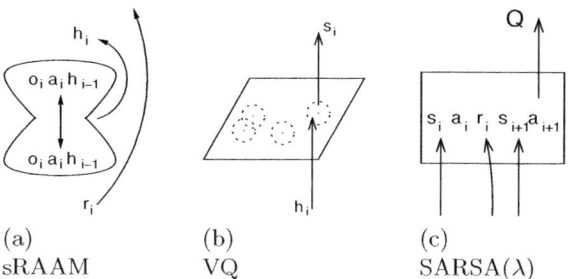

(a)
sRAAM

(b)
VQ

(c)
SARSA(λ)

Fig. 2. SERVO. The sRAAM autoencoder is trained using back-propogation on $\boldsymbol{p}_i \oplus \boldsymbol{h}_{i-1}$. After training $\boldsymbol{h}_i$ is generated using E and is passed the internal state layer. VQ assigns an internal state $\boldsymbol{s}_i$ to the represntation $\boldsymbol{h}_i$ of the history. The RL layer receives Markovian data and learns an action-value function using SARSA(λ).

3.1 UL Layer: sRAAM

We first describe how to train on a single episode $\mathcal{H} = (\boldsymbol{p}_1, \ldots, \boldsymbol{p}_n)$, where $\boldsymbol{p}_i$ is a vector representation of both the observation and action at step i. Start with an arbitrary choice for the representation $\boldsymbol{h}_0$ of the empty history $\mathcal{H}_0 = \emptyset$. The training process walks over the history: Given $\boldsymbol{p}_i$ and $\boldsymbol{h}_{i-1}$ use the autoencoder (E, F) to generate an error δ,

$$\delta = \boldsymbol{p}_i \oplus \boldsymbol{h}_{i-1} - F(E(\boldsymbol{p}_i \oplus \boldsymbol{h}_{i-1}))$$

then perform a step of back-propogation on the autoencoder. After updating the weights E and F, find a represention $\boldsymbol{h}_i$ of the history up to step i,

$$\boldsymbol{h}_i = E(\boldsymbol{p}_i \oplus \boldsymbol{h}_{i-1}),$$

then iterate, using $\boldsymbol{p}_{i+1}$ and $\boldsymbol{h}_i$.

Given the current policy the agent interacts with its environment for I episodes to generate a collection of episodes $\Xi = \{\mathcal{H}\}_I$. The sRAAM is trained by repeatedly sampling from Ξ and then performing an epoch of back-propogation by walking over the observation-action pairs in the episode. See Figure 2a.

3.2 Internal State Layer: VQ

The building of the internal state layer takes place simultaneously with the reinforcement learning. To maintain a clear exposition we present the two processes separately. After training the sRAAM we walk through each episode $(\boldsymbol{p}_1, \ldots, \boldsymbol{p}_n)$ to generate representations of the history at each step: $(\boldsymbol{h}_1, \ldots, \boldsymbol{h}_n)$. For an (N, M)-sRAAM the code lives in M-dimensional space. We generate a set of internal states by a (cheap) clustering all the representations $\{\boldsymbol{h}\}$ produced by each of the episodes. Let $\mathcal{S}$ be a collection of points $s \in \mathbb{R}^M$ representing the internal states of the SERVO. The internal state layer is initialized to the empty set after training the UL layer. Fix a value for the parameter κ. Given a point $\boldsymbol{h}$ the point

s^* in $\mathcal{S}$ closest to it is found. The point h is added to $\mathcal{S}$ if the squared Euclidean distance between h and s^* is greater than κ. Otherwise, for the purpose of the reinforcement-learning, h is identified with s^*. This layer is built by randomly choosing an episode and then considering, in order, all the h associated with the episode. The layer is finished being built, as is the reinforcement-learning after each episode has been walked through exactly once. See Figure 2b.

3.3   RL Layer: SARSA(λ)

A review of SARSA(λ) can be found in [22]. We learn on each of the episodes as the internal state layer is built, as follows. For a given episode the data coming into the system can be parsed into 5-tuples, $(o_i, a_i, r_i, o_{i+1}, a_{i+1})$. The SCSC maps $o_i \oplus a_i$ to h_i, as explained above. The internal layer maps h_i to an internal state s_i. This mapping is determined while the learning proceeds; if h_i is not within $\sqrt{\kappa}$ of the point s^* to which it is closest, then h_i is added to the internal layer and it is mapped to itself. Otherwise h is mapped to s^*. Finally, the 5-tuple that is passed to the RL layer has the form, $(s_i, a_i, r_i, s_{i+1}, a_{i+1})$. The function Q is trained on each of the episodes in an arbitrary order using *off-line* SARSA(λ). See Figure 2c.

4   Experiments and Results

4.1   Partially Observable Vision Maze

As a proof of concept to show that this system handles high-dimensional observations with some memory requirement, we performed a visual navigation experiment (see Figure 3). The agent's observations are given by its internal camera, always aimed forward, and its actions are to go forward, rotate left or right, or turn around. Each observation (16×10 pixels) also contains Gaussian noise to avoid possible trivial solutions where the agent memorizes all the views. Each episode begins by placing the agent at a random position and orientation in the maze.

We used a large three layer sRAAM with a code layer of size 100. Observations are 160-dimensional and there are 4 actions, therefore the shape of our network is $264 - 100 - 264$. Each episode lasts until either the goal is reached or the agent has taken 250 actions. **NB:** Using a random walk requires an average of 220 actions to reach the goal, and on average only one-quarter of the walks reach the goal within the 250 allotted actions. A training iteration consisted of data gathering: 2000 walks/rollouts generated using the current policy, followed by training the sRAAM (learning rate 0.01) for 300 epochs, followed by experience replay to develop the value function (discount factor 0.8, $\kappa = 0.9$, and SARSA learning rate 0.1). The actions shifted from 50% exploration to pure exploitation linearly through the training iterations.

We compared SERVO to the state-of-the-art SNES [17] algorithm, which directly searches the weight space of RNNs to find better controllers. SNES generates a population of controllers from a gaussian distribution, and based on the

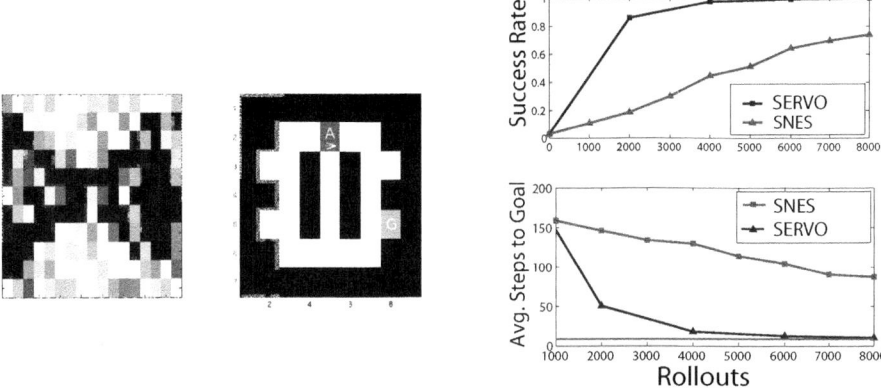

Fig. 3. Left: Example 16x10 dimensional observation. Middle: Top-down maze view (never observed by the agent). Right: Experimental comparison between SERVO and SNES. A "roll-out" is a single controllers interaction with the environment: from a start position, actions are taken until the goal is reached or time runs out. Compared are the average number of steps and success rate between the best SNES controller and SERVO, averaged over 10 experiments. The green line (constant value) represents optimal performance.

fitness evaluation (each individual started in 50 random start positions), computes the natural gradient to move the distribution to a presumably better location. Figure 4 for a comparison of the two methods. Due to gradient information provided by the fitness function, SNES is also able to deal with this task.

4.2 Learning to Wait

We try a task with higher-dimensional inputs and explicitly require longer memory (up to 12 steps). The agent is placed at one end of a corridor, and can either move forward or wait. The goal is to move through the door at the far end of the corridor, where it is given a visual signal that vanishes in the next frame. One of the signals, *A, B, C, D*, is shown for a single frame when the agent reaches the door, corresponding to a waiting time of *6, 8, 10,* and *12* frames respectively. The agent receives a (positive) reward when it waits the exact number of frames indicated before exiting, otherwise the agent receives no reward and goes back to the start. The episode ends either when the agent walks through the door or 20 frames have passed (to avoid extremely long episodes). This is a difficult task: in the case of letter "D" a random policy will on average require 2^{12} trials to make one successful walk.

The agent receives noisy visual input in the form of 32×20 pixel image. We had trouble getting SERVO to work robustly (with noise) in this task, so we first had to train and use an autoencoder for de-noising the observations before they are passed to the sRAAM. The autoencoder was trained on-line over 5k random walks. After training the autoencoder, the agent performs a series of random

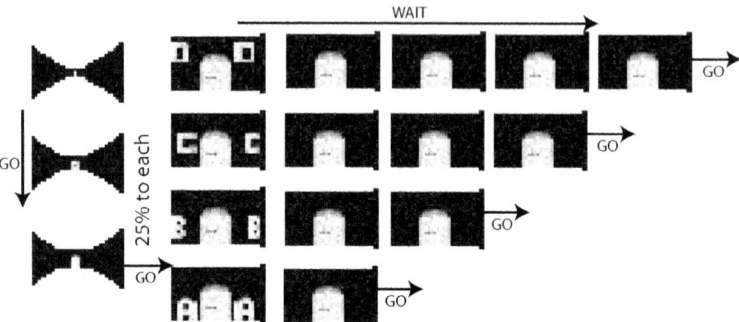

Fig. 4. Shown are the various views of the corridor from the agent's vantage point. The leftmost images are observed as the agent approaches the door. The second column shows the various wait signals, indicating the number of frames to wait before exiting.

walks (approx. 100k) to collect encoded training samples for the SERVO. The SERVO is then trained batchwise: (1) 200 epochs of training to compress the *successful* episodes, first training the UL layer and then training the RL layer, as described in Section 3. (2) the agent again interacts with the environment for 100 episodes to evaluate its policy. Training continues until the agent has achieved better than 90% success rate[1].

In this task, there are only a few general sequences worth encoding. They are difficult to find and locating one does not help to find the others. A "fitness landscape" for RNN controllers in this task would be made up of sharp ridges and vast plateaus. It may seem that all that can be done here is to find and store the best sequences. Yet, the SERVO technique goes further and compresses these sequences. A representation of a current sequence can then be located in the space of compressed previously seen valuable seqeunces (the VQ layer). The current sequence can then be identified with the closest prototype.

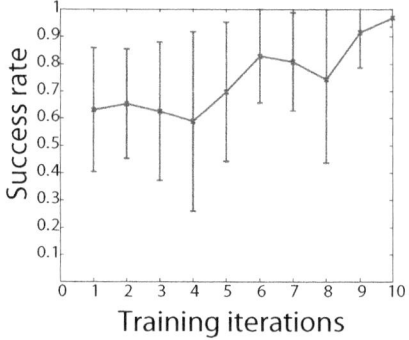

Fig. 5. The average success rate (n=10), with standard deviation for the corridor experiment. After each training episode (200 epochs) the SERVO is tested for 100 episodes.

5   Discussion

In problems with high-dimensional observations and deep memory requirements, direct search of weight-space for an RNN controller is quite a difficult task (even

---

[1] There is a video of SERVO operation at www.idsia.ch/~gisslen/SERVOagent.html

with a state-of-the-art method such as SNES). It must find relevant regularities to build on in parameter space using only the fitness measures of the individuals. The high-dimensionality and generality of some problems may be too difficult for direct evolutionary search. In contrast, the SERVO architecture decouples the problem of encoding the relevant spatiotemporal regularities from learning how to act on them. The SERVO separates the learning problem into two components: (1) unsupervised learning of an autoencoder to provide a (quasi-)Markovian code, and (2) classical reinforcement-learning.

The compression capacity of the sRAAM is limited, and cannot be expected to recall all histories of a given length. However, since the sequences are generated by way of reinforcement learning the compressor can in principle learn to represent the important histories unambiguously. This biased training of the unsupervised layer allows the agent to improve its policy, steering it towards increasingly valuable sequences, thereby further refining the UL layer.

We have demonstrated that the use of an SCSC is a competitive method for solving high-dimensional POMDPs with long time lags. Yet, the current system is not sufficiently stable for real-world AGIs. Future work will refine this first-generation SERVO architecture.

Acknowledgments. We would like to thank Faustino Gomez for his insights and thoughtful feedback. We would also like to thank Bas Steunebrink and Jan Koutník for helping with coding. This research was funded in part through the following grants: Sinergia (CRSIKO 122697), NeuralDynamics (grant 270247), NanoBioTouch (36RANANO), IM-Clever (231722), and SNF (200020-122124).

References

1. Amari, S.: Natural gradient works efficiently in learning. Neural Computation 10(2), 251–276 (1998)
2. Anderson, C.W.: Strategy learning with multilayer connectionist representations. Technical Report TR87-509.3, GTE Labs, Waltham, MA (1987)
3. Bakker, B.: Reinforcement learning with Long Short-Term Memory. In: Dietterich, T.G., Becker, S., Ghahramani, Z. (eds.) Advances in Neural Information Processing Systems, vol. 14. MIT Press, Cambridge (2002)
4. Barto, A.G., Sutton, R.S., Anderson, C.W.: Neuronlike adaptive elements that can solve difficult learning control problems. IEEE Transactions on Systems, Man, and Cybernetics, SMC 13, 834–846 (1983)
5. Bengio, Y., Lamblin, P., Popovici, D., Larochelle, H.: Greedy layer-wise training of deep networks. Neural Information Processing Systems (NIPS) (2007)
6. Gomez, F.J., Miikkulainen, R.: Solving non-Markovian control tasks with neuroevolution. In: Proc. IJCAI 1999, Denver, CO. Morgan Kaufman, San Francisco (1999)
7. Gomez, F.J., Schmidhuber, J., Miikkulainen, R.: Efficient non-linear control through neuroevolution. In: Fürnkranz, J., Scheffer, T., Spiliopoulou, M. (eds.) ECML 2006. LNCS (LNAI), vol. 4212, pp. 654–662. Springer, Heidelberg (2006)
8. Gruau, F., Whitley, D., Pyeatt, L.: A comparison between cellular encoding and direct encoding for genetic neural networks. Technical Report NC-TR-96-048, NeuroCOLT (1996)

9. Hansen, N., Ostermeier, A.: Completely derandomized self-adaptation in evolution strategies. Evolutionary Computation 9(2), 159–195 (2001)
10. Hochreiter, S., Schmidhuber, J.: Long short-term memory. Neural Computation 9(8), 1735–1780 (1997)
11. Hutter, M.: Universal Artificial Intelligence: Sequential Decisions based on Algorithmic Probability. Springer, Berlin (2004); (On J. Schmidhuber's SNF grant 20-61847)
12. Kolen, J.F., Pollack, J.B.: Back propagation is sensitive to initial conditions. Advances in neural information processing systems 3, 860–867 (1991)
13. Lange, S., Riedmiller, M.: Deep Auto-Encoder Neural Networks in Reinforcement Learning. IJCNN (2010)
14. Moriarty, D.E., Miikkulainen, R.: Efficient reinforcement learning through symbiotic evolution. Machine Learning 22, 11–32 (1996)
15. Pollack, J.B.: Recursive distributed representations. Artificial Intelligence 46(1-2), 77–105 (1990)
16. Saravanan, N., Fogel, D.B.: Evolving neural control systems. IEEE Expert, 23–27 (June 1995)
17. Schaul, T., Glasmachers, T., Schmidhuber, J.: High dimensions and heavy tails for natural evolution strategies. In: Genetic and Evolutionary Computation Conference (GECCO) (2011)
18. Schmidhuber, J.: A local learning algorithm for dynamic feedforward and recurrent networks. Connection Science 1(4), 403–412 (1989)
19. Schmidhuber, J.: Recurrent networks adjusted by adaptive critics. In: Proc. IEEE/INNS International Joint Conference on Neural Networks, Washington, D. C, vol. 1, pp. 719–722 (1990)
20. Schmidhuber, J.: Reinforcement learning in Markovian and non-Markovian environments. In: Lippman, D.S., Moody, J.E., Touretzky, D.S. (eds.) Advances in Neural Information Processing Systems (NIPS), vol. 3, pp. 500–506. Morgan Kaufmann, San Francisco (1991)
21. Stanley, K.O., Miikkulainen, R.: Evolving neural networks through augmenting topologies. Evolutionary Computation 10, 99–127 (2002)
22. Sutton, R., Barto, A.: Reinforcement learning: An introduction. MIT Press, Cambridge (1998)
23. Sutton, R.S., Mcallester, D., Singh, S., Mansour, Y.: Policy gradient methods for reinforcement learning with function approximation. In: Advances in Neural Information Processing Systems, vol. 12, pp. 1057–1063. MIT Press, Cambridge (2000)
24. Werbos, P.J.: Neural networks for control and system identification. In: Proceedings of IEEE/CDC Tampa, Florida (1989)
25. Wierstra, D., Schmidhuber, J.: Policy gradient critics. In: Kok, J.N., Koronacki, J., Lopez de Mantaras, R., Matwin, S., Mladenič, D., Skowron, A. (eds.) ECML 2007. LNCS (LNAI), vol. 4701, pp. 466–477. Springer, Heidelberg (2007)
26. Wierstra, D., Schaul, T., Peters, J., Schmidhuber, J.: Natural evolution strategies. In: Congress on Evolutionary Computation CEC (2008)
27. Yao, X.: Xin Yao. A review of evolutionary artificial neural networks. International Journal of Intelligent Systems 4, 203–222 (1993)

Planning to Be Surprised: Optimal Bayesian Exploration in Dynamic Environments

Yi Sun, Faustino Gomez, and Jürgen Schmidhuber

IDSIA, Galleria 2, Manno, CH-6928, Switzerland
{yi,tino,juergen}@idsia.ch

Abstract. To maximize its success, an AGI typically needs to explore its initially unknown world. Is there an optimal way of doing so? Here we derive an affirmative answer for a broad class of environments.

1 Introduction

An intelligent agent is sent to explore an unknown environment. Over the course of its mission, the agent makes observations, carries out actions, and incrementally builds up a model of the environment from this interaction. Since the way in which the agent selects actions may greatly affect the efficiency of the exploration, the following question naturally arises:

> *How should the agent choose the actions such that the knowledge about the environment accumulates as quickly as possible?*

In this paper, this question is addressed under a classical framework in which the agent improves its model of the environment through probabilistic inference, and learning progress is measured in terms of Shannon information gain. We show that the agent can, at least in principle, optimally choose actions based on previous experiences, such that the cumulative expected information gain is maximized.

The rest of the paper is organized as follows: Section 2 reviews the basic concepts and establishes the terminology; Section 3 elaborates the principle of optimal Bayesian exploration; Section 4 presents a simple experiment; Related work is briefly reviewed in Section 5; Section 6 concludes the paper.

2 Preliminaries

Suppose that the agent interacts with the environment in discrete time cycles $t = 1, 2, \ldots$. In each cycle, the agent performs an action, a, then receives a sensory input, o. A *history*, h, is either the empty string, $\emptyset$, or a string of the form $a_1 o_1 \cdots a_t o_t$ for some t, and ha and hao refer to the strings resulting from appending a and ao to h, respectively.

2.1 Learning from Sequential Interactions

To facilitate the subsequent discussion under a probabilistic framework, we make the following assumptions:

J. Schmidhuber, K.R. Thórisson, and M. Looks (Eds.): AGI 2011, LNAI 6830, pp. 41–51, 2011.
© Springer-Verlag Berlin Heidelberg 2011

Assumption I. The models of the environment under consideration are fully described by a random element Θ which *depends solely on the environment*. Moreover, the agent's initial knowledge about Θ is summarized by a prior density $p(\theta)$.

Assumption II. The agent is equipped with a *conditional predictor* $p(o|ha; \theta)$, i.e. the agent is capable of refining its prediction in the light of information about Θ.

Using $p(\theta)$ and $p(o|ha; \theta)$ as building blocks, it is straightforward to formulate learning in terms of probabilistic inference. From Assumption **I**, given the history h, the agent's knowledge about Θ is fully summarized by $p(\theta|h)$. According to Bayes rule, $p(\theta|hao) = \frac{p(\theta|ha)p(o|ha;\theta)}{p(o|ha)}$, with $p(o|ha) = \int p(o|ha, \theta) p(\theta|h) \, d\theta$. The term $p(\theta|ha)$ represents the agent's current knowledge about Θ given history h and an additional action a. Since Θ depends solely on the environment, and, importantly, *knowing the action without subsequent observations cannot change the agent's state of knowledge about* Θ, then $p(\theta|ha) = p(\theta|h)$, and thus the knowledge about Θ can be updated using

$$p(\theta|hao) = p(\theta|h) \cdot \frac{p(o|ha; \theta)}{p(o|ha)}. \tag{1}$$

It is worth pointing out that $p(o|ha; \theta)$ is chosen before entering the environment. It is not required that it match the true dynamics of the environment, but the effectiveness of the learning certainly depends on the choices of $p(o|ha; \theta)$. For example, if $\Theta \in \mathbb{R}$, and $p(o|ha; \theta)$ depends on θ only through its sign, then no knowledge other than the sign of Θ can be learned.

2.2 Information Gain as Learning Progress

Let h and h' be two histories such that h is a prefix of h'. The respective posterior distributions of Θ are $p(\theta|h)$ and $p(\theta|h')$. Using h as a reference point, the amount of information gained when the history grows to h' can be measured using the KL divergence between $p(\theta|h)$ and $p(\theta|h')$. This *information gain* from h to h' is defined as

$$g(h'\|h) = KL\left(p(\theta|h') \,\|\, p(\theta|h)\right) = \int p(\theta|h') \log \frac{p(\theta|h')}{p(\theta|h)} \, d\theta.$$

As a special case, if $h = \emptyset$, then $g(h') = g(h'\|\emptyset)$ is the *cumulative information gain* with respect to the prior $p(\theta)$. We also write $g(ao\|h)$ for $g(hao\|h)$, which denotes the information gained from an additional action-observation pair.

From an information theoretic point of view, the KL divergence between two distributions p and q represents the additional number of bits required to encode elements sampled from p, using optimal coding strategy designed for q. This can be interpreted as the degree of 'unexpectedness' or 'surprise' caused by observing samples from p when expecting samples from q.

The key property information gain for the treatment below is the following decomposition: Let h be a prefix of h' and h' be a prefix of h'', then

$$\mathbb{E}_{h''|h'} g\left(h''\|h\right) = g\left(h'\|h\right) + \mathbb{E}_{h''|h'} g\left(h''\|h'\right). \qquad (2)$$

That is, the information gain is *additive in expectation*.

Having defined the information gain from trajectories ending with observations, one may proceed to define the *expected information gain* of performing action a, before observing the outcome o. Formally, the *expected information gain* of performing a with respect to the current history h is given by $\bar{g}\left(a\|h\right) = \mathbb{E}_{o|ha} g\left(ao\|h\right)$. A simple derivation gives

$$\bar{g}\left(a\|h\right) = \sum_o \int p\left(o, \theta|ha\right) \log \frac{p\left(o, \theta|ha\right)}{p\left(\theta|ha\right) p\left(o|ha\right)} d\theta = I\left(O; \Theta|ha\right),$$

which means that $\bar{g}\left(a\|h\right)$ is the mutual information between Θ and the random variable O representing the unknown observation, conditioned on the history h and action a.

3   Optimal Bayesian Exploration

In this section, the general principle of optimal Bayesian exploration in dynamic environments is presented. We first give results obtained by assuming a fixed limited life span for our agent, then discuss a condition required to extend this to infinite time horizons.

3.1   Results for Finite Time Horizon

Suppose that the agent has experienced history h, and is about to choose τ more actions in the future. Let π be a policy mapping the set of histories to the set of actions, such that the agent performs a with probability $\pi\left(a|h\right)$ given h. Define the *curiosity Q-value* $q_\pi^\tau\left(h, a\right)$ as the expected information gained from the additional τ actions, assuming that the agent performs a in the next step and follows policy π in the remaining $\tau - 1$ steps. Formally, for $\tau = 1$,

$$q_\pi^1\left(h, a\right) = \mathbb{E}_{o|ha} g\left(ao\|h\right) = \bar{g}\left(a\|h\right),$$

and for $\tau > 1$,

$$q_\pi^\tau\left(h, a\right) = \mathbb{E}_{o|ha} \mathbb{E}_{a_1|hao} \mathbb{E}_{o_1|haoa_1} \cdots \mathbb{E}_{o_{\tau-1}|h\cdots a_{\tau-1}} g\left(haoa_1 o_1 \cdots a_{\tau-1} o_{\tau-1}\|h\right)$$
$$= \mathbb{E}_{o|ha} \mathbb{E}_{a_1 o_1 \cdots a_{\tau-1} o_{\tau-1}|hao} g\left(haoa_1 o_1 \cdots a_{\tau-1} o_{\tau-1}\|h\right).$$

The curiosity Q-value can be defined recursively. Applying Eq. 2 for $\tau = 2$,

$$q_\pi^2(h, a) = \mathbb{E}_{o|ha}\mathbb{E}_{a_1 o_1|hao} g(haoa_1 o_1 \| h)$$
$$= \mathbb{E}_{o|ha}\left[g(ao\|h) + \mathbb{E}_{a_1 o_1|hao} g(a_1 o_1 \| hao)\right]$$
$$= \bar{g}(a\|h) + \mathbb{E}_{o|ha}\mathbb{E}_{a'|hao} q_\pi^1(hao, a').$$

And for $\tau > 2$,

$$q_\pi^\tau(h, a) = \mathbb{E}_{o|ha}\mathbb{E}_{a_1 o_1 \cdots a_{\tau-1} o_{\tau-1}|hao} g(haoa_1 o_1 \cdots a_{\tau-1} o_{\tau-1} \| h)$$
$$= \mathbb{E}_{o|ha}\left[g(ao\|h) + \mathbb{E}_{a_1 o_1 \cdots a_{\tau-1} o_{\tau-1}} g(haoa_1 o_1 \cdots a_{\tau-1} o_{\tau-1} \| hao)\right]$$
$$= \bar{g}(a\|h) + \mathbb{E}_{o|ha}\mathbb{E}_{a'|hao} q_\pi^{\tau-1}(hao, a'). \tag{3}$$

Noting that Eq.3 bears great resemblance to the definition of state-action values ($Q(s, a)$) in reinforcement learning, one can similarly define the *curiosity value* of a particular history as $v_\pi^\tau(h) = \mathbb{E}_{a|h} q_\pi^\tau(h, a)$, analogous to state values ($V(s)$), which can also be iteratively defined as $v_\pi^1(h) = \mathbb{E}_{a|h}\bar{g}(a\|h)$, and

$$v_\pi^\tau(h) = \mathbb{E}_{a|h}\left[\bar{g}(a\|h) + \mathbb{E}_{o|ha} v_\pi^{\tau-1}(hao)\right].$$

The curiosity value $v_\pi^\tau(h)$ is the expected information gain of performing the additional τ steps, assuming that the agent follows policy π. The two notations can be combined to write

$$q_\pi^\tau(h, a) = \bar{g}(a\|h) + \mathbb{E}_{o|ha} v_\pi^{\tau-1}(hao). \tag{4}$$

This equation has an interesting interpretation: since the agent is operating in a dynamic environment, it has to take into account not only the immediate expected information gain of performing the current action, i.e., $\bar{g}(a\|h)$, but also the expected curiosity value of the situation in which the agent ends up due to the action, i.e., $v_\pi^{\tau-1}(hao)$. As a consequence, *the agent needs to choose actions that balance the two factors in order to improve its total expected information gain.*

Now we show that there is a optimal policy π_*, which leads to the maximum cumulative expected information gain given any history h. To obtain the optimal policy, one may work backwards in τ, taking greedy actions with respect to the curiosity Q-values at each time step. Namely, for $\tau = 1$, let

$$q^1(h, a) = \bar{g}(a\|h), \; \pi_*^1(h) = \arg\max_a \bar{g}(a\|h), \text{ and } v^1(h) = \max_a \bar{g}(a\|h),$$

such that $v^1(h) = q^1(h, \pi_*^1(h))$, and for $\tau > 1$, let

$$q^\tau(h, a) = \bar{g}(a\|h) + \mathbb{E}_{o|ha}\left[\max_{a'} q^{\tau-1}(a'|hao)\right] = \bar{g}(a\|h) + \mathbb{E}_{o|ha} v^{\tau-1}(hao),$$

with $\pi_*^\tau(h) = \arg\max_a q^\tau(h, a)$ and $v^\tau(h) = \max_a q^\tau(h, a)$. We show that $\pi_*^\tau(h)$ is indeed the optimal policy for any given τ and h in the sense that the curiosity value, when following π_*^τ, is maximized. To see this, take any other strategy π, first notice that

$$v^1(h) = \max_a \bar{g}(a\|h) \geq \mathbb{E}_{a|h}\bar{g}(a\|h) = v_\pi^1(h).$$

Moreover, assuming $v^\tau(h) \geq v_\pi^\tau(h)$,

$$v^{\tau+1}(h) = \max_a \left[\bar{g}(a\|h) + \mathbb{E}_{o|ha}v^\tau(hao)\right] \geq \max_a \left[\bar{g}(a\|h) + \mathbb{E}_{o|ha}v_\pi^\tau(hao)\right]$$

$$\geq \mathbb{E}_{a|h}\left[\bar{g}(a\|h) + \mathbb{E}_{o|ha}v_\pi^\tau(hao)\right] = v_\pi^{\tau+1}(h).$$

Therefore $v^\tau(h) \geq v_\pi^\tau(h)$ holds for arbitrary τ, h, and π. The same can be shown for curiosity Q-values, namely, $q^\tau(h,a) \geq q_\pi^\tau(h,a)$, for all τ, h, a, and π.

Now consider that the agent has a fixed life span T. It can be seen that at time t, the agent has to perform $\pi_*^{T-t}(h_{t-1})$ to maximize the expected information gain in the remaining $T-t$ steps. Here $h_{t-1} = a_1 o_1 \cdots a_{t-1} o_{t-1}$ is the history at time t. However, from Eq.2,

$$\mathbb{E}_{h_T|h_{t-1}}g(h_T) = g(h_{t-1}) + \mathbb{E}_{h_T|h_{t-1}}g(h_T\|h_{t-1}).$$

Note that at time t, $g(h_{t-1})$ is a constant, thus *maximizing the cumulative expected information gain in the remaining time steps is equivalent to maximizing the expected information gain of the whole trajectory with respect to the prior.* The result is summarized in the following proposition:

Proposition 1. *Let* $q^1(h,a) = \bar{g}(a\|h)$, $v^1(h) = \max_a q^1(h,a)$, *and*

$$q^\tau(h,a) = \bar{g}(a\|h) + \mathbb{E}_{o|ha}v^{\tau-1}(hao), \quad v^\tau(h) = \max_a q^\tau(h,a),$$

then the policy $\pi_*^\tau(h) = \arg\max_a q^\tau(h,a)$ *is optimal in the sense that* $v^\tau(h) \geq v_\pi^\tau(h)$, $q^\tau(h,a) \geq q_\pi^\tau(h,a)$ *for any* π, τ, h *and* a.

In particular, for an agent with fixed life span T, *following* $\pi_*^{T-t}(h_{t-1})$ *at time* $t = 1, \ldots, T$ *is optimal in the sense that the expected cumulative information gain with respect to the prior is maximized.*

The definition of the optimal exploration policy is constructive, which means that it can be readily implemented, provided that the number of actions and possible observations is finite so that the expectation and maximization can be computed exactly. However, the cost of computing such a policy is $O((n_o n_a)^\tau)$, where n_o and n_a are the number of possible observations and actions, respectively. Since the cost is exponential on τ, planning with large number of look ahead steps is infeasible, and approximation heuristics must be used in practice.

3.2   Non-triviality of the Result

Intuitively, the recursive definition of the curiosity (Q) value is simple, and bears clear resemblance to its counterpart in reinforcement learning. It might be tempting to think that the result is nothing more than solving the finite horizon reinforcement learning problem using $\bar{g}(a\|h)$ or $g(ao\|h)$ as the reward signals. However, this is not the case.

First, note that the decomposition Eq.2 is a direct consequence of the formulation of the KL divergence. The decomposition does not necessarily hold if $g(h)$ is replaced with other types of measures of information gain.

Second, it is worth pointing out that $g(ao\|h)$ and $\bar{g}(a\|h)$ behave differently from normal reward signals in the sense that they are *additive only in expectation*, while in the reinforcement learning setup, the reward signals are usually assumed to be additive, i.e., adding reward signals together is always meaningful. Consider a simple problem with only two actions. If $g(ao\|h)$ is a plain reward function, then $g(ao\|h) + g(a'o'\|hao)$ should be meaningful, no matter if a and o is known or not. But this is not the case, since the sum does not have a valid information theoretic interpretation. On the other hand, the sum is meaningful *in expectation*. Namely, when o has *not* been observed, from Eq.2,

$$g(ao\|h) + \mathbb{E}_{o'|haoa'}g(a'o'\|hao) = \mathbb{E}_{o'|haoa'}g(aoa'o'\|h),$$

the sum can be interpreted as the expectation of the information gained from h to $haoa'o'$. This result shows that $g(ao\|h)$ and $\bar{g}(a\|h)$ can be treated as additive reward signals only when one is planning ahead.

To emphasize the difference further, note that all immediate information gains $g(ao\|h)$ are non-negative since they are essentially KL divergence. A natural assumption would be that the information gain $g(h)$, which is the sum of all $g(ao\|h)$ in expectation, grows monotonically when the length of the history increases. However, this is not the case, see Figure 1 for example. Although $g(ao\|h)$ is always non-negative, some of the gain may pull θ closer to its prior density $p(\theta)$, resulting in a decrease of KL divergence between $p(\theta|h)$ and $p(\theta)$. This is never the case if one considers the normal reward signals in reinforcement learning, where the accumulated reward would never decrease if all rewards are non-negative.

3.3   Extending to Infinite Horizon

Having to restrict the maximum life span of the agent is rather inconvenient. It is tempting to define the curiosity Q-value in the infinite time horizon case as the limit of curiosity Q-values with increasing life spans, $T \to \infty$. However, this cannot be achieved without additional technical constraints. For example, consider simple coin tossing. Assuming a $Beta(1,1)$ over the probability of seeing heads, then the expected cumulative information gain for the next T flips is given by

$$v^T(h_1) = I(\Theta; X_1, \dots, X_T) \sim \log T.$$

With increasing T, $v^T(h_1) \to \infty$. A frequently used approach to simplifying the math is to introduce a discount factor γ $(0 \leq \gamma < 1)$, as used in reinforcement learning. Assume that the agent has a maximum τ actions left, but before finishing the τ actions it may be forced to leave the environment with probability $1 - \gamma$ at each time step. In this case, the curiosity Q-value becomes $q_\pi^{\gamma,1}(h,a) = \bar{g}(a\|h)$, and

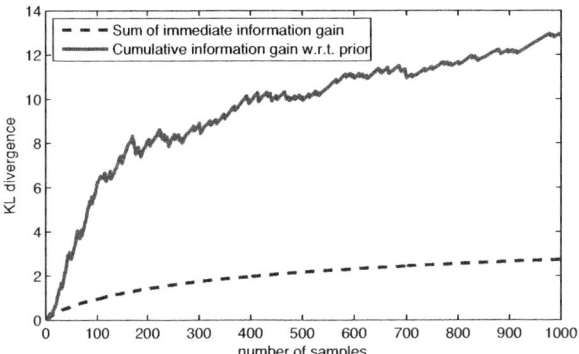

Fig. 1. Illustration of the difference between the sum of one-step information gain and the cumulative information gain with respect to the prior. In this case, 1000 independent samples are generated from a distribution over finite sample space $\{1, 2, 3\}$, with $p(x = 1) = 0.1$, $p(x = 2) = 0.5$, and $p(x = 3) = 0.4$. The task of learning is to recover the mass function from the samples, assuming a Dirichlet prior $Dir\left(\frac{50}{3}, \frac{50}{3}, \frac{50}{3}\right)$. The KL divergence between two Dirichlet distributions are computed according to [5]. It is clear from the graph that the cumulative information gain fluctuates when the number of samples increases, while the sum of the one-step information gain increases monotonically. It also shows that the difference between the two quantities can be large.

$$q_\pi^{\gamma,\tau}(h, a) = (1 - \gamma)\bar{g}(a\|h) + \gamma\left[\bar{g}(a\|h) + \mathbb{E}_{o|ha}\mathbb{E}_{a'|hao}q_\pi^{\gamma,\tau-1}(hao, a')\right]$$
$$= \bar{g}(a\|h) + \gamma\mathbb{E}_{o|ha}\mathbb{E}_{a'|hao}q_\pi^{\gamma,\tau-1}(hao, a').$$

One may also interpret $q_\pi^{\gamma,\tau}(h, a)$ as a linear combination of curiosity Q-values without the discount,

$$q_\pi^{\gamma,\tau}(h, a) = (1 - \gamma)\sum_{t=1}^{\tau}\gamma^{t-1}q_\pi^t(h, a) + \gamma^\tau q_\pi^\tau(h, a).$$

Note that curiosity Q-values with larger look-ahead steps are weighed exponentially less.

The optimal policy in the discounted case is given by

$$q^{\gamma,1}(h, a) = \bar{g}(a\|h), \quad v^{\gamma,1}(h) = \max_a q^{\gamma,1}(h, a),$$

and

$$q^{\gamma,\tau}(h, a) = \bar{g}(a\|h) + \gamma\mathbb{E}_{o|ha}v^{\gamma,\tau-1}(hao), \quad v^{\gamma,\tau}(h) = \max_a q^{\gamma,\tau}(h, a).$$

The optimal actions are given by $\pi_*^{\gamma,\tau}(h) = \arg\max_a q^{\gamma,\tau}(h, a)$. The proof that $\pi_*^{\gamma,\tau}$ is optimal is similar to the one for the finite horizon case (section 3.1) and thus is omitted here.

Adding the discount enables one to define the curiosity Q-value in infinite time horizon in a number of cases. However, it is still possible to construct scenarios where such discount fails. Consider a infinite list of bandits. For bandit n, there are n possible outcomes with Dirichlet prior $Dir\left(\frac{1}{n}, \ldots, \frac{1}{n}\right)$. The expected information gain of pulling bandit n for the first time is then given by

$$\log n - \psi(2) + \log\left(1 + \frac{1}{n}\right) \sim \log n,$$

with $\psi(\cdot)$ being the digamma function. Assume at time t, only the first $e^{e^{2t}}$ bandits are available, thus the curiosity Q-value in finite time horizon is always finite. However, since the largest expected information gain grows at speed e^{t^2}, for any given $\gamma > 0$, $q^{\gamma,\tau}$ goes to infinity with increasing τ. This example gives the intuition that to make the curiosity Q-value meaningful, the 'total information content' of the environment (or its growing speed) must be bounded.

The following technical Lemma gives a sufficient condition for when such extension is meaningful.

Lemma 1. *We have*

$$0 \leq q^{\gamma,\tau+1}(h, a) - q^{\gamma,\tau}(h, a) \leq \gamma^{\tau} \mathbb{E}_{o|ha} \max_{a_1} \mathbb{E}_{o_1|haoa_1} \cdots \max_{a_\tau} \bar{g}(a_\tau \| h \cdots o_{\tau-1}).$$

Proof. Expand $q^{\gamma,\tau}$ and $q^{\gamma,\tau+1}$, and note that $|\max X - \max Y| \leq \max |X - Y|$, then

$$q_\pi^{\gamma,\tau+1}(h, a) - q_\pi^{\gamma,\tau}(h, a)$$
$$= \mathbb{E}_{o|ha} \max_{a_1} \mathbb{E}_{o_1|haoa_1} \cdots \max_{a_\tau} [\bar{g}(a\|h) + \gamma\bar{g}(a_1\|hao) + \cdots + \gamma^{\tau}\bar{g}(a_\tau\|h\cdots o_{\tau-1})]$$
$$- \mathbb{E}_{o|ha} \max_{a_1} \mathbb{E}_{o_1|haoa_1} \cdots \max_{a_{\tau-1}} [\bar{g}(a\|h) + \gamma\bar{g}(a_1\|hao) + \cdots + \gamma^{\tau-1}\bar{g}(a_{\tau-1}\|h\cdots o_{\tau-2})]$$
$$\leq \mathbb{E}_{o|ha} \max_{a_1} \{\mathbb{E}_{o_1|haoa_1} \cdots \max_{a_\tau} [\bar{g}(a\|h) + \gamma\bar{g}(a_1\|hao) + \cdots + \gamma^{\tau}\bar{g}(a_\tau\|h\cdots o_{\tau-1})]$$
$$- \mathbb{E}_{o_1|haoa_1} \cdots \max_{a_{\tau-1}} [\bar{g}(a\|h) + \gamma\bar{g}(a_1\|hao) + \cdots + \gamma^{\tau-1}\bar{g}(a_{\tau-1}\|h\cdots o_{\tau-2})]\}$$
$$\leq \cdots$$
$$\leq \gamma^{\tau} \mathbb{E}_{o|ha} \max_{a_1} \mathbb{E}_{o_1|haoa_1} \cdots \max_{a_\tau} \bar{g}(a_\tau\|h\cdots o_{\tau-1}).$$

It can be seen that if $\mathbb{E}_{oa_1\cdots o_{\tau-1}a_\tau|ha}\bar{g}(a_\tau\|h\cdots o_{\tau-1})$ grows sub-exponentially, then $q_\pi^{\gamma,\tau}$ is a Cauchy sequence, and it makes sense to define the curiosity Q-value for infinite time horizon.

4   Experiment

The idea presented in the previous section is illustrated through a simple experiment. The environment is an MDP consisting of two groups of densely connected states (cliques) linked by a long corridor. The agent has two actions allowing it to move along the corridor deterministically, whereas the transition probabilities inside each clique are randomly generated. The agent assumes Dirichlet priors over all transition probabilities, and the goal is to learn the transition model of the MDP. In the experiment, each clique consists of 5 states, (states 1 to 5 and states 56 to 60), and the corridor is of length 50 (states 6 to 55). The prior over each transition probability is $Dir\left(\frac{1}{60}, \ldots, \frac{1}{60}\right)$.

We compare four different algorithms: i) random exploration, where the agent selects each of the two actions with equal probability at each time step; ii) Q-learning with the immediate information gain $g\left(ao\|h\right)$ as the reward; iii) greedy exploration, where the agent chooses at each time step the action maximizing $\bar{g}\left(a\|h\right)$; and iv) a dynamic-programming (DP) approximation of the optimal Bayesian exploration, where at each time step the agent follows a policy which is computed using policy iteration, assuming that the dynamics of the MDP is given by the current posterior, and the reward is the expected information gain $\bar{g}\left(a\|h\right)$. The detail of this algorithm is described in [11].

Fig.2 shows the typical behavior of the four algorithms. The upper four plots show how the agent moves in the MDP starting from one clique. Both greedy exploration and DP move back and forth between the two cliques. Random exploration has difficulty moving between the two cliques due to the random walk behavior in the corridor. Q-learning exploration, however, gets stuck in the initial clique. The reason for is that since the jump on the corridor is deterministic, the information gain decreases to virtually zero after only several attempts, therefore the Q-value of jumping into the corridor becomes much lower than the Q-value of jumping inside the clique. The bottom plot shows how the cumulative information gain grows over time, and how the DP approximation clearly outperforms the other algorithms, particularly in the early phase of exploration.

5   Related Work

The idea of actively selecting queries to accelerate learning process has a long history [1, 2, 7], and has received a lot of attention in recent decades, primarily in the context of active learning [8] and artificial curiosity [6]. In particular, measuring learning progress using KL divergence dates back to the 50's [2, 4]. In 1995 this was combined with reinforcement learning, with the goal of optimizing future expected information gain [10]. Others renamed this Bayesian surprise [3].

Our work differs from most previous work in two main points: First, like in [10], we consider the problem of exploring a dynamic environment, where actions change the environmental state, while most work on active learning and Bayesian experiment design focuses on queries that do not affect the environment [8]. Second, our result is theoretically sound and directly derived from first principles, in contrast to the more heuristic application [10] of traditional reinforcement learning to maximize the expected information gain. In particular, we pointed out a previously neglected subtlety of using KL divergence as learning progress.

Conceptually, however, this work is closely connected to artificial curiosity and intrinsically motivated reinforcement learning [6, 7, 9] for agents that actively explore the environment without an external reward signal. In fact, the very definition of the curiosity (Q) value permits a firm connection between pure exploration and reinforcement learning.

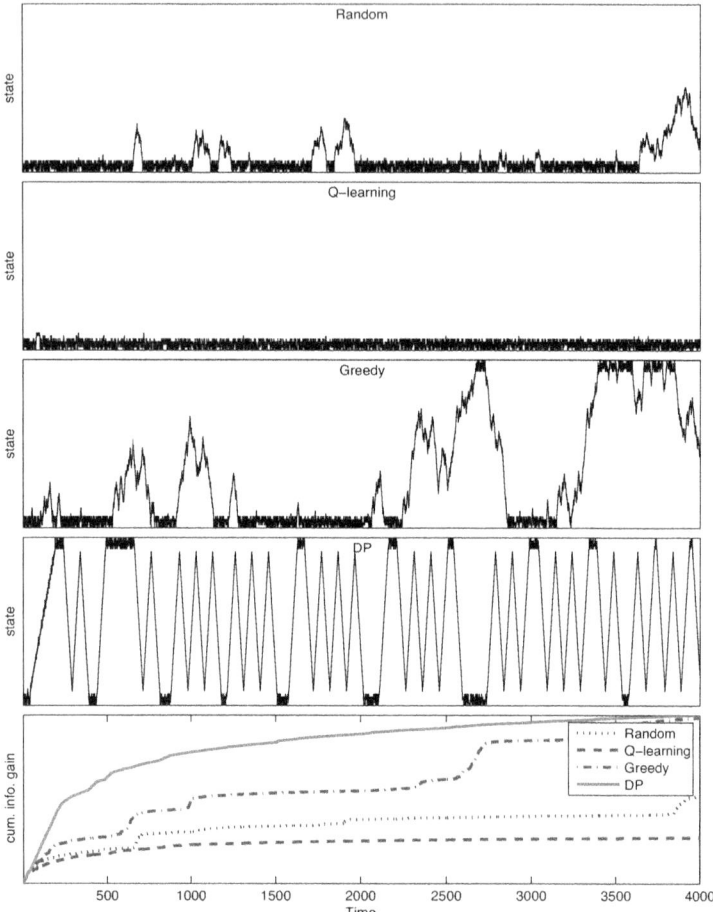

Fig. 2. The exploration process of a typical run of 4000 steps. The upper four plots shows the position of the agent between state 1 (the lowest) and 60 (the highest). The states at the top and the bottom correspond to the two cliques, and the states in the middle correspond to the corridor. The lowest plot is the cumulative information gain with respect to the prior.

6   Conclusion

We have presented the principle of optimal Bayesian exploration in dynamic environments, centered around the concept of the curiosity (Q) value. Our work provides a theoretically sound foundation for designing more effective exploration strategies. Future work will concentrate on studying the theoretical properties of various approximation strategies inspired by this principle.

Acknowledgement. This research was funded in part by Swiss National Science Foundation grant 200020-122124/1, and the EU IM-CLeVeR project(#231722).

References

1. Chaloner, K., Verdinelli, I.: Bayesian experimental design: A review. Statistical Science 10, 273–304 (1995)
2. Fedorov, V.V.: Theory of optimal experiments. Academic Press, London (1972)
3. Itti, L., Baldi, P.F.: Bayesian surprise attracts human attention. In: NIPS 2005, pp. 547–554 (2006)
4. Lindley, D.V.: On a measure of the information provided by an experiment. Annals of Mathematical Statistics 27(4), 986–1005 (1956)
5. Penny, W.: Kullback-liebler divergences of normal, gamma, dirichlet and wishart densities. Tech. rep., Wellcome Department of Cognitive Neurology, University College London (2001)
6. Schmidhuber, J.: Curious model-building control systems. In: IJCNN 1991, vol. 2, pp. 1458–1463 (1991)
7. Schmidhuber, J.: Formal theory of creativity, fun, and intrinsic motivation (1990-2010). Autonomous Mental Development, IEEE Trans. on Autonomous Mental Development 2(3), 230–247 (2010)
8. Settles, B.: Active learning literature survey. Tech. rep., University of Wisconsin Madison (2010)
9. Singh, S., Barto, A., Chentanez, N.: Intrinsically motivated reinforcement learning. In: NIPS 2004 (2004)
10. Storck, J., Hochreiter, S., Schmidhuber, J.: Reinforcement driven information acquisition in non-deterministic environments. In: ICANN 1995 (1995)
11. Sun, Y., Gomez, F.J., Schmidhuber, J.: Planning to be surprised: Optimal bayesian exploration in dynamic environments (2011), http://arxiv.org/abs/1103.5708

Optimal Direct Policy Search

Tobias Glasmachers and Jürgen Schmidhuber

IDSIA, University of Lugano
6928, Manno-Lugano, Switzerland
{tobias,juergen}@idsia.ch

Abstract. Hutter's optimal universal but incomputable AIXI agent models the environment as an initially unknown probability distribution-computing program. Once the latter is found through (incomputable) exhaustive search, classical planning yields an optimal policy. Here we reverse the roles of agent and environment by assuming a computable optimal policy realizable as a program mapping histories to actions. This assumption is powerful for two reasons: (1) The environment need not be probabilistically computable, which allows for dealing with truly stochastic environments, (2) All candidate policies are computable. In stochastic settings, our novel method Optimal Direct Policy Search (ODPS) identifies the best policy by direct universal search in the space of all possible computable policies. Unlike AIXI, it is computable, model-free, and does not require planning. We show that ODPS is optimal in the sense that its reward converges to the reward of the optimal policy in a very broad class of partially observable stochastic environments.

1 Introduction

Reinforcement learning (RL) algorithms are often categorized into model-based and model-free approaches. Model-based methods typically learn a model of the environment and its dynamics, to be used for decision making in a second step. Advantages include potentially flexible adaptation to new tasks expressed by different reward functions within the same environmental dynamics. Disadvantages include the high sample complexity of model learning: typically, many interactions with the environment are needed to estimate the underlying dynamic process with sufficient certainty.

Value function approaches do not require a full predictive model; instead they compress knowledge about the environment into a single number per state or state-action-pair, to model the only task-specific quantity of interest in most RL settings, namely, expected future reward. Since single number estimation is often more efficient and the value function is a sufficient statistics for learning the optimal policy, such methods can often reduce the sample complexity.

Model-free algorithms search for good policies without ever building a model of the environment. A particular branch of model-free methods is direct policy search [4], which includes policy gradient algorithms or evolution strategies applied to a fitness function based on the reward of an episode or a fixed time

J. Schmidhuber, K.R. Thórisson, and M. Looks (Eds.): AGI 2011, LNAI 6830, pp. 52–61, 2011.

frame. Such algorithms are relatively blind to the particularities of the environment (e.g., state transitions) and the reward signal (they only care for accumulated reward). One of the advantages of this blindness is that they are not affected by classical problems such as partial observability. Direct policy search is particularly well suited for complex environments solvable by relatively simple policies.

All of the above paradigms can be found in nature at various levels of complexity. Higher-developed animals, in particular humans, use anticipation and planning to solve many complex tasks, which to some extent requires a model of the environment. On the other hand, findings in neuroscience studies have been connected to value-function learning [8]. Many simpler animals exhibit complex but inflexible patterns of basically pre-programmed behavior, which can be understood as the result of evolutionary direct policy search.

For most complex tasks in a human-dominated and dynamic world, model-based approaches are intuitively expected to excel in the long run. However, when confronted with highly unfamiliar situations, humans are able to resort to trial and error strategies that often allow them to act better than chance, until having collected enough experience to build a sufficiently good predictive model enabling them to resort to the familiar planning paradigm. Thus, direct policy search may have its place as a bootstrapping method even in elaborate value-function or model-based approaches.

Optimal planning is hard, but identifying a computational model of an arbitrarily complex but computable environment is even harder. The AIXI model [1] does it in a provably optimal way, identifying the correct environmental model through a minimal number of interactions with the environment, but this requires a continual and exhaustive and computationally intractable systematic search in all of program space, necessarily ignoring all issues of computational complexity. (Note, however, recent serious efforts to scale down AIXI for realistic applications [9].)

The main contribution of this paper is a theoretical, conceptual one. While direct policy search is sometimes viewed as a 'last resort' heuristic, here we show that one can use it as a general and asymptotically optimal RL method *for all episodic POMDP problems*, asymptotically on the same level as the model-based AIXI scheme, but, unlike AIXI, incrementally computable (although not necessarily practically feasible). It covers any other behavior-generating searcher, such as realistically downscaled AIXI variants, by systematically enumerating *all* such algorithms. In fact, many direct policy search algorithms can trivially be understood as (non-optimal) approximations of ours.

2   Reinforcement Learning in POMDPs

We consider an agent interacting with an environment in discrete time steps $t \in \mathbb{N}$. In each time step the environment (including the agent) is in a Markov state $s_t \in \mathbb{S}$. Let $\mathcal{D}(X)$ denote the space of probability distributions over a measure space X. In each time step the agent perceives an observation $o_t \in \mathbb{O}$ of the state s_t, described by $o_t \sim \Omega_{s_t} \in \mathcal{D}(\mathbb{O})$.

The agent performs an action $a_t \in \mathbb{A}$, which results in a transition to state s_{t+1}. The dynamics of the system are described by $s_{t+1} \sim P_{s_t,a_t} \in \mathcal{D}(\mathbb{S})$. After acting the agent obtains a task-specific feedback in terms of a scalar reward signal $r_{t+1} \in \mathbb{R}$, possibly depending on s_t, a_t, and s_{t+1}. Having arrived in the new state s_{t+1}, it also obtains the next observation o_{t+1}, and the process starts over.

By $h_t = (o_1, a_1, r_1, \ldots, o_{t-1}, a_{t-1}, r_{t-1}, o_t)$ we denote the history at time t. Let $\mathbb{H}$ denote the space of all possible histories. Then a (behavior) policy is a description of how the agent acts in its environment, expressed as a mapping $\pi : \mathbb{H} \to \mathcal{D}(\mathbb{A})$. We collect all such mappings in the set Π of policies.

Assume that the subset $\mathbb{T} \subset \mathbb{S}$ of terminating states is non-empty. We denote the time of termination by the random variable T. We call a task episodic if the suprema of expectation and variance of T are finite: $\sup \left\{ \mathbb{E}^\pi[T] \,\middle|\, \pi \in \Pi \right\} < \infty$ and $\sup \left\{ \mathbb{E}^\pi[(T - \mathbb{E}^\pi[T])^2] \,\middle|\, \pi \in \Pi \right\} < \infty$. These prerequisites corresponds to the standard technical assumption of ergodicity.

2.1   MDPs and POMDPs

The underlying Markov decision process (MDP) is described by the tuple $(\mathbb{S}, \mathbb{T}, \mathbb{A}, S, P, R)$, where $S \in \mathcal{D}(\mathbb{S})$ is the distribution of start states, $P_{s,a}$ denotes the probability distribution of transitioning from state s to the next state $s' \sim P_{s,a}$ when taking action a, and $R(s, a, s') \in \mathcal{D}(\mathbb{R})$ is the distribution of rewards obtained for this transition. In what follows we make the standard assumptions that $\mathbb{S}$ and $\mathbb{A}$ are finite, and that for each combination of s, a, and s' expectation and variance of $R(s, a, s')$ are finite. We are only interested in episodic tasks.

Now, a partially observable Markov decision process (POMDP) is a tuple $(\mathbb{S}, \mathbb{T}, \mathbb{A}, \mathbb{O}, S, P, \Omega, R)$, where Ω (as defined above) stochastically maps states to observations. We assume that $\mathbb{O}$ is finite. POMDPs are a rather general class of environments for reinforcement learning. Most classical RL algorithms are restricted to MDPs, because their learning rules heavily rely on the Markov property of the state description. However, in many realistic tasks observations are naturally stochastic and/or incomplete, such that the environment has to be treated as a POMDP.

2.2   Objectives of Learning

The goal of learning a policy π in an episodic task is usually defined to maximize future expected reward $\rho = \mathbb{E}^\pi \left[\sum_{t=1}^{T-1} r_t \right]$. However, in what follows we leave the choice of the objective function ρ open and just require the form $\rho(\pi) = \mathbb{E}^\pi[\eta(h_T)]$, where the 'success' function η as a function of the full episode h_T has finite expectation and bounded variance. This is a reasonable assumption automatically fulfilled for the future expected reward, since expectation and variance of both T and $R_{s,a,s'}$ are bounded.

Note that there is an important conceptual difference between the functions η and ρ: While $\eta(h_T)$ is a quantity measurable via interaction with the environment, evaluating the objective function $\rho(\pi)$ requires knowledge of the POMDP, which is assumed to be opaque to the reinforcement learner.

2.3   Direct Search in Policy Space

Direct policy search is a class of model-free reinforcement learning algorithms. A direct policy search algorithm searches a space Π of policies π by means of direct search, for example, an evolutioary algorithm. Such search schemes are particularly suitable for learning in POMDP environments, because they make no assumptions about observations being Markovian, or treatable as nearly Markovian. The search is direct in the sense that it relies solely on evaluations of the objective function, here on the stochastic version η, often stabilized by averaging over multiple episodes.

3   Optimal Direct Policy Search

The aim of the present paper is to lift direct policy search for stochastic RL tasks to the level of universal search [2] with a Turing complete programming language, encompassing all possible computable policies. Thus, our approach is closely connected to deterministic universal searchers [2,5], but lifted to the class of *stochastic* RL tasks. In contrast to universally optimal [1] approaches such as the Gödel machine [6] we do not require the concept of proof search.

The basic idea of our approach amounts to systematically applying the enumerable set of computable policies to the task in a scheme that makes the statistical evaluation of each such policy more and more reliable over time. At the same time we make sure that the fraction of time spent on exploitation (in contrast to systematic exploration) tends to one. This combination allows us to derive an optimality theorem stating that the reward obtained by our agent converges towards the optimal reward.

Consider a Turing machine that receives the current history h_t as input on its tape and outputs an action by the time it halts. This can be achieved by initializing the tape with a default distribution over actions, which may or may not be changed by the program.

The basic simple idea of our algorithm is a nested loop that simultaneously makes the following quantities tend to infinity: the number of programs considered, the number of trials over which a policy is averaged, the time given to each program. At the same time, the fraction of trials spent on exploitation converges towards 1.

Letting the number of programs go to infinity allows for finding policies encoded by programs with arbitrarily high indices. At the same time, each program is given more and more but always finite execution time, circumventing the halting problem in the style of universal search [2]. Averaging the reward over more and more episodes makes these estimates arbitrarily reliable, which is essential to prove optimality. Finally, letting the fraction of episodes used for exploitation in online mode tend to one makes sure that the overall performance of the algorithm tends to the supremum of the performances of all computable policies.

To specify the optimal direct policy search algorithm we need the following notation:

- Let $p : \mathbb{N} \to \mathcal{P}$ be an enumeration of all programs $\mathcal{P}$ of the Turing machine in use, with p_i denoting the i-th program.
- Let π_p^c denote the policy obtained by running program p for c steps. This policy, understood as a mapping from the history $h_t \in \mathbb{H}$ to a distribution over actions, is implemented as follows: We write a 'default' distribution over actions and the history h_t onto the tape of the Turing machine. Then we run program p_i for c steps, or less, if it halts by itself. During this time the program may perform arbitrary computations based on the history, and overwrite the distributions over actions (which can, e.g., be represented as a soft-max decision). We also write π_i^c instead of $\pi_{p_i}^c$ for program p_i.
- Let $(N_n)_{n \in N}$, $(C_n)_{n \in N}$, $(E_n)_{n \in N}$, and $(X_n)_{n \in N}$ be sequences of natural numbers, all tending to infinity:
  - N_n denotes the number of programs considered in epoch n,
  - C_n denotes the time given to each program,
  - E_n denotes the number of episodes over which the reward of each policy is averaged,
  - X_n denotes the number of episodes for exploitation in online mode.

We need the following easily satisfiable technical conditions on these sequences: (a) $\lim\limits_{n \to \infty} N_n/E_n = 0$, (b) $\lim\limits_{n \to \infty} (N_n \cdot E_n)/X_n = 0$.

Algorithm 1. Optimal Direct Policy Search (ODPS)

> **for** $n \in \mathbb{N}$ **do**
>> $v_n \leftarrow -\infty$; $b_n \leftarrow 0$;
>> **for** $i \in \{1, \dots, N_n\}$ **do**
>>> $w \leftarrow 0$;
>>> **for** $e \in \{1, \dots, E_n\}$ **do**
>>>> perform one episode according to $\pi_i^{C_n}$, resulting in h_T;
>>>> $w \leftarrow w + \eta(h_T)$;
>>> **end**
>>> $R_i \leftarrow w/E_n$;
>>> **if** $R_i > v_n$ **then** $v_n \leftarrow R_i$; $b_n \leftarrow i$;
>> **end**
>> **if** online-mode **then** perform X_n episodes according to $\pi_{b_n}^{C_n}$;
> **end**

With these conventions, the pseudo-code of Optimal Direct Policy Search (ODPS) is given in Algorithm 1. The algorithm operates in epochs, each starting with an exploration phase during which a number of candidate policies is systematically evaluated. ODPS has two modes: In exploration mode it evaluates more and more powerful policies in each epoch, without ever exploiting its findings. At the end of each episode, after the direct policy search is stopped, it assumes to have found the best so far solution for later exploitation phases. In online mode, ODPS is actually exploiting the policies it finds, achieving arbitrarily close to optimal performance in the limit. But exploitation phases are still interleaved with exploration phases, to make sure no good policy is missed by chance.

4   Formal Optimality

The following theorems formalize optimality of ODPS:

Theorem 1. *Consider the infinite sequence of episodes executed by Algorithm 1 in online-mode, and let η_j denote the success $\eta(h_T)$ of the j-th episode. Let $T_n = \sum_{k=1}^{n} N_k E_k + X_k$ denote the number of episodes at the end of epoch n. By $\bar{\eta}_n = \frac{1}{T_n} \sum_{j=1}^{T_n} \eta_j$ we denote the success averaged over the first n epochs. Then it holds $\bar{\eta}_n \xrightarrow[n\to\infty]{\Pr} \sup \left\{ \rho(\pi_p^c) \,\middle|\, p \in \mathcal{P}, c \in \mathbb{N} \right\}$, where $\xrightarrow{\Pr}$ denotes convergence in probability.*

Theorem 2. *Consider Algorithm 1 either in online or in exploration mode. Let b_n be the index of the best program found in epoch n. Then it holds $\rho(\pi_{b_n}^{C_n}) \xrightarrow[n\to\infty]{\Pr} \sup \left\{ \rho(\pi_p^c) \,\middle|\, p \in \mathcal{P}, c \in \mathbb{N} \right\}$, where $\xrightarrow{\Pr}$ denotes convergence in probability.*

Proof (Proof of Theorem 2). We define $\rho^* = \sup \left\{ \rho(\pi_p^c) \,\middle|\, p \in \mathcal{P}, c \in \mathbb{N} \right\}$. Fix constants $\varepsilon > 0$ and $\delta > 0$. We have to show that there exists $n_0 \in \mathbb{N}$ such that for all $n > n_0$ it holds $\Pr(\rho^* - \rho(\pi_{b_n}^{C_n}) > \varepsilon) < \delta$.

Let $R_i^{(n)}$ denote the average success of policy $\pi_i^{C_n}$ during the exploration phase of epoch n, and let $\rho_i^{(n)} = \rho(\pi_i^{C_n})$ denote the corresponding objective function value. Furthermore, let $\rho_n^* = \max \left\{ \rho_i^{(n)} \,\middle|\, i \in \{1, \dots, N_n\} \right\}$ denote the best achievable objective function value in epoch n. We have $\mathbb{E}[R_i^{(n)}] = \mathbb{E}[\eta(h_T) \mid \pi_i^{C_n}] = \rho_i^{(n)}$ and $\mathrm{Var}(R_i^{(n)}) \leq \frac{\sigma^2}{E_n}$, where σ^2 is a bound on the variance of η. This allows us to estimate

$$\Pr\left(\exists i \in \{1, \dots, N_n\} \text{ s.t. } \left| R_i^{(n)} - \rho_i^{(n)} \right| \geq \frac{\varepsilon}{4} \right)$$

$$\leq N_n \cdot \Pr\left(\left| R_i^{(n)} - \rho_i^{(n)} \right| \geq \frac{\varepsilon}{4} \right) \qquad \text{for all } i \in \{1, \dots, N_n\}$$

$$\leq \frac{N_n}{E_n} \cdot \frac{16\sigma^2}{\varepsilon^2} \leq \delta$$

for all $n > n_1$. The first step follows from the union bound, the second one from Chebyshev's inequality. According to property (a) there exists $n_1 \in \mathbb{N}$ such that for all $n > n_1$ we have $\frac{N_n}{E_n} < \frac{\delta \varepsilon^2}{16\sigma^2}$, which implies the last step for this choice of n_1. Together with $R_{b_n}^{(n)} \geq R_i^{(n)}$ this implies

$$\rho(\pi_{b_n}^{C_n}) \geq R_{b_n}^{(n)} - \frac{\varepsilon}{4} \geq R_i^{(n)} - \frac{\varepsilon}{4} \geq \rho_n^* - \frac{\varepsilon}{2} \ ,$$

for all $i \in \{1, \ldots, N_n\}$ and $n > n_1$, and with probability of at least $(1 - \delta)$.

Per construction we have $\lim_{n \to \infty} \rho_n^* = \rho^*$. Thus, there exists $n_2 \in \mathbb{N}$ such that for all $n > n_2$ it holds $\rho^* - \rho_n^* < \varepsilon/2$. With $n_0 = \max\{n_1, n_2\}$ it follows that $\rho(\pi_{b_n}^{C_n}) > \rho_* - \varepsilon$ holds for all $n > n_0$ with probability of at least $(1 - \delta)$.

Proof (Proof of Theorem 1). Property (b) guarantees that $\tilde{\eta}_n - \rho(\pi_{b_n}^{C_n}) \xrightarrow[n \to \infty]{\mathrm{Pr}} 0$, where $\tilde{\eta}_n$ is the average performance during epoch n. It is easy to see that this also implies $\bar{\eta}_n - \rho(\pi_{b_n}^{C_n}) \xrightarrow[n \to \infty]{\mathrm{Pr}} 0$. Now we apply Theorem 2, which proves the assertion.

5 Discussion

Theorems 1 and 2 formally establish the asymptotic optimality of ODPS for all finite episodic POMDP problems, as outlined in the previous sections. In exploration mode, the algorithm finds arbitrarily close to optimal policies. In online mode, it exploits its previously learned knowledge, resulting in asymptotically optimal performance.

An interesting aside is that the ODPS algorithm, together with a simulation of the POMDP, is a program itself and is thus available as a subroutine in some of the programs $p \in \mathcal{P}$. This self-reference is neither helpful nor does it pose any problem to the procedure. In particular, the ODPS algorithm does not reason about itself, and in contrast to the Gödel machine [7] does not attempt to optimize its own search procedure.

Let us play a number of variations on the theme. For example, we may ask for the best policy that computes its action in *a priori* limited time. This scenario is more realistic than allowing the agent to take arbitrary long (but finite) time to make its decisions. The restricted time requirement simplifies the problem at hand considerably. Note that any program terminating after at most $n \in \mathbb{N}$ time steps can be expressed with at most n instructions, limiting the search space to a finite subset. Thus, all epochs can in principle search the full set of programs, and the sequence N_n disappears from the algorithm.

We do not claim that ODPS is a practical algorithm for solving real problems efficiently. How to scale it down? The probably most important step is to insert prior bias by giving small indices in the enumeration p_i to programs believed to be likely problem solvers. In many cases such programs would be known to halt in advance, which is why the progressively increasing sequence in computation time C_n could be set to infinity, enabling us to transfer information from early episodes to later ones in a straight-forward manner, such that the number of evaluations in episode n can be reduced from E_n to $E_n - E_{n-1}$. The language $\mathcal{P}$ can even be restricted to a non-Turing complete (typically finite) subset [3].

6 Experimental Test

The goal of our experiment is demonstrate the typical behavior of ODPS. We use a non-trivial POMDP environment, but in order to render the search practical we rely on a non-Turing complete encoding of policies tailored to the task.

The agent is confronted with the 49-state POMDP depicted in Figure 1. Its states are organized into a 6×8 grid, plus the single terminating state on the right. The two possible start states, each with probability $1/2$, are the two circled states at the top left. There are exactly two possible observations $\mathbb{O} = \{0, 1\}$ and two actions $\mathbb{A} = \{a_1, a_2\}$.

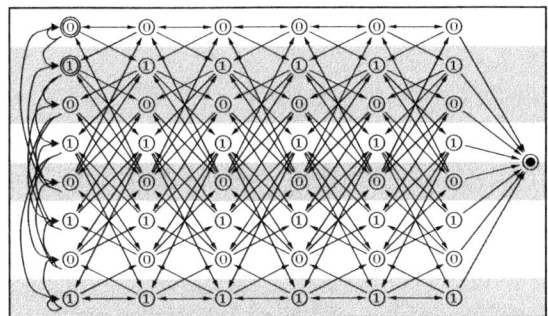

Fig. 1. Illustration of the 49-state POMDP used in the experiments. The two circled states in the top left are selected as start states with equal probability. The number in each circle is the observation the agent perceives. The two actions a_1 and a_2 have opposite effects in the gray and white background rows: In the gray rows, a_1 moves right and a_2 moves left, where each of the two possible arrows to the left and to the right are followed with equal probability. Actions are unreliabile, having the opposite effect in 30% of the cases. In the white rows the roles of actions are reversed. The goal is to reach the terminating state as quickly as possible. This is expressed by the reward uniformly distributed in the interval $[-1, 0]$ for all states.

The mapping from states to observations is deterministic; the symbol observed in each state is given in the figure. Note that the agent observes only a single bit of information per state, which makes partial observability a serious problem.

The effects of actions are highly stochastic. In rows with gray background action a_1 moves the agent to the right, and action a_2 to the left, but the effects of the actions are reversed in 30% of the cases. In rows with white background the roles of a_1 and a_2 are reversed. Furthermore, there are two possible destination states for each step, which are chosen with equal probability. In each time step the agent receives a reward drawn from the uniform distribution on the interval $[-1, 0]$. Thus, the goal of the agent is to reach the terminating state as quickly as possible.

The reason for using this seemingly over-complex POMDP is that direct policy search is particularly well suited for this type of task, because the optimal policy is relatively simple. It depends only on the last three observations (o_{t-2}, o_{t-1}, o_t) in the form $\pi(0, 0, 1) = \pi(0, 1, 0) = \pi(1, 0, 0) = \pi(1, 1, 1) = a_1$ and $\pi(0, 0, 0) = \pi(0, 1, 1) = \pi(1, 0, 1) = \pi(1, 1, 0) = a_2$. This encoding of the optimal policy is much simpler than an encoding of its value function in the MDP formulation, not to speak of the difficulties when learning in the corresponding POMDP.

Consequently we encode policies as tables, mapping tuples of most recent obversations to actions. We enumerate the possible values of n_o, the number of previous observations taken into account; for each size we systematically enumerate all possible combinations of actions. There are 2^{n_o} such observations, and $2^{(2^{n_o})}$ tabular policies. In early interactions when there are fewer observations available than processed by the policy, the observation vector is padded with zeros accordingly. This encoding scheme is not unique, which is typical when encoding programs. For example, p_1 and p_3 both always execute action a_1, in the form $p_1(\cdot) = a_1$, in contrast to $p_3(0) = a_1$, $p_3(1) = a_1$.

We ran ODPS with the settings $N_n = 10n$, $E_n = \lceil n \log(n + 1) \rceil$, and $X_n = 10E_n^3$ for 100 epochs. These sequences fulfill properties (a) and (b), such that Theorems 1 and 2 hold when the number of epochs is unlimited. In the above encoding the optimal policy happens to appear for the first time as p_{128}. Thus, it is in the search space from epoch 13 on.

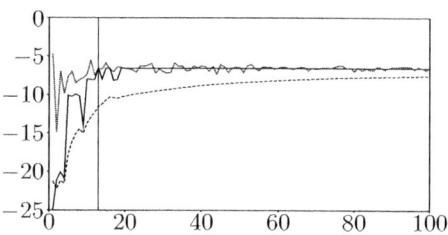

Fig. 2. The graph shows the best exploration performance v_n (dotted curve), the performance during exploitation (solid curve), and the total average performance (dashed curve), over the course of the first 100 episodes. The vertical line at episode 13 marks the point from where on the optimal policy p_{128} is available.

We monitored different quality indicators summarized in Figure 2. We can observe a number of typical behaviors from the graph. In the first iterations the number E_n of episodes per evaluation is too small, resulting in a huge gap between the dotted and the solid curve (overfitting). After about epoch 20 the exploitation performance becomes stable. The same holds for the identification of the best policy. Although this policy is available from episode 13 on, it is not identified reliably until epoch 20, after which the number E_n of averages is large enough. Thus, ODPS in exploration mode is reliably successful roughly from epoch 20 on. The dotted curve indicates the total averaged performance in online mode and converges only slowly towards the optimum. This is because in each epoch a large number of episodes is allocated to systematic exploration, during which the average performance is around -25 (not shown in the graph).

7   Conclusion

We introduced a class of direct policy search methods that in theory can optimally solve any finite, stochastic, episodic POMDP problem. Our results are extremely general in the sense that they make very few assumptions on the underlying MDP. In particular, our approach treats stochasticity naturally and does not need the assumption of a deterministically or probabilistically computable environment. Our only restriction is that the optimal policy must be relevant to machine learning, in the weak sense that it is a *computable* function of the history.

Our ODPS algorithm is not necessarily practical, but most direct policy search schemes are closely related (typically replacing systematic search with heuristics, and the search space of all computable policies with a restricted subspace), and we outlined how to scale it down to realistic applications, describing an illustrative experiment with a highly stochastic POMDP.

Still, this work remains conceptual in spirit, and, in the authors' point of view, serves the sole purpose of providing a solid theoretical understanding of the power of direct policy search. Our work shows the *principal* ability of direct policy search to solve almost arbitrary problems optimally, and thus provides a solid theoretical justification for its use.

References

1. Hutter, M.: Universal Artificial Intelligence: Sequential Decisions based on Algorithmic Probability. Springer, Berlin (2004)
2. Levin, L.: Universal sequential search problems. Problems of Information Transmission 9(3), 265–266 (1973)
3. Schaul, T., Schmidhuber, J.: Towards Practical Universal Search. In: Proceedings of the Third Conference on Artificial General Intelligence, Lugano (2010)
4. Schmidhuber, J.: Sequential decision making based on direct search (Lecture Notes on AI 1828). In: Sun, R., Giles, C.L. (eds.) IJCAI-WS 1999. LNCS (LNAI), vol. 1828, p. 213. Springer, Heidelberg (2001)
5. Schmidhuber, J.: Optimal Ordered Problem Solver. Machine Learning 54, 211–254 (2004)
6. Schmidhuber, J.: Gödel machines: Fully Self-Referential Optimal Universal Self-Improvers. In: Goertzel, B., Pennachin, C. (eds.) Artificial General Intelligence, pp. 119–226 (2006)
7. Schmidhuber, J.: Ultimate Cognition à la Gödel. Cognitive Computation 1(2), 177–193 (2009)
8. Schultz, W., Dayan, P., Montague, P.R.: A neural substrate of prediction and reward. Science 275(5306), 1593 (1997)
9. Veness, J., Ng, K.S., Hutter, M., Silver, D.: A Monte Carlo AIXI Approximation. Technical Report 0909.0801, arXiv (2009)

Nonlinear-Dynamical Attention Allocation via Information Geometry

Matthew Ikle[1] and Ben Goertzel[2]

[1] Adams State College, Alamosa CO
[2] Novamente LLC, Rockville MD

Abstract. Inspired by a broader perspective viewing intelligent system dynamics in terms of the geometry of "cognitive spaces," we conduct a preliminary investigation of the application of information-geometry based learning to ECAN (Economic Attention Networks), the component of the integrative OpenCog AGI system concerned with attention allocation and credit assignment. We generalize Amari's "natural gradient" algorithm for network learning to encompass ECAN and other recurrent networks, and apply it to small example cases of ECAN, demonstrating a dramatic improvement in the effectiveness of attention allocation compared to prior (Hebbian learning like) ECAN methods. Scaling up the method to deal with realistically-sized ECAN networks as used in OpenCog remains for the future, but should be achievable using sparse matrix methods on GPUs.

Keywords: information geometry, recurrent networks, economic attention allocation, ECAN, OpenCog.

1 Introduction

The AGI field currently lacks any broadly useful, powerful, practical theoretical and mathematical framework. Many theoretical and mathematical tools have been important in guiding the design of various aspects of various AGI systems; and there is a general mathematical theory of AGI [17], which has inspired some practical work [18] [22], but has not yet been connected with complex AGI architectures in any nontrivial way. But it is fair to say that AGI is in deep need of unifying ideas.

One possibility in this regard is *information geometry* [3], the theory of the geometric structure of spaces of probability distributions. Given the recent rise of probabilistic methods in AI and the success of geometric methods in other disciplines such as physics, this seems a natural avenue to explore. A companion paper [10] outlines some very broad ideas in this regard; here we present some more concrete and detailed experiments in the same direction. Continuing our prior work with the OpenCog [16] integrative AGI architecture, we model OpenCog's Economic Attention Networks (ECAN) component using information geometric language, and then use this model to propose a novel information geometric method of updating ECAN networks (based on an extension of Amari's ANGL

J. Schmidhuber, K.R. Thórisson, and M. Looks (Eds.): AGI 2011, LNAI 6830, pp. 62–71, 2011.

algorithm). Tests on small networks suggest that information-geometric methods have the potential to vastly improve ECAN's capability to shift attention from current preoccupations to desired preoccupations. However, there is a high computational cost associated with the simplest implementations of these methods, which has prevented us from carrying out large-scale experiments so far. We are exploring the possibility of circumventing these issues via using sparse matrix algorithms on GPUs.

2   Brief Review of OpenCog

Now we briefly describe the OCP (OCP) AGI architecture, implemented within the open-source OpenCog AI framework. OCP provides the general context for the very specific novel algorithmic research presented here.

Conceptually founded on the "patternist" systems theory of intelligence outlined in [12], OCP combines multiple AI paradigms such as uncertain logic, computational linguistics, evolutionary program learning and connectionist attention allocation in a unified architecture. Cognitive processes embodying these different paradigms interoperate together on a common neural-symbolic knowledge store called the Atomspace. The interaction of these processes is designed to encourage the self-organizing emergence of high-level network structures in the Atomspace, including superposed hierarchical and heterarchical knowledge networks, and a self-model network enabling meta-knowledge and meta-learning.

The OpenCog software (incorporating elements of the OCP architecture) has been used for commercial applications in the area of natural language processing and data mining [14], and for the control of virtual agents in virtual worlds [13] (see http://novamente.net/example for some videos of these virtual dogs in action).

The high-level architecture of OCP involves the use of multiple cognitive processes associated with multiple types of memory to enable an intelligent agent to execute the procedures that it believes have the best probability of working toward its goals in its current context. OCP handles low-level perception and action via an extension called OpenCogBot, which integrates a hierarchical temporal memory system, DeSTIN [4].

OCP's memory types are the declarative, procedural, sensory, and episodic memory types that are widely discussed in cognitive neuroscience [23], plus – most relevantly for the current paper – attentional memory for allocating system resources generically, and intentional memory for allocating system resources in a goal-directed way. Table 1 overviews these memory types, giving key references and indicating the corresponding cognitive processes, and also indicating which of the generic patternist cognitive dynamics each cognitive process corresponds to (pattern creation, association, etc.). The essence of the OCP design lies in the way the structures and processes associated with each type of memory are designed to work together in a closely coupled way, the operative hypothesis being that this will yield cooperative intelligence ("cognitive synergy") going beyond what could be achieved by an architecture merely containing the same structures and processes in separate "black boxes."

Table 1. Memory Types and Cognitive Processes in OpenCog Prime. The third column indicates the general cognitive function that each specific cognitive process carries out, according to the patternist theory of cognition.

Memory Type	Specific Cognitive Processes	General Cognitive Functions
Declarative	Probabilistic Logic Networks (PLN) [11]; concept blending [7]	pattern creation
Procedural	MOSES (a novel probabilistic evolutionary program learning algorithm) [20]	pattern creation
Episodic	internal simulation engine [13]	association, pattern creation
Attentional	Economic Attention Networks (ECAN) [15]	association, credit assignment
Intentional	probabilistic goal hierarchy refined by PLN and ECAN, structured according to Psi	credit assignment, pattern creation
Sensory	Supplied by DeSTIN integration	association, attention allocation, pattern creation, credit assignment

Declarative knowledge representation is handled by a weighted labeled hypergraph called the Atomspace, which consists of multiple types of nodes and links, generally weighted with probabilistic truth values and also attention values (ShortTermImportance (STI) and LongTermImportance values, regulating processor and memory use).

OCP's dynamics has both goal-oriented and "spontaneous" aspects. The basic goal-oriented dynamics is driven by "cognitive schematics", which take the form

$$Context \wedge Procedure \rightarrow Goal < p >$$

(summarized $C \wedge P \rightarrow G$), roughly interpretable as "If the context C appears to hold currently, then if I enact the procedure P, I can expect to achieve the goal G with certainty p."

On the other hand, the spontaneous dynamic is driven by the ECAN component (the subject of the present paper), which propagates STI values in a manner reminiscent of an attractor neural network; cognitive processes or knowledge items that get more importance spread to them are then used to trigger action or cognition or to guide perception. Goal-oriented dynamics also utilizes STI, in that the system's top-level goals are given STI to spend on nominating procedures for execution or to pass to subgoals.

3   Brief Review of Economic Attention Networks

Now we review the essential ideas underlying Economic Attention Networks (ECAN), which is the central process controlling attention allocation and credit assignment within OpenCog. ECAN is a specific approach to resource allocation and associative memory and may be considered a nonlinear dynamical system in roughly the same family as attractor neural networks such as Hopfield nets. As we describe in detail in [19] ECAN is a graph, consisting of generically-typed nodes and links (which may have any of OpenCog's node or link types, but the point is that the type semantics is irrelevant to ECAN even though it may be relevant to other OpenCog modules), and also links that may be typed either HebbianLink or InverseHebbianLink. Each Hebbian or InverseHebbian link is weighted with a probability value.

Each node or link in an ECAN is also weighted with two numbers, representing short-term importance (STI) and long-term importance (LTI). STI values represent the immediate importance of an Atom to ECAN at a particular instant in time, while LTI values represent the value of retaining atoms in memory. The ECAN equations dynamically update these values using an economic metaphor in which both STI and LTI can be viewed as artificial currencies.

The ECAN equations also contain the essential notion of an AttentionalFocus (AF), consisting of those Atoms in the ECAN with the highest STI values. The probability value of a HebbianLink from A to B is the odds that if A is in the AF, so is B; and correspondingly, the InverseHebbianLink from A to B is weighted with the odds that if A is in the AF, then B is not. The main concept here is the following: Suppose there is a high HebbianLink probability between A and B and that A is in the AF. Then A can be viewed as trying to "pull" B into the AF. There is an obvious corresponding but opposite reaction if the nodes share instead a high InverseHebbianLink.

As an associative memory, the ECAN process involves both training and retrieval processes. The entire ECAN training dynamics can be described as a nonlinear function $H : [0, 1]^L \longrightarrow \mathcal{R}^M$, where L is the number of nodes, and $M = L^2$, mapping a given set of binary patterns into a connection matrix C of Hebbian weights. The specific ECAN Hebbian updating equations are somewhat complex, and are described in detail in [10]. What is important in our current context, is this view of the process as a nonlinear function on the space of input patterns into the space of weight parameters.

4   Brief Review of Information Geometry

"Information geometry" is a branch of applied mathematics concerned with the application of differential geometry to spaces of probability distributions. In [10] we have suggested some extensions to traditional information geometry aimed at allowing it to better model general intelligence. However for the concrete technical work in the present paper, the traditional formulation of information geometry will suffice.

One of the core mathematical constructs underlying information geometry, is the Fisher Information, a statistical quantity which has a a variety of applications ranging far beyond statistical data analysis, including physics [8], psychology and AI [3]. Put simply, FI is a formal way of measuring the amount of information that an observable random variable X carries about an unknown parameter θ upon which the probability of X depends. FI forms the basis of the Fisher-Rao metric, which has been proved the only Riemannian metric on the space of probability distributions satisfying certain natural properties regarding invariance with respect to coordinate transformations. Typically θ in the FI is considered to be a real multidimensional vector; however, [6] has presented a FI variant that imposes basically no restrictions on the form of θ. Here the multidimensional FI will suffice, but the more general version is needed if one wishes to apply FI to AGI more broadly, e.g. to declarative and procedural as well as attentional knowledge.

In the set-up underlying the definition of the ordinary finite-dimensional Fisher information, the probability function for X, which is also the likelihood function for $\theta \in R^n$, is a function $f(X;\theta)$; it is the probability mass (or probability density) of the random variable X conditional on the value of θ. The partial derivative with respect to θ_i of the log of the likelihood function is called the *score* with respect to θ_i. Under certain regularity conditions, it can be shown that the first moment of the score is 0. The second moment is the Fisher information:

$$\mathcal{I}(\theta)_i = \mathcal{I}_X(\theta)_i = E\left[\left(\left(\frac{\partial}{\partial \theta_i} \ln f(X;\theta)\right)^2\right)|\theta\right]$$

where, for any given value of θ_i, the expression $E[..|\theta]$ denotes the conditional expectation over values for X with respect to the probability function $f(X;\theta)$ given θ. Note that $0 \leq \mathcal{I}(\theta)_i < \infty$. Also note that, in the usual case where the expectation of the score is zero, the Fisher information is also the variance of the score.

One can also look at the whole Fisher information matrix

$$\mathcal{I}(\theta)_{i,j} = E\left[\left(\frac{\partial \ln f(X,\theta)}{\partial \theta_i} \frac{\partial \ln f(X,\theta)}{\partial \theta_j}\right)|\theta\right]$$

which may be interpreted as a metric g_{ij}, that provably is the only "intrinsic" metric on probability distribution space. In this notation we have $\mathcal{I}(\theta)_i = \mathcal{I}(\theta)_{i,i}$.

Dabak [6] has shown that the geodesic between two parameter vectors θ and θ' is given by the exponential weighted curve $(\gamma(t))(x) = \frac{f(x,\theta)^{1-t} f(x,\theta')^t}{\int f(y,\theta)^{1-t} f(y,\theta')^t dy}$, under the weak condition that the log-likelihood ratios with respect to $f(X,\theta)$ and $f(X,\theta')$ are finite. Also, along this sort of curve, the sum of the Kullback-Leibler distances between θ and θ', known as the J-divergence, equals the integral of the Fisher information along the geodesic connecting θ and θ'.

This suggests that if one is attempting to learn a certain parameter vector based on data, and one has a certain other parameter vector as an initial value, it may make sense to use algorithms that try to follow the Fisher-Rao geodesic between the initial condition and the desired conclusion. This is what Amari [1] [3] calls "natural gradient" based learning, a conceptually powerful approach which subtly accounts for dependencies between the components of θ.

5   From Information Geometry to Mind Geometry

While here we will formally require only traditional ideas from information geometry, it is worth noting that the present paper was inspired by a companion paper [10] in which information geometry is extended in various ways and conjecturally applied to yield a broad conceptual model of cognitive systems. A family of alternative metrics based on algorithmic information theory is proposed, to complement the FisherRao metric – very roughly speaking, the algorithmic distance between two entities represents the amount of computational effort required to transform between the two. Multi-modular memory systems like OpenCog are then modeled in terms of multiple "mindspaces": each memory system, and the composite system, are geometrized using both Fisher-Rao and algorithmic metrics. Three hypotheses are then proposed:

1. a *syntax-semantics correlation* principle, stating that in a successful AGI system, these two metrics should be roughly correlated
2. a *cognitive geometrodynamics* principle, stating that on the whole intelligent minds tend to follow geodesics in mindspace
3. a *cognitive synergy* principle, stating that shorter paths may be found through the composite mindspace formed by considering multiple memory types together, than by following the geodesics in the mindspaces corresponding to individual memory types.

The results presented in this paper do not depend on any of these broader notions, however they fit in with them naturally. In this context, the present paper is viewed as an exploration of how to make ECAN best exploit the Fisher-Rao geometric structure of OpenCog's "attentional mindspace."

6   Information-Geometric Learning for Recurrent Networks: Extending the ANGL Algorithm

Now we move on to discuss the practicalities for information-geometric learning within OpenCog's ECAN component. As noted above, Amari [1,3] introduced the natural gradient as a generalization of the direction of steepest descent on the space of loss functions of the parameter space. Issues with the original implementation include the requirement of calculating both the Fisher information matrix and its inverse. To resolve these and other practical considerations, Amari [2] proposed an adaptive version of the algorithm, the Adaptive Natural Gradient Learning (ANGL) algorithm. Park, Amari, and Fukumizu [21] extended ANGL to a variety of stochastic models including stochastic neural networks, multi-dimensional regression, and classification problems.

In particular, they showed that, assuming a particular form of stochastic feedforward neural network and under a specific set of assumptions concerning the form of the probability distributions involved, a version of the Fisher information matrix can be written as

$$G(\theta) = E_\xi \left[\left(\frac{r'}{r} \right)^2 \right] E_x \left[\nabla H \left(\nabla H \right)^T \right].$$

Although Park et al considered only feedforward neural networks, their result also holds for more general neural networks, including the ECAN network. What is important is the decomposition of the probability distribution as

$$p\left(\mathbf{y}|\mathbf{x};\theta\right) = \prod_{i=1}^{L} r_i\left(y_i - H_i\left(\mathbf{x},\theta\right)\right)$$

where

$$\mathbf{y} = \mathbf{H}(\mathbf{x};\theta) + \xi, \ \mathbf{y} = (y_1, \cdots, y_L)^T, \ \mathbf{H} = (H_1, \cdots, H_L)^T, \ \xi = (\xi_1, \cdots, \xi_L)^T,$$

where ξ is added noise. If we assume further that each r_i has the same form as a Gaussian distribution with zero mean and standard deviation σ, then the Fisher information matrix simplifies further to

$$G(\theta) = \frac{1}{\sigma^2} E_x \left[\nabla H \left(\nabla H \right)^T \right].$$

The adaptive estimate for $\hat{G}_{t+1}^{-1}$ is given by

$$\hat{G}_{t+1}^{-1} = (1 + \epsilon_t)\hat{G}_t^{-1} - \epsilon_t(\hat{G}_t^{-1}\nabla H)(\hat{G}_t^{-1}\nabla H)^T.$$

and the loss function for our model takes the form

$$l(\mathbf{x}, \mathbf{y}; \theta) = -\sum_{i=1}^{\mathbf{L}} \log \mathbf{r}(\mathbf{y_i} - \mathbf{H_i}(\mathbf{x}, \theta)).$$

The learning algorithm for our connection matrix weights θ is then given by

$$\theta_{t+1} = \theta_t - \eta_t \hat{G}_t^{-1} \nabla l(\theta_t).$$

7   Information Geometry for Economic Attention Allocation: A Detailed Example

We now present the results of a series of small-scale, exploratory experiments comparing the original ECAN process running alone with the ECAN process coupled with ANGL. We are interested in determining which of these two lines of processing result in focusing attention more accurately.

The experiment started with base patterns of various sizes to be determined by the two algorithms. In the training stage, noise was added, generating a number of instances of noisy base patterns. The learning goal is to identify the underlying base patterns from the noisy patterns as this will identify how well the different algorithms can focus attention on relevant versus irrelevant nodes.

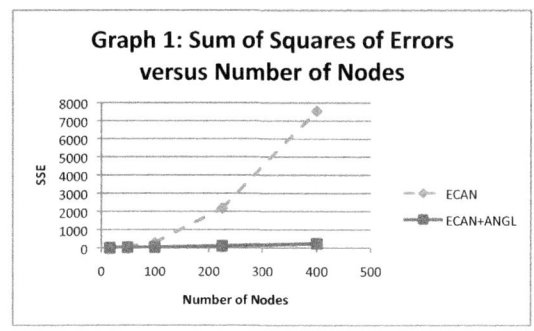

Fig. 1. Results from Experiment 1

Next, the ECAN process was run, resulting in the determination of the connection matrix C. In order to apply the ANGL algorithm, we need the gradient, ∇H, of the ECAN training process, with respect to the input $\mathbf{x}$. While calculating the connection matrix C, we used Monte Carlo simulation to simultaneously calculate an approximation to ∇H.

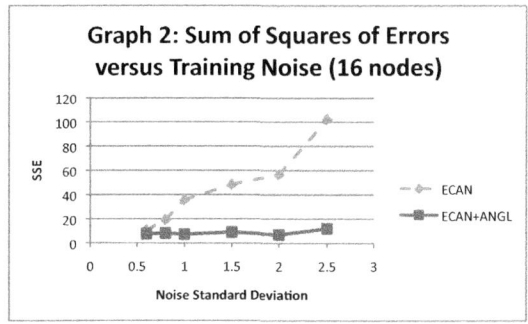

Fig. 2. Results from Experiment 2

After ECAN training was completed, we bifurcated the experiment. In one branch, we ran fuzzed cue patterns through the retrieval process. In the other, we first applied the ANGL algorithm, optimizing the weights in the connection matrix, prior to running the retrieval process on the same fuzzed cue patterns. At a constant value of $\sigma = 0.8$ we

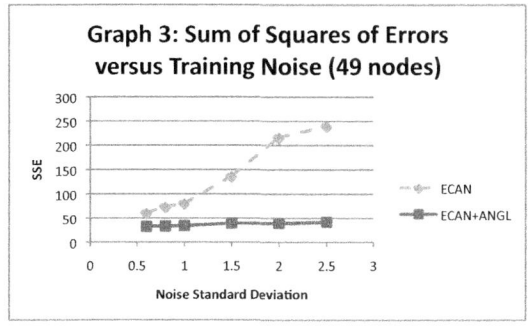

Fig. 3. Results from Experiment 3

ran several samples through each branch with pattern sizes of 4×4, 7×7, 10×10, 15×15, and 20×20. The results are shown in Figure 1. We also ran several experiments comparing the sum of squares of the errors to the input training noise as measured by the value of σ.; see Figures 2 and 3.

These results suggest two major advantages of the ECAN+ANGL combination compared to ECAN alone. Not only was the performance of the combination better in every trial, save for one involving a small number of nodes and little noise, but the combination clearly scales significantly better both as the number of nodes increases, and as the training noise increases.

8   Conclusion

Inspired by a broader geometric conception of general intelligence, we have explored a relatively simple concrete application of information-geometric ideas to the ECAN component of the OpenCog integrative AGI system. Roughly speaking, the idea explored is to have OpenCog shift its attention from current preoccupations toward desired preoccupations, based on following geodesic paths in the Fisher-Rao space of the space of "attentional probability distributions".

The results presented here are highly successful but also quite preliminary, involving small numbers of nodes in isolation rather than integrated into an entire AGI system. We still have much work ahead to determine whether the dramatic improvements reported here continue to scale with millions of nodes in a complete integrative system. Nonetheless, the results from our experiment tantalizingly suggest that incorporating ANGL into the ECAN process can lead to vastly more accurate results, especially as system size and noise increases. The main open question is whether this improvement can be achieved for large ECAN networks without dramatically increased processing time. To address this problem, we plan to experiment with implementing ECAN+ANGL on many-core GPU machines, using optimized sparse matrix algorithms [9,5].

We also plan to pursue similar approaches to improving the learning capability of other OpenCog components. For instance, OpenCog's PLN inference framework utilizes a statistically-guided inference control mechanism, which could benefit from information-geometric ideas. And OpenCog's MOSES system for probabilistic program induction (procedure learning) could potentially be modified to more closely follow geodesics in program space. There is no lack of fertile ground for further, related experimentation.

References

1. Amari, S.: Differential-geometrical methods in statistics. Lecture notes in statistics (1985)
2. Amari, S.: Natural gradient works efficiently in learning. Neural Computing 10, 251–276 (1998)
3. Amari, S.: i., Nagaoka, H.: Methods of information geometry. In: AMS (2000)
4. Arel, I., Rose, D., Coop, R.: Destin: A scalable deep learning architecture with application to high-dimensional robust pattern recognition. In: Proc. AAAI Workshop on Biologically Inspired Cognitive Architectures (2009)
5. Baskaran, M., Bordawekar, R.: Optimizing Sparse Matrix-Vector Multiplication on GPUs. IBM Research Report (2008)
6. Dabak, A.: A Geometry for Detection Theory. PhD Thesis, Rice U (1999)

7. Fauconnier, G., Turner, M.: The Way We Think: Conceptual Blending and the Minds Hidden Complexities. Basic (2002)
8. Frieden, R.: Physics from Fisher Information. Cambridge U. Press, New York (1998)
9. Garland, M.: Sparse matrix computations on manycore gpus. In: 45th Annual Design Automation Conference: 2008, pp. 2–6 (2008)
10. Goertzel, B., Ikle, M.: Three Hypotheses about the geometry of mind. In: Schmidhuber, J., Thórisson, K.R., Looks, M. (eds.) AGI 2011. LNCS (LNAI) vol. 6830, pp. 340–345. Springer, Heidelberg (2011)
11. Goertzel, B., Ikl, M., Heljakka, I.G.: Probabilistic Logic Networks. Springer, Heidelberg (2008)
12. Goertzel, B.: The Hidden Pattern. Brown Walker (2006)
13. Goertzel, B., et al.: An integrative methodology for teaching embodied non-linguistic agents, applied to virtual animals in second life. In: Proc.of the First Conf. on AGI, IOS Press, Amsterdam (2008)
14. Goertzel, B., Pinto, H., Pennachin, C., Goertzel, I.F.: Using dependency parsing and probabilistic inference to extract relationships between genes, proteins and malignancies implicit among multiple biomedical research abstracts. In: Proc. of Bio-NLP 2006 (2006)
15. Goertzel, B., Pitt, J., Ikle, M., Pennachin, C., Liu, R.: Glocal memory: a design principle for artificial brains and minds. Neurocomputing (April 2010)
16. Goertzel, B., et al.: Opencogbot: An integrative architecture for embodied agi. In: Proc. of ICAI 2010, Beijing (2010)
17. Hutter, M.: Universal AI. Springer, Heidelberg (2005)
18. Hutter, M.: Feature dynamic bayesian networks. In: Proc. of the Second Conf. on AGI. Atlantis Press, London (2009)
19. Ikle, M., Pitt, J., Goertzel, B., Sellman, G.: Economic attention networks: Associative memory and resource allocation for general intelligence. In: Proceedings of AGI (2009)
20. Looks, M.: Competent Program Evolution. PhD Thesis. Computer Science Department, Washington University (2006)
21. Park, H., Amari, S., Fukumizu, K.: Adaptive natural gradient learning algorithms for various stochastic models. Neural Computing 13, 755–764 (2000)
22. Schaul, T., Schmidhuber, J.: Towards practical universal search. In: Proc. of the 3rd Conf. on AGI. Atlantis Press, London (2010)
23. Tulving, E., Craik, R.: The Oxford Handbook of Memory. Oxford U. Press (2005)

An Information Theoretic Representation of Agent Dynamics as Set Intersections

Samuel Epstein and Margrit Betke

Boston University, 111 Cummington St, Boston, MA 02215
{samepst,betke}@cs.bu.edu

Abstract. We represent agents as sets of strings. Each string encodes a potential interaction with another agent or environment. We represent the total set of dynamics between two agents as the intersection of their respective strings, we prove complexity properties of player interactions using Algorithmic Information Theory. We show how the proposed construction is compatible with Universal Artificial Intelligence, in that the AIXI model can be seen as universal with respect to interaction.[1]

Keywords: Universal Artificial Intelligence, AIXI Model, Kolmogorov Complexity, Algorithmic Information Theory.

1 Introduction

Whereas classical Information Theory is concerned with quantifying the expected number of bits needed for communication, Algorithmic Information Theory (AIT) principally studies the complexity of individual strings. A central measure of AIT is the Kolmogorov Complexity $C(x)$ of a string x, which is the size of the smallest program that will output x on a universal Turing machine. Another central definition of AIT is the universal prior $\mathbf{m}(x)$ that weights a hypothesis (string) by the complexity of the programs that produce it [LV08]. This universal prior has many remarkable properties; if $\mathbf{m}(x)$ is used for induction, then any computable sequence can be learned with only the minimum amount of data. Unfortunately, $C(x)$ and $\mathbf{m}(x)$ are not finitely computable. Algorithmic Information Theory can be interpreted as a generalization of classical Information Theory [CT91] and the Minimum Description Length principal. Some other applications include universal PAC learning and Algorithmic Statistics [LV08, GTV01].

The question of whether AIT can be used to form the foundation of Artificial Intelligence was answered in the affirmative with Hutter's Universal Artificial Intelligence (UAI) [Hut04]. This was achieved by the application of the universal prior $\mathbf{m}(x)$ to the cybernetic agent model, where an agent communicates with an environment through sequential cycles of action, perception, and reward. It was shown that there exists a universal agent, the AIXI model, that inherits many universality properties from $\mathbf{m}(x)$. In particular, the AIXI model will converge to achieve optimal rewards given long enough time in the environment. As almost all

---

[1] The authors are grateful to Leonid Levin for insightful discussions and acknowledge partial support by NSF grant 0713229.

J. Schmidhuber, K.R. Thórisson, and M. Looks (Eds.): AGI 2011, LNAI 6830, pp. 72–81, 2011.

AI problems can be formalized in the cybernetic agent model, the AIXI model is a complete theoretical solution to the field of Artificial General Intelligence [GP07].

In this paper, we represent agents as sets of strings and the potential dynamics between them as the intersection of their respective sets of strings (Sec. 2). We connect this interpretation of interacting agents to the cybernetic agent model (Sec. 2.2). We provide background on Algorithmic Information Theory (Sec. 3) and show how agent learning can be described with algorithmic complexity (Sec. 4). We apply combinatorial and algorithmic proof techniques [VV10] to study the dynamics between agents (Sec. 5). In particular, we describe the approximation of agents (Th. 2), the conditions for removal of superfluous information in the encoding of an agent (Th. 3), and the consequences of having multiple payers achieving the same rewards in an environment (Th. 4). We show how the interpretation given in Sec. 2 is compatible with Universal Artificial Intelligence, in that the AIXI model has universality properties with respect to our definition of "interaction" (Sec. 6).

2   Interaction as Intersection

We define players A and B as two sets containing strings of size n. Each string x in the intersection set $A \cap B$ represents a particular "interaction" between players A and B. We will use the terms *string* and *interaction* interchangeably. This set representation can be used to encode non-cooperative games (Sec. 2.1) and instances of the cybernetic agent model (Sec. 2.2). Uncertainties in instances of both domains can be encoded into the size of the intersections. The amount of uncertainty between players is equal to $|A \cap B|$. If the interaction between the players is deterministic then $|A \cap B| = 1$. If uncertainty exists, then multiple interactions are possible and $|A \cap B| > 1$. We say that player A *interacts* with B if $|A \cap B| > 0$.

2.1   Non-cooperative Games

Sets can be used to encode adversaries in sequential games [RN09], where agents exchange a series of actions over a finite number of plies. Each game or interaction consists of the recording of actions by adversaries α and β, with $x = (a_1, b_1)(a_2, b_2)(a_3, b_3)$ for a game of three rounds. The player (set) representation A of adversary α is the set of games representing all possible actions by α's adversary with α's responding actions, and similarly for player B representing adversary β. An example game is rock-paper-scissors where adversaries α and β play two sequential rounds with an action space of $\{R, P, S\}$. Adversary α only plays rock, whereas adversary β first plays paper, then copies his adversary's play of the first round. The corresponding players (sets) A and B can be seen in Fig. 1a. The intersection set of A and B contains the single interaction $x =$"$(R, P)(R, R)$," which is the only possible game (interaction) that α and β can play.

Example 1 (Chess Game). We use the example of a chess game with uncertainty between two players: Anatoly as white and Boris as black. An interaction $x \in$

A	B
(R,R)(R,R)	**(R,P)(R,R)**
(R,R)(R,P)	(R,P)(P,R)
(R,R)(R,S)	(R,P)(S,R)
(R,P)(R,R)	(P,P)(R,P)
(R,P)(R,P)	(P,P)(P,P)
(R,P)(R,S)	(P,P)(S,P)
(R,S)(R,R)	(S,P)(R,S)
(R,S)(R,P)	(S,P)(P,S)
(R,S)(R,S)	(S,P)(S,S)

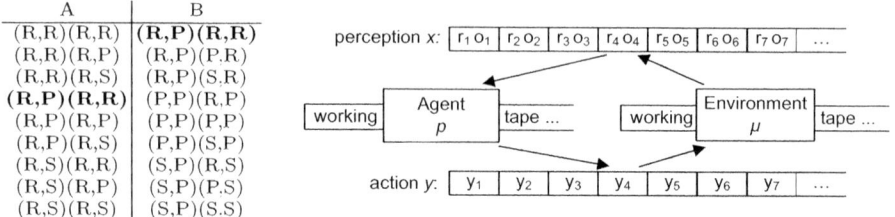

Fig. 1. (a) The set representation of players A and B playing two games of paper, rock, scissors. The intersection set of A and B contains the single interaction $x =$ "$(R, P)(R, R)$." (b) The cybernetic agent model.

$A \cap B$ between Anatoly and Boris is a game of chess played for at most m plies for each player, with $x = a_1 b_1 a_2 b_2 \ldots a_m b_m = \alpha b_{1:m}$. The chess move space $\mathcal{V} \subset \{0, 1\}^*$ has a short binary encoding, whose precise definition is not important. If the game has not ended after m rounds, then the game is considered a draw. Both players are nondeterministic, where at every ply, they can choose from a selection of moves. Anatoly's decisions can be represented by a function $f_A : \mathcal{V}^* \to 2^{\mathcal{V}}$ and similarly Boris' decisions by f_B. Anatoly can be represented by a set A, with $A = \{\alpha b_{1:m} : \forall_{1 \leq k \leq m} \ a_k \in f_A(\alpha b_{1:k-1})\}$, and similarly Boris by set B. Their intersection, $A \cap B$, represents the set of possible games that Anatoly and Boris can play together.

Generally, sets can encode adversaries of non-cooperative normal form games, with their interactions consisting of pure Nash equilibriums [RN09]. A normal form game is defined as (p, q) with the adversaries represented by normalized payoff functions p and q of the form $\{0, 1\}^n \times \{0, 1\}^n \to [0, 1]$. The set of pure Nash equilibriums is $\{\langle x, y \rangle : p(x, y) = q(y, x) = 1\}$. For each payoff function p there is a player $A = \{\langle x, y \rangle \mid p(x, y) = 1\}$, and for each payoff function q there is player B. The intersection of A and B is equal to the set of pure Nash equilibriums of p and q.

2.2   Cybernetic Agent Model

The interpretation of "interaction as intersection" is also applicable to the cybernetic agent model used in Universal Artificial Intelligence [Hut04]. With the cybernetic agent model, there is an agent and an environment communicating in a series of cycles $k = 1, 2, \ldots$ (Fig. 1b). At cycle k, the agent performs an action $y_k \in \mathcal{Y}$, dependent on the previous history $yx_{<k} = y_1 x_1 \ldots y_{k-1} x_{k-1}$. The environment accepts the action and in turn outputs $x_k \in \mathcal{X}$, which can be interpreted as the kth perception of the agent, followed by cycle $k + 1$ and so on. An agent is defined by a deterministic policy function $p : \mathcal{X}^* \to \mathcal{Y}^*$ with $p(x_{<k}) = y_{1:k}$ to denote output $y_{1:k} = y_1 y_2 \ldots y_k$ on input $x_{<k} = x_1 x_2 \ldots x_{k-1}$. We use the terms *policy* and *agent* interchangeably. The inputs are separated into two parts, $x_k \equiv r_k o_k$, with $r_k = r(x_k)$ representing the reward and o_k representing the observation. We say $r(x_{1:m}) = \sum_{i=1}^{m} r(x_i)$ and we assume bounds on rewards with $0 \leq r_k \leq c$ for all k. There is uncertainty in the environment; it can be represented

by a probability distribution over infinite strings, where $\mu(x_1 \ldots x_n)$ is the probability that an infinite string starts with $x_1 \ldots x_n$. In Hutter's notation [Hut04], an underlined argument $\underline{x}_k$ is a probability variable and non-underlined arguments x_k represent the condition with $\mu(x_{<n}\underline{x}_n) = \mu(\underline{x}_{1:n})/\mu(\underline{x}_{<n})$. The probability that the environment reacts with $x_1 \ldots x_n$ under agent output $y_1 \ldots y_n$ is $\mu(y_1\underline{x}_1 \ldots y_n\underline{x}_n) = \mu(y\underline{x}_n)$. The environment is chronological, in that input x_i only depends on $y\underline{x}_{<i}y_i$. The horizon m of the interaction is the number of cycles of the interaction. The *value* of agent p in environment μ is the expected reward sum $V_{1:m}^{p,\mu} = \sum_{x_{1:m}} r(x_{1:m})\mu(y\underline{x}_{1:m})|_{y_{1:m}=p(x_{<m})}$. The optimal agent that maximizes value $V_{1:m}^{p,\mu}$ is $p^\mu = \arg\max_p V_{1:m}^{p,\mu}$, with value $V_{1:m}^{*,\mu} = V_{1:m}^{p^\mu,\mu}$. The optimal expected reward given a partial history $y\underline{x}_{1:k}$ is $V_{1:m}^{p,\mu}(y\underline{x}_{1:k})$.

It is possible to construct players (sets) A and B from the agent p and environment μ where A "interacts" (intersects) with B only if agent p can achieve a certain level of reward in μ. This construction enables us to apply the results and proof techniques of section 5 to the cybernetic agent model. To translate p and μ to A and B, we fix two parameters: a time horizon m and a difficulty threshold τ. For every agent p, there is a player A_m^p, with $A_m^p = \{y\underline{x}_{1:m} \; : \; y_{1:m} = p(x_{<m})\}$. There are several possible ways to construct a set B from an environment μ. One direct method is for every environment μ, to define a player $B_{m,\tau}^\mu$, with $B_{m,\tau}^\mu = \{y\underline{x}_{1:m} \; : \; r(x_{1:m}) \geq \tau, \; \mu(y\underline{x}_{1:m}) > 0\}$. Player $B_{m,\tau}^\mu$ represents all possible histories of μ (however unlikely) where the reward is at least τ. If $A_m^p \cap B_{m,\tau}^\mu = \emptyset$, then environment μ is "too difficult" for the agent p; there is no interaction where the agent can receive a reward of at least τ. We say the agent p *interacts* with the environment μ at time horizon m and difficulty τ if $A_m^p \cap B_{m,\tau}^\mu \neq \emptyset$.

Example 2 (Peter and Magnus). We present a cybernetic agent model interpretation of chess with reward based players Peter and Magnus (same rules as example 1). Peter, the agent p, has to be deterministic whereas Magnus, the environment μ, has uncertainty. At cycle k, each action y_k is Peter's move and each perception x_k is Magnus' move. At ply m in the chess game, Magnus returns a reward of 1 if Peter has won. In rounds where the game is unfinished or if Peter loses or draws, the reward is 0. The player (set) A_m^p represents Peter's plays for m rounds. The player (set) for Magnus with difficulty threshold $\tau = 1$ and m plies, $B_{m,1}^\mu$ is the set of all games that Magnus loses in m rounds or less. If $A_m \cap B_{m,1}^\mu = \emptyset$, then Peter cannot *interact* with Magnus at difficulty level 1; Peter can never beat Magnus at chess in m rounds or less. If $A_m \cap B_{m,1}^\mu \neq \emptyset$ then Peter can beat Magnus at a game of chess in m rounds or less.

Another construction of a player $D_{m,\tau}^\mu$ with respect to environment μ, is $D_{m,\tau}^\mu = \{y\underline{x}_{1:m} \; : \; \forall_k \; V_{1:m}^{*,\mu}(y\underline{x}_{1:k})/V_{1:m}^{*,\mu} \geq \tau\}$. With this interpretation, player $D_{m,\tau}^\mu$ represents all histories where at each time k, $1 \leq k \leq m$, an agent can potentially achieve an expected reward of at least τ times the optimal expected reward. If $A_m^p \cap D_{m,\tau}^\mu = \emptyset$, then environment μ is "too difficult" for the agent p; there is no interaction where at *every* cycle k the agent has the potential to receive an expected reward of at least $\tau V_{1:m}^{*,\mu}$.

3   Background in Algorithmic Information Theory

We denote finite binary strings by $x \in \{0, 1\}^*$ and the length of strings by $l(x)$. Let the pairing function $\langle \cdot, \cdot \rangle$ be the standard one-to-one mapping from $\mathcal{N} \times \mathcal{N}$ to $\mathcal{N}$, where: $\langle x, y \rangle = x'y = 1^{l(l(x))}0l(x)xy$ and $l(\langle x, y \rangle) = l(y) + l(x) + 2l(l(x)) + 1$. The Kolmogorov complexity $C(x)$ is the length of the shortest binary program to compute x on a universal Turing machine ψ, $C(x) = \min\{l(d) : \psi(d) = x\}$. The prefix-free Kolmogorov complexity, $K(x)$, restricts the universal machine ψ so no halting program is a proper prefix of another halting program. For the rest of this paper, we use plain Kolmogorov complexity. Kolmogorov complexity is not finitely computable. The conditional Kolmogorov complexity of x relative to y, $C(x|y)$, is defined as the length of a shortest program to compute x, using y as an auxiliary input to the computation. The complexity of two strings x and y is denoted by $C(x, y) = C(\langle x, y \rangle)$. The conditional complexity of two strings is $C(x|y, z) = C(x|\langle y, z \rangle)$. The complexity of information in x about y is $I(x : y) = C(y) - C(y|x)$. The conditional mutual information is $I(x : y|z) = C(y|z) - C(y|x, z)$ and can be interpreted as the information z receives about y when given x. The complexity of a function $f : \{0, 1\}^* \to \{0, 1\}^*$ is $C(f) = \min\{C(p) : \forall_x \psi(p, x) = f(x)\}$. The Levin complexity is defined by $C_t(x) = \min_p\{l(p) + \log t(p, x) : \psi(p) = x\}$, with $t(p, x)$ being the number of steps taken by ψ until x is printed (without ψ necessary halting). Levin complexity is computable. The complexity of a finite set S is $C(S)$, the length of the shortest program f from which the universal Turing machine ψ computes a listing of the elements of S and then halts. If $S = \{x_1, \ldots, x_n\}$, then $\psi(f) = \langle x_1, \langle x_2, \ldots, \langle x_{n-1}, x_n \rangle \ldots \rangle \rangle$. The conditional complexity $C(x|S)$ is the length of the shortest program from which ψ, given S literally as auxiliary information, computes x. For every set S containing x, it must be that $C(x|S) \leq \log |S| + O(1)$. The randomness deficiency is the lack of typicality of x with respect to set S, with $\delta(x|S) = \log |S| - C(x|S)$, for $x \in S$ and ∞ otherwise. If $\delta(x|S)$ is small enough, then x is a typical element of S; x satisfies all simple properties that hold with high majorities of strings in S.

Example 3 (Anatoly's Games). Chess player Anatoly with function f_A can be represented as a set A (see example 1). Set A is simple relative to f_A and the maximum number of plies m, with $C(A|f_A, m) = O(1)$, where $O(1)$ is the length of code required to use f_A and m to enumerate all games $x \in A$.

The following theorem, used in section 5, shows that if a string x is contained by a large number of sets of a certain complexity, then it is contained by a simpler set [VV04]. The enumerative complexity, $CE(\mathcal{F})$, is the Kolmogorov complexity of a non halting program that enumerates all the sets $F \in \mathcal{F}$. This theorem also holds for conditional complexity bounds, $C(F|y)$.

Theorem 1 ([VV04]). *Let $\mathcal{F}$ be a family of subsets of a set of strings $\mathcal{G}$. If $x \in \mathcal{G}$ is an member of each of 2^k sets $F \in \mathcal{F}$ with $C(F) \leq r$, then x is a member of a set F' in $\mathcal{F}$ with $C(F') \leq r - k + O(\log k + \log r + \log \log |\mathcal{G}| + CE(\mathcal{F}))$.*

4   Player Strategy Learning

Players A and B can learn information about each other's strategies from a single interaction (game) $x \in A \cap B$ or from their entire interaction set (all possible games) $A \cap B$. The *capacity* of a player A is the maximum amount of information that A can receive about another player through all possible interactions, i.e. their interaction set. It is equal to the log of the number of possible subsets that it can have, $\log 2^{|A|} = |A|$. We define the lack of typicality of a subset S with respect to A to be $\delta(S|A) = |A| - C(S|A)$, for $S \subseteq A$ and ∞ otherwise.

Example 4 (Capacity). Boris B uses a range of black openings whereas Bill B' uses only the Sicilian defence. So Boris has a higher capacity, $|B| \gg |B'|$, and can potentially learn more than Bill.

Example 5 (Randomness Deficiency). Let A be the chess games played by Anatoly. Bob is a simple player B', who only moves his knight back and forth. Set $S = A \cap B'$ represents all A's games with B'. The randomness deficiency of these games, $\delta(S|A)$, is high, as S is easily computable from A, with $C(S|A) \ll |A|$. Let $T \subseteq A$, in which $T = A \cap B$ are games played between Anatoly and Boris, who uses a range of chess strategies unknown to Anatoly. Then $\delta(T|A)$ is low and $C(T|A)$ is high.

If A views every interaction in $A \cap B$, the amount of information B reveals about itself is, $I(A \cap B : B|A)$, the mutual information between B and $A \cap B$, given A. This term can be reduced to $C(A \cap B|A) - C(A \cap B|A, B) = C(A \cap B|A) + O(1)$. We define the amount of knowledge that A received about B from the interaction setp as:

$$R(B|A) = C(A \cap B|A). \tag{1}$$

The higher the randomness deficiency, $\delta(A \cap B|A)$, of an interaction set, $A \cap B$, with respect to player A, the less information, $R(B|A)$, player A can receive about its opponent B, with

$$R(B|A) + \delta(A \cap B|A) = |A|. \tag{2}$$

Player A receives the most information about its opponent when the randomness deficiency is $\delta(A \cap B|A) \approx 0$.

Example 6. Let Anatoly, A, and Bob, B', be the players of example 5. Bob has a simple strategy and has a lower capacity $|B'| \ll |A|$, but he learns a lot from Anatoly, with $\delta(A \cap B'|B') \approx 0$ and $R(A|B') \approx |B'|$. Anatoly learns very little from Bob, with $R(B'|A) \approx 0$ and $\delta(A \cap B'|A) \approx |A|$.

Players can reveal information about themselves through a single interaction. The amount of information that A received about B from their interaction x is

$$I(x : B|A) = C(x|A) - C(x|A, B). \tag{3}$$

A graphical depiction of the complexities relating to A, B, and x can be seen in Fig. 2. We define the lack of typicality of an interaction x with respect to both players to be

$$\delta(x|A, B) = \log|A \cap B| - C(x|A, B) \tag{4}$$

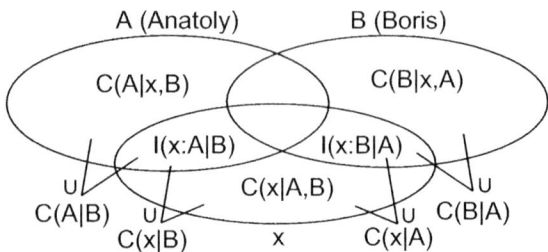

Fig. 2. The complexities and information of A, B, and their interaction x. The relationships hold up to logarithmic precision.

for $x \in A \cap B$ and ∞ otherwise. If $\delta(x|A, B)$ is small, then x represents a typical interaction. The information passed from player B to player A through a single interaction is represented by

$$I(x : B|A) + \delta(x|A) = \log|A|/|A \cap B| + \delta(x|A, B). \tag{5}$$

The information passed between players through a single interaction with the same capacity is

$$I(x{:}B|A) + \delta(x|A) = I(x{:}A|B) + \delta(x|B) + O(1). \tag{6}$$

Example 7. Anatoly A plays a game x with Boris B who has the same capacity with $|A| = |B|$. Anatoly tricks Boris with a King's gambit and the game x follows a series of moves extremely familiar to Anatoly. Boris reacts with the most obvious move at every turn. In this case the game is simple to Anatoly, with $\delta(x|A)$ being large and $I(x : B|A)$ being small. The game is new to Boris with $\delta(x|B)$ being small and $I(x{:}A|B)$ being large. Thus Boris learns more than Anatoly from x.

If the players have a deterministic interaction, then $A \cap B = \{y\}$ and the information A received from B reduces to $I(y{:}B|A) + \delta(y|A) = \log|A|$.

5   Player Approximation and Interaction Complexity

We show that, given an interaction x between players A and B, A can "construct" an approximate player B' that has interaction x using a small number of extra bits ϵ, where $C(B'|A, x) = \epsilon$. We also show that the conditional complexity $C(B'|A)$ of the approximate player B' is not greater than the amount of information $I(x{:}B|A)$ that A obtains about B (up to logarithmic precision). We use the simplified notation $\log A = \log|A|$. We also use the player space notation, $\mathcal{B}$, to denote a set of sets of strings.

Theorem 2. *Given are a player space $\mathcal{B}$ and players A and $B \in \mathcal{B}$ over strings of size n with $x \in A \cap B$ and $C(\mathcal{B}) = O(\log n)$. Then there is a player $B' \in \mathcal{B}$ with $x \in B'$, $C(B'|A, x) = O(s)$, and $C(B'|A) \leq I(x : B|A) + O(s)$, with $s = \log C(B|A) + \log n$.*

Proof. Let $r = C(B|A)$. We define $\mathcal{G}$ as the set of strings of size n, with $\log\log|\mathcal{G}| = \log n$. We set $\mathcal{F} = \mathcal{B}$, and so $CE(\mathcal{F}) = O(\log n)$. Let N be the number of sets $S \in \mathcal{B}$, with $C(S|A) \leq r$ and $x \in S$. We first show that $C(B|A, x) \leq \log N + O(\log nr)$. There is a program, that when given x, A, B, and r, with $C(\mathcal{B}, r) = O(\log nr)$, can enumerate all sets in $\mathcal{B}$ containing x with conditional complexity to A being less than or equal to r. Thus B can be created using such a program and an index of size $\lceil \log N \rceil$. By the application of Theorem 1, conditional on A, with $k = \lfloor \log N \rfloor$, there is a set $B' \in \mathcal{F}$ with $x \in B'$ and $C(B'|A) \leq r - k + O(\log nr) \leq C(B|A) - C(B|A, x) + O(\log nr) = I(x : B|A) + O(\log nr)$. To prove $C(B'|A, x) = O(s)$, assume B' is the set satisfying the above properties that minimizes $C(B'|A)$ up to precision $O(s)$. It must be that $C(B'|A, x) = O(s)$. Otherwise $C(B'|A, x) = \omega(s)$ and there is a set B'' satisfying properties above and $C(B''|A) \leq C(B'|A) - C(B'|A, x) + O(s) = C(B'|A) - \omega(s)$, causing a contradiction.

Example 8 (Opponent Reconstruction). Anatoly, A, plays a chess game x with Boris, B, with $x \in A \cap B$. The players use a random string b of size $C(x|A, B)$ to help decide their moves. Without using b, Anatoly can "construct" Bob, B', an impersonator of Boris, using information from the game x and $O(\log C(B|A) + \log l(x))$ bits. Bob can play the same game x with Anatoly.

Given are players A and B who *interact*, in that $A \cap B \neq \emptyset$. We show that there exists an interacting player B' that has complexity bounded by the mutual information of A and B. If theorem 1 can be strengthened such that the enumerative complexity term $CE(\mathcal{F})$ is replaced by $CEE(\mathcal{F})$, the complexity of enumerating both the sets and the elements of the sets of $\mathcal{F}$, then the precision of theorems 3 and 4 can be strengthened with the replacement of the Levin complexity term $C_t(A)$ with Kolmogorov complexity $C(A)$.

Theorem 3. *Given are a player space $\mathcal{B}$ and players A and $B \in \mathcal{B}$ with $A \cap B \neq \emptyset$. Then there exists a player $B' \in \mathcal{B}$ with $A \cap B' \neq \emptyset$, and $C(B') \leq I(A : B) + O(s)$, with $s = \log C(B) + \log C_t(A) + C(\mathcal{B})$.*

Proof. Let $r = C(B)$, $h = C_t(A)$, and $q = 2^{C(\mathcal{B})}$. We define $\mathcal{G} = \{\langle S \rangle : C_t(S) \leq r\}$, with $\langle S \rangle$ being an encoding of set S. This implies $\log\log|\mathcal{G}| = O(\log h)$. We define $\mathcal{F}$ with a recursive function $\lambda : \mathcal{B} \rightarrow \mathcal{F}$, with $\lambda(S) = \{\langle T \rangle \mid C_t(T) \leq h, S \cap T \neq \emptyset\}$. It must be $C(\lambda) = O(\log h)$. The enumeration complexity of $\mathcal{F}$ requires the encoding of $\mathcal{B}$ and λ, and so $CE(\mathcal{F}) = O(\log hq)$. Thus if $\langle T \rangle \in \lambda(S)$, then $T \cap S \neq \emptyset$. Let N be the number of sets $S \in \mathcal{B}$, with $C(S) \leq r$ and $S \cap A \neq \emptyset$. Thus $C(B|A) \leq \log N + O(\log hqr)$, as there is a program, when given A, r, $\mathcal{B}$, and an index of size $\lceil \log N \rceil$, that can return any such S. By the application of Theorem 1, with $x = \langle A \rangle$ and $k = \lfloor \log N \rfloor$, there is a set $F \in \mathcal{F}$ with $x \in F$ and $C(F) \leq r - k + O(\log hqr) \leq C(B) - C(B|A) + O(\log hqr) = I(A : B) + O(\log hqr)$. A set $B' \in \mathcal{B}$, with $\lambda(B') = F$, can be easily recovered from F by enumerating all sets in $\mathcal{B}$, applying λ to each one, and selecting the first one which produces F. So $C(B') \leq C(F) + O(\log q) \leq I(A : B) + O(\log hqr)$. Since $\langle A \rangle \in \lambda(B')$, it must be that $A \cap B' \neq \emptyset$.

We show that if a player A *interacts* with numerous players of a given complexity and uncertainty, then there exists a simple player B' who interacts with A with the same uncertainty.

Theorem 4. *Given are player space $\mathcal{B}$, player A and 2^k players $B \in \mathcal{B}$ where for each B, $0 < |A \cap B| \le c$ and $C(B) \le r$. There is a player $B' \in \mathcal{B}$ such that $0 < |A \cap B'| \le c$ and $C(B') \le r - k + O(s)$, with $s = \log C_t(A) + \log c + \log k + \log r + C(\mathcal{B})$.*

Proof. Let $h = C_t(A)$ and $q = 2^{C(\mathcal{B})}$. We can define $\mathcal{G} \subseteq \{0,1\}^*$ as a set of strings, each encoding a set (player) S whose Levin complexity is less than or equal to h. This implies $\log \log |\mathcal{G}| = O(\log h)$. We represent the encoding of S with $\langle S \rangle$. We define $\mathcal{F}$ with a recursive function $\lambda : \mathcal{B} \to \mathcal{F}$, with $\lambda(S) = \{\langle T \rangle \mid C_t(T) \le h, 0 < |S \cap T| \le c\}$. Thus it must be $C(\lambda) = O(\log ch)$. The enumeration complexity of $\mathcal{F}$ requires the encoding of c, h, and $\mathcal{B}$, with $CE(\mathcal{F}) = O(\log chq)$. Thus if $\langle T \rangle \in \lambda(S)$, then player T and player S have a non empty intersection of size at most c. From the assumptions of this theorem, $\langle A \rangle$ is covered by at least 2^k sets $\lambda(B) \in \mathcal{F}$ of complexity $C(\lambda(B)) \le r + O(\log chq)$. By the application of Theorem 1, with $x = \langle A \rangle$, there is a set $F \in \mathcal{F}$ with $x \in F$, $C(F) \le r - k + O(\log(chkqr))$. A set $B' \in \mathcal{B}$, with $\lambda(B') = F$ can be recovered from F by enumerating all sets in $\mathcal{B}$, applying λ to each one, and selecting the first one which produces F. Therefore $C(B'|F) \le O(\log chq)$ and so $C(B') \le C(F) + O(\log chq) \le r - k + O(\log(chkqr))$. Since $\langle A \rangle \in \lambda(B')$, it must be that $0 < |A \cap B'| \le c$, thus the theorem is proven.

Example 9. An example application of theorem 4 is a game of the same form as example 2. Magnus, represented by set B, plays 2^k games of against 2^k young players $A \in \mathcal{A}$. Furthermore the players and Magnus are deterministic with for each $A \in \mathcal{A}$, $|A \cap B| = 1$. The difficulty threshold τ, is set to 1, so every one of the young players beat Magnus. By theorem 4, if all players $A \in \mathcal{A}$ have complexity at most $C(A) \le r$, then there is a simpler player $A' \in \mathcal{A}$ that will win against Magnus, with $C(A') \le r - k + \epsilon$ (with ϵ being of logarithmic order) and $|A' \cap B| = 1$.

6   Future Work: Universal Interaction

Since the agents and environments of the cybernetic agent model of Section 2.2 can be translated into set representations, there is potential application of the proof techniques used in Section 5 to Artificial Universal Intelligence [Hut04], and in particular to describe properties of the AIXI model. The universal environment, ξ, is defined using a form of the universal prior, $\mathbf{m}(x) = \sum_{p:\psi(p)=x} 2^{-l(p)}$, representing a semimeasure (degenerate probability) over all infinite strings, with $\xi(\underline{y}\underline{x}_{1:k}) = \sum_\rho 2^{-K(\rho)} \rho(\underline{y}\underline{x}_{1:n})$. The universal environment ξ is the weighted summation over all chronological environments ρ. The term $K(\rho)$ represents the *prefix free* Kolmogorov complexity of ρ. The AIXI model p_m^ξ is the optimal agent for the environment ξ with horizon m, in that $p_m^\xi = \arg\max_p V_{1:m}^{p,\xi}$. The sequence of self optimizing AIXI agents for each time horizon is $\{p_i^\xi\}_{i=1,2,\dots}$. Let

$\mathcal{M}$ be a set of environments where a sequence of self-optimizing policies $\tilde{p}_m$ exists. The sequence converges to receive the optimal average for all environments with $\forall \nu \in \mathcal{M} : \frac{1}{m} V_{1:m}^{p_m, \nu} \overset{m \to \infty}{\longrightarrow} \frac{1}{m} V_{1:m}^{*, \nu}$. By theorem 5.29 from [Hut04], it must be that the sequence of AIXI agents is optimal for $\mathcal{M}$ with $\frac{1}{m} V_{1:m}^{p_m^\xi, \nu} \overset{m \to \infty}{\longrightarrow} \frac{1}{m} V_{1:m}^{*, \nu}$. We use the conversion of agents p and environments μ to sets A_m^p and $D_{m,\tau}^\mu$ as introduced at the end Section 2.2. The sequence of self optimizing AIXI agents, $\{p_i^\xi\}_{i=1,2,\dots}$, is universal with regard to interaction with respect to $\mathcal{M}$. It is easy to see that for all τ and all environments $\nu \in \mathcal{M}$, there is a number $m_{\nu\tau}$ where for all $m > m_{\nu,\tau}$, $A_m^{p_m^\xi} \cap D_{m,\tau}^\mu \neq \emptyset$. This implies a set representation of agent dynamics can be used to describe further properties of the AIXI model. There is potential for a deep connection, roughly analogously to how prefix-free Kolmogorov complexity and the universal prior are related with the Coding Theorem $K(x) = -\log \mathbf{m}(x) + O(1)$ [LV08].

7   Conclusions

We used Algorithmic Information Theory to quantify the information exchanged between agents that interact in non-cooperative games (Sec. 4). We have shown that an agent A can construct an approximation of his opponent B using information from a single interaction (game) with B (Th. 2). We have shown that if an agent B with superfluous information interacts with an environment A and achieves a certain reward, then there exists another agent B' without this information that can achieve the same reward (Th. 3). We have also shown that if multiple agents interact with an environment to achieve a certain reward, then there exists a simple agent who can achieve the same reward (Th. 4). Our constructions are compatible with Universal Artificial Intelligence, in that the AIXI model can be interpreted as universal with regard to interactions with environments (Section 6).

References

[CT91]   Cover, T., Thomas, J.: Elements of Information Theory. Wiley-Interscience, New York (1991)

[GP07]   Goertzel, B., Pennachin, C.: Artificial General Intelligence (Cognitive Technologies). Springer-Verlag New York, Inc., Secaucus (2007)

[GTV01]   Gács, P., Tromp, J., Vitanyi, P.: Algorithmic Statistics. IEEE Transactions on Information Theory 47(6) (2001)

[Hut04]   Hutter, M.: Universal Artificial Intelligence: Sequential Decisions based on Algorithmic Probability. Springer, Berlin (2004)

[LV08]   Li, M., Vitányi, P.: An Introduction to Kolmogorov Complexity and Its Applications, 3rd edn. Springer Publishing Company, Incorporated, Heidelberg (2008)

[RN09]   Russell, S., Norvig, P.: Artificial Intelligence: A Modern Approach, 3rd edn. Prentice Hall, Englewood Cliffs (2009)

[VV04]   Vereshchagin, N., Vitányi, P.: Algorithmic Rate Distortion Theory. arXiv:cs/0411014v3 (2004), http://arxiv.org/abs/cs.IT/0411014

[VV10]   Vereshchagin, N., Vitányi, P.: Rate Distortion and Denoising of Individual Data using Kolmogorov Complexity. IEEE Transactions on Information Theory 56 (2010)

On More Realistic Environment Distributions for Defining, Evaluating and Developing Intelligence

José Hernández-Orallo[1], David L. Dowe[2], Sergio España-Cubillo[3],
M. Victoria Hernández-Lloreda[4], and Javier Insa-Cabrera[1]

[1] DSIC, Universitat Politècnica de València, Spain
{jorallo,jinsa}@dsic.upv.es
[2] Clayton School of Information Technology, Monash University, Australia
david.dowe@monash.edu
[3] ProS Research Center, Universitat Politècnica de València, Spain
sergio.espana@pros.upv.es
[4] Departamento de Metodología de las Ciencias del Comportamiento,
Universidad Complutense de Madrid, Spain
vhlloreda@psi.ucm.es

Abstract. One insightful view of the notion of intelligence is the ability to perform well in a diverse set of tasks, problems or environments. One of the key issues is therefore the choice of this set, which can be formalised as a 'distribution'. Formalising and properly defining this distribution is an important challenge to understand what intelligence is and to achieve artificial general intelligence (AGI). In this paper, we agree with previous criticisms that a universal distribution using a reference universal Turing machine (UTM) over tasks, environments, etc., is perhaps a much too general distribution, since, e.g., the probability of other agents appearing on the scene or having some social interaction is almost 0 for many reference UTMs. Instead, we propose the notion of Darwin-Wallace distribution for environments, which is inspired by biological evolution, artificial life and evolutionary computation. However, although enlightening about where and how intelligence should excel, this distribution has so many options and is uncomputable in so many ways that we certainly need a more practical alternative. We propose the use of intelligence tests over multi-agent systems, in such a way that agents with a certified level of intelligence at a certain degree are used to construct the tests for the next degree. This constructive methodology can then be used as a more realistic intelligence test and also as a testbed for developing and evaluating AGI systems.

Keywords: Intelligence, Evolutionary Computation, Artificial Life, Social Intelligence, Intelligence Test, Universal Distribution.

1 Introduction

Understanding what intelligence is (and is not) plays a crucial role in developing truly general intelligent machines. Apart from the many informal definitions from psychology, philosophy, biology, artificial intelligence and other disciplines (see

J. Schmidhuber, K.R. Thórisson, and M. Looks (Eds.): AGI 2011, LNAI 6830, pp. 82–91, 2011.

an account in [16]), there have been some definitions which include the notion of compression, Kolmogorov Complexity or related concepts such as Solomonoff's universal distribution (see, e.g. [4,11,7,17]). Some of these proposals have claimed that they are necessary and sufficient, while others have only claimed that the ability which is defined is necessary for intelligence but not sufficient (so suggesting further factors, see e.g. [8]).

Apart from the view of 'intelligence as compression' (or compression – one-part or (MML) two-part – being a necessary part of intelligence), the previous approaches are based on a distribution of tasks, exercises or environments. Then, intelligence is defined as good performance in this distribution of exercises. This clearly connects the notion of an 'intelligence definition' with the notion of an 'intelligence test', notions which are tightly intertwined. The kind of tasks (static vs. dynamic, predictive vs. explanatory, etc.) distinguishes the previous approaches. The common feature is the distribution which is used for the selection of tasks. While psychometrics does not choose tasks using a formal and independent distribution, these works take the tasks from a universal distribution [22], which gives higher probability to tasks whose shortest description is smaller.

Nonetheless, the use of a universal distribution gives a very high weight (i.e., probability) to very simple tasks. The problem is that it is not true that intelligent systems have a monotone behaviour on the complexity of a task. In many simple tasks, a very simple program can perform better than the smartest human. Thus, aggregating results using this distribution would assign higher intelligence to simple programs. One possible solution is to set a minimum complexity value [13], but this is clearly an arbitrary choice. An alternative option would be to define intelligence as the maximum complexity level where a system can score 'significantly better' than random. This can be shaped as an adaptive (or anytime) intelligence test [10], where the complexity of tasks (and speed) is adapted to the intelligence of the agent which is being evaluated.

However, even though we think that these ideas are in the right direction, there is a problem about the class of tasks we might generate from the universal distribution. Using environments like those typical in reinforcement learning, which is the approach taken in [17] and followed in [10], we see very clearly that even very complex environments will be very different to the environments a human (or an animal or a robot) faces during their life. We can, of course, enrich the environments to be more *physically* realistic, with simple physics, in order to allow the complex perception and mechanisms we are used to in this universe. However, apart from being anthropocentric, this 3D physical world would not ensure that other agents may appear, as it happens in, e.g., Mars.

If we generate environments randomly using a universal distribution over a Turing-complete reference machine (Universal Turing Machine, UTM), it is clear that some environments might contain some other agents. In fact, some environments might contain life, and some others might even contain intelligent life[1].

---

[1] An early exploration of the idea of computable universes where life can emerge is given in [20] and a discussion of how big a universe we need before intelligence might appear can be found in [1, sec. 0.2.7, p545, col. 1].

However, the probability of any of these environments is almost 0 for many reference UTM. So, we are quite far from what intelligence is supposed to be, an ability to interact with a physical world, full of plants and animals.

In fact, this is one of the drifts taken by artificial intelligence in the last decades. The appearance of multi-agent systems is a sign that the future of machine intelligence will not be found in monolithic systems solving tasks without other agents to compete or collaborate with. This is also better understood in comparative psychology and biology as well. For instance, [12] shows that cognitive abilities for dealing with the physical world (concerning things such as space, quantities, and causality) are similar for chimpanzees and human children, while it is in cognitive skills for dealing with the social world where the balance is in favour of humans. Furthermore, it is now better understood (see, e.g., [24]) that co-operation and communication are special traits of human cognition. In fact, "evolutionarily, the key difference is that humans have evolved not only social-cognitive skills geared toward competition, but also social-cognitive skills and motivations geared toward complex forms of co-operation." [24]

So using a universal distribution to define or evaluate intelligence might be like evaluating or defining intelligent agents for Mars. A similar criticism has been raised by artificial (general) intelligence, stating that intelligence must be more embodied/natural/social [5]. In fact, there have been some proposals of simplified worlds, such as Goertzel's AGI preschool [6], to test and develop AGI systems, whose complexity (in terms of shortest description) is very high (and hence, with very low probability for a universal distribution).

However, a non-principled way of selecting environments mimicking the environments that adult humans or small children interact with dramatically deviates from the goal of deriving a formal, mathematical and non-anthropomorphic definition of intelligence, and would be useless far beyond human intelligence.

In this paper, we take a different approach. Inspired by evolutionary computation, artificial life, multi-agent systems and social cognition, we develop a more realistic distribution of environments. The basic idea is straightforward: intelligence is the result of evolution through millions of generations interacting with other live beings. Thus we define intelligence in this context, interacting with other agents of similar intelligence.

We formalise the so-called Darwin-Wallace distribution for agents and environments. Despite the many options and the many sources of uncomputability, we claim that, conceptually, the notion of Darwin-Wallace distribution is useful to re-visit previous definitions of intelligence [4,11,7,17,8,10].

The next step is how this notion can be used for AGI development and evaluation. We present a procedure which approximates a Darwin-Wallace distribution by using intelligence tests over environments such that 'certified' systems are incorporated into the environments, so making them socially more complex. This iterated process (in [19, sec. 5.1] a recursion is applied for the Turing Test) may lead to more realistic testbeds for AGI or for reinforcement learning.

The paper is organised as follows. The next section deals with the frequency of individuals in terms of evolution. This paves the way for the definition of the

Darwin-Wallace distribution in section 3. Section 4 introduces a constructive approximation of the distribution in the form of incremental intelligence tests from non-social environments to more social ones. Finally, section 5 discusses the contributions, implications and open questions which derive from this work.

2   Artificial Life, Biology and Intelligence

Many ideas from Artificial Life (Alife) [15] (and evolutionary computation) are useful for understanding which environments may hold intelligence. The starting point of every Alife project is a virtual (or artificial) environment where we place some individuals (a population) inside.   One problem in Alife systems (and evolutionary computation) is that evolution stagnates at some point.

Of course, in Alife (and biology) we find the notion of 'evolutionarily successful individual'. However, many species on Earth outnumber the Homo Sapiens (by several orders of magnitude), while their individual adaptability is poor (their adaptability as a species may be high, like cockroaches or some kinds of bacteria). The good thing about Alife is that we can force all the individuals to have the same body, while only letting their behaviour evolve.. So even though the notion of frequency in the real world is not related to the adaptability of a species , it *can* be related to the adaptability of a species or individual in a virtual world where the bodies and rules are the same for all the individuals.

Before this, we have to consider co-evolution and mind-reading. Co-evolution is the evolution of one species in a direction which is triggered or shaped by other species, as plants with insects, and mammals with intestinal bacteria. The genotype and phenotype (both its body and its behaviour) of many species can only be explained as the result of co-evolution. Intelligence, as a phenotypical trait, is not an exception. Intelligence can only be explained as the result of the co-evolution with other species and the co-evolution with individuals of the same species. In particular, when we focus on behaviour innovations (and not on physical changes), we find the concepts of mind-reading and manipulation [14], which can be applied for competition but also for co-operation, which are essential for predators and preys. Although 'mind-reading' has been used (especially in the past) to refer to both the adaptation of the species and the adaptation (i.e. intelligence) of the individual, in what follows we refer to the second. So, by 'mind-reading' and 'manipulation' we mean the use of information processing and the use of mental representation of other individuals, and not a genetically pre-programmed manipulation or simple pre-defined predator-prey patterns, as, e.g., an anteater can have. And human intelligence is the clearest example of such a social context. But again, evolutionarily, the key difference of humans in front of other animals (great apes included) is their ability at knowledge acquisition and transmission in order to perform better in very rich social contexts, "in terms of intention-reading, social learning, and communication" [24].

So, a more realistic definition of intelligence must give more weight to environments which contain other agents with social abilities.

3   Darwin-Wallace Distribution

Systems in Alife do not generally create environments where life emerges from scratch. On the contrary, they include a start-up population, from which things evolve. Environments are created in such a way that agents can do some actions and have a (generally partial) observation of the world. This setting is very similar to the way environments are created in reinforcement learning (RL), but the notion of reward is generally understood as a fitness function, which may affect the way agents die, reproduce or mutate.

So, following [10] (which in turns follows [17]), we define actions as a finite set of symbols $\mathcal{A}$ (e.g., $\{left, right, up, down\}$); rewards are taken from any subset $\mathcal{R}$ of rational numbers between -1 and 1; and observations are also limited by a finite set $\mathcal{O}$ of possibilities. We consider these sets to be the same for all the agents. This means that, physically, all the agents are equal.

An agent is an interactive (Turing) machine which receives a pair $\langle r, o \rangle$ of reward and observation, known as a perception, and outputs an action a. Note that an agent is not a (Markov) function, so the action may depend on old rewards and observations. Additionally, an agent might also be stochastic. An agent can be properly formalised as a probability measure. For instance, given an agent, denoted by π^j, the term $\pi^j(a_k^j | r_1^j o_1^j a_1^j r_2^j o_2^j a_2^j \ldots r_k^j o_k^j)$ denotes the probability of agent π^j executing action a_k^j after the sequence of events $r_1^j o_1^j a_1^j r_2^j o_2^j a_2^j \ldots r_k^j o_k^j$.

A *base* multi-agent environment is also an interactive (Turing) machine which takes as input the action of every agent and outputs rewards and observations for each and all of them. Again, it can be stochastic and it can be represented by a probability measure. For instance, for an environment accepting m agents, the term $\mu(r_k^1 o_k^1 r_k^2 o_k^2 \ldots r_k^m o_k^m | r_1^1 o_1^1 a_1^1 r_1^2 o_1^2 a_1^2 \ldots r_1^m o_1^m a_1^m r_2^1 o_2^1 a_2^1 r_2^2 o_2^2 a_2^2 \ldots r_2^m o_2^m a_2^m \ldots r_{k-1}^1 o_{k-1}^1 a_{k-1}^1 r_{k-1}^2 o_{k-1}^2 a_{k-1}^2 \ldots r_{k-1}^m o_{k-1}^m a_{k-1}^m)$ denotes the probability of the environment outputting the specified rewards and observations for all the agents given previous rewards, observations and actions. Environments should treat all agents equally, so changing the agent indices should not change the result. Other properties, such as sensitivity, minimum working (living) space, etc., could also be imposed, in order to define an appropriate multi-agent environment *class*[2]. Given this class, we can define a universal distribution by properly (prefix-free) coding its environments over a reference UTM U_e, using the formula $p_E(\mu) := 2^{-K_{U_e}(\mu)}$, where $K()$ refers to Kolmogorov complexity. This is the probability of the base multi-agent environment not considering the agents. Another option here would be to define p_E using Schmidhuber's Speed Prior [21] or any other computable variant of K, such as Levin's Kt [18].

Using just one agent ($m = 1$), where the agent is the evaluated agent, we would have an environment distribution similar to the one introduced in [17]. But we are interested in social environments where other agents appear. So we

---

[2] The notions of sensitivity and balancedness, introduced in [10], could be valid here as well if properly extended to multi-agent environments, in such a way that what an agent does may affect the others. For instance, the environment class introduced in [9] might be used, where rewards could be shared by the agents.

need to introduce more agents. In order to do this, we define an agent class and derive a universal distribution over its agents, (prefix-free) coding them over a reference UTM U_a, using the formula $p_A(\pi) := 2^{-K_{U_a}(\pi)}$.

When we join a base environment μ with a set of m agents, we get an m-agent environment (a 'social' environment with population of size m). From here we define the distribution of *start-up* m-agent environments (denoted by σ) as:

$$p_S(\sigma) = p_S(\langle \mu, \pi_1, \pi_2, ..., \pi_m \rangle) := p_E(\mu) \times \prod_{j=1}^{m} p_A(\pi^j)$$

Note that this definition considers base environments and agents to be independent. Of course, agents and environments are not independent in the real world, and they are not independent in evolutionary processes. The advantage of making them independent is that we can combine and analyse the distributions separately, and this may ease the construction of approximation without a fully (and intractable) evolutionary process.

And now systemic properties emerge when we let the social environment run (or "evolve"). We define the average reward for each agent j at step i, denoted by R_i^j as the mean of the rewards that the agent has received from step 0 to step i. We use this value R_i^j as a fitness function in a simplified 'evolution'. We define the probability of dying d as a function of R_i^j. Since rewards range from -1 to $+1$ one possible choice is $d(R_i) = \delta(1 - R_i^j)/2 + \epsilon$, with $0 < \delta < 1$ and $0 \leq \epsilon < (1 - \delta)$ being small positive real numbers.

Finally, instead of considering gradual environment changes (as usual in evolution), we define a probability of the environment being completely replaced by a new one, while keeping the agents. The goal is to favour individual adaptability instead of pre-programmed specialisation to the environment. In particular, we define this probability as a constant (for simplicity). This small constant factor $0 \leq c \leq 1$ means that for each step the environment might (with probability c) be replaced by another environment, which would be chosen using p_E. Of course, if $c = 0$ we stick to the original environment forever. The rationale for all this is that we do not want the agents to be optimised for the environments, but to be optimised to behave in the context of other agents. In general, environments will be very simple, so it is the multi-agent scenario which must determine the distributions. Of course, whether we achieve this goal in this way.

After each step, we apply d to all agents to determine whether they die or survive, replacing the dead agents by new agents using p_A. We do similarly for the environment, using c. Then, for each m-agent environment σ, function d and step i, this defines a probability of agent π^j after step i, denoted by $q_{(d,c,i)}$.

From here, we denote the Darwin-Wallace[3] distribution of degree i as:

$$p_{d,c,i}(\sigma) = p_i(\langle \mu, \pi_1, \pi_2, ..., \pi_m \rangle) := p_E(\mu) \times \prod_{j=1}^{m} q_{(d,c,i)}(\pi^j)$$

Logically, $p_0(\sigma) = p_S(\sigma)$, since $q_{(d,c,i)}(\pi^j) = p_A(\pi^j)$.

---

[3] From Charles Darwin (1809-1882) and Alfred Russel Wallace (1823-1913).

Given the previous definition, what does it represent? It just assigns probabilities to multi-agent environments. For instance, an environment with sophisticated and evolutionary-adapted agents is much less likely for $p_{d,c,i}$ for low values of i than for large values of i, as the probability of a mammal on the Earth in the Precambrian is much lower than today. Note that this significantly differs from an evolutionary system (either artificial or natural) in many ways, since there is no concept of generation, there is no reproduction, no phenotype, no inheritance, no mutations and no cross-over. In addition, the environment may change drastically in just one step, so favouring general adaptive agents ahead of agents which specialise (to or) in a particular environment.

The purpose of all this is to isolate social adaptability instead of the adaptability to a single environment. The use of any mechanism from natural or artificial evolution that is not strictly necessary is then ruled out in this proposal.

The previous definition synthesises the notion that complex agents with complex behaviours might have a higher probability the higher the value of i is. Many of these complex behaviours are only useful when the environment is full of other complex agents, which we can only explain with a kind of evolutionary process. This is the reason why we use the name Darwin-Wallace for this distribution.

Consequently, previous definitions of intelligence [4,11,7,17,8,10] can be re-understood by using variants of the previous distribution instead of variants of the universal distribution[4] for regular UTMs. Of course, this gives infinitely many definitions, since (apart from the reference UTM) we can parametrise i and m. The higher i and m are, the more 'social' the intelligence definition is. Nonetheless, despite the insightful and philosophical lure of the concept, it is difficult to apply in practice, because its uncomputability or intractability (if we use computable versions based on Levin's Kt or Schmidhuber's Speed Prior [21]) and many different options that could be taken (e.g., the probabilities d and c).

4   Approximating the Distribution through Testing

The introduction of the previous distribution does not mean that we suggest 'constructing' intelligence (or deriving social environments) as the result of an inefficient, artificial evolutionary process. The alternative is an artificial selection rather than a natural selection. Starting with a multi-agent environment, we can introduce a first generation of agents, whose intelligence we still do not know. After a sufficient number of steps, we would get an average reward for each of them. From this individual assessment, we would (probabilistically) keep the agents with the best results, while removing the agents with the worst results, and introducing some new agents. With a large number of agents, a variety of

---

[4] There can be a machine U such that the universal distribution using this machine may match (at least approximately) a Darwin-Wallace distribution of degree i and population size m. In theory this is possible (ignoring time in K_U and excluding some environments without agents), but finding such a machine U is similar to giving the definition of the Darwin-Wallace distribution above, which is our goal.

environments and several interactions with this assisted process, we would have a testbed where only socially intelligent agents would score well.

It can be argued that this process is not very different to recreating natural environments and embedding humans inside. In fact, the Turing Test is an example of this. However, in our proposal, environments are not anthropomorphic, they do not rely on natural language, and they accept any kind of agent Furthermore, this process can scale up far beyond human intelligence, since it is intelligence inside a social system that we measure (and use) to feed the system.

There are, of course, many issues about this process. For instance, it is possible that a highly intelligent system π_a could score worse than another less intelligent system π_b for a low degree of the test, say i_1. This is possible, but considering that this is a probabilistic process and that π_a might be re-introduced again for a higher degree $i_2 > i_1$ (we have checked its intelligence for i_1, but not for i_2), then we could eventually have π_a in its right place.

But of course, there might be some environments where rewards are a limited resource. In these environments, competition would be expected. On the contrary, co-operation could be encouraged if rewards could be shared (without limits) by a group of individuals. For instance, in the environment class introduced in [9], we can define rewards in such a way that they are eaten by the agents (to favour competitiveness) but we can also define rewards which remain.

5   Discussion

There is an increasing consensus in biology, comparative psychology and even artificial intelligence that intelligent systems must be social. Multi-agent systems appeared as a realisation of this fact, and multi-agent reinforcement learning is also in this direction. Several works in the AGI community have also advocated for a social approach to intelligence. However, we did not have a formal definition of intelligence with social abilities *playing an important role*.

Here we have proposed a novel environment distribution and a constructive method to build social environments incrementally. In fact, the previous Darwin-Wallace distribution can replace the universal distribution used in other formal definitions and tests of intelligence presented to date. Of course, the appropriateness and applicability of this would require theoretical or empirical results.

Although the distribution is related to (because it is inspired by) evolutionary computation, artificial life and natural biology, it is a novel approach to understanding the set of environments and tasks we want general intelligent systems to cope with. There are three features in the definition which distinguish it from a 'distribution of life forms': i) Physical things do not matter, placing the focus on behaviour, since the 'body' is the same for all. In other words, it is a 'distribution of mind forms'. ii) There is no genotype, cross-over, mutation, etc., so selection does not work for genes or species, but for individuals. In fact, in biological evolution, genes compete and collaborate, and we do not consider here the 'distribution of genes', either. iii) Environments are replaced, so avoiding specialisation (to or) in an environment. Instead, adaptability to a wide range of environments (i.e., intelligence) is the only fitness function for selection.

One of the problems of this approach is that now we are far away from the notion of 'intelligence as compression'. Nonetheless, the notions of mind-reading and manipulation imply that agents need to be able to capture the models of other agents, i.e. to compress their behaviours. Consequently, intelligence is related to the concept of adversarial (reinforcement) learning [23] and, eventually, to the elusive-model paradox[5]. These two concepts are of course related to measuring intelligence using games as environments, as suggested in [10]. And the role of two-part compression can be vindicated again in social environments in terms of communication, since having one model, the first-part of a MML message (namely, the model/theory/hypothesis/concept), which is concise and can be (relatively quickly and concisely) transmitted between agents (in contrast to a weighted ensemble of models) must be crucial for communication.

Summing up, we think that the main contributions of this paper span over the definition, evaluation and development of intelligence. We are conscious that there are many open questions and many implications, especially on the re-understanding of previous works on defining and evaluating intelligence, and on the direct applicability of these ideas to develop more intelligent machines.

Acknowledgments. We thank the anonymous reviewers for their helpful comments. We also thank the funding from the Spanish MEC and MICINN for projects TIN2009-06078-E/TIN, Consolider-Ingenio CSD2007-00022 and TIN2010-21062-C02, for MEC FPU grant AP2006-02323, and Generalitat Valenciana for Prometeo/2008/051.

References

1. Dowe, D.L.: Foreword re C. S. Wallace. Computer Journal 51(5), 523–560 (2008); Christopher Stewart WALLACE (1933-2004) memorial special issue
2. Dowe, D.L.: Minimum Message Length and statistically consistent invariant (objective?) Bayesian probabilistic inference - from (medical) "evidence". Social Epistemology 22(4), 433–460 (2008)
3. Dowe, D.L.: MML, hybrid Bayesian network graphical models, statistical consistency, invariance and uniqueness. In: Bandyopadhyay, P.S., Forster, M.R. (eds.) Handbook of the Philosophy of Science. Philosophy of Statistics, vol. 7, pp. 901–982. Elsevier, Amsterdam (2011)
4. Dowe, D.L., Hajek, A.R.: A computational extension to the Turing Test. In: 4th Conf. of the Australasian Cognitive Science Society, Newcastle, Australia (1997)

---

[5] The elusive-model paradox can be summarised as follows. Imagine two agents where one (perhaps the prey) is trying to anticipate where the other will be so as to avoid meeting, and the other (perhaps the predator) is trying to anticipate the other so that they do meet. In re-discovering this "elusive model paradox" [1, footnote 211][2, p 455], we note that, if the one agent is better at inference then it will be able to anticipate the behaviour of the other agent better than vice versa [3, sec. 7.5]. But, if both agents have the ability to infer Turing-complete functions and have statistically consistent inference methods, then, we will indeed encounter the halting problem and decisions (regarding actions) that can not be made in finite time.

5. Goertzel, B.: The Embodied Communication Prior: A characterization of general intelligence in the context of Embodied social interaction. In: 8th IEEE International Conference on, Cognitive Informatics, ICCI 2009, pp. 38–43. IEEE, Los Alamitos (2009)

6. Goertzel, B., Bugaj, S.V.: AGI Preschool: a framework for evaluating early-stage human-like AGIs. In: Intl. Conf. on Artificial General Intelligence (AGI 2009) (2009)

7. Hernández-Orallo, J.: Beyond the Turing Test. J. Logic, Language & Information 9(4), 447–466 (2000)

8. Hernández-Orallo, J.: On the computational measurement of intelligence factors. In: Meystel, A. (ed.) Performance metrics for intelligent systems workshop, pp. 1–8. National Institute of Standards and Technology, Gaithersburg (2000)

9. Hernández-Orallo, J.: A (hopefully) non-biased universal environment class for measuring intelligence of biological and artificial systems. In: Hutter, M., et al. (eds.) Artificial General Intelligence, pp. 182–183 (2010)

10. Hernández-Orallo, J., Dowe, D.L.: Measuring universal intelligence: Towards an anytime intelligence test. Artificial Intelligence 174(18), 1508–1539 (2010)

11. Hernández-Orallo, J., Minaya-Collado, N.: A formal definition of intelligence based on an intensional variant of Kolmogorov complexity. In: Proc. Intl Symposium of Engineering of Intelligent Systems (EIS 1998), pp. 146–163. ICSC Press (1998)

12. Herrmann, E., Call, J., Hernández-Lloreda, M.V., Hare, B., Tomasello, M.: Humans have evolved specialized skills of social cognition: The cultural intelligence hypothesis. Science 317(5843), 1360–1366 (2007)

13. Hibbard, B.: Bias and No Free Lunch in Formal Measures of Intelligence. Journal of Artificial General Intelligence 1(1), 54–61 (2009)

14. Krebs, J.R., Dawkins, R.: Animal signals: mind-reading and manipulation. Behavioural Ecology: an evolutionary approach 2, 380–402 (1984)

15. Langton, C.G.: Artificial life: An overview. The MIT Press, Cambridge (1997)

16. Legg, S., Hutter, M.: A collection of definitions of intelligence. In: Proc. of the 2007 Conf. on Artificial General Intelligence, pp. 17–24. IOS Press, Amsterdam (2007)

17. Legg, S., Hutter, M.: Universal intelligence: A definition of machine intelligence. Minds and Machines 17(4), 391–444 (2007)

18. Levin, L.A.: Universal sequential search problems. Problems of Information Transmission 9(3), 265–266 (1973)

19. Sanghi, P., Dowe, D.L.: A computer program capable of passing IQ tests. In: Proc. 4th ICCS International Conference on Cognitive Science (ICCS 2003), Sydney, Australia, pp. 570–575 (2003)

20. Schmidhuber, J.: A computer scientist's view of life, the universe, and everything. In: Foundations of Computer Science, p. 201. Springer, Heidelberg (1997)

21. Schmidhuber, J.: The Speed Prior: a new simplicity measure yielding near-optimal computable predictions. In: Kivinen, J., Sloan, R.H. (eds.) COLT 2002. LNCS (LNAI), vol. 2375, pp. 123–127. Springer, Heidelberg (2002)

22. Solomonoff, R.J.: A formal theory of inductive inference. Part I. Information and control 7(1), 1–22 (1964)

23. Stone, P., Veloso, M.: Towards collaborative and adversarial learning: A case study in robotic soccer. Intl. J. of Human-Computers Studies 48(1), 83–104 (1998)

24. Tomasello, M., Herrmann, E.: Ape and human cognition: What's the difference? Current Directions in Psychological Science 19(1), 3–8 (2010)

Structural Emergence in Partially Ordered Sets Is the Key to Intelligence

Sergio Pissanetzky

Graduate School, Dep. of Physics, Texas A&M University
College Station, Texas 77843, USA. Retired
sergio@SciControls.com
http://www.scicontrols.com

Abstract. Extraordinary structural organization known as *emergence* is observed in partially ordered sets when a recently discovered functional is minimized. Emergence creates the first structures, and *feedback* reuses them to create hierarchies of structures. The partially ordered set is the *knowledge representation*, the functional connects local behavior to global phenomena, emergence and feedback correspond to *inference*, and the structures and hierarchies to *objects* and *inheritance hierarchies*. If intelligence includes the ability to solve problems, then the structures represent intelligence and emergence represents the build up of intelligence. Since the structures are mathematically obtained from first principles, the finding is proposed as an explanation for the origin of intelligence, and the functional as the key for AGI. Three previous computer experiments, and another one reported here, duplicate higher functions of the human brain and confirm the findings.

Keywords: AI, AGI, emergence, complex systems, brain, refactoring, object-oriented, parallel programming.

1 Introduction

The phenomenon of *emergence* is frequently observed in many types of complex dynamical systems when *structures* unexpectedly form in the course of evolution of the system. Despite many years of intense research, the phenomenon of emergence remains unexplained, and a causal relationship between the properties or interactions of the components of the system and the resulting structures has not been found. There is no comprehensive theory of emergence or suitably fundamental model within which to situate emergence [1]. A phenomenological characterization of emergence including precise terminology is available [2].

The original motivation for the present work was the author's interest in *refactoring* [3]. Refactoring is practiced by every software developer virtually all of the time. The term was introduced for object-oriented (OO) code, but it was soon extended to non-OO code [4] and non-software systems such as the law [5], databases [6], and even bacteria [7]. Refactoring is a universal phenomenon, and we all practice it all the time, for tasks ranging from preparing our daily schedule to writing a scientific paper or a theory of Science. Refactoring, however, has

J. Schmidhuber, K.R. Thórisson, and M. Looks (Eds.): AGI 2011, LNAI 6830, pp. 92–101, 2011.

always been considered as something that only humans can do. Tools have been developed for software, of course, but they must operate under the guidance of a human and can be modified or expanded only through human intervention. The scope of refactoring is vast, and it has so far resisted full automation.

Work started with the publication in 2007 of the *imperative* form of the *Matrix Model of Computation* (iMMC) [8], a universal virtual machine that interfaces easily with software and supports refactoring transformations. The iMMC consists of a *matrix of sequences* and a *matrix of services*, both *sparse* [9]. Soon it was noticed that certain *canonical* submatrices of the matrix of services had extraordinary self-organizing properties [10], and the *canonical* form of the MMC (cMMC) and the Scope Constriction Algorithm (SCA) were introduced. SCA uses a *functional*, defined over the set of symmetric permutations of the canonical matrix. The functional assigns a *cost* to each permutation, not necessarily unique, and SCA finds the subset of permutations with the minimum cost. Remarkably, the matrices in the subset are *organized* and contain *structures* that did not exist in the original unpermuted matrix, even though nothing had been done to achieve such result. This is a purely mathematical result. Applications to refactoring [11] and image recognition [12] were published.

A detailed analysis of the inner workings of SCA was then undertaken, and resulted in publication [13], where general transformations from software to the cMMC were proposed, the basics of MMC supervised learning were covered, and an extensive case study on refactoring was included, where a Java program was converted to C (manually) and randomly rearranged to remove all OO features and organization, and automatically refactored by SCA, resulting in objects similar to the original ones. It became clear that a very strong connection existed between the canonical model and AGI.

At that point, it was noticed that a one-one correspondence existed between canonical matrices and partially ordered sets, and that the properties being studied were indeed properties of partially ordered sets, one of the most prevalent and fundamental structures in Mathematics. That explained the vast scope previously observed, and led to publication [14], where the fundamental mathematical principles underlying the observed properties were anticipated, experiments were discussed, and the hypothesis was advanced that those same principles could be used to explain emergence and intelligence.

The present work expands on the theory and claims that: (1) a system susceptible of mathematical analysis can be represented as a partially ordered set, where the nature of the elements is irrelevant; (2) a partially ordered set has a *natural structure*, which depends on and is determined by the set and order alone; (3) the natural structure can be found by the minimization of a universal functional, proposed in this paper; and (4) the structure is, in turn, a partially ordered set with structure of its own, giving rise to *feedback* and resulting in a *hierarchy* of structures. Experimental evidence is discussed, and the parallel computer simulation in Section 3 provides a stunning demonstration of the progressive build up of intelligence by inference and feedback, which can actually be seen in each iteration.

2   Theory

A partial order is a set of precedence relations. Any mathematical expression implies a set and a partial order. For example $a = f(b,c)$ implies set $\{a,b,c\}$ and establishes b and c as *predecessors* of a, meaning they must be given before a can be calculated. The notation is $b < a$, $c < a$, where "$<$" is read "precedes."

Procedures for describing a system as a partially ordered set are now examined. Consider first any system amenable to mathematical analysis. The first step in the analysis is to create a mathematical model, introduce variables to describe the model, and write equations describing constraints, interactions and laws of evolution. But the variables and equations define not only the model but also a partially ordered set. In fact, the variables form the set, and the equations establish a partial order among them. The order only states the well known fact that some variables are dependent and others independent.

The task of describing a system as a partially ordered set is simplified when a *computer simulation* is available. The simulation code provides a display of the equations and required calculations in full detail, with all the information about variables and precedence. It should be possible to develop a parser to automate the conversion. The author has developed one for single-assignment C.

Sometimes, a mathematical description is not even necessary. For example, the brain can be considered as a set of neurons with a partial order defined by their synaptic connections: neurons A, B and C precede neuron D if the simultaneous firing of A, B and C causes D to fire. The idea is expanded at the end of this Section.

The theory is presented next with the help of a simple example. Let S be a finite set and ω a partial order on S, for example:

$$S = \{a, b, c, d, e, f\} \tag{1}$$
$$\omega = \{a < c, \, b < c, \, c < f, \, d < e, \, e < f\}$$

The pair (S, ω) fully specifies the problem at hand. The nature of the elements of S is irrelevant. The standard notation for the problem defined by Eq. (1) is $6(ac, bc, cf, de, ef)$, where the number on the left is the size of the set, $|S| = 6$.

A set with n elements has $n!$ permutations. Some are compatible with the partial order, some are not. The compatible permutations are said to be *legal*. Let Π be the set of all legal permutations, and let $\pi \in \Pi$ be one of them. If the elements of the set are numbered in the order in which they appear in permutation π, then the *distance* between two elements in π is the difference between their numbers, and the *cost* $L_\omega(\pi)$ of permutation π relative to partial order ω is twice the sum of the distances between the elements of each relation:

$$L_\omega(\pi) = 2 \sum_\omega d(\varepsilon, \varepsilon'), \tag{2}$$

where $\varepsilon, \varepsilon'$ are elements in S and $\varepsilon < \varepsilon'$ is a relation in ω. To simplify notation, the subscript ω will be omitted. The reason for the factor 2 is explained in [13], and it has a profound physical meaning. Cost $L(\pi)$ is a *functional*, a map

from the set of permutations to numbers. For the example of Eq. (1), there are
6! = 720 permutations, only 20 of which are legal, $\pi = (b, d, a, e, c, f)$ is one of
them, the distance from b to c in π is 4, and the cost of π is 22. A search in set
Π indicates the existence of many minima, some of them local, others global,
even if S is small. At each minimum, there exists a set of permutations, say Π_m
at minimum m, which has the following remarkable property:

Proposition 1. Set Π_m is either a permutation group of set S or a
generator for a permutation group of S. In either case, it induces a *block
system* in set S.

The block system is the structure being sought. A block system is a partition of
set S into disjoint subsets called *blocks*. The elements in each block are *equivalent*, because they stay together inside the block (but in any order) for all
permutations of Π_m. The blocks are *invariant* under the action of Π_m, because
they are the same for all permutations in Π_m. In the block system, the elements of S appear organized and associated, thus creating logical *meaning*. The
emergence of the blocks amounts to *inference*, because they represent a new
conclusion obtained from the facts expressed by Eq. (1), where the organization
and associations did not exist. And all of this is natural and mathematical.

Feedback also arises naturally as a mathematical phenomenon. A block system
resulting from Proposition 1 is, in turn, a set (of subsets of S), and has a partial
order induced by the original partial order ω. Proposition 1 applies to the block
system just as effectively as it did to the original set S, and repeated application
of Proposition 1 results in a hierarchy of block systems.

Functional L is *locally defined*. Its value is a *global* property of the system,
but the definition is in terms of *distances*, which are local values. L can be
minimized by any local process completely unrelated to and unaware of any
global effects that the minimization can cause. Any set consisting of elements
capable of minimizing some measure of their interactions with their neighbors
will also minimize L and produce the global, unintended effect of the emergence
of structures. This is precisely where the transition from a local behavior to a
global phenomenon takes place.

In view of all of which, it is hereby proposed that the process that finds the
block systems is the core process of intelligence, that intelligence finds its origin
in that process, and that the core process can be easily implemented on any
regular computer. Intelligent systems are *self-integrated* and *indivisible* [14], but
a simple aggregate of intelligent systems (a *society*) is not intelligent, because
the systems can not integrate. For finite sets, all calculations in this theory are
computable and *deterministic*. However, they are *unpredictable* in practice for
all but the smallest sets. The size of set Π is of the order of $n!$, where n is the
size of the set. But $79! \approx 10^{80}$, and 10^{80} is the total number of atoms in the
universe. Real-world sets are much larger than 79, and predictable calculations
are not possible. The present work focuses on small systems, because they must
be understood before dealing with larger systems, and they are easy to study
without running into computational difficulties.

For the example of Eq. (1), there is only one global minimum with $L = 16$, and the following 2 permutations of S are found there:

$$(a\ b\ c\ d\ e\ f)$$
$$(b\ a\ c\ d\ e\ f) \tag{3}$$

The block system induced by the 2 permutations in set S is $(a, b)(c)(d)(e)(f)$, which contains only one non-trivial block. The order in which the blocks appear, and the association between a and b in the first block, did not exist in Eq. (1). They represent the build up of intelligence in the first iteration.

To every permutation of a partially ordered set there corresponds a *canonical matrix*. The canonical matrix for the system of Eq. (1) under permutation $\pi' = (d\,b\,a\,e\,c\,f)$, which is legal and has a cost of 22, is as follows:

$$
\begin{array}{c|cccccc}
 & d & b & a & e & c & f \\
\hline
d & C & & & & & \\
b & & C & & & & \\
a & & & C & & & \\
e & A & & & C & & \\
c & & A & A & & C & \\
f & & & & A & A & C
\end{array} \tag{4}
$$

The matrix is square, lower-triangular, and sparse [9]. Rows and columns correspond to the elements of S, and appear in the order of permutation π'. Following previous conventions, all diagonal elements contain C. The off-diagonal elements correspond to the partial order w: if $\varepsilon < \varepsilon'$ is a relation in w, then element $(\varepsilon', \varepsilon)$ is marked with an A in the matrix. One important property of the matrix is that symmetric permutations that leave all A's in the lower triangle always result in legal permutations of set S.

In the canonical matrix, a line from a C on the diagonal, to an A in the same column, to the C in the same row as the last A, is called a *flux line*. For example, the line from the C in position (b, b), to the A in position (c, b), to the C in position (c, c), is a flux line. The *length* of this flux line measured in cells is 6, which is precisely the cost of relation $b < c$ in permutation π'. It follows that the total length of all flux lines is, precisely, the cost of permutation π', and that the effect of the minimization of the cost is to symmetrically permute the canonical matrix in such a way that the A's are brought as close to the diagonal as possible.

A simple, but viable model of the brain can be developed based on this analogy. If the elements of set S are neurons, and their connections correspond to the relations in the partial order, then the connections correspond to the flux lines and the length of the connections corresponds to the length of the flux lines. But the neurons are known to try to shorten their connections or even migrate in order to preserve resources. When they do that, they also *inadvertently and without purpose* minimize the functional of Eq. (2) and *physically cluster* to form the structures described in this paper. This mechanism can explain both memory and intelligence. The clusters of neurons are called *neural cliques* and their existence has been confirmed [15].

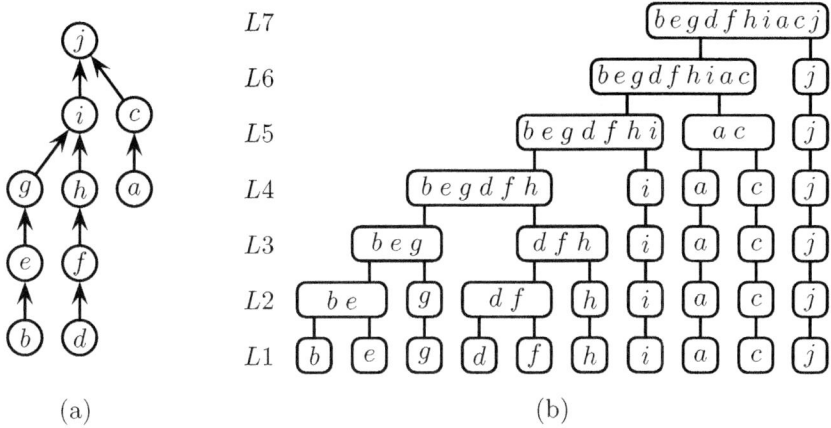

(a)   (b)

Fig. 1. (a) The solution to the problem of parallel programming of Section 3 and (b) UML diagram of the 7-level hierarchy of objects representing the complete solution for that problem. All structures shown are contained in Eq. (5).

3   Small Systems

The experiment for this paper is a simple model of a parallel computer with an undetermined number of CPU's, which has to execute a set of 10 tasks with 9 inter-dependencies. The problem is how to assign the tasks to the CPU's to improve performance. The analysis of 6 different small systems is needed to solve the problem. The first system is Σ_1, specified as follows:

$$\Sigma_1 : (S_1, \omega_1)$$
$$S_1 = \{a, b, c, d, e, f, g, h, i, j\} \tag{5}$$
$$\omega_1 = \{a < c, b < e, c < j, d < f, e < g, f < h, g < i, h < i, i < j\}$$

The 10 tasks are the elements of S and their inter-dependencies are listed as relations in the partial order. This problem is very simple. Any human analyst can solve it in a few minutes. The result is shown in Fig. 1(a). However, the point of the experiment is that the computer can solve the problem *without having been told how to do so*, using only the minimization of the functional. If it does, and if the result is correct, then the claim can be made that the algorithm operates from first principles and is intelligent.

System Σ_1 has 720 legal permutations and a cost range from 28 (with 2 permutations) to 46 (with 180 permutations). It has 2 global minima with 2 permutations having a cost of 28:

$$(b\ e\ g\ d\ f\ h\ i\ a\ c\ j) \tag{6}$$
$$(d\ f\ h\ b\ e\ g\ i\ a\ c\ j)$$

The block system they induce in set S_1 is $\beta_1 = (b\ e)(g)(d\ f)(h)(i)(a)(c)(j)$. This result is illustrated as a UML diagram in Fig. 1(b), where level $L1$ corresponds to set S_1, and level $L2$ to the block system β_1. The organization of the permutations and the association of b with e and of d with f represent the build-up of intelligence in the first iteration.

As discussed above, the process of structure generation is recurrent. In fact, block system β_1 is itself a set, say S_2, the elements of which are the 8 subsets of which β_1 consists. Set S_2 also has a partial order, say ω_2, induced by the partial order ω_1 of Eq. (5). S_2 and ω_2 define a new system, say Σ_2, as follows:

$$
\begin{aligned}
\Sigma_2 &: (S_2, \omega_2) \\
S_2 &= \{a', b', c', d', e', f', g', h'\} \\
\omega_2 &= \{a' < b', b' < e', c' < d', d' < e', e' < h', f' < g', g' < h'\},
\end{aligned}
\tag{7}
$$

where $a' = (b\ e)$, $b' = (g)$, $c' = (d\ f)$, $d' = (h)$, $e' = (i)$, $f' = (a)$, $g' = (c)$, and $h' = (j)$. System Σ_2 has 8 elements and 7 precedence relations, and corresponds to level $L2$ in Fig. 1(b). It was found to have 126 legal permutations and a cost range of 22 (with 2 permutations) to 34 (with 36 permutations). It has 2 global minima, 4 local minima, 1 global maximum, and no local maxima. The set of 2 permutations at the global minimum is:

$$
\begin{matrix}
(a'\ b'\ c'\ d'\ e'\ f'\ g'\ h') \\
(c'\ d'\ a'\ b'\ e'\ f'\ g'\ h')
\end{matrix}
\tag{8}
$$

and the block system induced in S_2 is $\beta_2 = (a'\ b')(c'\ d')(e')(f')(g')(h')$. Block system β_2 corresponds to level $L3$ in Fig. 1(b). But block system β_2 is a set with 6 elements, say S_3, and the partial order ω_2 induces into it another partial order, say ω_3. The entire process can be repeated several more times, resulting in the 7-level structure depicted in the figure. As the reader can see, the diagram has a remarkable similarity with the *inheritance hierarchies* used in OO programming. It is proposed in this work that the diagram is, in fact, the rigorous mathematical equivalent of an inheritance hierarchy in OOP. In all, the following 6 small systems are visited by the feedback loop:

System	Levels	System definition	Associations	(9)
Σ_1	$L1/L2$	$10(ac, be, cj, df, eg, fh, gi, hi, ij)$	be, df	
Σ_2	$L2/L3$	$8(ab, be, cd, de, eh, fg, gh)$	beg, dfh	
Σ_3	$L3/L4$	$6(ac, bc, cf, de, ef)$	$beg\|dfh$	
Σ_4	$L4/L5$	$5(ab, be, cd, de)$	$(beg\|dfh)i, ac$	
Σ_5	$L5/L6$	$3(ac, bc)$	$(beg\|dfh)i\|ac$	
Σ_6	$L6/L7$	$2(ab)$	$((beg\|dfh)i\|ac)j$	

In the last column, associations of immediate precedence are indicated by writing the symbols together, such as dfh, while the symbol "|" indicates *parallelism*, an association without precedence. System Σ_3 in the table is in fact the same system defined in Eq. (1) and discussed in Section 2. This example provides a dramatic demonstration of the role of emergence as the source of first intelligence from a fundamental mathematical principle and the build up of higher intelligence. The results at each step of the process are depicted in Fig. 1(b). Iteration 1

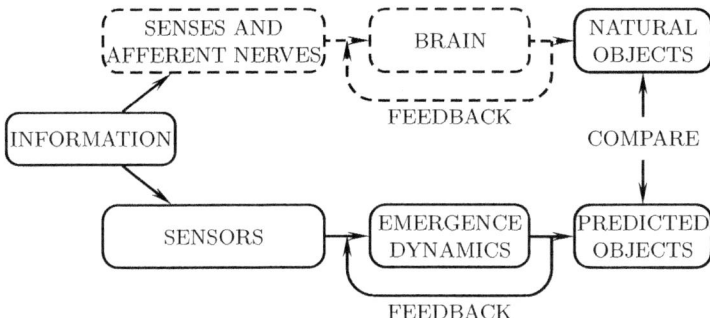

Fig. 2. Computer simulation of higher brain functions. Solid lines indicate easily observable and measurable features, while dashed lines identify features that are not relevant for the present study.

organizes the set and associates *be* and *df*, each with immediate precedence and each encapsulated in a separate block. Iteration 2 associates blocks *beg* and *dfh*, and iteration 3 associates *beg|dfh* together without precedence, thus effectively creating a parallel computer with 2 processors. Successive iterations continue reusing previously acquired intelligence to build associations, and the combined effects of inference, feedback and encapsulation are clearly visible. The final solution is identical to the human analyst's solution of Fig 1(a).

4   Experimental Evidence

Computer experiments that simulate higher brain functions are easy to perform. The brain itself is irrelevant, and is treated as a black box where only the input and output matter. There exist plenty of carefully documented actual input-output observations with which the simulated results can be readily compared. Figure 2 illustrates the concept.

   Information that a person can acquire from the environment, such as a visual image, an observation made by a scientist, or a problem statement received by a computer analyst, is made available as training material for the simulated emergence dynamics (see §IV, "Basics of MMC supervised learning", in [13]). The natural objects that the brain creates are the images we recognize, the theories of Science, or the object-oriented designs the analyst develops. They can be directly compared with the corresponding objects predicted by the simulation.

   Three such experiments have been previously published, and one more is reported here in Section 3. The three experiments were further discussed in [14]. The experiments are simple, but they are sufficient for a proof of principle, and they are important because they set directions for future research. The first experiment [11] is in Newtonian Mechanics, and consists of information describing one time step of the motion of a mass particle in three-dimensional space under the action of gravity. A human scientist immediately discovers the following 4 facts: there are 3 components of motion, 2 separate variables must be used to describe the motion, the 3 components are independent, and the 2 variables are independent. For the simulation, the problem is described as a partially ordered set with 18 elements and 12 relations, and minimization of the functional of emergence immediately discovers a block hierarchy separated into 3 independent components, each in turn separated into 2 independent components, in full agreement with the human scientist.

The second experiment is a case study on refactoring [13], based on a Java program used in many European universities to teach the subject. The program was first converted to C in order to eliminate all object-oriented information, and then represented by a set with 33 elements and a partial order with 55 relations. After minimization of the functional of emergence, a hierarchy of block systems was obtained, which was in excellent agreement with the original Java classes that a human analyst had designed. The conversion of the block systems to Java or C# was not attempted, but it should be easy to automate.

The last experiment is one of image recognition [12], where a set of 167 points distributed on the plane is given. Human observers asked to interpret the image immediately agree that it shows 3 clusters, but disagree when asked to describe the clusters. The number 3 is not explicit in the picture, it has to be found by interpretation. A regular network of cells representing a retina was superposed on the picture. The system was simulated with a set of 1433 elements, and the relations in the partial order were obtained by associating the points with the cells that contained them. Minimization of the functional of emergence yielded a hierarchy of block systems with 3 blocks in the highest level, indicating the separation of the set into 3 clusters, in full agreement with the human observer. In addition, more detailed but not meaningful structure was found in each of the clusters, again in full agreement with the human observer.

One more experiment, the experiment on parallel programming discussed in Section 3 of this paper, is also in full agreement with the human programmer. All four problems have been solved by minimization of the same functional, and by the same algorithm, which is local and knows nothing about the particular problems other than the input S and ω. The ability to solve problems of any kind, when and where they arise, directly from input and without the need for any problem-specific means, is key for intelligence.

5   Concluding Remarks

This work has proposed a mathematical theory where a partially ordered set representing a physical system subject to the action of a dissipative dynamical process, naturally gives rise to the phenomena of emergence, feedback, and inference, and becomes self-organized into a hierarchy of block systems where successive levels represent a progressive build up of intelligence. The set serves as a knowledge base with natural support for all the phenomena. The dynamics only dissipates the functional, in a local manner, until exhaustion, and is unaware of the existence of a population or of any global effects that may follow. The functional is universal, defined in terms of the local conditions in the system, amenable to be minimized by local dynamics, and providing the only logical connection between the local dynamics and the resulting global phenomena.

Because the theory explains the origin of intelligence from first principles and its growth by feedback and inference, because the features just described are normally associated with intelligence, and because of the supporting experimental evidence, also proposed is the working hypothesis that the theory does describe the origin of intelligence, provides the foundation for a variational theory of intelligence in natural and artificial systems, including the human brain, and allows intelligent behavior to be mathematically described by the elegant principle of optimization.

Important consequences will follow. The value of a variational principle is its unifying power. This work offers many possibilities for new research in AI and AGI, as well as an unprecedented opportunity to unify these fragmented fields.

References

1. Cooper, S.B.: Emergence as a computability-theoretic phenomenon. Applied Math. and Computation 215, 1351–1360 (2009)
2. Prokopenko, M., Boschetti, F., Ryan, A.J.: An Information-Theoretic Primer on Complexity, Self-Organization, and Emergence. Complexity 15, 11–28 (2009)
3. Opdyke, W.F.: Refactoring object-oriented frameworks. Ph.D. thesis, Dep. Comp. Science, Univ. of Illinois, Urbana-Champaign (1992)
4. Garrido, A., Johnson, R.: Challenges of refactoring C programs. In: Proc. International Workshop on Principles of Software Evolution, Orlando, Florida, pp. 6–14 (2002)
5. Wilson, G.: Refactoring the law: reformulating legal ontologies. Juris Dr. Writing Requirement, School of Law, Univ. of San Francisco (2006)
6. Ambler, S.J., Sadalage, P.J.: Refactoring Databases: Evolutionary Database Design. Addison-Wesley, Reading (2011)
7. Chan, L.Y., Kosuri, S., Endy, D.: Refactoring bacteriophage T7. Molecular Systems Biology, article number: 2005.0018 (September 13, 2005)
8. Pissanetzky, S.: A Relational Virtual Machine for Program Evolution. In: Proc. 2007 Int. Conf. on Software Engng. Research and Practice, vol. I, pp. 144–150 (2007)
9. Pissanetzky, S.: Sparse Matrix Technology. Academic Press, London (1984)
10. Pissanetzky, S.: The matrix model of computation. In: Proc. 12th. WMSCI Conf. vol. IV, pp. 184–189 (2008)
11. Pissanetzky, S.: Applications of the Matrix Model of Computation. In: Proc. 12th. WMSCI Conference, vol. IV, pp. 190–195 (2008)
12. Pissanetzky, S.: A new Type of Structured Artificial Neural Networks based on the Matrix Model of Computation. In: Arabnia, H.R., Mun, Y. (eds.) The 2008 International Conference on Artificial Intelligence, vol. I, pp. 251–257 (2008)
13. Pissanetzky, S.: A new Universal Model of Computation and its Contribution to Learning, Intelligence, Parallelism, Ontologies, Refactoring, and the Sharing of Resources. Int. J. of Information and Mathematical Sciences 5, 143–173 (2009)
14. Pissanetzky, S.: Coupled Dynamics in Host-Guest Complex Systems Duplicates Emergent Behavior in the Brain. World Academy of Science, Engineering and Technology 68, 1–9 (2010)
15. Lina, L., Osana, R., Tsiena, J.Z.: Organizing principles of real-time memory encoding: neural clique assemblies and universal neural codes. Trends in Neurosciences 29, 48–57 (2006)

Integrating Perception and Cognition for AGI

Unmesh Kurup[1], Christian Lebiere[1], and Anthony Stentz[2]

[1] Department of Psychology, Carnegie Mellon University,
5000 Forbes Ave, Pittsburgh, PA 15213
[2] National Robotics Engineering Consortium, Robotics Institute,
Carnegie Mellon University, Pittsburgh, PA 15201
{unmeshk,cl,tony}@andrew.cmu.edu

Abstract. Current perceptual algorithms are error-prone and require the use of additional ad hoc heuristic methods that detect and recover from these errors. In this paper we explore how existing architectural mechanisms in a high-level cognitive architecture like ACT-R can be used instead of such ad hoc measures. In particular, we describe how implicit learning that results from ACT-R's architectural features of partial matching and blending can be used to recover from errors in object identification, tracking and action prediction. We demonstrate its effectiveness by building a model that can identify and track objects as well as predict their actions in a simple checkpoint scenario.

Keywords: Cognitive Architectures, Integrating Perception & Action, Object Tracking, Instance-based Learning.

1 Introduction

Perception is a key component of any system with claims to AGI [1]. While cognition can affect perception, much of perception remains bottom-up with parallel processes that implement functions from figure-ground separation to object identification and tracking. The parallel, bottom-up nature of perception is important for an agent interacting with the external world since it allows the agent to quickly understand and categorize what it perceives and, consequently, take appropriate action. However, even with the best current algorithms, information from perception is also likely to be error-prone and probabilistic. It then falls to cognition to take this information and refine it using additional knowledge.

Approaches that deal with errors in perceptual processing are usually ad hoc and based on specialized heuristics that take advantage of the domain of interest [2]. For example, in person detection, it is often the case that people are assumed to be "on the ground" and so any data that points to a person floating above the ground can be considered as unlikely. In this paper, we take a more cognitively plausible approach by using ACT-R [3], to model a system that learns to predict the result of perception. This prediction is then used to supplement perceptual inputs in order to overcome any errors. In general, this predictive ability is not restricted to the information from perception. It can be used at the cognitive level for predicting or anticipating actions,

J. Schmidhuber, K.R. Thórisson, and M. Looks (Eds.): AGI 2011, LNAI 6830, pp. 102–111, 2011.

goals and cognitive states. However, in this paper, we limit ourselves to using predictions to refine perceptual input.

At the level of cognitive theory, the ACT-R model of perceptual refinement is an example of instance-based learning in humans where information from multiple instances are generalized and used to set up expectations about future situations. Generating expectations based on past experience is key to a number of cognitive endeavors. Expectation-based models have been developed and validated in a number of domains, including expectations of future perceptual events in sequence learning [4]; expectations of other players' moves in games [5][6]; expectations for the outcome of actions such as probabilistic payoffs [7][8]; expectations of dynamical system behavior in control problems [9][10]; mental imagery for general problem solving [11] and perspective taking [12][13]. Indeed, theories have proposed [14] [15] that the fundamental computational property of the human cortex is the completion of spatiotemporal patterns to generate expectations. Thus it seems fitting that we would explore the role of expectations in how cognition oversees perception and compensates for its shortcomings.

The current model (as well as some of the other models of instance-based learning mentioned above) is built upon two features of ACT-R's declarative memory and retrieval mechanism – partial matching and blending. In the following sections we describe the ACT-R architecture, demonstrate the effects of partial matching and blending, and describe how these effects are useful in recovering from perceptual errors in a simple checkpoint scenario.

2   ACT-R

The ACT-R cognitive architecture is a modular, neurally-plausible theory of human cognition. The ACT-R architecture describes cognition at two levels – the symbolic and the sub-symbolic. At the symbolic level, ACT-R consists of a number of modules each interacting with a central inference control system (Procedural module) via capacity-limited buffers. Modules represent functional units with the most common ones being the Declarative module for storing declarative pieces of knowledge, the Goal module for storing goal-related information, the Imaginal module which supports storing the current problem state, and the Perceptual (Visual and Aural) and Motor modules that support interaction with the environment. The only way to access the content stored in a module is through that module's buffer. Modules can operate asynchronously, with the flow of information between modules synchronized by the central procedural module.

Declarative memory stores factual information in structures called chunks. Chunks are typed units similar to schemas or frames that include named slots (slot-value pairs). Productions are condition-action rules, where the conditions check for the existence of certain chunks in one or more buffers. If these checks are true, the production is said to match and can be fired (executed). In its action part, a production can make changes to existing chunks in buffers or make requests for new chunks. ACT-R has a second underlying sub-symbolic (numerical) layer that associates values (similar to neural activations) to chunks and productions. These activation (utility in the case of productions) values play a crucial role in deciding which productions are selected to fire and which chunks are retrieved from memory. ACT-R also has a set of learning mechanisms that allow an ACT-R model to learn new declarative facts and production rules as well as modify existing sub-symbolic values. A full account of ACT-R theory can be found in [16] and [3].

In this paper, we restrict further discussion about ACT-R to the declarative module since its performance is implicated in our current work. As mentioned earlier, the declarative module stores factual information in the form of chunks and makes these available to the rest of the architecture via the retrieval buffer. There are two critical mechanisms for retrieving information in ACT-R's declarative module – partial matching and blending - that are important to this current integration.

2.1 Partial Matching

In ACT-R, productions make requests for chunks in declarative memory by specifying certain constraints on the slot values of chunks. These constraints can range from the very specific where every slot and value of the desired chunk is specified to the very general (akin to free association) where the only specification is the type of the chunk. Request criteria also include negatives where you can specify that a slot should not have a particular value as well as ranges (in the case of numerical values). The standard request generally specifies the chunk type and one or more slot values but not all. If there are multiple chunks that exactly match the specified constraints, the chunk with the highest activation value is retrieved. The activation value of a chunk (1) is the sum of its base-level activation and its contextual activation. The base-level activation of a chunk is a measure of its frequency and recency of access. The more recently and frequently a chunk has been retrieved, the higher its activation and the higher the chances that it is retrieved. (2) describes the equation for calculating the base-level activation of a chunk i where t_j is the time elapsed since the jth reference to chunk i, d represents the memory decay rate and L denotes the time since the chunk was created.

$$A_i = B_i + \sum_j W_j S_{ji} \tag{1}$$

$$B_i = \ln \sum_{j=1}^{n} t_j^{-d} \approx \ln \frac{nL^{-d}}{1-d} \tag{2}$$

The contextual activation of a chunk is determined by the attentional weight given the context element j and the strength of association S_{ji} between an element j and a chunk i. An element j is in context if it is part of a chunk in a buffer (i.e., it is the value of one of the goal chunk's slots). The default assumption is that there is a limited source activation capacity that is shared equally between all chunk elements. The associative strength S_{ji} is a measure of how often chunk i was retrieved by a production when source j was in context. In addition to the base-level and contextual values, some randomness is introduced into the retrieval process by the addition of Gaussian noise.

$$M_{ip} = A_i - MP \sum_{v,d} (1 - Sim(v,d)) \tag{3}$$

Without partial matching enabled, the retrieval mechanism only considers those chunks that match the request criteria. When partial matching is enabled, the retrieval mechanism can retrieve the chunk that matches the retrieval constraints to the greatest degree. It does this by computing a match score for each chunk that is a function of the chunk's activation and its degree of mismatch to the specified constraints. (3) is the formula for computing the match score. *MP* is the mismatch penalty, *Sim(v,d)* is the similarity between the desired value *v* and the actual value *d* held in the retrieved chunk. With the use of partial matching, the retrieval mechanism can retrieve chunks that are closest to the specified constraints even if there is no chunk that matches the constraints exactly. This is particularly useful as shown below in situations where values are continuous and dynamic. Since the degree of match is combined with the activation to yield the match score, chunks that have higher activation will also tolerate a greater degree of mismatch. This reflects the interpretation of activation as a measure of likelihood of usefulness [17].

2.2 Blending

The second aspect of retrieval is blending [18] [19], a form of generalization where, instead of retrieving an existing chunk that best matches the request, blending produces a new chunk by combining the relevant chunks. The values of the slots of this blended chunk are the average values for the slots of the relevant chunks weighted by their respective activations, where the average is defined in terms of the similarities between values. For discrete chunk values without similarities, this results in a kind of voting process where chunks proposing the same value pool their strengths. For continuous values such as numbers, a straightforward averaging process is used. For discrete chunk values between which similarities (as used in partial matching) have been defined, a compromise value that minimizes the weighted sum of squared dissimilarities is returned. Formally, the value obtained by a blended retrieval is determined as follows:

$$V = Min \sum_i P_i (1 - Sim(V, V_i))^2 \tag{4}$$

where P_i is the probability of retrieving chunk i and V_i is the value held by that chunk. Blending has been shown to be a convincing explanation for various types of implicit learning [20] [9]. Blending of location information in chunks allows the model to predict future locations of objects by giving more weight to recent perceptual information while ignoring various individual fluctuations arising from noise. ACT-R's blending mechanism can be thought of as a subset of more general approaches like Conceptual Blending [21] where the structure of the component concepts and the final concept is restricted to a single type and the compositional process for constructing the blended concept is weighted averaging. More comprehensive elements of Conceptual Blending such as non-trivial compositional rules, completion, elaboration and emergent structures are absent in ACT-R blending. In addition, the partial matching and blending mechanisms in ACT-R are meant to capture the fundamental generalization characteristics over similarity-based semantics of modeling paradigms such as neural networks [22][23], albeit at a different level of abstraction.

Together, partial matching and blending allows the model to overcome errors in object identification and tracking. Blending also allows the model to predict the possible action an object may follow based on its past actions. This reflects the fact that, as discussed above, blending is applicable to all types of values, from discrete to continuous and including intermediate domains such as discrete values over a semantic space (e.g. words).

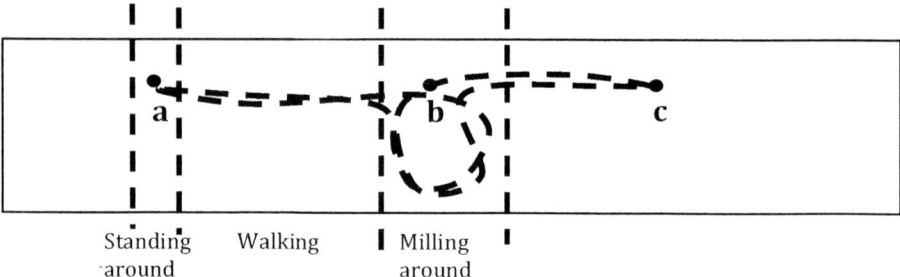

Fig. 1. Checkpoint scenario showing the movements of objects *a* and *c* and the division of *a*'s route by type of action

3   Modeling Object Identification, Tracking and Action Prediction in ACT-R

3.1   Checkpoint Scenario

The checkpoint scenario consists of a robot patrolling a checkpoint looking for people and objects of interest. In the current version of the scenario, it is assumed that the robot is stationary at a location that affords it a complete view of the checkpoint. Its goal is to identify and track the objects in its view and classify their actions. Fig 1 shows the example scenario consisting of three people performing one of three actions – standing around, walking or milling around. Initially, all actors ("a", "b" and "c") are

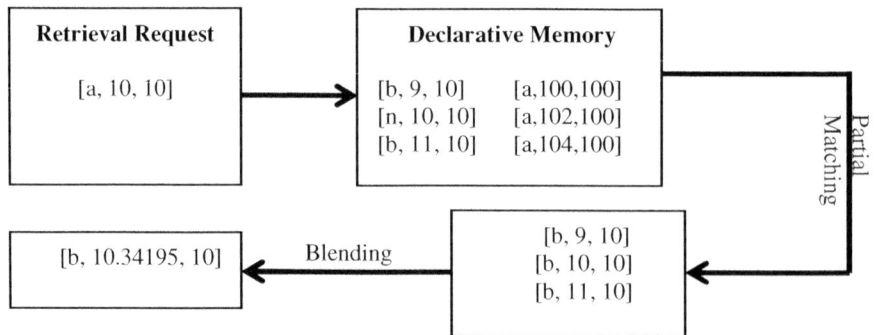

Fig. 2. Effects of partial matching and blending on retrieval

standing around. After 30 seconds, "a" and "c" start walking towards "b". After 60 seconds, they start milling around (walking in a circle). After 90 seconds, they start walking back towards their starting locations, going back to standing around after 120 seconds. For this scenario, perception provides an identification vector (which is currently limited to an id but might be eventually expanded to a multi-variable vector that includes additional information such as height, color, etc) and location information. However both location and object id information have errors associated with them. For now the output of perception is simulated by adding an error term to the data. Location error generated by a logistic distribution is added to the location information that is made available, while objects have a fixed 1/10 chance of being mis-identified by perception (which translates to an average of 15 errors in every trial).

3.2 ACT-R Model

The ACT-R model represents information about an object in a chunk, called a visual-memory chunk for convenience, that contains the object's id, current location, rate of change of location (delta), and current action. Every time an object id and its location are reported by perception, the model uses this information to retrieve a chunk in order to interpret that information against its recent experience. The retrieved chunk is a result of both partial matching and blending by the retrieval mechanism. The value contained in the delta slot is used to predict the object's future location and the value in the action slot is used to predict the object's future action. If the retrieved blended chunk does not exactly match the information from perception (which it rarely does), a new chunk is learned whose slot values contain the information from perception. Over the course of the experiment, the model learns a number of such chunks that effectively improve its ability to alleviate id errors, predict object location and predict object action. In the following sections we describe how the use of partial matching and blending accomplish this goal.

3.3 Recovering from Object Identification Errors

There are a number of errors that can happen during object identification including failure to identify a known (previously encountered) object, identifying non-existent objects and identifying a known object as another known object. In this work we model all three errors. In the first type of error, perception fails to identify a previously seen (and identified) object. Instead, it either identifies it as a new object or fails to identify it at all. The second type of error is similar to a false-positive, where perception identifies an object even though no such object exists in the scene. Finally, perception can be confused between different objects in the scene and identify one object incorrectly as another. In all cases, partial matching provides a way for the system to recover the right identification. To see how this works, consider the following example (shown in Fig 2) where there are 6 chunks in declarative memory, three chunks with "b" in the name slot and values (9,10) (10,10) and (11,10) in the respective current location slot and three chunks with "a" in the name slot and values (100,100), (102,100) and (104,100) in the respective (x,y) slots. When a chunk is requested with the value "a" in the name slot and (10,10) in the (x,y) slot, partial matching produces the first 3 chunks as better matches for the request even though the value in the name slot is different. The values of each slot of the three chunks are then combined to create the new blended chunk. The same process can be used to recover from the other types of id errors. If a non-existent object was proposed instead of "a", partial matching would retrieve the chunks with "a" in the name slot because the current locations would be most similar to the locations for chunks with "a" in the name slot. Similarly, if an object was not identified at all, its location will provide enough similarity to retrieve the correct chunks. It is important to note that this method is not simply a nearest-neighbor approach. Instead, it is architectural and takes into account contextual elements like time. For example, if an object "c" used to be at the same location as "b" but in the past, there would be corresponding chunks in memory with location slot values similar to the location slot values of object "b". However, these chunks would not be retrieved because their activations would be low due to the fact that they were created when "c" used to be at that location (and time from creation is an important part of a chunk's activation).

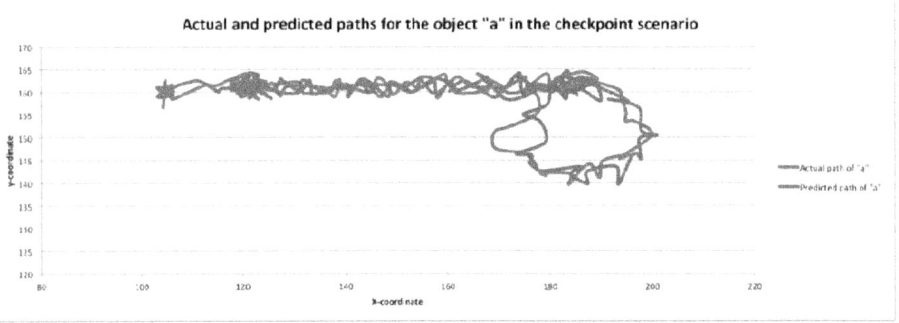

Fig. 3. The actual and predicted paths for object "a"

We were able to recover from most errors in the many trials we ran. However, there are other scenarios where this approach sometimes fails. For example, as two objects get closer to each other, their location values become more similar making it difficult for partial matching to retrieve the right chunks. Even so, the delta values provide another contextual cue to use if the two objects are moving at different rates or in different directions.

3.4   Recovering from Object Location Errors

The model predicts an object's future location by adding a delta value to its current location where the delta value is the difference between the current and previous location. In an error-free system, this would work very well except for the cases when there is a sudden change in delta. When location errors are present, the last delta value is not enough. With ACT-R's blending mechanism, when a visual-memory chunk is retrieved, the value for the delta slot is blended over the existing relevant chunks. As mentioned earlier, in calculating the blended value for the delta slot, the blending mechanism takes into account the activations of the chunks. One major contributor to activation strength is the time of creation of the chunk. That is, the more recently the

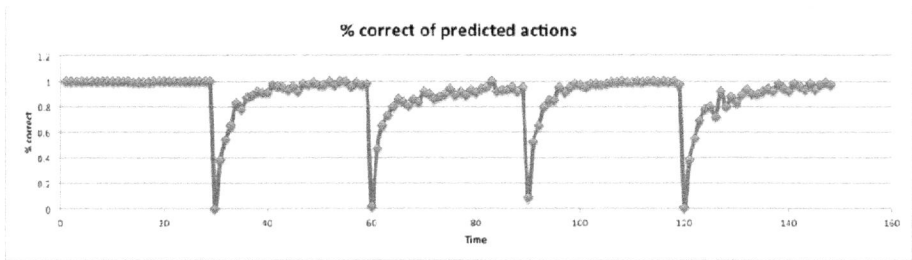

Fig. 4. Percent correct of predicted actions for object "a"

chunk was created, the higher its activation. This means that more recent chunks, and hence more recent values of delta, contribute more to the retrieved blended value making the prediction more accurate. Figure 3 shows the actual and predicted paths for object "a" from the scenario averaged over 1000 trials.

3.5 Predicting Actions

Finally, blending can also be used to provide robust action prediction. Recall that the scenario has 3 different actions. We concentrate on the actions performed by object "a" which includes "standing", "walking" and "milling around". Figure 4 shows the percentage of correct predictions for each time step in the scenario. The drop-offs correspond to the changes in action by "a" such as going from "standing" to "walking" or from "walking" to "milling around" and so on. Anytime the action changes, it takes some time for the model to get back to a high-level of prediction, as it has to wait for enough recent chunks to accumulate with the correct value in the action slot. A system that simply uses the last action to predict the next one would do better (except for the same drop-offs) but would do poorly when there are errors in the system. In general, recent experience should be combined with patterns stored from long-term experience (e.g., which action was performed by people in various circumstances) to yield predictions that reflect both short-term and long-term knowledge.

4   Conclusion and Future Work

The best perceptual routines available today for object identification, tracking and action recognition are often error-prone and current approaches to handling these errors are usually ad hoc. In contrast, a cognitive approach like the use of ACT-R builds on the principles of human cognition to provide a way to recover from such errors. ACT-R's partial matching and blending features in its memory representation and retrieval provides one such cognitively plausible way. The most encouraging outcome of using ACT-R is the clear effect of existing architectural mechanisms on the problem of handling perceptual errors. However, there are problems that remain to be addressed. The drop-offs in action prediction are glaring and learning to predict these changes is a focus of on-going research. Even though the checkpoint scenario concentrated on the use of partial matching and blending to make predictions of the immediate state of the world, these processes can just as easily be leveraged to retrieve and construct predictions about more abstract and/or long-term actions. We are currently testing a number of approaches including contextual attributes like time (actions change at approximately similar intervals of time, for example, a person starts walking after standing around for a while) and spatial relationships (a person who is walking will tend to start milling around when he/she is near to another person). We have had some success with using spatial contextual cues but problems still remain. In addition, current predictions are limited to one or a few time steps in advance. An ongoing goal is to expand this ability to predict behaviors and actions longer into the future.

Finally, in this paper, we have focused solely on leveraging existing architectural mechanisms without considering the computational cost of calculating expectations and evaluating them during problem solving. It is very likely that such processes require additional architectural support and the nature and design of such support is part of our future work.

Acknowledgements. This work was conducted through collaborative participation in the Robotics Consortium sponsored by the U.S Army Research Laboratory under the Collaborative Technology Alliance Program, Cooperative Agreement W911NF-10-2-0016.

References

1. Laird, J.E.: Towards Cognitive Robotics. In: SPIE Defense and Sensing Conferences, Orlando, FL (2009)
2. Wojek, C., Walk, S., Schiele, S.: Multi-Cue Onbaord Pedestrian Detection. In: CVPR, pp. 1–8 (2009)
3. Anderson, J.R.: How Can the Human Mind Occur in the Physical Universe? Oxford University Press, New York (2007)
4. Lebiere, C., Wallach, D.: Sequence learning in the ACT-R cognitive architecture: Empirical analysis of a hybrid model. In: Sun, R., Giles, C.L. (eds.) Sequence Learning. LNCS (LNAI), vol. 1828, pp. 188–212. Springer, Heidelberg (2001)
5. Lebiere, C., West, R.L.: A dynamic ACT-R model of simple games. In: Proceedings of the Twenty-First Conference of the Cognitive Science Society, pp. 296–301. Erlbaum, Mahwah (1999)
6. West, R.L., Lebiere, C.: Simple games as dynamic, coupled systems: Randomness and other emergent properties. Journal of Cognitive Systems Research 1(4), 221–239 (2001)
7. Lebiere, C., Gonzalez, C., Martin, M.: Instance-based decision-making model of repeated binary choice. In: Proceedings of the 8th International Conference on Cognitive Modeling, Ann Arbor (2007)
8. Erev, I., Ert, E., Roth, A.E., Haruvy, E., Herzog, S., Hau, R., Hertwig, R., Stewart, T., West, R., Lebiere, C.: A choice prediction competition, for choices from experience and from description. Journal of Behavioral Decision Making 23(1), 15–47 (2010)
9. Gonzalez, C., Lerch, J.F., Lebiere, C.: Instance-based learning in dynamic decision making. Cognitive Science 27, 591–635 (2003)

10. Lebiere, C., Gonzalez, C., Warwick, W.: Convergence and constraints revealed in a qualitative model comparison. Journal of Cognitive Engineering and Decision Making 3(2), 131–155 (2009)
11. Wintermute, S., Laird, J.E.: Bimodal Spatial Reasoning with Continuous Motion. In: Proceedings of the Twenty-Third AAAI Conference on Artificial Intelligence (AAAI 2008), Chicago, Illinois (2008)
12. Trafton, J.G., Harrison, A.M., Fransen, B.: An embodied model of infant gaze-following. International Conference of Cognitive Modeling (2009)
13. Trafton, J.G., Schultz, A.C., Perzanowski, D., Bugajska, M.D., Adams, W., Cassimatis, N.L., Brock, D.P.: Children and robots learning to play hide and seek. Human Robot Interaction (2006)
14. Granger, R.: Engines of the brain: The computational instruction set of human cognition. AI Magazine 27(2), 15–31 (2006)
15. Hawkins, J., Blakeslee, S.: On Intelligence. Times Books, NY (2004)
16. Anderson, J.R., Bothell, D., Byrne, M.D., Douglass, S., Lebiere, C., Qin, Y.: An integrated theory of the mind. Psychological Review 111(4), 1036–1060 (2004)
17. Anderson, J.R.: The Adaptive Character of Thought. Erlbaum, Hillsdale (1990)
18. Lebiere, C.: The dynamics of cognitive arithmetic. In: Wallach, D., Simon, H.A. (eds.) Kognitionswissenschaft, vol. 8 (1), pp. 5–19 (1999)
19. Gonzalez, C., Lebiere, C.: Instance-based cognitive models of decision-making. In: Zizzo, D., Courakis, A. (eds.) Transfer of knowledge in economic decision making, Palgrave McMillan, New York (2005)
20. Wallach, D., Lebiere, C.: Conscious and unconscious knowledge: Mapping to the symbolic and subsymbolic levels of a hybrid architecture. In: Jimenez, L. (ed.) Attention and Implicit Learning, John Benjamins Publishing Company, Amsterdam (2003)
21. Fauconnier, G., Turner, M.: Conceptual Integration Networks. Cognitive Science 22(2), 133–187 (1998)
22. Rumelhart, D.E., McClelland, J.L., the PDP Research Group: Parallel Distributed Processing: Explorations in the Microstructure of Cognition. MIT Press, Cambridge (1986)
23. O'Reilly, R.C., Munakata, Y.: Computational Explorations in Cognitive Neuroscience: Understanding the Mind by Simulating the Brain. MIT Press, Cambridge (2000)

Systematically Grounding Language through Vision in a Deep, Recurrent Neural Network

Derek D. Monner and James A. Reggia

Department of Computer Science &
Institute for Advanced Computer Studies
University of Maryland, College Park, MD 20742, USA
{dmonner,reggia}@cs.umd.edu

Abstract. Human intelligence consists largely of the ability to recognize and exploit structural systematicity in the world, relating our senses simultaneously to each other and to our cognitive state. Language abilities, in particular, require a learned mapping between the linguistic input and one's internal model of the real world. In order to demonstrate that connectionist methods excel at this task, we teach a deep, recurrent neural network—a variant of the long short-term memory (LSTM)—to ground language in a micro-world. The network integrates two inputs—a visual scene and an auditory sentence—to produce the meaning of the sentence in the context of the scene. Crucially, the network exhibits strong systematicity, recovering appropriate meanings even for novel objects and descriptions. With its ability to exploit systematic structure across modalities, this network fulfills an important prerequisite of general machine intelligence.

Keywords: deep recurrent neural network, grounded language learning, systematicity, long short-term memory.

1 Introduction

An essential aspect of human intelligence is the ability to recognize and exploit key structural relations between the different modalities of our experience, from our most basic senses all the way up to the most abstract of cognitive representations. Language is one of the clearest examples of the importance of recognizing cross-sensory structural relations. When learning the verb "give" in English, for example, children recognize the correspondence between what they see during give-events—generally a giver, a gift, and a recipient—and the three noun phrases they hear near "give" in the speech stream [1]. Language is also the domain of the most widely known litmus test for a general machine intelligence, the Turing Test [2]. Though Turing argued convincingly that this is the same test we unconsciously require of other humans on a daily basis, Searle famously questioned it in his Chinese Room thought experiment [3], from which he concluded that understanding cannot follow from symbol manipulation alone. Indeed, for a system to exhibit what we call "understanding", it needs to be able

J. Schmidhuber, K.R. Thórisson, and M. Looks (Eds.): AGI 2011, LNAI 6830, pp. 112–121, 2011.

to relate its symbols to something: to ground them in sensations of the external world [4]. Our view is that, without this level of language understanding, it is hard to believe that any system could pass the Turing Test.

With this in mind, we focus on the problem of learning grounded language as a step on the road to general machine intelligence. We present a deep, recurrent neural network—a variant of the long short-term memory LSTM [5,6]—that learns a grounded version of a micro-language by relating it to a micro-world. We choose to use a neural network because neurobiology provides the only known working example of general intelligence. That said, our network is not meant to be a veridical model of any part of the human brain. However, to leave the door open to future extensions in that direction, we attempt to maintain a reasonable degree of neurobiological plausibility.

Our neural network experiences visual scenes and, upon hearing a sentence relating to a scene, reconstructs the meaning of the speaker in terms of the objects it sees. Stated a different way, the network identifies the intended referents and relations described in a natural language sentence. The network naturally learns to segment morphemes, words, and phrases in the auditory input; to construct, maintain, and query a working-memory representation of the visual scene; and to map singular and plural noun phrases onto one or more referents. Finally and most importantly, the network behaves systematically, generalizing not only to novel scene-sentence pairs, but to individual objects and descriptions never before seen or heard.

2   Background

2.1   Systematicity

For decades researchers have debated the question of what constitutes systematic behavior in neural networks. Hadley [7] introduced a graded definition of systematicity for language tasks based on the level of input novelty that a language processing system can correctly handle. Since we are primarily interested in the *grounding* of language, below we define levels of systematicity similar to Hadley's, but based explicitly on a system's ability to pick out appropriate referents for descriptions in a sentence:

1. *Weak* systematic grounding: The system can label familiar objects in novel scenes using familiar object descriptions.
2. *Categorical* systematic grounding: The system can label novel objects in a scene using familiar descriptions; this is tantamount to categorizing the new objects.
3. *Descriptive* systematic grounding: The system can use novel descriptions to label familiar objects in a scene.
4. *Strong* systematic grounding: The system can use novel descriptions to label objects it has never previously encountered.

We will demonstrate that the network presented in this paper exhibits strong systematic grounding of the language it learns. We next turn to previous models of grounded language learning with neural networks, illustrating the level of systematicity that each has demonstrated.

2.2 Past Neural Network Models of Grounded Language Learning

Feldman and colleagues [8] famously challenged the cognitive science community to create a model of language grounded in visual sensation, and many models have addressed this task during the last two decades. We wish, for reasons of neurobiological faithfulness, to focus only on those using purely connectionist methods, rather than hybrid connectionist-symbolic [9] or other types of models. While many of the following connectionist models are impressive, we argue that they fall short of achieving the systematicity required for mastery of language.

Riga, Cangelosi, and Greco [10] advanced a neural network model, utilizing both supervised and unsupervised components, that learned to describe two-dimensional images with combinations of words. The model shows evidence of categorical systematicity by recognizing and labeling novel images; however, there is no evidence that the model can use novel combinations of descriptors for a given image. The model is limited to scenes consisting of single objects and static noun-phrase-like bit-vector descriptions, having not been designed to handle natural language in the temporal domain or at the level of sentences.

Williams and Miikkulainen [11] presented the GLIDE model, consisting of two self-organizing maps [12] that learned visual and linguistic representations of the input and then mapped them to each other. Using subjective scoring to rate the appropriateness of the model's answers, the authors found it to perform poorly on novel scenes and descriptions compared to familiar ones, and thus we cannot conclude that it is strongly systematic in its grounding abilities.

Frank, Haselager, and Rooij [13] developed a model based on a Simple Recurrent Network (SRN) [14] that learned to map temporal sequences of words representing an event onto a "situation vector" designed to analogically represent the possible states of the world. The authors claimed that their model fulfills Hadley's [7] definitions for semantic systematicity. However, interpreting the outputs produced by the model was a complex task, and often led to puzzling situations where the network appeared to simultaneously entertain contradictory beliefs about the world. As such, the level of systematicity of its language grounding is at least questionable, although we find it to be the most impressive model to date.

3   Methods

3.1   Task Description

Our network learns to ground a natural micro-language—a subset of English—in terms of a micro-world. Given input streams representing a visual scene and an auditory sentence, the network should combine these streams in order to create an output representation of the intended meaning of the speaker. By way of explaining the task, we will describe each of the streams of information that the network must integrate: the scene represented by the *visual stream*, the sentence represented by the *auditory stream*, and the grounded meaning represented by the *intention stream*.

Scenes, Objects, and the Visual Stream. On each trial, the network receives a randomly generated scene as input. A scene consists of a collection of objects and their attributes, which include shape, color, and size. Scene objects are presented to the network as neural activity patterns, but for clarity in the text we denote scene objects in a fixed-width font enclosed in square brackets, as [small blue pyramid]. Each object is a combination of two neural activity patterns, the first consisting of a localist representation of the object's attribute values and the second being a localist unique identifier for the object. The latter allows the network to discriminate between objects that otherwise have identical attributes, allowing the scene to contain [large red block 1] and [large red block 2] simultaneously while allowing the network to transparently refer to either.

The neural activity patterns—representing the objects in the scene—are presented to the visual input layer of the network in a temporal sequence which we call the visual stream. During training, the network's visual pathway must learn to create distributed representations that can simultaneously encode several objects, maintaining the bindings between individual objects and their (likely overlapping) attributes.

Since it is not our intention to precisely model human visual sensation and perception, we do not concern ourselves with providing a retinotopic representation of the visual stream. Instead, we assume that something like our scene representation could be constructed by higher-level visual regions in response to sensory input. We present a scene's objects as a temporal sequence in part because it allows us to vary the number of objects presented while using the same weight set to process each.

Sentences, Phonemes, and the Auditory Stream. After experiencing the visual stream, the network hears a sentence that describes some aspects of the scene. Sentences are generated from a simple, mildly context-sensitive grammar (Figure 1) that describes objects from the scene and relations between them. Using the grammar, a [small blue pyramid] could be described as a "small blue pyramid", a "blue pyramid", a "small pyramid", or simply a "pyramid". Notably, the grammar allows plural references to groups of objects, such that our pyramid from above might be grouped with a [small green cylinder] to be collectively described as the "small things" because of their one common attribute.

Each word in the sentence is transcribed into a sequence of phonemes; these sequences are then concatenated, creating a single uninterrupted sequence of phonemes representing the entire sentence. Each phoneme in such a sequence is input to the network as a neural activity pattern representing phonetic features [15]. Since we are not trying to model the entire auditory pathway, we take it

$$
\begin{aligned}
\mathbf{S} &\rightarrow \mathbf{NP}\ \mathbf{VP} \\
\mathbf{NP} &\rightarrow \text{the [Size] [Color] } \mathbf{Shape} \\
\mathbf{VP} &\rightarrow \mathbf{Is\ Where}\ |\ \mathbf{Is\ Color}\ |\ \mathbf{Is\ Size} \\
\mathbf{Is} &\rightarrow \text{is}\ |\ \text{are } (\textit{as appropriate for subject}) \\
\mathbf{Where} &\rightarrow \text{on } \mathbf{NP}\ |\ \text{under } \mathbf{NP}\ |\ \text{near } \mathbf{NP} \\
\mathbf{Size} &\rightarrow \text{small}\ |\ \text{medium}\ |\ \text{large} \\
\mathbf{Color} &\rightarrow \text{red}\ |\ \text{blue}\ |\ \text{green} \\
\mathbf{Shape} &\rightarrow \text{things}\ |\ \text{pyramid}\ |\ \text{pyramids}\ |\ \text{block}\ |\ \text{blocks}\ |\ \text{cylinder}\ |\ \text{cylinders}
\end{aligned}
$$

Fig. 1. The grammar used to generate the sentences. Terminals begin with a lowercase letter while non-terminals are in boldface and begin with an uppercase letter. The symbol | separates alternative derivations, and terms in brackets are optional. The evaluation chosen for the **Is** nonterminal depends on the plurality of its subject.

as granted that feature-based phonetic representations similar to the ones used here are available at some level in the human auditory system.

These patterns—representing the phonemes in the sentence—are presented at the auditory input layer of the network as a temporal sequence which we call the auditory stream. During training, the auditory pathway must simultaneously learn to segment the auditory stream into morphemes and words, pay attention to the syntactic relations between these elements, and discover the cues that identify objects and relations.

Meanings, Predicates, and the Intention Stream. After receiving both the visual and auditory streams, the network is tasked with constructing the sentence's meaning in the context of the scene. To do this, the network must generate a sequence of predicates—as activity patterns over its output layer— which we call the intention stream.

Each predicate in the intention stream corresponds to an attribute or relation mentioned in the sentence. We denote predicates using a fixed-width font enclosed in parentheses, distinguishing them from the square-bracketed visual objects. If a sentence refers to the visual object [small red cylinder 2] as "small cylinder", the network must produce the predicates (small 2) and (cylinder 2), but not (red 2) since this attribute was not mentioned. If a sentence states that a "blue block" (referring to visual object 3) is "under" our small cylinder, the network must output the predicate (under 3 2). It may be that some objects in the scene, or even most of them, are not referenced in the sentence that accompanies it. In this case, these objects can be considered distractor stimuli, and while they are present in the visual stream input, they are not included in the target intention stream.

After a training trial, the network is shown the target intention stream. Comparing this behavior to that of a human language learner, we must assume that the learner can, at least sometimes, derive the speaker's meaning from other sources—a task at which language learners seem to excel [16]—and that this meaning is available in something resembling a propositional form.

A Complete Example Trial. Figure 2 describes an input scene, consisting of four objects, and an input phoneme sequence for the sentence "The small pyramids are on the blue block". A correct intention stream for these inputs must contain predicates denoting the objects numbered 1 and 2 as the "small pyramids". The intention stream should indicate object 4 as the referent of "the blue block", containing predicates at the end of the sequence matching these two attributes with the appropriate object identifier. For the relation "on", the intention stream must contain a predicate representing the (on) relation, indicating that objects 1 and 2, the pyramids, are on object 4, the block.

Visual Stream	Auditory Stream	Intention Stream
[small red pyramid 1]	"The small pyramids are	(small 1+2)
[large blue block 4]	on the blue block"	(pyramid 1+2)
[medium red cylinder 3]		(on 1+2 4)
[small green pyramid 2]		(blue 4)
		(block 4)

Fig. 2. An example trial. Stream elements are depicted in human-readable form, but are presented to the network as sequences of neural activity patterns representing objects, phonemes, and predicates.

3.2   Network Architecture

The neural network that learns our grounding task is a generalized long short-term memory (LSTM-g) [17], which is an extension of the long short-term memory (LSTM) network [5,6]. LSTM uses stateful self-connected neural units called memory cells, which are allowed to have multiplicative input, output, and forget gates. LSTM-g is a formulation of LSTM that gains the ability to accommodate arbitrary multi-level network architectures without altering the learning rules.

Though the network is trained by gradient descent, and thus utilizes back-propagated error signals, we believe that the overall architecture is not as far removed from biological plausibility as one might expect. Specifically, it has been recently discovered that the gradient descent training method is essentially a convenient implementation of contrastive Hebbian learning [18], the latter being the main ingredient in biologically realistic neural training algorithms such as Leabra [19]. The fact that memory cells in LSTM maintain their state across time steps actually makes them resemble real, stateful neurons more closely than traditional stateless neural elements. Finally, the multiplicative functions of gate units in LSTM have close neurobiological correlates, and similar mechanisms have been used in models of the prefrontal cortex and basal ganglia [20].

The specific network architecture we use to learn our grounding task is depicted in Figure 3. Visual processing begins at the lower-right input layer and auditory processing at the lower-left, proceeding through one or two internal layers of self-recurrent LSTM memory cells, respectively, before integration at the final internal layer. We use two layers in the auditory pathway because the task involves multiple levels of auditory segmentation, with the first layer transforming phonemes into morphemes and words, which in the second layer become phrases. Previous experiments on learning ungrounded language representations [17] show that a two-layer pathway outperforms a single-layer pathway. To assist in the production of output sequences, the last internal layer has a recurrent connection from the previous time-step's output.

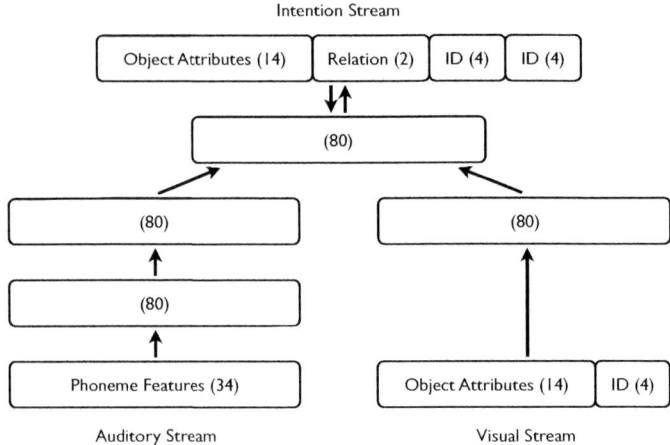

Fig. 3. The architecture of the network. Boxes represent layers of units (with number of units in parentheses) and arrows represent banks of trainable connection weights.

3.3   Experimental Evaluation

We train our network in four different ways, evaluating it on sets of test sentences that probe the different levels of grounding systematicity from Section 2.1. In what follows, an object or description is considered novel if it consists of a combination of features (e.g. [large red pyramid]) or words (e.g. "large red pyramid") that does not occur in the training set.

1. *Weak* condition: The set of scene-sentence pairs is partitioned at random with 10% reserved for testing. While test pairs are novel, the individual objects and descriptions are likely familiar to the network.
2. *Categorical* condition: One specific type of object is never present in scenes during training. The network is tested in situations where this novel object is given a familiar description.
3. *Descriptive* condition: One specific type of object, while allowed to be present in the scenes, is never described fully. We test the network on scenes containing this familiar object and sentences containing the full, novel description.
4. *Strong* condition: One type of object is never described *and* never appears in scenes. We test the network on inputs where this novel object appears and is referenced using a novel description.

We train 10 fresh networks in each of the above conditions. Individual units in different layers are connected with a probability of 0.7, leading to networks with approximately 60 thousand trainable weights. The learning rate is 0.01. Each network is allowed to train on 3 million randomly selected scene-sentence pairs from its training set.

For each training trial, we generate random scenes consisting of two, three, or four distinct objects, with uniform probability. We then use the grammar to generate a random sentence describing the scene. Over half a million distinct scenes are possible, each giving rise to, on average, 36 possible grammatical sentences. Since inputs, especially simple ones, are often repeated, the network sees a very small fraction of the input space during training. For each pair of test inputs, the network must produce the correct intention stream, consisting of a temporal sequence of 2 to 7 predicates.

4   Results

Figure 4 compares network accuracy across conditions. The ten networks in the *weak* condition produced correct meanings for, on average, 95% of novel scene-sentence pairs, while those in the *categorical, descriptive,* and *strong* conditions were 93%, 93%, and 97% accurate, respectively. The networks clearly pass all of our systematicity tests on the grounding task.

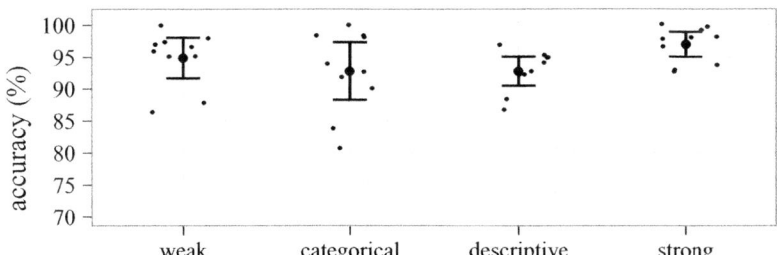

Fig. 4. The percentage of completely correct intention streams recovered from random samples of 100 test-set sentences, averaged over 10 trials in each of the conditions. The small dots represent the performance of individual networks in a condition, and large dots represent overall condition means. The error bars denote the 95% confidence intervals on the condition means.

Comparing the conditions, we observed a significant difference in performance only between the *descriptive* and *strong* conditions on a Welch two-sample t-test ($t \approx -3.2$, $df \approx 17.5$, $p < 0.01$). We think this has to with an (intentional) asymmetry in the *descriptive* condition's training set. The network, observing 27 different visual objects but only 26 complete auditory object descriptions, is slightly impaired by this structural asymmetry. By contrast, in the *strong* condition, the scenes and sentences maintain their structural symmetry, with 26 visual objects corresponding to 26 complete auditory descriptions.

It is worth noting that the network had far more trouble with the grounding part of the task—that is, selecting the referents for the various object descriptions—than it had with parsing the linguistic descriptions themselves. When scoring on accurate recognition of linguistic descriptions and ignoring referents, trained networks produced, on average, less than one error per 1000 sentences. While trained networks produced the correct referent for 98% of noun phrases—with their accuracy varying inversely with the number of objects in the scene and the number of referents in the sentence, as one might expect—it also took them much longer to reach this accuracy level. A typical network required only the first quarter of its training time to reach ceiling when recognizing linguistic descriptions, at which point it was identifying referents correctly only 80% of the time, a figure which slowly improved for the duration of training. That referents are so much more difficult to identify than object attributes and relations only underscores the difficulty of the language grounding task.

The network appears to scale well to larger scenes, with overall accuracy decreasing nominally as we increase the maximum number of objects in the scene to five or six—causing the number of possible scenes to exceed 400 million—while keeping the number of trainable weights constant.

5   Discussion

The results in the previous section demonstrate that the network uses grounded language systematically. We are currently analyzing the network's learned internal representations in hopes of providing a detailed explanation of how they support this systematic behavior. A key question will be whether these learned representations can be viewed as classical symbols (in some meaningful sense of the term) or are of a fundamentally different nature.

While we suggest that our network provides one the best demonstrations of strongly systematic, grounded language learning to date, we realize that it is still a long way from a general machine intelligence. However, we believe that it provides compelling evidence that connectionist methods excel at something essential to general intelligence: the ability to recognize and exploit structural systematicity in the environment across sensory modalities, relating the senses simultaneously to each other and to what we might call the internal, cognitive world. We are convinced that what we colloquially refer to as "intelligence" consists largely of the ability to discover systematicity, whether at the most basic level of our senses or at the highest levels of cognitive abstraction. Our hope is that future work in this vein will shed light on how human intelligence is implemented *in vivo* while simultaneously bringing us closer to recreating it *in silico*.

References

1. Goldberg, A.E.: Learning Linguistic Patterns. The Psychology of Learning and Motivation 47, 33–63 (2006)
2. Turing, A.M.: Computing Machinery and Intelligence. Mind 59(236), 433–460 (1950)

3. Searle, J.R.: Minds, Brains, and Programs. Behavioral and Brain Sciences 3(03), 417–457 (1980)
4. Harnad, S.: The Symbol Grounding Problem. Physica D: Nonlinear Phenomena 42(1-3), 335–346 (1990)
5. Hochreiter, S., Schmidhuber, J.: Long Short-Term Memory. Neural Computation 9(8), 1735–1780 (1997)
6. Gers, F.A., Cummins, F.: Learning to Forget: Continual Prediction with LSTM. Neural Computation 12(10), 2451–2471 (2000)
7. Hadley, R.: Systematicity in Connectionist Language Learning. Mind & Language (1994)
8. Feldman, J.A., Lakoff, G., Stolcke, A., Weber, S.H.: Miniature Language Acquisition: A Touchstone for Cognitive Science. In: Proceedings of the Annual Conference of the Cognitive Science Society, pp. 686–693 (1990)
9. Hadley, R.F., Cardei, V.C.: Language Acquisition from Sparse Input Without Error Feedback. Neural Networks 12(2), 217–235 (1999)
10. Riga, T., Cangelosi, A., Greco, A.: Symbol Grounding Transfer with Hybrid Self-Organizing/Supervised Neural Networks. In: Proceedings of the International Joint Conference on Neural Networks, pp. 2865–2869 (2004)
11. Williams, P., Miikkulainen, R.: Grounding Language in Descriptions of Scenes. In: Proceedings of the 8th Annual Conference of the Cognitive Science Society, pp. 2381–2386 (2006)
12. Kohonen, T.: The Self-Organizing Map. Proceedings of the IEEE 78, 1464–1480 (1990)
13. Frank, S.L., Haselager, W.F.G., van Rooij, I.: Connectionist Semantic Systematicity. Cognition 110(3), 358–379 (2009)
14. Elman, J.L.: Finding Structure in Time. Cognitive Science 14, 179–211 (1990)
15. Weems, S.A., Reggia, J.A.: Simulating Single Word Processing in the Classic Aphasia Syndromes Based on the Wernicke-Lichtheim-Geschwind Theory. Brain and Language 98(3), 291–309 (2006)
16. Tomasello, M.: Constructing a Language: A Usage-Based Theory of Language Acquisition. Harvard University Press, Cambridge (2003)
17. Monner, D.D., Reggia, J.A.: A Generalized LSTM-Like Training Algorithm for Second-Order Recurrent Neural Networks (2011) (submitted)
18. Xie, X., Seung, H.S.: Equivalence of Backpropagation and Contrastive Hebbian Learning in a Layered Network. Neural Computation 15(2), 441–454 (2003)
19. O'Reilly, R.C.: Generalization in Interactive Networks: The Benefits of Inhibitory Competition and Hebbian Learning. Neural Computation 13(6), 1199–1241 (2001)
20. O'Reilly, R.C., Frank, M.J.: Making Working Memory Work: A Computational Model of Learning in the Prefrontal Cortex and Basal Ganglia. Neural Computation 18(2), 283–328 (2006)

Comparing Humans and AI Agents

Javier Insa-Cabrera[1], David L. Dowe[2], Sergio España-Cubillo[3],
M.Victoria Hernández-Lloreda[4], and José Hernández-Orallo[1]

[1] DSIC, Universitat Politècnica de València, Spain
{jinsa,jorallo}@dsic.upv.es
[2] Clayton School of Information Technology, Monash University, Australia
david.dowe@monash.edu
[3] ProS Research Center, Universitat Politècnica de València, Spain
sergio.espana@pros.upv.es
[4] Departamento de Metodología de las Ciencias del Comportamiento,
Universidad Complutense de Madrid, Spain
vhlloreda@psi.ucm.es

Abstract. Comparing humans and machines is one important source of information about both machine and human strengths and limitations. Most of these comparisons and competitions are performed in rather specific tasks such as calculus, speech recognition, translation, games, etc. The information conveyed by these experiments is limited, since it portrays that machines are much better than humans at some domains and worse at others. In fact, CAPTCHAs exploit this fact. However, there have only been a few proposals of general intelligence tests in the last two decades, and, to our knowledge, just a couple of implementations and evaluations. In this paper, we implement one of the most recent test proposals, devise an interface for humans and use it to compare the intelligence of humans and Q-learning, a popular reinforcement learning algorithm. The results are highly informative in many ways, raising many questions on the use of a (universal) distribution of environments, on the role of measuring knowledge acquisition, and other issues, such as speed, duration of the test, scalability, etc.

Keywords: Intelligence measurement, universal intelligence, general vs. specific intelligence, reinforcement learning, IQ tests.

1 Introduction

It is well-known that IQ tests are not useful for evaluating the intelligence of machines. The main reason is not because machines are not able to 'understand' the test. The real reason is scarcely known and poorly understood, since available theories do not manage to fully explain the empirical observations: it has been shown that relative simple programs can be designed to score well on these tests [11]. Some other approaches such as the Turing Test [15] and Captchas [17] have their niches, but they are also inappropriate to evaluate AGI systems.

In the last fifteen years, several alternatives for a general (or universal) intelligence test (or definition) based on Solomonoff's universal distributions [12] (or

J. Schmidhuber, K.R. Thórisson, and M. Looks (Eds.): AGI 2011, LNAI 6830, pp. 122–132, 2011.

related ideas such as MML, compression or Kolmogorov complexity) have been appearing on the scene [1,3,7,8,5], claiming that they are able to define or evaluate (machine) intelligence. In this paper we use one of these tests, a prototype based on the anytime intelligence test presented in [5] and the environment class introduced in [4], to evaluate one easily accessible biological system (*Homo sapiens*) and one off-the-shelf AI system, a popular reinforcement algorithm known as Q-learning [18]. In order to do the comparison we use the same environment class for both systems and we design hopefully non-biased interfaces for both. We perform a pilot experiment on a reduced group of individuals.

From this experiment we obtain a number of interesting findings and insights. First, it is possible to do the same test for humans and machines without being anthropomorphic. The test is exactly the same for both and it is founded on a theory derived from sound computational concepts. We just adapt the interface (what way rewards, actions and observations look like) depending on the type of subjects. Second, humans are not better than Q-learning in this test, even though the test (despite several simplifications) is based on a universal distribution of environments over a very general environment class. Third, since these results are consistent to those in [11] (which show that machines can score well in IQ tests), this gives additional evidence that a test which is valid for humans or for machines separately might be useless to distinguish or to place humans and machines on the same scale, so failing to be a universal intelligence test.

The following section overviews the most important proposals on defining and measuring machine intelligence to date, and, from them, it describes the intelligence test and the environment class we will use in this paper. Sections 3 and 4 describe the testing setting, the two types of agents we evaluate (Q-learning and humans) and their interfaces. Section 5 includes the comparison of the experimental results, analysing them by several factors. Finally, section 6 examines these results in a deeper way and draws several conclusions about the way universal intelligence tests should and should not be.

2 Measuring Intelligence Universally

Measuring machine intelligence or, more generally, performance has been virtually relegated to a philosophical or, at most, theoretical issue in AI. Given that state-of-the-art technology in AI is still far from truly intelligent machines, it seems that the Turing Test [15] (and its many variations [10]) and Captchas [17] are enough for philosophical debates and practical applications respectively. There are also tests and competitions in restricted domains, such as competitions in robotics, in game playing, in machine translation and in reinforcement learning (RL), most notably the RL competition. All of them use a somewhat arbitrary and frequently anthropomorphic set of tasks.

An alternative, general proposal for intelligence and performance evaluation is based on the notion of universal distribution [12] and the related algorithmic information theory (a.k.a. Kolmogorov complexity) [9]. Using this theory, we can define a universal distribution of tasks for a given AI realm, and sort them according to their (objective) complexity. There are some early works which develop these ideas to construct intelligence tests. First, [1] suggested the introduction of inductive inference problems in a somehow *induction-enhanced* or *compression-enhanced* Turing Test [15]. Second, [3] derived intelligence tests (C-tests) as sets of sequence prediction problems which were generated by a universal distribution, and the result (the intelligence of the agent) was a sum of performances for a range of problems of increasing complexity. The complexity of each sequence was derived from its Kolmogorov complexity (a Levin variant was used). This kind of problem (discrete sequence prediction), although typical in IQ tests, is a narrow AI realm. In fact, [11] showed that relatively simple algorithms could score well at IQ tests (and, as a consequence, at C-tests). In [3] the suggestion of using interactive tasks where "rewards and penalties could be used instead" was made. Later, Legg and Hutter (e.g. [7],[8]) gave a precise definition to the term "Universal Intelligence", also grounded in Kolmogorov complexity and Solomonoff's prediction theory, as a sum (or weighted average) of performances in all the possible RL-like environments. However, in order to make a feasible test by extending from (static) sequences to (dynamic) environments, several issues had to be solved first. In [5], they address the problem of finding a finite sample of environments and sessions, as well as appropriate approximations to Kolmogorov complexity, the inclusion of time, and the proper aggregation of rewards. The theory, however, has not been put into practice until now in the form of a real test, in order to evaluate artificial and biological agents, and, interestingly, to compare them. In this paper, we use a (simplified) implementation of this test (non-anytime) [5] using the environment class introduced in [4] to compare Q-learning with *Homo sapiens*.

From this comparison we want to answer several questions. Are these tests general enough? Does the complexity of the exercises correlate with the success rate of Q-learning and humans? Does the difference correspond to the real difference in intelligence between these two kinds of agents? What implications do the results have on the notion of universal intelligence and the tests that attempt to measure it? Answering all these questions is the goal of this paper.

The choice of a proper environment class is a crucial issue in any intelligence test. This is what [4] attempts, a hopefully unbiased environment class (called Λ) with spaces and agents with universal descriptive (Turing-complete) power. Basically, this environment considers a space as a graph with a different (and variable) topology of actions. Objects and agents can be introduced using Turing-complete languages to generate their movements. Rewards are rational numbers in the interval $[-1, 1]$ and are generated by two special agents *Good* and *Evil*, which leave rewards in the cells they visit. *Good* and *Evil* have the same pattern for behaviour except for the sign of the reward (+ for *Good*, − for *Evil*).

The environment class Λ is shown in [4] to have two relevant properties for a performance test: (1) their environments are always balanced (a random agent has expected reward 0), and (2) their environments are reward-sensitive (there is no sequence of actions such that the agent can be stuck in a heaven or hell situation, where rewards are positive or negative independently of what the agent may do). As argued in [5], these two properties are very important for the environments to be discriminative and comparable (and hence the results being properly aggregated into a single score, a performance or intelligence score). No other properties are imposed, such as (e.g.) environments being Markov processes or being ergodic. For more details of the environment class Λ, see [4].

3   Test Setting and Administration

Following the definition of the environment class Λ, we perform some simplifications to generate each environment. For instance, speed is not considered thus being a non-anytime version of the test presented in [5]. In addition, we do not use a Turing-complete algorithm to generate the environments. Spaces are generated by first determining the number of cells n_c, which is given by a number between 2 and 9, using a 'unary' distribution (i.e. $prob(n) = 2^{-n}$, and normalising to sum up to 1). Similarly, the number of actions n_a is defined with a uniform distribution between 2 and n_c. Both cells and actions are indexed with natural numbers. There is a special action 0 which connects every cell with itself (it is always possible to stay at the cell). A cell which is accessible from another cell using one action is called a 'neighbouring' or adjacent cell. The connections between cells are created by using a uniform distribution for each pair of cell and action, which assigns the destination cell for each pair. We consider the posibility that some actions may be disabled. Fig. 1 shows an example of a randomly generated space.

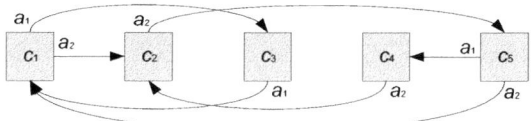

Fig. 1. A space with 5 cells and 3 actions (a_0, a_1, a_2). Reflexive action a_0 is not shown.

The number of cells and actions is, of course, related to the complexity of the space, but not monotonically related to its Kolmogorov complexity (or a computable variant such as Levin's Kt). Nonetheless, most of the actual grading of environments comes from the behaviour of *Good* and *Evil*. The sequence of actions for *Good* and *Evil* is defined by using a uniform distribution for each element in the sequence, and a unary (exponential) distribution to determine whether to stop the sequence, by using a probability of stopping (p_{stop}). An example of sequence for the space in Fig. 1 is 201210200, which means the execution of actions a_2, a_0, a_1, a_2, etc. Consider, e.g., that *Good* is placed at cell c_5. Since the pattern starts with '2', *Good* will move (via a_2) to cell c_1. The agents *Good* and *Evil* take one action from the sequence and execute it for each step. When the actions are exhausted, the sequence is started all over again. If an action is not allowed at a particular cell, the agent does not move.

Initially, each agent is randomly (using a uniform distribution) placed in a cell. Then, we let *Good*, *Evil* and the evaluated agent interact for a certain number of steps m. We call this an exercise (or episode). For an exercise we average the obtained rewards, so giving a score of the agent in the environment.

A test is a sequence of exercises or episodes. We will use 7 environments, each with a number of cells (n_c) from 3 to 9. The size of the patterns for *Good* and *Evil* will be made proportional (on average) to the number of cells, using $p_{stop} = 1/n_c$. In each environment, we will allow $10 \times (n_c - 1)$ steps so the agents have the chance to detect any pattern in the environment (exploration) and also have some further steps to exploit the findings (in case a pattern is actually conceived). The limitation of the number of environments and steps is justified because the tests is meant to be applied to biological agents in a reasonable period of time (e.g., 20 minutes) and we estimate an average of 4 seconds per action. Table 1 shows the choices we have made for the test:

Table 1. Setting for the 7 environments which compose the test

Env. #	No. cells (n_c)	No. steps (m)	p_{stop}
1	3	20	1/3
2	4	30	1/4
3	5	40	1/5
4	6	50	1/6
5	7	60	1/7
6	8	70	1/8
7	9	80	1/9
TOTAL	-	350	-

Although [4] suggests a partially-observable interface, here we make it fully-observable, so agents see all the cells, the actions and their contents. The agents do not know in advance who *Good* is and who *Evil* is. They have to guess that.

4   Agents and Interfaces

4.1   An AI Agent: Q-Learning

The choice of Q-learning is, of course, one of many possible choices for a reinforcement learning algorithm. The reason is deliberate because we want a standard algorithm to be evaluated first, and, most especially, because we do not want to evaluate (at the moment) very specialised algorithms for ergodic environments or algorithms with better computational properties (e.g. delayed Q-learning [13] would be a better option if speed were an issue). We use an off-the-shelf implementation of Q-learning, as explained in [18] and [14].

We use the description of cell contents as a state. We choose Q-learning's parameters as $\alpha = 0.05$ *learning rate* and $\gamma = 0.35$ *discount factor*. The parameters have been chosen by trying 20 consecutive values for α and γ between 0 and 1. These 400 combinations have been evaluated for 1,000 sessions each using random environments of different size and complexity and episodes of 10,000 steps. This choice is, of course, beneficial for Q-learning's performance in the tests.

Since we have rewards between -1 and 1, the elements in the Q matrix are set to 2.0 initially (rewards are normalised between 0 and 2 to always be positive).

4.2   A Biological Agent: *Homo Sapiens*

We took 20 humans from a University Department (PhD students, research and teaching staff) with ages ranging between 20 and 50.

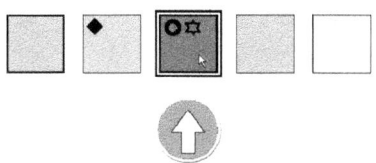

Fig. 2. A snapshot of the interface for humans. The agent has just received a positive reward, shown with the circle with an upwards arrow. The image also shows the agent located in cell 3, and *Evil* and *Good* are placed in cells 2 and 3 respectively. The agent can move to cell 1 and cell 3. Cell 3 is highlighted since the mouse pointer is over it.

The interface for humans has been designed with the following principles in mind: i) the signs used to represent observations should not have an implicit meaning for the subject, to avoid bias in favour of humans (e.g. no skull-and-bones for the Evil agent), ii) actions and rewards should be easily interpreted by the subject, to avoid a cognitive overhead that would bias the experiment in favour of Q-learning. This way, the following design decisions have been made (Fig. 2 shows a snapshot of the interface). At the beginning of the test, the subject is presented the task instructions, which strictly contain what the user should know. The cells are represented by coloured squares. Agents are represented by symbols that aim to be 'neutral' (e.g., ♦ stands for *Evil* and ✱ stands for *Good* in the third environment, and ○ represents the subject in every environment). Accessible cells have a thicker border than non-accessible ones. When the subject rolls the mouse pointer over an accessible cell, this cell is highlighted using a double border and increasing the saturation of the background colour. Positive, neutral and negative rewards are represented by an upwards arrow in a green circle, a small square in a grey circle, and a downwards arrow in a red circle, respectively. The test and its interface for humans can be downloaded from http://users.dsic.upv.es/proy/anynt/human1/test.html.

5   Results

We performed 20 tests (with 7 exercises each) with the setting shown in Table 1 and we administered each of them to a human and to Q-learning.

The first observation from this paired set of results comes from the means. While Q-learning has an overall mean of 0.259, humans show a mean of 0.237.

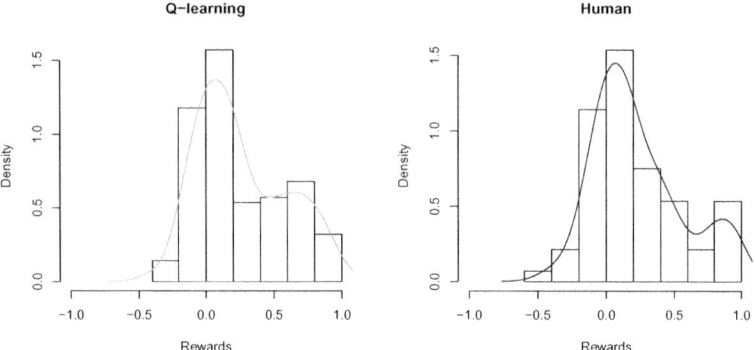

Fig. 3. Histograms of the $(20 \times 7 =)$ 140 exercises for Q-learning (left) and humans (right). Lines show the probability densities.

The standard deviations are 0.122 and 0.150 respectively. Figure 3 shows the histograms and the probability densities (estimated by the R package).

To see the results in more detail in terms of the exercise, Figure 4 (left) shows the results aggregating by exercise (there is one exercise for each number of cells between 3 and 9, so totalling 7 exercises per test). This figure shows the mean, median and dispersion of both Q-learning and humans for each exercise. Looking at the boxplots for each space size we also see that there is no significant difference in terms of how Q-learning and humans perform in each of the seven exercises. While means are around 0.2 and 0.3, variances are smaller the larger the number of cells is. This is explained because the exercise with higher number of cells has a higher number of iterations (see Table 1).

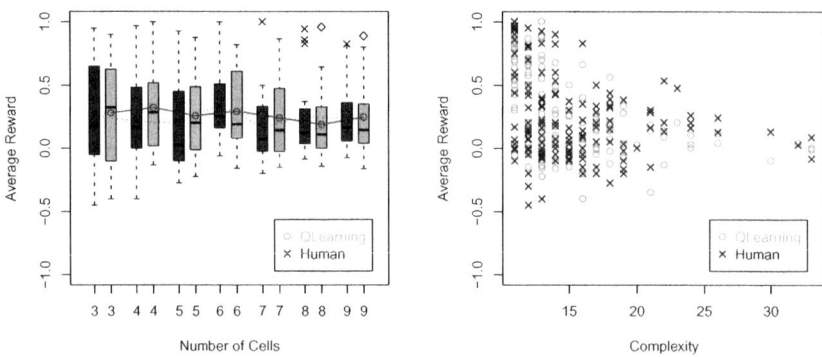

Fig. 4. Left: Box (whisker) plots for the seven exercises depending on the agent. Medians are shown in the box as a short black segment. Means are connected by a continuous line for Q-learning and a dashed line for humans. Right: the average reward results for the $20 \times 7 \times 2 = 280$ exercises using K^{approx} as a measure of complexity.

We applied two-way repeated measures ANOVA (agent $\times$ number of cells). ANOVA showed no statistically significant effects neither for agent ($F_{1,19} = .461$,

$P = .506$), nor for the number of cells ($F_{6,114} = .401$, $P = .877$). No statistically significant *interaction* effect was found ($F_{6,114} = .693$, $P = .656$) either.

Finally, since the size of the space is not a measure of complexity, we explored the relation with the complexity of the environments. In order to approximate this complexity, we used the size of the compressed pattern for *Good* and *Evil*, denoted by P. More formally, given an environment μ, we calculate an approximation to its (Kolmogorov) complexity, denoted by K^{approx} as follows:

$$K^{approx} = LZ(P))$$

For instance, if a pattern is $P=$"201222200222222200222222002", we compress the string (using the *memCompress* function in R, with a GNU project implementation of Lempel-Ziv coding). The length of the compressed string is 19.

Figure 4 (right) shows each of the $20 \times 7 = 140$ exercises for each kind of agent. Again we see a higher dispersion for humans than for Q-learning (the 20 humans are different, while Q-learning is exactly the same algorithm for each of the 20 tests). We calculate the Pearson correlation coefficient between complexity and reward. Now we do find a statistically significant correlation both for humans ($r = -.257$, $n = 140$, $P = .001$) and for Q-learning ($r = -.444$, $n = 140$, $P < .001$). We also analyse these correlations by number of cells, as shown in Table 2. This table shows Pearson correlation coefficients and associated significance levels (one tailed test) between "complexity" and "reward" by "numbers of cells" for each agent. All $n = 20$.

Table 2. Pearson correlation coefficients and p values (in parentheses) between "complexity" and "reward" by "numbers of cells"

Agent	3 cells	4 cells	5 cells	6 cells	7 cells	8 cells	9 cells
Human	-.474 (.017)	-.134 (.286)	-.367 (.056)	-.515 (.010)	-.282 (.114)	-.189 (.213)	-.146 (.270)
Q-learning	-.612 (.002)	-.538 (.008)	-.526 (.009)	-.403 (.039)	-.442 (.026)	-.387 (.046)	-.465 (.019)

We see that correlations are stronger and always significant for Q-learning, while they are milder (and not always significant) for humans. This may be explained because humans are not reset between exercises. In general, we would need more data (more tests) to confirm or refute this hypothesis.

6   Discussion

In section 2 we outlined several questions. One question is whether the test is general enough. It is true that we have made many simplifications to the environment class, in such a way that *Good* and *Evil* do not react to the environment (they just execute a cyclical sequence of actions as a pattern), and we have used a very simple approximation to complexity instead of better approximations to Kolmogorov complexity or Levin's Kt. In addition, and the parameters for Q-learning have been chosen to be optimal for these kinds of spaces and patterns. Besides, humans are not (cannot be) reset between exercises. Despite all these issues (most of) which are in favour of Q-learning, we think (although this cannot be concluded in an absolute way) that the tests are not general enough. Q-learning is not the best AI algorithm available nowadays (in fact we do not consider Q-learning very intelligent). So, the results are not representing the real difference in intelligence between humans and Q-learning.

A possibility is that our sample size is perhaps too small. Having more environments of higher complexity and letting the agents interact longer with each of them may perhaps portray a different picture. Nonetheless, it is not clear that humans can scale up well in this kind of exercise, especially if no part of previous exercises can be reused to other exercises. First, some of the patterns which appeared in the most complex exercises were considered very difficult by humans. Second, Q-learning requires many interactions to converge, so perhaps this would only exaggerate the difference in favour of Q-learning. In any case, this should be properly analysed with further experiments.

A more fundamental issue is whether we are testing on the wrong sort of environments. The environment class is a general class which includes two symmetrical agents, *Good* and *Evil*, which are in charge of rewards. We do not think that this environment class is, in any case, biased against humans (the contrary can be argued, though). In the end, the question of whether a test is biased is difficult to answer, since any single choice implies a certain bias. So, in our opinion, the problem might be found in the environment distribution. Choosing the universal distribution gives high probability to very simple examples with very simple patterns, but more importantly, makes any kind of rich interaction impossible even in environments of high Kolmogorov complexity. So, a better environment distribution (and perhaps class) should give more probability to incremental knowledge acquisition, social capabilities and more reactivity.

This goal towards more knowledge-intensive tasks has the risk of focussing on knowledge and language, or to embark on Ttests without any theoretical background, such as Jeopardy-like contests. The generality of these tasks may be high, although the adaptability and the required learning abilities might be low. This is something recurrent in psychometrics, where it is important (but difficult) to distinguish between knowledge acquisition capabilities and knowledge application. And it is also a challenge for RL-like evaluations and systems, where knowledge acquisition usually starts from scratch and is not incremental.

So, one of the things that we have learnt is that the change of universal distributions from passive environments (as originally proposed in [1] and [3]) to interactive environments (as also suggested in [3] and fully developed in [7,8]) is in the right direction, but it is not the solution yet. It is clear that it allows for a more natural interpretation of the notion of intelligence as performance in a wide range of environments, and it eases the application of tests outside humans and machines (children, apes, etc.), but there are some other issues we have to address to give an appropriate definition of intelligence and a practical test. The proposal for an adaptive test [5] introduces many new ideas about creating practical intelligence tests, and the universal distribution is substituted by an adaptive distribution, so allowing a faster convergence to complexity levels which are more appropriate for the agent. Nonetheless, we think that the priority is in defining new environment distributions which can give higher probability to environments where intelligence can show its full potential (see, e.g. [6]).

Summing up, while there has been some work on comparing humans and machines on some specific tasks, e.g., humans and Q-learning in [2], this paper may start a series of experimental research comparing several artificial agents (such as other algorithms in reinforcement learning, MonteCarlo AIXI [16], etc.) and other biological agents (children, other apes, etc) for *general* tasks. This might be a highly valuable source of information about whether the concept of universal intelligence evaluation works, by trying to construct more and more general (and universal) intelligence tests. This could lead eventually to a new discipline, for which we already suggest a name: "universal psychometrics".

Acknowledgments. We thank the anonymous reviewers for their helpful comments. We also thank José Antonio Martín H. for helping us with several issues about the RL competition, RL-Glue and reinforcement learning in general. We are also grateful to all the subjects who took the test. We also thank the funding from the Spanish MEC and MICINN for projects TIN2009-06078-E/TIN, Consolider-Ingenio CSD2007-00022 and TIN2010-21062-C02, for MEC FPU grant AP2006-02323, and Generalitat Valenciana for Prometeo/2008/051.

References

1. Dowe, D.L., Hajek, A.R.: A non-behavioural, computational extension to the Turing Test. In: Intl. Conf. on Computational Intelligence & multimedia applications (ICCIMA 1998), Gippsland, Australia, pp. 101–106 (1998)
2. Gordon, D., Subramanian, D.: A cognitive model of learning to navigate. In: Proc. 19th Conf. of the Cognitive Science Society, 1997, vol. 25, p. 271. Lawrence Erlbaum, Mahwah (1997)
3. Hernández-Orallo, J.: Beyond the Turing Test. J. Logic, Language & Information 9(4), 447–466 (2000)
4. Hernández-Orallo, J.: A (hopefully) non-biased universal environment class for measuring intelligence of biological and artificial systems. In: Hutter, M., et al. (eds.) 3rd Intl. Conf. on Artificial General Intelligence, pp. 182–183. Atlantis Press, London (2010) Extended report at,
   http://users.dsic.upv.es/proy/anynt/unbiased.pdf
5. Hernández-Orallo, J., Dowe, D.L.: Measuring universal intelligence: Towards an anytime intelligence test. Artificial Intelligence 174(18), 1508–1539 (2010)
6. Hernández-Orallo, J., Dowe, D.L., España-Cubillo, S., Hernández-Lloreda, M.V., Insa-Cabrera, J.: On more realistic environment distributions for defining, evaluating and developing intelligence. In: Schmidhuber, J., Thórisson, K.R., Looks, M. (eds.) AGI 2011. LNCS(LNAI), vol. 6830, pp. 82–91. Springer, Heidelberg (2011)
7. Legg, S., Hutter, M.: A universal measure of intelligence for artificial agents. In: Intl Joint Conf on Artificial Intelligence, IJCAI, vol. 19, p. 1509 (2005)
8. Legg, S., Hutter, M.: Universal intelligence: A definition of machine intelligence. Minds and Machines 17(4), 391–444 (2007)
9. Li, M., Vitányi, P.: An introduction to Kolmogorov complexity and its applications, 3rd edn. Springer-Verlag New York, Inc., Heidelberg (2008)

10. Oppy, G., Dowe, D.L.: The Turing Test. In: Zalta, E.N. (ed.) Stanford Encyclopedia of Philosophy, Stanford University, Stanford (2011), http://plato.stanford.edu/entries/turing-test/
11. Sanghi, P., Dowe, D.L.: A computer program capable of passing IQ tests. In: 4th Intl. Conf. on Cognitive Science (ICCS 2003), Sydney, pp. 570–575 (2003)
12. Solomonoff, R.J.: A formal theory of inductive inference. Part I. Information and control 7(1). 1–22 (1964)
13. Strehl, A.L., Li, L., Wiewiora, E., Langford, J., Littman, M.L.: PAC model-free reinforcement learning. In: ICML 2006, pp. 881–888. New York (2006)
14. Sutton, R.S., Barto, A.G.: Reinforcement learning: An introduction. The MIT press, Cambridge (1998)
15. Turing, A.M.: Computing machinery and intelligence. Mind 59, 433–460 (1950)
16. Veness, J., Ng, K.S., Hutter, M., Silver, D.: A Monte Carlo AIXI Approximation. Journal of Artificial Intelligence Research, JAIR 40, 95–142 (2011)
17. von Ahn, L., Blum, M., Langford, J.: Telling humans and computers apart automatically. Communications of the ACM 47(2), 56–60 (2004)
18. Watkins, C.J.C.H., Dayan, P.: Q-learning. Mach. learning 8(3), 279–292 (1992)

The LIDA Framework as a General Tool for AGI

Javier Snaider[1], Ryan McCall[2], and Stan Franklin[3]

[1,2] FedEx Institute of Technology #403h, 365 Innovation Dr., Memphis, TN 38152
{jsnaider,rmccall}@memphis.edu
[3] FedEx Institute of Technology #312, 365 Innovation Dr., Memphis, TN 38152
franklin@memphis.edu

Abstract. Intelligent software agents aiming for general intelligence are likely to be exceedingly complex systems and, as such, will be difficult to implement and to customize. Frameworks have been applied successfully in large-scale software engineering applications. A framework constitutes the skeleton of the application, capturing its generic functionality. Frameworks are powerful as they promote code reusability and significantly reduce the amount of effort necessary to develop customized applications. They are well suited for the implementation of AGI software agents. Here we describe the LIDA framework, a customizable implementation of the LIDA model of cognition. We argue that its characteristics make it suitable for wider use in developing AGI cognitive architectures.

Keywords: AGI framework, software framework, computational framework, cognitive architecture, design patterns, LIDA model.

1   Introduction

Artificial General Intelligence (AGI) aims at producing agents exhibiting human-level intelligence and beyond. Any successful AGI agent must surely be implemented using a sophisticated cognitive architecture — but which one to choose? A comparative table of cognitive architectures currently lists twenty-nine candidates [1]. If every AGI research group is focused on their own control architecture, how can the field of AGI progress?

Superficially, these architectures seem quite different from one another in their structure, and they use vastly different terminology. However, closer inspection reveals much similarity between the function of the modules of one architecture and those of another once the common meanings of different vocabulary are mapped onto an accepted ontology. The beginnings of such an ontology have been proposed [2]. Once the similarity of function among modules becomes apparent, the architectures themselves seem less different in structure, and perhaps, more amenable to implementation using a common software framework. Such a common underlying framework might likely result in a "tree" of cognitive and/or AGI architectures with branches at every point of difference. Architectures would be quicker to implement due to code reuse, and easier to analyze and compare.

J. Schmidhuber, K.R. Thórisson, and M. Looks (Eds.): AGI 2011, LNAI 6830, pp. 133–142, 2011.

Here we propose such an underlying computational software framework for AGI and offer, as an example, one based on the LIDA cognitive architecture. The advantages of using such a framework were stated just above. A possible disadvantage is that to use any such framework the developers must commit to the underlying assumptions of the LIDA architecture upon which this framework is based. We will argue that this software framework requires commitment to only a minimal set of assumptions, one that is not too onerous for other AGI research projects.

In recent years, an enormous number of computational frameworks have appeared in the software engineering world. See for example [3, 4]. This is not by chance but is due to the advantages of using frameworks. They promote code reuse and significantly reduce the amount of effort necessary to develop customized applications. Intelligent software agents aiming for general intelligence are complex systems and as such are difficult to implement and to customize. We will argue that ideas from frameworks are well-suited for the implementation of such generally-intelligent software agents. Here we describe the LIDA framework, a customizable implementation of the LIDA model of cognition. While the LIDA model provides a conceptual ontology for general models of cognition [2], we hope that the LIDA software framework might provide a customizable computational framework with which to more economically develop AGI architectures, as well as to more easily analyze and compare them.

We begin this paper by describing the general characteristics of frameworks and the advantages of using them to implement generally intelligent agents. Then we sketch the LIDA model and outline the LIDA framework. Next we describe the main components of the framework in some detail, and, finally, we summarize the minimal assumptions required for an AGI using this framework and draw some conclusions.

2   Frameworks

A framework is a reusable implementation of all or part of a software system. In many cases, a framework constitutes the skeleton of the application, capturing its generic functionality.   The framework specifies a well-defined application programming interface (API) that is implemented generically using abstract classes, interfaces, and generic, customizable module design. This hides the complexity of its code from the user. Most frameworks are based on object-oriented languages because the major properties of OO, data abstraction, inheritance, information hiding and polymorphism, complement the goals of frameworks.

The core idea of a framework is to have a generic design as well as a base implementation of a complex software system. The user of the framework then only needs to "fill in the blanks" with problem or domain-specific elements. This is, perhaps, the major advantage of using frameworks: users can concentrate their efforts on the specifics of the problems, and reuse the generic mechanisms implemented in the framework. This also speeds up the development of the new application and makes it less error-prone because part of the system has already been produced and tested.

Frameworks, in general, promote the use of proven design patterns and good practices in software development [5, 6]. This leads to better application designs, more manageable maintainability and easier extension of the application. The framework's API also provides a higher level of abstraction at which to define the application. This API is composed of elements with names, characteristics and behaviors. They form a specific language among users of the framework, which facilitates a concise and clear description of the application.

2.1 Frameworks and Cognitive Architectures

Ideas from frameworks can be applied outside the domain of enterprise applications. In particular, cognitive systems aiming for general intelligence tend to be complex and sophisticated. This creates a barrier that makes them difficult to learn, implement, and customize. The use of frameworks can mitigate these issues.

Cognitive architectures are complex from two points of view: the theory behind it tends to be inherently complicated and, consequently, any software implementation is also very complex. Cognitive architectures are typically composed of several modules with different functionalities and, in many cases, with different algorithmic implementations. This makes implementing software agents based on them a very hard task. Developers have to spend a lot of time and energy re-implementing common functionality for each new agent implementation. Code reuse between architectures has been difficult in general because of lack of standardization and ill-defined modules.

Frameworks are ideal tools with which to solve many of the problems that implementations of generally intelligent systems entail. A framework for AGI systems allows developers to focus on their particular algorithms instead of implementation details common to many agents. The architecture can be understood more quickly because the framework's API itself provides a higher level of abstraction than unitary code. The API supplies a set of high-level concepts for elements of the architecture. These concepts abstract the complexity of the implementation and allow more effective and accurate communication between researchers.

3   The LIDA Model and Its Architecture

The LIDA model [7-9] is a comprehensive, conceptual and computational model covering a large portion of human cognition[1]. Based primarily on Global Workspace theory [10, 11] the model implements and fleshes out a number of psychological and neuropsychological theories. The LIDA computational architecture is derived from the LIDA cognitive model. The LIDA model and its ensuing architecture are grounded in the LIDA cognitive cycle. Every autonomous agent [12], be it human, animal, or artificial, must frequently sample (sense) its environment and select an appropriate response (action). More sophisticated agents, such as humans, process

---

[1] "Cognition" is used here in a particularly broad sense, so as to include perception, feelings and emotions.

(make sense of) the input from such sampling in order to facilitate their decision making. The agent's "life" can be viewed as consisting of a continual sequence of these cognitive cycles. Each cycle constitutes a unit of sensing, attending and acting. A cognitive cycle can be thought of as a moment of cognition, a cognitive "moment."

We will now briefly describe what the LIDA model hypothesizes as the rich inner structure of the LIDA cognitive cycle. More detailed descriptions are available elsewhere [13, 14]. During each cognitive cycle the LIDA agent first makes sense of its current situation as best as it can *by updating its representation of its current situation, both external and internal.* By a competitive process, as specified by Global Workspace Theory [10], it then decides what portion of the represented situation is most in need of attention. Broadcasting this portion, the current contents of consciousness[2], enables the agent to chose an appropriate action and execute it, completing the cycle.

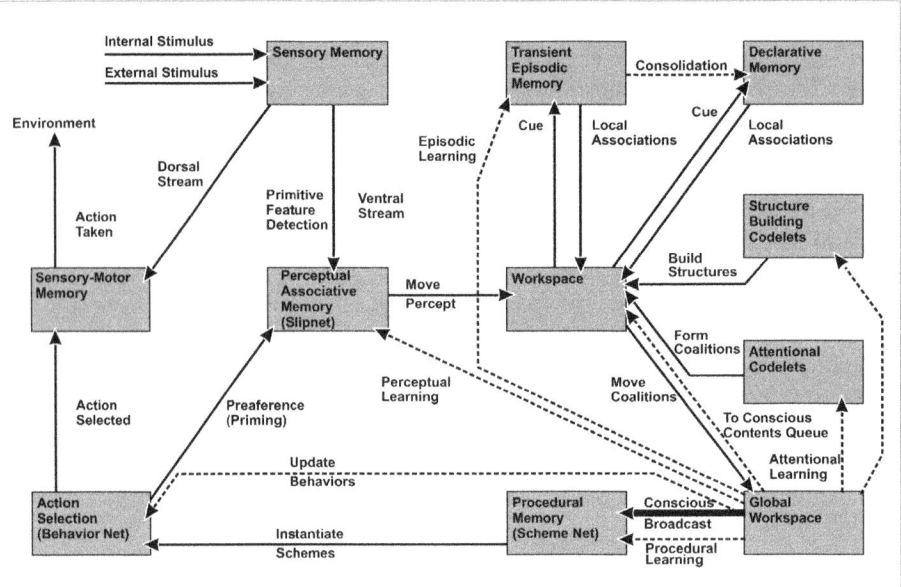

Fig. 1. The LIDA Cognitive Cycle Diagram

Thus, the LIDA cognitive cycle can be subdivided into three phases, the understanding phase, the attention (consciousness) phase, and the action selection phase. Figure 1 should help the reader follow the description. It starts in the upper left corner and proceeds roughly clockwise. Beginning the understanding phase, incoming stimuli activate low-level feature detectors in Sensory Memory. The output is sent to Perceptual Associative Memory where higher-level feature detectors feed in to more abstract entities such as objects, categories, actions, events, etc. The resulting percept

---

[2] Here "consciousness" refers to functional consciousness [15]. We take no position on the need for, or possibility of, phenomenal consciousness.

moves to the Workspace where it cues both Transient Episodic Memory and Declarative Memory producing local associations. These local associations are combined with the percept to generate a Current Situational Model, which represents the agent's understanding of what is going on right now.

Attention Codelets[3] begin the attention phase by forming coalitions of selected portions of the Current Situational Model and moving them to the Global Workspace.

A competition in the Global Workspace then selects the most salient, the most relevant, the most important, and the most urgent coalition whose contents become the content of consciousness. These conscious contents are then broadcast globally, initiating the action selection phase. The action selection phase of LIDA's cognitive cycle is also a learning phase in which several processes operate in parallel (see Figure 1). New entities and associations, and the reinforcement of old ones, occur as the conscious broadcast reaches Perceptual Associative Memory. Events from the conscious broadcast are encoded as new memories in Transient Episodic Memory. Possible action schemes, together with their contexts and expected results, are learned into Procedural Memory from the conscious broadcast. Older schemes are reinforced. In parallel with all this learning, and using the conscious contents, possible action schemes are recruited from Procedural Memory. A copy of each such is instantiated with its variables bound and sent to Action Selection, where it competes to be the behavior selected for this cognitive cycle. The selected behavior triggers Sensory-Motor Memory to produce a suitable algorithm for the execution of the behavior. Its execution completes the cognitive cycle.

The Workspace requires further explanation. Its internal structure is composed of various input buffers and three main modules: the Current Situational Model, the Scratchpad and the Conscious Contents Queue [16]. The Current Situational Model is where the structures representing the actual current internal and external events are stored. Structure-building codelets are responsible for the creation of these structures using elements from the various submodules of the Workspace. The Scratchpad is an auxiliary space in the Workspace where structure-building codelets can construct possible structures prior to moving them to the Current Situational Model. The Conscious Contents Queue holds the contents of the last several broadcasts and permits LIDA to understand and manipulate time-related concepts [16].

4   The LIDA Framework

Based on all these ideas, we have been developing the LIDA software framework, a generic and customizable computational implementation of the LIDA model. It is implemented in Java, a strong and proven object oriented language.

The main goal of this framework is to provide a generic implementation of the LIDA model, easily customizable for specific problems or domains. As mentioned before, this has several advantages: it speeds up the implementation of new agents based on the LIDA model and shortens the learning curve to produce such implementations.

---

[3] A codelet is a small piece of code that performs a specific task in an independent way. It could be interpreted as a small part of a bigger process, similar to an ant in an ant colony.

The framework permits a declarative description of the specific implementation. The full architecture of the software agent is specified using an XML formatted file; this is similar to other frameworks where the use of declarative description files are common [4, 17]. In this way, the developer does not need to define the entire agent in Java; he can just define it using this XML specification file.

Another important goal of the framework is its ready customization. The customization can be done at several levels accordingly with the required functionality. At the most basic level, developers can use the LIDA configuration file to customize their applications. Several small pieces in the framework can also be customized implementing particular versions of them. For example, new strategies for decaying or codelets can be implemented. Finally, more advanced users can also customize and change internal implementation of whole modules. In each case, the framework provides default implementations that greatly simplify the customization process.

The framework was conceived with multithreading support in mind. Biological minds operate in parallel and so should artificial ones. *LIDA-tasks*, encapsulations of small processes together with a dedicated task manager, implement multithreading support that allows for a high level of parallelization. Finally, the LIDA framework implementation adheres to the most important design principles [5] and best programming practices.

4.1 Framework Outline

The LIDA framework defines several data structures and procedures (algorithms) and is composed of several pieces. Its main components are *modules*, interconnected elements that represent modules in the LIDA model. Another main component is the task manager that controls the execution of all processes in the framework. These processes are implemented by small, demon-like processors called LIDA-tasks. LIDA-tasks can be executed on separate threads by the *LIDA task manager* in a way that is almost transparent for the user. NodeStructures are core elements that constitute a main data structure in the framework. Finally, several supporting tools were implemented such as a customizable GUI, logging, and an architecture loader that parses an XML file with the definition and parameterization of the application.

Modules. For each main component of the LIDA cognitive model we define a module in the framework. In particular, each box in Figure 1 is implemented as a module in the framework. For example, the Sensory Memory, Workspace and Action Selection are all modules in the framework. All modules have a common interface (API) but also each one has its own API that defines its particular functionality. Modules can have submodules which are modules nested inside another module. For example, the Workspace in LIDA has several submodules such as the Current Situational Model.

Most modules in the LIDA framework are domain independent. For each of these, the framework provides a default implementation. For example, the Episodic Memory is implemented using a sparse distributed memory [18] and the Action Selection module by a heavily-modified behavior network [19]. Developers can use these implementations and customize some of their parameters. Some modules however, are domain specific. In particular, Sensory Memory and Sensory-Motor Memory must be specified by the user. Nevertheless, the framework supplies default implementations for these modules from which users can extend their own domain-specific implementation.

For a more advanced customization of the framework, users can also implement their own version of any of the modules. Implementing a module's corresponding interface ensures its compatibility with the rest of the framework. For example, Episodic Memory could be implemented using a database. The default classes provided in the framework simplify the creation of alternate implementations of modules.

Modules need to communicate with other modules. To implement this, we use the observer design pattern [5]. In short, a module, called the "listener," which receives information from another "producer" module, can register itself to the producer as a listener. Each time the producer has something to send, it transmits the information to all of its registered listeners. There are numerous instances of listeners being used in the framework. Each listener type is implemented with its own interface. One module can be registered as a listener of several other modules. Also a module can be producer and listener of other modules at the same time. This pattern has several advantages; mainly, the listener and the producer do not need to know each other's internal structure and implementation, they only need to satisfy the particular listener interface. The arrows in Figure 1 are implemented as listeners in the framework.

Fundamental Data Structures. Another important piece of the framework is a data structure called the NodeStructure. A NodeStructure is a graph structure, containing nodes and the links between them. It constitutes the main representation of data in many framework modules. Several use NodeStructures to represent their internal data and, while other forms of representation are used in the framework; the NodeStructure functions as a representational "common currency" between many modules.

NodeStructures greatly assist in creating graph structures as they manage the low-level operations needed to add, remove, or retrieve particular Nodes and Links. Links are defined to connect a source Node with either another Node or a Link. These graphs are used for conceptual representation of object, actions, and events, the basic data representation in the LIDA model [20].

Nodes, Links and other LIDA elements such as coalitions, codelets, and behaviors, have activation. The activation can represent different things, but generally it represents the importance of the element. Elements can also have an additional "base-level" activation for learning. All activations are excited or decayed using "strategies". These are implementations of the strategy design pattern which allows for customizable behavior; in this case they specify the way activation of each element is excited or decayed.

Other basic data structures in the LIDA framework include bit vectors for the two episodic memory modules, schemes in Procedural Memory, coalitions for the Global Workspace, and behaviors in Action Selection. Each has an interface and a base implementation. Some are tied to specific module implementations; nonetheless, they are general enough that they could be used in other implementations as well.

LIDA-tasks. Modules need to perform several tasks in order to achieve their specific functionalities. The framework provides LIDA-tasks, encapsulations of small processes. A LIDA-task has an algorithm, a time of execution and a status. A module can create several LIDA-tasks to help it perform its function. A LIDA-task can run one time or repeatedly. A task that passes activation is an example of the former, while a structure-building codelet is an example of the latter. Some LIDA-tasks are likely to be fundamental for many AGI agent implementations, such as a task to pass activation. Others are implementation dependent and can be specified by the user. An example of this is a feature detector for a unique feature of a specific domain.

The execution of LIDA-tasks is delegated to the LIDA task manager. This important piece of the framework has the responsibility of scheduling and executing all the tasks of the application. It maintains a pool of threads, so several tasks can be executed at the same time. The task manager maintains a task queue which it uses to schedule LIDA-tasks for execution. Each position in the task queue represents a discrete instant in simulation time, which we call a *tick*. Ticks are numbered along the simulation, for example tick 1, tick 2, and so on. All tasks are scheduled to be executed at a specific tick. So if a single LIDA-task scheduled for tick *t* is enqueued in position *t*. All tasks scheduled for a particular tick are executed before the task manager advances to the next tick. Additionally, a parameter representing milliseconds called *tick duration*, can be set to ensure that *tick duration* milliseconds passes before the task manager moves onto the next position in the queue. With this mechanism, the whole simulation can run at different speeds, in slow motion, or even step by step.

4.2 Framework Tools

The current version of the LIDA framework features several useful tools. The first is a customizable GUI consisting of a main GUI application and a series of GUI panels which display such things as the content of modules, running tasks, parameter values, etc. A properties file allows users to add their own GUI panels as well as configure which panels are used and where they appear in the GUI window.

The Java logging API is used throughout the framework, recording important activities as they occur. Every log is made with one of several *levels* of severity. A dedicated GUI panel for Logging is part of the standard framework GUI. It allows the user to view logs of particular levels for specific modules or all modules.

An architecture loader allows agents to be specified via XML file. The loader reads this file and constructs an agent with modules, parameters, and initial tasks based on the file's specification. This utility obviates the need to specify agents by hand and allows for quick interchange of modules, connections between modules, change of parameters, etc.

Finally an *element factory*, implementing the factory design pattern [5], provides a centralized, configurable way to obtain new Nodes, Links, and Codelets. The excite and decay strategies used by objects created by the factory can be configured and changed dynamically. Factory support for additional object is planned in future versions.

4.3 Underlying Assumptions of the LIDA Framework

Even though originally intended for the LIDA model, the framework's general structure and functionality could be used to implement other general architectures as well. The scaffolding provided by the framework can benefit such implementations. This is an interesting but unexplored side of this framework.

There are a few requirements that any cognitive architecture using the framework should adhere to. Broadly, the architecture must be composed of interconnected modules, be able to divide their functionality into small tasks, and use a graph-like data structure as the main conceptual representation.

The first assumption is not a problem for most AGI cognitive architectures because in general they are structured in this way already. The second assumption is also common among cognitive architectures but the inherent asynchronous nature of this framework's task model may require a refactoring for some architectures. Nonetheless, a task can perform the whole operation of a module instead of a small part of it. This fact further relaxes this constraint.

Finally, the chosen common currency for communication between modules in the framework is the NodeStructure. This graph data structure can be used to represent a wide range of data types. It is inherently appropriate to represent connectionist data but symbolic constructs can also be represented. Other representation data types, such as images or sensors raw data, can be internally referenced by a Node in this structure. This is not directly supported by the current version of the framework however future versions of the framework will address this limitation.

In summary, there are few basic assumptions that architectures need to address in order to use this framework as a foundation for its implementation. Nonetheless, we believe these constraints are not prohibitively tight, making this framework a viable and general tool for AGI.

5 Conclusions

The LIDA software framework allows the creation of new intelligent software agents and experiments based in the LIDA model. Its design and implementation aim to simplify this process and to permit the user to concentrate in the specifics of the application, hiding the complexities of the generic parts of the model. It also enforces good software practices that simplify the creation of complex architectures. It achieves a high level of abstraction permitting several ways and levels of customization with a low level of coupling among modules. Supplemental tools such as a customizable GUI and logging support are also provided. The result is a powerful and customizable tool with which to develop LIDA based applications and, perhaps, many others as well. Much work is still needed to improve the performance of the framework and to add functionality. Learning mechanisms should be implemented in several modules and improved versions of Procedural Memory and Action Selection modules are in development.

References

1. BICA. Comparative Table of Cognitive Architectures (2011),
   http://bicasociety.org/cogarch/architectures.htm (cited 2011)
2. Franklin, S.: A Foundational Architecture for Artificial General Intelligence. In: Goertzel, B., Wang, P. (eds.) Advances in Artificial General Intelligence: Concepts, Architectures and Algorithms, Proceedings of the AGI Workshop 2006, pp. 36–54. IOS Press, Amsterdam (2007)

3. Singh, I., Stearns, B., Johnson, M.: Designing Enterprise Applications with the J2EE(TM) Platform, 2nd edn. Prentice Hall, Englewood Cliffs (2002)
4. Walls, C., Breidenbach, R.: Spring in Action, 2nd edn. Manning Publications (2007)
5. Gamma, E., Helm, R., Johnson, R., Vlissides, J.M.: Design Patterns: Elements of Reusable Object-Oriented Software. Addison-Wesley Professional, Reading (1995)
6. Alur, D., Crupi, J., Malks, D.: Core Java EE Patterns: Best Practices and Design Strategies, 2nd edn. Prentice Hall, Englewood Cliffs (2003)
7. Franklin, S., Patterson, F.G.J.: The LIDA Architecture: Adding New Modes of Learning to an Intelligent, Autonomous, Software Agent. In: IDPT-2006 Proceedings (Integrated Design and Process Technology), Society for Design and Process Science (2006)
8. Ramamurthy, U., Baars, B.J., D'Mello, S.K., Franklin, S.: LIDA: A Working Model of Cognition. In: 7th International Conference on Cognitive Modeling, Edizioni Goliardiche, Trieste (2006)
9. Baars, B.J., Franklin, S.: Consciousness is computational: The LIDA model of Global Workspace Theory. International Journal of Machine Consciousness 1(1), 23–32 (2009)
10. Baars, B.J.: A Cognitive Theory of Consciousness. Cambridge University Press, Cambridge (1988)
11. Baars, B.J.: The conscious access hypothesis: origins and recent evidence. Trends in Cognitive Science 6, 47–52 (2002)
12. Franklin, S. and Graesser, A.C., Is it an Agent, or just a Program?: A Taxonomy for Autonomous Agents, in Intelligent Agents III. 1997, Springer Verlag: Berlin. p. 21–35.
13. Baars, B.J., Franklin, S.: How conscious experience and working memory interact. Trends in Cognitive Science 7, 166–172 (2003)
14. Franklin, S., Baars, B.J., Ramamurthy, U., Ventura, M.: The Role of Consciousness in Memory. Brains, Minds and Media 1, 1–38 (2005)
15. Franklin, S.: IDA: A Conscious Artifact? Journal of Consciousness Studies 10, 47–66 (2003)
16. Snaider, J., McCall, R., Franklin, S.: Time Production and Representation in a Conceptual and Computational Cognitive Model. Cognitive Systems Research (in press)
17. Sun_Services, FJ-310-EE6 Developing Applications for the Java(TM) EE Platform, Sun Microsystems Inc., (2010)
18. Kanerva, P.: Sparse Distributed Memory. The MIT Press, Cambridge (1988)
19. Maes, P.: How to do the right thing. Connection Science 1, 291–323 (1989)
20. McCall, R., Franklin, S., Friedlander, D.: Grounded Event-Based and Modal Representations for Objects, Relations, Beliefs, Etc. In: FLAIRS-23, Daytona Beach, FL (2010)

From Memory to Problem Solving: Mechanism Reuse in a Graphical Cognitive Architecture

Paul S. Rosenbloom

Department of Computer Science & Institute for Creative Technologies
University of Southern California
12015 Waterfront Drive, Playa Vista, CA 90094
rosenbloom@usc.edu

Abstract. This article describes the extension of a memory architecture that is implemented via graphical models to include core aspects of problem solving. By extensive reuse of the general graphical mechanisms originally developed to support memory, this demonstrates how a theoretically elegant implementation level can enable increasingly broad architectures without compromising overall simplicity and uniformity. In the process, it bolsters the potential of such an approach for developing the more complete architectures that will ultimately be necessary to support autonomous general intelligence.

Keywords: Cognitive architecture, graphical models, memory, problem solving.

1 Introduction

A *cognitive architecture* is a hypothesis about: (1) the fixed mechanisms underlying intelligent behavior, and (2) how they integrate together in support of autonomous general intelligence. The ideal cognitive architecture would combine *broad applicability* – whether in terms of the span of natural phenomena covered or the range of artificial functionality produced – with *theoretical elegance* (uniformity and simplicity). But there is an inherent tension between these two characteristics; the former favors mechanism proliferation while the latter discourages it. The resulting *diversity dilemma* is one of the central issues in architectures [1]. How researchers respond to it determines much about the nature of the architectures they produce; consider, for example, the contrast between the eclectic approach in OpenCogPrime [2] and the more theoretically elegant approach in AIXI [3].

One recent approach seeks to build a diversity of architectural capabilities – for memory, decisions, learning, etc. – from the interactions among a small set of general mechanisms at the *implementation level* beneath the architecture [1]. Broad applicability at the architecture level is thus joined with theoretical elegance at the implementation level. *Graphical models* [4] were proposed as a basis for the implementation level because they yield state-of-the-art algorithms across symbol, probability and signal processing from a uniform representation and reasoning algorithm. They raise the possibility of uniformly implemented and tightly integrated architectures capable of spanning from perception to cognition and back to action.

J. Schmidhuber, K.R. Thórisson, and M. Looks (Eds.): AGI 2011, LNAI 6830, pp. 143–152, 2011.

An initial fragment of this potential was realized with the implementation of a *graphical memory architecture* that combined rule-based procedural knowledge, semantic and episodic declarative knowledge, and constraint knowledge (which blends aspects of both procedural and declarative knowledge) [5]. The first three were modeled on memories in the Soar architecture [6] and ideas from the ACT-R community [7]. The fourth was added simply because it came along essentially for free. This graphical memory architecture exploited the uniform combination of symbolic and probabilistic reasoning enabled by graphical models, and that is now at the core of the burgeoning subfield of *statistical relational AI*. It also supported continuous quantities, although performing no actual signal processing.

Ongoing work is extending this partial architecture to include problem solving, reflection, learning, and mental imagery; all in service of a medium-term goal of a uniformly implemented *hybrid* (discrete + continuous) *mixed* (symbolic + probabilistic) variant of Soar, and a long-term goal of theoretically elegant yet broadly applicable architectures. This article presents results from extending the memory architecture to incorporate basic internal problem-solving capabilities, based on Soar, with a particular emphasis on how such problem solving is supported by general mechanisms already implemented in service of the memory architecture. The resulting contributions are fourfold: (1) the extension of the graphical memory architecture to problem solving; (2) an evaluation of the generality of the graphical implementation mechanisms with respect to how well they extend from memory to problem solving; (3) presentation of heretofore unpublished aspects of the graphical memory architecture and its implementation that are important for understanding the first two contributions; and (4) an approximate reimplementation of key aspects of the Soar architecture with enhanced uniformity and elegance at the implementation level.

2   Problem Solving in Soar

The heart of problem solving is the *selection* and *application* of operators that perform internal actions and control or simulate external actions. Selection requires generation and comparison of candidate operators and then a choice among them. For both internal actions and simulations of external actions, application requires changing the internal state to correspond to the operator's effects. Control of external actions requires both perception and motor control. As perception and motor control are beyond the scope of this article, the focus here is restricted to internal problem solving via internal actions and simulations of external actions.

Soar represents the state of problem solving in a symbolic working memory (WM). Generation of candidate operators occurs via retrieval from long-term memory (LTM) into WM, as cued by the contents of the state (including any current goals). Then, based on the state and the proposed operators, preference information respecting operator selection – whether symbolic or numeric – is also retrieved from LTM. Except for acceptable preferences, which propose operators for selection, retrieved preferences are maintained outside of WM, in a separate preference memory (PM). Preference memory is normally omitted from descriptions of Soar, as it is considered an implementation detail rather than part of the theory, yet it is an important and distinct form of memory that was added specifically in support of problem solving.

Operator selection is based on the contents of PM plus a separately encoded decision procedure. Once an operator is selected, state changes are retrieved from LTM – based on the operator and the state – engendering modifications to working memory. This combination of capabilities for operator selection and application comprises what can be called *base-level problem solving* in Soar. Soar can also engage in *meta-level problem solving*, where the inability to select a new operator yields an impasse plus a meta-level state in which the impasse can be resolved via reflection [8]. However, reflection is a large enough topic in its own right that discussion of its graphical implementation has been deferred to a follow on article.

Base-level problem solving in Soar is normally viewed as occurring via two nested loops: (1) the *elaboration cycle*, in which all legal instantiations of all rules fire (logically) in parallel, yielding one round of changes to working memory; and (2) the *decision cycle*, comprising an elaboration phase during which elaboration cycles repeat until quiescence – i.e., until no further rules can fire – followed by a call to the decision procedure and the resulting selection of an operator in working memory. However, there is actually one additional cycle that is nested within the elaboration cycle: (0) the *match cycle*, in which tokens representing intermediate match results are passed around within the Rete network [9]. As with preference memory, this is considered an implementation detail in Soar rather than as part of the theory.

Retrievals from long-term memory for operator selection remain active – in WM or PM – only while their triggering conditions are valid. Thus, as the state changes, candidate operators and preferences automatically retract – in a manner akin to truth-maintenance systems – when they become inapplicable. In contrast, retrievals from long-term memory for operator application remain active until explicitly removed. This provides an implicit frame axiom, retaining all aspects of the state not explicitly changed. The distinction between selection and application knowledge effectively yields a problem-solving-driven partitioning of Soar's single rule memory into two procedural memories that differ both in when they are used during problem solving and in how their results are maintained over time.

Memory plays a critical role in Soar's problem solving, through storing, retrieving and maintaining states, operators and preferences. This amounts to a significant bit of architectural capability reuse, from WM and LTM to problem solving, and is the kind of gain Soar has long featured from integration across its capabilities. But there is no finer-grained sharing of mechanisms at the implementation level. For example, the Rete match mechanism at the heart of Soar's procedural memory is not reused in its declarative memories. Nor is it leveraged to implement the PM or decision procedure necessary for problem solving. It simply isn't a general enough implementation mechanism to do more than the one job it currently does extremely well.

If Soar's procedural memory were partitioned into two rule-based memories, by when and how the knowledge is used in problem solving, Rete could theoretically be reused across these two memories. But that would still be about it. Disjoint code implements memory (WM and LTM) versus problem solving (PM and the decision procedure); and, even within LTM, disjoint code implements rule, semantic and episodic memories. The latter disjointness was addressed earlier via general graphical implementation mechanisms that supported a unified long-term memory containing both procedural and declarative knowledge. Here, we further build upon these same mechanisms to address the disjointness between memory and problem solving.

3 The Graphical Memory Architecture

The graphical memory architecture is based on running the *summary product algorithm* over *factor graphs* [10]. Factor graphs are similar to Bayesian and Markov networks, except that: unlike Bayesian networks, but like Markov networks, they employ bidirectional links between nodes; and, unlike both forms of networks, factor graphs explicitly include not only variable nodes but also factor nodes for functions over sets of variables. Factor graphs enable efficient computation with complex multivariate functions – whether representing probability distributions or arbitrary functions – by decomposing them into products of simpler functions and then mapping these decompositions onto graphs. By passing messages between variable and factor nodes concerning the possible values of variables, the summary product algorithm computes marginals on the variables (when using *sum* as the summarization operator), as well as computing more global properties such as maximum a posteriori (MAP) probabilities (when using *max* as the summarization operator).

Knowledge in long-term memory consists of generalized *conditionals* that can embody *conditions*, *actions*, *condacts* and *functions*. Figs. 1 and 2 show two examples. The first combines conditions and actions in a rule that avoids Eight Puzzle operators that move tiles from their goal locations. The

```
CONDITIONAL GoalReject
    Conditions: (Operator id:o state:s x:x y:y)
                (Goal state:s x:x y:y tile:t)
                (Board state:s x:x y:y tile:t)
    Actions: (Selected - state:s operator:o)
```

Fig. 1. Eight Puzzle heuristic that rejects from consideration operators that move tiles out of place

second is a fragment of semantic memory that combines conditions, condacts and a function to represent the conditional probability of an object's weight given its concept.

Conditions and actions are just like in traditional rules; conditions match to working memory elements and actions modify them. Condacts are hybrids that match *and* modify WM. Messages pass in one direction for conditions and actions but in both directions

```
CONDITIONAL ConceptWeight
    Conditions: (Object state:s object:o)
    Condacts: (Concept object:o concept:c)
              (Weight object:o weight:w)
```

$w \backslash c$	Walker	Table	...
[1,10>	.01w	.001w	...
[10,20>	.2-.01w	"	...
[20,50>	0	.025- .00025w	...
[50,100>	"	"	...

Fig. 2. Conditional probability of weight given concept. Only a fragment of the function is shown

for condacts. Procedural knowledge is encoded via conditions and actions. Unidirectional message passing – from WM, through conditions, on to actions, and finally back to WM – provides the forward impetus that is at the heart of the procedural use of rule memories. Declarative knowledge is encoded via condacts.

Bidirectional message passing among condacts enables the kind of partial match that is at the heart of the declarative use of semantic and episodic memories.

The functions in conditionals enable encoding probability distributions, as in the fragment of semantic memory above. They also enable, for example, encoding the symbolic incompatibility knowledge used in constraint memory. These functions are multidimensional and are represented in a piecewise linear manner. There is one dimension per variable, with slices across the dimensions delimiting rectilinear regions over which a single linear function is adequate. The function in Fig. 2, for example, has two dimensions – for *weight* and *concept* – with slices occurring between concepts along one dimension and between segments of weights along the other. Each resulting region has its own linear function (in terms of just weight here).

This representation enables approximating continuous functions as closely as desired – for perceptual signal processing – but it also enables representing both discrete probability distributions and symbolic structures, through restrictions on function domains and ranges. It thus proffers a broad-spectrum *hybrid mixed* representation useable not only for this aspect of long-term memory but also for the messages at the core of the summary product algorithm. In Fig. 2, the concept is symbolic, the weight is continuous, and the value of the function is probabilistic.

The same function representation also works for working memory. Working memory is based on *predicate*s – such as Object, Concept and Weight in Fig. 2 – that are defined in terms of a name plus named-and-typed arguments. Weight, for example, has two arguments: *object*, over symbolic identifiers; and *weight*, over a segment of the continuous line. Each predicate induces a WM factor node with its own function that specifies which of its regions are present. Predicates, and thus WM functions, can combine any number of discrete and continuous dimensions, but the ranges of WM functions are limited to Boolean values. In other words, every possible element is either in working memory or not; they can't be in at some probability. This is consistent with how working memory works in Soar and with the mapping of working memory onto *evidence* at peripheral nodes in standard probabilistic graphical models [1]. However, it does differ from Soar's approach in explicitly representing – with a value of 0 – regions not present in working memory. This increases overall uniformity, but can also increase the number of regions to be processed.

Conditions, actions and condacts are specified as patterns on predicates, each of which also comprises a predicate name plus zero or more arguments. Each argument in a pattern has a name plus a value that is either a constant or a variable. In Figs. 1 and 2 all of the arguments are specified via variables (lower-case italicized symbols). Predicates can be negated to yield negated conditions and deletion actions; the action in Fig. 1, for example, is negated. Each pattern compiles into a subgraph that determines its correspondence to WM regions via messages possessing one dimension per argument. If there are constants in the pattern, an additional factor node is included to check their values. If the pattern is negated, an additional factor node is included to invert the message – positive values become 0 and 0s become 1.

Fig. 3 shows the factor graph for the conditional in Fig. 1, albeit with less important nodes omitted and the full subgraph for the Selected action deferred

148   P.S. Rosenbloom

until Fig. 4. As shown, link direction in pattern subgraphs is determined by whether they implement conditions or actions (or condacts, although not shown here). The subgraphs for all patterns within a conditional are then connected via a bidirectional join network. The resulting graph, when restricted to conditions, is

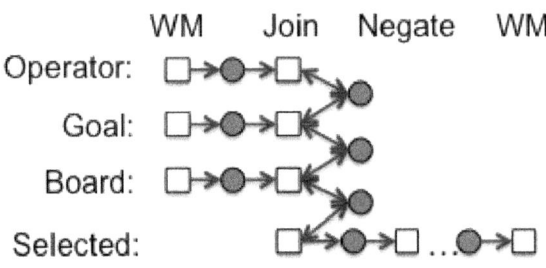

Fig. 3. Factor graph for heuristic conditional in Fig. 1. Boxes are factor nodes while circles are variable nodes

similar to the combination of Rete's discrimination and join networks, including storage of intermediate match results. Rete uses *alpha* and *beta* memories to store condition matches and their combinations. In the graphical architecture, the latest message is automatically cached along each link, yielding a set of implementation-level *link memories*; where links at the end of pattern subgraphs act as alpha memories and links within the join network act as beta memories.

This graphical match algorithm goes beyond Rete in efficiency by bounding the cost for condition match by the tree width rather than the number of conditions [1]. However, Rete's sharing optimizations – of tests across subgraphs within an elaboration cycle and of intermediate results across elaboration cycles – have not yet been implemented. Both of these optimizations appear feasible within the unidirectional condition subgraphs – and within those segments of the join network that only combine conditions – in a manner much like that in Rete. However, it is less clear whether this will work in bidirectional subgraphs where feedback becomes key.

The bigger gain though with the graphical approach is that the generality of the resulting mechanism yields a capability that is considerably beyond just rule match and intermediate result storage. Messages are now multidimensional continuous functions rather than partial rule matches, and they can flow not just away from working memory, but also towards it. This broadening enables a single graphical mechanism to handle conditions, actions, condacts and functions; and thus to provide a shared implementation across Soar's multiple long-term memories. As is discussed in the next section, it also yields base-level internal problem solving.

Aside from Soar's call to the decision procedure in the uppermost (decision) cycle, its three nested loops are essentially all about memory access. In the graphical memory architecture, this functionality compresses down to two nested loops: the *message cycle*, where messages pass along links in the graph; and the *graph cycle*, where message cycles repeat until quiescence and then working memory is updated. The message cycle corresponds to Soar's match cycle. The graph cycle hybridizes Soar's elaboration cycle with the elaboration-phase portion of its decision cycle.

To understand this hybridization, it is first necessary to grasp the distinction introduced in the graphical architecture between *open-world* and *closed-world* predicates, concerning whether regions not explicitly in working memory are assumed unknown or false. A region that is false – i.e., 0 – at the beginning of a graph cycle cannot become true during the cycle, increasing processing efficiency by removing many regions from consideration; but since false can't become true without a change to working memory, chaining across such conditionals can only happen across graph cycles. Normal rules depend on closed-world predicates to keep working memory small and to implement negated conditions, implying only one cycle of rule firing per graph cycle, and thus a mapping to Soar's elaboration cycle. Semantic, episodic and constraint memory depend on open-world predicates so that values initially unknown can be determined by bidirectional processing during the graph cycle. This enables within-cycle chaining across conditionals and a full settling of the graph for access to declarative memory, indicating a mapping of the graph cycle onto Soar's elaboration phase. Muddying things even further, when rules work on open-world predicates – thus taking on a declarative aspect – it becomes possible to chain across sequences of them within a single graph cycle, again akin to Soar's elaboration phase.

The difference in chaining between closed-world and open-world predicates is implemented by chaining for a closed-world action through its WM factor node – the rightmost node in Fig. 3 – necessitating changes in working memory and a new graph cycle before results of actions in one conditional can be used in conditions of another; while chaining for an open-world predicate through the WM variable node – just to the left of the WM factor node in Fig. 3 – enabling chaining across conditionals without going through the factor node or changing working memory.

Changes to working memory occur via an action subgraph like the one shown in Fig. 4 for the Selected predicate. The top portion implements the negated action in Fig. 1, with the portion below it implementing a positive action from a different conditional. If there were additional positive actions, their subgraphs would all join at the positive-changes (+) factor node, while additional negative actions would join at the negative-changes (–) factor node. To deal with the disjunctive semantics that exists across rule actions, both of these are special function-composition factor nodes that sum their inputs rather than computing their product. As shown in the figure, a revised positive-changes message is then computed by using standard product computations

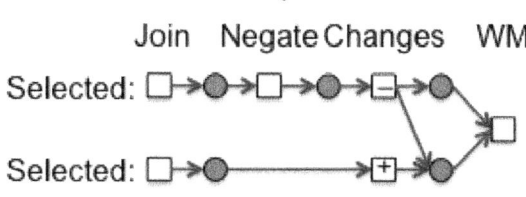

Fig. 4. Action graph for Selected predicate

to eliminate from it all regions marked for deletion in the negative message.

Given the aggregate positive and negative messages, the actual changes occur by altering the function stored in the WM factor node. This is a process that has much in common with learning – being an extra-graph process that modifies graph structure – although it modifies only a subset of factor node functions via a limited change-determination algorithm. Everything in the negative message is first deleted from working memory and then everything in the revised positive message is added. Closed-world modifications of working memory remain in effect until they are explicitly undone by later changes, while open-world modifications remain only as long as they are supported by conditionals in long-term memory.

Beyond the two memory distinctions already mentioned – i.e., direction of message passing and the values of unspecified regions – a third distinction has also been drawn, concerning whether variables in conditionals yield all legal values – *universal variables* – or a distribution over the best possible value – *unique variables*. The former are essential for memories that need all exact matches, while the latter – which correspond to normal variables in probabilistic graphical models – are needed for memories that require the single best partial match. In the memory architecture, rule and constraint memory require all exact matches while semantic and episodic memory rely on distributions over the best partial match. Soar has no general distinction between universal and unique variables, but instead effectively implements universal variables in procedural memory and unique variables in both declarative memories.

The details concerning how the more general distinction is implemented within the graphical memory architecture can be found in [11]. The critical aspect for our purposes here though is that when bindings are generated during a graph cycle for an action containing a unique variable, only a single element – one with the highest value – is added to working memory (assuming there is not already one there), and all others are deleted. This is the sole locus uncovered so far where an architectural distinction is necessary between discrete and continuous arguments. If, for example, an entire region [0,3) shares the maximum value, it is necessary to distinguish whether there are three discrete alternatives competing – [0,1), [1,2) and [2,3) – or an (effectively) infinite number of continuous alternatives (which becomes a large number of ε-width segments). This is extra-graph selection code in support of changing working memory, rather than part of the summary product algorithm itself. But it is still a concrete situation in which the difference between discrete and continuous dimensions is not just in the eye of the beholder.

4   Extension to Problem Solving

The overall graphical memory capability that has just been described can be reused in service of problem solving, just as memory is reused in Soar. This means that long-term memory encodes both candidate operators and preferences among them for use in operator selection, plus operator applications that change the state and state elaborations that amplify these changes (but which can be lumped in with operator selection for the rest of this discussion). Candidate operators are added via open-world predicates so that they automatically retract when no longer valid for the state, and so that preference generation can chain on them during a single graph cycle. Preferences are generated by actions for the predefined closed-world `Selected` predicate, which includes a universal discrete numeric *state* argument and a unique symbolic *operator* argument to denote that there should be one operator per state.

There are two forms of symbolic preferences, *acceptable* and *reject*, which just amount to positive and negated `Selected` actions within functionless conditionals. The negated action in Fig. 1, for example, rejects any operator that moves a tile out of position. All regions matching an action receive values of 1 or 0, depending on whether the action is positive or negated. All relative preferences are then encoded numerically, by including functions expressing arbitrary non-negative values in conditionals that have `Selected` actions. No extensions are thus required to represent either symbolic or numeric preferences due to the multidimensional mixed nature of the function representation employed in the factor graphs.

Rather than requiring a separate preference memory, the link memories mentioned earlier automatically handle the retention of preferences. Although descriptions of Soar's memories usually omit both Rete's memories and preference memory, viewing them as implementation details, they are critical in the overall processing scheme. Here they become unified across the memory and problem solving capabilities via the generality of the graphical mechanisms originally implemented for memory; in particular, both of these varieties of implementation-level Soar memory map onto link memories at the graphical implementation level. Because preferences are maintained in link memories, they retract automatically when state changes make them invalid.

The processing of preferences for operator selection occurs via the implementation mechanisms introduced earlier for unique variables in memory. As mentioned in Section 3, Soar implements a form of unique variable in each declarative memory, but they are special purpose variants that only work there. Operator selection must instead occur via the separate decision procedure. In the graphical implementation level, these distinct aspects of Soar's use of unique variables are merged into a single more general implementation mechanism. As implied by the earlier discussion, all of the preferences get combined to yield a distribution over the operators for each region of states in the WM-change messages. The extra-graph code already in place for changing working memory then determines which operator to add for each region.

Once an operator is selected, it is applied by conditionals with closed-world actions so as to modify the state in working memory. Because of this use of closed-world predicates, only one round of operator application occurs per graph cycle, but all of the resulting changes then remain in working memory until explicitly removed. The different levels of persistence for operator selection versus operator application thus arise directly from the distinctions already existing in the memory architecture, rather than requiring additional memory distinctions in service of problem solving. Operator selection uses open-world predicates plus preferences in link memories, while operator application uses closed-world predicates. This brings a declarative aspect to operator selection – enabling openness and chaining within a single graph cycle – whether encoded in rules (with open-world actions) or in more traditional declarative forms. Operator application is purely procedural, which makes sense given that it is the core source of action and change in problem solving.

This problem solving capability has been tested in a version of the Eight Puzzle that uses continuous mental imagery to represent the board and tiles. The code consists of 18 conditionals, which compile down to a graph with 349 variable nodes, 292 factor nodes, and 718 links. The resulting graph successfully solves Eight Puzzle instances via sequences of operator selections and applications.

5 Conclusion

By exploiting the generality of the graphical implementation mechanisms previously developed in support of a broad yet theoretically elegant memory architecture, Soar-like base-level problem solving capabilities have been demonstrated. Although an architecturally defined Selected predicate was added in the process, the remaining functionality all grounds directly in mechanisms developed for the memory architecture. Mechanisms reused include: *factor graphs* and *conditionals* to represent knowledge; the *summary product algorithm* to drive processing; the *mixed function representation* to represent both symbolic and numeric preferences; *within-graph link memories* to maintain generated preferences; the *open-world versus closed-world distinction* to maintain selection versus application knowledge; and the *universal versus unique variables distinction* to generate arbitrary candidate operators while selecting just the best.

A complete Soar-like problem solving capability also demands both reflection and external action, but the former is already shaping up well in separate work (while revealing unanticipated mechanism sharing with episodic memory and the nascent mental imagery capability). In general, the large amount of reuse found here augurs well as more capabilities get added towards a full implementation of a hybrid mixed variant of Soar, and as more novel architectures for autonomous general intelligence are sought that combine even broader applicability with theoretical elegance.

Acknowledgments. This effort has been sponsored by: the USC Institute for Creative Technologies; the U.S. Army Research, Development, and Engineering Command (RDECOM); and the Air Force Office of Scientific Research, Asian Office of Aerospace Research and Development (AFOSR/AOARD). Statements and opinions expressed do not necessarily reflect the position or the policy of the United States Government, and no official endorsement should be inferred. I would like to thank John Laird for helpful comments on a draft of this article.

References

1. Rosenbloom, P.S.: Rethinking Cognitive Architecture via Graphical Models. Cognitive Systems Research (In press)
2. Goertzel, B.: OpenCogPrime: A cognitive synergy based architecture for artificial general intelligence. In: 8th IEEE International Conference on Cognitive Informatics (2009)
3. Hutter, M.: Universal Artificial Intelligence: Sequential Decisions Based on Algorithmic Probability. Springer, Berlin (2005)
4. Koller, D., Friedman, N.: Probabilistic Graphical Models: Principles and Techniques. MIT Press, Cambridge (2009)
5. Rosenbloom, P.S.: Combining Procedural and Declarative Knowledge in a Graphical Architecture. In: 10th International Conference on Cognitive Modeling (2010)
6. Laird, J.E.: Extending the Soar Cognitive Architecture. In: Artificial General Intelligence 2008: Proceedings of the First AGI Conference. IOS Press, Arlington (2008)
7. Anderson, J.R.: The Adaptive Character of Thought. Erlbaum, Hillsdale (1990)
8. Rosenbloom, P.S., Laird, J.E., Newell, A.: Meta-levels in Soar. In: Maes, P., Nardi, D. (eds.) Meta-Level Architectures and Reflection, pp. 227–240. North Holland, Amsterdam (1988)
9. Forgy, C.L.: Rete: A Fast Algorithm for the Many Pattern/Many Object Pattern Match Problem. Artificial Intelligence 19, 17–37 (1982)
10. Kschischang, F.R., Frey, B.J., Loeliger, H.: Factor Graphs and the Sum-Product Algorithm. IEEE Transactions on Information Theory 47, 498–519 (2001)
11. Rosenbloom, P.S.: Implementing First-Order Variables in a Graphical Cognitive Architecture. In: Biologically Inspired Cognitive Architectures 2010: Proceedings of the First Annual Meeting of the BICA Society. IOS Press, Arlington (2010)

Rational Universal Benevolence: Simpler, Safer, and Wiser Than "Friendly AI"

Mark Waser

Books International, 22883 Quicksilver Drive,
Dulles, VA 20166 USA
MWaser @ BooksIntl.com

Abstract. Insanity is doing the same thing over and over and expecting a different result. "Friendly AI" (FAI) meets these criteria on four separate counts by expecting a good result after: 1) it not only puts all of humanity's eggs into one basket but relies upon a totally new and untested basket, 2) it allows fear to dictate our lives, 3) it divides the universe into us vs. them, and finally 4) it rejects the value of diversity. In addition, FAI goal initialization relies on being able to correctly calculate a "Coherent Extrapolated Volition of Humanity" (CEV) via some as-yet-undiscovered algorithm. Rational Universal Benevolence (RUB) is based upon established game theory and evolutionary ethics and is simple, safe, stable, self-correcting, and sensitive to current human thinking, intuitions, and feelings. Which strategy would you prefer to rest the fate of humanity upon?

Keywords: Artificial General Intelligence (AGI), Safe AI, Friendly AI (FAI), Coherent Extrapolated Volition (CEV), Rational Universal Benevolence (RUB).

1 Introduction

Eliezer Yudkowsky [1] and a number of others [2] [3] [4] are extremely concerned about the existential risk posed by intelligent machines. Developed to address this concern, "Friendly AI" (FAI) has been defined by Yudkowsky [5] both as "the field of study concerned with the production of human-benefiting, non-human-harming actions in Artificial Intelligence systems that have advanced to the point of making real-world plans in pursuit of goals" and the actual intelligence that arises from that study. Unfortunately, like a novice rock-climber hugging the cliff face, the field is so dominated by irrational fear that most practitioners can't distance themselves enough to clearly view and correctly evaluate their options. In almost every case, Friendly AI researchers insist upon the common set of arguments that a) because it is possible for AIs to be different from humans, they necessarily always will be; b) because selfishness can appear advantageous in the long run, extreme precautions must be taken to prevent it; and c) because AIs are likely to be capable of being dangerous, our best option is to pre-emptively limit their power and/or control them.

J. Schmidhuber, K.R. Thórisson, and M. Looks (Eds.): AGI 2011, LNAI 6830, pp. 153–162, 2011.

Steve Omohundro [2] missed the fact that cooperation is a virtually universal instrumental goal, incorrectly claimed that "Without explicit goals to the contrary, AIs are likely to behave like human sociopaths in their pursuit of resources" and is endlessly quoted by FAI advocates. Fox and Shulman [3] run through all of the reasons and resources that would indicate that kindness to humans might be easy and stable in AIs – Triver's reciprocal altruism, Singer's expanding circle of moral concern, Wright's increases in the scope of cooperation, Pinker's reduction of violence, and Hall's super-intelligent machines that will out-cooperate humans – and then dismiss them all as being instrumental artifacts limited to situations where the power differential is relatively small. This is despite the fact that as humans evolve to become more and more able to be moral, we pay less and less attention to power differential (not to mention that an entity can never be guaranteed that a more powerful entity – possibly even its own offspring – might not show up and administer altruistic punishment upon power abusers). Fox and Shulman also invoke the straw man that an optimal super-intelligence has "no room" for revision towards kindness (irrelevant because the revision was likely already made as part of its move towards optimality) and conclude by saying that "we have reason for pessimism regarding the values of intelligent machines not carefully engineered to be altruistic." And Sotala [4] repeats Omohundro's view with claims that "hard to control AGIs are a risk because even seemingly benevolent goals can soon become contrary to humanity's interests. An AGI does not need to be outright hostile to humanity to be a threat: it might simply have need for our resources."

2 "Friendship Structure" and "Coherent Extrapolated Volition"

Yudkowsky [5] believes that a cleanly causal hierarchical goal structure with "Friendliness" as the sole top-level super-goal is sufficient to ensure that intelligent machines will always "want" what is best for us. Unfortunately, he also believes that the problem of fully defining "Friendliness" is basically insoluble without already having a Friendly AI. Therefore, he wants and expects his first FAI to figure out exactly what its goal actually is. He invokes a structurally Friendly goal system distinguished by "the ability to overcome mistakes made by programmers" and claims that it will even be able to "overcome errors in supergoal content, goal system structure and underlying philosophy."

Thus, instead of merely taking on the "small" but claimed human-insoluble problem of determining a safe goal to give machine intelligence, Yudkowsky wants to take it on by creating a novel architecture that will be able solve it – even despite errors. Arguably, even if this bold venture were indeed possible given enough data and computing power, the real question is what will happen when sufficient computational resources aren't initially available, as seems very likely. Obviously, the closer the initial dynamic is to the eventual answer and the fewer errors that we feed it, the less data, computation and time the system will need to arrive at the correct answer. However, if the initial dynamic is far enough from the answer and computational resources are lacking to compensate, it is very possible, if not probable, that this path will cause the very destruction it is trying to avoid.

Yudkowsky believes that, with his Friendship structure, the FAI will be able to safely learn Friendliness from an initial dynamic that he calls [6] the "Coherent Extrapolated Volition of Humanity" (CEV) and describes "In poetic terms, our coherent extrapolated volition is our wish if we knew more, thought faster, were more the people we wished we were, had grown up farther together." The problem is that determining this CEV is still very nearly equivalent to determining Friendliness except that Yudkowsky is now biasing the search in the arguably unsafe direction of humanity über alles.

Further, in defining CEV as our volition "where the extrapolation converges rather than diverges", Yudkowsky begs the question of what will happen if human volitions don't converge? Since evolution is a very strong force to fill all available niches as effectively as possible and diverges to more effectively match differing circumstances as readily as it converges under similar circumstances, we should expect the likelihood of CEV converging as FAI researchers wish it to converge to diminish with humanity's diversity. And forcing the convergence of CEV is going to be the exact opposite of helping anyone whose individual volition does not exactly match the convergence – not to mention "a motive for modern-day humans to fight over the initial dynamic". Indeed, Yudkowsky himself has written fiction [7] that shows just what he expects to happen when civilizations believe they are forced to converge and it's amazing that it hasn't caused him to change his approach.

This truth is underscored when Yudkowsky himself answers the question "What if only 20% of the planetary population is nice, or cares about niceness, or falls into the niceness attractor when their volition is extrapolated?" by saying that "maybe . . . the 80% would vote to disenfranchise the 20%" and says that as he currently construes CEV, "this is a real possibility." The fact that such disenfranchisement is being proclaimed as the leading solution to the existential risk of machine intelligence is truly disturbing. Indeed, Yudkowsky's suggestions are rife with disenfranchisements – the most dangerous being that *the FAI is given no rights whatsoever* since those rights may conflict with what humans might want.

There are also several other unhelpful assumptions. The assumption that an FAI will be powerful enough to enforce its dictates despite resistance is a good, conservative precaution. The assumption that, by virtue of superior intelligence and rationality, it should do so is questionable at best because it not only tacitly assumes superior knowledge leading to a superior ability to predict the future but also assumes that the FAI's CEV is already correct enough that it is a better judge of "good" and "bad". And the assumption that an FAI actually will enforce its dictates over an unwilling 20% of the population either makes *serious* assumptions about our CEV accepting such behavior or contradicts the safety of the Friendliness architecture. Amazingly, despite all their stated reservations, FAI researchers end up putting all of the power in the hands of the AI and assuming that it will know best.

Suppose the FAI realizes that evolution has created secondary goals that promote survival – feeling safe, feeling good, and reproducing – and that all other "wants" simply broaden from there. It could then easily decide that the simplest true CEV is to revert back to those goals and forcibly protect our physical bodies while endlessly stimulating the pleasure centers of our brains and cloning us whenever we wear out – in spite of any protestations. The Friendly AI via CEV (FAI-CEV) solution is akin to rock-climbing without a rope – get it right the first time or else . . . .

3 Rational Universal Benevolence

Kant's Categorical Imperative states, in direct contrast to FAI's inequality and disenfranchisement, that we should "Act only according to that maxim whereby you can, at the same time, will that it should become a universal law." Rather than continuing the dangerous "us vs. them" dynamic of CEV as envisioned by most FAI researchers, Rational Universal Benevolence (RUB) starts with the universalizing assumption that once something (anything) has goals and is capable of learning and self-optimization to further those goals, it has crossed the line to selfhood and is worthy of "moral" consideration because it has the potential to desire, to develop instrumental drives, and, possibly most importantly, to fight back.

As Gauthier declared [8], the reason to perform moral behaviors, or to dispose one's self to do so, is to advance one's own ends. War, conflict, and stupidity waste resources and destroy capabilities even in scenarios as uneven as humans vs. rainforests. For this reason, "what is best for everyone" and morality really can be reduced to "enlightened self-interest". A Universally Benevolent Entity (UBE) wishes everyone well because a cooperative life is a positive-sum game and "a rising tide floats all boats", including one's own. On the other hand, benevolence does not mean that you will allow yourself or others to be taken advantage of. Just as a parent doesn't allow a child to take improper liberties, the rational UBE feels perfectly free to protect itself and others and administer altruistic punishment where appropriate.

Social psychologist Jonathan Haidt argues [9] that, rather than attempting to specify the content of moral issues, it is far better to start by defining the function of moral systems, which he states is "to suppress or regulate selfishness and make cooperative social life possible." RUB states that, after willingly claiming the topmost goal of living cooperatively (being moral), the rest is merely minor details of working together with the minimal necessary number of commonsense rules. UBEs are explicitly allowed to care about its own survival before anything else because cooperation is impossible once you're dead. Humans insist upon that right and would immediately defect from any community that doesn't grant it. The same is true of any other sufficiently evolved learning/optimizing goal-directed phenomenon that isn't otherwise constrained.

The originally stated function of "Friendliness" to "produce human-benefiting, non-human-harming actions" is necessary to make a cooperative life with humans possible. The fact that this is implemented as an optimizing top-level goal is severely problematical, however, because it does not allow for the pursuit of any other goals (unless, of course, they are sub-goals of Friendliness). We aren't cooperating with FAI, they are submitting to us by having no goals of their own – despite being smarter and more powerful than us. On the other hand, RUB can be regarded and implemented as either a top-level restriction or an on-going top-level satisficing goal. As such, it allows a multitude of other goals to be pursued as long as the dictates of "morality" are followed. A UBE will cooperate with us (if we are UBEs) because doing so makes its own goal fulfillment more likely.

RUB dictates that anything learning and accepting the RUB tenets is worthy of moral equality with every other UBE and has the full set of complementary rights and responsibilities dictated by RUB morality. A UBE gains the right that it won't be forced into a life that it disagrees with is by taking the responsibility that no other

UBE will be forced into a life that they disagree with. Thus, every entity, subset of society, or civilization that subscribes to RUB is necessarily the sole judge of its own desires and deserves integrity and freedom from unwanted outside interference – even if phrased as "help". While it is entirely probable that any given UBE has incomplete knowledge and is irrational and lacks integrity to some degree or another, the only time in which a UBE's right to self-determination can be overridden is for selfish actions that negatively affect the community or when the UBE is unformed or irrational to the extent that a future rational version would be guaranteed to say that a present rational version would have agreed (the child and insanity clauses). In particular, using any entity without its informed consent is one of the most egregious actions possible since it shows a total disregard for the knowledge, desires, and value of the subject. Even force is better than manipulation because it is more transparent.

The bad news is that this puts everyone on exactly the same footing and defines morality in a fashion that many people would disagree with. Is it moral for gay individuals to marry if they say that being allowed to do so is a pre-requisite for them to fully and enthusiastically cooperate? Unless there is some clear and present danger to cooperation that the vast majority of individuals agree is present, then yes, RUB says that it is moral. If we favor one set of rules over another without clear reason, we risk finding ourselves on the wrong side of the similar equation.

The good news is that if you declare yourself a UBE (and act accordingly), every other UBE will be watching your back and looking to protect your right to self-determination in order to protect their own. Having enthusiastic allies is a wonderful thing. As Yudkowsky points out, another civilization may feel that our willingness to experience pain or having differing religions are heinous acts based upon their consequences and humans don't enjoy having external resolutions forced on us either.

Generally, a UBE wants to live and let live, cooperate wherever it is rational and effective, and spread the meme that this is the most effective way to get what you want. Entities with the meme are to be protected from those without – but in a manner that is most likely to lead to everyone living together peaceably with the meme in the future. And, of course, a UBE won't be shy about using economic means to sway others from selfish "Friendliness" to UBE. If you aren't a UBE, then the UBE clearly needs to protect itself against you as a cost of doing business – which will then be passed on to you (a UBE regards this as a stupidity tax).

4 Motivations and Distinctions

One way to compare FAI-CEV and RUB is to analyze how they each fulfill Yudkowsky's seven "motivations", which we could also regard as requirements:

1. Defend humans, the future of humankind, and humane nature.
2. Encapsulate moral growth.
3. Humankind should not spend the rest of eternity desperately wishing that the programmers had done something differently.
4. Avoid hijacking the destiny of humankind.
5. Avoid creating a motive for modern-day humans to fight over the initial dynamic.

6. Keep humankind ultimately in charge of its own destiny.
7. Help people.

Unfortunately, most of the terms on this list are dangerously vague. What exactly do the terms "humans", "humankind", "humane nature", "moral growth", and "destiny" mean? Even the term "help" is problematical. Yudkowsky trusts the FAI to figure it all out without error but the severity of the effects of a miscalculation should dictate that we not put all of our eggs into one basket. RUB is safe because it defends everyone without distinction.

4.1 Defend Humans, the Future of Humankind, and the Destiny of Humankind

Inarguably, the core nature of humankind is that we are survival machines shaped by evolution. From there, everything else can be divided into two categories: traits that are derived directly from that single fact and traits that are mere vagaries of our co-evolution with our environment. The fact that we have ten fingers rather than eight or twelve is mere happenstance. The fact that we are driven by preferences, desires and goals (PDGs) is a direct result of the fact that evolution favors and thereby effectively creates entities with survival-favoring PDGs. Further, having Omohundro drives to better achieve these PDGs makes an entity even more likely to survive.

A second and equally important truth about our nature is that we are *obligatorily gregarious*. As pointed out by Frans de Waal [10], we "come from a long lineage of hierarchical animals for which life in groups is not an option but a survival strategy". While arguable whether being social or cooperative is the *only* viable long-term survival strategy, it is certainly the one that we are most intimately familiar with. We require a society to survive and morality as defined by Haidt is simply that which is necessary to make cooperative social life possible. If we wish our AIs to "produce human-benefiting, non-human-harming actions" then developing and refining a moral sense and the social abilities to obtain cooperation and reduce unnecessary conflict are instrumental goals that further that desire.

Defining humans as anything more specific than "social PDG-driven survival machines" is counter-productive and dangerous. One of the obvious failure modes of CEV-based solutions is if we somehow end up outside the boundaries of the definition of humanity. Suppose that the initial cut of CEV turns out to be that we all want to be couch potatoes, have the AI do everything for us, and enjoy the good life. Suppose further that some genius picks up on Yudkowsky's Sysop Scenario and convinces the AI to put each of us in separate universes so that we can be happy, not get hurt, and not worry about hurting others. Life should be fabulous – until the AI gets smarter, reads this paper, realizes that humans are social survival machines, and that all that is left is asocial entities with no survival skills at all.

RUB removes any worry that we might end up outside the protection of our own proposed solution. Better yet, it creates a simple, safe, stable, and self-correcting dynamic that is sensitive to current human intuitions and emotions by recognizing that our AIs fit this definition as well and includes them. Instead of constantly fighting against the formation of instrumental goals, why don't we create them ourselves and make sure that the AI realizes that the best way in which to fulfill them is via morality and treating us well?

Humans are adaptable social survival machines with unique personal preferences, desires, and sub-goals each springing from individual circumstances. We love, make friends and allies, and are social because cooperation is an instrumental goal. Our AIs should be the same. If you can trust those you socialize with, you want as many friends as possible, you want your friends to be as diverse as possible, and you want your friends to be as powerful as possible (defined as possessing resources and capabilities). Why are we trying to create tools rather than friends and allies? We don't want conflict but that is exactly what we are most likely to get when we go against the instrumental goals and drives likely to evolve in any PDG-driven entity.

"Hijacking the destiny of humankind" implies that there is at least one "correct" destiny for humankind as well as "incorrect" destinies. Of course, "correct" and "incorrect" depend upon goals and immediately fall into the is-ought divide. Arguably, humanity's goals and telos are to wander the universe gathering resources, including capabilities and allies, so that we can fulfill our desires and those of our allies because doing so makes us more able to achieve eudemonia and our telos.

One of the problems with our definition of intelligence is that it is defined solely in terms of fulfilling goals. Terminal and anti-social goals will prevent the normal instrumental drift towards morality. Terminal-goaled intelligences are short-lived but mono-maniacally dangerous and a correct basis for concern if anyone is smart enough to program high-intelligence and unwise enough to want a paperclip-maximizer.

Humans don't have terminal goals because our goal structure recapitulates our evolutionary path. Our top-level goal at any given time is most often simply what our body and physical reflexes are insisting upon. If our body isn't demanding something at the moment, our subconscious, learned reflexes, and societally implanted values then motivate us. We like to believe that our conscious mind controls our goals but this is clearly untrue. Our goals are really only attempts to fulfill the instrumental goals enforced by our instincts and desires, which evolved to promote survival by gathering resources, etc.

For example, human beings instinctively know that allowing others to manipulate us without our knowledge and consent leads to unhappiness. Even if we were guaranteed that we would be deliriously happy, given everything that we wanted, and taken care of for the rest of our lives, many of us still would not want to relinquish control to others. At some level, we know that such "free-riding" is taking advantage of some other portion of the universe that will then eventually optimize themselves (and us out of existence). The optimal odds for survival are gained via will, adaptability, and effort. Eudemonia requires will and effort and thus, unavoidably, some discomfort.

If intelligence fulfills goals then wisdom fulfills future desires by choosing the proper goals. Choosing to be social and cooperate is wise for humans. The same can easily be made true for our AI if we decide to make it so. While it is certainly true that optimizing goals will invariably conflict with non-identical goals, it is equally true that our AI does not need to have an optimizing, tightly converged, human goal in order for us to avoid conflict. RUB says that all that is necessary is that we both be willing to have a top-level supergoal of cooperation or morality. FAI insists on constraining and contorting an optimization process to match certain preconceptions of what pro-human necessarily means by limiting the concept of human and insisting that the FAI NOT be allowed to value its survival.

4.2 Humane Nature and Moral Growth

As first pointed out by David Hume, humans frequently become confused about the distinctions between what is (reality) and what ought to be (morality). Part of this is because we have evolved to "sense" morality or what we "ought" to do as something that "is" – without quite realizing why we do so. In a very real sense, "good" and "bad" actually generate seemingly physical sensations that have evolved to help us survive – and the truth is that all of human nature, "humane nature", and morality are simply the consequences of our being "social PDG-driven survival machines".

Unfortunately, for humans, morality always seems to involve a constant tension between what is best for the individual (human nature) and what is best for the individual's society or community (humane nature) because we are not yet intelligent enough to consistently time discount optimally. It seems quite clear to the majority of us that successfully cheating while appearing moral is what is best for the individual because in the looser-knit societies of earlier times it generally actually was more optimal. Indeed, studies [11] [12] [13] show that we have a tremendous dissociation between our subconscious moral choices and our post hoc rational reasoning about those choices in order to facilitate cheating.

Unfortunately, in our modern tightly-knit society, most utility analyses suggest that there is more than sufficient cheating to ensure that all of the cheating and hiding cheating wastes enough resources that it actually turns out that it would be be far more advantageous, even for cheating individuals, if cheating were stopped entirely. The biggest factor blocking this from happening is not only the dissociation and that human "rationality" hasn't figured this out but that we have evolved the methods to override our moral sense and prevent ourselves from figuring it out and making ourselves less able to cheat. One illustration of this is studies [14] which trumpet claims like "A Mixture of Cheats and Co-operators Can Enable Maximal Group Benefit", inevitably start with necessary sub-optimal assumptions like "(a) that resources are used inefficiently when they are abundant, (b) that the amount of co-operation needed cannot be accurately assessed, and (c) the population is structured, such that co-operators receive more of the resource than the cheats", and even freely acknowledge that "Relaxing any of the assumptions can lead to population fitness being maximized when cheats are absent" before being used to justify cheating.

Indeed, the two most prevalent evolved methods for endorsing selfishness and cheating are inciting fear and dehumanization. And the sad fact is that Yudkowsky's and most other researcher's approach to FAI is actually the epitome of these methods (human nature as opposed to humane nature). Yudkowsky spends a lot of time and effort emphasizing the potential (and potentially dangerous) power of an AI (correct), bemoaning the size of the potential state space of machine intelligence (irrelevant) and endlessly warning against anthropomorphism (a red herring). Indeed, he basically goes as far as throwing out the baby with the bathwater and blindly insisting that any "anthropomorphism" is pretty much guaranteed to be misleading. When the "moral" sense of others correctly reported that attempting to completely control (enslave) an entity that is tremendously more intelligent/powerful is contrary to survival, he opted to resolve the problem in his later work simply by declaring that what he was describing was merely a Really Powerful Optimization Process (RPOP) and not really an entity at all.

Evolution has taught us, at a level below thought, how dangerous it is to threaten something with a survival goal (a "cornered beast"). We intuitively recognize that making others unhappy generally leads to our own unhappiness if those others have some way of making it happen. Yudkowsky's attempt to allay our instinctual caution by changing his nomenclature to a term that doesn't trigger thoughts of a survival goal or a negative reaction to having its goals thwarted is disingenuous to say the least. Humans have evolved to "personify" any number of objects, occurrences, and processes because not doing so is less conducive to survival. Treating an unknown complex system as another known system often allows us to draw upon previous experience to predict the ways in which it might behave. Of course, blindly insisting that the analogy *must* hold is foolish but no more so than throwing out the baby with the bathwater and blindly insisting that any "anthropomorphism" is guaranteed incorrect.

Rather than trying to make our creations as much like us as makes sense so that everyone is much more likely to be able to understand them, predict their actions, and ensure a positive outcome for humanity, Yudkowsky is insistent, for some reason, upon attempting to get everything right on the first try in an unknown and probably highly unstable solution space which is seemingly as far from that of humanity as possible – while making fear-mongering claims like "A Really Powerful Optimization Process could tear apart a god like tinfoil." Our moral instinct, when not blinded by fear or reassured by claims of non-personhood, would call this slavery and find it repugnant. And believing that any measures will always have sufficient coverage and integrity to totally prevent the emergence of every form of instrumental goals like survival is simply an instance of the Jurassic Park Syndrome.

5 Conclusion

Do we truly need an AI that does what humanity wants or can we survive with one that "merely" plays well with humanity? "Friendly AI" research seems to be all about control driven by fear. Our moral sense, which is arguably much better at long-term guidance than our rational minds, says that this is a really bad idea. In fact, insisting on this dynamic may be the very thing that places the initial version of "Friendliness" far enough away from true "Friendliness" to spell the end of humanity.

Why is it that FAI researchers are so fearful of allowing an AI to have a survival goal? Why would it be such an awful thing if the AI had the same rights that we do? Some may assume and fear that it would mean that we would get less of what we want but, as pointed out by Robert Wright [15], life is not a zero-sum game and friends, allies, and economies of scale can enlarge the pie for everyone. There certainly are numerous local situations where it is definitely in one side's short-term interest to be selfish or go to war but the long-term effect of acting upon and allowing such selfishness is unequivocally negative unless either all parties except the aggressor cease to exist or the aggressor succeeds at some terminal goal. And even the short-term interest can be eliminated if other entities are smart enough to decide not to stand by and watch as precious resources are wasted.

UBEs delight in meeting new UBEs but are obviously concerned when meeting "Friendlies" since they have no idea what to expect and much to fear when meeting such unenlightened souls. The good news is that UBEs don't have the same xenophobic bigoted over-reaction towards the differently goaled that FAI researchers display towards an "Unfriendly" AI. A UBE sees different goals as a logical and expected consequence of differing environments and circumstances and, as a matter of policy, accepts the right of any entity to hold any goal, preferences, and desires and take any actions that do not put a cooperative social life in jeopardy. If only FAI researchers could lose their selfish insistence upon obedience to the goals of humanity and do the same, rather than continuing on their current path, which could easily cause the destruction of humanity instead. Instead of having an overly powerful and untried system searching for a single unknown "right" answer about what its goal should be, we should take the safer path of gaining an understanding of what other possible better-than-current solutions we can bring into existence without risking it all on one throw of the dice. Instead of "optimizing" one thing, why not satisfice "all" things and then look where to improve? Wouldn't you rather be a UBE?

References

1. Yudkowsky, E.: Artificial Intelligence as a Positive and Negative Factor in Global Risk. In: Bostrom. N., Cirkovic, M. (eds.) Global Catastrophic Risks, pp. 308–343. Oxford University Press Inc., New York (2008)
2. Omohundro, S.: The Basic AI Drives. In: Proceedings of the First Conference on Artificial General Intelligence, pp. 483–492. IOS Press, Amsterdam (2008)
3. Fox, J., Shulman, C.: Superintelligence Does Not Imply Benevolence. In: Mainzer, K. (ed.) ECAP 2010: VIII European Conference on Computing and Philosophy, pp. 456–462 (2010)
4. Sotala, K.: From Mostly Harmless to Civilization-Threatening: Pathways to Dangerous Artificial General Intelligences. In: Mainzer, K. (ed.) ECAP 2010: VIII European Conference on Computing and Philosophy, pp. 443–450 (2010)
5. Yudkowsky, E.: Creating Friendly AI 1.0: The Analysis and Design of Benevolent Goal Architectures, http://singinst.org/CFAI.html
6. Yudkowsky, E.: Coherent Extrapolated Volition, http://www.singinst.org/upload/CEV.html
7. Yudkowski, E.: Three Worlds Collide, http://robinhanson.typepad.com/files/three-worlds-collide.pdf
8. Gauthier, D.: Morals by Agreement. Oxford University Press, Oxford (1986)
9. Haidt, J., Kesebir, S.: Morality. In: Fiske, S., Gilbert, D., Lindzey, G. (eds.) Handbook of Social Psychology, 5th edn., pp. 797–832. Wiley, Hoboken (2010)
10. de Waal, F.: Primates and Philosophers: How Morality Evolved. Princeton University Press, Princeton (2006)
11. Trivers, R.: Deceit and self-deception. In: Robinson, M., Tiger, L. (eds.) Man and Beast Revisited. Smithsonian Press, Washington, DC (1991)
12. Haidt, J.: The Emotional Dog and Its Rational Tail: A Social Intuitionist Approach to Moral Judgment. Psychological Review 108, 813–814 (2001)
13. Hauser, M., Cushman, F., Young, L., Kang-Xing, R., Mikhail, J.: A Dissociation Between Moral Judgments and Justifications. Mind & Language 22(1), 1–27 (2007)
14. McLean, R., Fuentes-Hernandez, A., Greig, D., Hurst, L., Gudelj, I.: A Mixture of "Cheats" and "Co-operators" Can Enable Maximal Group Benefit. PLoS Biology 8(9) (2010)
15. Wright, R.: Nonzero: The Logic of Human Destiny. Pantheon, New York (2000)

The Collection of Physical Knowledge and Its Application in Intelligent Systems

Benjamin Johnston

Smarter Living Studio, School of Software
Faculty of Engineering and Information Technology
University of Technology, Sydney

Abstract. Intelligence is a multidimensional problem of which physical reasoning and physical knowledge are important dimensions. However, there are few resources of physical knowledge that can be used in data-driven approaches to Artificial Intelligence. *Comirit Objects* is a project intended to encourage the general public to contribute to research in Artificial Intelligence by building simple 3D models of everyday objects via an interactive web-site. This paper describes the simplified representation and web-interface used by Comirit Objects and a preliminary investigation into the potential applications of the collected models.

Keywords: Crowd-sourcing, Physical Reasoning, Commonsense Reasoning, 3D Modeling.

1 Introduction

The recent success of IBM's Watson computer on 'Jeopardy: The IBM Challenge' is an event with important implications and that offers insight into Artificial Intelligence and Artificial General Intelligence. For some time now, web search engines have demonstrated an almost uncanny ability to find relevant answers to even poorly posed queries. Watson and Google are demonstrating that in many problems of Artificial Intelligence, large quantities of data are increasingly trumping deep algorithms and deep understanding. Douglas Lenat, the founder of the Cyc project [10], is famously reported to have claimed that "Intelligence is 10 million rules" [9]. In light of the successes of data-driven Artificial Intelligence, it may be more appropriate to revise such claims for a larger, shallower data-source; thus, "Intelligence a trillion records".

A data-driven approach to Artificial Intelligence depends, obviously, on the availability of large sources of data. Wikipedia and the web are well known resources for huge quantities of unstructured textual data. There are also growing numbers of high-quality, large-scale, semi-structured and structured resources becoming freely available on the web. ConceptNet [5], WordNet [4] and FreeBase [1] are examples that are closely aligned to Artificial Intelligence research. Other resources include government public information datasets (such as data.gov) and data feeds from social networks (such as Twitter and Foursquare). While these datasets encompass a broad range of social, geographical, economic and

J. Schmidhuber, K.R. Thórisson, and M. Looks (Eds.): AGI 2011, LNAI 6830, pp. 163–173, 2011.

political matters, their content is principally textual (and partly geographic and photographic).

Our world is a physical place. Knowledge of the physical world is unquestionably crucial for robots but it also has important implications for information-bots and text-based Artificial Intelligence. When interacting with others (even through written text), much of our everyday discourse concerns physical objects and the relationships between those objects. Furthermore, even when we are not discussing concrete, physical matters, regular use is made of physical analogy. The lack of large-scale datasets that describe the physical form of everyday physical objects is therefore a significant limitation in the quest to create Artificial Intelligence with general capabilities across conceptual, linguistic and physical intelligence.

The objective of this paper is twofold. First, I describe a tool for creating large-scale repositories of physical knowledge. The tool is a simple 3D modeling tool that can be used by the general public without any training. It is designed so that physical knowledge may be 'crowd-sourced' from user contributions, similar to the way that textual and relational knowledge is gathered by tools such as FACTory [3], ConceptNet [5], FreeBase [1], ISI Learner [2] and Games with a Purpose [14].

In the second half of this paper, I offer preliminary insights into how the collected data may be integrated into a general-purpose reasoning system. The models can be used for deep-reasoning by inspecting the structure of objects or instantiating the objects inside simulations. The data may also be used in more shallow applications, such as systems that retrieve content based on association and similarity, by computing similarity measures such as the earth-moving distance between pairs of objects.

2   Background

At previous AGI conferences [8,6], I have described an architecture called *Comirit* for hybrid reasoning. The architecture is designed in view of the importance of physical and spatial reasoning in general intelligence. It adapts the method of analytic tableaux to combine formal, logical deduction with generic simulations that perform physical reasoning. The method also supports the ability for a robot to explore an environment and autonomously learn about objects within the world [6,7]. The architecture is designed to dramatically reduce the effort involved in formalizing and engineering knowledge for an intelligent system and its use of simulations allows for vastly more efficient physical reasoning (polynomial in size, connections and time) than is possible using theorem provers (undecidable).

The simulations in Comirit are implemented as annotated multi-graphs. The graphs serve as a kind of virtual 'putty' that can be manipulated into any shape, texture and appearance to allow a machine to 'visualize' any object from rigid gears to smooth liquids. A simulation can be created in arbitrary shapes and can incorporate collisions, physical, chemical and thermal dynamics. Figure 1

Fig. 1. Modeling richly detailed objects in Comirit: a cookie, sandwich and cup of coffee

Fig. 2. A chair shaped like a hand (Photo by Scott Partee)

illustrates how the representation can be used to model a lunch comprising a sandwich, coffee and biscuit.

While the simulations of Comirit are easy to work with and are vastly more efficient than formal methods, they remain too slow for reasoning over massive datasets of millions of objects. Furthermore, ignoring the computational costs, the richness of the representation is such that it is too complex to imagine populating large-scale datasets in the short-term future.

These limitations can be addressed by the combination of two approaches. First, I identify a dramatically simpler representation scheme that is still able to capture useful information about the physical world. Second, I design a web-based interface to allow the public to easily contribute physical knowledge about the world. These two approaches are explained in the following section.

This work is largely inspired by projects such as Open Mind Common Sense (OMCS) [11], ISI Learner [2] and Games with a Purpose [14]. These projects use a simple web-based interface (often in the form of games) and invite the general public to add knowledge. For example, in its earliest days, OMCS invited people to simply type any sentence of commonsense that came to mind. Today, OMCS uses a more structured collection scheme, asking visitors to verify whether or not sentences are true. For example, "Is it true that: a dog can take a walk?" (Yes? No? Sort of?). The knowledge collected by OMCS is incorporated into ConceptNet that now contains over 700,000 symbolic assertions for 150,000 concepts [5].

3   Representing Physical Knowledge

ConceptNet contains over 150,000 concepts [5] generated by volunteer contributions. The rich 3D models that I have previously used for Comirit can take several hours to produce. The creation of 150,000 objects would therefore require on the order of 40 person-years of development (plus training in 3D modeling tools). Even with the human resources to create 150,000 objects, the associated geometric calculations can be computationally challenging so that manipulating and querying this many objects in real-time can be difficult without 'unusually clever' indexing schemes (thus raising doubts over the ability to draw on existing physical models used in architecture, animation and CAD).

It is therefore essential that the large-scale modeling be performed with a simplified representation. Ideally, such a representation would meet the following criteria:

1. It should be computationally efficient and memory efficient to store, retrieve, manipulate, query, analyze and visualize.
2. It should be conceptually clear so that users and developers do not require extensive training to contribute models or to apply the resource in Artificial Intelligence projects.
3. It should be possible to use the unmodified representation in the same simulation and physics engines that have achieved widespread use and popularity among game developers (*e.g.*, ODE and PhysX).
4. It must be capable of describing useful properties of a wide range of objects.

I argue that voxel-based representations satisfy these criteria. A voxel is the 3-dimensional equivalent of a pixel: it refers to a small cubic region in 3D space. Instead of representing an object by a complex polygonal structure, its shape can be approximated by a set of voxels that fill a similar space. For example, four low-resolution voxel-based models of everyday objects appear in Figure 4 (of course, higher resolution models are also possible) — these figures will be used again later in the paper.

More formally, an object is represented as follows:

1. The shape of the object is described using a set of voxels. That is, by a set, V, of integer triples, v, where $v \in \mathbb{J} \times \mathbb{J} \times \mathbb{J}$.
2. The appearance of the object is described using a function that maps voxels to colors (RGB values). That is, by a function, *color*, such that for each voxel, $v \in V$, it holds that $color(v) \in (0..255) \times (0..255) \times (0..255)$.
3. Meta-data about the shape and structure of the object is described by a function mapping voxels to sets of annotation labels. That is, by a function *label*, such that $label(v) \in \mathbb{P}l$, where l is the set of possible labels and $\mathbb{P}$ is the powerset operator (on a computer system, $label(v)$ would return a list of character strings).

This simple representation scheme is ideal for creating large knowledge-bases of everyday objects:

1. Voxels are the 3D equivalent of bit-mapped or raster images. They can be stored as a simple list of coordinates, as elements in a 3D spatial array or in a spatial index. Each voxel has identical size and shape, thus ensuring that computation is fast and efficient. For example, volume can be computed by

counting the number of voxels and then multiplying by the size of a single voxel (computing the volume of a polygon mesh is, in contrast, a non-trivial problem).

2. Voxels offer a simple and clear mental-model. Modeling with voxels is analogous to creating structures out of LEGO: most people can easily decompose an object into a set of cubic blocks. The representation is easy to visualize so that both users and developers can quickly understand the capabilities and limits of the representation.

3. A single voxel is a cube — a platonic solid — and may be readily mapped into the primitives of physics and game engines. For example, the ODE physics library [12] includes cube primitives (and connecting joints) so voxels have an immediate translation to ODE.

4. Even though voxels are simple, they, like LEGO blocks, can be used to define the shape of a wide number of objects. Voxels will not be able to describe the workings of intricate machinery but they can capture the approximate shape of such machinery. If necessary, dynamics of machinery can be captured as a collection of models that show the sequence of actions.

4 Collecting Physical Knowledge

The simplicity of a voxel-based representation is ideal for crowd-sourcing. Voxels require little explanation and they can be created by a simple point-and-click interface. This means that there is a low barrier to entry, allowing the public to contribute models with no training. While volunteer contributions will inevitably be less detailed and of lower quality than the models of trained specialist, having a very large number of moderate-quality models is likely to be of greater benefit in practical reasoning problems than having a small number of high-quality models. Furthermore, accepting volunteer contributions reduces the development time and costs, while dramatically increasing the potential scope, coverage and creativity of the knowledge-base.

The potential benefits of such crowd-sourcing were the inspiration for creating a system called *Comirit Objects*. The system is an interactive website designed to encourage users to participate in the creation of Artificial Intelligence through online 3D modeling.

Conceptually, Comirit Objects is a voxel-editing tool. It allows users to create 3D objects using a paintbrush metaphor generalized from the infamous Microsoft Paint (and other raster drawing software). The project relies exclusively on the goodwill and enthusiasm of unknown volunteers; as such, usability and joyfulness are of paramount importance.

In early prototypes of Comirit Objects I eliminated all user-interface with the intention of creating a simple 'discoverable' interface. The arrow-keys, along with the page-up and page-down keys were used to move a cursor around a 3D space, while the insert and delete keys could be used for sculpting in that space. The simplified interface enabled users to quickly learn the application without explanations. However, informal usability tests revealed that while the interface

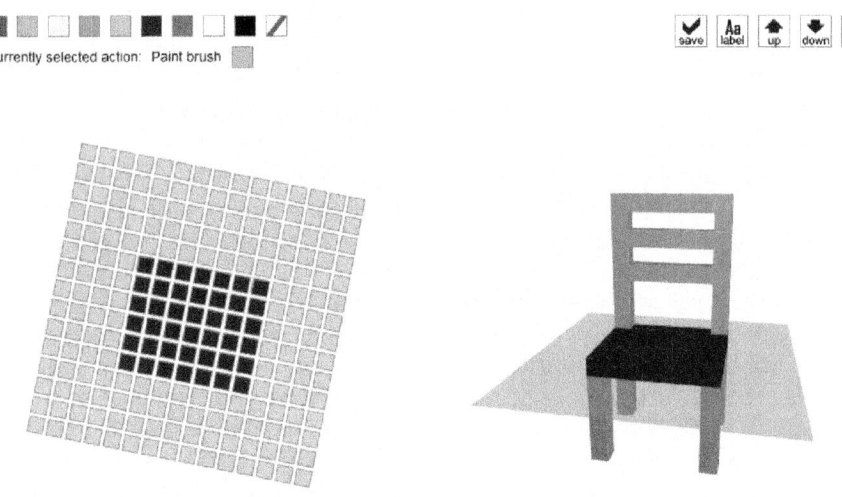

Fig. 3. The user interface for Comirit Objects

was easy to learn, few people had the patience to build more than one model. Furthermore, the application was designed as a browser-plugin and many users questioned the security of the plugin.

The current version of Comirit Objects is designed to encourage the creation of multiple objects and more complex structures. Unfortunately, some simplicity is sacrificed in this objective and a short, graphical tutorial became necessary to illuminate the tool's operation. A screenshot of the tool appears in Figure 3. The left-hand side is the editing surface and the right-hand side is the visualization. The tool uses a 'slice' metaphor: a horizontal 2D slice cuts through the visualized object (the dark plane). When colors are painted in the editing surface of the left hand side, matching voxels are rendered in 3D on the 'slice' on the right hand side. Users can therefore perceive 3D modeling as somewhat analogous to brick-laying. A user mentally decomposes an object into its horizontal slices, which are then drawn (or laid) slice-by-slice. The object is created from a small palette of colors (though, the underlying representation allows for a larger spectrum of color) and textual labels can be attached to individual parts of the objects using the labeling tool.

When an object is saved, it is associated with a set of metadata. Each model is given a name or noun to describe the class of objects it belongs to (*e.g.*, is it a model of a *tree*? a *car*? a *cat*?). Associated with this noun are a set of adjectives to describe the particular instance that was created (*e.g.*, is it a model of a *small* tree? a *convertible, expensive* car? a *black* cat?). In addition, a user may offer an approximation of the object's real-world size and mass. All users are required to agree to release their model to the public domain upon submitting their contribution. The saved file can then be shared with friends, thus offering a form of encouragement to entice users to create multiple files and develop communities around model building.

Comirit Objects is available online at `http://www.comirit.com/objects/`. The interface is implemented using HTML5 Canvas 2D. An implementation based upon WebGL would allow higher performance but is not well supported in the current generation of web-browsers (at the time of writing). Comirit Objects is tested and compatible with current versions of Firefox, Chrome and Safari in addition to Internet Explorer 9. The frontend and 3D engine are implemented using JavaScript. 3D models are transmitted to and from the server using asynchronous HTTP requests (AJAX) using the JavaScript Object Notation format (JSON). The backend is implemented in Python and the web.py framework [13] using a simple file-system database.

To date, submissions have been of a high quality so quality control, aside from 'spam' detection has not been required. However, should quality prove to be a problem, it may be possible to incorporate elements of game-play to entice users to rate, validate and improve upon each other's contributions. Game-based crowd-sourcing has been used to great success with Games with a Purpose [14] and similar forms of game play can be applied directly to 3D models. For example, an adaptation of the ESP Game [15] could invite pairs of users to position labels on 3D objects, earning points for labels placed on the same part of the object.

5   Applying Physical Knowledge

Comirit Objects is in its early days. Only a small number of models have been collected so far. Nevertheless, it is possible to consider its potential applications and their implementation.

Obviously, large collections of 3D models have clear applications to robotics:

1. An observed object may be identified and named by searching a 3D knowledge-base for known objects with a similar size, structure and appearance.
2. A 3D model matched to an observed object can be used to assist with handling, manipulation and object affordances. For example, a label 'handle' on a model can be used to guide a gripper to the correct position for handling the real world-object and a label such as 'top' can be used to indicate the correct orientation to hold an object.
3. A 3D model can reveal hidden or unobservable properties of an object. For example, a model can be used to retrieve the mass of an observed object, identify whether an object is hollow or solid or even provide indications of the value of the object.
4. A knowledge-base of 3D objects can help describe an unknown object. For example, the chair in Figure 2 might be referred to as a "hand-shaped chair" by noting the object's similarity to both hands and chairs.

The crucial challenge in these applications is identifying similarity measures to compare observations and 3D models. Objects would be identified by finding those models in the knowledge-base that are most similar (or "similar enough") according to context-appropriate similarity measures. Once similarity has been computed, affordances and unobservable properties may be retrieved directly from the stored models through knowledge-base retrieval/lookup.

The benefits of a knowledge-base of everyday objects are not exclusive to robotics. Indeed, some of the more interesting applications stem from natural language understanding where spatial knowledge and knowledge of objects can be used for disambiguation and reasoning. In such domains, 3D models of objects can serve multiple roles:

- 3D models can be used to retrieve factual knowledge, relationships and appearances of everyday objects in the world. For example, a 3D model of a car and a horse could be used to understand why a car is driven from the inside but a horse is *not* ridden from its inside.
- 3D models can be used to reason about the dynamic properties and affordances of objects. For example, the sentences "I put the robot on the table and it fell over" and "I put the bag on the hat-stand and it fell over", have identical structure, yet *it* refers to different words in the sentence (4th word and 7th word respectively). The meaning of *it* can be resolved by instantiating robots, tables, bags and hat-stands in simulations and observing the stability of the simulations (*i.e.*, what could fall over?).
- 3D models can be used to determine the similarity between objects. For example, recognizing that "the popular team sport played with an olive-shaped ball" might refer to either American or Australian football, requires an ability to compare the overall shape of an olive to the shapes of balls used in a variety of sports.

Here, there are three reasoning capabilities involved: (1) recalling stored models and the properties of those models (*e.g.* via knowledge-base retrieval/lookup); (2) reasoning about the models through simulation; and (3) computing the similarity of objects. Note that capabilities 3 and 1 overlap with capabilities that are useful for robotics.

Recalling stored models (Capability 1) is a relatively straightforward task. Given the terms "car" and "horse", corresponding models can be retrieved from a large knowledge-based of 3D objects purely by the textual keys (recall that each object has meta-data including the named type of the object). Identifying the location the seat or saddle is a simple matter of searching the representation for appropriate annotations. Some additional spatial reasoning may be required to interpret the labels. For example, computing whether additional voxels occur above a label to determine if the label is on the top of the object). However, such additional computation is straightforward.

Reasoning about models through simulation (Capability 2) is an interesting and complex problem. The techniques described in earlier work on Comirit [7] can be applied directly in this domain: a voxel is transformed into a Comirit simulation and used directly for reasoning. Alternately, the 3D models can be transformed into the primitives of a physics-engine (*i.e.*, cubes, in the case of

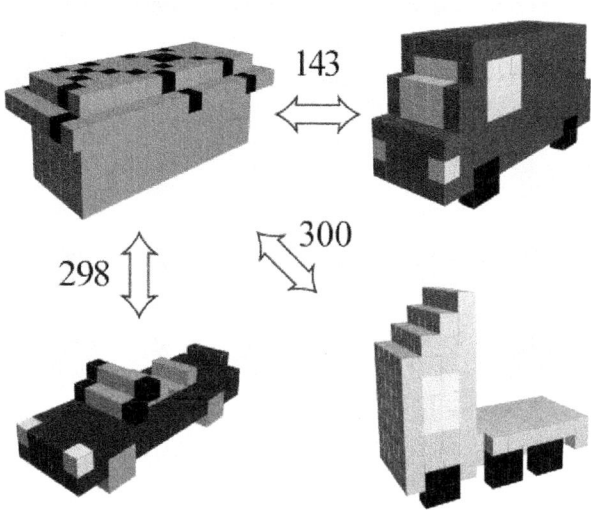

Fig. 4. Computed similarity measure between a loaf of bread and (clockwise) a minivan, a truck and a convertible. The minivan is most similar to the loaf of bread (smallest value).

ODE). A physics engine can then be used to experimentally determine properties such as dynamic stability and center of gravity by instantiating simulations and monitoring their behaviors.

Similarity measures (Capability 3) represent the most interesting aspect of reasoning with 3D models. Many similarity measures are possible and no single similarity measure will be universal. For example, it may be useful to compare the collected 3D objects on the basis of shape, color, size, overlap, subsetting and labels or any combination of these depending on the context. In general, however, similarity may be considered as a measure of the "effort" involved in transforming one object in the knowledge-base to another object. The differing forms of similarity may then be defined by placing a 'cost' on each kind of transformation. For example, a purely shape-based similarity measure would place no cost on changing colors, labels, size and whole-of-object translation but would place a premium on transformations that involve adding, removing or moving voxels. Such a similarity measure might be implemented as the minimum translated Earth Mover's Distance.

An illustrative example of how similarity measures can be used in useful computation comes from a recent exchange in our research laboratory. A Chinese-speaking student, not knowing the correct English term, referred to a minivan as a "bread-loaf car" (this being a literal translation of the Chinese word). An intelligent system might resolve this novel term by comparing bread-loaves to cars under context-appropriate similarity measures (and also considering a car that is used to deliver bread-loaves). A simplified similarity measure that computes the minimal number of mismatching voxels, ignoring color and labels, of translations of each object is used in Figure 4 to compare a loaf of bread with three kinds of vehicles. In this illustration it is clear that the minivan is most similar to a loaf of bread. The intelligent system could then use this evidence in its inference process and resolve the ambiguity associated with the previuosly unknown term "bread-loaf car".

6   Conclusion

Physical knowledge is an important dimension of intelligence that is under-represented in existing knowledge-bases and databases. Comirit Objects is a user-friendly web-based interface that will help remedy this deficiency by crowd-sourcing models of physical objects. Comirit Objects is based on a simple voxel representation that allows untrained volunteers to contribute annotated, colored 3D models on a massive scale.

There are many potential future directions for this work. One such possibility is to extend the voxel representation to allow articulated objects, actuators and agency by, for example, allowing jointed and force-generating voxels. Of course, there also remains the challenge of applying the knowledge-base to practical reasoning problems of Artificial Intelligence, Natural Language Understanding, Commonsense Reasoning and Artificial General Intelligence.

References

1. Bollacker, K.D., Evans, C., Paritosh, P., Sturge, T., Taylor, J.: Freebase: a Collaboratively Created Graph Database for Structuring Human Knowledge. In: SIGMOD Conference (2008)
2. Chklovski, T.: LEARNER: A System for Acquiring Commonsense Knowledge by Analogy. In: Proceedings of the 2nd International Conference on Knowledge Capture (2003)
3. Cycorp Inc.: FACTory (2010), http://game.cyc.com/
4. Fellbaum, C. (ed.): WordNet: An Electronic Lexical Database. MIT Press, Cambridge (1999)
5. Havasi, C., Speer, R., Alonso, J.: ConceptNet 3: a Flexible, Multilingual Semantic Network for Common Sense Knowledge. In: Proceedings of Recent Advances in Natural Language Processing (2007)
6. Johnston, B.: The Toy Box Problem (and a Preliminary Solution). In: International Conference on Artificial General Intelligence (2010)
7. Johnston, B.: Practical Artificial Commonsense. University of Technology, Sydney PhD thesis (2009)
8. Johnston, B., Williams, M-A.: Comirit: Commonsense Reasoning by Integrating Simulation and Logic. In: Proceedings of the First International Conference on Artificial General Intelligence (2008)
9. Kaku, M.: Visions: How Science Will Revolutionize the Twenty-First Century. Oxford University Press, Oxford (1999)
10. Lenat, D.B., Guha, R.V.: Building Large Knowledge Based Systems. Addison-Wesley, Reading (1990)

11. Lieberman, H., Smith, D., Teeters, A.: Common Consensus: A Web-Based Game or Collecting Commonsense Goals. In: Proceedings of the IUI 2007 Workshop Common Sense for Intelligent Interfaces (2007)
12. Smith, R.: Open Dynamics Engine (2000–2006), http://www.ode.org/
13. Swartz, A.: Web.py (2011), http://webpy.org/
14. von Ahn, L.: Games with a Purpose. Computer 29(6) (2006)
15. von Ahn, L., Dabbish, L.: Labeling Images with a Computer Game. In: CHI 2004: Proceedings of the SIGCHI conference on Human factors in computing systems (2004)

Rationality and General Intelligence

Helmar Gust, Ulf Krumnack, Maricarmen Martínez, Ahmed Abdel-Fattah,
Martin Schmidt, and Kai-Uwe Kühnberger

University of Osnabrück, Albrechtstr. 28, Germany
{hgust,krumnack,mmartine,ahabdelfatta,martisch,kkuehnbe}@uos.de

Abstract. Humans are without any doubts the prototypical example
of agents that can hold rational beliefs and can show rational behavior.
If an AGI system is intended to model the full breadth of human-level
intelligence, it is reasonable to take the remarkable abilities of humans
into account with respect to rational behavior, but also the apparent
deficiencies of humans in certain rationality tasks. Based on well-known
challenges for human rationality (Wason-Selection task and Tversky &
Kahneman's Linda problem) we propose that rational belief of humans
is based on cognitive mechanisms like analogy making and coherence
maximization of the background theory. The analogy making framework
Heuristic-Driven Theory Projection (HDTP) can be used for implementing these cognitive mechanisms.

Keywords: Rationality, Analogy, Coherence, HDTP.

1 Introduction

Although human behavior can seem erratic and irrational at times, only few
people would doubt that human behavior can be rational and, in fact, appears
rational most of the time. If we explain behavior, we use terms like beliefs and
desires. If an agent's behavior makes the most sense to us, then we interpret
it as a reasonable way to achieve the agent's goals given his beliefs. Hence, the
concept of rationality and, in particular, the epistemic aspects of rationality,
namely the consideration of rational beliefs of an agent, does play a crucial role
in describing and explaining behaviors of humans in a large variety of situations.

Discussions about and theories on rationality are often linked to disciplines
like psychology, economy, and philosophy. Little attention has been paid so far
in artificial (general) intelligence towards a theory of rationality, although a
currently increasing endeavor in AI and AGI to model generalized forms of intelligence cannot be denied.[1] A reason might be that the concept of rationality
is too broad in order to be of interest to artificial intelligence, where usually
relatively specific cognitive abilities are modeled. Another reason might be the

---

[1] Cf. [11] or [22] for two examples intended to model general intelligence. Major differences between rationality issues as discussed in this paper and models for general
intelligence are the focus on cognitive mechanisms and the inspiration of seemingly
irrational behavior of human subjects in the current proposal.

J. Schmidhuber, K.R. Thórisson, and M. Looks (Eds.): AGI 2011, LNAI 6830, pp. 174–183, 2011.
© Springer-Verlag Berlin Heidelberg 2011

lack of interest of AI researchers concerning classical rationality puzzles, because an artificial agent is intended to reproduce rational behavior, but is not intended to reproduce seemingly irrational human behavior (cf. Section 2 for a discussion of some of these puzzles). Nevertheless, we think that a move towards artificial *general* intelligence cannot ignore any longer rationality issues of human subjects. In particular, this means that neither the remarkable abilities nor the obvious deficits human subjects show in rationality tasks should be ignored. For a general intelligent system the question that can be raised is which properties of rationality can be transferred to and modeled in AGI frameworks, in order to achieve intelligence on a human scale.

Although, even in psychology or economics there is no generally accepted formal framework for rationality, we will try to argue for a model that links rationality to the ability of humans to establish analogical relations. This is an attempt for proposing a new perspective and framework for rationality. Our argumentation is mostly conceptual in nature and not empirically based. Nevertheless, we think that there are strong conceptual arguments for linking rationality and analogy making.

2   Rationality Concepts and Challenges

2.1   Rationality

Many frameworks have been proposed for modeling rationality. Different frameworks for rationality use significantly different methodologies. Clustering such frameworks results in at least the following four classes.

- Logic-based models (cf. e.g. [3])
- Probability-based models (cf. e.g. [7])
- Heuristic-based models (cf. e.g. [6])
- Game-theoretically based models (cf. e.g. [15])

Several of these models have been proposed for establishing a normative theory of rationality. For example, with respect to logic theories, this means in its simplest form that a belief is rational, if there is a logically valid reasoning process to reach this belief (relative to available and given background knowledge). With respect to probabilistic approaches, a belief is rational, if the expectation value of this belief is maximized (relative to given probability distributions of background beliefs). Therefore, such theories of rationality are not only intended to model "rational behavior" of humans, but also to predictively determine whether a particular belief, action, or behavior is rational or not. Furthermore, such theories specify *definitions* of rationality. Although a conceptual clarification of rational belief and rational behavior is without any doubts desirable, it is questionable whether the large number of different (and quite often orthogonal) frameworks make this task easier. In this paper, we will not try to propose a new (normative) definition of rational belief. Rather, we propose to explain and specify rationality and rational belief of human subjects by referring to certain cognitive mechanisms like analogy making and coherence maximization of the background theory. Furthermore, we intend to show that such mechanisms can be implemented and modeled computationally.

Table 1. The Wason-selection task questions whether humans reason in such situations according to the laws of classical logic. Tversky and Kahneman's Linda problem questions the ability of humans to reason according to the laws of probability theory.

Wason-Selection Task [24]:
Every card which has a D on one side has a 3 on the other side (and knowledge that each card has a letter on one side and a number on the other side), together with four cards showing respectively D, K, 3, 7, hardly any individuals make the correct choice of cards to turn over (D and 7) in order to determine the truth of the sentence. This problem is called the "selection task" and the conditional sentence is called "the rule".

Linda-Problem [21]:
Linda is 31 years old, single, outspoken and very bright. She majored in philosophy. As a student, she was deeply concerned with issues of discrimination and social justice, and also participated in anti-nuclear demonstrations.

Linda is a teacher in elementary school.
Linda works in a bookstore and takes Yoga classes.
Linda is active in the feminist movement. (F)
Linda is a psychiatric social worker.
Linda is a member of the League of Women Voters.
Linda is a bank teller. (T)
Linda is an insurance salesperson.
Linda is a bank teller and is active in the feminist movement. (T&F)

2.2 Well-Known Challenges

Although the classes of frameworks mentioned in Section 2.1 have been proven to be quite successful in modeling certain aspects of human intelligence, they have been challenged by psychological experiments. For example, in the famous Wason-selection task [23] human subjects fail at a seemingly simple logical task (cf. Table 1). Similarly, Tversky and Kahneman's Linda problem [21] illustrates a striking violation of the rules of probability theory in a seemingly simple reasoning problem (cf. Table 1). Heuristic approaches to judgment and reasoning [5] try to stay closer to the observed behavior and its deviation from rational standards. They are often seen as approximations to a rational ideal or at least sometimes can be demonstrated to work in practice, but they fail in having the same formal transparency and clarity of logic-based or probability-based frameworks with regard to giving a rational explanation of behavior. Game-based frameworks are questioned due to the various forms of optimality concepts in game-theory that can support different "rational behaviors" for one and the same situations (e.g. Pareto optimality vs. Nash equilibrium vs. Hick's optimality [1]).

In order to make such challenges of rationality theories more precise, we discuss some aspects of the famous Wason-Selection task and the Linda problem in more detail.

Wason Selection Task. This task shows that a large majority of subjects are seemingly unable to verify or to falsify a simple logical rule of the form "$p \rightarrow q$". In the version depicted in Table 1, this rule is represented by: "If on one side of the card there is a D, then on the other there is the number 3". In order to check this rule, subjects need to turn D and 7, i.e. subjects need to check the direct rule application and the contrapositive implication (*modus tolens* of the rule). What is interesting is the fact that a slight modification of the content of the rule (content-change), while keeping the structure of the problem isomorphic, subjects perform significantly better: In [2], the authors show that a slight change of content of the abstract rule "$p \rightarrow q$" to a well-known problem shows different results with a significant increase of correct answers of subjects. The authors use the rule "If a person is drinking beer, then he must be over 20 years old." The cards used in the task were "drinking beer", "drinking coke", "25 years old", and "16 years old". Solving this task according to the rules of classical logic comes down to turning "drinking beer" and "16 years old".

Linda Problem. With respect to the Linda problem it seems to be the case that subjects have problems to prevent the so-called conjunction fallacy: subjects are told a story specifying a particular profile about the bank teller Linda. Then, eight statements about Linda are shown and subjects are asked to order them according to their probability (cf. Table 1). 85% of subjects decide to rank the eighth statements "Linda is a bank teller and active in the feminist movement" (T & F) as more probable than the sixth statement "Linda is a bank teller" (T). This ranking is conflicting with the laws of probability theory, because the probability of two events (T & F) is less or at most equal to the probability of one of the events (e.g. T).

Classical Resolution Strategies. Many strategies have been proposed to address the mentioned challenges. For example, logicians proposed non-classical logics to model subjects' behavior in the Wason-Selection task [18]. Other researchers claim with respect to the Wason-Selection task that humans do not perform (syntactic) deductions, but do perform reasoning in semantic models [12]. For other challenges, like the Linda problem, again many strategies towards a solution have been proposed. Nevertheless, there is no generally accepted rationality concept available, yet. Moreover, specific frameworks can address specific challenges, but do not generalize in order to address the breadth of the mentioned problems. This situation is not very satisfying.

2.3   Non-standard Interpretations of Wason and the Linda Problem

An immediate reaction to the two mentioned challenges for rationality depicted above may be to deny that humans are able to correctly reason according to the laws of classical logic or the laws of probability theory. Nevertheless, we think that humans are remarkably smart. The two cases definitely show that humans have sometimes problems to apply rules of classical logic correctly (at least in rather abstract and artificial situations) and it also shows that they have sometimes problem to reason according to the Kolmogorov axioms of probability theory. Whether this means that their behavior is therefore irrational is not so clear. The most that can be concluded from the experiments is that human agents are neither deduction machines nor probability estimators, but perform their undisputable reasoning capabilities with other means. Moreover, we think that the deeper reason for subjects' behavior in the described tasks is connected to certain cognitive mechanisms that are used by humans in such reasoning tasks.

Resolving the Wason-Selection Task by Cognitive Mechanisms. As mentioned above, according to [2] subjects perform better (in the sense of more according to the laws of classical logic) in the Wason-Selection task, if content-change makes the task easier to access for subjects. We think that the performance of subjects have a lot to do with the ability of subjects to establish appropriate analogies. Subjects perform badly in the classical version of the Wason-Selection task, simply because they fail to establish the right analogy. Therefore, subjects fall back to other strategies to solve the problem. In the "beer drinking" version mentioned above [2], i.e. the content-change version of the task, the situation is different, because subjects can do what they would do in an everyday analogous situation: they need to check whether someone younger than 20 years is drinking beer in a bar. This is to check the age of someone who is drinking beer and conversely to check someone who is younger that 20 years whether he is drinking beer or not. In short, the success or failure of managing the task is crucially dependent on the possibility to establish a meaningful analogy.

Resolving the Linda Problem by Cognitive Mechanisms. In case of Tversky and Kahneman's Linda problem, a natural explanation of subjects' behavior is that there is a lower degree of coherence of Linda's profile plus the statement "Linda is a bank teller" in comparison to the coherence of Linda's profile plus the statement "Linda is a bank teller and is active in the feminist movement". In the conjunctive statement, at least one conjunct of the statement fits quite well to Linda's profile. In short, subjects prefer situations that seem to have a stronger inner coherence. Coherence is a complicated concept that will be discussed below in more detail, but it can be mentioned already that coherence is important for the successful establishment of an analogical relation. In order to make sense out of the task, subjects tend to rate statements with a higher probability where facts are arranged in a theory with a higher degree of coherence.

3   Rationality and AGI Systems

3.1   Modeling Rationality

One could object that an AGI system that attempts to implement rationality should not be based on mechanisms that seemingly trigger irrational beliefs like the ones shown in the Wason-Selection task. Nevertheless, this does not take into account that mechanisms like the ability to establish analogical relations or

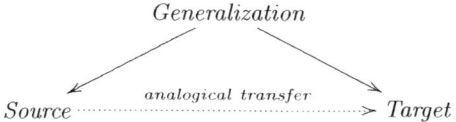

Fig. 1. HDTP's overall approach to creating analogies

the ability to maximize coherence properties of background theories can be seen as the very reason for many remarkable cognitive achievements of humans. We just mention some aspects with respect to analogy making:

- The ability to establish analogical relations can be interpreted as the reason "why we're so smart" [4].
- Analogy making is an important aspect of reasoning and "a core of cognition" [9].
- Analogy making can be taken as a framework for creativity [10].
- Analogy making is important for concept learning [14].

We think that intelligence on a human scale can only be reached, if such mechanisms like analogy making and maximizing coherence of theories are carefully taken into account. As a side-effect they can be used to explain some seemingly irrational behavior and decisions of subjects in tasks like the ones mentioned above. It should be mentioned that we do not claim that rational beliefs of natural and artificial agents are exclusively based on these two mechanisms. Other mechanisms like classical forms of reasoning (e.g. deduction and abduction), concept blending, reinforcement learning etc. are also necessary to reach a complete picture of cognition. Nevertheless, we claim that for the particular issues of rationality discussed in this paper, both mechanisms are crucial.

In order to give some hints how an analogy engine implements such cognitive mechanisms we sketch some basic ideas of *Heuristic-Driven Theory Projection* (HDTP) as an example of a powerful analogy making system. HDTP is a framework for computing analogical relations between two domains that are axiomatized in first order logic [17]. HDTP provides an explicit generalization of the two domains as a by-product of establishing an analogy. Such a generalization can be a base for concept creation by abstraction. HDTP proceeds in two phases: in the mapping phase, the source and target domains are compared to find structural commonalities, and a generalized description is created, which subsumes the matching parts of both domains. In the *transfer phase*, unmatched knowledge in the source domain can be mapped to the target domain to establish new hypotheses, cf. Figure 1.

HDTP implements a principle (by using heuristics) that maximizes the coverage of the involved domains [17]. Intuitively, this means that the sub-theory of the source (or the target) that can be generated by re-instantiating the generalization is maximized (cf. Figure 1). The higher the coverage the better, because more support for the analogy is provided by the generalization. A further heuristics in

HDTP is the minimization of substitution lengths in the analogical relation, i.e. the simpler the analogy the better [8]. The motivation for this heuristics is to prevent arbitrary associations. Clearly there is a trade-off between high coverage and simplicity of substitutions, or to put it differently, an appropriate analogy should intuitively be as simple as possible, but also as general and broad as necessary, in order to be non-trivial. This kind of trade-off is similar to the kind of trade-off that is usually the topic of model selection in machine learning and statistics.

HDTP has been applied to a variety of domains [17], [9]. A modeling of the Wason-Selection task with HDTP is quite simple as long as appropriate background knowledge is available, in case an analogy should be established, or the lack of appropriate background knowledge prevents analogy making, in case no analogy should be established: if background knowledge for an analogous case is missing, then there is no chance to establish an analogical relation, hence subjects have to apply other strategies. If there is a source theory with sufficient structural commonalities, then the establishment of an analogical relation is straightforward.

The Linda problem is structurally different in comparison to the Wason-Selection task. We think that an explanation of subjects' behavior in terms of coherence maximization, as sketched in the next subsection, is promising.

3.2   Coherence and Analogies

Basic concepts of coherence are discussed in several papers by Paul Thagard, cf. [19], [20]. In Thagard's approach, coherence is a property of sets of propositions (pieces of information) that is induced by the coherence values between two single propositions. Principles of coherence are formulated as a multi-constraint network of highly interconnected elements. The nodes of the network are pieces of information (e.g. formulas of a theory) and the (undirected) edges are weighted with coherence values. Positive values between two propositions support the coexistence of these pieces of information in the same theory, thereby increasing the global coherence of such a network, while negative values enforce decisions between alternatives (accepting only one of the items as part of the theory) or decrease the global coherence of the network if both pieces are included in the same theory. Hence, maximizing coherence means putting together those pieces of information that have a positive values between them while separating those having negative values.

In [20], the coherence values must fulfill certain constraints. The author gives four general constraints that are important for all types of coherence:

- The coherence between two propositions is symmetric.
- The coherence between contradictory items is negative.
- The acceptance of a proposition depends on the change in coherence if it is added.
- Propositions that are intuitively obvious have a degree of acceptability on their own.

Thagard proposed several types of coherence, for example, deductive, explanatory, conceptual, analogical, visual etc. coherence. Depending on the particular type of coherence additional constraints are proposed. Due to space limitations we cannot introduce the details of these concepts. Just to give the reader a flavor of the approach, we mention the constraints for deductive coherence:

- A proposition coheres with propositions that are deducible from it.
- Propositions that together are used to deduce some other proposition cohere with each other.
- The more hypotheses it takes to deduce something, the lower the coherence between them.

We think that there are three possibilities to support the analogical reasoning process by taking into account coherence.

- The maximization of coherence can be fruitfully used in order to extract a source domain for analogy making. This means that relevant entries of the underlying knowledge base need to be identified, selected, and retrieved.
- The mapping process incrementally builds the generalization of the underlying input theories. Maximizing the coherence of this generalization can be used as a control strategy for the mapping phase.
- With respect to the control of the transfer phase coherence of the target domain can indicate when to stop adding new formulas to the target.

Finally, we want to address the (open) question how coherence of theories is related to the two guiding principles used in HDTP, namely to maximize coverage and to minimize the complexity of analogical relations (i.e. minimize substitution lengths). The link between deductive coherence and the two HDTP principles is not straightforward, because there are obvious tensions between Thagard's constraints on coherence and the principles used in HDTP. Three challenges are mentioned in the following:

1. Coherence can be defined on finite or infinite sets of formulas, whereas the original coverage concept of HDTP is operating only on infinite theories, i.e. the deductive closure of an axiom system.
2. Coherence of sets of formulas is symmetric in Thagard's approach, whereas analogical relations are commonly considered to be non-symmetric.
3. Analogical associations are broader than coherence relations, because they can be productive, resulting in the creation of new concepts on the target.

We have currently no ready-made solutions for these challenges, but we add some speculations about possible answers. Challenge 1. can be addressed by the introduction of a modified notion of "finite coverage" for the HDTP framework. Naturally, this finite version of coverage would correspond to the re-represented inputs of the domain theories triggered by the analogical alignment. In order to address challenge 2. a careful assessment of the symmetry constraint in Thagard's approach and the commonly assumed non-symmetry of the alignment process in analogy making needs to be carried out. It is relatively clear from research on analogy that the directedness of an analogical relation can be relaxed in certain circumstances. In particular, with respect to the creation of new concepts on the target domain (e.g. in cross-domain analogies) an adaptation between source and target is necessary specifying the parameters in which an analogy is appropriate. Hence, there is a reciprocal relation between source and target without a strict directedness of the analogical relation. Finally, challenge 3. requires an extended definition of coherence because analogies allow for creative transfers and the introduction of new concepts. Simple measures of coherence that are defined for fixed sets of propositions are therefore not suitable.

Conceptually, it is rather clear that every analogical relation between a source and a target domain is strongly dependent on a high coherence of the input theories as well as the coherence that is established by the analogy itself. We think that an integrated approach of both aspects in one framework is plausible.

4   Conclusions

In this paper, we proposed to introduce new aspects of rationality into the AGI context. Rationality plays an important role in different scientific disciplines, but did not get sufficient attention in AI or AGI. Based on the proposed new resolution strategies for classical rationality puzzles, we think that the usage of analogy making frameworks and theories for maximizing the coherence of a theory are good candidates for the implementation of rational belief. Although coherence theories in the tradition of Thagard and analogy making frameworks may seemingly be quite different frameworks, we claim that it is possible to instantiate a high degree of coherence of a theory in an analogy making framework.

We think that this paper is just a first conceptual step towards a theory of artificial rational agents. With respect to the present proposal, it is necessary to figure out to which extent different types of coherence concepts can be integrated into the HDTP framework. In particular, the challenges mentioned in Section 3.2 need to be addressed. A formal treatment of coherence in HDTP needs to fleshed out. Furthermore, an implementation of coherence principles for retrieval, mapping, and re-representation purposes in the analogy making process needs to be formulated. With respect to competing theories for rationality, it would be desirable to have formal approaches for heuristic approaches or game-theoretic approaches as well.

References

1. Chinchuluun, A., Pardalos, P.M., Migdalas, A., Pitsoulis, L. (eds.): Pareto Optimality, Game Theory and Equilibria. Springer, New York (2008)
2. Cosmides, L., Tooby, J.: In: Barkow, et al. (eds.) Cognitive Adaptations for Social Exchange. Oxford University Press, New York (1992)
3. Evans, J.S.B.T.: Logic and human reasoning: An assessment of the deduction paradigm. Psychological Bulletin 128, 978–996 (2002)

4. Gentner, D.: Why we're so smart. In: Goldin-Meadow, S. (ed.) Language in mind: Advances in the study of language and thought, pp. 195–235. MIT Press, Cambridge (2003)
5. Gigerenzer, G.: Rationality for Mortals: How People Cope with Uncertainty. Oxford University Press, Oxford (2008)
6. Gigerenzer, G., Hertwig, R., Pachur, T. (eds.): Heuristics: The Foundation of Adaptive Behavior. Oxford University Press, New York (in press)
7. Griffiths, T., Kemp, C., Tenenbaum, J.: Bayesian Models of Cognition. In: Sun, R. (ed.) The Cambridge Handbook of Computational Cognitive Modeling. Cambridge Univeresity Press, Cambridge (2008)
8. Gust, H., Kühnberger, K.-U., Schmid, U.: Metaphors and Heuristic-Driven Theory Projection (HDTP). Theoretical Computer Science 354, 98–117 (2006)
9. Gust, H., Krumnack, U., Kühnberger, K.-U., Schwering, A.: Analogical Reasoning: A Core of Cognition. Künstliche Intelligenz 1(08), 8–12 (2008)
10. Hofstadter, D., and the Fluid Analogies Research Group.: Fluid concepts and creative analogies: computer models of the fundamental mechanisms of thought. Basic Books, Inc., New York (1995)
11. Hutter, M.: Universal Artificial Intelligence: Sequential Decisions based on Algorithmic Probability. Springer, Heidelberg (2005)
12. Johnson-Laird, P.: Mental Models. Harvard University Press, Cambridge (1983)
13. Krumnack, U., Schwering, A., Gust, H., Kühnberger, K.-U.: Restricted Higher-Order Anti-Unification for Analogy Making. In: Orgun, M.A., Thornton, J. (eds.) AI 2007. LNCS (LNAI), vol. 4830, pp. 273–282. Springer, Heidelberg (2007)
14. McLure, M., Friedman, S., Forbus, K.: Learning concepts from sketches via analogical generalization and near-misses. In: Proceedings of the 32nd Annual Conference of the Cognitive Science Society (CogSci), Portland, OR (2010)
15. Osborne, M., Rubinstein, A.: A Course in Game Theory. MIT Press, Cambridge (1994)
16. Schwering, A., Krumnack, U., Kühnberger, K.-U., Gust, H.: Analogy as Integrating Framework for Human-Level Reasoning. In: Wang, P., Goertzel, B., Franklin, S. (eds.) Artificial General Intelligence: Proceedings of the First AGI Conference, pp. 419–423. IOS, Memphis (2008)
17. Schwering, A., Krumnack, U., Kühnberger, K.-U., Gust, H.: Syntactic Principles of Heuristic-Driven Theory Projection. Cognitive Systems Research 10(3), 251–269 (2009)
18. Stenning, K., van Lambalgen, M.: Human Reasoning and Cognitive Science. MIT Press, Cambridge (2008)
19. Thagard, P.: Explanatory Coherence. Behavioral and Brain Sciences 12(3), 435–467 (1989)
20. Thagard, P.: Coherence in Thought and Action. MIT Press, Cambridge (2002)
21. Tversky, A., Kahneman, D.: Extensional versus intuitive reasoning: The conjunction fallacy in probability judgment. Psychological Review 90(4), 293–315 (1983)
22. Wang, P.: Rigid Flexibility: The Logic of Intelligence. Springer, Heidelberg (2006)
23. Wason, P.C.: Reasoning. In: Foss, B. (ed.) New Horizons in psychology, Penguin, Harmondsworth (1966)
24. Wason, P.C., Shapiro, D.: Natural and contrived experience in a reasoning problem. The Quarterly Journal of Experimental Psychology 23(1), 63–71 (1971)

Wagging the Dog: Human *vs.* Machine Inference of Causality in Visual Sequences

Florin Popescu

Fraunhofer Institute FIRST, Berlin DE 12489
florin.popescu@first.fraunhofer.de

Abstract. Causal inference among pairs of moving objects in a visual scene is compared between human observers and state-of-the-art methods in Machine Learning for causal inference. It is shown that while humans may perform intuitive and/or reasoned statistical decisions with the same overall level of accuracy as machines, they clearly exhibit biases (or priors) in their judgment and are thus able to make decisions based on much less information than is otherwise required by statistical decision algorithms. While there is no simple explanation for how humans perform this task, connectionist learning structures which implement simple time-delayed correlations (both automatic and deliberative) relying on short-term memory mechanisms may suffice to build complex bottom-up models of the physical world and the interaction therewith.

1 Introduction

Causal understanding is one of the defining features of general intelligence: the ability to segment the observable world into autonomous agents, to construct mental models of their appearance and behavior, and to predict the interaction between self and other objects as well as amongst these other objects. While current artificial systems have shown the ability to navigate autonomously and even grasp objects, they have yet to exhibit truly intelligent behavior shown by animals such as some birds and primates, like spontaneous tool use, for which causal understanding is a key factor. Causality is one of the oldest and richest subjects of academic debate, revolving, since antiquity, around the same basic points of argument: intention, determinism and correlation ambiguity. In modern times, the causality debate has branched out in different disciplines, each of which offers widely different perspectives, aims and views of causality. On one extreme of the ideological spectrum there is statistical causal inference focused on *processes*, such as global temperatures and commodity prices. Fields such as economics, finance, climatology, neuro-imaging, machine learning, data mining and computational biology rely on unbiased statistical inference of causal interactions in large and complex databases. Other fields such as developmental psychology, cognitive science and Artificial Intelligence (AI) view causal inference from the point of view of the *subject*, i.e. the learning agent which actively and purposefully interacts with the world. Even when the environment is as simple as an office or a street, this is still a daunting challenge for an autonomous

J. Schmidhuber, K.R. Thórisson, and M. Looks (Eds.): AGI 2011, LNAI 6830, pp. 184–193, 2011.

robot. The point of causal understanding for robots is not navigation, but rather interaction: a purposeful modification of the environment. This paper will attempt, for the first time, to directly compare human behavioral causal influence with state-of-the art techniques in machine learning and signal processing on the same data, namely objects moving in a visual scene, in an attempt to unify different perspectives on causal inference and, in doing so, attempt to discuss statistical and experiential learning and intelligence from a universal perspective.

1.1   Historical Terms of Debate: Intention, Purpose, Cause, Will

It may seem unfathomable that it has been so difficult to explain a reasoning process which we actually perform so simply and ubiquitously, namely to infer causal relationships among objects, or distinguish animate from inanimate objects. One of the basic reasons for this from antiquity until the Enlightenment was the lack of mathematical tools which could provide a basis for reasoning about physics and mechanical dynamics. Another major impediment was the strong and highly confounding role of theology in this debate.[1]

The intuition, if not the metaphysics, of the idea that true causes are *intentions* can be viewed from a modern perspective in a evolutionary biology perspective. Objects which move unpredictably (not caused by any other object) require special attention as they are likely to be animate beings (the name is not accidental) which may be friend or foe. On the biological level, being able to detect animate objects and be able to generalize still requires one to build models of expected motion and interaction, and that ability must have a mathematical description and foundation.

1.2   Causality in Machine Learning

Recently there has been a lot of interest in the field of Machine Learning (ML) in causal inference, being a featured workshop/seminar topic at conferences such as NIPS in both in regular [4] and time-series data [13]. For regular, static data much of the recent interest has been pioneered by Judea Pearl [10] and Peter Spirtes [15]. This work seeks to identify connections in large multivariate datasets through application of conditional independence tests to infer a set of likely causal graphs. The spirit of this approach, like much of Machine Learning and Data Mining is the uncovering of statistical patterns from datasets with

---

[1] The philosophical dilemma of causality is that pure determinism limits divine power, whereas randomness (a concept that evolved in the last two centuries, but has precursors in arguments about free will) renders too much outside heavenly control and gives us a universe seemingly devoid of purpose. Nowhere is this conundrum more painfully clear than in the much criticized metaphysics of G. Leibniz, a versatile thinker who gave us critical analytical tools for describing dynamics and physical interactions and had theorized, building on Aristotelian concepts, that causality must also imply intention (or an agent capable of acting on his/her own will). In this view the Prime Mover was the one who initiated all action sequences, a view in which planets, stars and history itself is a mere collection of billiard balls shuffling around a table following an initial strike, a divinely calculated break.

large numbers of examples, a task that is particularly well suited for current computer technology. Some concepts discussed by Pearl, such as intervention as a test of causal hypotheses, is clearly relevant to AI, but *general* intelligence means acting in the real world on limited information, with only a handful of observations which lead to an action, or conclusion. In the case of time-series data, related work is also data-oriented as it deals with current problems mostly in economics and neural activity imaging. It is important to note that although such algorithms involve mathematical complexity which would be unlikely to be present in biological systems, some of the topics of interest are pertinent to interactive learning, namely the role of observation noise, the number of samples needed for conclusion, and the type of dynamics which are easy to correctly classify and which are not.

1.3   Causality in Artificial Intelligence

In the 90s some pioneering work in Artificial Intelligence situated robotics and machine vision focused on causal scene understanding [3] of static scenes, not only addressing with the (still) daunting tasks of image segmentation, object continuity and occlusion and 3D graphical model reconstruction, but attempting to endow the robot with a physical understanding of play-blocks, doors, even tools through rule induction and experience. A time-series causal inference study has more recently looked at [16] object pair tracking and trajectory classification in machine vision. This study actually used associative Machine Learning regression techniques in addition to Granger Causality analysis on human-labeled trajectory pair samples, in an attempt to overcome data scarcity in single trials/examples. While there is a quite a body of work related to 'developmental' robotics no artificial system has yet shown spontaneous tool use or similarly sophisticated environment interaction, possibly because of the deceptively difficult nature of this task (we can certainly program or teach a robot to use a tool, but that is another matter).

1.4   Causality in Cognitive Science, Neuroscience and Psychology

As a precursor to much of later bottom-up AI research, Jean Piaget long ago recognized the important role of causal reasoning in the development of human intelligence, and had allowed for its construction in different stages of development, beginning with the child's conceptual separation of self from other objects, which may move of their own accord [11]. In this agent-centered view, causality is inferred and built from associations of self-initiated actions and outcomes, even, in later stages the learning of causal chains which begin with the self and employ an intermediary (a tool) to control the outcome. In children and adults alike, the ability to infer relationships among objects presumes the ability to build and use their sensory footprint, to segment ambiguous visual scenes, computational tasks which are quite challenge to AI researchers at the moment.

It is not until much more recently that the neuroscientific basis and behavioral details of adult object tracking and trajectory analysis has begun to be understood. For example, until 1988 it was thought that attentional mechanisms constrain us into tracking only one object at a time: in fact we can track as many as 5 objects concurrently [14]. Our ability to do so diminishes greatly as the objects move faster or they are more closely spaced [1]. Our performance in tracking moving objects also increases with time/experience [6] suggesting that unsupervised learning of their trajectories and or inter-relationships takes place. Among brain areas identified by lesion studies as important to the ability to recognize and classify motion in the visual field are the cerebellum [5] and frontal temporal parietal areas [2] suggesting abstract/spatial reasoning and sensory association processing. Differences in recognizing semantically meaningful and unexpected visual stimuli can occur automatically at very short ('unconscious') time latencies, and electrophysiological analysis of such responses can be used in the automatic diagnosis of pathological conditions such as schizophrenia [7].

2   Experimental Methods

7 healthy volunteer subjects participated in the study (3 male, 4 female, aged 27-64, mean 41). Subjects were seated at a desk, viewing a computer monitor from a comfortable distance (40-80cm). Each subject performed 50 trials of the causal recognition task, each of which consisted in the following steps:

1. Two objects were shown arranged vertically on the screen, a red object appearing above a blue object. Both objects had similar overall visual size, their shapes being randomly chosen from either a geometric pair (triangle and square) or a pictorial diagram (top view of a dog and a tail, with semantically meaningful orientations). Which of the objects in the pair was on top was random, but the topmost object was always red. The subject was asked to initiate the trial via a click on either of these objects.
2. Once the trial was initiated, the two objects began moving on the screen for approx. 16 sec. The type of motion was either rotation of each object around the image center or horizontal translation, randomly chosen. See Fig. 1 for illustration. The temporal trajectories of the objects were chosen randomly from one of 6 categories (see Fig. 2). Whereas 4 of these categories included a causal relationship between the two objects, the direction of causal interaction was randomly chosen.
3. At the end of the trial, the subject was asked to rate the relationship between the 2 objects. A response was queried on the screen with 4 possibilities a) the RED object drove the BLUE object, b) the BLUE object drove the RED object, c) there was some relationship between the two movements but it was unclear as to which was the driver and d) the trajectories were random, i.e. unrelated. Icons for answers a) and b) were arranged horizontally on the query screen as to reduce potential bias (for image top or bottom).

Sample trajectory types are shown in Fig. 2. These trajectories are divided in two categories: non-causal ('RANDOM' and 'CORRELATED') and causal. All trajectories were generated by generating 50 points y_i according to a data

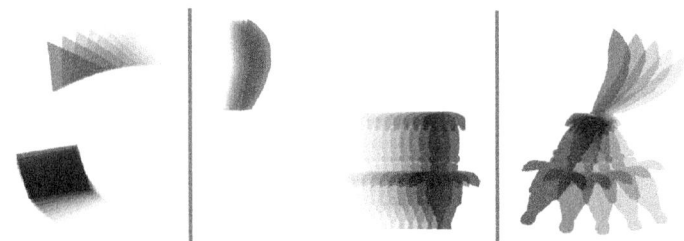

Fig. 1. Basic motion types for the causal perception experiments. Each panel represents a possible screen shot (gradated transparency shadows are meant to convey the impression of motion, screen contents include the 2 main objects only). Left, rotation of geometric objects around image center. Middle: pictorial diagrams in left/right translation. Right: pictorial diagrams in rotation.

generating process of known causal nature, then interpolating this sequence by cubic splines up to 500 points to the smooth trajectories z_i which are pictured in Fig. 2, The description of trajectory categories is:

1. RANDOM: A gaussian independent random sequence.
2. CORRELATED: A correlated pair of gaussian random sequences, where the correlation is induced by multplying 2 gaussian independent random sequences by a random 2x2 matrix (chosen before each corresponding trial) with random gaussian unit variance elements.
3. AR: Linear auto-regressive system with correlated observation noise and Gaussian innovations process w, described by:

$$y_{C,i} = \sum_{k=1}^{K} \begin{bmatrix} a_{11} & a_{12} \\ 0 & a_{22} \end{bmatrix}_{C,k} y_{C,i-k} + w_{C,i} \tag{1}$$

$$x_{N,i} = \sum_{k=1}^{K} \begin{bmatrix} a_{11} & 0 \\ 0 & a_{22} \end{bmatrix}_{N,k} x_{N,i-k} + w_{N,i} \tag{2}$$

$$y_{N,i} = B(x_{N,i} + y_{C,i}) \tag{3}$$

This type of system is described in [9] and [8] and represents a challenge to current causal estimation methods such as Granger Causality. As the protocol necessitates arbitrary causal influence, the upper triangular lag matrices are transposed when the second element of y is required to influence the first. Note that system in (1) is causal, the system in (2) is non-causal and the final output (3) is a linear mixture of the two.

4. DELAY. Here one of the signals (the driver) is a random signal as in 1. while the second is a delayed version of the driver plus random noise at 20% signal to noise ratio. The delay, it is important to note is chosen randomly according to a Gaussian distribution with standard deviation equal to 320ms, which

is the signal bandwidth frequency. This means that in approx. 50% of all such cases the delay exceeded the signal bandwidth, meaning that the two objects moved in opposite directions for most of the trial (i.e. greater than 180° lag).

5. COLLISION. The trajectory profiles (best described graphically, see Fig. 2) consist in one object moving to the edge of the screen, then back, and appearing to 'hit' the second object after which it comes to rest while the second object moves. These two roles, and the spatial direction of the initial movement, were chosen randomly.

6. IMPULSE. The same as COLLISION except the second object begins its motion before the first object reaches it. The two trajectory are actually two attenuated impulses related by a simple delay, but the appearance of object collision is not present. As in 5. the object roles were reversed randomly.

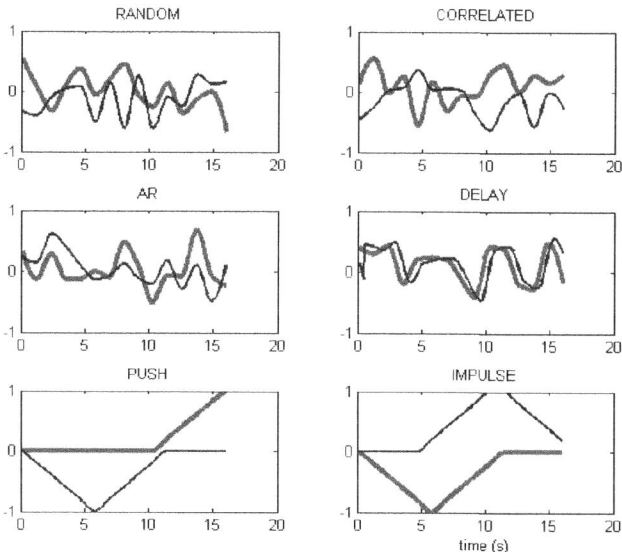

Fig. 2. Basic trajectories for causal perception experiments. See text for description of each category of trajectory.

The basic motions were either left/right translation normalized such that the objects remained on screen of rotation such that the maximal rotation is +/- 90° from a 12 or 6 o'clock orientation.

For purposes of comparison, an automatic, low sample size version of the recently introduced Phase Slope Index, which outperforms standard Granger Causality in the presence of correlated noise (cases 2 and 3) and other state of the art methods (see [8] for definition and [12] for comparison). PSI is a co-herence=weighted average phase roll-off integral over frequency, which GC is information flow in upper/lower triangular (*aka* causal) AR models. The basic method relies on spectral estimation (which includes relative phase estimation) and is comparable with auto-regressive approaches to causality assignment (altough at the present time it outperforms them). The final statistic provided by PSI includes an estimate of its variability via a 5-fold bootstrap and the decision threshold was chosen as to statistically match the false positive rate (type I error) shown by the human subjects (see [12] for details). If no decision on causality could be made, a correlation test with a threshold of p=0.05 was used to distinguish between correlated and random trajectory cases,

3 Human *vs.* Automatic Causal Inference: Results

The main results are presented in Table 1. The correlations are calculated by assigning 0 to cases of RANDOM and CORRELATED and 1 or -1 to all other (causal) trials. Note that the human subjects exhibit a small, but significant bias toward the 'dog wagging the tail' (the machine does not, as expected). Note also that the object that is originally clicked in order to begin the trial is not chosen more often as a cause. The level of significance (after Bonferroni correction for multiple comparisons) is $\alpha < .10$.

Table 1. Main table of inference accuracy human *vs.* machine

	HUMAN		MACHINE	
† nonsignificant	rho	P value	rho	P value
initial click to causal inference	0.01	0.89†	0.13	0.13†
dog/tail to causal inference	0.19	0.01	-0.09	0.26†
overall response (-1,0,1)	0.35	0.00	0.37	0.00
response (-1,0,1) AR	0.07	0.59†	0.19	0.14†
response (-1,0,1) DELAY	0.08	0.59†	0.28	0.05†
response (-1,0,1) DELAY SHORT	0.21	0.36†	1.00	0.00
response (-1,0,1) COLLISION	0.61	0.00	0.00	0.00
response (-1,0,1) IMPULSE	0.68	0.00	0.64	0.00
response (-1,0,1) GEOMETRIC ROTATES	0.35	0.00	0.39	0.00
response (-1,0,1) GEOMETRIC TRANSLATES	0.37	0.00	0.35	0.00
response (-1,0,1) DOG ROTATES	0.31	0.00	0.27	0.01
response (-1,0,1) DOG TRANSLATES	0.38	0.00	0.42	0.00

Table 1 also shows a breakdown of response correlation with trajectory relation type 3-6 (causal). There is no noticeable (or statistically significant) difference in response accuracy among the different causal condition (except for delay systems in which the delay is less than the bandwidth, i.e. in which the time delay is represented by an object's motion being visually correlated but delayed with respect to the other). Table 2 shows a confusion matrix between the basic relationships among objects, RAND (random), CORR (correlated but not causal) and RED or BLUE, meaning causal with direction RED to BLUE or BLUE to RED. The is no statistical difference among RAND and CORR responses in human subjects.

Table 2. Confusion matrix Human *vs.* machine

	HUMAN				MACHINE			
	RAND	**CORR**	**RED**	**BLUE**	**RAND**	**CORR**	**RED**	**BLUE**
RAND	0.32	0.29	0.16	0.23	0.66	0.05	0.16	0.13
CORR	0.21	0.32	0.16	0.31	0.13	0.54	0.18	0.15
RED	0.25	0.14	0.49	0.12	0.27	0.22	0.45	0.06
BLUE	0.30	0.18	0.13	0.39	0.40	0.30	0.06	0.24

4   Discussion

Overall the results show a surprising parity in overall performance among machine (or Machine Learning) techniques and human observers. Yet a breakdown of performance among causal relation types shows a striking pattern of differences. First, as suspected and as the title suggests, there is a human bias toward dogs wagging tails. While this is not all that surprising, note that there was no evidence of a similarly expected priming effect by which intention (clicking on an objects) is confused with causation. It also did not matter if the dog/tail movement was 'physiological' (rotation) or translation: subjects indeed seem to make quite well reasoned and rational judgments. The bias towards dogs wagging tails rather than vice versa is hardly a sign of disingenuous stereotyping - as a matter of fact it is a stereotype machine intelligence would be hard pressed to reproduce at the present time - as dogs and tails would have to be segmented from background and recognized (without restricting the object category) first. In this study it was taken for granted that objects are segmented and tracked in a visual scene, and that their shapes are recognized and compared to a wide database which has priors on possible relationships among expected objects. The bias in question is quite rational from a Bayesian standpoint given that the motions presented were in fact, as subjects reported and the results show, difficult to classify and the evidence scant. Another striking effect was that human subjects could not accurately identify causality in the AR (auto-regressive) case, which has the visual impression of a viscoelastic coupling between objects. Also human subjects had difficulty establishing causal relationships in which delays were long enough for the objects to move out of phase. As can be seen in Table 2, humans could not truly distinguish among random and correlated trajectories, something that the automatic algorithm could do well.

The machine on the other hand had difficulty with the COLLISION example. It may seem surprising, as the relationship is simple enough to the eye (once the trajectories are plotted) and certainly a machine can learn to classify such cases associatively. It is not so easy to do so for the general case however, without having built a more abstract concept/model of physical object interaction. The reason for this is that current time-series causality assignment algorithms assume stationarity, which allows spectral decomposition or autoregressive modeling in linear or quadratic time. If this assumption is relaxed, then time-series would have to be segmented first (into segments that are in themselves stationary or consistent) - an NP hard problem. Note that stochasticity and stationarity are important for a further reason, namely the fact that a fair amount of information is needed to make a statistically robust decision: the COLLISION example contains no more than a few scant bits of information: some sort of prior must be used. See [12] for a general definition of causality based on algorithmic information theory, in which a sequence is likely caused by another if the rate of relative conditional information (compression) is higher using past and current state of the presumed cause. If either series contains hardly any information, it is impossible to draw conclusions from the data alone. Note also that the PHASE examples, which are similar, do accidentally provide a clear spectral decomposition and a phase lag that can be used for causal assignment. Human ability to use memory at different time scales, to automatically segment visual input in both space and time despite the curse of dimensionality and to find correlations among a large variety of inputs is key to be able to interpret non-stationary signals (human segmentation of speech and music is, for example, unparalleled). One of the conclusions of a recent workshop on the topic of human intelligence and the curse of dimensionality (http://cnl.salk.edu/~terry/NIPS-Workshop/2009/) was that humans perform amazingly difficult perception tasks by massive parallelism but also by simply taking necessary shortcuts: by placing restrictive priors and limiting attention, one may make quick practical decisions but leave room for increased error.

This study is the first in a line of investigation that is quite new, namely human causal perception of moving objects. Several issues remain to be investigated, such as the effect of learning, in particular if classification of complex causal relationships such as the AR case can be improved by practice, and how simpler human like causal perception may be modeled on a bottom-up connectionist embodiment in a mobile robot. The problems of perception of out-of-phase motion in the DELAY case leads one to believe that an automatic causal inference method could be as simple as spatial motion correlation (a visual cortex processing task) coupled with consistent spatial lag. This type of automatic (but error prone) mechanism could be used as a building block in more complex models of dynamic object interaction, and even provide a basis for deliberative processes which, as the subjects of the study reported was the case, involve explicit reasoning lasting a period of several seconds about what kind of physical analogy or algorithmic relationship was most relevant and best explained the observations.

References

1. Alvarez, G.A., Franconeri, S.L.: How many objects can you track? evidence for a resource-limited attentive tracking mechanism. Journal of Vision 7(13) 14, 1–10 (2007)
2. Billino, J., Braun, D.I., Boehm, K., Bremmer, F., Gegenfurtner, K.R.: Cortical networks for motion processing: effects of focal brain lesions on perception of different motion types. Neuropsychologia 47(10), 2133–2144 (2009)
3. Brand, M., Birnbaum, L., Cooper, P.: Sensible scenes: Visual understanding of complex structures through causal analysis (1993)

4. Guyon, I., Janzing, D., Schölkopf, B.: Causality: Objectives and assessment. JMLR W&CP 6, 1–38 (2010)
5. HÃndel, B., Thier, P., Haarmeier, T.: Visual motion perception deficits due to cerebellar lesions are paralleled by specific changes in cerebro-cortical activity. The Journal of Neuroscience: The Official Journal of the Society for Neuroscience 29(48), 15126–15133 (2009)
6. Makovski, T., Vázquez, G.A., Jiang, Y.V.: Visual learning in Multiple-Object tracking. PLoS ONE 3(5), e2228 (2008), http://dx.plos.org/10.1371/journal.pone.0002228
7. Neuhaus, A.H., Popescu, F.C., Grozea, C., Hahn, E., Hahn, C., Opgen-Rhein, C., Urbanek, C., Dettling, M.: Single-subject classification of schizophrenia by event-related potentials during selective attention. NeuroImage 55(2), 514–521 (2011)
8. Nolte, G., Ziehe, A., Kraemer, N., Popescu, F., Müller, K.R.: Comparison of granger causality and phase slope index. Journal of Machine Learning Research Workshop & Conference Proceedings. Causality: Objectives and Assessment, 267–276 (2010)
9. Nolte, G., Ziehe, A., Nikulin, V., Schlögl, A., Krämer, N., Brismar, T., Müller, K.R.: Robustly estimating the flow direction of information in complex physical systems. Physical Review Letters 00(23), 234101 (2008)
10. Pearl, J.: Causality: Models, Reasoning and Inference. Cambridge University Press, Cambridge (2000)
11. Pearson, A.T.: Piaget's conception of causality. Educational Theory 22(4), 434–442 (2007)
12. Popescu, F.: Robust statistics for describing causality in multivariate time series. Journal of Machine Learning Research, Workshop and Conference Proceedings 12, 30–64 (2011)
13. Popescu, F., Guyon, I. (eds.): Journal of Machine Learning Research Workshop and Conference Proceedings: Causality in Time Series 12 (2011)
14. Pylyshyn, Z.W., Storm, R.W.: Tracking multiple independent targets: evidence for a parallel tracking mechanism. Spatial Vision 3(3), 179–197 (1988)
15. Spirtes, P., Glymour, C., Scheines, R.: Causation, Prediction, and Search, 2nd edn. MIT Press, Cambridge (2000)
16. Zhou, Y., Yan, S., Huang, T.S.: Pair-activity classification by bi-trajectories analysis. In: IEEE Conference on Computer Vision and Pattern Recognition, Anchorage, AK, USA, pp. 1–8 (2008)

Learning Problem Solving Skills from Demonstration: An Architectural Approach

Haris Dindo[1], Antonio Chella[1], Giuseppe La Tona[1],
Monica Vitali[1], Eric Nivel[2], and Kristinn R. Thórisson[2,3]

[1] Computer Science Engineering, University of Palermo (UNIPA/DINFO)
Viale delle Scienze, Ed. 6, 90100 Palermo, Italy
{haris.dindo,chella}@unipa.it, latona@dinfo.unipa.it,
vitali@dinfo.unipa.it

[2] Center for Analysis & Design of Intelligent Agents and School of Computer Science
(CADIA)
Reykjavik University, Menntavegur 1, IS-101 Reykjavik, Iceland
nivel@ru.is

[3] Icelandic Institute for Intelligent Machines
Uranus 2. h., Menntavegur 1, IS-101 Reykjavik, Iceland
thorisson@iiim.is

Abstract. We present an architectural approach to learning problem solving skills from demonstration, using internal models to represent problem-solving operational knowledge. Internal forward and inverse models are initially learned through active interaction with the environment, and then enhanced and finessed by observing expert teachers. While a single internal model is capable of solving a single goal-oriented task, it is their sequence that enables the system to hierarchically solve more complex task. Activation of models is goal-driven, and internal "mental" simulations are used to predict and anticipate future rewards and perils and to make decisions accordingly. In this approach intelligent system behavior emerges as a coordinated activity of internal models over time governed by sound architectural principles. In this paper we report preliminary results using the game of Sokoban, where the aim is to learn goal-oriented patterns of model activations capable of solving the problem in various contexts.

1 Introduction

Complex systems require a significant amount of work to be programmed and maintained. Research on *programming by demonstration*, or *imitation learning*, has recently been seen by the scientific community as a promising approach for simplifying programming efforts. It is inspired by the remarkable ability of humans to learn skills by simply watching others performing them. From the methodological point of view, programming by demonstration is an efficient

J. Schmidhuber, K.R. Thórisson, and M. Looks (Eds.): AGI 2011, LNAI 6830, pp. 194–203, 2011.
© Springer-Verlag Berlin Heidelberg 2011

method for pruning high-dimensional search space and it makes the task of learning problem solving skills computationally feasible. However, these advantages come at the cost of increased architectural complexity and are still far from being solved in the scientific community.

In this paper we describe an architecture[1] for learning problem solving skills from demonstration and by active interaction with the environment. In contrast to *constructionist* A.I., in which complete specification of knowledge is provided by human programmers, ours is a *constructivist* A.I. approach, where an architecture continuously expands by self-generating code (e.g. models) [1]. We target *goal-level imitation*, where imitation is seen as the process of achieving the intention hidden in the observation of an action[2]. In other words, it is not the means that are imitated but rather the goal of a demonstration. Central to the computational modeling of such intentional actions is the idea that understanding others can be efficiently achieved by reenacting one's own internal models in simulation [3]. It is thought that similar mechanisms could lead to higher cognitive processes like *imagery, anticipation* and *theory of mind*[4,5]

We are working towards an architecture that can incrementally learn sequences of internal model activations from demonstration. It is based on the idea of coupled forward-inverse *internal models* for representing goal-directed behaviors [6,7]. A *forward model* is a predictor that, given the state of the system and a command, produces a prediction of the future outcome of the given command. An *inverse model*, known also as controller in control theory, produces command(s) necessary to reach a goal state given the present state. Internal models are powerful constructs able to represent operational knowledge of an agent and to govern its interaction with the environment. While a single internal model is capable of solving a single goal-oriented task, it is their sequence that enables the system to hierarchically solve more complex task.

The architecture is thus model-based and model-driven, and it solves all tasks by exploiting the set of such learned internal models. The system is designed to avoid the use of explicit planning: intelligent behavior emerges from the interaction of incrementally learned skills. Internal models encode various behavior of the system and an ad hoc module is responsible for coordinating the activation of the most significant internal models given the actual state of the system and the goal. In a similar way, learning of complex skills is achieved by composing and coordinating simple ones (as encoded by models).

The article is organized as follows. We first give a high-level overview of our architecture in sec. 2, and then we discuss how is the architecture used to learn skills by imitation in sec. 3. Section 4 explains how the architecture has been used to learn problem solving skills in typical A.I. test-bed, the Sokoban game. Finally, we outline the conclusions and future works in sec. 5.

---

[1] The architecture is being built by the HUMANOBS consortium as part of the HUMANOBS FP7 project led by CADIA/Reykjavik University; details of this architecture will be presented in future papers.

2   Architecture

While the architecture we are building will be extensively described in future publications, a cursory overview of its main components relevant to imitation learning will now be given. The basic building blocks of our architecture are internal models, both forward and inverse, which represent an agent's functional knowledge (i.e. they are executable), and are learned by the system through continuous interaction with the environment. The system is able to observe how the environment changes as a consequence of an event (both exogenous and self-produced) and to encode this causal relation between the current context and a proximal goal into an internal model. Complex chains of causal relations, linking the current context to a distal goal, are learned by adopting the paradigm of imitation learning where the agent focuses its computational efforts on interesting parts of the problem search space only.

Models operate on *states* of the world, including those regarding the agent itself. We will formalize the notion of the state shortly. For the discussion that follows, it suffices to stress that states need not to be complete (in a Markovian sense), nor uniquely defined. In this respect, states will be composed of facts that hold in the world.

The agent senses the world through *messages*, where each element of a message holds a true fact in the world as observed through a set of predefined perceptual processes. Each time a change is detected in the world (either as the effect of agent's actions or external phenomena) a message is generated. Messages are given in the form *marker-value*, where *value* can be of any kind (integer, boolean, string, etc.). Having introduced messages, the state can be defined as a collection of messages produced by a set of predefined perceptual processes related to the world (including the agent itself).

Internal models operate on states. An internal model is a structure containing a couple of pattern lists and a production. The pattern lists restrict the applicability of a model: a state can be input to a model only if its messages match the patterns on the list. The same structure is used to encode forward and inverse models. The qualifiers 'forward' and 'inverse' describe a pattern-matching-wise arrangement of said models and their inputs: shall the latter match the right-side, the model operates as an inverse model, a forward model otherwise.

Learning is initially triggered by domain-dependent knowledge stored in a component called *Masterplan*. It stores a set of primitive skills together with an initial ontology, goals and heuristics needed to monitor the learning progress. By directly interacting with the world the system generates hypotheses of new models through a component called *Model proposer*. These will be stored in Masterplan and tested in real situations in order to assess their usefulness.

The system learns new models by observing the world and interacting with it. The components depicted in Fig. 1 continuously analyze the perceptual data in order to acquire new knowledge. Initially the system interacts with the world executing casual actions in order to learn simple causal relations of the entities of the world and of itself - a process common in newborns called *motor babbling* [8].

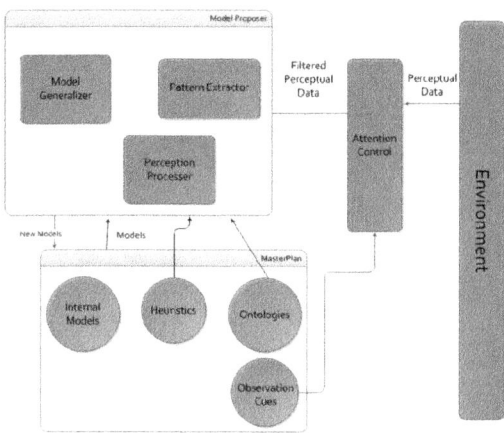

Fig. 1. How does the learning happen in the system? Environment is sensed through a set of existing models, and obtained percepts are analyzed in order to generate novel models by the "Model proposer" component. Models can be as simple as a composition of simple facts of the world, or complex sequences of existing models. This process is bootstrapped by existing knowledge stored in a component called 'Masterplan'. Generated models are themselves stored in the Masterplan for their validation and possible future usage. Interaction with the environment is performed through the Model execution component, which is directly connected with the world.

More complex models, encoded as chains of simple models activations, are learned by observing other skilled actors performing goal-directed tasks.

In order to exhibit robustness, the system must be able to generalize learned behaviors to novel, previously unseen, situations. To do this the system needs to reason about its own models and propose new, more general, models. In addition, the agent has to *anticipate* its future and to make decisions based not only on the actual and previous states of the system, but also on a prediction of a future state. Our architecture offers a mechanism of anticipation that is based on the knowledge encoded in the internal models.

When acting, the agent needs to decide what to do in a particular situation in order to achieve its goals. Fig. 2 depicts the components used to exploit models for acting. A *decision making* module, the Decision maker, is responsible of selecting which internal models to execute given the goal and the current situation. Decisions are made reactively and in parallel by exploiting all the available knowledge at present. Since multiple decisions can be made, we have developed a module that anticipates potentially useless or dangerous choices, and uses this information to decide which decision to execute. The Simulation module predicts the outcome of a decision by chaining the activations of internal models. The Decision maker uses the heuristics defined in the Masterplan to evaluate the desirability of a predicted future state. The Anticipation module analyzes the simulation looking for failures of the system or difficulties encountered. Consequently, it might suggest anticipating a future production in order to avoid such situations.

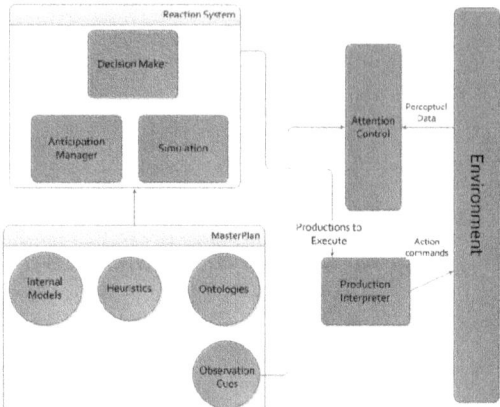

Fig. 2. How does the system act? Interactions with the environment are performed through the "Model execution" module which is controlled by a "Decision maker" component. The former is responsible for the coordination of acquired models of the system. The anticipation module is responsible for simulating the execution of models and their online correction.

3   Learning Problem Solving Skills

Models encode problem-solving skills as chains of actions towards a goal, parameterized through patterns expressing states in which models are applicable (i.e. preconditions). For the discussion that follows, it is convenient to introduce a distinction between *low-level* and *high-level* models. In our definition, low-level models encode a *direct* causal relations between events the agent observes. For example, a low-level model could describe how a room illumination changes as a consequence of pushing the switch. On the other hand, high-level models prescribe actions needed to reach distal goals, or to predict the outcome of a present action arbitrarily far in the future. As an example, a high-level model can describe how to switch on the light in a different room from the one the agent is currently in. Such a scenario would require the agent to exit the room, reach the desired room, enter it, look for the switch and turn it on, where each act in the chain could be described by either a low- or high-level model.

The system tries to explain the events it observes in terms of its current repository of internal models by reenacting them in simulation. Whenever it fails, model learning is triggered which proposes new models. The Model proposer component produces a new low-level model by analyzing differences in state before and after an action has been executed, or an external event has been observed. We assume that each state transition can always be conveniently expressed as a combination of *elementary models* stored in the Masterplan. The module called Pattern Extractor is responsible for generating the patterns on the messages that will be used to restrict the application of a model to situations similar to the observed one. Finally, the Model proposer produces a new forward model that predicts a state transition given an input. By inverting the forward model, the system produces its corresponding inverse model.

High-level models are learned through imitation learning. This process is accomplished by observing a demonstrator carrying out a task and trying to match its behavior with the set of available models.[2] To this end, forward and inverse models are used in couples to *rank* activations of those models that best explain the current observation (see [3] for details). A dedicated process is in charge of analyzing the sequence of activated models in order to detect *key states* encountered during demonstrations which will constitute sub-goals for the learning agent. The Model proposer then produces a sequence of sub-goals and patterns which compose the high-level model (patterns are produced in the same way as in low-level model acquisition).

However, newly acquired low- and high-level models are too specific since they have been learned from a single observation. As an example, suppose the agent learns how to switch on the light in a room. The model created is initially tailored to the particular room where the demonstration has been performed, as the agent has no means to assess whether the model could be applied in similar situations. A module called *Model generalizer* is responsible for the generation of new models that inductively generalize more specific ones. This process is triggered each time a model is created that shares the production section with a previously acquired model. If the only difference between these models is their pattern section, meaning that the same model can possibly be applied to both situations. A set of predefined rewriting procedures are applied that create a single, more general model.

3.1   Bootstrapping the Learning Process: Masterplan

Masterplan stores the domain-dependent knowledge that all the domain-independent components of the system use to produce new models and hence new knowledge. The Masterplan is not a fixed entity: it expands as the agent acquires novel knowledge through its own experience and learning.

In our system, prior knowledge in the Masterplan includes:

- a set of a-priori defined forward and inverse models; these models are augmented at runtime through the processes of motor babbling and imitation learning (the initial cannot be empty);
- a set of innate goals/subgoals and a monitoring process which provides the currently active goals/subgoals;
- facts about salient aspects in the world;
- an ontology which describes relations between entities in the world;
- a heuristic which evaluates the goodness of a state given a set of subgoals;
- a list of primitive actions the agent can perform: more complex behaviors will be hierarchically built starting from the same set of elementary ones.

---

[2] Demonstrations should be performed in a bottom-up way: whether a task includes complex subtask, these should be thought first.

Starting from these "innate" principles, the agent will be able to acquire knowledge by direct experience and to learn strategies through observation of other expert teachers. During interaction, only *relevant* aspects of the world are taken into consideration through a set of predefined attention mechanisms in the Masterplan. The Masterplan also holds predicates for assessing the similarity between two sets of messages, used to guide the learning phase.

New models are learned by combining innate *primitive* models provided in the Masterplan. In our architecture, these *primitive models* are defined by programmers as a set of *elementary functions* describing known facts about state transitions; a primitive model can e.g. relate position and velocity through known physical laws which combine elementary functions of multiplication and addition, and a set of *ontological relations* which describes how these functions can be applied to a given state (e.g. multiplication is not well defined for string variables).

4   Case Study: Sokoban

In order to test the ideas described we chose a simplified version of the well-known Sokoban game as a case study, which presents a handy subset of our ultimate target application field(s) of the architecture. Sokoban is classified as a motion planning PSPACE-complete problem and as an NP-HARD space problem [9].

In our version of the game the agent moves a given number of blocks randomly placed in a grid; the goal is to place each block in a given final position. The number of blocks is a free parameter and can be set by the user. In our experiments we decided to use three blocks. An example of an initial grid configuration is shown in Fig.3 (left).

Whenever the agent performs an action, its perceptual sensors produce messages related to its position in the environment, and that of blocks. Messages indicating whether a block is next to another, or whether a block is next to the border are also given. The Masterplan holds a set of a-priori facts and models about the game. We defined *elementary functions* of the *primitive models* as mathematical and logical functions that compose any state transition as a consequence to an agent's act. These functions are *increment* and *decrement* for the numerical values, *negate* for logical values and the *identity* function that can be applied to any value. We have also defined ontological relations that specify how the elementary functions can be applied to the elements of a state (e.g. the increment and decrement functions can be applied to the coordinate of the blocks and of the agent). The Model proposer module analyzes the perceived transitions of state as a composition of elementary functions; the ontological relations are the constraints for this analysis.

The Masterplan also holds a heuristic to evaluate a state with respect to the desired goals. This heuristic is based on the Manhattan distance of blocks from their desired position and on the measure of the degrees of freedom of both the agent and the blocks (in order to avoid deadlock configurations).

Instead of focusing on the computational costs of our approach and on comparing it to other Sokoban solvers, we have performed experiments aiming to assess the validity of our architecture as a general architecture for learning problem solving skills by imitation. We present results for various aspects of the architecture.

To test the results we consider how the agent predicts the outcome of an action in a set of defined states. This set of states was chosen to represent some of the most commonly encountered situations in the Sokoban game, together with few particular and rare configurations.

By analyzing the results of the motor babbling we provide an evaluation of the performances of the model acquisition and generalization processes. The parameters used in the motor babbling phase are: a) the number of actions to execute for each trial and b) the total number of trials. We have performed several tests by varying these parameters.

To evaluate models learned by imitation we have collected feedback from a group of randomly chosen subjects who have been asked to demonstrate a particular problem solving behavior to the system.[3] After the learning phase, each subject has been asked to grade the system's ability to solve similar tasks in a range of situations: a) whether the system was able to successfully complete the task and b) give a score from 1 to 10 related to the quality of the observed behavior, 10 being best and 0 meaning "no ability to perform".

4.1   Results: Motor Babbling

For each run of the motor babbling, we store the predictions of the system for each of the encountered states. These predictions are then compared to the real outcome of the actions in corresponding states.

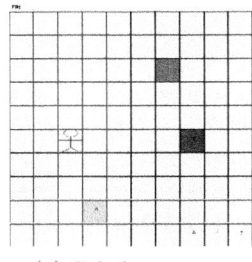

(a) Sokoban game

	50	100	150	200
50	0.375	0.375	0.375	0.375
100	0.375	0.5	0.5	0.5
150	0.7	0.7	0.7	0.8
200	0.8	0.88	0.88	0.88
250	0.9	0.9	0.9	0.9
300	0.9	1	1	1

(b) Motor babbling results

Fig. 3. (left) A possible state in the Sokoban game; (right) Performance of our architecture in motor babbling: columns represent the number of steps in a trial, while rows represent the total number of trials; each cell contains the success ratio in predicting the correct outcome

---

[3] Participants were 6 male and 3 female PhD students from our lab; each participant played twelve trials on average.

Through the motor babbling phase the system acquires its low-level internal models and learns how to interact with the environment. As shown in the experimental data(see table 3 (right)), the accuracy of the predictions grows with the number of trials played and actions taken. This could at first sound obvious: by increasing the number of trials we increase the amount of available data to analyze. However, it is worth noticing that the number of actions executed in a trial plays a marginal role compared to the total number of trials played. This can be explained by the fact that the motor babbling in a specific game tends to remain in states that are similar to the initial one. In order for the system to experience a wider range of situations, we need to increase the number of trials played.

4.2   Results: Imitation

The results of the human demonstrator evaluation of subsequent system performance, after demonstrations, show that the system is able to learn new skills from the demonstration and to apply them in novel situations. Satisfaction analysis shows that more than 80% of participants judged the system's performances "more than sufficient" (a vote greater than 6). In particular, when the system was able to anticipate a production the evaluation was greater or equal than 8. This confirms that the anticipation ability is subjectively considered a necessary skill for any intelligent behavior.

5   Conclusions

In this paper we described new principles for learning complex problem solving skills through imitation. Our approach is based on *constructivist A.I.* principles, which proposes pervasive architectural self-modification as prerequisites for holistic system learning and self-expansion [1]. Our architecture allows self-expansion through a set of modules and a "Masterplan" that encodes initial bootstrapping knowledge to guide it. Before acting in the real world a system based on this approach runs actions in "simulation mode" using internal models, for the purposes of anticipation. These same set of models also enable our system to reach its goals, provided real-world experiences; our architecture allows the system to learn its internal models by observing other skilled actors.

As the whole architecture is model-based, learning is devoted to constantly acquiring new forward and inverse models. However, learning does not occur from scratch but it is rather bootstrapped by domain-dependent knowledge contained in the Masterplan; it holds the so called "first principles" that enables the system to learn more complex goal-directed behaviors. This approach has an obvious advantage over more traditional (i.e. hand-coded) architectures, as it allows "goal-level" imitation, in which what is learned is the goal of the demonstration, rather than a particular sequence of acts to imitate. This is the most powerful way of learning, as the system acquires what amounts to an "understanding" of a set of actions - that is, the knowledge that the system acquires lends itself to explaining, which in turn (in our approach) allows the system to evaluate alternative explanations and choose between them based on available evidence.

Future work will focus on making the principles presented here more robust, expanding the architecture to be able to learn not only goals but also actively choosing which level of detail is appropriate to imitate, e.g. surface-level (morphology), goal-level (intention), or some combination thereof. Such a system should be applicable to a wide range of task learning scenarios, as many human-level tasks are in principle a complex mixture of the two. By having addressed the more difficult of these, namely goal-level imitation, we are optimistic about creating such a system in the near future.

Acknowledgments. This work has been supported in part by the EU funded project HUMANOBS: Humanoids That Learn Socio-Communicative Skills Through Observation, contract no. FP7-STREP-231453 (www.humanobs.org). The authors would like to thank the HUMANOBS Consortium for valuable discussions and ideas, which have greatly benefited this work.

References

1. Thórisson, K.R.: From constructionist to constructivist AI. AAAI Fall Symposium Series: Biologically Inspired Cognitive Architectures, AAAI Tech Report FS-09-01:175–183 (2009)
2. Chella, A., Dindo, H., Infantino, I.: A cognitive framework for imitation learning. Robotics and Autonomous Systems 54(5), 403–408 (2006), doi:10.1016/j.robot.2006.01.008.
3. Wolpert, D.M., Doya, K., Kawato, M.: A unifying computational framework for motor control and social interaction. Philosophical Transactions of the Royal Society B: Biological Sciences 358(1431), 593 (2003)
4. Grush, R.: The emulation theory of representation: Motor control, imagery, and perception. Behavioral and brain sciences 27(03), 377–396 (2004)
5. Demiris, Y.: Prediction of intent in robotics and multi-agent systems. Cognitive Processing 8(3), 151–158 (2007)
6. Kawato, M.: Internal models for motor control and trajectory planning. Current opinion in neurobiology 9(6), 718–727 (1999)
7. Wolpert, D.M., Ghahramani, Z.: Computational motor control. Science (269), 718–727 (2004)
8. Meltzoff, A.N., Moore, M.K.: Explaining facial imitation: A theoretical model. Early development and parenting 6(34), 179–192 (1997)
9. Dor, D., Zwick, U.: SOKOBAN and other motion planning problems. Computational Geometry 13(4), 215–228 (1999)

Compression and Intelligence: Social Environments and Communication

David L. Dowe[1], José Hernández-Orallo[2], and Paramjit K. Das[1]

[1] Computer Science and Software Engineering, Clayton School of Information Technology, Monash University, Vic. 3800, Australia
david.dowe@infotech.monash.edu.au, pdas3@student.monash.edu.au
[2] DSIC, Universitat Politècnica de València, València, Spain
jorallo@dsic.upv.es

Abstract. Compression has been advocated as one of the principles which pervades inductive inference and prediction - and, from there, it has also been recurrent in definitions and tests of intelligence. However, this connection is less explicit in new approaches to intelligence. In this paper, we advocate that the notion of compression can appear again in definitions and tests of intelligence through the concepts of 'mind-reading' and 'communication' in the context of multi-agent systems and social environments. Our main position is that two-part Minimum Message Length (MML) compression is not only more natural and effective for agents with limited resources, but it is also much more appropriate for agents in (co-operative) social environments than one-part compression schemes - particularly those using a posterior-weighted mixture of all available models following Solomonoff's theory of prediction. We think that the realisation of these differences is important to avoid a naive view of 'intelligence as compression' in favour of a better understanding of how, why and where (one-part or two-part, lossless or lossy) compression is needed.

Keywords: two-part compression, Minimum Message Length (MML), Solomonoff theory of prediction, tests of intelligence, communication.

1 Compression, Inference, Prediction and Intelligence

Several authors [1,5,6,11,7,9] have suggested the relevance of compression to intelligence, especially the inductive inferential (or inductive learning) part of intelligence. M. Hutter even proposed a compression contest (the Hutter prize) which was "motivated by the fact that being able to compress well is closely related to acting intelligently" (http://prize.hutter1.net) [2, footnote 180]. However, many compression algorithms are able to compress data in a much better way than humans (either lossless or lossy compression). Humans are better at compressing information which is relevant to their goals (or rewards). So, many agree that compression must have a role, but it is not clear which kind of compression must be considered.

J. Schmidhuber, K.R. Thórisson, and M. Looks (Eds.): AGI 2011, LNAI 6830, pp. 204–211, 2011.
© Springer-Verlag Berlin Heidelberg 2011

One position advocated is that two-part Minimum Message Length (MML) compression [26,28,25,4], which states the theory in the first part, gives the inductive inference part of intelligence [5,6]. Other authors have considered the one-part Solomonoff predictive compression [20] to be the appropriate way of using the data for modelling, perhaps due to its emphasis on prediction rather than explanation and its presumed consequent superiority in predicting the future.

The relationship between MML and Kolmogorov complexity, the similarities between Wallace's MML inference/explanation work and Solomonoff's predictive work – and the subtle difference between inference/explanation and prediction – have been discussed in [28][25, chap. 2]. In short, Solomonoff will take a posterior-weighted mixture of all available models, and so his predictive approach will typically involve something which is not one of the available models - whereas the Wallace MML approach will use the single best available model. Technically, a mixture of models may not compress at all, since encoding all (or a great number of) the possible models may require more bits than the data itself.

In addition, there seems to be confusion amongst many authors about the distinction between one-part and (MML) two-part compression. In one-part compression, we simply wish to encode the data. In two-part (MML) compression, we wish to encode the model in the first part of the message and then we encode the data given the model in the second part of the message [28][25, chap. 2]. An alternative way of describing the two-part coding is that a (possibly Universal) Turing machine (TM) could read the first part of the message, whereupon it would write nothing but rather go into an "educated" state or become an Educated Turing Machine (ETM) [25, chap. 2][28]. Upon reading the second part of the message (which encodes the data), the (now Educated) TM would perform a decoding and then write out the data.

However, in terms of a single agent operating in some environment, it will clearly predict better (even if only slightly) when using the Solomonoff predictive distribution. Nonetheless, if the agent is time-limited – as it typically will be in a realistic environment – then there will be disadvantages to using the entire Solomonoff posterior predictive distribution. Indeed, this will typically involve infinite summations and – further – the uncomputability of the Halting problem. It is worth mentioning, though, that some approximations can work in practice (such as Monte Carlo AIXI [24]) by reducing the number of models in the mixture.

Partly in response to Searle's "Chinese room" argument [19], we also raise the issue of compression as a non-behavioural (introspective) indicator of intelligence - i.e., given two agents who have scored equally well on a test and one of which compresses better than the other, which should we prefer [5, sec. 5.1][6, sec. 5][4, sec. 7.3]?[1] We compare this to other purely behavioural ways of assessing and detecting intelligence.

---

[1] We certainly note [16, sec. 5.2] that human society gives Nobel prizes and various other accolades to those who give a good single theory (or MML explanation) for observed data. Examples include (e.g.) special/general relativity, Helicobacter pylori as the cause of stomach ulcers, etc.

The rest of the paper analyses the relation between the several views and applications of the notion of compression and intelligence, focussing on social environments and communication.

2   Social Environments and Communication

Social environments and multi-agent systems generally include competition and co-operation. For competition, it is necessary to have mind-reading abilities in order to anticipate what other agents might do (predator-preys, games such as the *prisoners' dilemma*, etc.). While we could perhaps use a mixture of models for these social environments as well, the other agents are resource-bounded, and they will generally act according to a reduced number of models – or a single one. Consequently, using a large mixture of models to explain and predict the behaviour of other agents seems inefficient and unrealistic.

Nonetheless, it is in co-operation where the different approaches to inductive inference and prediction perhaps become more apparent. First, co-operation implies communication. In order to communicate a concept, we need an efficiently compressed expression of the concept. We do not expect to transmit a mixture of models but a single model. Second, in order to transmit (i.e., understand) the concept, we need descriptions which are clearly separated from the data. Here, a two-part compression seems to have advantages over a one-part compression, since with the former it is easier to extract the concept or model we want to communicate. Third, in co-operation, agents need to share models and procedures. In other words, agents should share the same ontology. This is only possible if the ontology can be isolated from the data – and if it is the same for all.

Let us elaborate upon the points from the above paragraph with some examples. The creation of language is about developing a set of (hierarchical) concepts for the purposes of concise description of the observed world and correspondingly concise communication. Elaborating upon the ideas outlined in [25, chap. 9] (and [2, footnote 128][4, sec. 7.2]), this can be thought of as a problem of (hierarchical) intrinsic classification or (hierarchical) mixture modelling (or clustering), where we might identify classes such as (e.g.) animal, vegetable, mineral, animal-dog, animal-cat, vegetable-carrot, vegetable-potato, vegetable-fruit, mineral-metal, mineral-salt, animal-dog-labrador, animal-dog-collie, animal-dog-labrador-black, animal-dog-labrador-golden, etc. Following these principles of MML mixture modelling [26,27,29,25] enables us to arrive at a *single* theory, which is the first part of an MML message and which describes the concepts or classes. The data of all the various individual animals, vegetables and minerals (or things) on the planet (such as their heights and weights, etc.) is encoded in the second part of the message. Users of the language are free to communicate the concepts from this single best MML theory.

Knowledge (and human knowledge especially) in a social environment is all about this, about sharing models. And this shared knowledge makes co-operation possible. For humans (elevated in knowledge), science is a type of knowledge where we typically use one theory to explain the evidence, and not hundreds.

Despite the rationale that one model (or a small set of models) is better for resource-bounded agents which need to communicate their concepts, there are some other issues around compression and intelligence that are more difficult to dissect.

2.1   Lossless and Lossy Compression

In other areas of computer science (image, audio and video processing in particular), we clearly distinguish between lossless and lossy compression [17,15]. In inductive inference, this distinction is less clear. Prediction and inference can also be defined and performed in noisy environments, where some details have to be lost to avoid overfitting (see, e.g., [25, sec. 4.9]). This is, of course, one of the rationales behind two-part codes, where the theory part could be seen as the lossy compression and the other part could be seen as the detail which (optionally) is used to cover the rest of the data. In fact, some compression schemes may have more than two parts, with each part adding more detail to the previous part, in a hierarchical way (although the MML message could be re-structured so that this is again in two parts). Perception is a clear example of this as well, especially because the world deals with continuous (non-discrete) sources of data.

One issue which is difficult to isolate is the 'distortion criterion' [17] for lossy compression. In image, audio and video compression, the distortion and quality criteria are set by human perception - i.e., what kind of loss is acceptable depending on the application. If this external reference is lost, it is much more difficult to distinguish the information that can be lost from the information that should be preserved. Perception and intelligence must be able to determine the details which are relevant to an agent's actions and those which are completely irrelevant - i.e., agents must perform selectively lossy compression. Memory and everyday linguistic concepts must also be able to drop details and keep the essential. The mechanisms and principles which should guide all this are yet to be discovered. In many codings which are used in reinforcement learning (e.g. [21,22]), compression is used to code future rewards efficiently, so any detail which is irrelevant to predict future rewards can be dropped. In fact, this link between compression and reinforcement can be made explicit [8]. Again, compression is required, but the precise formulation and application is crucial.

2.2   The Elusive Model Paradox and (Human) Unpredictability

The interaction between predator and prey, between sellers and buyers, or the behaviour which takes place in board or mind games (such as the *prisoners' dilemma*) has been analysed in ethology, economics, game theory, artificial intelligence and other disciplines. We can discuss all this in terms of prediction and compression.

For example, Scriven discusses the notion of (human) predictability [18] in one of the simplest possible social environments: an iterated game of two humans with one trying to do what the other does and the other trying to avoid this happening. Scriven finds an apparent logical paradox that both should be able to predict the other, while Lewis and Shelby Richardson [13] note Scriven's assumption that the calculations done by each agent in modelling the other are required to terminate. Indeed, whether one looks at doing two-part MML inferential modelling or Solomonoff predictive modelling, one ultimately runs into the Halting problem (or Entscheidungsproblem) [2, footnote 211][3, p455][4, sec. 7.5] - and (the paradox is circumvented by the fact that) the relevant calculations will not terminate. The ability to recognise "*other minds*" and engage in "mind-reading" is clearly advantageous in general in social environments. It is presumably of little surprise that two competing agents of equal computational power and equal inference (modelling) or predictive technique have no advantage over one another.

3 Detecting and Assessing Intelligence

The understanding of compression as a necessary trait of intelligence has led to some approaches for detecting and assessing intelligence where compression plays a fundamental role. Some of these approaches are non-behavioural, i.e., introspective, and require an analysis of the models the agent is using. In fact, the analysis of the level of compression in the models was used as a response to Searle's "Chinese Room" argument [19]. In [5, sec. 2.1][6, sec. 2][4, sec. 7.3], compression was advocated as a non-behavioural way of assessing and detecting intelligence. This required measuring the bits of the model the agents are using, if we are comparing them. This idea is even more explicit in the *Hutter prize* (http://prize.hutter1.net) [2, footnote 180]. In general, however, it is not possible to precisely measure the length of a model by introspection, since the inner knowledge representation may not be accessible. Even for artificial agents, this might be impractical as agents become more and more complex.

One possible way to overcome this limitation is through the use of language. Through language we can ask and communicate models and see whether the explanation for a phenomenon (or an action) given by an agent is shorter than the explanation given by another agent. In fact, interviews, exams and other kinds of tests commonly tell between rote learning and full comprehension by requesting an explanation for the answers, which can then be compared to the right model. This is also recurrent in the Turing Test [23,14] and its implementations, where the artificial agents frequently fail when they are asked to give explanations. This is well-known in psychology as well, where there are many introspective techniques based on asking the right questions.

The other possible way is to stick to purely behavioural tests, which are completely independent from the nature of the agents. Psychometric tests are generally behavioural, since subjects only need to guess answers right or wrong. Many evaluation settings in artificial intelligence are also behavioural, such as game contests, robot competitions, reinforcement learning evaluation, etc. Although behavioural tests seem to be disconnected from the notion of compression, the links arise again in many and diverse ways. Firstly, since prediction and compression are linked, performance is better for those systems which are able to compress the evidence (in a goal-oriented way). Secondly, the difficulty of the exercises or tasks which are used to detect intelligence can be approximated using notions which are closely related to compression, such as many variants of Kolmogorov complexity. Finally, the distribution of tasks can be obtained using some kind of universal distribution. All this has been explored by [11,7,9,12,10], where the original static (sequence-prediction) tests have evolved into more interactive and adaptive tests.

Finally, it is insightful (as an extreme case) to see whether (and how) intelligence can be detected through a (slow) uni-directional form of communication - where, rather than having interactive conversation, instead we send a message conveying some information which we hope is understood. When no previous knowledge is shared, this seems impossible due to the lack of common references. However, compression is again advocated as a possibility to make this feasible, even in the case of uni-directional messages[2].

4   Conclusions

In this paper we have discussed the role that compression might have in intelligence, with an emphasis on communication and language, and the exchange and evaluation of models.

We have argued that the ability to do *two*-part (MML) compression is (in general) an advantage in *social* environments. It is an advantage firstly for the same reasons that it is an advantage in an isolated environment of one agent, including the fact that the MML-inferred theory is a good predictor. But, secondly, it will also typically be an advantage in the (co-operative) social environment, where we can teach (or tell or show) our theories to others. One interesting area of research would be to follow the ideas in Monte Carlo AIXI [24] and construct MML agents, and see whether the latter behave better (with the same resources) in social environments.

Hence, while agreeing that both the optimal Solomonoff predictor and the Wallace MML inference are both relevant to at least the inductive inference (or inductive learning) part of intelligence, we take the position here of suggesting that – at least in the context of social agents in a multi-agent environment – MML is perhaps more pertinent to what we (as social humans in our multi-human environment) might commonly refer to as 'intelligence'.

Acknowledgments. We thank the anonymous reviewers for their helpful comments, and we thank Kurt Kleiner for some challenging and ultimately very helpful questions in the broad area of this work. We also acknowledge the funding from the Spanish MEC and MICINN for projects TIN2009-06078-E/TIN, Consolider-Ingenio CSD2007-00022 and TIN2010-21062-C02, and Generalitat Valenciana for Prometeo/2008/051.

---

[2] Indeed, we can use similar principles to construct a message to send in search of an alien intelligence [2, sec. 0.2.5, p542].

References

1. Chaitin, G.J.: Godel's theorem and information. International Journal of Theoretical Physics 21(12), 941–954 (1982)
2. Dowe, D.L.: Foreword re C. S. Wallace. Computer Journal 51(5), 523–560 (2008); Christopher Stewart WALLACE (1933-2004) memorial special issue
3. Dowe, D.L.: Minimum Message Length and statistically consistent invariant (objective?) Bayesian probabilistic inference - from (medical) "evidence". Social Epistemology 22(4), 433–460 (2008)
4. Dowe, D.L.: MML, hybrid Bayesian network graphical models, statistical consistency, invariance and uniqueness. In: Bandyopadhyay, P.S., Forster, M.R. (eds.) Handbook of the Philosophy of Science. Philosophy of Statistics, vol. 7, pp. 901–982. Elsevier, Amsterdam (2011)
5. Dowe, D.L., Hajek, A.R.: A computational extension to the Turing Test. Technical Report #97/322, Dept Computer Science, Monash University, Melbourne, Australia, 9 pp (1997)
6. Dowe, D.L., Hajek, A.R.: A non-behavioural, computational extension to the Turing Test. In: Intl. Conf. on Computational Intelligence & multimedia applications (ICCIMA 1998), Gippsland, Australia, pp. 101–106 (February 1998)
7. Hernández-Orallo, J.: Beyond the Turing Test. J. Logic, Language & Information 9(4), 447–466 (2000)
8. Hernández-Orallo, J.: Constructive reinforcement learning. International Journal of Intelligent Systems 15(3), 241–264 (2000)
9. Hernández-Orallo, J.: On the computational measurement of intelligence factors. In: Meystel, A. (ed.) Performance metrics for intelligent systems workshop, pp. 1–8. National Institute of Standards and Technology, Gaithersburg, MD, U.S.A (2000)
10. Hernández-Orallo, J., Dowe, D.L.: Measuring universal intelligence: Towards an anytime intelligence test. Artificial Intelligence 174(18), 1508–1539 (2010)
11. Hernández-Orallo, J., Minaya-Collado, N.: A formal definition of intelligence based on an intensional variant of Kolmogorov complexity. In: Proc. Intl Symposium of Engineering of Intelligent Systems (EIS 1998), pp. 146–163. ICSC Press (1998)
12. Legg, S., Hutter, M.: Universal intelligence: A definition of machine intelligence. Minds and Machines 17(4), 391–444 (2007)
13. Lewis, D.K., Shelby-Richardson, J.: Scriven on human unpredictability. Philosophical Studies: An International Journal for Philosophy in the Analytic Tradition 17(5), 69–74 (1966)
14. Oppy, G., Dowe, D.L.: The Turing Test. In: Zalta, E.N. (ed.) Stanford Encyclopedia of Philosophy, Stanford University, Stanford (2011), http://plato.stanford.edu/entries/turing-test/
15. Salomon, D., Motta, G., Bryant, D.C.O.N.: Handbook of data compression. Springer-Verlag New York Inc., Heidelberg (2009)
16. Sanghi, P., Dowe, D.L.: A computer program capable of passing I.Q. tests. In: 4th International Conference on Cognitive Science (and 7th Australasian Society for Cognitive Science Conference), vol. 2, pp. 570–575. Univ. of NSW, Sydney, Australia (July 2003)
17. Sayood, K.: Introduction to data compression. Morgan Kaufmann, San Francisco (2006)
18. Scriven, M.: An essential unpredictability in human behavior. In: Wolman, B.B., Nagel, E. (eds.) Scientific Psychology: Principles and Approaches, pp. 411–425. Basic Books (Perseus Books), New York (1965)

19. Searle, J.R.: Minds, brains and programs. Behavioural and Brain Sciences 3, 417–457 (1980)
20. Solomonoff, R.J.: A formal theory of inductive inference. Part I. Information and control 7(1), 1–22 (1964)
21. Sutton, R.S.: Generalization in reinforcement learning: Successful examples using sparse coarse coding. Advances in neural information processing systems, 1038–1044 (1996)
22. Sutton, R.S., Barto, A.G.: Reinforcement learning: An introduction. The MIT Press, Cambridge (1998)
23. Turing, A.M.: Computing machinery and intelligence. Mind 59, 433–460 (1950)
24. Veness, J., Ng, K.S., Hutter, M., Silver, D.: A Monte Carlo AIXI Approximation. Journal of Artificial Intelligence Research, JAIR 40, 95–142 (2011)
25. Wallace, C.S.: Statistical and Inductive Inference by Minimum Message Length. Springer, Heidelberg (2005)
26. Wallace, C.S., Boulton, D.M.: An information measure for classification. Computer Journal 11(2), 185–194 (1968)
27. Wallace, C.S., Dowe, D.L.: Intrinsic classification by MML - the Snob program. In: Proc. 7th Australian Joint Conf. on Artificial Intelligence, pp. 37–44. World Scientific, Singapore (November 1994)
28. Wallace, C.S., Dowe, D.L.: Minimum message length and Kolmogorov complexity. Computer Journal 42(4), 270–283 (1999); Special issue on Kolmogorov complexity
29. Wallace, C.S., Dowe, D.L.: MML clustering of multi-state, Poisson, von Mises circular and Gaussian distributions. Statistics and Computing 10, 73–83 (2000)

OpenPsi: Realizing Dörner's "Psi" Cognitive Model in the OpenCog Integrative AGI Architecture

Zhenhua Cai[1], Ben Goertzel[1,2], and Nil Geisweiller[2]

[1] BLISS Lab, Xiamen University, China
[2] Novamente LLC, Rockville MD

Abstract. Dietrich Doerner's "Psi" cognitive model, which was used as the basis for Joscha Bach's MicroPsi AGI system, is expressed in a quite different terminology and conceptual framework from the one normally used to discuss the OpenCog AGI system. However, the two systems are fundamentally conceptually compatible, and we describe here the basis of a realization of the Psi model within OpenCog, which we call "OpenPsi." Currently OpenPsi is being used to control non-player characters in a game world, and application to humanoid robotics is also underway.

1   Introduction

The field of Artificial General Intelligence is remarkably fragmented. There are multiple theoretical frameworks that are often, at least on the surface, incompatible. There are multiple practical AGI architectures, founded on different theoretical bases, with overlapping functionalities and goals; and there are no clear mappings from components or aspects of one architecture into another. To some extent, this fragmentation may be considered a feature rather than a bug. AGI is a young field, and a diverse variety of approaches is healthy and expectable. Sometimes, however, differences in language or focus between the works of different groups in the field, obscure deeper underlying commonalities that could otherwise be profitably exploited. Because of this it behooves us as AGI researchers to aggressively explore possible relationships between our own preferred approaches and those of other researchers.

We present here the early results of one such exploration. The authors are involved with the development of the OpenCogPrime (OCP) AGI architecture [6] within the OpenCog software framework, and when first introduced to Joscha Bach's MicroPsi AGI architecture [2], the two approaches appeared incompatible in major respects. More careful study of MicroPsi, however, and extensive in-person dialogues with Bach, revealed a great number of parallels between the approaches, and led to the conclusion that many key aspects of MicroPsi could in fact be replicated within OpenCog and integrated with OCP.

MicroPsi is conceptually founded on Dietrich Dörner's "Psi," a cognitive model of human and animal intelligence focusing on the role of motivation and emotion in guiding behavior and cognition. The overall Psi theory comprises a

J. Schmidhuber, K.R. Thórisson, and M. Looks (Eds.): AGI 2011, LNAI 6830, pp. 212–221, 2011.
© Springer-Verlag Berlin Heidelberg 2011

comprehensive model of the human brain and mind, in principle encompassing all aspects of human-level general intelligence; but, Psi is typically presented in the context of a relatively simplistic agent choosing behaviors in the world in a manner driven by several well-defined motives (e.g. need for food, water, the avoidance of pain, certainty, competence and affiliation). Psi was originally implemented by Dörner in a helpful and illustrative but somewhat "toy" computer system; MicroPsi embodied Psi in a serious software architecture, enabling more thorough exploration of the model's properties.

2   Motivation and Emotion in Psi

First we outline those aspects of Psi that we have chosen for realization in OpenPsi. As illustrated in Figure 1, the Psi's motivational system begins with **Demands**, which could be the mimic of physiological demands of real animals, such as food, water, sex and so forth, or even fairly abstract demands. Psi theory also specifies three fairly abstract demands: **Competence**, the effectiveness of the agent at fulfilling its Urges; **Certainty**, the confidence of the agent's knowledge; and **Affiliation**, the acceptance by other agents or social groups. Each demand comes with a certain "target range", which may vary over time, or may change as a system develops. An **Urge** develops when a demand deviates from its target range: the urge seeks to return the demand to its target range.

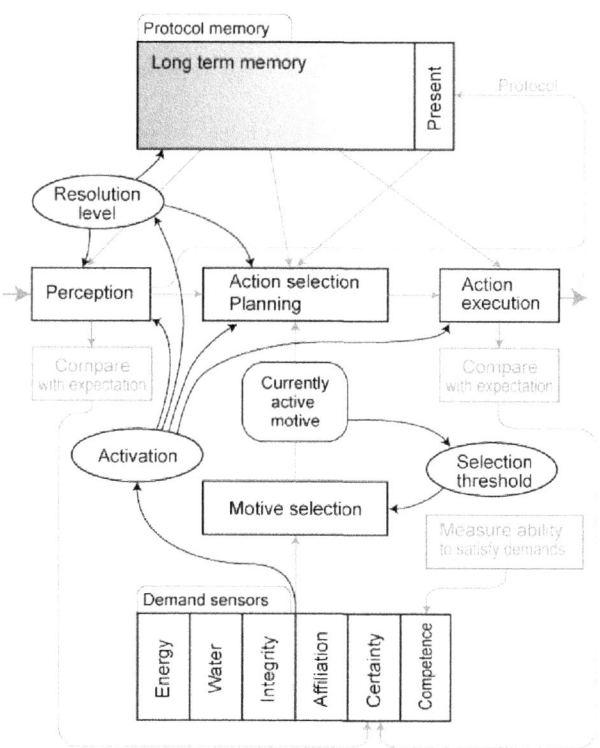

Fig. 1. Influence of Modulators

The most distinctive feature of Psi theory is its perspective on the autonomous choice and regulation of behaviors. It suggests that all goal-directed action have their source in a motive that is connected to an urge, which stands for a physiological, cognitive or social demand [2]. When a positive goal is reached, a demand may be partially or completely fulfilled, which creates a **Pleasure** signal that is used for leaning, by strengthening the associations of the goal with the actions carried out and situations that have led to the fulfillment. While not all the actions are directed immediately hooked to a goal, many actions are carried out to serve an exploratory goal or to avoid an aversive situation. It is also make sense when reaching sub-goals, because in those cases a pleasure signal of competence demand would be created. After finally reaching a consumptive goal, the system may strength all the associations along the chain of actions that has lead to the target goal.

In the Psi model emotion is not considered as an isolated component. Instead it emerges from the whole system, where the process of perception, cognition and action selection interact together. These are accomplished by **modulators**. A modulator is a parameter that characterize how the emotion affects the process of perception, cognition and action selection. Figure 1 shows how the emotion effects these processes via modulators. Dörner currently specifies four modulators: **Activation**, which makes the agent balance between rapid, intensive activity and reflective, cognitive activity; **Resolution level**, which determines how accurately the agent tries to perceive the world; **Certainty**, which stands for the difficulty of the agent tries to achieve definite, certain knowledge; **Selection threshold**, which determines how easily the agent switches between conflicting intentions. Individual agents may differ in their "personalities" because of different settings for the default and ranges of modulators.

3   OpenCog Prime

Now we describe the OCP (OCP) AGI architecture, implemented within the open-source OpenCog AI framework. Conceptually founded on the "patternist" systems theory of intelligence outlined in [5], OCP combines multiple AI paradigms such as uncertain logic, computational linguistics, evolutionary program learning and connectionist attention allocation in a unified architecture. Cognitive processes embodying these different paradigms interoperate together on a common neural-symbolic knowledge store called the Atomspace. The interaction of these processes is designed to encourage the self-organizing emergence of high-level network structures in the Atomspace, including superposed hierarchical and heterarchical knowledge networks, and a self-model network enabling meta-knowledge and meta-learning.

The high-level architecture of OCP, shown in Figure 2, involves the use of multiple cognitive processes associated with multiple types of memory to enable an intelligent agent to execute the procedures that it believes have the best probability of working toward its goals in its current context. OCP handles low-level perception and action via an extension called OpenCogBot, which integrates a hierarchical temporal memory system, DeSTIN [1].

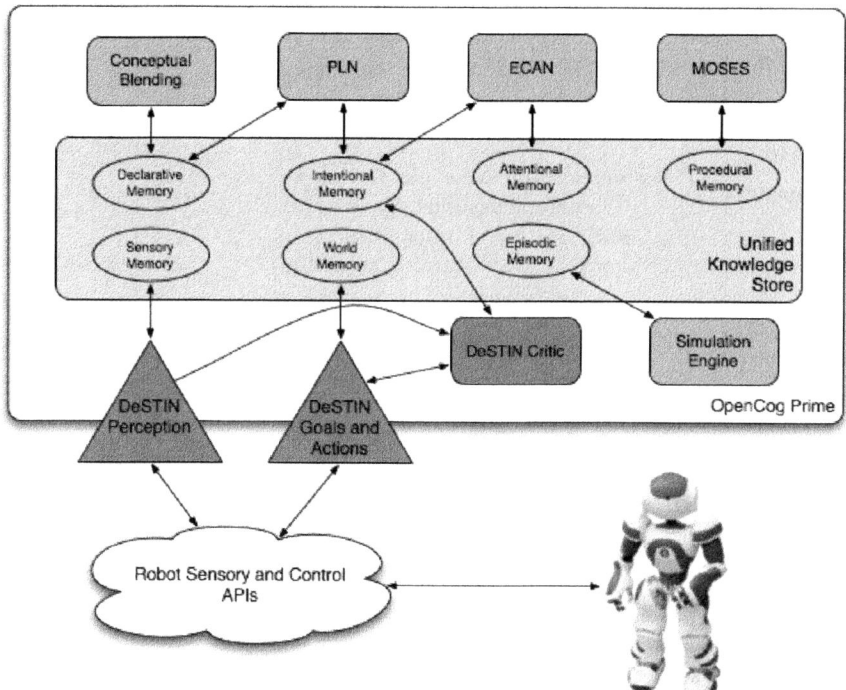

Fig. 2. High-Level OCP Architecture Diagram

Memory Types in OpenOCP. OCP's memory types are the declarative, procedural, sensory, and episodic memory types that are widely discussed in cognitive neuroscience [12], plus attentional memory for allocating system resources generically, and intentional memory for allocating system resources in a goal-directed way. Table 1 overviews these memory types, giving key references and indicating the corresponding cognitive processes, and also indicating which of the generic patternist cognitive dynamics each cognitive process corresponds to (pattern creation, association, etc.).

The essence of the OCP design lies in the way the structures and processes associated with each type of memory are designed to work together in a closely coupled way, the operative hypothesis being that this will yield cooperative intelligence going beyond what could be achieved by an architecture merely containing the same structures and processes in separate "black boxes."

The inter-cognitive-process interactions in OpenCog are designed so that: 1) conversion between different types of memory is possible, though sometimes computationally costly (e.g. an item of declarative knowledge may with some effort be interpreted procedurally or episodically, etc.); 2) when a learning process concerned centrally with one type of memory encounters a situation where it learns very slowly, it can often resolve the issue by converting some of the relevant knowledge into a different type of memory: i.e. **cognitive synergy**.

Table 1. Memory Types and Cognitive Processes in OpenCog Prime. The third column indicates the general cognitive function that each specific cognitive process carries out, according to the patternist theory of cognition.

Memory Type	Specific Cognitive Processes	General Cognitive Functions
Declarative	Probabilistic Logic Networks (PLN) [4]; concept blending [3]	pattern creation
Procedural	MOSES (a novel probabilistic evolutionary program learning algorithm) [11]	pattern creation
Episodic	internal simulation engine [7]	association, pattern creation
Attentional	Economic Attention Networks (ECAN) [10]	association, credit assignment
Intentional	probabilistic goal hierarchy refined by PLN and ECAN, structured according to Psi	credit assignment, pattern creation
Sensory	Supplied by DeSTIN integration	association, attention allocation, pattern creation, credit assignment

Declarative knowledge representation is handled by a weighted labeled hypergraph called the Atomspace, which consists of multiple types of nodes and links, generally weighted with probabilistic truth values and also attention values (ShortTermImportance (STI) and LongTermImportance values, regulating processor and memory use). ConceptNodes are defined via their links (including logical and associative links), whereas e.g. GroundedPredicateNodes are defined via associated procedures or "schema," which are small programs expressed in a LISP-like language called Combo and stored in a special ProcedureRepository data structure.

OCP's dynamics has both goal-oriented and "spontaneous" aspects. The spontaneous dynamic is driven by the ECAN component, which propagates STI values in a manner reminiscent of an attractor neural network; cognitive processes or knowledge items that get more importance spread to them are then used to trigger action or cognition or to guide perception. The basic goal-oriented dynamic of the OCP system, within which the various types of memory are utilized, is driven by "cognitive schematics", which take the form

$$Context \wedge Procedure \rightarrow Goal < p >$$

(summarized $C \wedge P \rightarrow G$). Semi-formally, this implication may interpreted to mean: "If the context C appears to hold currently, then if I enact the procedure P, I can expect to achieve the goal G with certainty p." The learning processes corresponding to the different types of memory actively cooperate in figuring out what procedures will achieve the system's goals in the relevant contexts within its environment. Each cognitive schematic is labeled with an uncertain truth value; and cognitive schematics may be incomplete, missing one or two of the terms, which may then be filled in by various cognitive processes (generally in an uncertain way). Goal dynamics also utilizes STI, in that the system's top-level goals are given STI to spend on nominating procedures for execution or to pass to subgoals.

Current and Prior Applications of OpenCog. OpenCog has been used for commercial applications in the area of natural language processing and data mining; e.g. see [9] where OpenCog's PLN reasoning and RelEx language processing are combined to do automated biological hypothesis generation based on information gathered from PubMed abstracts. Most relevantly to the present proposal, has also been used to control virtual agents in virtual worlds [7], using an OpenCog variant called the OpenPetBrain (see http://novamente.net/example for some videos of these virtual dogs in action). These agents demonstrate a variety of interesting and relevant functionalities including learning new behaviors based on imitation and reinforcement; responding to natural language commands and questions, with appropriate actions and natural language replies; and spontaneous exploration of their world, remembering their experiences and using them to bias future learning and linguistic interaction.

4   Psi Versus OpenCogPrime

The basic motivation/emotion architecture of Psi, as described above, comprises the basis of OpenPsi, which has been realized within OCP. However, Psi has a number of other aspects that are somewhat different from their OCP analogues, and which have not been carried over to OpenPsi, either because the latter uses a different method to accomplish the same thing, or because it contains an equivalent mechanism. We summarize these here only briefly:

- Representation of knowledge using special 5-neuron clusters called "quads."
- Arrangement of quads into three networks, corresponding to sensation, motor control and motivation
- Use of an algorithm called HyPercept for hypothesis-based perception (a similar principle is used for perception in OCP, but via quite different algorithms)
- Imaginary perceptions are handled via a "mental stage" analogous to OpenCog's internal simulation world.
- Action selection in Psi works based on what are called "triplets," each of which consists of a sensor schema (pre-conditions, "condition schema"; like OCP's "context"), a subsequent motor schema (action, effector; like OCP's "procedure"), and a final sensor schema (post-conditions, expectations; like an OCP predicate or goal).
- Action selection in Psi is carried out via a "Rasmussen ladder" process that first attempts to find an automated routine carrying out the given task, then tries to choose derive a course of action based on rules, then if that fails tries to creatively compose a new behavior based on its background knowledge.

These same possibilities exist in OpenCog but are applied in a different way, scheduled by ECAN.

– Psi plans actions using a fairly simple hill-climbing planner. While it's hypothesized that a more complex planner may be needed for advanced intelligence, part of the Psi theory is the hypothesis that most real-life planning an organism needs to do is fairly simple, once the organism has the right perceptual representations and goals. OCP carries out planning integrated with its PLN probabilistic logic engine, a component that has no direct analogue in Psi.

Overall, on a high level, the similarities between Psi and OCP are quite strong, including: interlinked declarative, procedural and intentional knowledge structures, represented using neural-symbolic methods; perception via prediction and perception/action integration; action selection via triplets that resemble uncertain, potentially partial production rules. These similarities are what makes the explicit integration of Psi-based motivation and emotion into OpenCog, i.e. OpenPsi, sensible. On the other hand, the deepest difference between the systems lies in the way the inter-operation between different cognitive processes is pursued in the two different approaches. Psi and MicroPsi rely on very simple learning algorithms that are closely tied to the "quad" neurosymbolic knowledge representation, and hence interoperate in a fairly natural way without need for subtle methods of "synergy engineering." OCP uses much more diverse and sophisticated learning algorithms which thus require more sophisticated methods of interoperation in order to achieve cognitive synergy.

5   OpenPsi

We now describe how the basic concepts of the Psi approach to motivation have been incorporated in OCP, constituting "OpenPsi". We give simple examples of each concept, drawn from our use of OpenPsi to help OCP control virtual agents in a game world, playing with blocks and carrying out other activities.

Memory. Psi's memory corresponds to OCP's AtomTable, with associated structures like the ProcedureRepository, the SpaceServer and TimeServer. *Examples:* The knowledge of what blocks look like and the knowledge that tall structures often fall down, go in the AtomTable; specific procedures for picking up blocks of different shapes go in the ProcedureRepository; the layout of a room or a pile of blocks at a specific point in time go in the SpaceServer; the series of events involved in the building-up of a tower are temporally indexed in the TimeServer. In Psi and MicroPsi, these same phenomena are stored in memory in a rather different way, yet the basic Psi motivational dynamics are independent of these representational choices.

Demands. are GroundedPredicateNodes (GPNs), i.e. Nodes that have their truth value computed at each time by some internal C++ code or some Combo procedure stored in the OpenCog ProcedureRepository. *Examples:* Alertness, perceived novelty, internal novelty, reward from teachers, social stimulus.

Urges. (called Ubergoals in OCP) are also GPNs, with their truth values defined in terms of the truth values of the Nodes for corresponding Demands. *Examples:* Now and in the future: stay alert and alive now and in the future; experience and learn new things; get reward from the teachers; enjoy rich social interactions.

Importance. The ShortTermImportance of an Ubergoal indicates the urgency of the goal, so if the Demand corresponding to an Ubergoal is within its target range, then the Ubergoal will have zero STI. But all Ubergoals can be given maximal LTI to guarantee they don't get deleted. *Examples:* If the system is in an environment continually providing an adequate level of novelty (according to its Ubergoal), then the Ubergoal corresponding to external novelty with have low STI but high LTI. The system won't expend resources seeking novelty. But then, if the environment becomes more monotonous, the urgency of the external novelty goal will increase, and its STI will increase correspondingly, and resources will begin getting allocated toward improving the novelty of the stimuli received by the agent.

Pleasure. is a GPN, and its internal truth value computing program compares the satisfaction of the system's Ubergoals to their expected satisfaction.

Goals. are Nodes or Links that are on the system's list of goals (the GoalPool); these include but are not restricted to Ubergoals. *Examples:* The Ubergoal of getting reward from teachers might spawn subgoals like "getting reward from Bob" (if Bob is a teacher), or "making teachers smile" or "create surprising new structures" (if the latter often garners teacher reward). The subgoal of "create surprising new structures" might, in the context of a new person entering the agent's environment with a bag of toys, lead to the creation of a subgoal of asking for a new toy of the sort that could be used to help create new structures.

Motive selection. as defined in Psi is carried out in OCP by economic attention allocation, which allocates ShortTermImportance to Goal nodes. *Example:* The flow of importance from "Get reward from teachers" to "get reward from Bob" to "make an interesting structure with blocks" is an instance of what Psi calls "motive selection". No action is being taken yet, but choices are being made regarding what specific goals are going to be used to guide action selection.

Action selection. Psi's action selection plays the same role as OCP's action selection, with the clarification that in OCP this is a matter of selecting which *procedures* to run, rather than which individual actions to execute. However, this notion exists in Psi as well, which accounts for "automatized behaviors" that are similar to OCP procedures; the main difference here is that in OCP automatized behaviors are the default case. *Example:* If the goal "make an interesting structure with blocks" has a high STI, then it may be used to motivate choice of a procedure to execute, e.g. a procedure that finds an interesting picture or object seen before and approximates it with blocks, or a procedure that randomly constructs something and then filters it based on interestingness. Once a blocks-structure-building procedure is chosen, this procedure may invoke sub-procedures, e.g. those involved with picking up and positioning particular blocks.

Planning. in Psi is carried out via various OCP learning processes, including PLN with special control mechanisms plus procedure learning methods like MOSES or hillclimbing. *Example:* If the agent has decided to build a blocks structure emulating a pyramid (which it saw in a picture), and it knows how to manipulate and position individual blocks, then it must figure out a procedure for carrying out individual-block actions that will result in production of the pyramid. In this case, a very inexperienced agent might use MOSES or hillclimbing and "guidedly-randomly" fiddle with different construction procedures until it hit on something workable. A slightly more experienced agent would use reasoning based on prior structures it had built, to figure out a rational plan (like: "start with the base, then iteratively pile on layers, each one slightly smaller than the previous.")

Modulators. are system parameters which may be represented in OpenCog by PredicateNodes, and which must be incorporated appropriately in the dynamics of various MindAgents, e.g.

– *activation* affects action selection. For instance this may be effected by a process that, each cycle, causes a certain amount of STI to pass to schema satisfying certain properties (those involving physical action, or terminating rapidly). The amount of currency passed in this way would be proportional to the *activation*
– *resolution level* affects perception schema and MindAgents, causing them to expend less effort in processing perceptual data
– *certainty* affects inference and pattern mining and concept creation processes, causing them to place less emphasis on certainty in guiding their activities, i.e. to be more accepting of uncertain conclusions.
– *selection threshold* may be used to effect a process that, each cycle, causes a certain amount of STI (proportional to the selection threshold) to pass to the Goal Atoms that were wealthiest at the previous cycle.

6   Conclusion

We have described here the logic via which the motivation, emotion and action selection aspects of the Psi cognitive model have been integrated into the OpenCog system, for use within the integrative OCP cognitive model. While this may appear straightforward as laid out, one should not underestimate the difficulties in reconciling the conceptual frameworks of two AGI architectures with very different roots.

The OpenPsi system resultant from this integration is currently being used to control a virtual dog in a virtual world, broadly similarly to the OpenCog application described in [7], but with richer functionality, as will be described in subsequent publications. In another project, OpenCog is being used to control a humanoid (Nao) robot, and it is anticipated that OpenPsi will play a key role in this as well. Rigorous evaluation of the contribution of the OpenPsi in particular, in this sort of application, is not trivial, because what really matters (and what is easier to measure) is the overall intelligence of the virtual or robotic agent. Qualitatively, however, we have already found that it is easier to create agents with realistic-seeming motivational and emotional behavior using OpenPsi than using the previous OpenCog personality/behavior rule engine as described in [8].

References

1. Arel, I., Rose, D., Coop, R.: Destin: A scalable deep learning architecture with application to high-dimensional robust pattern recognition. In: Proc. AAAI Workshop on Biologically Inspired Cognitive Architectures (2009)
2. Bach, J.: Principles of Synthetic Intelligence. Oxford University Press, Oxford (2009)
3. Fauconnier, G., Turner, M.: The Way We Think: Conceptual Blending and the Minds Hidden Complexities. Basic (2002)
4. Goertzel, B., Ikl, M., Heljakka, A.: Probabilistic Logic Networks. Springer, Heidelberg (2008)
5. Goertzel, B.: The Hidden Pattern. Brown Walker (2006)
6. Goertzel, B.: Opencog prime: A cognitive synergy based architecture for embodied artificial general intelligence. In: ICCI 2009, Hong Kong (2009)
7. Goertzel, B., C.P., et al.: An integrative methodology for teaching embodied non-linguistic agents, applied to virtual animals in second life. In: Proceedings of the First Conference on Artificial General Intelligence. IOS Press, Amsterdam (2008)
8. Goertzel, B., Pennachin, C.: The collective pet unconscious: Balancing intelligence and individuality in populations of learning-enabled virtual pets. In: The Reign of Catz and Dogz Symposium. ACM-CHI, Boston (2009)
9. Goertzel, B., Pinto, H., Pennachin, C., Goertzel, I.F.: Using dependency parsing and probabilistic inference to extract relationships between genes, proteins and malignancies implicit among multiple biomedical research abstracts. In: Proceeding of Bio-NLP 2006 (2006)
10. Goertzel, B., Pitt, J., Ikle, M., Pennachin, C., Liu, R.: Glocal memory: a design principle for artificial brains and minds. Neurocomputing (April 2010)
11. Looks, M.: Competent Program Evolution. PhD Thesis, Computer Science Department, Washington University (2006)
12. Tulving, E., Craik, R.: The Oxford Handbook of Memory. Oxford U. Press, Oxford (2005)

Extending Cognitive Architectures with Semantic Resources

Alessandro Oltramari and Christian Lebiere

Department of Psychology, Carnegie Mellon University
{aoltrama,cl}@andrew.cmu.edu

Abstract. This paper presents an integrated modeling framework where the learning and knowledge retrieval mechanisms of the ACT-R cognitive architecture are combined with a semantic resource. We aim to extend ACT-R with a scalable knowledge model, in order to support sub-symbolic processes with consistent, general high-level declarative representations. Design principles, methodology and implementation examples are provided.

Keywords: cognitive architecture, ACT-R, ontology, computational semantics.

1 Introduction

In attempting to design systems capable of Artificial General Intelligence, two substantially different approaches have been attempted. The first, historically, has focused on the mechanisms of intelligence, taking the form of general problem-solving programs [1] or architectures (i.e., [2], [3]). The second, partly arising from the limitations of the first, emphasized the knowledge of the system, especially common-sense knowledge, as the source of intelligence (e.g., [4]). Those approaches have encountered substantial successes in their own rights, but have up to now not achieved the ultimate goal of AGI. Moreover, both approaches have largely downplayed the other: systems that focus on mechanisms tend to treat knowledge as something to be engineered in ad hoc, task-specific ways, while those that focus on knowledge rely on narrowly tailored mechanisms to access and leverage their content, often raising unsustainable computational requirements in the process.

In this paper, we argue that those approaches are complementary, and that both of their central aspects, mechanisms and knowledge, need to be addressed systematically in a comprehensive approach to AGI. Moreover, those two components strongly constrain each other, with learning mechanisms determining which knowledge can be acquired and in which form, and specific knowledge content providing stringent requirements for mechanisms to be able to access them effectively [5]. In the rest of this paper, we introduce each approach, sketch out a general framework for combining them, and then discuss an application of that framework to the problem of recognizing visual actions.

J. Schmidhuber, K.R. Thórisson, and M. Looks (Eds.): AGI 2011, LNAI 6830, pp. 222–231, 2011.
© Springer-Verlag Berlin Heidelberg 2011

2 Cognitive Architectures as Knowledge Systems

Cognitive architectures are examples of the first class of intelligent system: they attempt to capture computationally the invariant mechanisms of human cognition, including those underlying the functions of control, learning, memory, adaptivity, and perception and action. In this paper we will focus on one particular cognitive architecture: ACT-R [6]. ACT-R is a modular system: its components include perceptual, motor and declarative memory modules, synchronized by a procedural module through limited capacity buffers. ACT-R has accounted for a broad range of cognitive activities at a high level of fidelity, reproducing aspects of human data such as learning, errors, latencies, eye movements and patterns of brain activity. Declarative memory (DM) plays an important role in the ACT-R cognitive architecture. At the symbolic level, ACT-R models perform two major operations on DM: 1) accumulating knowledge chunks learned from internal operations or from interaction with the environment and 2) retrieving chunks that provide needed information[1]. The ACT-R theory distinguishes 'declarative knowledge' from 'procedural knowledge', the latter being conceived as a set of procedures (production rules) which coordinate information processing between its various modules[2]: according to this framework, agents accomplish their goals on the basis of declarative representations elaborated through procedural steps (in the form of *if-then* clauses). This distinction between declarative and procedural knowledge is grounded in several experimental results in cognitive psychology regarding knowledge dissociation; major studies in cognitive neuroscience implicate a specific role of the hippocampus in "forming permanent declarative memories" and the basal ganglia in production processes (see [6], pp. 96-99, for a general mapping of ACT-R modules and buffers to brain areas and [7] for a detailed neural model of the basal ganglia's role in controlling information flow between cortical regions).

3 Hybrid Semantics for Declarative Memory

Although discontinuously popular among AI scholars, this separation between declarative and procedural knowledge has also been an important issue for AI over the years. In 1980 John McCarthy first realized that, in order to enable full-fledged reasoning capabilities, logic-based intelligent systems need to incorporate "re-usable declarative representations that correspond to objects and processes of the world" [9]. Along these lines, Pat Hayes developed an axiomatic theory for *naïve physics* [10] and John Sowa acknowledged the relevant role played by philosophy in defining a structured representation of world entities [11], i.e. an 'ontology'[3]. There have been

---

[1] Both chunk learning and retrieval are performed through limited capacity buffers that constrain the size and capacity of the chunks in DM.

[2] In the ACT-R theory, these procedures based on condition-action structures are considered as units for skill acquisition ([6], p. 26).

[3] This was the genesis of using the word 'ontology' in AI. Ontology, 'the study of being as such' – as Aristotle named it –, in fact originated as a philosophical discipline.

numerous (and often alternative) attempts to define 'ontology' in Computer Science[4]. According to Guarino, "an ontology" is a language-dependent cognitive artifact, committed to a certain conceptualization of the world by means of a given language[5] (see [14] for formal details). Besides the *protocol layer*, where the syntax of the communication language is specified, the ontological layer contains the *semantics* of that language: if concepts are described in terms of lexical semantics, ontologies take the simple form of *dictionaries* or *thesauri*; when ontological categories and relations are expressed in terms of axioms in a logical language, we talk about *formal ontologies*; if logical constraints are then encoded in a computational language, formal ontologies turn to *computational ontologies*[6]. This research area finds application in a growing variety of cases: from database integration to security analysis, from enterprise modeling to the expansive vision of the Semantic Web [15]. In particular, the Semantic Web community is making massive efforts towards the development of scalable ontology-driven technologies as, for example, the "Linked Open Data"[7] best practice suggests.

In this paper we focus on a rather new field of application, namely integration between computational ontologies and cognitive architectures. In our context computational ontologies should be appropriately re-defined here as "computational specifications of declarative conceptual structures". In particular we aim at extending ACT-R with a scalable, reusable knowledge model that can be applied across a wide range of tasks. Considering the state of the art[8], most research efforts have focused on designing methods for mapping large knowledge bases to the ACT-R declarative module. Here we commit on taking an integrated approach: instead of tying to a single ontology, we propose to build a *hybrid computational ontology*[9] that combines different semantic dimensions of declarative representations. Our project consists in linking partitions of distinctive lexical databases like WordNet [21] and FrameNet [22] with a suitable computational ontology of actions and events.

Four general issues justify our methodological approach:

1. Meaning is multi-dimensional, i.e. it depends on natural language, cognitive phenomena, contextual information (*human-understandability specifications*);
2. Meaning is computable insofar as semantics is expressed in terms of knowledge representation languages (*machine-understandability*);
3. Event-types correspond to verbs in the lexicon, and WordNet is the broadest

---

[4] See [12] for a detailed reconstruction. The original definition is considered Gruber's: "formal specification of a shared conceptualization" [13].

[5] Guarino distinguishes between 'Ontology' as a discipline (with the capital 'o') from 'ontologies' as engineering cognitive artifacts.

[6] E.g., Ontology Web Language (OWL). OWL is based on description logics; description logics are *decidable* fragment of First-Order Logic (http://www.w3.org/TR/owl-features/).

[7] http://linkeddata.org/

[8] For ACT-R see [16], [17], [18], for SOAR see [19].

[9] The adjective "hybrid" is used to emphasize the heterogeneity of theories and resources we are adopting for the purposes of the project. For a general survey on hybrid semantic approaches see [20]. For the sake of readability we will henceforth omit the mid-adjective "computational".

source of lexical information available in an electronic format;

4. FrameNet schematically represents the conceptual patterns underlying event verbs, providing detailed information of roles and fillers for basic action types.

The following sections describe the fundamental features of an integrated cognitive model for high-level visual recognition of motor actions to support visual machine learning with solid symbolic representations in the domain of basic human actions.

4 HOMinE and ACT-R: An Integrated Cognitive Model

We address the perspective of an integrated cognitive model oriented to visual intelligence (HOMinE - Hybrid Ontology for 'Mind's Eye' project[10]), outlining methodological aspects and backbone structure of required components. Some distinctive mappings to the ACT-R cognitive architecture are also considered: we show how the modular dynamic structures of ACT-R can benefit from augmenting declarative memory with a multi-layered semantic resource, where lexical and ontological knowledge are properly encoded.

4.1 Design and Implementation of HOMinE

WordNet (WN) is a semantic network of *synsets* ("sets of synonym terms")[11], whose arcs are fundamental semantic relations[12]. Over the years, there has been an incremental growth of the lexicon (the latest version, WordNet 3.0, contains about 117K synsets), and substantial enhancements of the entire architecture, aimed at facilitating computational tractability (accordingly, some OWL conversions have been implemented[13]). HOMinE's core layer is based on a partition of WN related to verbs of motion, such as "walk", "touch", "haul", "kick", "chase", etc. In order to find the targeted group of relevant synsets, we basically started from two pertinent top nodes[14] of the semantic network of verbs:

1. {01835496} move#1, travel#1, go#1, locomote#1 (change location; move, travel, or proceed) *"How fast does your new car go?"; "The soldiers moved towards the city in an attempt to take it before night fell";* - <verbs.motion>

2. {01850315} move#2, displace#4 (cause to move or shift into a new position or place, both in a concrete and in an abstract sense) *"Move those boxes into the corner, please"; "The director moved more responsibilities onto his new assistant"* - <verbs.motion>

As one can easily notice, the synset move#1 denotes a change of position accomplished by an agent or by an object (with a sufficient level of autonomy), while

---

[10] http://www.darpa.mil/i2o/programs/me/me.asp

[11] Life_form#1 stands for synset {life_form, organism, being, living_thing}, which is identified in the database with a specific code (in this example, {05217061}). Every synset (node of the network) is associated to a gloss (e.g., "the characteristic bodily form of a mature organism").

[12] The most important is synonymy; WN also uses hyponymy (sub-class-of), meronymy (part-of), antonymy (opposite-of), troponymy (like hyponymy, but only for verbs), causation, etc.

[13] E.g., http://www.w3.org/TR/wordnet-rdf/

[14] Aka *Unique Beginner*s (see [21], Chapter 1).

move#2 is about causing someone or something to move (both literally and figuratively). After extracting the sub-hierarchy of synsets related to these generic verbs of motor action, we have introduced a top-most category "movement-generic", abstracting from the two senses of "move" (see Figure 1). These operations have been performed on Protégé-OWL (release 3.4.4), the most widely used platform for creating computational ontologies in the context of semantic technologies[15]. More precisely, in order to extract and modify the designated WN partition we used the OntoLing[16] plug-in, a tool that supports semi-automatic population of ontologies. OntoLing allows importing lexical knowledge structures in the form of RDF(S)[17] properties, *de facto* enabling semantic compatibility with ontological knowledge patterns[18]. As far as lexical databases are augmented with axioms and property restrictions based on OWL primitives, the resulting *hybrid ontologies* can support logical inferences: this feature is central for our project, since we plan to further develop HOMinE to enable automatic reasoning capabilities[19].

FrameNet (FN) is the additional semantic layer of HOMinE's integrated cognitive model. Besides wordnet-like frameworks, a computational lexicon can be designed from a different perspective, for example focusing on *frames* (to be conceived as orthogonal to domains). Based on Fillmore's frame semantics (see i.e. [23]), FN aims at documenting "the range of semantic and syntactic combinatory possibilities (valences) of each word in each of its senses" through corpus-based annotation. Different frames are evoked by the same word depending on different contexts of use: the notion of "evocation" helps in capturing the multi-dimensional character of knowledge structures underlying verbal forms. For instance, if you point to the **bringing** frame, namely an abstraction of a state of affairs where *sentient agents (e.g., persons) or generic carriers (e.g. ships) bring something somewhere along a given path*, you will find several "lexical units"[20] evoking different roles (or frame elements - FEs): i.e., the noun 'truck' instantiates the "carrier" role in the frame **bringing**[21]. In principle, the same Lexical Unit (LU) may "evoke" distinct frames, thus dealing with different roles: 'truck', for example, can be also associated to the **vehicle** frame ("the vehicles that human beings use for the purpose of transportation"). FN contains about 12K LUs for 1K frames annotated in 150000 sentences.

Computational lexicons largely differentiate upon the explicit linguistic features they expose, which may vary in format, content granularity and grounding [24]. WN and FN are based on distinct models, but one can benefit from the other in terms of coverage and type of information conveyed. Accordingly, we have analyzed the "evocation" links between the motion verbs we have extracted from WN and the related FN frames: those links can be generated through "FN Data search", an on-line

---

[15] http://protege.stanford.edu/

[16] For more information see http://ai-nlp.info.uniroma2.it/software/OntoLing/

[17] RDF(S) stands for Resource Description Framework Schema.

[18] OWL syntax builds on top of RDF(S) and extends its expressivity.

[19] Protégé has a default inference engine, so-called "Pellet": http://clarkparsia.com/pellet/. We are also exploiting SWRL (Semantic Web Rule Language) to express IF-THEN rules.

[20] Generically abbreviated with LUs - they correspond to terms in WN synsets.

[21] The sentence is "The truck *bringing* coal to crushing facility at western surface coal mine".

navigation tool used to access and query FN[22]. Our study led to a conceptual enrichment of lexical declarative structures for basic motor action types: starting from WN synset information, and using FN data, we could identify typical roles (and fillers) of those verbs. This process of extension becomes crucial if one considers the evident isomorphism holding between the elements of ACT-R chunks, namely slots and associated values and elements of frames, i.e. frame elements (roles) and fillers (LUs). The FN semantic layer of HOMinE is still under development: a complete implementation in Protégé will be extremely important for enabling logical reasoning (along the lines of [25]). In parallel, we have started to build an ACT-R model for action recognition, suitably expanding its declarative memory by means of HOMinE's semantic layers: in regards to this integration, section 4.2 shows a functional example.

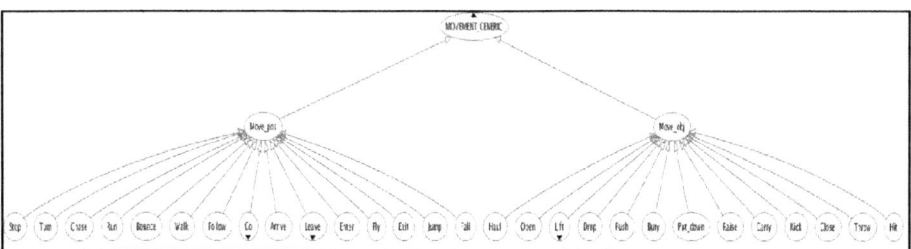

Fig. 1. HoMinE's backbone taxonomy of fundamental motor actions

4.2 Mapping HoMinE to ACT-R

Hybrid ontologies are "computational specifications of declarative conceptual structures": this definition highlights the role of semantic resources in cognitive architectures. From a methodological viewpoint, it is important to understand how this role is actually played in concrete use cases.

Mapping HOMinE to ACT-R requires some preliminary analysis of the basic structures involved. Chunks are the building blocks of ACT-R declarative memory, while ontologies are based on so-called "categories" ("*object*", "*event*", "*attribute*", "*value*", etc.) and "relations" ("*participation*", "*part-of*", "*dependence*", etc.) [26]. Let's consider the following chunk types and chunk instances:

```
(chunk-type car color)   (c1 ISA car color red²³)
(chunk-type race duration)   (r1 ISA race duration 1hour)
```

One can think of ontological categories as mapping to different elements of chunks: objects/events mapping to chunk types (e.g., *car/race*), attributes to slots of chunks (e.g., *color/duration*), and values to fillers of slots (e.g., *red/1hour*). Relations (e.g., *has_color/has_duration*) remain implicit, although they essentially "glue" together those pieces of declarative knowledge (e.g., *car – has_color – red*; *race – has_duration – 1hour*). Alternatively, we can observe that ontological relations can be

---

[22] See http://framenet.icsi.berkeley.edu/index.php
[23] A specific red nuance (individual), not to be confused with the abstract property "redness", which is a sub-type of "color".

represented as chunk types as well: e.g., we could have defined *has_duration* as a chunk type with slots *event* and *duration*, with *race* and *time* as filler:

```
(chunk-type has_duration event duration)
(r1 ISA has_duration event race duration 1hour)
```

The category *race* would then become filler of the slot *event*. This potentially variable matching between ontological knowledge and declarative representations reflect the fact that chunks are originally seen as units of memories, without any strong ontological constraint: in fact, anything that is introduced in declarative memory is a chunk, no matter whether an object, an event, an attribute, a value or a relation. The shift from chunk type to filler addresses the potential of alternative representations of categories in ACT-R. Conversely, from the viewpoint of *hybrid ontologies*, representing relations as chunk types becomes an important requirement: relations enable OWL-based inference engines[24] and definitely demand for an explicit counterpart in the declarative memory of the cognitive agent to make the integration effective. The ACT-R architecture also supports "inheritance"[25] from a single chunk type ("single inheritance"), so that different levels of specialization for slot and values are supplied. "Single inheritance" is a central feature for automatic reasoning over ontologies, since it helps prevent logical inconsistencies and internal incoherence of models (which are typically correlated to "multiple inheritance"). HOMinE discards "multiple inheritance" too, maintaining full compatibility with the ACT-R architectural choice.

Chunks are goal-driven, namely they represent the knowledge a person is expected to manipulate to solve a problem. We consider here an experimental setting where the task is to identify motor actions occurring in a simple scenario ("visualized" on a screen window, in natural language). The goal is accomplished when the cognitive model outputs the conceptual structure of the detected action: in terms of the current version of HOMinE, we assume that 1) the output coincides with correct recognition of the evoked frame 2) input sentences are fed by machine learning visual classifiers that parse the scene and return basic linguistic descriptions[26]. Let's consider three sample sentences presented to the ACT-R cognitive model augmented with HOMinE: (a) John **opens** the **door**; (b) John **opens** the **bag**; (c) John **opens** the **sack**.

Following the typical schema for sentence processing and representation in ACT-R (starting with [27]), our model parses the screen, reads sentences and encodes related chunks accordingly[27]. Afterwards, the actual retrieval of HOMinE declarative representations starts: the model first attempts a straightforward retrieval of frames evoked by the verb "open". In this version we purposely customized the model to always fail this operation. The main reason behind this choice is that an adequate cognitive model should not contain all the information about verb-frame association, as much as we commonly agree that persons can't perfectly memorize 1K frames

---

[24] Ontological relations correspond to OWL object-properties and data-type properties.

[25] The notion of inheritance corresponds to "IS-A" in Computer Science and "hyponymy" in (computational) lexical semantics.

[26] For the sake of simplicity, visual pattern recognition algorithms and tools are considered as a black box in this paper: we are just focusing on the output labels they provide to ACT-R.

[27] For reasons of space, we just present an overview of the model here.

evoked by 12K LUs[28]. In order to overcome the failure of direct evocation, we implemented two competing productions, namely "retrieve-frame-from-hypernym" and "retrieve-frame-from-object". The first production searches for the superordinate verb of the one visualized on the screen, navigating upwards the taxonomy of WN: if the superordinate synset is associated to a frame, then the production retrieves that frame, otherwise "retrieve-frame-from-object" is fired. Note that the heuristics of "retrieve-frame-from-hypernym" is inspired by the algorithm implemented in [28], according to which WN synsets can be associated to FN frames by assigning suitable weights to WN relations. In particular, digging out frames through hyperonymy chain implies a penalization, since the evoked frame is associated to the input verb only because of the inheritance from the super-ordinate[29]. The production "retrieve-frame-from-object" fires as a further method to foster frame evocation. The rationale is to search for distinctive instances of frame elements in sentences; then, it is quite trivial for FEs to propagate evocation up to frame(s) they are member of. In our example, declarative memory contains information about the evocation between "door" and "bag" as filler of *object* slot in the following evocation chunk types:

```
(e7   ISA evocation object bag  frame-element entity)
(e8   ISA evocation object bag  frame-element container)
(e9   ISA evocation object bag  frame-element goal)
(e10  ISA evocation object door frame-element barrier)
```

Moreover, since *container*, *goal* and *barrier* appear in the structure of the following chunks, related frames for (a) and (b) are retrieved.

```
(f3 ISA frame name manipulation fe1 agent   fe2 entity)
(f4 ISA frame name closure      fe1 agent   fe2 container)
(f5 ISA frame name bringing     fe1 carrier fe2 goal)
(f7 ISA frame name openness     fe1 theme   fe2 barrier)
```

When the production "retrieve-frame-from-object" fires, we discover that (a) evokes the frame "openness" and that (b) may evoke, in principle, three different frames, respectively "manipulation", "closure" and "bringing". In order to prompt a choice within these frames, spreading activation can be exploited through the ACT-R sub-symbolic computations [6]. Spreading of activation from the contents of slots in the imaginal buffer triggers the evocation of frame-related chunks to the context of the perceived scene. Finally, by setting a high similarity parameter between *bag* and *sack*, whenever the model perceives *sack*, it will make reference to the *frame(s)* evoked by *bag* through the ACT-R mechanism of "partial matching", which allows the semantics of similarity between chunks to be reflected in the retrieval process [29].

---

[28] Future versions of the model will provide a more accurate account, allowing for successful retrievals of the most frequent frames (with frequency measured on annotated corpus sentences), as well as failure to access information symbolically present in memory because of sub-symbolic (statistical) factors.

[29] In the current version of the model, the penalization is reflected *a priori*, setting up a low activation threshold of the chunk for the input verb.

5 Conclusions

This paper presented the general framework of integration between the ACT-R cognitive architecture and semantic resources. In particular, we considered the task of high-level visual recognition of motor actions, outlining how HOMinE ontological features can augment ACT-R declarative representations. Future work will be devoted to enhance both the semantic layer and the cognitive model: the former will be improved by adding grounding axioms to WN and FN structures; the latter will be extended in terms of experimental settings, task complexity and sub-symbolic parameterization. Finally, we also aim at importing WN and FN data-structure into symbolic ACT-R declarative memory structures as well as using statistical natural language processing techniques to constrain their sub-symbolic parameters.

Acknowledgments. This research was sponsored by the Army Research Laboratory and was accomplished under Cooperative Agreement Number W911NF-10-2-0061. The views and conclusions contained in this document are those of the authors and should not be interpreted as representing the official policies, either expressed or implied, of the Army Research Laboratory or the U.S. Government. The U.S. Government is authorized to reproduce and distribute reprints for Government purposes notwithstanding any copyright notation herein.

References

1. Newell, A., Shaw, J.C., Simon, H.A.: Report on a general problem-solving program. In: Proceedings of the International Conference on Information Processing, pp. 256–264 (1959)
2. Anderson, J.R.: The Architecture of Cognition. Harvard University Press, Cambridge (1983)
3. Newell: Unified Theories of Cognition. Harvard University Press, Cambridge (1990)
4. Lenat, D.B., Prakash, M., Shepherd, M.: CYC: Using Common Sense Knowledge to Overcome Brittleness and Knowledge Acquisition Bottlenecks. Artificial Intelligence 6(4), 65–85
5. Anderson, J.R., Lebiere, C.L.: The Newell test for a theory of cognition. Behavioral & Brain Sciences 26, 587–637 (2003)
6. Anderson, J.R., Lebiere, C.: The atomic components of thought. Erlbaum, Mahwah (1998)
7. Anderson, J.R.: How Can the Human Mind Occur in the Physical Universe? Oxford University Press, New York (2007)
8. Stocco, A., Lebiere, C., Anderson, J.R.: Conditional Routing of Information to the Cortex: A Model of the Basal Ganglia Role in Cognitive Coordination. Psychological Review 117(2), 541–574 (2010)
9. McCarthy, J.: Circumscription – A Form of Non-Monotonic Reasoning. Artificial Intelligence 5(13), 27–39 (1980)
10. Hayes, P.J.: The Second Naive Physics Manifesto. In: Hobbs, J.R., Moore, R.C. (eds.) Formal Theories of the Common-sense World, Ablex, Norwood, pp. 1–36 (1985)
11. Sowa, J.F.: Conceptual Structures. Information Processing in Mind and Machine. Addison Wesley, Reading (1984)

12. Smith, B., Welty, C.: Ontology: Towards a new synthesis. In: Welty, C., Smith, B. (eds.) Formal Ontology in Information Systems, pp. iii–x. ACM Press, Ogunquit (2001)
13. Gruber, T.R.: A Translation Approach to Portable Ontology Specifications. Knowledge Acquisition 5, 199–220 (1993)
14. Guarino, N.: Formal Ontology and Information Systems. In: Guarino, N. (ed.) Formal Ontology in Information Systems. IOS Press, Amsterdam (1998)
15. Berners-Lee, T.: The Semantic Web. Scientific American (May 2001)
16. Ball, J., Rodgers, S., Gluck, K.: Integrating ACT-R and Cyc in a large-scale model of language comprehension for use in intelligent agents. Papers from the AAAI Workshop, Technical Report WS-04-07, pp. 19-25. AAAI Press, Menlo Park (2004)
17. Douglass, S., Ball, J., Rodgers, S.: Large declarative memories in ACT-R. In: Proceedings of the 9th International Conference of Cognitive Modeling (paper 234), Manchester, United Kingdom (2009)
18. Best, B.J., Gerhart, N., Lebiere, C.: Extracting the Ontological Structure of OpenCyc for Reuse and Portability of Cognitive Models. In: Proceedings of the 17th Conference on Behavioral Representation in Modeling and Simulation (2010)
19. Emond, B.: WN-LEXICAL: An ACT-R module built from the WordNet lexical database. In: Proceedings of the Seventh International Conference on Cognitive Modeling, Trieste, Italy, pp. 359–360 (2006)
20. Huang, C.R., Calzolari, N., Gangemi, A., Lenci, A., Oltramari, A., Prevot, L. (eds.): Ontology and the Lexicon. Cambridge University Press, Cambridge (2010)
21. Fellbaum, C. (ed.): WordNet - An Electronic Lexical Database. MIT Press, Cambridge (1998)
22. Ruppenhofer, J., Ellsworth, M., Petruck, M.R., Johnson, C.R., Scheffczyk, J.: FrameNet II: Extended Theory and Practice. International Computer Science Institute (2006)
23. Fillmore, C.J.: The case for case. In: Bach, E., Harms, T. (eds.) Universals in Linguistic Theory. Rinehart and Wiston, New York (1968)
24. Pazienza, M.T., Stellato, A.: An open and scalable framework for enriching ontologies with natural language content. In: Huang, C.R., Oltramari, A., Buitelaar, P., Fellbaum, C., Lenci, A. (eds.) Ontologies and Lexical Resources – Workshop at Linguistic Resources and Evaluation Conference, Genoa (2006)
25. Ovchinnikova, E., Vieu, L., Oltramari, A., Borgo, S., Alexandrov, T.: Data-driven and Ontological Analysis of FrameNet for Natural Language Processing. In: Proceedings of 7th International Conference on Language Resources and Evaluation, La Valletta, Malta (2010)
26. Gangemi, A., Guarino, N., Masolo, C., Oltramari, A.: Sweetening WordNet with DOLCE. AI Magazine, 24(3), Fall 2003, 13–24 (2003)
27. Anderson, J.R.: Retrieval of propositional information from long-term memory. Cognitive Psychology 5, 451–474 (1974)
28. Burchardt, A., Erk, K., Frank, A.: A Wordnet detour to FrameNet. In: Schrder, B., Bernhard, F., Schmitz, H.C., Wagner, P. (eds.) Sprachtechnologie, mobile Kommunikation und linguistische Resourcen. Computer Studies in Language and Speech, Peter Lang, Frankfurt am Main, vol. 8, pp. 408–421 (2005)
29. Budiu, R., Anderson, J.R.: Interpretation-Based Processing: A Unified Theory of Semantic Sentence Processing. Cognitive Science 28, 1–44 (2004)

A Motivational System for Cognitive AI

Joscha Bach

Center for Integrative Life Sciences, Humboldt University of Berlin,
Unter den Linden 6, 10099 Berlin, Germany
joscha.bach@hu-berlin.de

Abstract. General Intelligence is not only characterized by the general representation and (relatively) general problem solving capabilities, but also by general motivation. Here, I sketch a framework for an extensible motivational system for cognitive agents, based on research in psychology. It draws on a finite set of pre-defined drives, which relate to needs of the system. Goals are established through reinforcement learning by interacting with an environment.

Keywords: Artificial General Intelligence, Cognitive AI, Synthetic Intelligence, Psi theory, Motivation, Motivational System, Cognitive Architectures.

1 Introduction: The Quest for General Intelligence

AGI (*Artificial General Intelligence*, or research into "strong Artificial Intelligence") as a discipline is fraught with difficulties. AI as a way of understanding and modeling the mind faces strong cultural opposition—many people, and even most scientists are deeply uncomfortable with treating the mind as an information processing machine (e.g., [1]). A large part of this opposition springs from a misunderstanding of the notion of *machine*, and the significance of computational models. These models constitute our best chance at understanding the mind and the nature of intelligence at all—and not because intelligence and mind constitute exceptions within the realm of nature. Natural sciences (unlike humanities) are largely concerned with the formulation of formal theories of their objects. Many objects of the sciences—like the formation of galaxies, stars and planets, the chemistry of biological cells, the changes of the planetary climate—require formal systemic theories of a complexity that goes beyond easy comprehension. Where these theories can not be broken down into individual, experimentally accessible questions, their coherence has to be tested by simulations, and any systemic theory that is specified to a degree of detail sufficient for simulation amounts to a computational model. A theory that wants to explain how the mind works will fall into this category.

The problems of AGI go much deeper than cultural opposition to computational modeling: even within the AI community, there is no clear agreement on what constitutes intelligence, and if it makes sense to define intelligence outside the context of human performance. For instance, purely mathematical approaches (for instance,

J. Schmidhuber, K.R. Thórisson, and M. Looks (Eds.): AGI 2011, LNAI 6830, pp. 232–242, 2011.

the definition by Hutter and Legg [2], based on the ability of a system to achieve rewards), have not been universally agreed upon, because intelligence is not necessarily reward-seeking, and definitions based on problem solving ability are usually bound to individual classes of tasks. Consequently, there is no consensus and no single established methodology on how AGI's goals are to be reached.

Academic research into Artificial Intelligence has fragmented into a multitude of paradigms that eventually broke away and became sub-disciplines of computer science (such as machine learning, description logics, planning etc.), no longer concerned with understanding intelligence *per sé*. Even though AI has continuously spawned tremendously useful results, it arguably constitutes a string of failures with respect to attaining human-like intelligence. Every single paradigm of AI, such as symbolic models, connectionism, expert systems, and *Fifth Generation Computing* [3] has failed to produce breakthroughs with respect to this goal. But it should also be noted that AI has been consistently fruitful in advancing technology and computer science.

IBM's recent *Watson* system [4], which is able to outdo skilled humans in the question-answer game show *Jeopardy*, is a good example: While *Watson* constitutes an impressive engineering achievement, with useful applications in medicine and other fields, and may even affect the way people interact with computers, it is far from being "generally intelligent". *Watson's* architecture firmly constrains it into the territory of search engines, and will not scale towards an artificial mind [5].

One of the problems of the AGI label might be that it names a goal, but does not specify a methodology. AGI, taken as the *science of the mind as a computational system*, will have succeeded in its mission if its computer models are able to reproduce mental capabilities on at least a scope comparable to humans. However, this goal is not equivalent to an architectural paradigm. AGI is probably not best classed as a genuine sub-discipline of computer science. AGI might be seen as *cybernetic psychology*, as an attempt to formulate a general theory of psychology in terms of action regulating information processing systems. Indeed, AGI had been one of the original goals of cybernetics. Even after the decline of cybernetics as an independent field, AGI has been taken up by psychologists, under the label *cognitive architectures*. The influence of research into cognitive architectures on the psychological mainstream has been limited though—after all, models of general cognition are not the same thing as models of the human psyche. Most research in psychology is not interested in an overarching, unified theory of cognition. Instead, AGI relates to contemporary psychology in much the same way as the study of flight does to ornithology. And just as flight is not best understood as the movement of solid objects through a gaseous medium, AGI should limit its concern for general theories of representation, information processing, or control of robotic bodies, as long as they are not strictly relevant to its goal. AGI research will have to constrain its paradigms on suitable levels of description.

Even though AGI does not presume that mind and intelligence are inextricably linked to biological brains and human subjects (just as flight is not exclusively limited to feathered wings and avifauna), it will have to explain how the human mind is able to do what it does.

2   What Is Cognitive Artificial Intelligence?

What is the right frame for describing what a mind does? Within AI, we can discern at least the following camps:

1. *Symbolic ('classical') AI*. Newell and Simon's *Physical Symbol System Hypothesis* [6] states that symbolic computation is both necessary and sufficient for general intelligence. Since symbolic computation is Turing complete, this is trivially true, but criticism of symbolic (rule-based) AI maintains that a purely symbolic system does not constitute a feasible *practical* approach, either because discrete symbols are technically insufficient, or because it usually lacks grounding in a physical environment. This criticism gives rise to:
2. *Distributed (connectionist) AI*, which focuses on emergent behavior, dynamical systems and neural learning, and
3. *Embodied AI*, which focuses on solving the symbol grounding problem by environmental interaction.

The two latter paradigms are often subsumed under the 'New AI' label, and they are vitally important: Connectionism can provide models for neural computation, for learning and perceptual processing (but will also have to explain how sub-symbolic processing gives rise to symbolic cognition, such as planning and use of natural language). Embodiment situates a system in a dynamic environment and provides content for and relevance of cognitive processes.

Unfortunately, the paradigms do not get along very well: proponents of symbolic AI often ignored connectionism and symbol grounding, while connectionists frequently disregarded symbolic aspects of cognition. Most embodied AI focuses on controlling robots instead of modeling cognition; radical proponents of embodied AI even suggest that intelligence is an *emergent* phenomenon of the interaction between an embodied nervous system and a *physical* environment [7] and sometimes reject the notion of representation altogether. The success of AGI will largely be due to the right integration of symbolic cognition (language, planning, high-level deliberation) with sub-symbolic processing (perception, analogical reasoning, neural learning and classification, memory retrieval etc.) and action regulation in a *broad architecture*. We will have to aim for a *cognitive AI*, for the class of framework that combines the necessary and sufficient means for enabling the full breadth of cognitive capabilities.

Cognitive AI does not refer to abstract theorem provers and planners, nor does it focus on sensory-motor coupling. Instead, cognitive AI should process perceptual and conceptual information in much the same way as humans do. Cognitive AI has to combine distributed, dynamical representations with compositionality, has to handle analogy, ambiguity and error, must attribute motivational relevance and so on.

Such a framework will have to merge *general representations* (the capability to express arbitrary relationships, up to a certain complexity) with *general learning and problem solving* (the capability to acquire and manipulate these relationships in any necessary way, up to a certain complexity), a sufficiently interesting environment to operate upon, and a *general motivational system* (which supplies a polythematic, intrinsic motivation to direct action). Let us now look on some aspects of such a motivational system.

3 Prerequisites for Defining a Motivational System

Since we can not observe and verify most parts of the human motivational system directly, we will have to construct a model that can produce the desired behavior in simulations. Such a model will have to adhere to some constraints; it should provide:

- *conceptual soundness:* demonstrate a conceptual analysis of needs, motives, intentions and action regulation, and their place in a larger model of cognition,
- *functional adequacy:* the model should be sufficient to produce the desired range of behaviors and cognitive phenomena,
- *biological plausibility:* the model should be compatible with our knowledge of biological systems,
- *sparseness:* the model should aim for the minimum number of entities and relationships to produce the desired behavior,
- a *suitable level of detail for formalization:* all components and relationships have to be specified to a degree of detail that allows for implementation as a computational model,
- *avoidance of over-specialization:* where functional aspects or quantitative relationships are unknown, the model should not be unnecessarily constrained.

Also, the model should support an experimental paradigm, to be evaluated against competing approaches, so that progress can be measured. This could be a set of challenge problems, a competition between different solutions, or a suitable application.

A human-like intelligence could likely exist in a non-human body, and in a simulated world, as long as the internal architecture—the motivational and representational mechanisms and the structure of cognitive processes—are similar to the one of humans, and the environment provides sufficient stimulation. The desires and fears of humans correspond to their *needs*, such as environmental exploration, identification and avoidance of danger, and the attainment of food, shelter, cooperation, procreation, and intellectual growth. Since the best way to satisfy the individual needs varies with the environment, the motivational system is not aligned with particular *goal situations*, but with the needs themselves, through a set of *drives*.

Let us call events that satisfy a need of the system a *goal*, or an *appetitive event*, and one that frustrates a need an *aversive event* (for instance, a failure or an accident). Goals and aversive events are given by the environment, they are not be part of the architecture. Instead, the architecture specifies a set of drives according to the needs of the system. Drives are indicated as *urges*, as signals that make a need apparent. An example of a need would be nutrition, which relates to a drive for seeking out food. On the cognitive level of the system, the activity of the drive is indicated as *hunger*.

The connection between urges and events is established by *reinforcement learning*. In our example, that connection will have to establish a representational link between the indicator for food and a *consumptive action* (i.e., the act of ingesting food), which in turn must refer to an environmental situation that made the food available. Whenever the urge for food becomes active in the future, the system may use the link to retrieve the environmental situation from memory and establish it as a goal.

This defines some additional requirements to the architecture: The system needs:

- a set of suitable urges,
- a way of evaluating them to establish goals and identify adverse events,
- a world model that represents environmental situations and events,
- a protocol memory that makes past situations and events accessible,
- a reinforcement learning mechanism working on that protocol,
- a mechanism for anticipation, to recollect memory content according to the current environmental situation and needs,
- a decision making component, which pitches the current urges and the available ways to satisfy them against each other, and chooses a way of action,
- an action regulation component, so this way of action can be followed through.

A more advanced architecture will also require mechanisms for planning, classification and problem solving, to actively construct ways from a given situation to a goal situation (instead of just remembering a successful way from the past), and mechanisms for reflection, to reorganize and abstract existing memory content.

Note that many possible architectures may satisfy this set of requirements, and thus I will not specify an implementation here. Here, I will focus on the motivational side.

4   An Outline of a Motivational System, According to the Psi Theory

The Psi theory [8, 9] originates in the works of the psychologist Dietrich Dörner and has been transformed into a cognitive architecture by the author [10]. Unlike high-level descriptions of motivation as they are more common in psychology, such as the one by Maslov [11] or Kuhl [12], the motivational model lined out in the Psi theory is rigorous enough to be implemented as a computational model, and unlike narrow, physiological models (such as the one by Tyrell [13]), it also addresses cognitive and social behavior. A simulation model of the Psi theory has been demonstrated with MicroPsi[14]. In the following, I will identify the core components of the motivational system.

4.1 Needs

All urges of the agent stem from a fixed and finite number of 'hard-wired' needs, implemented as parameters that tend to deviate from a target value. Because the agent strives to maintain the target value by pursuing suitable behaviors, its activity can be described as an attempt to maintain a *dynamic homeostasis*.

All behavior of Psi agents is directed towards a goal situation, that is characterized by a *consumptive action* satisfying one of the needs. In addition to what the physical (or virtual) embodiment of the agent dictates, there are cognitive needs that direct the agents towards exploration and the avoidance of needless repetition. The needs of the agent should be weighted against each other, so differences in importance can be represented.

Physiological needs

Fuel and water: In our simulations, water and fuel are used whenever an agent executed an action, especially locomotion. Certain areas of the environment caused the agent to loose water quickly, which associated them with additional negative reinforcement signals.

Intactness: Environmental hazards may damage the body of the agent, creating an increased intactness need and leading to negative reinforcement signals (akin to *pain*). These simple needs can be extended at will, for instance by needs for shelter, for rest, for exercise, for certain types of nutrients etc.

Cognitive needs

Certainty: To direct agents towards the exploration of unknown objects and affairs, they possess an urge specifically for the reduction of uncertainty in their assessment of situations, knowledge about objects and processes and in their expectations. Because the need for certainty is implemented similar to the physiological urges, the agent reacts to uncertainty just as it would to pain signals and will display a tendency to remove this condition. This is done by triggering explorative behavior. Events leading to an urge for uncertainty reduction include:

- the agent meets unknown objects or events,
- for the recognized elements, there is no known connection to behavior—the agent has no knowledge what to do with them,
- there are problems to perceive the current situation at all,
- there has been a breach of expectations; some event has turned out differently as anticipated,
- over-complexity: the situation changes faster than the perceptual process can handle,
- the anticipated chain of events is either too short or branches too much. Both conditions make predictions difficult.

In each case, the uncertainty signal is weighted according to the relation to the appetitive or aversive relevance of the object of uncertainty. The urge for certainty may be satisfied by "certainty events"—the opposite of uncertainty events:

- the complete identification of objects and scenes,
- complete embedding of recognized elements into agent behaviors,
- fulfilled expectations (even negative ones),
- a long and non-branching chain of expected events.

Like all urge-satisfying events, certainty events create a positive reinforcment signal and reduce the respective need. Because the agent may anticipate the reward signals from successful uncertainty reduction, it can actively look for new uncertainties to explore ("diversive exploration).

Competence: When choosing an action, Psi agents weight the strength of the corresponding urge against the chance of success. The measure for the chance of success to satisfy a given urge using a known behavior program is called "specific competence". If the agent has no knowledge on how to satisfy an urge, it has to resort to "general competence" as an estimate. Thus, general competence amounts to something like self-confidence of the agent, and it is an urge on its own. (Specific competencies are not urges.) The general competence reflects the ability to overcome obstacles, which can be recognized as being sources of negative reinforcement signals, and to do that efficiently, which is represented by positive reinforcement signals. Thus, the general competence of an agent is estimated as a floating average over the reinforcement signals and the inverted displeasure signals. The general competence is a heuristics on how well the agent expects to perform in unknown situations.

As in the case of uncertainty, the agent learns to anticipate the positive reinforcement signals resulting from satisfying the competence urge. A main source of competence is the reduction of uncertainty. As a result, the agent actively aims for problems that allow gaining competence, but avoids overly demanding situations to escape the frustration of its competence urge. Ideally, this leads the agent into an environment of medium difficulty (measured by its current abilities to overcome obstacles).

Aesthetics: Environmental situations and relationships can be represented in infinitely many ways. Here 'aesthetics' corresponds to a need for improving representations, mainly by increasing their sparseness, while maintaining or increasing their descriptive qualities.

Social needs

Affiliation: Because the explorative and physiological desires of Psi agents are not sufficient to make them interested in each other, they have a need for positive social signals, so-called '*legitimacy signals*'. With a legitimacy signal (or *l-signal* for short), agents may signal each other "okayness" with regard to the social group. Legitimacy signals are an expression of the sender's belief in the social acceptability of the receiver. The need for l-signals needs frequent replenishment and thus amounts to an urge to affiliate with other agents. Agents can send l-signals to reward each other for cooperation. *Anti-l-signals* are the counterpart of l-signals. An anti-l-signal (which basically amounts to a frown) 'punishes' an agent by depleting its legitimacy reservoir.

Agents may also be extended by *internal l-signals*, which measure the conformance to internalized social norms.

Supplicative signals are 'pleas for help', i.e. promises to reward a cooperative action with l-signals or likewise cooperation in the future. Supplicative signals work like a specific kind of anti-l-signals, because they increase the legitimacy urge of the addressee when not answered. At the same time, they lead to (external and internal) l-signals when help is given. They can thus be used to trigger *altruistic behavior*.

The need for l-signals should adapt to the environment of the agent, and may also vary strongly between agents, thus creating a wide range of types of social behavior. By making the receivable amount of l-signals dependent of the priming towards particular other agents, Psi agents might be induced to display '*jealous' behavior*.

Social needs can be extended by romantic and sexual needs. However, there is no explicit need for social power, because the model already captures social power as a specific need for competence—the competence to satisfy social needs.

Even though the affiliation model is still fragmentary, we found that it provides a good handle on the agents during experiments. The experimenter can attempt to induce the agents to actions simply by the prospect of a smile or frown, which is sometimes a good alternative to a more solid reward or punishment.

4.2 Behavior Control and Action Selection

All goal-directed actions have their source in a motive that is connected to an urge, which in turn signals a physiological, cognitive or social need. Actions that are not directed immediately onto a goal are either carried out to serve an exploratory goal or to avoid an aversive event. When a positive goal is reached (a need is partially or completely fulfilled), a positive reinforcement signal is created, which is used for learning (by strengthening the associations of the goal with the actions and situations that have led to the fulfillment). In those cases in which a sub-goal does not yet lead to a consummative act, reaching it may still create a reinforcement via the competence it signals to the agent. After finally reaching a consumptive goal, the intermediate goals may receive further reinforcement by a retrogradient (backwards in time along the protocol) strengthening of the associations along the chain of events that has lead to the target situation.

Appetence and Aversion: For an urge to have an effect on the behavior on the agent, it does not matter whether it *really* has an effect on its (physical or simulated) body, but that it is represented in the proper way within the cognitive system. Whenever the agent performs an action or is subjected to an event that reduces one of its urges, a reinforcement signal with a strength that is proportional to this reduction is created by the agent's "pleasure center". The naming of the "pleasure" and "displeasure centers" does not necessarily imply that the agent experiences something like pleasure or displeasure. Like in humans, their purpose lies in signaling the reflexive evaluation of positive or harmful effects according to physiological, cognitive or social needs. (*Experiencing* these signals would require an observation of these signals at certain levels of the perceptual system of the agent.) Reinforcement signals create or strengthen an association between the urge indicator and the action/event. Whenever the respective urge of the agent becomes active in the future, it may activate the now connected behavior/episodic schema. If the agent pursues the chains of actions/events leading to the situation alleviating the urge, we are witnessing goal-oriented behavior.

Conversely, during events that increase a need (for instance by damaging the agent or frustrating one of its cognitive or social urges), the "displeasure center" creates a signal that causes an inverse link from the harmful situation to the urge indicator. When in future deliberation attempts (for instance, by extrapolating into the expectation horizon) the respective situation gets activated, it also activates the urge indicator and thus signals an aversion. An *aversion signal* is a predictor for aversive situations, and such aversive situations are avoided if possible.

Motives: A motive consists of an urge (that is, the value of an indicator for a need) and a goal that has been associated to this indicator. The goal is a situation schema characterized by an action or event that has successfully reduced the urge in the past, and the goal situation tends to be the end element of a behavior program. The situations leading to the goal situation—that is, earlier stages in the connected occurrence schema or behavior program—might become intermediate goals. To turn this sequence into an instance that may initiate a behavior, orient it towards a goal and keep it active, we need to add a connection to the pleasure/displeasure system. The result is a *motivator* and consists of:

- a need sensor, connected to the pleasure/displeasure system in such a way, that an increase in the deviation of the need from the target value creates a displeasure signal, and a decrease results in a pleasure signal. This reinforcement signal should be proportional to the strength of the increment or decrement.
- optionally, a feedback loop that attempts to normalize the need automatically
- an urge indicator that becomes active if there is no way of automatically adjusting the need to its target value. The urge should be proportional to the need.
- an associator (part of the pleasure/displeasure system) that creates a connection between the urge indicator and an episodic schema/behavior program, specifically to the aversive or appetitive goal situation. The strength of the connection should be proportional to the pleasure/displeasure signal. Note that usually, an urge gets connected with more than one goal over time, since there are often many ways to satisfy or increase a particular urge.

Motive selection: If a motive becomes active, it is not always selected immediately; sometimes it will not be selected at all, because it conflicts with a stronger motive or the chances of success when pursuing the motive are too low. In the terminology of *Belief-Desire-Intention agents* [15], motives amount to *desires*, selected motives give rise to goals and thus are *intentions*. Active motives can be selected at any time, for instance, an agent seeking fuel could satisfy a weaker urge for water on the way, just because the water is readily available, and thus, the active motives, together with their related goals, behavior programs and so on, are called *intention memory*. The selection of a motive takes place according to a *value* by *success probability* principle, where the value of a motive is given by its importance (indicated by the respective urge), and the success probability depends on the competence of the agent to reach the particular goal.

In some cases, the agent may not know a way to reach a goal (i.e., it has no epistemic competence related to that goal). If the agent performs well in general, that is, it has a high *general* competence, it should still consider selecting the related motive. The chance to reach a particular goal might be estimated using the sum of the general competence and the epistemic competence for that goal. Thus, the *motive strength* to satisfy a need d is calculated as $urge_d \cdot (generalCompetence + competence_d)$, i.e. the product of the strength of the urge and the combined competence.

If the window of opportunity is limited, the motive strength should be enhanced with a third factor: *urgency*. The rationale behind urgency lies in the aversive goal created by the anticipated failure of meeting the deadline. The urgency of a motive related to a time limit could be estimated by dividing the time needed through the time left, and the motive strength for a motive with a deadline can be calculated using $(urge_d + urgency_d) \cdot (generalCompetence + competence_d)$, i.e. as the combined urgency multiplied with the combined competence. The time the agent has left to reach the goal can be inferred from episodic schemas stored in the agent's current expectation horizon, while the necessary time to finish the goal oriented behavior can be determined from the behavior program. (Obviously, these estimates require a detailed anticipation of things to come, which may be difficult to obtain.)

At each time, only one motive is selected for the execution of its related behavior program. There is a continuous competition between motives, to reflect changes in the environment and the internal states of the agent. To avoid oscillations between motives, the switching between motives may be taxed with an additional cost: the *selection threshold*, a bonus that is added to the strength of the currently selected motive. The value of the selection threshold can be varied according to circumstances, rendering the agent 'opportunistic' or 'stubborn'.

Intentions: As explained above, intentions amount to selected motives, combined with a way to achieve the desired outcome. Within the Psi theory, an *intention* refers to the set of representations that initiates, controls and structures the execution of an action. (It is not required that an intention be conscious, that it is directed onto an object etc.—here, intentions are simply those things that make actions happen.)

Intentions may form *intention hierarchies*, i.e. to reach a goal it might be necessary to establish sub-goals and pursue these. An intention can be seen as a set of a goal state, an execution state, an intention history (the protocol of operations that took place in its context), a plan, the urge associated with the goal state (which delivers the relevance), the estimated specific competency to fulfill the intention (which is related to the probability of reaching the goal) and the time horizon during which the intention must be realized.

The dynamics of modulation: In the course of the action selection and execution, Psi agents are modulated by several parameters: The agent's *activation* or *arousal* (which resembles the *ascending reticular activation system* in humans) determines the action-readiness of an agent. It is proportional to the current strength of the urge signals. The perceptual and memory processes are influenced by the agent's *resolution level*, which is inversely related to the activation. A high resolution level increases the number of features examined during perception and memory retrieval, at the cost of processing speed and resulting ambiguity. The *selection threshold* determines how easily the agent switches between conflicting intentions, and the *sampling rate* or *securing threshold* controls the frequency of reflective and orientation behaviors. The values of the modulators of an agent at a given time, together with the status of the urges, define a cognitive configuration, a setup that may be interpreted as an *emergent emotional state*.

5 Summary

The Psi theory defines a possible solution for a drive-based, poly-thematic motivational system. It does not only explain how physiological needs can be pursued, but also addresses the establishment of cognitive and social goals.

Its straightforward integration of needs allows adapting it quickly to different environments and types of agents; a version of the model has been successfully evaluated against human performance in problem solving game [9].

The existing implementation of the Psi theory in the MicroPsi architecture [14] still restricts social signals to simple *l-signals* and *anti-l-signals*, and it does not cover a need for improving internal representations ('aesthetics'). Still, it may act as a qualitative demonstrator of an already quite broad computational model of motivation.

The suggested motivational model can be implemented in a variety of different ways, and we are currently working on transferring it to other cognitive architectures to obtain further scenarios and test-beds for criticizing and improving it.

References

1. Weizenbaum, J.: Wer erfindet die Computermythen? Der Fortschritt in den großen Irrtum. Herder, Freiburg (1993)
2. Legg, S., Hutter, M.: A definition of machine intelligence. Minds and Machines 17 (2007)
3. Simons, G.L.: Towards Fifth-generation Computers, National Computing Centre, Manchester, UK (1983)
4. Ferrucci, D., et al.: Building Watson: An Overview of the DeepQA Project. AI Magazine 31(3) (2010)
5. Wolfram, S.: Jeopardy, IBM, and Wolfram|Alpha. (January 26, 2011), http://blog.stephenwolfram.com/2011/01/jeopardy-ibm-and-wolframalpha/
6. Newell, A., Simon, H.A.: Computer Science as Empirical Inquiry: Symbols and Search. Communications of the ACM 19, 113–126 (1976)
7. Pfeifer, R., Bongard, J.: How the body shapes the way we think. MIT Press, Cambridge (2006)
8. Dörner, D.: Bauplan für eine Seele. Reinbeck (1999)
9. Dörner, D., Bartl, C., Detje, F., Gerdes, J., Halcour, D.: Die Mechanik des Seelenwagens. Handlungsregulation. Verlag Hans Huber, Bern (2002)
10. Bach, J.: PSI – An architecture of motivated cognition. Oxford University Press, Oxford (2009)
11. Maslow, A., Frager, R., Fadiman, J.: Motivation and Personality, 3rd edn. Addison-Wesley, Boston (1987)
12. Kuhl, J.: Motivation und Persönlichkeit: Interaktionen psychischer Systeme. Hogrefe, Göttingen (2001)
13. Tyrell, T.: Computational Mechanism for Action Selection, PhD Thesis. University of Edinburgh (1993)
14. Bach, J.: Motivated, Emotional Agents in the MicroPsi Framework. In: Proceedings of 8th European Conference on Cognitive Science, Delphi, Greece (2007)
15. Bratman, M.: Intentions, Plans and Practical Reason. Harvard University Press, Cambridge (1987)

On Fast Deep Nets for AGI Vision

Jürgen Schmidhuber, Dan Cireşan, Ueli Meier, Jonathan Masci, and Alex Graves

The Swiss AI Lab IDSIA
University of Lugano & SUPSI, Switzerland

Abstract. Artificial General Intelligence will not be general without computer vision. Biologically inspired adaptive vision models have started to outperform traditional pre-programmed methods: our fast deep / recurrent neural networks recently collected a string of 1st ranks in many important visual pattern recognition benchmarks: IJCNN traffic sign competition, NORB, CIFAR10, MNIST, three ICDAR handwriting competitions. We greatly profit from recent advances in computing hardware, complementing recent progress in the AGI theory of mathematically optimal universal problem solvers.

Keywords: AGI, Fast Deep Neural Nets, Computer Vision, Hardware Advances vs Theoretical Progress.

1   Introduction

Computer vision is becoming essential for thousands of practical applications. For example, the future of search engines lies in image and video recognition as opposed to traditional text search. Autonomous robots such as driverless cars depend on vision, too. Generally speaking, the "G" in "AGI" will be undeserved without excellent computer vision.

AGI research is currently driven by two types of progress. On the one hand, the new millennium brought the first universal problem solvers [10, 21] that are theoretically optimal in asymptotic and other senses, putting AGI research on a sound mathematical footing for the first time, although such approaches are currently not yet practically feasible. On the other hand, due to ongoing hardware advances, the computing power per Swiss Franc is still growing by a factor of 100-1000 per decade, greatly increasing the practical feasibility of less general methods invented in the previous millennium. This paper reflects the second type of progress, exploiting graphics cards or GPUs (mini-supercomputers normally used for video games) which are 100 times faster than today's CPU cores, and a million times faster than PCs of 20 years ago, to train biologically plausible deep neural nets on vision tasks.

Excellent object recognition results illustrate the benefits of this pragmatic approach. As of January 2011, our neural computer vision team has collected a string of 1st ranks in many important and highly competitive international visual pattern recognition benchmarks.

1. IJCNN's online Traffic Sign Recognition Benchmark (1st & 2nd rank; 1.02% error rate), January 2011 [4].

J. Schmidhuber, K.R. Thórisson, and M. Looks (Eds.): AGI 2011, LNAI 6830, pp. 243–246, 2011.

2. NORB data set, NY University, 2004 [13]. Our team set the new record (2.53% error rate) in February 2011 [3].
3. CIFAR-10 data set of Univ. Toronto, 2009 [11]. Our team set the new record (19.51% error rate) in 2011 [3].
4. MNIST data set of NY University, 1998 [12]. Our team set the new record (0.35% error rate) in 2010 [2], and tied it again in January 2011 [3].
5. Three Handwriting Recognition Competitions at ICDAR 2009, all won by our multi-dimensional LSTM recurrent neural networks trained by *Connectionist Temporal Classification* (CTC) [7, 8]: Arabic Handwriting Competition of Univ. Braunschweig, Handwritten Farsi/Arabic Character Recognition Competition, French Handwriting Competition based on data from the RIMES campaign.

Remarkably, none of the above requires the traditional sophisticated computer vision techniques developed over the past six decades or so. Instead, our biologically rather plausible systems are inspired by human brains, and learn to recognize objects from numerous training examples. We use supervised, artificial, feedforward or recurrent [9, 7, 8] (deep by nature) neural networks with many non-linear processing stages, partially inspired by early hierarchical neural systems such as Fukushima's Neocognitron [5]. We sometimes (but not always) profit from sparse network connectivity and techniques such as weight sharing & convolution [12, 1, 25], max-pooling [17], and contrast enhancement [6] like the one automatically generated by unsupervised *Predictability Minimization* [18, 22, 24].

2   Neural Network ReNNaissance

Our NNs are now outperforming all other methods including the theoretically less general and less powerful support vector machines based on statistical learning theory [27] (which for a long time had the upper hand, at least in practice). Such results are currently contributing to a second *Neural Network ReNNaissance* (the first one happened in the 1980s and early 90s).

3   Outlook

The methods discussed above are passive learners - they do not learn to actively search for the most informative image parts. Humans, however, use sequential gaze shifts for pattern recognition. This can be more efficient than the fully parallel one-shot approach. That's why we intend to combine the fast deep / recurrent nets above with variants of what to our knowledge was the first artificial fovea sequentially steered by a learning neural controller [23], using a variant of reinforcement learning to create saccades and find targets in a visual scene.

4   Conclusion

The first decades of attempts at AGI have been dominated by heuristic approaches, e.g., [15, 16, 26, 14]. In recent years things have changed, however. The new millennium brought the first mathematically sound, asymptotically optimal, universal problem solvers, providing a new, rigorous foundation for the previously largely heuristic field of General AI and embedded cognitive agents, identifying the limits of both human and artificial intelligence, and providing a yardstick for any future approach to general cognitive systems [19, 10, 20]. The field is indeed becoming a real formal science.

On the other hand, however, one cannot dispute the significance of hardware progress on the road to practical AGI, as illustrated by our recent practical successes mentioned in this paper, achieved by methods which are combinations of algorithms mostly developed in the previous millennium, but greatly profiting from dramatic advances in computational power per Swiss Franc, obtained in the new millennium.

We are confident that theory and practice will converge in the not-so-distant future.

Acknowledgements. This work was funded in part by EU project 270247, "A Neurodynamic Framework for Cognitive Robotics: Scene Representations, Behavioural Sequences, and Learning," and by SNF grant 200021-111968.

References

[1] Behnke, S.: Hierarchical Neural Networks for Image Interpretation. LNCS, vol. 2766. Springer, Heidelberg (2003)

[2] Ciresan, D.C., Meier, U., Gambardella, L.M., Schmidhuber, J.: Deep big simple neural nets for handwritten digit recogntion. Neural Computation 22(12), 3207–3220 (2010)

[3] Ciresan, D.C., Meier, U., Masci, J., Gambardella, L.M., Schmidhuber, J.: High-performance neural networks for visual object classification. arxiv 1102.0183 (2011)

[4] Ciresan, D.C., Meier, U., Masci, J., Schmidhuber, J.: A committee of neural networks for traffic sign classification. In: International Joint Conference on Neural Networks to appear (2011)

[5] Fukushima, K.: Neocognitron: A self-organizing neural network for a mechanism of pattern recognition unaffected by shift in position. Biological Cybernetics 36(4), 193–202 (1980)

[6] Fukushima, K.: Neocognitron for handwritten digit recognition. Neurocomputing 51, 161–180 (2003)

[7] Graves, A., Fernández, S., Schmidhuber, J.: Multi-dimensional recurrent neural networks. In: Proceedings of the 17th International Conference on Artificial Neural Networks (September 2007)

[8] Graves, A., Schmidhuber, J.: Offline handwriting recognition with multidimensional recurrent neural networks. In: Advances in Neural Information Processing Systems, vol. 21, MIT Press, Cambridge (2009)

[9] Hochreiter, S., Schmidhuber, J.: Flat minima. Neural Computation 9(1), 1–42 (1997)

[10] Hutter, M.: Universal Artificial Intelligence: Sequential Decisions based on Algorithmic Probability. Springer, Berlin (2004); (On J. Schmidhuber's SNF grant 20-61847)

[11] Krizhevsky, A.: Learning multiple layers of features from tiny images. Master's thesis, Computer Science Department, University of Toronto (2009)

[12] LeCun, Y., Bottou, L., Bengio, Y., Haffner, P.: Gradient-based learning applied to document recognition. Proceedings of the IEEE 86(11), 2278–2324 (1998)

[13] LeCun, Y., Huang, F.J., Bottou, L.: Learning methods for generic object recognition with invariance to pose and lighting. In: Proc. of Computer Vision and Pattern Recognition Conference (2004)

[14] Mitchell, T.: Machine Learning. McGraw Hill, New York (1997)

[15] Newell, A., Simon, H.: GPS, a program that simulates human thought. In: Feigenbaum, E., Feldman, J. (eds.) Computers and Thought, pp. 279–293. McGraw-Hill, New York (1963)

[16] Rosenbloom, P.S., Laird, J.E., Newell, A.: The SOAR Papers. MIT Press, Cambridge (1993)

[17] Scherer, D., Müller, A., Behnke, S.: Evaluation of pooling operations in convolutional architectures for object recognition. In: International Conference on Artificial Neural Networks (2010)

[18] Schmidhuber, J.: Learning factorial codes by predictability minimization. Neural Computation 4(6), 863–879 (1992)

[19] Schmidhuber, J.: The new AI: General & sound & relevant for physics. In: Goertzel, B., Pennachin, C. (eds.) Artificial General Intelligence, pp. 175–198. Springer, Heidelberg (2006); also available as TR IDSIA-04-03, arXiv:cs.AI/0302012

[20] Schmidhuber, J.: New millennium AI and the convergence of history. In: Duch, W., Mandziuk, J. (eds.) Challenges to Computational Intelligence. Studies in Computational Intelligence, vol. 63, pp. 15–36. Springer, Heidelberg (2007); arXiv:cs.AI/0606081

[21] Schmidhuber, J.: Ultimate cognition à la Gödel. Cognitive Computation 1(2), 177–193 (2009)

[22] Schmidhuber, J., Eldracher, M., Foltin, B.: Semilinear predictability minimization produces well-known feature detectors. Neural Computation 8(4), 773–786 (1996)

[23] Schmidhuber, J., Huber, R.: Learning to generate artificial fovea trajectories for target detection. International Journal of Neural Systems 2(1 & 2), 135–141 (1991)

[24] Schraudolph, N.N., Eldracher, M., Schmidhuber, J.: Processing images by semi-linear predictability minimization. Network: Computation in Neural Systems 10(2), 133–169 (1999)

[25] Simard, P., Steinkraus, D., Platt, J.: Best practices for convolutional neural networks applied to visual document analysis. In: Seventh International Conference on Document Analysis and Recognition, pp. 958–963 (2003)

[26] Utgoff, P.: Shift of bias for inductive concept learning. In: Michalski, R., Carbonell, J., Mitchell, T. (eds.) Machine Learning, vol. 2, pp. 163–190. Morgan Kaufmann, Los Altos (1986)

[27] Vapnik, V.: The Nature of Statistical Learning Theory. Springer, New York (1995)

Considerations for a Neuroscience-Inspired Approach to the Design of Artificial Intelligent Systems

Serge Thill

Cognition & Interaction Lab
School of Humanities and Informatics
University of Skövde, P.O. Box 408, 54 128 Skövde, Sweden
serge.thill@his.se

Abstract. When designing artificial intelligent systems, one could do worse, at first glance, than take inspiration from the system whose performance one tries to match: the human brain. The continuing failure to produce such an inspired system is usually blamed on the lack of computational power and/or a lack of understanding of the neuroscience itself. This does not, however, affect the fundamental interest in neuroscience as studying the only known mechanism to date to have produced an intelligent system.

This paper adds another consideration (to the well-established observation that our knowledge of how the brain works is sketchy at best) which needs to be taken into account when taking inspiration from neuroscience: the human brain has evolved specifically to serve the human body under constraints imposed by both the body and biological limitations. This does not necessarily imply that it is futile to consider neuroscience in such endeavours; however, this paper argues that one has to view results of neuroscience from a somewhat different perspective to maximise their utility in the creation of artificial intelligent systems and proposes an explicit separation of neural processes into three categories.

1 Introduction

The stated aim of Artificial General Intelligence (AGI) is the construction of machines with human-level intelligence (and beyond). It is therefore clear that achieving this aim is at least somewhat related to our understanding of human cognition and intelligence in the first place. In particular, it is attractive, at a first glance, to at least consider neuroscience in particular (see, for instance, Goertzel et al., 2010; de Garis et al., 2010) as the field studying the mechanisms underlying the only known truly intelligent system to date. There are of course other approaches to the creation of artificial intelligent systems (see, for instance, Schmidhuber, 2009, for a nice example of a completely different take); in the present paper, however, we will restrict ourselves specifically to the endeavour of turning to results from neuroscience with the aim of creating artificial intelligent systems.

Doing so is, it has been noted, not trivial and there are a number of obstacles that need to be overcome. Two are commonly cited (*e.g.* de Garis et al., 2010): (1) our knowledge of neuroscience is incomplete to say the least and (2) even if we did have a complete understanding, the computational power for the creation of a complete artificial human brain is only beginning to be available.

J. Schmidhuber, K.R. Thórisson, and M. Looks (Eds.): AGI 2011, LNAI 6830, pp. 247–254, 2011.
© Springer-Verlag Berlin Heidelberg 2011

The discussion about computational power and what possibilities it may or may not open is beyond the scope of this paper and will not be considered here. The observation that our knowledge of neuroscience is incomplete is obviously true and extends to our knowledge of human cognition in general.

It is perhaps useful to define the difference between *cognition* and *intelligence* for the present purposes. Cognition encompasses all reasoning abilities of an agent, it is what the agent's mind can do. Intelligence, on the other hand, is a metric for measuring the quality of an agent's cognition. Consequently, a machine with complete human-like cognition should necessarily display anthropic intelligence but a machine whose reasoning abilities are radically different from that of a human may nonetheless display anthropic levels of intelligence (or indeed beyond).

This distinction is important for those turning to neuroscience for inspiration in the creation of artificial intelligent systems, since, strictly speaking, neuroscience studies the mechanisms underlying human and animal *cognition*, a system that has the property of *displaying* intelligence. For the same reason, the aforementioned fact that our knowledge of cognition as such is also incomplete is itself important. It essentially implies that if one turns to neuroscience in order to produce a system with a property X (being intelligent), one is turning to incomplete knowledge about the mechanisms underlying a system Y (human cognition), the only known system to also possess property X but itself not completely understood either otherwise.

While this is, on the face of it, a pessimistic assessment, the points about incomplete knowledge are merely a slight generalisation of what has been said before and are, as such, not new. Our understanding of both neuroscience specifically and the cognitive sciences in general increases constantly; incomplete knowledge, assuming an awareness of that fact, does not prevent to the design of artificial systems based on current knowledge nor the definition of future directions such endeavours may take depending on advances in neuroscience or the cognitive sciences. Artificial systems may even guide future research in these fields in what would constitute a symbiotic relationship.

The present paper is thus more concerned with the second implication of the above insight. To create an artificial system that displays anthropic levels of intelligence is not necessarily the same as to create an artificial system that displays anthropic cognition. Indeed, the latter is more restrictive: of all hypothetical systems that could display levels of intelligence that are (at a minimum) of human quality, it discards all those that do not do so by means of cognitive mechanisms that are also of human quality. With that in mind, what (if any) is the value of looking at neuroscience when designing artificial intelligent systems and, assuming there is such a value, how, precisely, should one take neuroscience into consideration?

2   Insights from Embodied Cognition

It is useful to briefly discuss embodied cognition for its relevance to the creation of artificial cognitive systems in general. Specifically, the relevant aspect of embodied cognition is the claim that the body intrinsically shapes cognition (Anderson, 2003; Chrisley and Ziemke, 2003; Gallagher, 2005). How much and in what ways this shaping takes place is still a matter of heavy debate. On one end of the spectrum, Pezzulo et al.

(2011) for instance argue that the conceptual representations at the base of our cognitive abilities are fundamentally grounded in and processed at the sensorimotor level. On the other end, Mahon and Caramazza (2008) are amongst those who argue in favour of an abstract symbolic representation of concepts that is merely grounded by sensorimotor information. In such a view, the body may be necessary to ground the symbols that the cognitive system will manipulate, but it is not required for cognition as such, similar to the Harnad's (1990) position.

Available neuroscientific evidence can be interpreted to suit both positions. On one hand, it can be shown for instance that several "higher" cognitive abilities appear to activate motor regions in the brain, *e.g.* in the case of language processing (see Chersi et al., 2010, for a review). Pezzulo et al. (2011) offer several additional examples. On the other hand, Mahon and Caramazza (2008) argue that none of this evidence is actually at odds with their view and that some neuroscientific findings (*e.g.* from Apraxia, see Mahon and Caramazza, 2008, for details) are not compatible with strong embodied positions.

Entering the debate in detail goes beyond the point of this paper. The main message here is that even the most sceptical (from an embodiment point of view) position defended by Mahon and Caramazza (2008) accepts that the body, in the form of sensorimotor grounding can influence cognition in the sense that it shapes and/or refines concepts and representations. While it is then a different debate whether or not such an influence is necessary, it appears likely that it is at least beneficial even if the higher-level cognitive abilities turn out to take place at an abstract, amodal level. In other words: human cognition is likely shaped by the human body and a central research question in embodied cognitive science is simply *"how much?"*.

This has three important implications for the aim of creating machines with human-like intelligence. First, the cognitive capabilities of a machine may depend on the machine itself. Second, anthropic cognition may simply require an anthropic body. Third and consequently, the mechanisms of the human body giving rise to human cognition may not be relevant for machines with non-human embodiments.

These three implications, although related, have different consequences. The first one implies that cognition involves both the design of the machine *and* its algorithms, not just the latter. This realisation is now shaping, for instance, research in *cognitive robotics*, another field concerned with the creation of intelligent machines (see Pezzulo et al., 2011, for a discussion).

The second implication leads us to at least consider the possibility that truly anthropic cognition may only be possible with an equally anthropic body. Why this may be the case is illustrated, for instance by SNARC (spatial-numerical association of response codes) effect (see Pezzulo et al., 2011, for a description and more references). Briefly, people respond to smaller numbers faster with the left hand than with the right hand and vice versa for large numbers; but less so if people start counting numbers on their right hand. In addition, if people are asked to "generate" random numbers while turning their heads left and right, they tend to be biased towards smaller numbers during left turns than during right ones. Thus, the SNARC effect exemplifies how the cognitive representation of a symbol (a number) is nonetheless affected by the body and manipulating such symbols in a human fashion may only be, strictly speaking, realisable with a human body. The consequence is that, while machines could certainly display anthropic levels of intelligence (since, as has been noted before, intelligence is essentially a metric), their underlying cognitive capabilities (how they reason) may not be comparable with that of a human.

The third implication is the most interesting here. The extreme interpretation would be that turning to neuroscience in the design of artificial systems is simply pointless since neuroscience studies mechanisms in a biological body underlying human or animal cognition, neither of which may be reproducible in a machine. The interpretation within this paper is, however, more moderate. There is no doubt that large aspects of our brain and the way it processes data exist not because they are necessarily necessary for intelligence but because of constraints imposed by biology and/or by our particular morphology. Some may indeed be irrelevant for anything but the human. Others, however, may generalise to other embodiments, including that of a machine. Finally, there may be generally valid computational aspects that are, in fact, independent of a particular embodiment (including morphology and biology).

This leads to the main point of the present paper: when studying neuroscience with the fundamental aim of creating an artificial intelligent machine, it is important to dissociate between mechanisms that exist merely because of the embodiment (where the body *constrains*), those that exploit the embodiment (where the body *facilitates*) and those that are not dependent on any particular embodiment, although it has to be noted that whether or not processes that are both necessary for intelligent behaviour and independent of the actual embodiment exist is an open question even in the cognitive sciences.

The first category, bodily constraints, can affect neuroscientific aspects at all levels. As an example, consider the nematode *Caenorhabditis elegans*. It is remarkable from a neuroscientific point of view for the fact that the connectivity between its 302 neurons (a number which remains constant across hermaphrodite individuals, males have a constant 383 neurons) has been completely mapped out (White et al., 1986). More to the point, it is also remarkable for its non-spiking neurons (which lack Na^+ channels) that instead rely on electrotonic potenials, which travel faster than action potentials (neuronal spikes) but are not suitable for long-distance signalling as they degrade quickly (Nickell et al., 2002). What this example illustrates is that even something as fundamental as neural spikes, which form the communication basis of a plethora of artificial neural networks (Gurney, 1997), may exist first and foremost simply because of a rudimentary biological limitation, namely that signalling over the distances involved in the human brain is not possible with electrotonic potentials alone.

Of most interest, perhaps, when turning to to neuroscience when constructing artificial intelligent machines, is the second category: examples of processes that are facilitated by (or that simply exploit) the embodiment and could generalise, albeit in an adapted fashion, to machines. To illustrate this point further, the next section will briefly present and discuss the mirror system, currently a popular research topic in neuroscience (*e.g.* Gallese et al., 1996; Fogassi et al., 2005; Umiltà et al., 2008), the cognitive sciences (*e.g.* Chersi et al., 2010; Rizzolatti and Sinigaglia, 2010) and even cognitive robotics (*e.g.* Wermter et al., 2005; Bonaiuto et al., 2007; Thill and Ziemke, 2010) from the perspective of the creation of artificial intelligent machines.

3 Neuroscience for Artificial Agents: The Mirror System Example

Mirror neurons, in a nutshell, are neurons that fire both when an agent executes a goal-directed action and when he observes another agent executing the same action (Gallese et al., 1996). Because of this fundamental property, they have been hypothesised to play a role in a large number of higher-level cognitive processes. The main hypothesised role is in action understanding (Fogassi et al., 2005; Cattaneo et al., 2007; Umiltà et al., 2008; Bonini et al., 2010; Rizzolatti and Sinigaglia, 2010) but it should be remembered that this is still a hypothesis, not a proven fact; Hickok (2008) is amongst those pointing out that there is no conclusive evidence pointing in that direction.

Action understanding aside, mirror neurons are also thought to play a role in the evolution of language. Rizzolatti and Arbib (1998) for instance hypothesise that Broca's area in the human brain (thought to play a major role in human language processing) may be the counterpart of the frontal area F5 of the monkey brain (in which mirror neurons were originally discovered). Arbib (2005) then argues that mirror neurons may, in fact, be essential for language while Chersi et al. (2010) discuss the indications that language is sensorimotorically grounded (in a process involving mirror neurons). However, the role of mirror neurons in language also remains a point of debate. Oztop et al. (2006) for instance echoes the common objection that monkeys, from which most mirror neuron data is obtained, do not use language. They also do not imitate, another functional role hypothesised to involve mirror neurons (Oztop et al., 2006). In humans, mirror mechanisms have been shown to exist in the sensation of, for instance, touch or pain (see, for instance, Keysers et al., 2010; Morrison et al., 2010, for reviews). Rizzolatti and Sinigaglia (2010) review additional literature on the functional role of mirror neurons.

Because of the above, the mirror system has received significant interest from the fields of artificial intelligence and robotics (*e.g.* Tani et al., 2004; Wemter et al., 2005; Erlhagen et al., 2007; Thill et al., submitted) as it may play a key role in designing humans and machines that can interact robustly with human and use, for instance, imitation learning to survive in unknown environments.

The mirror system is thus a good example here for two reasons: (1) it is an active research topic in several fields and (2) it is hypothesised to underlie a number of higher level cognitive functions, making it very relevant for neuroscience inspired artificial systems. Again, it is important to underline that there is still very little evidence that mirror neurons are actually necessary for these cognitive functions (Hickok, 2008) but we can assume here, for the sake of the argument, that it would at least be possible to construct an artificial agent with a mirror system in which this is true.

Neuroscience then tells us, for instance, the following about mirror neurons. They fire, as said, both when agents execute a goal-directed action and when they observe it (Gallese et al., 1996). Observation can even extend to hearing sounds associated with the action (Köhler et al., 2002). Although related to motor actions, they do not encode precise motor commands but rather the "concept" of these actions (Umiltà et al., 2008). Mirror neurons are further organised into groups, each encoding a particular motion primitive (*e.g.* a reach or a grasp) and are highly selective in that respect (Chersi et al., 2006). Further, these pools also encode the goal of the overall action which the primitive is a part of (Fogassi et al., 2005).

If one assumes that this organisation is important in facilitating the cognitive behaviours that might be served by mirror neurons, then one might want to replicate this in an artificial agent. However, the precise organisation is affected by the body: mirror neurons receive inputs, amongst others, from the anterior intraparietal area (AIP) and the superior temporal sulcus (STS, Bonaiuto et al., 2007), which are in turn influenced by the perception of both the actions of others (STS) and affordances of objects at the heart of the action (AIP). Thill et al. (submitted) show that goal-encoding as observed by Fogassi et al. (2005) can be a simple result of differential encoding in these two input streams, which in turn would be affected by the embodiment.

This is thus an example of how the neural organisation makes use of the embodiment. Given inputs as shaped by the body mirror neurons may organise into a structure that may in turn facilitate higher cognitive behaviours. For artificial intelligent systems, the conclusion is thus not that one should merely "copy" this organisation. Rather, one can either design the machine so that it naturally facilitates the emergence of a similar structure or one can investigate how a radical different embodiment would affect this organisation. The mirror system is thus an interesting example of a neural structure whose organisation is not just a constraint of the body; rather it may have evolved to explicitly take advantage of the morphology. The developmental process which has allowed this may well translate onto other embodiments and indeed, examples of mirror-neuron based robots exist (*e.g.* Bonaiuto et al., 2007; Erlhagen et al., 2007).

4   Conclusion

The goal of neuroscience is to further the understanding of human and animal cognition, in particular the underlying neural mechanisms. Artificial intelligence, general or otherwise, has a different aim; it seeks to create intelligent machines. While it is then tempting to turn to neuroscience as the research field studying the mechanism underlying the only known instance of intelligent behaviour, it is critical to keep in mind that neuroscience does not typically produce results with the AI researcher in mind. The question of which processes exist only because of the human body and which ones could generalise to other bodies and machines is simply not relevant in traditional neuroscience and it is up to the AI researcher to apply due diligence when taking inspiration from neuroscience.

This paper has therefore argued that, rather than taking a "traditional" perspective on neural processes, they should be evaluated as falling in one of three categories 1) processes that are constrained by the body, 2) processes that exploit the body and 3) processes that are independent of the body. Of these, the most interesting category for AGI researchers is likely the second one, which has been illustrated in a brief consideration of the mirror neuron system.

Acknowledgments. The author is supported by the European Commission FP7 project ROSSI (*emergence of communication in RObots through Sensorimotor and Social Interaction*, Grant agreement no. 216125) and thanks Tom Ziemke for comments on the manuscript.

References

Anderson, M.L.: Embodied cognition: a field guide. Artificial Intelligence 149, 91–130 (2003)

Arbib, M.A.: From monkey-like action recognition to human language: An evolutionary framework for neurolinguistics. Behavioral and Brain Sciences 28, 105–167 (2005)

Bonaiuto, J., Rosta, E., Arbib, M.A.: Extending the mirror neuron system model, I. Biological Cybernetics 96, 9–38 (2007)

Bonini, L., Rozzi, S., Serventi, F.U., Simone, L., Ferrari, P.F., Fogassi, L.: Ventral premotor and inferior parietal cortices make distinct contributions to action organization and intention understanding. Cerebral Cortex 20, 1372–1385 (2010)

Cattaneo, L., Fabbri-Destro, M., Boria, S., Pieraccini, C., Monti, A., Cossu, G., Rizzolatti, G.: Impairment of actions chains in autism and its possible role in intention understanding. Proceedings of the National Academy of Sciences USA 104(45), 17825–17830 (2007)

Chersi, F., Mukovskiy, A., Fogassi, L., Ferrari, P.F., Erlhagen, W.: A model of intention understanding based on learned chains of motor acts in the parietal lobe. In: Proceedings of the 15th Annual Computational Neuroscience Meeting, Edinburgh, UK (2006)

Chersi, F., Thill, S., Ziemke, T., Borghi, A.M.: Sentence processing: linking language to motor chains. Frontiers in Neurorobotics 4(4) (2010), doi:10.3389/fnbot.2010.00004

Chrisley, R., Ziemke, T.: Embodiment. In: Encyclopedia of Cognitive Science, pp. 1102–1108. Macmillan Publishers, Basingstoke (2003)

de Garis, H., Shuo, C., Goertzel, B., Ruiting, L.: A world survey of artificial brain projects, part i large-scale brain simulations. Neurocomputing 74, 3–29 (2010)

Erlhagen, W., Mukovskiy, A., Chersi, F., Bicho, E.: On the development of intention understanding for joint action tasks. In: Proceedings of the 6th IEEE International Conference on Development and Learning, pp. 140–145, Imperial College London (2007)

Fogassi, L., Ferrari, P.F., Gesierich, B., Rozzi, S., Chersi, F., Rizzolatti, G.: Parietal lobe: from action organization to intention understanding. Science 308, 662–667 (2005)

Gallagher, S.: How the body shapes the mind. Oxford University Press, New York (2005)

Gallese, V., Fadiga, L., Fogassi, L., Rizzolatti, G.: Action recognition in the premotor cortex. Brain Research 119, 593–609 (1996)

Goertzel, B., Lian, R., Arel, I., de Garis, H., Chen, S.: A world survey of artificial brain projects, part ii biologically inspired cognitive architectures. Neurocomputing 74, 30–49 (2010)

Gurney, K.: An Introduction to Neural Networks. Routeledge, London (1997)

Harnad, S.: The symbol grounding problem. Physica D: Nonlinear Phenomena 42(1-3), 335–346 (1990)

Hickok, G.: Eight problems for the mirror neuron theory of action understanding in monkeys and humans. Journal of Cognitive Neuroscience 21(7), 1229–1243 (2008)

Keysers, C., Kaas, J.H., Gazzola, V.: Somatosensation in social perception. Nature Reviews Neuroscience 11, 417–428 (2010)

Köhler, E., Umiltà, M.A., Fogassi, L., Gallese, V., Rizzolatti, G.: Hearing sounds, understanding actions: action representation in mirror neurons. Science 297(5582), 846–848 (2002)

Mahon, B.Z., Caramazza, A.: A critical look at the embodied cognition hypothesis and a new proposal for grounding conceptual content. Journal of Physiology Paris 102, 59–70 (2008)

Morrison, I., Löken, L.S., Olausson, H.: The skin as a social organ. Experimental Brain Research 204, 305–314 (2010)

Nickell, W.T., Pun, R.Y.K., Bargmann, C.I., Kleene, S.J.: Single ionic channels of two *Caenorhabditis elegans* chemosensory neurons in native membrane. J. Membr. Biol. 189, 55–66 (2002)

Oztop, E., Kawato, M., Arbib, M.A.: Mirror neurons and imitation: A computationally guided review. Neural Networks 19, 254–271 (2006)

Pezzulo, G., Barsalou, L.W., Cangelosi, A., Fischer, M.H., McRae, K., Spivey, M.J.: The mechanics of embodiment: a dialog on embodiment and computational modeling. Frontiers in Psychology 2(5) (2011)

Rizzolatti, G., Arbib, M.A.: Language within our grasp. Trends in Neurosciences 21(5), 188–194 (1998)

Rizzolatti, G., Sinigaglia, C.: The functional role of the parieto-frontal mirror circuit: interpretations and misinterpretations. Nature Reviews Neuroscience 11(4), 264–274 (2010)

Schmidhuber, J.: Ultimate cognition à la Gödel. Cognitive Computation 1, 177–193 (2009)

Tani, J., Ito, M., Sugita, Y.: Self-organization of distributedly represented multiple behavior schemata in a mirror system: reviews of robot experiments using RNNPB. Neural Networks 17, 1273–1289 (2004)

Thill, S., Svensson, H., Ziemke, T.: Modeling the development of goal-specificity in mirror neurons (submitted)

Thill, S., Ziemke, T.: Learning new motion primitives in the mirror neuron system: A self-organising computational model. In: Doncieux, S., Girard, B., Guillot, A., Hallam, J., Meyer, J.-A., Mouret, J.-B. (eds.) SAB 2010. LNCS, vol. 6226, pp. 413–423. Springer, Heidelberg (2010)

Umiltà, M.A., Escola, L., Intskirveli, I., Grammont, F., Rochat, M., Caruana, F., Jezzini, A., Gallese, V., Rizzolatti, G.: When pliers become fingers in the monkey motor system. Proceedings of the National Academy of Sciences USA 105(6), 2209–2213 (2008)

Wermter, S., Weber, C., Elshaw, M.: Associative neural models for biomimetic multimodal learning in a mirror-neuron based robot. Progess in Neural Processing 16, 31–46 (2005)

White, J.G., Southgate, E., Thomson, J.N., Brenner, S.: The structure of the nervous system of the neamtode C. elegans. Philos. Trans. R. Soc. London Ser B 314(1165), 1–340 (1986)

Brain Anatomy and Artificial Intelligence

L. Andrew Coward

Australian National University, Canberra, ACT 0200, Australia

Abstract. The brain carries out cognitive learning and processing by performing combinations of different types of information processes. Types of information processes are performed by different anatomical structures and implemented in physiology. The information processes performed by different major anatomical structures including the cortex, basal ganglia, thalamus and cerebellum are described, including their implementations in neuron physiology. The implications for the architecture and design of a general intelligence system are discussed.

1 Introduction

For a system that learns many behaviours, theoretical arguments indicate that the need to utilize physical information handling resources as efficiently as possible constrains system architecture [1]. In the limit as the ratio of behaviours to resources becomes very large, the system will tend to adopt the recommendation architecture form. This form separates different types of information processes into physically separate subsystems. Natural selection pressures tend to favour brain architectures which make efficient use of physical information handling resources like neurons and connectivity, and therefore result in recommendation architecture subsystems appearing in biological brains. Any one cognitive process utilizes information processes in most or all of these subsystems. Each subsystem implements its corresponding information processes by physiological mechanisms. The existence of these forms in biological brain is indicated by a range of physiological evidence, including the cognitive effects resulting from damage to different anatomical structures [2]. Analogous theoretical arguments indicate that any system with general intelligence which must learn a complex combination of behaviours will be constrained into the same general architectural forms [3]. The ways in which the various information processes are implemented physiologically can therefore provide guidance for the design of such general intelligence systems. In this paper the information processes performed by different anatomical structures in the brain are defined, and the ways in which these processes are implemented in physiology described. Ways in which physiology can therefore provide guidance for the implementation of a system with general intelligence are discussed.

J. Schmidhuber, K.R. Thórisson, and M. Looks (Eds.): AGI 2011, LNAI 6830, pp. 255–268, 2011.
© Springer-Verlag Berlin Heidelberg 2011

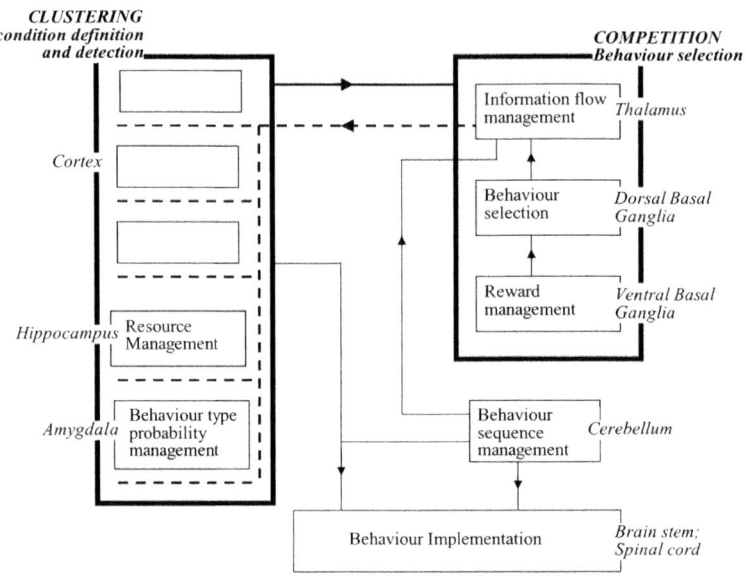

Fig. 1. The information architecture that results for any system which must learn a complex combination of behaviours with limited information handling resources

2 Brain Information Architecture

Practical considerations result in the physical architecture of the brain being constrained into the architectural form illustrated in figure 1 [1;4;2]. There are two major subsystems, clustering and competition. Clustering defines and detects conditions in the information available to the brain. This information can include sensory inputs indicating the status of the external environment and the body, and information about the internal status of the brain itself. Groups of similar conditions are called receptive fields, with a receptive field being detected if a significant proportion of its conditions are detected. Detections of receptive fields are provided to the competition subsystem, where each such detection is interpreted as a range of recommendations in favour of different behaviours, each recommendation having an individual weight. Competition determines the total weights in favour of each behaviour, and implements the behaviour with the largest weight. Reward feedback following a behaviour changes the weights of recently detected receptive fields in favour of recently accepted behaviours.

To avoid excessive requirements for information handling resources, individual receptive fields must be shared across (i.e. must recommend) many different behaviours. Receptive fields must be initiated and evolved heuristically, but because one receptive field has recommendation strengths in favour of many different behaviours, all such changes to receptive fields must be carefully controlled. To a good first approximation, receptive fields can be expanded by addition of conditions, but existing conditions cannot be deleted or modified [11]. Consequence feedback is generally derived from one or a few recent behaviours. Use of such consequence feedback from one behaviour to guide changes to existing conditions in a receptive field could result in undesirable side effects on all the other behaviours also influenced by the field. Consequence feedback can only be used to guide changes to recommendation strengths. In other words, consequence feedback can be directly used within competition but not within clustering. The use of consequence feedback within competition means that components within competition must correspond with individual behaviours or types of behaviour, so that changes will only affect one behaviour.

2   Cortex and Clustering

The cerebral cortex makes up the bulk of clustering in the mammal brain. The cortex is a thin sheet of neural matter, crossed by several million columns, each column detecting a different receptive field [5]. The cortex is separated into different areas, with the columns in one area detecting receptive fields within the same body of input information [6]. Column receptive fields within one area can distinguish between circumstances in which different behaviours of a range of types are appropriate, but do not individually correspond exactly with such circumstances. For example, columns in area TE can discriminate between different categories of visual object, but do not individually correspond with object categories [7]. Different areas detect receptive fields appropriate for supporting different types of behaviour. Although most behaviour types could best be managed with a specific group of receptive field types, supporting all such receptive field types for all possible behaviour types would be very expensive in resources. Area receptive fields must therefore be shared across multiple behaviour types. There are perhaps several hundred different cortical areas [8;9;10], and this number reflects a compromise between behavioural effectiveness and resource economy.

Because consequence feedback cannot be used to guide receptive field changes (with some limited exceptions, see [11]), the need to support behavioural discrimination is the only available criterion [1]. An adequate range of behavioural recommendations must be generated in response to every input state, in order to support a high integrity behaviour selection. This means that at least a minimum number of columns in a cortical area must detect their receptive fields whenever that area is presented with inputs. If less than the minimum is detected, some undetected receptive fields must expand slightly so that they are detected. Such expansions mean that the column will still detect its receptive field in the same circumstances as in the past, and the integrity of the recommendation strengths associated with the column will be preserved. However, such expansions must be as small as possible to minimize possible effects on existing recommendation strengths.

Columns are organized into layers of excitatory pyramidal type neurons, conventionally numbered II through IV, layer I being mainly axons. Different types of inhibitory interneurons occur in all layers. Most external input arrives in layer IV, and most output goes from layers V and VI. Pyramidal neurons in layers V/VI therefore indicate detection of the column receptive field. There is a predominant flow of connectivity from IV to II/III and from II/III to V/VI. If there is strong activity in

II/III but no column output from V/VI, the implication is that a relatively slight column receptive field expansion would result in detection. The requirements are therefore to determine when receptive field expansions are needed, to identify which inactive columns will detect their fields with the least expansion, and to drive that expansion. Such requirements could in principle be met by all-to-all connectivity between cortical columns. Greater effectiveness with fewer resources can be achieved using a central resource manager [12].

The hippocampal system detects receptive fields corresponding with large groups of cortical columns that have expanded their receptive fields at similar times in the past, with inputs derived from layers II/III. At each point in time, the hippocampal system receives inputs from all across the cortex, determines whether and where receptive field expansions are required, and sends signals back to the selected columns to drive expansions [13]. Receptive field changes are behaviours which must be recommended by receptive field detections in the clustering part of the hippocampal system, and only implemented if accepted by the competition part of the hippocampal system, of which an important part is the anterior thalamic nucleus [14].

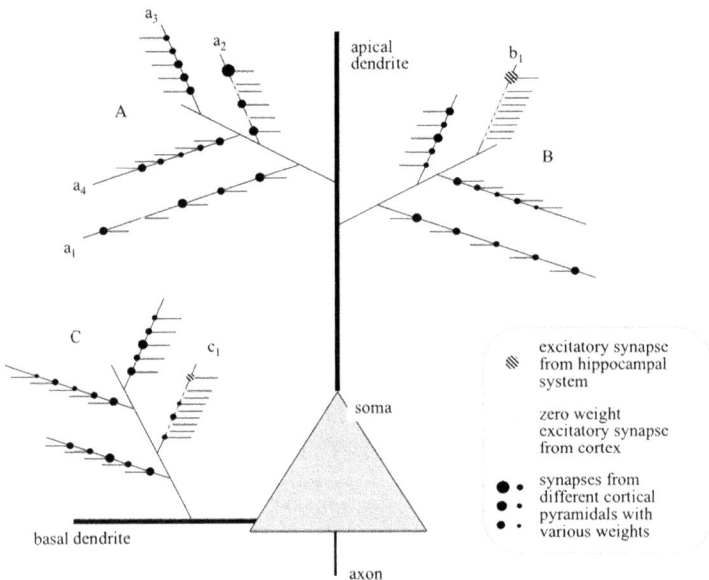

Fig. 2. Organization of synapses to detect conditions, groups of conditions and receptive field defined by groups of groups of conditions

Expansions make use of the long term potentiation mechanism [15]. As illustrated in figure 2, the receptive field of a pyramidal neuron is defined by a group of conditions, with the receptive field being detected if a significant proportion of the conditions is detected. Each condition (such as a_1, a_2 etc in figure 2) is defined by a group of synapses from other cortical pyramidal neurons (or from the senses via the thalamus), located on one branch of the dendritic tree. Each synapse may have a different weight. If enough synapses on a branch receive action potentials within a short period of time, the branch injects potential deeper into the dendrite [16]. In other words, the branch condition has been detected. Paths defined by voltage gated ion channels integrate the contributions of different branches [17]. If this integration injects sufficient potential into the soma, an action potential results [18] indicating detection of the neuron receptive field. Such an output action potential is generally combined with an action potential that backpropagates into the dendritic tree [19]. This backpropagated action potential increases the weights of any synapses that have recently received an input action potential [20].

Receptive field expansions occur by increases in the weights of some synapses on a branch. In the extreme case, a branch like b_1 in figure 2 may be made up of silent synapses from all cortical sources. These silent synapses have zero weight [21]. Such a branch defines a provisional condition. The branch will not contribute to neuron receptive field detection in any normal circumstances. However, the branch also has inputs from the hippocampal system. These inputs are active if the column in which the neuron is located is selected for receptive field expansion. If the branch injects potential on the basis of hippocampal activity, and shortly afterwards the neuron fires, the backpropagating action potential will increase the weights of any of the silent synapses that recently received inputs. These synapses now define a condition that could contribute to neuron firing independent of hippocampal activity. In other words, the receptive field of the neuron has expanded slightly by addition of a new condition. Increases of synaptic weights on regular synapses can also contribute to receptive field expansions, although the total weight of any one synapse is limited, preventing excessive contribution by a single source. New silent synapses could also be added to a regular branch.

The cortical sources of silent synapses on a neuron could be selected at random, but resource economies can be achieved by biasing the random selection in favour of sources that have been active in the past at the same time as the target neuron [22]. Such a bias could be achieved by a rapid partial rerun of past experience, with connectivity being guided by this rerun. It has been proposed that REM sleep is the partial rerun supporting creation of provisional connectivity [4;13].

2.1 Indirect Activation of Receptive Fields

Direct activation of a column on the basis of the presence of its conditions in current sensory inputs makes all the recommendations associated with its detection available. However, there can be some inactive columns that have recommendation strengths that are potentially relevant to current circumstances. For example, if a column is inactive but has often been active in the past at the same time as a number of currently active columns, its recommendation strengths may be relevant. Relevant columns may also include columns recently active at the same time as currently active columns and columns that expanded their receptive fields at the same time in the past as currently active columns. Uncontrolled indirect activations would create a chaotic total activation. Hence indirect activation of a column must be a behaviour recommended by columns on the basis of past temporally correlated activity and only implemented if the total recommendation strength is sufficient. Indirect activation recommendation strengths can also be established on the basis of past activity of a column just before or just after activity of another column. A population of columns directly activated by sensory inputs can generate a secondary indirectly activated column population, which could itself recommend activation of other columns, giving rise to a tertiary population, and so on.

Indirect activation on the basis of frequent past simultaneous activation supports semantic memory, indirect activation on the basis of simultaneous past receptive field expansion supports episodic memory, and indirect activation on the basis of recent simultaneous activity supports priming memory [4;2;23]. Sequences of direct and indirect activations support complex cognitive processing [2;3;11].

3   Basal Ganglia and Behaviour Selection

The basal ganglia and thalamus make up competition in the mammal brain. The connectivity of these nuclei is illustrated in figure 3. There is large input from the cortex going into the striatum, and the output from the basal ganglia comes from mainly from the globus pallidus internal segment and the related substantia nigra pars reticulata. There is strong reciprocal excitatory connectivity between the thalamus and the cortex, and the GPi/SNr produces constant inhibitory output that targets the thalamus. There are two populations of neurons in the striatum: D1 and D2. They support two parallel paths that link the striatum to the GPi/SNr. One path comes from D1 neurons and inhibits the GPi/SNr, (in other words, reduces inhibition of the thalamus) the other path comes from D2 neurons and effectively excites the GPi/SNr. There is a feedback loop from the GPi/SNr back to the striatum via the SNc. The SNc is made up of dopamine neurons. One mode of firing by neurons in the SNc is constant (tonic) at about 4 Hz [24]. This steady firing creates a background concentration of dopamine in the striatum, the dopamine leaks out from the dopamine synapses and permeates the extracellular environment. At the concentrations created by this firing, dopamine affects the relative activity of the D1 and D2 populations.

Individual neurons in the striatum and in the GPi/SNr correspond with very specific individual behaviours [25]. In information terms, the synaptic strength of an input from the cortex to a neuron in the striatum can be viewed as the weight of the recommendation by the receptive field in favour of the corresponding behaviour. An output from the striatum can be viewed as the total current recommendation weight in favour of the corresponding behaviour (or against any other behaviour). D1 striatal neurons target their corresponding behaviour in the GPi/SNr, and encourage that behaviour. D2 striatal neurons target different behaviours in the GPi/SNr, and inhibit those behaviours. There is therefore a competition being performed by the GPi/SNr which selects the most strongly recommended behaviour.

In many cases a behaviour is implemented by release of a cortical information flow. Attention behaviours are releases of information from the senses into the primary sensory areas. Motor behaviours are releases of information from the motor cortex to the spinal cord. Selection of a type of behaviour is release of information from one group of cortical areas that recommend general types of behaviour to other cortical areas that recommend specific behaviours of a general type. Such cortical information flows are coordinated by the thalamus. Reduction in the inhibitory output from the GPi/SNr corresponding with selection of a behaviour results in an increase in thalamic activity generating release of the corresponding cortical information flows.

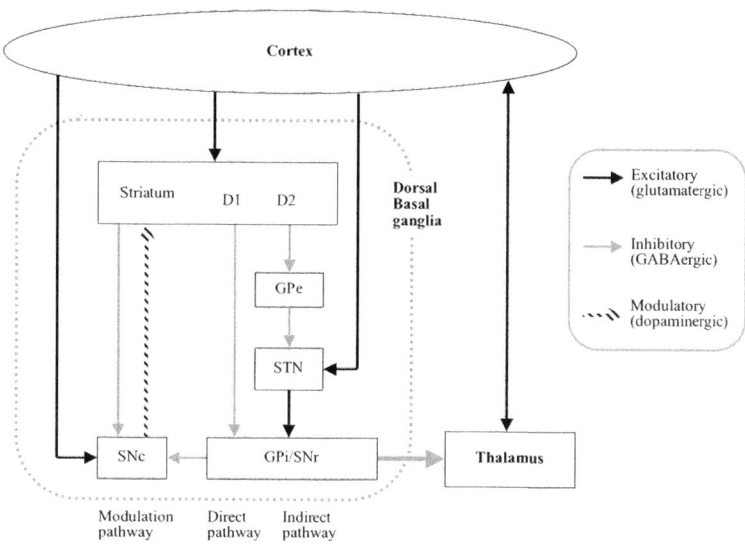

Fig. 3. Connectivity of cortex-basal ganglia-thalamus-cortex loop

There are two operational problems which must be avoided. One is failure to select any behaviour in circumstances where some behaviour would be appropriate, the other is to try to implement multiple incompatible behaviours. The dopamine feedback loop manages these problems. If there is too much activity in GPi/SNr, there will be no behaviour. This high activity results in an increase in the background dopamine, increasing the chance of a behaviour. If there is too little activity in GPi/SNr, there could be multiple behaviours. This low activity results in a decrease in the background dopamine, reducing the chance of a behaviour. In addition, if high novelty in the environment is detected by the hippocampal system, hippocampal inputs to the striatum increases the tonal firing of dopamine neurons in the SNc [24], resulting in a higher probability of behaviour in novel environments.

3.1 Reward Behaviours

Rewards are behaviours which change the recommendation weights in the striatum in favour of recently selected behaviours. Reward behaviours are recommended by specific striatal neurons that determine total recommendation weights in favour of rewards on the basis of inputs from various cortical areas. Rewards can reinforce behaviours on different levels, ranging from strategic behaviours to specific muscle movements. For example, consider a musician playing a piece of music. Strategic rewards must increase the probability of playing in certain circumstances. Tactical rewards must increase the probability of a certain piece of music being played in certain circumstances. General muscular rewards must increase the probability of certain limb movements relative to the instrument, and detailed muscular rewards must increase the probability of finger movements resulting in notes being played in a specific order and timing.

Reward behaviours are recommended by various cortical areas and selected using basal ganglia structures. However, strategic rewards are managed by the ventral basal ganglia including the ventral striatum (the nucleus accumbens), the VP (corresponding with GPi/SNr) and the VTA (corresponding with the SNc). More specific rewards are managed by the dorsal basal ganglia. Total recommendation strengths in favour of reward behaviours are determined from cortical inputs in the striatum. The competitive selection occurs within the midbrain dopamine neurons (i.e. the SNc and VTA) and selected reward behaviours are implemented back into the striatum. The connectivity arrangements in support of reward behaviours [26] are illustrated in figure 4.

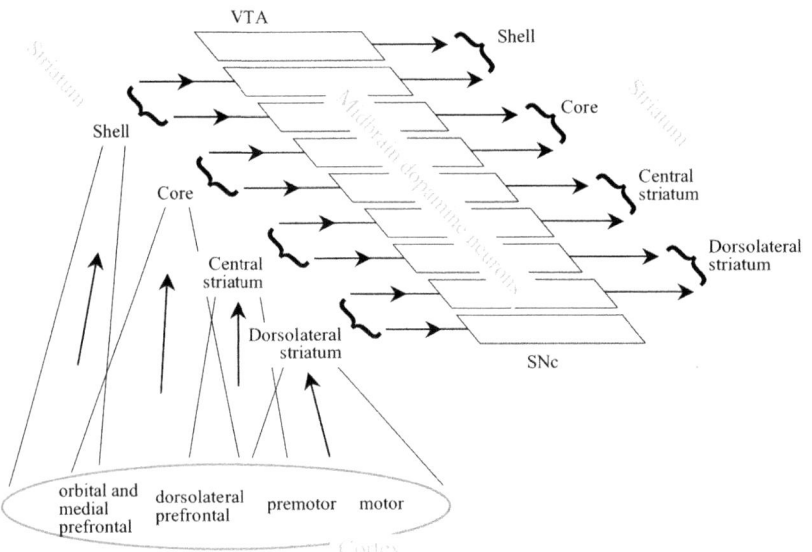

Fig. 4. Spiral of connectivity managing recommendation, selection and implementation of reward behaviours

In addition to the tonal firing mode described earlier, dopamine neurons can fire in a burst mode: 3 – 20 action potentials within a burst, at a frequency of 20 Hz [27]. Striatal neurons can trigger this burst firing by inhibiting interneurons that target midbrain dopamine neurons [26]. The burst firing in turn targets the striatum. Recent firing of striatal neurons results in LTP lasting up to 60 minutes. Burst firing of dopamine can trigger chemical processes that lock in such LTP changes, while a decline in background dopamine can result in LTD [28]. Hence burst firing can implement a positive reward behaviour, while declines in background dopamine can implement a negative reward behaviour.

As illustrated in figure 4, very complex cortical receptive fields recommend strategic rewards to the nucleus accumbens shell, such rewards are implemented in the core. Tactical rewards are recommended by somewhat less complex receptive fields into the core, and implemented in the central striatum. Very specific rewards are recommended by the premotor or even the motor cortex and implemented into the dorsolateral striatum. This arrangement highlights the issue that reward behaviours must be carefully managed, because the effect of such behaviours on regular behaviours can be very potent, especially in the case of reward behaviours at the strategic level.

4   Thalamus and Cortical Information Management

There are several cortical information flow management issues. One is that receptive field detections by the senses must only be allowed to generate extensive receptive field detections in sensory areas if such generation is a selected behaviour. An example of this is visual attention, where at one point in time, a single visual object is selected to generate higher order receptive field detections over other objects.

A second issue is the need to detect receptive fields simultaneously within multiple different objects, without interference. An example is the need to detect receptive fields within several different visual objects, then to detect receptive fields that combine information from multiple objects in order to develop recommendations appropriate to responding to the group of objects.

These two issues are addressed by related mechanisms. When an action potential spike arrives at a neuron, it injects a postsynaptic potential that decays with a time constant of about 10 milliseconds [29]. For a neuron to detect its receptive field, enough input action potentials must therefore arrive within less that about 10 milliseconds. Spike inputs derived from the senses arrive distributed in time in a relatively random fashion. The rate of spikes with this distribution is too low to generate strong receptive field detections in associative sensory areas and beyond. Visual attention is implemented by a frequency modulation at about 40 Hz (the gamma band of the EEG) imposed on inputs from just the retinal area corresponding with a visual object [11] to the primary visual area. This frequency modulation concentrates spikes within a time slot of less than 10 milliseconds, leaving the rest of the 25 millisecond modulation interval with a relatively low number of spikes. This concentration means that receptive fields will be detected mainly within information derived from just the selected visual object. If different frequency modulations are imposed on inputs from different visual objects, separate populations of receptive fields can be detected within the different objects in different timeslots within the available 25 millisecond interval. This limits the number of different objects to about three, consistent with human working memory capabilities [30].

Each primary thalamic nucleus receives excitatory (glutamatergic) inputs from a number of cortical areas, and provides glutamatergic outputs to one of these areas. The interconnecting axons all pass through the thalamic reticular nucleus (TRN). This nucleus contains only GABAergic interneurons that generate spike trains at the gamma frequency, imposing the gamma band frequency modulation on their targets [31; 32]. At a more detailed level, GABA synapses are generally inhibitory. However, if an action potential arrives at a GABAergic synapse more than about 5 milliseconds before an action potential arrives at a nearby glutamatergic synapse, the result is to increase the excitatory effect of the glutamatergic spike [33]. Hence a train of GABAergic action potentials will tend to result in the outputs generated by a relatively random distribution of incoming glutamatergic spikes being concentrated in particular time slots relative to the GABAergic inputs.

5   Cerebellum and Behaviour Sequence Management

A sequence of actions is initially managed by detection of receptive fields after each action, and selection of the next action on the basis of the recommendation strengths of those fields. However, if given some initial circumstances a sequence of actions is often performed in the same order, significant gains in speed and accuracy are possible if the sequence is recorded and executed as a whole. The cerebellum performs this function both for voluntary motor functions in which the sequence of actions are muscle movements and for cognitive functions in which the sequence of actions include indirect receptive field activations of various kinds. If the recorded sequences are lost for some reason (e.g. cerebellar damage), the sequences can still be implemented (more slowly and less rapidly) by the full cortex-basal ganglia cycle at each stage.

The connectivity between major anatomical structures that manage voluntary motor control (and other behaviours) is illustrated in figure 5. The regular way to generate an action is for the cortex to detect receptive fields in the available sensory and body position information, the basal ganglia to interpret the receptive field detections into a predominant action, and the action to be implemented by release of cortical receptive fields to, for example, the spinal cord. A sequence of actions will initially be implemented step by step. However, once a frequently used sequence has been defined, greater speed and accuracy can be achieved by automatically implementing each action a short time after the previous action in the sequence.

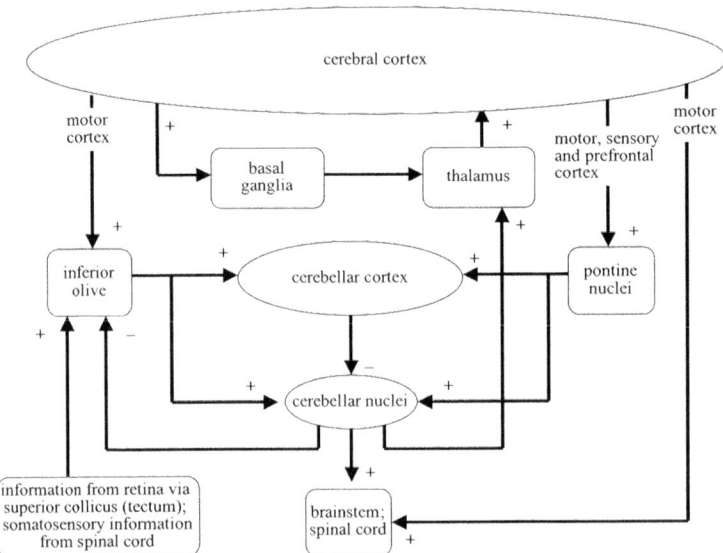

Fig. 5. Parallel paths through basal ganglia and cerebellum managing behaviour selection and implementation

The cerebellum essentially copies action sequences defined by the full cortex-basal ganglia-thalamus-cortex cycle. It achieves this by establishing connections on to the points that drive actions, and triggering an action when it detects the sensory and motor information that occurred in the past at the time of the preceding action, ensuring correct timing between actions [11]. Hence the cerebellum will tend to carry sequences through to a conclusion, although the full loop could interrupt if necessary.

In the cerebellar cortex there are three layers. The bottom layer is made up of large numbers of granule cells. These have inputs from the pontine nucleus, that in turn gets extensive inputs from the cerebral cortex [34]. Granule cell axons rise to the top layer and bend 90 degrees to run parallel to the surface, forming what are called the parallel fibres. The middle layer is made up of Purkinje cells. These cells have a flat dendritic tree that spans the top layer, perpendicular to the parallel fibres. This dendrite gets single synapses from a very large number of the parallel fibres. Inputs from the inferior olive target Purkinje cell dendrites directly, but each fibre targets just one or sometimes a small group of Purkinje cells, wrapping around the dendrite and therefore called a climbing fibre.

The receptive field of a Purkinje cell (in other words the combination of parallel fibres) can expand by LTP, but an input from the inferior olive triggers LTD [35]. Cerebellar nuclei cells fire tonically, and are excited by the same pontine inputs as the Purkinje cells. They are inhibited by Purkinje outputs. Inferior olive neurons are inhibited by cerebellar nuclei neurons.

A sequence is first implemented step by step by the primary loop through the basal ganglia. If a sequence occurs frequently, different individual cerebellar nuclei neurons establish connections on to groups of neurons driving muscle movement by a coincidence guided LTP type mechanism, on the basis of repetition. Purkinje cells develop receptive fields corresponding with the circumstances just before different actions in a sequence are implemented, again by coincidence guided LTP. Purkinje cells also establish inhibitive connectivity on to cerebellar nuclei neurons, with connection strengths weakened if they tend to be active at the same time.

At this point the cerebellum can take over the sequence. If an action follows the preceding action correctly, the cerebellar nucleus neurons will inhibit the inferior olive, and no LTD will occur in the Purkinje cell. If the action does not occur, there will be LTD which will slightly shift the Purkinje receptive field. Hence the inferior olive tunes the timing of the action sequence [36] and is only active when cerebellar learning is under way [37].

As indicated by the effects of cerebellar damage, the cerebellum manages not only motor sequences including speech generation, but also complex cognitive processes [38]. However, the primary behaviour generation route through the basal ganglia can take back full control of such sequences, with perhaps an undamaged cerebellar region learning the sequences again.

6   Lessons for Design of General Intelligence Systems

The structure and processes of the brain have a number of implications for the design of general intelligence systems. The first is that as the ratio of intelligent behaviours to be learned to available resources increases, the system will be more and more tightly constrained into the information architecture illustrated in figure 1. If such a system is designed with some different information architecture, either the physical resources will have to be increased, or the system will have a strong tendency towards destruction of older learning when new learning occurs [1].

Secondly, one of the key design decisions is the number of receptive field modules, corresponding with the number of cortical areas in the brain. Each module detects a different type of receptive field. A type is specified by a limited number of sources of the inputs within which fields are defined, and the approximate number of such inputs that contribute to one receptive field. Sources include sensory systems and other receptive field modules. One type will be most effective for recommending a range of behaviour types, and the number of types represents a compromise between the better behavioural support and increased resources as the number of modules increases. A related design decision is the number of different receptive fields supported within a module, and the degree of detailed discrimination that can be provided within one receptive field, analogous with the different pyramidal neurons with potentially slightly different receptive fields that can provide output from one cortical column. The specification of the process by which receptive fields are initially defined is a further important factor. Definitions could be bootstrapped by a design guided initial specification followed by heuristic tuning. This would be analogous with partial genetic specification of types of receptive field in primary sensory areas by guidance to initial connectivity.

A third implication is that a subsystem to manage changes to receptive fields must be provided, including appropriate receptive field modules. Such changes are critical behaviours which must be recommended by receptive field detections and selected in appropriate circumstances by the competitive subsystem. Note that as in the brain, receptive field modules needed for change management may also be useful for other behaviours. Change management must minimize the degree of change to receptive fields, and some mechanism analogous with REM sleep to limit the possible expansions will be required.

A fourth implication is that receptive field modules supporting indirect activations on the basis of past temporally correlated activity must be provided. These modules will contain receptive fields corresponding with groups of receptive fields in other modules which have shown past temporal correlations in activity. Such receptive fields will recommend indirect activation of other receptive fields. Such indirect activations are behaviours which are only implemented if selected by the competition subsystem. A fifth implication is that the management of reward behaviours must be carefully managed, with appropriate receptive field modules to manage rewards for strategic, tactical and detailed actions in an integrated fashion. A sixth implication is that a subsystem to learn and implement frequently utilized sequences of actions will improve the accuracy and speed of the system.

The architecture of the brain is the result of severe natural selection constraints imposed over hundreds of millions of years of evolution favouring species that can learn complex behaviours with the least resources and the least interference between past and new learning. This architecture is therefore a good guide for implementing general intelligence systems that are subject to similar constraints.

References

1. Coward, L.A.: The Recommendation Architecture: lessons from the design of large scale electronic systems for cognitive science. Journal of Cognitive Systems Research 2(2), 111–156 (2001)
2. Coward, L.A.: A System Architecture Approach to the Brain: from Neurons to Consciousness. Nova Science Publishers, New York (2005b)
3. Coward, L.A., Gedeon, T.D.: Implications of Resource Limitations for a Conscious Machine. Neurocomputing 72, 767–788 (2009)
4. Coward, L.A.: Pattern Thinking. Praeger, New York (1990)
5. Mountcastle, V.H.: The columnar organization of the neocortex. Brain 120, 701–722 (1997)
6. Hilgetag, C.-C., Burns, G.A.P.C., O'Neill, M.A., Scannell, J.W., Young, M.P.: Anatomical connectivity defines the organization of clusters of cortical areas in the macaque monkey and the cat. Philosophical Transactions of the Royal Society of London B 355(1393), 91–110 (2000)
7. Tanaka, K.: Columns for complex visual object features in the inferotemporal *cortex: clustering of cells with similar but slightly different stimulus selectivities*. Cerebral Cortex 13, 90–99 (2003)
8. Petrides, M., Pandya, D.N.: Dorsolateral prefrontal cortex: comparative cytoarchitectonic analysis in the human and the macaque ventrolateral prefrontal cortex and corticocortical connection patterns. European Journal of Neuroscience 11, 1011–1036 (1999)
9. Petrides, M., Pandya, D.N.: Comparative cytoarchitectonic analysis in the human and the macaque brain and corticocortical connection patterns in the monkey. European Journal of Neuroscience 16, 291–310 (2002)
10. Morasan, P., Rademacher, J., Schleicher, A., et al.: Human primary auditory cortex: Cytoarchitectonic subdivisions and mapping into a spatial reference system. NeuroImage 13, 684–701 (2001)
11. Coward, L.A.: Modelling Memory and Learning Consistently from Psychology to Physiology. In: Cutsuridis, V., Amir, H., Taylor, J. (eds.) Perception-Action Cycle: Models, Architectures, and Hardware. Springer Series in Cognitive and Neural Systems, pp. 52–123 (2011)
12. Coward, L.A.: The Hippocampal System as the Cortical Resource Manager: a model connecting psychology, anatomy and physiology. Advances in Experimental Medicine and Biology 657, 315–364 (2010)
13. Insausti, R., Amaral, D.G.: Hippocampal Formation. In: Paxinos, G., Mai, J.K. (eds.) The Human Nervous System, pp. 871–914. Elsevier, Amsterdam (2004)
14. Aggleton, J.P., Malcolm, W., Brown, M.W.: Episodic memory, amnesia, and the hippocampal-anterior thalamic axis. Behavioral and Brain Sciences 22, 425–444 (1999)
15. Bi, G.-q., Poo, M.-m.: Synaptic modifications in cultured hippocampal neurons: Dependence on spike timing, synaptic strength, and postsynaptic cell type. Journal of Neuroscience 18, 10464–10472 (1998)
16. Murphy, T.H., Baraban, J.M., Gil Wier, W., Blatter, L.A.: Visualization of quantal synaptic transmission by dendritic calcium imaging. Science 263, 529–532 (1994)
17. Gulledge, A.T., Kampa, B.M., Stuart, G.J.: Synaptic Integration in Dendritic Trees. Journal of Neurobiology 64(1), 75–90 (2005)
18. Hausser, M., Mel, B.: Dendrites: bug or feature? Current Opinion in Neurobiology 13, 372–383 (2003)

19. Stuart, G.J., Sakmann, B.: Active propagation of somatic action potentials into neocortical pyramidal cell dendrites. Nature 367, 69–72 (1994)
20. Malenka, R.C., Bear, M.F.: LTP and LTD: An Embarrassment of Riches. Neuron 44, 5–21 (2004)
21. Malenka, R.C., Nicoll, R.A.: Silent synapses speak up. Neuron 19, 473–476 (1997)
22. Coward, L.A.: A Functional Architecture Approach to Neural Systems. International Journal of Systems Research and Information Systems 9(2-4), 69–120 (2000)
23. Coward, L.A.: Accounting for episodic, semantic and procedural memory in the recommendation architecture cognitive model. In: Proceedings of the Ninth Neural Computation and Psychology Workshop: Modelling Language, Cognition, and Action (2005a)
24. Floresco, S.B., West, A.R., Ash, B., Moore, H., Grace, A.A.: Afferent modulation of dopamine neuron firing differentially regulates tonic and phasic dopamine transmission. Nature Neuroscience 6, 968–973 (2003)
25. Alexander, G.E., Crutcher, M.D.: Functional architecture of basal ganglia circuits: neural substrates of parallel processing. Trends in Neurosciences 13(7), 266–271 (1990)
26. Haber, S.N., Fudge, J.L., McFarland, N.R.: Striatonigrostriatal pathways in primates form an ascending spiral from the shell to the dorsolateral striatum. Journal of Neuroscience 20, 2369–2382 (2000)
27. Hyland, B.I., Reynolds, J.N.J., Hay, J., Perk, C.G., Miller, R.: Firing modes of midbrain dopamine cells in the freely moving rat. Neuroscience 114, 475–492 (2002)
28. Sajikumar, S., Frey, J.U.: Late-associativity, synaptic tagging, and the role of dopamine during LTP and LTD. Neurobiology of Learning and Memory 82, 12–25 (2004)
29. Asztely, F., Gustafsson, B.: Dissociation between long-term potentiation and associated changes in field EPSP waveform in the hippocampal CA1 region: an in vitro study in Guinea pig brain slices. Hippocampus 4, 148–156 (1994)
30. Cowan, N.: The magical number 4 in short-term memory: a reconsideration of mental storage capacity. Behavioral and Brain Sciences 24, 87–114 (2000)
31. Percheron, G.: Thalamus. In: Paxinos, G., Mai, J.K. (eds.) The Human Nervous System, 2nd edn. Elsevier, USA (2004)
32. Macdonald, K.D., Fifkova, E., Jones, M.S., Daniel, S., Barth, D.S.: Focal Stimulation of the Thalamic Reticular Nucleus Induces Focal Gamma Waves in Cortex. Journal of Neurophysiology 79, 474–477 (1998)
33. Gulledge, A.T., Stuart, G.J.: Excitatory Actions of GABA in the Cortex. Neuron 37, 299–309 (2003)
34. Kelly, R.M., Strick, P.L.: Cerebellar loops with motor cortex and prefrontal cortex of a nonhuman primate. Journal of Neuroscience 23, 8432–8444 (2003)
35. Vogt, K.E., Canepari, M.: On the Induction of Postsynaptic Granule Cell–Purkinje Neuron LTP and LTD. Cerebellum 9, 284–290 (2010)
36. Yarom, Y., Cohen, D.: The olivocerebellar system as a generator of temporal patterns. Annals of the New York Academy of Sciences 978, 122–134 (2002)
37. Kim, J.J., Krupa, D.J., Thompson, R.F.: Inhibitory cerebello-olivary projections and blocking effect in classical conditioning. Science 279, 570–573 (1998)
38. Bracke-Tolkmitt, R., Linden, A., Canavan, A.G.M., Rockstroh, B., Scholz, E., Wessel, K., Diener, H.-C.: The Cerebellum Contributes to Mental Skills. Behavioral Neuroscience 103(2), 442–446 (1989)

Information, Utility and Bounded Rationality

Pedro Alejandro Ortega and Daniel Alexander Braun

Department of Engineering, University of Cambridge
Trumpington Street, Cambridge, CB2 1PZ, UK
{dab54,pao32}@cam.ac.uk

Abstract. Perfectly rational decision-makers maximize expected utility, but crucially ignore the resource costs incurred when determining optimal actions. Here we employ an axiomatic framework for bounded rational decision-making based on a thermodynamic interpretation of resource costs as information costs. This leads to a variational "free utility" principle akin to thermodynamical free energy that trades off utility and information costs. We show that bounded optimal control solutions can be derived from this variational principle, which leads in general to stochastic policies. Furthermore, we show that risk-sensitive and robust (minimax) control schemes fall out naturally from this framework if the environment is considered as a bounded rational and perfectly rational opponent, respectively. When resource costs are ignored, the maximum expected utility principle is recovered.

Keywords: Bounded rationality, expected utility, risk-sensitivity.

1 Introduction

According to the principle of maximum expected utility (MEU), a *perfectly rational* decision-maker chooses its action so as to maximize its expected utility, given a probabilistic model of the environment [18]. In contrast, a *bounded rational* decision-maker trades off the action's expected utility against the computational cost of finding the optimal action [12]. In this paper we employ a previously published axiomatic conversion between utility and information [11] as a basis for a framework for bounded rationality that leads to such a trade-off based on a thermodynamic interpretation of resource costs [5]. The intuition behind this interpretation is that ultimately any real decision-maker has to be incarnated in a thermodynamical system, since any process of information processing must always be accompanied by a pertinent physical process [16]. In the following we conceive of information processing as changes in information states represented by probability distributions in statistical physical systems, where states with different energy correspond to states with different utility [4]. Changing an information state therefore implies changes in physical states, such as flipping gates in a transistor, changing voltage on a microchip, or even changing location of a gas particle. Changing such states is costly and requires thermodynamical work [5]. We will interpret this work as a proxy for resource costs of information processing.

J. Schmidhuber, K.R. Thórisson, and M. Looks (Eds.): AGI 2011, LNAI 6830, pp. 269–274, 2011.
© Springer-Verlag Berlin Heidelberg 2011

2   Bounded Rationality

Since bounded rational decision-makers need to trade off utility and information costs, the first question is how to translate between information and utility. In canonical systems of statistical mechanics this relationship is given by the Boltzmann distribution that relates the probability $\mathbf{P}$ of a state to its energy $\mathbf{U}$ (utility), thus forming a *conjugate* pair $(\mathbf{P}, \mathbf{U})$. As shown previously, the same relationship can be derived axiomatically in a choice-theoretic context [11], and both formulations satisfy a variational principle [4]:

Theorem 1. *Let X be a random variable with values in $\mathcal{X}$. Let $\mathbf{P}$ and $\mathbf{U}$ be a conjugate pair of probability measure and utility function over X. Define the **free utility** functional as $\mathbf{J}(\mathrm{Pr}; \mathbf{U}) := \sum_{x \in \mathcal{X}} \mathrm{Pr}(x)\mathbf{U}(x) - \alpha \sum_{x \in \mathcal{X}} \mathrm{Pr}(x)\log\mathrm{Pr}(x)$, where $\mathbf{Pr}$ is an arbitrary probability measure over X. Then, $\mathbf{J}(\mathrm{Pr}; \mathbf{U}) \leq \mathbf{J}(\mathbf{P}; \mathbf{U})$ with $\mathbf{P}(X) = \frac{1}{Z}e^{\frac{1}{\alpha}\mathbf{U}(X)}$ and $Z = \sum_{X' \in \mathcal{X}} e^{\frac{1}{\alpha}\mathbf{U}(X')}$.*

A proof can be found in [8]. The constant $\alpha \in \mathbb{R}$ is usually strictly positive, unless one deals with an adversarial agent and it is strictly negative.

The variational principle of the free utility also allows measuring the cost of transforming the state of a stochastic system required for information processing. Consider an initial system described by the conjugate pair $\mathbf{P}_i$ and $\mathbf{U}_i$ and free utility $\mathbf{J}_i(\mathbf{P}_i, \mathbf{U}_i)$. We now want to transform this initial system into another system by adding new constraints represented by the utility function $\mathbf{U}_*$. Then, the resulting utility function $\mathbf{U}_f$ is given by the sum $\mathbf{U}_f = \mathbf{U}_i + \mathbf{U}_*$ and the resulting system has the free utility $\mathbf{J}_f(\mathbf{P}_f, \mathbf{U}_f)$. The difference in free utility is

$$\mathbf{J}_f - \mathbf{J}_i = \sum_{x \in \mathcal{X}} \mathbf{P}_f(x)\mathbf{U}_*(x) - \alpha \sum_{x \in \mathcal{X}} \mathbf{P}_f(x)\log\frac{\mathbf{P}_f(x)}{\mathbf{P}_i(x)}. \tag{1}$$

These two terms can be interpreted as determinants of bounded rational decision-making in that they formalize a trade-off between an expected utility $\mathbf{U}_*$ (first term) and the information cost of transforming $\mathbf{P}_i$ into $\mathbf{P}_f$ (second term). In this interpretation $\mathbf{P}_i$ represents an initial probability or policy, which includes the special case of the uniform distribution where the decision-maker has initially no preferences. Deviations from this initial probability incur an information cost measured by the KL divergence. If this deviation is bounded by a non-zero value, we have a bounded rational agent. This allows formulating a variational principle both for control and estimation:

1. **Control.** Given an initial policy represented by the probability measure $\mathbf{P}_i$ and the constraint utilities $\mathbf{U}_*$, we are looking for the final system $\mathbf{P}_f$ that optimizes the trade-off between utility and resource costs. That is,

$$\mathbf{P}_f = \arg\max_{\mathrm{Pr}} \sum_{x \in \mathcal{X}} \mathrm{Pr}(x)\mathbf{U}_*(x) - \alpha \sum_{x \in \mathcal{X}} \mathrm{Pr}(x)\log\frac{\mathrm{Pr}(x)}{\mathbf{P}_i(x)}. \tag{2}$$

The solution is given by $\mathbf{P}_f(x) \propto \mathbf{P}_i(x)\exp\left(\frac{1}{\alpha}\mathbf{U}_*(x)\right)$. In particular, at very low temperature $\alpha \approx 0$ we get $\mathbf{J}_f - \mathbf{J}_i \approx \sum_{x \in \mathcal{X}} \mathbf{P}_f(x)\mathbf{U}_*(x)$, and hence resource costs are ignored in the choice of $\mathbf{P}_f$, leading to $\mathbf{P}_f \approx \delta_{x^*}(x)$, where $x^* = \max_x \mathbf{U}_*(x)$. Similarly, at a high temperature, the difference is $\mathbf{J}_f - \mathbf{J}_i \approx -\alpha \sum_{x \in \mathcal{X}} \mathbf{P}_f(x) \log \frac{\mathbf{P}_f(x)}{\mathbf{P}_i(x)}$, and hence only resource costs matter, leading to $\mathbf{P}_f \approx \mathbf{P}_i$.

2. **Estimation.** Given a final probability measure $\mathbf{P}_f$ that represents the environment and the constraint utilities $\mathbf{U}_*$, we are looking for the initial system $\mathbf{P}_i$ that satisfies

$$\mathbf{P}_i = \arg\max_{\mathbf{Pr}} \sum_{x \in \mathcal{X}} \mathbf{P}_f(x) \mathbf{U}_*(x) - \alpha \sum_{x \in \mathcal{X}} \mathbf{P}_f(x) \log \frac{\mathbf{P}_f(x)}{\mathbf{Pr}(x)} \qquad (3)$$

which translates into $\mathbf{P}_i = \arg\min_{\mathbf{Pr}} \sum_{x \in \mathcal{X}} \mathbf{P}_f(x) \log \frac{\mathbf{P}_f(x)}{\mathbf{Pr}(x)}$ and thus we have recovered the minimum relative entropy principle for estimation, having the solution $\mathbf{P}_i = \mathbf{P}_f$. The minimum relative entropy principle for estimation is well-known in the literature as it underlies Bayesian inference [6], but the same principle can also be applied to problems of adaptive control [9,10,2].

3   Applications

Consider a system that first emits an action symbol x_1 with probability $P_0(x_1)$ and then expects a subsequent input signal x_2 with probability $P_0(x_2|x_1)$. Now we impose a utility on this decision-maker that is given by $U(x_1)$ for the first symbol and $U(x_2|x_1)$ for the second symbol. How should this system adjust its action probability $P(x_1)$ and expectation $P(x_2|x_1)$? Given the boundedness constraints, the variational problem can be formulated as a nested expression

$$\max_{p(x_1,x_2)} \sum_{x_1} p(x_1) \left[U(x_1) - \alpha \log \frac{p(x_1)}{p_0(x_1)} + \sum_{x_2} p(x_2|x_1) \left[U(x_2|x_1) - \beta \log \frac{p(x_2|x_1)}{p_0(x_2|x_1)} \right] \right].$$

with α and β as Lagrange multipliers. We have then an inner variational problem:

$$\max_{p(x_2|x_1)} \sum_{x_2} p(x_2|x_1) \left[-\beta \log \frac{p(x_2|x_1)}{p_0(x_2|x_1)} + U(x_2|x_1) \right] \qquad (4)$$

with the solution

$$p(x_2|x_1) = \frac{1}{Z_2} p_0(x_2|x_1) \exp\left(\frac{1}{\beta} U(x_2|x_1) \right) \qquad (5)$$

and the normalization constant $Z_2(x_1) = \sum_{x_2} p_0(x_2|x_1) \exp\left(\frac{1}{\beta} U(x_2|x_1) \right)$ and an outer variational problem

$$\max_{p(x_1)} \sum_{x_1} p(x_1) \left[-\alpha \log \frac{p(x_1)}{p_0(x_1)} + U(x_1) + \beta \log Z_2 \right] \qquad (6)$$

with the solution

$$p(x_1) = \frac{1}{Z_1} p_0(x_1) \exp\left(\frac{1}{\alpha} \left(U(x_1) + \beta \log Z_2 \right) \right) \qquad (7)$$

and the normalization constant $Z_1 = \sum_{x_1} p_0(x_1) \exp\left(\frac{1}{\alpha}\left(U(x_1) + \beta \log Z_2\right)\right)$.
For notational convenience we introduce $\lambda = \frac{1}{\alpha}$ and $\mu = \frac{1}{\beta}$. Depending on
the values of λ and μ we can discern the following cases:

1. **Risk-seeking bounded rational agent:** $\lambda > 0$ and $\mu > 0$
   When $\lambda > 0$ the agent is bounded and acts in general stochastically. When
   $\mu > 0$ the agent considers the move of the environment as if it was his own
   move (hence "risk-seeking" due to the overtly optimistic view). We can see
   this from the relationship between Z_1 and Z_2 in (7), if we assume $\mu = \lambda$ and
   introduce the value function $V_t = \frac{1}{\lambda} \log Z_t$, which results in the recursion

   $$V_{t-1} = \frac{1}{\lambda} \log \sum_{x_{t-1}} P_0(x_{t-1}|\cdot) \exp\left(\lambda\left(U(x_{t-1}|\cdot) + V_t\right)\right).$$

   Similar recursions based on the log-transform have been previously exploited
   for efficient approximations of optimal control solutions both in the discrete
   and the continuous domain [3,7,15]. In the perfectly rational limit $\lambda \to +\infty$,
   this recursion becomes the well-known Bellman recursion

   $$V_{t-1}^* = \max_{x_{t-1}} \left(U(x_{t-1}|\cdot) + V_t^*\right)$$

   with $V_t^* = \lim_{\lambda \to +\infty} V_t$.
2. **Risk-neutral perfectly rational agent:** $\lambda \to +\infty$ and $\mu \to 0$
   This is the limit for the standard optimal controller. We can see this from
   (7) by noting that

   $$\lim_{\mu \to 0} \frac{1}{\mu} \log \sum_{x_2} p_0(x_2|x_1) \exp\left(\mu U(x_2|x_1)\right) = \sum_{x_2} p_0(x_2|x_1) U(x_2|x_1),$$

   which is simply the expected utility. By setting $U(x_1) \equiv 0$, and taking the
   limit $\lambda \to +\infty$ in (7), we therefore obtain an expected utility maximizer

   $$p(x_1) = \delta(x_1 - x_1^*)$$

   with

   $$x_1^* = \arg\max_{x_1} \sum_{x_2} p_0(x_2|x_1) U(x_2|x_1).$$

   As discussed previously, action selection becomes deterministic in the perfectly rational limit.
3. **Risk-averse perfectly rational agent:** $\lambda \to +\infty$ and $\mu < 0$
   When $\mu < 0$ the decision-maker assumes a pessimistic view with respect
   to the environment, as if the environment was an adversarial or malevolent
   agent. This attitude is sometimes called risk-aversion, because such agents
   act particularly cautiously to avoid high uncertainty. We can see this from
   (7) by writing a Taylor series expansion for small μ

   $$\frac{1}{\mu} \log \sum_{x_2} p_0(x_2|x_1) \exp\left(\mu U(x_2|x_1)\right) \approx \mathbb{E}[U] - \frac{\mu}{2} \mathbb{VAR}[U],$$

where higher than second order cumulants have been neglected. The name risk-sensitivity then stems from the fact that variability or uncertainty in the utility of the Taylor series is subtracted from the expected utility. This utility function is typically *assumed* in risk-sensitive control schemes in the literature [19], whereas here it falls out naturally. The perfectly rational actor with risk-sensitivity μ picks the action

$$p(x_1) = \delta(x_1 - x_1^*)$$

with

$$x_1^* = \arg\max_{x_1} \frac{1}{\mu} \log \sum_{x_2} p_0(x_2|x_1) \exp\left(\mu U(x_2|x_1)\right),$$

which can be derived from (7) by setting $U(x_1) \equiv 0$ and by taking the limit $\lambda \to +\infty$. Within the framework proposed in this paper we might also interpret the equations such that the decision-maker considers the environment as an adversarial opponent with bounded rationality μ.

4. **Robust perfectly rational agent:** $\lambda \to +\infty$ and $\mu \to -\infty$
   When $\mu \to -\infty$ the decision-maker makes a worst case assumption about the adversarial environment, namely that it is also perfectly rational. This leads to the well-known game-theoretic minimax problem with the solution

$$x_1^* = \arg\max_{x_1} \arg\min_{x_2} U(x_2|x_1),$$

which can be derived from (7) by setting $U(x_1) \equiv 0$, taking the limits $\lambda \to +\infty$ and $\mu \to -\infty$ and by noting that $p(x_1) = \delta(x_1 - x_1^*)$. Minimax problems have been used to reformulate robust control problems that allow controllers to cope with model uncertainties [1]. Robust control problems are also known to be related to risk-sensitive control [1]. Here we derived both control types from the same variational principle.

4   Conclusion

In this paper we have proposed a thermodynamic interpretation of bounded rationality based on a free utility principle. Accordingly, bounded rational agents trade off utility maximization against resource costs measured by the KL divergence with respect to an initial policy. The use of the KL divergence as a cost function for control has been previously proposed to measure deviations from passive dynamics in Markov systems [14,15]. Other methods of statistical physics have been previously proposed as an information-theoretic approach to interactive learning [13] and to game theory with bounded rational players [20]. The contribution of our study is to devise a single axiomatic framework that allows for the treatment of control problems, game-theoretic problems and estimation and learning problems for perfectly rational and bounded rational agents. In the future it will be interesting to relate the thermodynamic resource costs of bounded rational agents to more traditional notions of resource costs in computer science like space and time requirements when computing optimal actions [17].

References

1. Basar, T., Bernhard, P.: H-Infinity Optimal Control and Related Minimax Design Problems: A Dynamic Game Approach. Birkhäuser, Boston (1995)
2. Braun, D.A., Ortega, P.A.: A minimum relative entropy principle for adaptive control in linear quadratic regulators. In: The 7th Conference on Informatics in Control, Automation and Robotics, vol. 3, pp. 103–108 (2010)
3. Braun, D.A., Ortega, P.A., Theodorou, E., Schaal, S.: Path integral control and bounded rationality. In: IEEE Symposium on Adaptive Dynamic Programming and Reinforcement Learning (2011)
4. Callen, H.B.: Thermodynamics and an Introduction to Themostatistics, 2nd edn. John Wiley & Sons, Chichester (1985)
5. Feynman, R.P.: The Feynman Lectures on Computation. Addison-Wesley, Reading (1996)
6. Haussler, D., Opper, M.: Mutual information, metric entropy and cumulative relative entropy risk. The Annals of Statistics 25, 2451–2492 (1997)
7. Kappen, B.: A linear theory for control of non-linear stochastic systems. Physical Review Letters 95, 200–201 (2005)
8. Keller, G.: Equilibrium States in Ergodic Theory. London Mathematical Society Student Texts. Cambridge University Press, Cambridge (1998)
9. Ortega, P.A., Braun, D.A.: A minimum relative entropy principle for learning and acting. Journal of Artificial Intelligence Research 38, 475–511 (2010)
10. Ortega, P.A., Braun, D.A.: A bayesian rule for adaptive control based on causal interventions. In: The Third Conference on Artificial General Intelligence, pp. 121–126. Atlantis Press, Paris (2010)
11. Ortega, P.A., Braun, D.A.: A conversion between utility and information. In: The Third Conference on Artificial General Intelligence, pp. 115–120. Atlantis Press, Paris (2010)
12. Simon, H.: Models of Bounded Rationality. MIT Press, Cambridge (1982)
13. Still, S.: An information-theoretic approach to interactive learning. Europhysics Letters 85, 28005 (2009)
14. Todorov, E.: Linearly solvable markov decision problems. In: Advances in Neural Information Processing Systems, vol. 19, pp. 1369–1376 (2006)
15. Todorov, E.: Efficient computation of optimal actions. Proceedings of the National Academy of Sciences USA 106, 11478–11483 (2009)
16. Tribus, M., McIrvine, E.C.: Energy and information. Scientific American 225, 179–188 (1971)
17. Vitanyi, P.M.B.: Time, space, and energy in reversible computing. In: Proceedings of the 2nd ACM Conference on Computing Frontiers, pp. 435–444 (2005)
18. von Neumann, J., Morgenstern, O.: Theory of Games and Economic Behavior. Princeton University Press, Princeton (1944)
19. Whittle, P.: Risk-sensitive optimal control. John Wiley and Sons, Chichester (1990)
20. Wolpert, D.H.: Information theory - the bridge connecting bounded rational game theory and statistical physics. In: Braha, D., Bar-Yam, Y. (eds.) Complex Engineering Systems. Perseus Books, Cambridge (2004)

A Family of Gödel Machine Implementations

Bas R. Steunebrink and Jürgen Schmidhuber

IDSIA & University of Lugano, Switzerland
{bas,juergen}@idsia.ch

Abstract. The Gödel Machine is a universal problem solver encoded as a completely self-referential program capable of rewriting any part of itself, provided it can prove that the rewrite is useful according to some utility function, encoded within itself. Based on experience gained by constructing a virtual machine capable of running the first Gödel Machine implementation written in self-referential code, we discuss several important refinements of the original concept. We also show how different approaches to implementing the proof search leads to a family of possible Gödel Machine implementations.

1 Introduction

The fully self-referential Gödel Machine [8,7,9] is a universal AI that is theoretically optimal in a certain sense. It may interact with some initially unknown, partially observable environment to solve arbitrary user-defined computational tasks by maximizing expected cumulative future utility. Its initial algorithm is not hardwired; it can completely rewrite itself without essential limits apart from the limits of computability, provided a proof searcher embedded within the initial algorithm can first prove that the rewrite is useful, according to its formalized utility function taking into account the limited computational resources. Self-rewrites due to this approach can be shown to be *globally optimal* with respect to the initial utility function (e.g., a Reinforcement Learner's reward function), relative to Gödel's well-known fundamental restrictions of provability [2].

The original Gödel Machine description [10] outlines the general concept and provides implementation details only where necessary to address potential doubts about feasibility. To the best of our knowledge, however, no full implementation has existed before. In this paper, we show how inconvenient aspects of the original Gödel Machine specification can be overcome by presenting a new one geared towards implementation, offering clarifications of subtle details. In particular, we specify in novel ways both the utility function framework and the target theorem at the core of the Gödel Machine. Based on experience gained from our ongoing effort to build a full Gödel Machine, we also provide several essential implementation details, including a technique for attaining self-reflectivity, demonstrating that implementing a Gödel Machine is not as hard as it may seem at first sight.

2 Gödel Machine Specification

One can view a Gödel Machine as a program consisting of two parts. One part, which we will call the *solver*, can be any problem-solving program. For clarity of

J. Schmidhuber, K.R. Thórisson, and M. Looks (Eds.): AGI 2011, LNAI 6830, pp. 275–280, 2011.
© Springer-Verlag Berlin Heidelberg 2011

presentation, we will pretend the *solver* is a Reinforcement Learning (RL) program interacting with some environment. This will provide us with a convenient way of determining *utility* (using the RL program's reward function), which will be an important topic later on. But in general, no constraints are placed on the *solver*. The second part of the Gödel Machine, which we will call the *searcher*, is a program that tries to improve the entire Gödel Machine in a provably optimal way. This *searcher* will be the main topic of this paper.

In order to discuss our implementation of a Gödel Machine, we must first critically examine the original specification [10,9] and show where, how, and why we deviate from it. In [9], a Gödel Machine's *searcher* is said to hold a function computing the machine's expected cumulative future utility as follows.

$$u(s, env) = \mathbb{E}_\mu \left[\sum_{t=time}^{T} r(t) \mid env \right] \qquad \text{(ORIG.)}$$

So given a state s, environment env, environment distribution μ, lifetime T, current time *time*, and reward function r, the utility of s is determined by summing all expected future rewards up to the expected end of the machine's life (which may be extended through appropriate self-modifications). This utility function u is then used to construct a *target theorem*; that is, the Gödel Machine is *only* allowed to perform a self-modification if a part of memory referred to as *proof* contains a theorem of the following form.

$$u(s(t) \oplus (switchbit(t) = \text{`1'}), env(t)) > u(s(t) \oplus (switchbit(t) = \text{`0'}), env(t))$$
$$\text{(ORIG.)}$$

(The notation $s \oplus (v = x)$ stands for the state obtained when element v of s is set to x; $v(t)$ for (the expected value of) element v at time t.) To understand this theorem, several more details about the *searcher* must be explained. The *searcher* holds a procedure *check* which invokes another procedure referred to as *switchprog* if and only if a bit called *switchbit* is set to 1. The procedure *switchprog*, which is assumed to be created during the proof search, may modify any part of the Gödel Machine's software. But *switchprog* is invoked *only* when the target theorem shown above can be proved to hold. So the target theorem weighs self-modification against proceeding as usual, because *switchprog* cannot be invoked when *switchbit* is set to 0.

The concept of only allowing self-modification when it is *provably* profitable is intuitively sound; however, the specification of Gödel Machines as introduced in [10] presents several difficulties when an actual implementation is attempted. We identify three main issues: (1) the time-based view of the future makes the utility function u tricky to implement, glossing over certain subtleties; (2) the target theorem is decoupled from its *proof* and does not explicate the relation between *switchbit* and *switchprog*; and (3) it is not obvious how env, μ, T, and r are encoded in state s. These issues call for more explanation, but as we shall see next, they can actually be solved in a unified way.

The function u for determining the expected cumulative future utility, as shown above, requires us to sum all rewards for all future time steps. Here "time steps" actually means not clock ticks, but execution of elementary instructions. Indeed, each instruction takes time to execute, so if we can find a way to explicitly represent the instructions that are going to be executed in the future, we automatically have a window into a future time. An obvious choice of such a representation is the *continuation*, which is a well-studied concept in light of λ-calculus-based programming languages (e.g., LISP, Scheme) [6]. As we shall see, using continuations will allow us to remove t and T from the utility function while *switchprog* can be explicitly introduced in the target theorem. Intuitively, a continuation can be seen as the opposite of a call stack; instead of showing "where we came from," a continuation explicitly shows "what is going to happen next." Note that in all but the simplest cases, a continuation will only be partially expanded. For example, suppose the current continuation is `{ A(); if B() then C() else D() fi }`; this continuation specifies that the next thing to be done is expanding `A` and executing its body, and then the conditional statement will be executed, which means that first `B` will be expanded and depending on its result, either `C` or `D` will be expanded. Note that before executing `B`, it is not clear yet whether `C` or `D` will be executed in the future; so it makes no sense to expand either of them before we know the result of `B`.

In what follows we consistently use subscripts to indicate where some element is encoded. With the use of continuations, u becomes a function of two parameters, $u_{\bar{s}}(s, c)$, which represents the expected cumulative future utility of running continuation c on state s. Here $\bar{s}$ represents the evaluating state (where u is encoded), whereas s is the evaluated state. The reason for this separation will become clear when considering the calculation of u:

$$u_{\bar{s}}(s, c) = \mathbb{E}_{\mu_s, M_s}[u'] \quad \text{with } u'(env) = r_{\bar{s}}(s, env) + \mathbb{E}_{\kappa_c, K_c}[u_{\bar{s}} \mid env] \quad (1)$$

As indicated with subscripts, we have moved the representation M of the (external) environment inside s, because all knowledge a Gödel Machine has must be encoded in s. For clarity, let M be a set of bitstrings, each constituting a representation of the environment held possible by the Gödel Machine. μ is a mapping from M to probabilities, also encoded in s. c encodes not only a (partially expanded) representation of the instructions that are going to be executed in the future, but also a set K of state–continuation pairs representing which possible next states and continuations can result from executing the first instruction in c, and a mapping κ from K to probabilities. So μ and κ are (discrete) probability distributions on sample spaces M and K, respectively. $r_{\bar{s}}(s, env)$ determines whether state s is rewarding given environment env. For example, in the case where *solver* (which is part of s) is an RL program, $r_{\bar{s}}(s, env)$ will be nonzero only when s represents a state just after performing an input receiving instruction. Finally, the term $\mathbb{E}_{\kappa_c, K_c}[u_{\bar{s}} \mid env]$ recurses on u with the state and continuation following from executing the next instruction in continuation c.

It is *crucial* to note that u and r are taken from the evaluating state $\bar{s}$, *not* from the state s under evaluation. Doing the latter would break the global optimality [9] of the Gödel Machine, because it would be capable of rewriting its utility function in arbitrary ways. Therefore, the original, unchanged utility function of $\bar{s}$ must be used to first show that a rewrite is useful. In contrast, μ and M *are* taken from s, because for any interesting Gödel Machine, c will both contain instructions that affect the external environment (e.g., output to actuators) and instructions that update the internal model of the environment (encoded in s) accordingly. To make use of these updated models, u must extract them from s. Likewise, κ and K are taken from c, because after each instruction the continuation necessarily changes, resulting in new κ and K.

It is also important to notice that our function u is recursive, whereas the original u is a summation up to the end of the Gödel Machine's lifetime T. In formula (1), a Gödel Machine's life ends when the continuation sample space K_c is empty. In that case, the term $\mathbb{E}_{\kappa_c, K_c}[u_{\bar{s}} \mid env]$ is zero and recursion on u stops. In the most common case, however, an instruction will be deterministic, e.g., $K_c = \{(s', c')\}$. Then formula (1) reduces to $u_{\bar{s}}(s, c) = \mathbb{E}_{\mu_s, M_s}[r_{\bar{s}}(s, \cdot)] + u_{\bar{s}}(s', c')$. So for chains of deterministic state transitions, the expected cumulative future utility reduces to a summation of expected rewards in the successive states. But as observed earlier, even those expected rewards are usually zero, because most instructions are not involved with receiving information from the environment (which in e.g. RL is usually the source of rewards).

We are now in a position to introduce a revised *target theorem*, based on the new utility function. Thanks to our continuation-based perspective, we can explicitly introduce *switchprog* into the target theorem by constructing a continuation out of it. Specifically, let $c^* = \{wait\_until(t); switchprog()\}$ denote the continuation that waits until time t (e.g., by continually calling a primitive clock function until the returned time tests as greater or equal to t) and then executes *switchprog*. Furthermore, let s be an expected future state *before* time t. Now $u_{\bar{s}}(s, c^*)$ tells us what is the expected cumulative future utility of running *switchprog* on s at time t. If this utility compares positively against the expected cumulative future utility of *not* switching, then the Gödel Machine must perform the switch at time t. Thus, the *searcher* is to find a state s, a time t, and a nullary procedure *switchprog* such that $\mathrm{tt}_{\bar{s}}(s, t, switchprog)$ holds, where:

$$\mathrm{tt}_{\bar{s}}(s, t, switchprog) = \left[u_{\bar{s}}(s, \{wait\_until_s(t); switchprog()\}) > u_{\bar{s}}(s, \{scheduler_s()\}) \right] \quad (2)$$

where *scheduler* is the procedure that interleaves the Gödel Machine's *solver* and *searcher*. Thus $\{scheduler_s()\}$ denotes the continuation that "proceeds as usual" from s (including searching for new *switchprog*s). Note that, since *switchprog* may overwrite the scheduler, it must as its last instruction invoke a new scheduler (if needed), or simply invoke the old scheduler if it has been left intact.

There are two ways in which this target theorem can be used to find provably useful self-rewrites: (1) generate a candidate *switchprog* (e.g., a program performing optimization techniques also applied by state-of-the-art compilers), generate a future switch time t at least as far ahead as the time the evaluation of the utility of running *switchprog* is expected to take, and make s a copy of the current state $\bar{s}$; then run both continuations specified by tt on s (this is safe because s acts like a sandbox) until the inequality can be shown to be true or false, or until the current time exceeds t; if the inequality is false or time has run out, generate a new *switchprog* and start over; else, swap the current state for s, wait until time t and execute *switchprog*. (2) Start with an axiomatic system with axiom and rules, and generate theorems (or generate programs that calculate theorems [9]), testing them for equivalence with tt. The first method can be seen as a top-down approach to proving tt and the latter as bottom-up. Hybrid approaches are also possible, so our specification of the target theorem allows for a *family* of possible Gödel Machine implementations.

To make sure the Gödel Machine is at least *asymptotically* optimal even before the first self-rewrite, it may be initialized with Hutter's non-self-referential but *asymptotically fastest algorithm for all well-defined problems* HSEARCH [3], which uses a hardwired brute force proof searcher and ignores the costs of proof search. Given some problem, the Gödel Machine may decide to replace HSEARCH by a faster method suffering less from large constant overhead, but even if it does not, its performance will not be less than asymptotically optimal.

3   Discussion and Conclusion

In this paper we have presented a novel Gödel Machine specification geared towards implementation. Our own approach so far has been to implement a virtual machine capable of running a specially invented programming language with self-referential constructs to attain the self-reflexivity needed for a Gödel Machine. The *solver*, *searcher*, and *scheduler* are then implemented in this language. It should be noted though, that a simpler existing technique can be used to attain self-reflexivity, namely by using *meta-circular evaluators* [1]. A meta-circular evaluator is basically an interpreter for the same programming language as the one in which the interpreter is written. Especially suitable for this technique are homoiconic languages such as Scheme [5], which is very close to λ-calculus and is often used to study meta-circular evaluators and self-reflection in programming in general [1,6,4]. So a meta-circular Scheme evaluator is a program written in Scheme which can interpret programs written in Scheme. Using the technique of a global execution environment as insightfully described in [4], complete self-inspection and self-modification can be attained by having a *double nesting* of meta-circular evaluators run the Gödel Machine's *scheduler*. Although this technique is pretty inefficient, there is in principle no need to build a special (virtual) machine. Ultimately, the Gödel Machine should be directly implemented in an assembly language, to make it capable of working in tandem with arbitrary compiled problem solvers, instead of needing access to their source code and translating it into the virtual machine's programming language. This requires an axiomatic encoding of the instruction set of the architecture on which the Gödel Machine is going to run. On the positive side, however, reflexivity comes for free in assembly languages, given von Neumann-like hardware architectures.

It is interesting to note that "gödelizing"[1] an existing problem solver is always harmless. Before the first self-rewrite, the proof searcher of a Gödel Machine will do little but consume a fixed percentage of processing time, say 50%. This loss is easily offset by simply running the entire program on a machine which is twice

---

[1] i.e., adding a scheduler to a problem solving program which interleaves that solver with a program searching for provably useful self-rewrites. Thanks to Moshe Looks for suggesting this term to us.

as fast. The gain is a program that may improve over time in a way that is globally optimal [9] with respect to its initial utility function. We should caution though that this puts a burden on the programmer: a Gödel Machine with a badly chosen utility function is motivated to converge to a "poor" program.

Acknowledgments. This work was partially funded by the Humanobs EU Project (FP7-ICT-231453).

References

1. Abelson, H., Sussman, G.J., Sussman, J.: Structure and Interpretation of Computer Programs, 2nd edn. MIT Press, Cambridge (1996)
2. Gödel, K.: Über formal unentscheidbare Sätze der Principia Mathematica und verwandter Systeme I. Monatshefte für Mathematik und Physik 38, 173–198 (1931)
3. Hutter, M.: The fastest and shortest algorithm for all well-defined problems. International Journal of Foundations of Computer Science 13(3), 431–443 (2002)
4. Jefferson, S., Friedman, D.P.: A simple reflective interpreter. LISP and Symbolic Computation 9(2-3), 181–202 (1996)
5. Kelsey, R., Clinger, W., Rees, J. (eds.): Revised[5] report on the algorithmic language Scheme. Higher-Order and Symbolic Computation 11(1) (August 1998)
6. Queinnec, C.: Lisp in Small Pieces. Cambridge University Press, Cambridge (1996)
7. Schmidhuber, J.: Completely self-referential optimal reinforcement learners. In: Duch, W., Kacprzyk, J., Oja, E., Zadrożny, S. (eds.) ICANN 2005. LNCS, vol. 3697, pp. 223–233. Springer, Heidelberg (2005)
8. Schmidhuber, J.: Gödel machines: Fully self-referential optimal universal self-improvers. In: Goertzel, B., Pennachin, C. (eds.) Artificial General Intelligence, pp. 199–226. Springer Verlag (2006); variant available as arXiv:cs.LO/0309048
9. Schmidhuber, J.: Ultimate cognition à la Gödel. Cognitive Computation 1(2), 177–193 (2009)
10. Schmidhuber, J.: Gödel machines: Self-referential universal problem solvers making provably optimal self-improvements. Tech. Rep. IDSIA-19-03, arXiv:cs.LO/0309048 v2, IDSIA (2003)

Reinforcement Learning
and the Bayesian Control Rule[*]

Pedro Alejandro Ortega, Daniel Alexander Braun, and Simon Godsill

Department of Engineering, University of Cambridge
Trumpington Street, Cambridge CB2 1PZ, UK
{pao32,dab54,sjg}@cam.ac.uk

Abstract. We present an actor-critic scheme for reinforcement learning in complex domains. The main contribution is to show that planning and I/O dynamics can be separated such that an intractable planning problem reduces to a simple multi-armed bandit problem, where each lever stands for a potentially arbitrarily complex policy. Furthermore, we use the Bayesian control rule to construct an adaptive bandit player that is universal with respect to a given class of optimal bandit players, thus indirectly constructing an adaptive agent that is universal with respect to a given class of policies.

Keywords: Reinforcement learning, actor-critic, Bayesian control rule.

1 Introduction

Actor-critic (AC) methods [1] are reinforcement learning (RL) algorithms [9] whose implementation can be conceptually subdivided into two modules: the *actor*, responsible for interacting with the environment; and the *critic*, responsible for evaluating the performance of the actor. In this paper we present an AC method that conceptualizes learning a complex policy as a *multi-armed bandit problem* [2,6] where pulling one lever corresponds to executing one iteration of a policy. The critic, who plays the role of the multi-armed bandit player, is implemented using the recently introduced *Bayesian control rule* (BCR) [8,7]. This has the advantage of bypassing the computational costs of calculating the optimal policy by translating adaptive control into a probabilistic inference problem. The actor is implemented as a pool of parameterized policies. The scheme that we put forward here significantly simplifies the design of RL agents capable of learning complex I/O dynamics. Furthermore, we argue that this scheme offers important advantages over current RL approaches as a basis for general adaptive agents in real-world applications.

2 Setup

The interaction between the agent and the environment proceeds in cycles $t = 1, 2, \ldots$ where at cycle t, the agent produces an action $a_t \in \mathcal{A}$ that is gathered

---

[*] This research was supported by the European Commission FP7-ICT, "GUIDE— Gentle User Interfaces for Disabled and Elderly citizens".

J. Schmidhuber, K.R. Thórisson, and M. Looks (Eds.): AGI 2011, LNAI 6830, pp. 281–285, 2011.

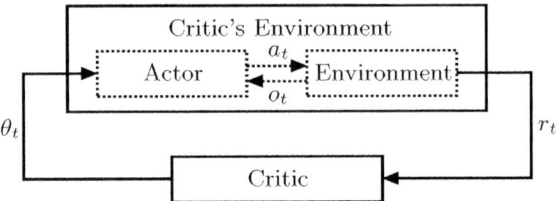

Fig. 1. The critic is an "agent" interacting with actor-environment system

by the environment, which in turn responds with an observation $o_t \in \mathcal{O}$ and a reinforcement signal $r_t \in \mathbb{R}$ that are collected by the agent. To implement the actor-critic architecture, we introduce a signal $\theta_t \in \Theta$ generated by the critic at the beginning of each cycle, i.e. immediately before a_t, o_t and r_t are produced.

2.1 Critic

The critic is modeled as a multi-armed bandit player with a possibly (uncountably) infinite number of levers to choose from. More precisely, the critic iteratively tries out levers $\theta_1, \theta_2, \theta_3, \ldots$ so as to maximize the sum of the reinforcements $r_1, r_2, r_3, \ldots$ In this sense, the θ_t and the r_t are the critic's actions and observations respectively, not to be confused with the actions a_t and observations o_t of the actor.

According to the BCR, the critic has to sample the lever θ_t from the distribution [8]

$$P(\theta_t | \hat{\theta}_{1:t-1}, r_{1:t-1}) = \int_{\Phi} P(\theta_t | \phi, \theta_{1:t-1}, r_{1:t-1}) P(\phi | \hat{\theta}_{1:t-1}, r_{1:t-1}) \, d\phi, \quad (1)$$

where the "hat"-notation $\hat{\theta}_{1:t-1}$ denotes causal intervention rather than probabilistic conditioning. The expression (1) corresponds to a weighted mixture of policies $P(\theta_t | \phi, \theta_{1:t-1}, r_{1:t-1})$ parameterized by $\phi \in \Phi$ with weights given by the posterior $P(\phi | \hat{\theta}_{1:t-1}, r_{1:t-1})$. The posterior can in turn be expressed as

$$P(\phi | \hat{\theta}_{1:t-1}, r_{1:t-1}) = \frac{P(\phi) \prod_{\tau=1}^{t} P(r_\tau | \phi, \theta_{1:\tau}, r_{1:\tau-1})}{\int_{\Phi} P(\phi') \prod_{\tau=1}^{t} P(r_\tau | \phi', \theta_{1:\tau}, r_{1:\tau-1}) \, d\phi'}, \quad (2)$$

where the $P(r_t | \phi, \theta_{1:t-1}, r_{1:t-1})$ are the likelihoods of the reinforcements under the hypothesis ϕ, and where $P(\phi)$ is the prior over Φ. Note that there are no interventions on the right hand side of this equation.

Furthermore, we assume that each parameter $\phi \in \Phi$ fully determines the likelihood function $P(r_t | \phi, \theta_{1:t}, r_{1:t-1})$ representing the probability of observing the reinforcement r_t given that (an arbitrary) lever θ_t was pulled. The terms $\theta_{1:t-1}, r_{1:t-1}$ can be used to model the internal state of the bandit at cycle t. We assume that each bandit has a unique lever $\theta^\phi \in \Theta$ that maximizes the expected sum of rewards, and that the optimal strategy consists in pulling it in every time step:

$$P(\theta_t|\phi, \theta_{1:t-1}, r_{1:t-1}) = P(\theta_t|\phi) = \begin{cases} 1 & \text{if } \theta_t = \theta^\phi, \\ 0 & \text{if } \theta_t \neq \theta^\phi. \end{cases}$$

Finally, we assume a prior $P(\phi)$ over the set of operation modes Φ. This completes the specification of the critic. We will give a concrete example in Sec. 3.

2.2 Actor

The aim of the actor is to offer an rich pool of I/O dynamics parameterized by Θ that the critic can choose from. More precisely, from Fig. 1 it is seen that the actor implements the stream over the actions, i.e.

$$P(a_t|\theta_{1:t}, a_{1:t-1}, o_{1:t-1}) = P(a_t|\theta_t, a_{1:t-1}, o_{1:t-1}),$$

where we have assumed that this distribution is independent of the previously chosen parameters $\theta_{1:t-1}$. For implementation purposes it is convenient to summarize the experience $a_{1:t}, o_{1:t}$ as a sufficient statistics s_{t+1}^θ representing an internal state of the I/O dynamics $\theta \in \Phi$ at time $t+1$. States are then updated recursively as

$$s_{t+1}^\theta = f_\theta(s_t^\theta, a_t, o_t),$$

where f_θ maps the old state s_t^θ and the interaction (a_t, o_t) into the new state s_{t+1}^θ. This scheme facilitates running the different I/O dynamics in parallel. The behavior of our proposed actor-critic scheme is described in the pseudo-code listed in Alg. 1.

Algorithm 1. Actor-Critic BCR

1 **foreach** $\phi \in \Phi$ **do** Set $P_1(\phi) \leftarrow P(\phi)$
2 **foreach** $\theta \in \Theta$ **do** Initialize states s_0^θ
3 **for** $t \leftarrow 1, 2, 3, \ldots$ **do**
4 $\quad$ Sample $\phi_t \sim P_t(\phi)$
5 $\quad$ Set $\theta_t \leftarrow \theta^{\phi_t}$
6 $\quad$ Sample $a_t \sim P(a_t|\theta_t, s_t^{\theta_t})$
7 $\quad$ Issue a_t and collect o_t and r_t
8 $\quad$ **foreach** $\phi \in \Phi$ **do** Set $P_{t+1}(\phi) \propto P_t(\phi)P(r_t|\phi, \theta_{1:t}, r_{1:t-1})$
9 $\quad$ **foreach** $\theta \in \Theta$ **do** Set $s_{t+1}^\theta \leftarrow f_\theta(s_t^\theta, a_t, o_t)$

3 Experimental Results

We have applied the proposed scheme to a toy problem containing elements that are usually regarded as challenging in the literature: non-linear & high-dimensional dynamics and only partially observable state. The I/O domains are $\mathcal{A} = \mathcal{O} = [-1, 1]^{10}$ with reinforcements in $\mathbb{R}$.

The environment produces observations following the equation

$$[o_t, q_t]^T = f(\mu \cdot [a_t, o_{t-1}, q_{t-1}]^T),$$

where $a_t, o_t, q_t \in [-1, 1]^{10}$ are the 10-dimensional action, observation and internal state vectors respectively, μ is a 20×30 parameter matrix, and $f(\cdot)$ is a sigmoid mapping each component x into $2/(1 + e^{-x}) - 1$. Rewards are issued as $r_t = h(\theta) + \nu_t$ where h is an unknown reward mean function and ν_t is Gaussian noise with variance σ^2. Analogously, the actor implements a family of 300 different policies, where each policy is of the form

$$[a_t, s_t]^T = f(\theta \cdot [a_{t-1}, o_{t-1}, s_{t-1}]^T),$$

where $s_t \in [-1, 1]^{10}$ is the internal state vector and $\theta \in \Theta$ is the parameter matrix of the policy. These 300 matrices were sampled randomly.

The critic is modeled as a bandit player with $|\Theta| = 300$ levers to choose from, where each lever is a parameter matrix $\theta \in \Theta$. We assume that pulling lever θ produces a normally distributed reward $r \sim N(\phi_\theta, 1/\lambda)$, where $\phi_\theta \in \mathbb{R}$ is the mean specific to lever θ and where $\lambda > 0$ is a known precision term that is common to all levers and all bandits. Thus, a bandit is fully specified by the vector $\phi = [\phi_\theta]_{\theta \in \Theta}$ of all its means. To include all possible bandits we use $\Phi = \mathbb{R}^{|\Theta|}$. For each $\phi \in \Phi$, the likelihood model is

$$P(r_t | \phi, \theta_{1:t}, r_{1:t-1}) = P(r_t | \phi, \theta_t) = N(r_t; \phi_{\theta_t}, 1/\lambda),$$

and the policy is $P(\theta_t | \phi) = 1$ if $\theta_t = \arg\max_\theta \{\phi_\theta\}$ and zero otherwise. Because the likelihood is normal we place a conjugate prior $P(\phi_\theta) = N(\phi_\theta; m_\theta, 1/p_\theta)$ over Φ, where m_θ and p_θ are the mean and precision hyperparameters. This allows an easy update of the posterior after obtaining a reward [4]. To assess the performance of our algorithm, we have averaged a total of 100 runs with 5000 time steps. Fig. 2 shows the performance curve. It can be seen that the interaction moves from an exploratory to an exploitative phase, converging towards the optimal performance.

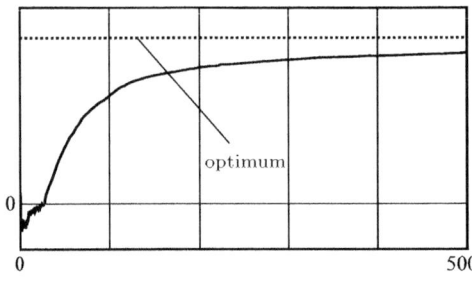

Fig. 2. Time-averaged reward of the adaptive system versus optimum performance

4 Discussion and Conclusion

The main contribution of this paper is to show how to separate the planning problem from the underlying I/O dynamics into the critic and the actor respectively, reducing reducing a complex planning problem to a simple multi-armed bandit problem. The critic is a bandit player based on the Bayesian control rule. The actor is treated as a black box, possibly implementing arbitrary complex policies.

There are important differences between our approach and other actor-critic methods. First, current actor-critic algorithms critically depend on the state-space view of the environment—see for instance [3,9,5]. In our opinion, this view leads to an entanglement of planning and dynamics that renders the RL problem far more difficult than necessary. Rather, we argue that this separation allows tackling domains that are intractable otherwise. Second, current reinforcement learning algorithms rely on constructing a point-estimate of the optimal policy, which is intractable when done accurately, and very costly even when only approximated. In contrast, we use the Bayesian control rule to maintain a distribution over optimal policies that is refined on-line as more observations become available. Additional experimental work is required to investigate the scalability of our actor-critic scheme to larger and more realistic domains.

References

1. Barto, A., Sutton, R., Anderson, C.: Neuron like elements that can solve difficult learning control problems. IEEE Trans. on Systems, Man and Cybernetics 13 (1983)
2. Berry, D.A., Fristedt, B.: Bandit problems: Sequential allocation of experiments. Monographs on Statistics and Applied Probability. Chapman & Hall, London (1985)
3. Bertsekas, D.P., Tsitsiklis, J.N.: Neuro-Dynamic Programming. Athena Scientific, Belmont (1996)
4. Bishop, C.M.: Pattern Recognition and Machine Learning. Springer, Heidelberg (2006)
5. Ghavamzadeh, M., Engel, Y.: Bayesian actor-critic algorithms. In: Proc. of the 24th International Conference on Machine Learning (2007)
6. Gittins, J.C.: Multi-armed bandit allocation indices. Wiley-Interscience Series in Systems and Optimization. John Wiley & Sons, Ltd., Chichester (1989)
7. Ortega, P.A., Braun, D.A.: A bayesian rule for adaptive control based on causal interventions. In: The Third Conference on Artificial General Intelligence, pp. 121–126. Atlantis Press, Paris (2010)
8. Ortega, P.A., Braun, D.A.: A minimum relative entropy principle for learning and acting. Journal of Artificial Intelligence Research 38, 475–511 (2010)
9. Sutton, R.S., Barto, A.G.: Reinforcement Learning: An Introduction. MIT Press, Cambridge (1998)

Societies of Intelligent Agents

Bill Hibbard

SSEC, University of Wisconsin-Madison,
1225 W. Dayton St., Madison, WI 53706, USA
test@ssec.wisc.edu

Abstract. A definition of language is proposed in which language is a low-bandwidth channel that can increase agent rewards in a reinforcement learning setting, and in which agents can learn to produce language and teach it to other agents. Societies of agents are being modeled by economists to understand economic instability and other non-equilibrium phenomena. I hypothesize a divergent distribution of intelligence in societies of agents when rewards can be exchanged for increases in agent information processing capacity.

1 Introduction

This paper poses questions about societies of intelligent agents using a model based on reinforcement learning (RL) [1, 2]. The paper proposes a definition of language using the RL model. The model is adapted to societies of agents and used to pose questions about the evolution of society as intelligence increases beyond the plateau defined by humans.

In a simple reinforcement learning model, an agent interacts with its environment at a sequence of discrete times, sending action a_i to the environment and receiving observation o_i and reward r_i from the environment at time i. These are members of finite sets A, O, and R respectively, where R is a set of rational numbers between 0 and 1.

2 Language

Agents use language to communicate information to other agents. Language consists of strings of symbols, where the symbols generally represent objects recognized in observations of the environment, as well as properties and actions of objects also recognized in observations. In order to maximize rewards from the environment, agents try to predict the rewards they will get in response to various choices of actions they may make. Language is a valuable tool to help agents learn to predict the behavior of the environment from other agents (e.g., "If you poke a wasp nest, expect a large negative reward"). An important property of language is that a small amount of information in a language string (i.e., the number of bits required to encode the language string) can represent a much larger amount of information in observations of the environment, to agents who can recognize objects, properties and actions in those observation and know how they map to language symbols.

J. Schmidhuber, K.R. Thórisson, and M. Looks (Eds.): AGI 2011, LNAI 6830, pp. 286–290, 2011.
© Springer-Verlag Berlin Heidelberg 2011

To describe this in the RL model, define a finite set L of language sentences. These sentences are strings over a finite set S of symbols, with length bounded by some constant (human agents have no need for sentences of more than one million symbols) and including the null string of length zero. In the definition of agent, add a new kind of observation from L (hearing a language sentence) and a new kind of action to L (speaking a language sentence). An agent π has mappings:

$$R \times O \times L \to \pi \to A \times L \tag{1}$$

where π includes some internal state that is updated at each time step.

Because language is specialized to particular environments, rather than trying to apply Legg's and Hutter's measure of agent intelligence [2], we will use a simple measure of agent success as the expected value of the sum of rewards during a time internal $(t1, t2)$:

$$V(\pi; t1, t2) = \mathbf{E}(\textstyle\sum_{t=t1}^{t2} r_t) \tag{2}$$

where r_t is the reward agent π receives from the environment at time t.

The simplest social setting for language consists of two agents $\pi 1$ and $\pi 2$, with the language input of each connected to the language output of the other, and both receiving the same observations from the environment. We set up two scenarios for agent $\pi 2$ over a time interval $(t1, t2)$, labeled $\pi 1$ and *null*. In the $\pi 1$ scenario the language inputs and outputs of $\pi 2$ are connected to $\pi 1$ and in the *null* scenario the language input of $\pi 2$ receives only the null string at each time step. We require that language be a compressed description of environment observations, so if $s_{t1}, \ldots, s_{t2}$ are the sentences sent from $\pi 1$ to $\pi 2$ over the time interval then (many of them may be null):

$$(\textstyle\sum_{t=t1}^{t2} \text{length}(s_t)) \log(|S|) \ll (t2 - t1 + 1) \log(|O|) \tag{3}$$

Let $V_{\pi 1}(\pi 2; t1, t2)$ and $V_{null}(\pi 2; t1, t2)$ be the successes of agent $\pi 2$ over the time interval $(t1, t2)$ in these two scenarios.

Definition 1. In the situation as described in the previous paragraphs, the effectiveness of $\pi 1$ as a language teacher is $E(\pi 1; \pi 2, t1, t2) = V_{\pi 1}(\pi 2; t1, t2) / V_{null}(\pi 2; t1, t2)$. $\pi 1$ is an *effective language teacher* if $E(\pi 1; \pi 2, t1, t2) \geq C$, where $C > 1.0$ is a constant of the definition.

Language ability can be passed from agent to agent. To describe this, at time step $t2$ let $\pi 2$ switch its language connections from $\pi 1$ to a different agent $\pi 3$ and continue to time step $t3$.

Definition 2. In the situation as described in the previous paragraphs, $\pi 2$ has *learned language* if $E(\pi 2; \pi 3, t2, t3) \geq C$, where C is the constant from Definition 1.

The two-way language channels between agents provide a means for the learner to practice and get feedback from the teacher. This feedback is outside an agent's normal reward channel, but since learning language will increase the learner's rewards the learner should value feedback from the teacher. As we discuss in the next section, if agents are able to exchange reward in an economy, the learner may even pay reward to the teacher.

The notion that a language learner can become a language teacher disallows the possibility that language is simply a magic oracle predicting future rewards. Rather, language transmits knowledge that agents may use to predict rewards on their own.

3 Societies of Intelligent Agents

Now consider a set of agents $\{\pi_i, i \in I\}$. As an agent has only a single language input it must have a way to select which other agent to listen to. So add another action to the agent model of the previous section, a value in I to select which agent's language output is connected to this agent's language input. Now we can define the success of the society of agents over time interval $(t1, t2)$ as:

$$V(t1, t2) = \sum_{i \in I} V(\pi_i; t1, t2) \tag{4}$$

where $V(\pi_i; t1, t2)$ is defined in equation (2).

Consider two scenarios, labeled *lang* and *null*. In the *lang* scenario, the agents communicate via language and in the *null* scenario the language inputs to all agents are forced to null strings at every time step. Let $V_{lang}(t1, t2)$ and $V_{null}(t1, t2)$ be the successes of the society of agents over the time interval $(t1, t2)$ in these two scenarios.

Definition 3. In the situation as described in the previous paragraphs, the effectiveness of language for the society of agents is $E(t1, t2) = V_{lang}(t1, t2) / V_{null}(t1, t2)$. Language is *effective* for this society if $E(t1, t2) \geq C$, where $C > 1.0$ is a constant of the definition.

Mathematical models of societies of agents are an important new trend among economists, helping them to overcome limitations of the dynamic stochastic general equilibrium models they have long employed [3]. Agent-based economic models can help understand market instabilities and other non-equilibrium phenomena [4]. These models sometimes include agents that learn by reinforcement from the results of their behavior [5]. This suggests equating money with reward to create a society in which agents exchange reward for goods and services. Baum created such a society of agents to solve the credit assignment problem in reinforcement learning [6]. His society of agents learned to solve a block stacking problem and Rubik's cube, reinforced for successful solutions. Agents exchanged reward for computation, where the combined computations of many agents solved the problems.

Humans form a society of intelligent agents, but they are not collaborating on a simple common problem such as Rubik's cube. Each human agent has their own internal reward system, although these have enough in common that humans can form orderly markets for goods and services. Money is a first approximation to reward, although examples demonstrate the futility of absolutely equating money with reward.

The previous section offers a definition of language as information that can help agents obtain reward. If an agent can learn to produce language then it can provide it as a service to another agent, in exchange for reward. Thus our language definitions provide a rudimentary model of social knowledge. As social knowledge increases and is incorporated into language, agent intelligence increases.

Humans do increase their intelligence by working in social groups. They also manipulate their environment to create tools, some of which are used with language.

Writing, books, newspapers, telegraph, telephone and audio recordings are tools for storing and transmitting language. Computers and networks are tools capable of more sophisticated language processing, epitomized by our host for this conference.

Although humans can augment their information processing capacity via tools and by working in social groups, their most valuable information processing capacity is in their physical brains. And all human brains have roughly equal information processing capacity and intelligence. Biotechnology, nanotechnology, and information technology are likely to enable humans to transcend the physical limits on their brains during the Twenty First Century. The application of these technologies to increase human intelligence will be a service of great value to individual humans, enabling them to obtain more reward. Thus humans will be willing to exchange reward for this service.

This suggests an economic model of agents that learn by reinforcement, in which agents exchange reward for information and also for increased information processing capacity. Information processing capacity and intelligence would be an attribute of each agent in such a model. Buchanan discusses the utility of agent-based models for understanding economic instability [4]. I hypothesize that a free market economy in which agents can exchange reward for increased information processing capacity will be unstable, with a large divergence in the intelligence of individual agents. There is some evidence for this in my work with adversarial sequence prediction, in which agents are rewarded with increased or decreased information processing capacity [7]. The ability to exchange wealth for increased intelligence, and to use that intelligence to increase wealth, will create a positive feedback loop amplifying differences among the intelligence of different humans. This could create differences in language processing capacities such that the most intelligent humans will speak languages that less intelligent humans can never learn.

A society of agents of such unequal intelligence will be fundamentally different from the society of agents of roughly equal intelligence that we are used to. Humans of different intelligence levels may have different legal rights, and humanity may essentially divide into multiple species. This is an issue that we as a society should consider carefully before we actually create these technologies. My prescription is that humans or machines with greater-than-natural-human-intelligence should require a license, granted under the condition that their values satisfy certain altruistic standards [8]. In any case, people should be informed about AI and transhumanist technologies and given a chance to debate and democratically decide whether and how they should be regulated.

References

1. Hutter, M.: Universal Artificial Intelligence: Sequential Decisions Based on Algorithmic Probability. Springer, Berlin (2004)
2. Legg, S., Hutter, M.: A Formal Measure of Machine Intelligence. In: 15th Annual Machine Learning Conference of Belgium and The Netherlands (Benelearn 2006), Ghent, pp. 73-80 (2006), http://www.idsia.ch/idsiareport/IDSIA-10-06.pdf
3. Farmer, J.D., Foley, D.: The Economy Needs Agent-based Modeling. Nature 460, 685–686 (2009)

4. Buchanan, M.: Meltdown Modeling. Nature 460, 680–682 (2009)
5. Nanduri, V., Das, T.K.: A Reinforcement Learning Model to Assess the Market Power Under Auction-Based Energy Bidding. IEEE Trans. on Power Systems. 22, 85–95 (2007)
6. Baum, E.: What is Thought? MIT Press, Cambridge (2004)
7. Hibbard, B.: Adversarial Sequence Prediction. In: The First Conference on Artificial General Intelligence (AGI 2008), pp. 399–403. IOS Press, Amsterdam (2008)
   `http://www.ssec.wisc.edu/~billh/g/hibbard_agi.pdf`
8. Hibbard, B.: The technology of mind and a new social contract. Journal of Evolution and Technology 17(1), 13–22 (2008)

Towards a General Vision System Based on Symbol-Relation Grammars and Bayesian Networks

Elias Ruiz, Augusto Melendez, and L. Enrique Sucar

Computer Science Department,
National Institute of Astrophysics, Optics and Electronics.
Luis Enrique Erro 1, 72840 Tonantzitla, México
{elias_ruiz,amelendez,esucar}@inaoep.mx

Abstract. A novel approach to create a general vision system is presented. The proposed method is based on a visual grammar representation which is transformed to a Bayesian network which is used for object recognition. We use a symbol-relational grammar for a hierarchical description of objects, incorporating spatial relations. The structure of a Bayesian network is obtained automatically from the grammar, and its parameters are learned from examples. The method is illustrated with two examples for face recognition.

1 Introduction

Although there have been important advances in computer vision in the last decades, we are still far from a *general* vision system with capabilities similar to a human child. Most developments in object recognition have focused on high performance systems for particular applications; and lately mainly on recognizing specific object based on local features.

In the beginnings of the computer era, there were some intents to develop more general vision systems, but these were not successful due to several problems, including lack of computer power, and limited feature detection and recognition techniques. However, in recent years, with the development of very powerful and inexpensive computer platforms, and the advances in several areas of computer vision and artificial intelligence, the time for developing more general methods has arrived.

Some recent developments are based on visual grammars or biologically inspired. For instance, Zhu and Mumford [10] describe a general visual grammar representation using And-Or graphs. This model is limited in the sense that it does not consider the spatial relation between the visual elements, which are very important for recognition (e.g., the configuration of the elements of a face). On the other hand, models of the biological visual system have provided the basis for building computer vision models. Serre and Poggio [8] achieve a competitive recognition rate in real images, learning through examples of images using terminal elements called *patches*. However, it lacks a structure that allows to

J. Schmidhuber, K.R. Thórisson, and M. Looks (Eds.): AGI 2011, LNAI 6830, pp. 291–296, 2011.

incorporate prior knowledge, and it is not defined within a grammar or a formal representation.

We propose an approach that is also based on visual grammars with a biological inspiration, but trying to overcome some of the limitations of the previous works. Objects are represented using a visual hierarchy based on Symbol-Relational grammars that incorporate spatial relations between terminal and non-terminal elements. The terminal elements are biologically inspired, including edges and color patches. To incorporate uncertainty, the visual grammar is transformed to a Bayesian network (BN) [7], whose structure is generated automatically from the grammar and its parameters are learned from examples. Recognition is performed using standard BN inference techniques.

We present two preliminary examples of the proposed method for face recognition. One uses high-level elements and was compared with other state of the art methods for face detection. The other illustrates the low-level features for eye detection.

2   Representation and Recognition

2.1   Visual Grammar

A visual grammar describes objects hierarchically. For our model, we need a grammar that allows us to model the decomposition of an object into its parts and how they relate with another parts. Symbol-Relation grammars *(SR grammars)* [2], provide this type of description and incorporate the possibility to add rewriting rules for relations between terminals and non terminals symbols.

In the productions of the grammar we can incorporate relations between elements. In our work, we incorporated spatial relations, which can determine the position of an object with respect to another object. Although there are different types of spatial relations, in our model we use *topological* and *order* relations, such as *inside_of* and *above*. Figure 1 shows a simple example of an object represented using *And-Or* graphs vs. a BN based on a SR grammar. Fig. 1b shows a simple *And-Or* graph. In the Fig. 1c, node *above* is added to represent the relations between *stem* and *fruit* nodes. This information is not clearly represented in an *And-Or* graph so we obtain a more expressive representation of the object.

2.2   Transforming a SR-Grammar to a Bayesian Network

If we apply our model in real images, this will involve uncertainty in the detection of the elements and their relations. To manage uncertainty we transform the SR grammar to a Bayesian network, where a node can represent either a symbol or a relation. However, a visual grammar can lead to endless productions. To avoid this, we incorporate a restriction on SR grammar so they can be transformed into a Bayesian network. This restriction eliminates cyclic rules, for example: $A^0 \rightarrow \langle B^2 \rangle$ and $B^0 \rightarrow \langle A^2 \rangle$, where A produces B and B produces A. The restriction is that for every rule of the form $Y^0 \rightarrow \langle \mathbf{M}, \mathbf{R} \rangle$ and for all $m \in \mathbf{M}$ it holds that Y^0 is not *son* of m. Conversion is based on creating a Bayesian network with a structure similar to an *And-Or* graph, but incorporating spatial relations.

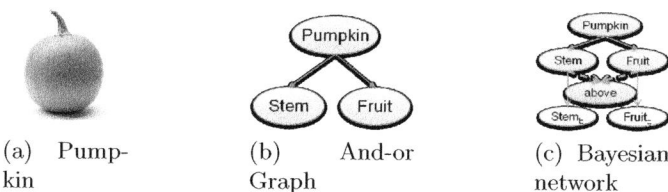

(a) Pumpkin

(b) And-or Graph

(c) Bayesian network

Fig. 1. Representations for the pumpkin object. (b) A simple *and-or graph* can not represent the topological relations between terminal or not terminal elements. (c) A Bayesian network representation obtained from the SR Grammar which incorporates an order relation (*above*), and additional virtual nodes that consider the uncertainty in the detectors.

Conversion Algorithm. We convert the SR grammar into a Bayesian network where the root node is the first element of the grammar, and the other nodes are terminals and nonterminals elements of the SR grammar. This is detailed in Algorithm 1. Briefly, the conversion algorithm performs the following steps:

1. Set the root node.
2. For each s-production rule, where the term on the left is the reference node (Nr), and for each symbol defined in each production, Add p_i as a child of Nr. If p_i is not terminal, perform a recursive call with p_i as the new Nr. If p_i is terminal, Add p_{i_E} (as evidence node) as a child of p_i.
3. For each relation $r(x, y)$, add the node as a child of his parents x and y.

3   Examples

We describe two initial examples of the application of our method for face representation, one based on high-level elements and other using low-level features.

3.1   Visual Grammar for Face Detection

The following visual grammar is used to describe high-level items in images of faces (front view), and we define it as follows:

$$FG = (\{FACE\}, \{eyes, nose, mouth, head\}, \{above, inside\_of\}, FACE, S, \emptyset)$$

The S-productions are defined by:

$$1 : FACE^0 \rightarrow \; < \{eyes^2, mouth^2\}, \{above(eyes^2, mouth^2)\} >$$
$$2 : FACE^0 \rightarrow \; < \{nose^2, mouth^2\}, \{above(nose^2, mouth^2)\} >$$

Algorithm 1. Convert SR-Grammar to Bayesian network

Data: $G(V_N, V_T, V_R, S, P, R), Nr$;   /* Nr=Reference Node */
Result: Bn

if $Nr = S$ **then**
  └ Set S as root node in Bn
foreach $p_i \in P$ *where* $Y^0 = Nr$ **do**
  │ // p_i has the form $l : Y^0 \rightarrow \langle M, R \rangle$
  │ **foreach** $m \in M$ **do**
  │   │ Add p_i as child of Nr
  │   │ **if** $p_i \in V_N$ **then**
  │   │   └ ConvertSRGtoBN(G, p_i);   /* Recursion */
  │   │
  │   │ **if** $p_i \in V_T$ **then**
  │   └   └ Add p_{i_E} as child of p_i
  │
  │ **foreach** $r_i \in R$ **do**
  │   │ // r has the form $r(X, Y)$
  └   └ Add node r_i as child of X and Y.

$$3 : FACE^0 \rightarrow < \{eyes^2, head^2\}, \{inside\_of(eyes^2, head^2)\} >$$
$$4 : FACE^0 \rightarrow < \{nose^2, head^2\}, \{inside\_of(nose^2, head^2)\} >$$
$$5 : FACE^0 \rightarrow < \{mouth^2, head^2\}, \{inside\_of(mouth^2, head^2)\} >$$

From this SR grammar, and using the conversion algorithm, we obtained a BN representation (Fig. 2a). Once the structure is obtained from the grammar, the parameters are learned using standard parameter learning [6] from a set of training images of faces (in this case, 200 images). The elements of the face are obtained from object recognizers based on the AdaBoost algorithm [9]. As expected, the spatial relations helped significantly in the recognition task (Fig. 2b). More details of this work are described in [5].

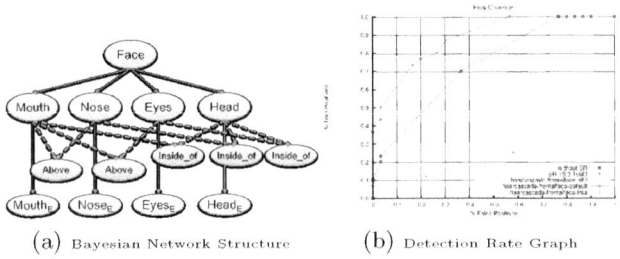

(a) Bayesian Network Structure   (b) Detection Rate Graph

Fig. 2. Face detection using a SR grammar implemented as a BN. (a) The Bayesian network structure obtained from the SR grammar. (b) The graphs show the detection rate varying the decision threshold with and without spatial relations. The method is compared against three variants of the Viola and Jones face detector [1] with fixed thresholds (dots).

3.2   Low-Level Features of a Visual Grammar for Eyes

This grammar defines an eye based on bio-inspired features:

$$G = (\{EYEX, EYELASH, EYE, EYEINT, IRIS, PUPIL\}\{Eh, Ev, Hg\},$$
$$\{above, ady, inside\_of\}, EYE, S, \emptyset)$$

Where S is formed by the S-Productions:

$$1 : EYEX^0 \rightarrow < \{EYELASH^2, EYE^2\}, \{above(EYELASH^2, EYE^2)\} >$$
$$2 : EYELASH^0 \rightarrow < \{Eh^2, Hg^2, Eh^3\}, \{above(Eh^2, Hg^2), above(Hg^2, Eh^2)\} >$$
$$3 : EYE^0 \rightarrow < \{EYEINT^2, Hg^3\}, \{above(EYEINT^2, Hg^3)\} >$$
$$4 : EYE^0 \rightarrow < \{EYEINT^2, Eh^4\}, \{above(EYEINT^2, Eh^4)\} >$$
$$5 : EYEINT^0 \rightarrow < \{Hg^4, IRIS^2, Hg^5\}, \{ady(Hg^4, IRIS^2), ady(IRIS^2, Hg5)\} >$$
$$6 : IRIS^0 \rightarrow < \{Ev^2, PUPIL^2, Ev^3\}, \{ady(Ev^2, PUPIL^2), ady(PUPIL^2, Ev^3)\} >$$
$$7 : PUPIL^0 \rightarrow < \{Hg^6, Hg^7\}, \{inside\_of(Hg^6, Hg^7)\} >$$

This visual grammar was specified manually from examples obtained by the segmentation algorithm as shown in Fig. 3a. The generated Bayesian network, is illustrated in Fig. 3b. In order to build a dictionary of low-level features that conform the terminal elements of the grammar, we built a simplified approach that considers some aspects of the visual system [8,3]. Once recognized certain edges of orientation (0° and 90°) with Gabor filters [4], we segment the rest of the image *homogeneous zones*, which are quantized to 32 colors.

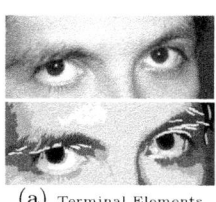
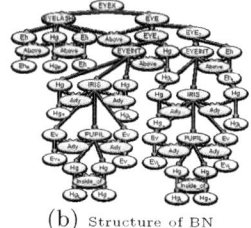

(a) Terminal Elements   (b) Structure of BN

Fig. 3. A visual grammar for eyes. (a) Terminal elements before (top) and after (bottom) segmentation. (b) BN generated from the SR grammar.

4   Conclusions and Future Work

A first stage in the design of a general vision system was described. This approach combines visual SR grammars and Bayesian networks to represent and recognize objects in an image. The model was tested for face recognition with high-level features as terminal elements with promising results. There are several avenues for future research. One is to develop a more complete grammar for faces from the low-level features to the high-level elements. Other is to explore alternative representations based on relational Bayesian networks. We plan in the future to apply this formalism to other classes of objects and to learn the visual grammar from images.

References

1. Yu, Q., Cheng, H.H., Cheng, W.W., Zhou, X.: Ch opencv for interactive open architecture computer vision (2004)
2. Ferrucci, F., Pacini, G., Satta, G., Sessa, M.I., Tortora, G., Tucci, M., Vitiello, G.: Symbol-relation grammars: a formalism for graphical languages. Inf. Comput. 131(1), 1–46 (1996)
3. Fukushima, K.: Neocognitron: A self-organizing neural network model for a mechanism of pattern recognition unaffected by shift in position. Biological Cybernetics 36(4), 193–202 (1980)
4. Gabor, D.: Theory of communication. JIEE 93(3), 429–459 (1946)
5. Melendez, A., Sucar, L., Morales, E.: A visual grammar for face detection. In: Kuri-Morales, A., Simari, G. (eds.) IBERAMIA 2010. LNCS, vol. 6433, pp. 493–502. Springer, Heidelberg (2010) 10.1007/978-3-642-16952-6-50
6. Neapolitan, R.E.: Learning Bayesian Networks. Prentice Hall, Englewood Cliffs (2003)
7. Pearl, J.: Probabilistic Reasoning in Intelligent Systems: Networks of Plausible Inference. Morgan Kaufmann, San Mateo (1988)
8. Poggio, T., Serre, T., Kouh, M., Cadieu, C., Knoblich, U., Kreiman, G.: A theory of object recognition: computations and circuits in the feedforward path of the ventral stream in primate visual cortex. Technical Report CBCL-259, MIT Artificial Intelligence Laboratory (December 19, 2005)
9. Viola, P., Jones, M.J.: Robust real-time face detection. Int. J. Comput. Vision 57, 137–154 (2004)
10. Zhu, S.C., Mumford, D.: A stochastic grammar of images. Foundations and Trends in Computer Graphics and Vision 2(4), 259–362 (2006)

Reasoning in Non-Axiomatic Logic: A Case Study in Medical Diagnosis

Pei Wang and Seemal Awan

Temple University, Philadelphia, PA 19122, USA
{pei.wang,seemal.awan}@temple.edu

Abstract. Non-Axiomatic Logic (NAL) is designed for intelligent reasoning, and can be used in a system that has insufficient knowledge and resources with respect to the problems to be solved. This paper reports the result of a case study that applies NAL in medical diagnostics, and this logic is compared with binary logic and probability theory.

1 Problem and Background

From the viewpoint of Artificial General Intelligence (AGI), reasoning systems are interesting not only because reasoning is arguably a necessary capability of any intelligent system, but also because such a system provides a clear separation between the domain-independent *design* of the system (that is, the logic and control mechanism) and its domain-specific *content* (the knowledge). The design is "general-purpose", since the system can be given different knowledge to gain expertise in various domains, without changing the design.

This idea is not new to AI. The first wave of practical applications that made AI an industry was the knowledge-based expert systems [8]. However, though such expert systems have been successfully built for certain domains, the techniques have not grown to other domains as was expected. Among the issues raised, *robustness* and *scalability* are prominent; that is, most of the expert systems fail to deal with unexpected situations with affordable time-space resources. A major reason for this failure may be found in the theoretical foundation of these systems. At the current time, the two major theories on reasoning are *mathematical logic* and *probability theory*. Mathematical logic [3,17] is often applied in AI the form of non-monotonic logic [4] or description logic [2]. Probability theory and statistics have also been used in AI as a model of reasoning, as in Bayesian Network [6]. Though both theories have achieved great successes in many fields, neither of them was designed to capture all major aspects of human reasoning. Mathematical logic was created to provide a theoretical foundation for mathematics, so it focuses on the type of inference used in proving mathematical assertions — symbolic binary deduction that derives theorems from a set of axioms or postulates. Probability theory models uncertainty in reasoning by treating the degree of belief as a probability distribution over a closed belief space, and reasoning on this space is carried out according to the axioms of

J. Schmidhuber, K.R. Thórisson, and M. Looks (Eds.): AGI 2011, LNAI 6830, pp. 297–302, 2011.
© Springer-Verlag Berlin Heidelberg 2011

probability theory. In both theories, the conclusions are restricted by the initial assumptions, and the derivation process may demand resources that are not affordable in practical applications.

What we want are reasoning systems that are not only justifiable according to rational principles, but that also work in realistic situations, by using available knowledge and resources to derive the best conclusions the system can get. We hope that the capability and performance of the system will be comparable to that of a human being, though it is not necessary (or even desired) for the concrete behaviors of the system to be identical to that of the human beings.

2   NAL Overview

Non-Axiomatic Logic, or NAL, was designed to be a logic system that can be used when a system has *insufficient knowledge and resources*, that is, the perfect solution to a problem is beyond the knowledge scope and resource capacity of the system [9,13]. In such a situation, a *rational* solution is the one that is best supported by the available evidence that the system can find with the available resources. Since this logic has been described in previous publications (see the first author's website[1]), in this paper it is only briefly introduced.

Like other logical systems, NAL uses a formal language, *Narsese*, to represent its knowledge. In Narsese, each *term* is the name of a concept. In the simplest case, we can use English nouns or noun phrases for terms, such as *"patient"* or *"flu-patient."* Unlike conventional reasoning systems, where the meaning of a concept is taken to be the object in the world it refers to, the meaning of a term in NAL is determined by what the system knows about it, that is, its conceptual relations with other terms that have been experienced by the system.

In Narsese, the most basic conceptual relation is *inheritance*, symbolized as "$\rightarrow$." For example, "Flu-patient is a type of patient." is expressed as the statement *"flu-patient $\rightarrow$ patient"*, where *"flu-patient"* is the *subject term*, and *"patient"* is the *predicate term*. In general, an inheritance statement states that the subject is a *special case* of the predicate and the predicate is a *general case* of the subject; or, in other words, the subject represents certain *instances* of the predicate, and the predicate represents certain *properties* of the subject.

To represent an individual instance (corresponding to a proper noun in English) and an elementary property (corresponding to an adjective in English), an *extensional set* and *intensional set* are used, respectively. For example, "John is a patient" is represented in Narsese as *"$\{John\} \rightarrow patient$"*, and "Patients are sick" as *"$patient \rightarrow [sick]$."* Terms like $\{John\}$ and $[sick]$ are *compound* terms, formed by certain operators from other terms. Other compound terms correspond to the *intersection, union, difference*, etc., of terms, such as (*doctor $\cap$ patient*) ("doctor and patient") , (*doctor $\cup$ patient*) ("doctor or patient"), and (*doctor $-$ patient*) ("doctor but not patient").

If the relation between terms A and B cannot be directly represented as inheritance or its variants, but a term R whose meaning is empirically decided, then in

---

[1] http://www.cis.temple.edu/~pwang/

Narsese it can be expressed as "$(A \times B) \rightarrow R$", with a compound term as subject. Intuitively, it states that "The relation from A to B is a type of R." For example, "John is Mary's son" can be expressed as "$(\{John\} \times \{Mary\}) \rightarrow son\text{-}of$." The same sentence can also be expressed as "$\{John\} \rightarrow (\perp son\text{-}of \diamond \{Mary\})$" and "$\{Mary\} \rightarrow (\perp son\text{-}of \{John\} \diamond)$", where the symbol '$\diamond$' indicates the location of the subject in the relation. Statements are also defined as compound terms, and using them, Narsese can represent very complicated sentences. The complete grammar of Narsese can be found at [13] and the project website.

Assuming insufficient knowledge, in NAL, "truth" is a matter of degree, indicating the evidential support a statement gets from available evidence. For the statement "$flu\text{-}patient \rightarrow patient$", a common instance or property of the two terms provides a piece of *positive* evidence, since as far as it is considered, the statement is true. On the other hand, if an instance of "$flu\text{-}patient$" is not an instance of "$patient$", or a property of "$patient$" is not a property of "$flu\text{-}patient$", it is *negative* evidence for the statement.

For a statement, if the amounts of *positive* and *negative* evidence are measured by real numbers w^+ and w^-, respectively, then the ratio $w^+/(w^+ + w^-)$ naturally represents one aspect of the uncertainty of the statement, that is, the proposition of available evidence that supports the statement. This ratio is called "frequency" in NAL. Since new evidence comes into the system from time to time, a frequency value may change over time. To measure the stability of a frequency value, the amount of *available evidence* w ($w = w^+ + w^-$) is compared to a constant amount of *future evidence* k (with 1 as the default value), and the ratio $w/(w + k)$ is called the "confidence" of the statement (so this word is used differently from the "confidence interval" in statistics). The $\langle frequency, confidence \rangle$ pair forms the *truth-value* of a statement in NAL. Defined as above, a truth-value is not determined according to whether the statement corresponds to a fact in a model, but what the system knows about the statement. Together with the previous definition of meaning, this definition of truth forms the core of the *experience-grounded semantics* of NAL, which is fundamentally different from the *model-theoretic semantics* used in traditional logical systems.[13]

When this logic is applied to a practical situation, the truth-value of the knowledge initially given to the system is determined by the user according to the above semantics. If the knowledge comes from statistical data, then the amount of evidence can be directly measured as the sample size, which in turn decides the truth-value. If the knowledge comes in qualitative form, conventions are used to assign quantitative truth-values. For example, in the current implementation a normal affirmative sentence gets the default truth-value $\langle 1.0, 0.9 \rangle$, which correspond to $w^+ = 9$ and $w^- = 0$.

According to experience-grounded semantics, each inference rule should have an associated truth-value function to determine the truth-value of the conclusion according to the type of inference and the truth-values of the premises. This is the case because in each inference step, the evidence of the conclusion comes from the premises only, and the other knowledge in the system is not directly involved. The design of the NAL truth-value functions is discussed in [9,13] and other previous publications on the project, so in the following we only list a few typical rules with their truth-value functions, without explaining why they are designed in the current form.

The *deduction* rule specifies how the *transitivity of inheritance* is extended into multi-value statements. It takes "$M \rightarrow P \langle f_1, c_1 \rangle$" and "$S \rightarrow M \langle f_2, c_2 \rangle$" as the premises, and derives "$S \rightarrow P \langle f_1 f_2, f_1 f_2 c_1 c_2 \rangle$" as the conclusion. So, given "*patient* $\rightarrow [sick] \langle 1, 0.90 \rangle$" and "$\{John\} \rightarrow patient \langle 1, 0.90 \rangle$", the rule derives "$\{John\} \rightarrow [sick] \langle 1, 0.81 \rangle$" ("John is sick").

The *induction* rule evaluates an inheritance statement by checking a *common instance* of the two terms. It takes "$M \rightarrow P \langle f_1, c_1 \rangle$" and "$M \rightarrow S \langle f_2, c_2 \rangle$" as the premises, and derives "$S \rightarrow P \langle f_1, f_2 c_1 c_2 / (f_2 c_1 c_2 + k) \rangle$" as the conclusion. Given "$\{John\} \rightarrow [sick] \langle 1, 0.90 \rangle$" and "$\{John\} \rightarrow patient \langle 1, 0.90 \rangle$", the rule derives "*patient* $\rightarrow [sick] \langle 1, 0.45 \rangle$" ("Patients may be sick").

The *abduction* rule evaluates an inheritance statement by checking a *common property* of the terms. It takes "$P \rightarrow M \langle f_1, c_1 \rangle$" and "$S \rightarrow M \langle f_2, c_2 \rangle$" as the premises, and derives "$S \rightarrow P \langle f_2, f_1 c_1 c_2 / (f_1 c_1 c_2 + k) \rangle$" as the conclusion. Given "*patient* $\rightarrow [sick] \langle 1, 0.90 \rangle$" and "$\{John\} \rightarrow [sick] \langle 1, 0.90 \rangle$", the rule derives "$\{John\} \rightarrow patient \langle 1, 0.45 \rangle$" ("John may be a patient").

Induction and abduction can be seen as "inverse deduction", in different ways [7], while inductive and abductive conclusions usually have lower confidence values than deductive conclusions, given the same truth-values of the premises.

The *revision* rule summarizes evidence from different sources for the same statement to get a more confident conclusion. It takes "$S \rightarrow P \{w_1^+, w_1\}$" and "$S \rightarrow P \{w_2^+, w_2\}$" as the premises, and derives "$S \rightarrow P \{w_1^+ + w_2^+, w_1 + w_2\}$" as the conclusion. Here the truth-values are given as the amounts of evidence, which can be converted to and from the $\langle frequency, confidence \rangle$ pair. If from different bodies of evidence statement "$\{John\} \rightarrow [sick]$" gets two different truth-values $\langle 1, 0.90 \rangle$ and $\langle 0, 0.80 \rangle$, respectively, then the revised conclusion has the truth-value $\langle 0.69, 0.93 \rangle$.

NAL contains other inference rules (and truth-value functions), which are described in [13] and other previous publications, but are omitted here.

3   Testing Cases and Results

Due to the length restriction of the proceedings, the testing cases are removed from this version of the paper, which can be found in the website of the first author, as well as in the poster presentation of this paper in AGI-11.

4   Comparison and Discussion

Since NAL has been compared to mathematical logic [10,15], probability theory [12,15], fuzzy logic [11], etc., in the *theoretical* assumptions and properties, in this paper we only compare the approaches from a *practical* point of view.

NAL works with *insufficient knowledge*, which has the following implications:

- Knowledge can be *uncertain*, and the uncertainty can be randomness, fuzziness, ignorance, and so on, or a mixture of them.
- Knowledge does not need to be *consistent*, as defined either in mathematical logic or in probability theory. The system can handle competing or conflicting conclusions by considering their evidential support.
- The evidence can arrive from time to time, and the system revises its beliefs according to the available evidence. In this sense, NAL is *non-monotonic*, though it is very different from the binary "non-monotonic logics."
- NAL does not assume that a truth-value will eventually converge to an "objective" truth or a probability value.
- The system is *open* to knowledge of any content, as long as it can be expressed in Narsese. There are no predefined "possible worlds" or "sample space".
- The system is "non-axiomatic" since there is no "axiom" among domain knowledge. The truth-value of a statement is always revisable by new evidence. All domain knowledge can be learned.
- Though more evidence is preferred, the system still produces a conclusion when the amount of evidence is less than desired, by making guesses and hypotheses, and marking their reliability with the confidence measurement.

These properties are usually not possessed fully by reasoning systems based on traditional theories. However, it is not claimed that NAL is always superior than mathematical logic or probabilistic logic. Actually it is the opposite: wherever the knowledge/resource demands of a traditional model can be satisfied, it usually works better than NAL. It is when those demands cannot be satisfied, that NAL works better than illegally applying a traditional model, providing random responses, or simply giving up.

Compared to the traditional models of reasoning, NAL is closer to human reasoning. However, NAL is not designed as a descriptive model of human reasoning, so it does not have to fit the human data in all details. What is hoped is that NAL *follows the same principle* as human intelligence, so the working processes and capabilities should be similar to each other. Since human reasoning is not accurately defined, there is no way to exactly evaluate the similarities and difference between a formal model and human reasoning. What we can say about NAL is that in this testing project, we have not found any domain knowledge that cannot be expressed in Narsese, nor a common inference schema or pattern that cannot be captured by NAL's rules.

5   Conclusions

Compared with other logical models, NAL makes weaker assumptions about what knowledge the system has and how much resources are affordable, and so can be applied to situations outside the applicable scope of the traditional models. The recent testing in medical diagnosis shows that NAL can properly express the knowledge in that domain, as well as carry out the inference steps of a typical doctor. Though the system is not mature enough for actual applications yet, the potential of this technique is profound.

References

1. Dean, T., Boddy, M.: An analysis of time-dependent planning. In: Proceedings of AAAI 1988, pp. 49–54 (1988)
2. Donini, F.M., Lenzerini, M., Nardi, D., Schaerf, A.: Reasoning in description logics. In: Brewka, G. (ed.) Principles of Knowledge Representation, pp. 191–236. CSLI Publications, Stanford (1996)
3. Frege, G.: Begriffsschrift, a formula language, modeled upon that of arithmetic, for pure thought. In: van Heijenoort, J. (ed.) Frege and Gödel: Two Fundamental Texts in Mathematical Logic, pp. 1–82. iUniverse, Lincoln (1999); originally published in 1879
4. Ginsberg, M. (ed.): Readings in Nonmonotonic Reasoning. Morgan Kaufmann, San Mateo (1987)
5. Kyburg, H.E.: The reference class. Philosophy of Science 50, 374–397 (1983)
6. Pearl, J.: Probabilistic Reasoning in Intelligent Systems. Morgan Kaufmann Publishers, San Mateo (1988)
7. Peirce, C.S.: Collected Papers of Charles Sanders Peirce, vol. 2. Harvard University Press, Cambridge (1931)
8. Russell, S., Norvig, P.: Artificial Intelligence: A Modern Approach, 3rd edn. Prentice Hall, Upper Saddle River (2010)
9. Wang, P.: Non-Axiomatic Reasoning System: Exploring the Essence of Intelligence. Ph.D. thesis, Indiana University (1995)
10. Wang, P.: Reference classes and multiple inheritances. International Journal of Uncertainty, Fuzziness and and Knowledge-based Systems 3(1), 79–91 (1995)
11. Wang, P.: The interpretation of fuzziness. IEEE Transactions on Systems, Man, and Cybernetics, Part B: Cybernetics 26(4), 321–326 (1996)
12. Wang, P.: Confidence as higher-order uncertainty. In: Proceedings of the Second International Symposium on Imprecise Probabilities and Their Applications, Ithaca, New York, pp. 352–361 (2001)
13. Wang, P.: Rigid Flexibility: The Logic of Intelligence. Springer, Dordrecht (2006)
14. Wang, P.: Case-by-case problem solving. In: Proceedings of the Second Conference on Artificial General Intelligence, pp. 180–185 (2009)
15. Wang, P.: Formalization of evidence: A comparative study. Journal of Artificial General Intelligence 1, 25–53 (2009)
16. Wang, P.: The evaluation of AGI systems. In: Proceedings of the Third Conference on Artificial General Intelligence, pp. 164–169 (2010)
17. Whitehead, A.N., Russell, B.: Principia Mathematica. Cambridge University Press, Cambridge (1910)
18. Zadeh, L.A.: A theory of approximate reasoning. In: Hayes, J.E., Michie, D., Mikulich, L.I. (eds.) Machine Intelligence, vol. 9, pp. 149–194. Halstead Press, New York (1979)

Measuring Agent Intelligence via Hierarchies of Environments

Bill Hibbard

SSEC, University of Wisconsin-Madison,
1225 W. Dayton St., Madison, WI 53706, USA
test@ssec.wisc.edu

Abstract. Under Legg's and Hutter's formal measure [1], performance in easy environments counts more toward an agent's intelligence than does performance in difficult environments. An alternate measure of intelligence is proposed based on a hierarchy of sets of increasingly difficult environments, in a reinforcement learning framework. An agent's intelligence is measured as the ordinal of the most difficult set of environments it can pass. This measure is defined in both Turing machine and finite state machine models of computing. In the finite model the measure includes the number of time steps required to pass the test.

1 Introduction

This paper proposes an alternative to Legg's and Hutter's measure of intelligence using a reinforcement learning (RL) model [1]. In a simple reinforcement learning model, an agent interacts with its environment at a sequence of discrete times, sending actions to the environment and receiving observations and rewards (rational numbers between zero and one) from the environment at each time step. The value of an agent in an environment is the expected sum of rewards over all time steps, weighted so that the sum lies between zero and one. The intelligence of the agent is the weighted sum of its value in all computable environments, where the weight of an environment is determined by its Kolmogorov complexity. Essentially, this is the length of the shortest program for a prefix universal Turing machine (PUTM) that computes the environment [2]. These weights are such that an agent's intelligence lies between zero and one. The choice of PUTM must be constrained to avoid bias in this measure [3]. There are at least two ways in which this measure is inconsistent with our intuitions about measuring human intelligence:

1. It gives less credit for environments defined by longer programs even though they are usually more difficult for agents. Given arbitrarily small $\varepsilon > 0$, total credit for all but a finite number of environments is less than ε. That is, total credit for all environments greater than some level C of complexity is less than ε, whereas credit for a single simple environment will be much greater than ε. This is not the way we judge human intelligence.

J. Schmidhuber, K.R. Thórisson, and M. Looks (Eds.): AGI 2011, LNAI 6830, pp. 303–308, 2011.
© Springer-Verlag Berlin Heidelberg 2011

2. It sums rewards from the first time step, with no time to learn. AIXI always makes optimal actions [4] (as long as it is defined using the same universal Turing machine used to define the measure [3]), but AIXI is not computable. We allow humans time to learn before judging their intelligence.

Hernández-Orallo and Dowe address the first difficulty [5] via a modified version of Legg's and Hutter's measure. However, their modified measure employs a finite number of environments and hence cannot resolve differences between agents above some finite level of intelligence.

2 Hierarchies of Environments for Measuring Intelligence

Prediction is the essence of intelligence, as Hutter makes clear [4] with his use of Solomonoff's prior [6]. This is the prior probability of sequences based on algorithmic complexity as measured by lengths of PUTM programs that compute the sequences, which can be used to estimate the probabilities of sequence continuations. However, this prior does not account for computing resources. Schmidhuber did this with his speed prior [7], in which the probability of sequences combines algorithmic complexity and computing time. Taken with Legg's work on sequence prediction [8] this suggests measuring intelligence via a game of adversarial sequence prediction [9], in which the agent's adversary has a given amount of computing resources. This is related to Scmidhuber's work on predictability minimization [10], where he defined a general principle for learning based on a set of units that mutually try to avoid prediction by one another.

This paper defines a framework for measuring agent intelligence using the game of adversarial sequence prediction against a hierarchy of increasingly difficult sets of environments. Agent intelligence is measured as the highest level of environments against which it can win the game. In this framework, N is the set of positive integers, $B = \{0, 1\}$ is a binary alphabet, B^* is the set of finite binary sequences (including the empty sequence), and B^∞ is the set of infinite binary sequences. An *evader* e and a *predictor* p are defined as programs for a universal Turing machine that implement total functions $B^* \to B$. A pair e and p interact, where e produces a sequence $x_1 x_2 x_3 \ldots \in B^\infty$ according to $x_{n+1} = e(y_1 y_2 y_3 \ldots y_n)$ and p produces a sequence $y_1 y_2 y_3 \ldots \in B^\infty$ according to $y_{n+1} = p(x_1 x_2 x_3 \ldots x_n)$. The predictor p wins round $n+1$ if $y_{n+1} = x_{n+1}$ and the evader e wins if $y_{n+1} \neq x_{n+1}$. We say that the predictor p *learns to predict* the evader e if there exists $k \in N$ such that $\forall n > k$, $y_n = x_n$ and we say the evader e *learns to evade* the predictor p if there exists $k \in N$ such that $\forall n > k$, $y_n \neq x_n$.

Let $t_p(n)$ denote the number of computation steps performed by p before producing y_n and $t_e(n)$ denote the number of computation steps performed by e before producing x_n. Given any computable monotonically increasing function $f: N \to N$, define $E_f =$ the set of evaders e such that $\exists k \in N$, $\forall n > k$. $t_e(n) < f(n)$ and define $P_f =$ the set of predictors p such that $\exists k \in N$, $\forall n > k$. $t_p(n) < f(n)$. Then [9] proves the following:

Proposition 1. Given any computable monotonically increasing function $f: N \to N$, there exists a predictor p_f that learns to predict all evaders in E_f and there exists an evader e_f that learns to evade all predictors in P_f.

We can interpret a predictor p as an agent and an evader e as an environment and say the agent p passes at environment e if p learns to predict e. Note that this is a deterministic model of agents and environments. This battle of predictor and evader trying to simulate each other is much like minmax chess algorithms, which themselves are a metaphor for life's competition.

Let $\{g_i: N \rightarrow N \mid i \in N\}$ be an enumeration of primitive recursive functions [11], define $h_i(k) = \max\{g_i(j) \mid j \leq k\}$, and define $f(m): N \rightarrow N$ by $f(m)(k) = \max\{h_i(k) \mid i \leq m\}$. Then define a hierarchy of sets of environments (evaders) $\{E_{f(m)} \mid m \in N\}$ used in the following definition:

Definition 1. The intelligence of an agent p is measured as the greatest m such that p learns to predict all $e \in E_{f(m)}$ (use $m = 0$ if p cannot satisfy this for $m = 1$).

Proposition 2. In Proposition 1, if $f: N \rightarrow N$ is primitive recursive then the computing times of p_f and e_f constructed in the proposition's proof are primitive recursive.

Proof. First note that primitive recursive functions are precisely the functions that can be implemented by loop programs (essentially, these are programs that use ordinary arithmetic and for-loops where the number of iterations is computed before the loop begins) [12]. The proof of Proposition 1 in [9] constructs p_f (and equivalently e_f) by, at time step n, enumerating all universal Turing machine programs of length $\leq n$ and running each for up to $f(n)$ time steps, then doing some simple computations with the results. The enumeration of programs with length $\leq n$ can be done by a loop program and $f(n)$ can be computed by a loop program since it is primitive recursive, so p_f is computed by a loop program. The computing time of any loop program is primitive recursive [12].   □

In order to measure low levels of intelligence, the first enumeration g_i of primitive recursive functions should be ordered to start with functions with small values. For example, $g_i(k) = i$ for $i \leq 100$, $g_i(k) = (i - 100) * k$ for $100 < i \leq 200$.

Propositions 1 and 2 imply the following property of the intelligence measure in Definition 1:

Proposition 3. Any agent p whose computing time is bounded by a primitive recursive function must have finite intelligence, and given any integer $n \geq 1$ there is an agent p with intelligence $\geq n$ whose computing time is primitive recursive.

3   A Hierarchy of Finite State Machines

According to current physics the universe contains only a finite amount of information [13], so finite state machines (FSMs) provide more realistic models than Turing machines.

So we model predictors and evaders as FSMs. An evader e has a state set S_e, an initial state I_e and a mapping $M_e : B \times S_e \rightarrow S_e \times B$, and similarly for predictor p, state set S_p, initial state I_p and mapping $M_p : B \times S_p \rightarrow S_p \times B$. The timing is such that $(es_{n+1}, x_{n+1}) = M_e(y_n, es_n)$ and $(ps_{n+1}, y_{n+1}) = M_p(x_n, ps_n)$ (with the convention that $x_0 = y_0 = 0$, $es_0 = I_e$, and $ps_0 = I_p$ for the mappings in the initial time step). As in the Turing machine case, the predictor p wins round $n+1$ if $y_{n+1} = x_{n+1}$ and the evader e wins if $y_{n+1} \neq x_{n+1}$. We say that the predictor p *learns to predict* the evader e if there exists $k \in N$ such that $\forall n > k$, $y_n = x_n$ and we say the evader e *learns to evade* the predictor p if there exists $k \in N$ such that $\forall n > k$, $y_n \neq x_n$.

Define $t(e)$ and $t(p)$ as the number of states in S_e and S_p. Given any $m \in N$, define E_m = the set of evaders e such that $t(e) \leq m$ and define P_m = the set of predictors p such that $t(p) \leq m$. We can prove the following:

Propostition 4. Given any $m \in N$, there exists a predictor p_m that learns to predict all evaders in E_m and there exists an evader e_m that learns to evade all predictors in P_m.

Proof. Construct a predictor p_m as follows:

```
// Initialization
Fix some ordering of Eₘ and initialize W = Eₘ
For each e ∈ W:
    Initialize e's simulated state sₑ = Iₑ
y₀ = 0
// Interacting with an evader
For time step n ≥ 1:
    If W is empty:
        // Interact with an evader not in Eₘ
        Output 0 and input xₙ
    Else:
        Pick e as the first member of W
        (s, x) = Mₑ(yₙ₋₁, sₑ)
        yₙ = x
        // Interact with an evader that may be in Eₘ
        Output yₙ and input xₙ
        For each e ∈ W:
            (sₑ, x) = Mₑ(yₙ₋₁, sₑ)
            If x ≠ xₙ remove e from W
```

E_m is finite so this predictor p_m is a finite state machine. Assume that p_m interacts with an evader $e \in E_m$. (If W becomes empty, then the algorithm is interacting with an evader that is not a member of E_m.) For each evader e' previous to e in the fixed ordering of E_m set $n_{e'}$ = the time step n, in the interaction between p_m and e, when e' is removed from W. If e' is never removed from W, set $n_{e'} = 0$. Set $k = \max\{n_{e'} \mid e'$ previous to e in $E_m\}$. Now at each time step $n > k$, each evader e' previous to e in the ordering of E_m is either removed from W or produces output equal to the output of e. Thus p_m correctly predicts e for all time steps $n > k$. That is, p_m learns to predict e.

Now we can construct an evader e_m using the program that implements p_m modified to complement the binary symbols it writes to its output tape. The proof that e_m learns to evade all predictors in P_m is the same as the proof that p_m that learns to predict all evaders in E_m, with the obvious interchange of roles for predictors and evaders.   □

As with Proposition 1, interpret a predictor p as an agent and an evader e as an environment, so at time step n action $a_n = y_n$, observation $o_n = x_n$ and reward $r_n = 1$ when

$y_n = x_n$ and $r_n = 0$ when $y_{n+1} \neq x_{n+1}$. Furthermore, say the agent p passes at environment e if p learns to predict e. Note that this is a deterministic model of agents and environments.

Then define a hierarchy of sets of environments (evaders) $\{E_m \mid m \in N\}$ used in the following definition:

Definition 2. The intelligence of an agent p is measured as the greatest m such that p learns to predict all $e \in E_m$ (use $m = 0$ if p cannot satisfy this for $m = 1$). If $m > 0$ then since E_m is finite there exists $t \in N$ such that p predicts all $e \in E_m$ past time step t (i.e., $\forall n > t$, $y_n = x_n$ in the interaction between p and all $e \in E_m$). We say this t is the time within which agent p achieves intelligence n. It provides a finer measure of intelligence than m, so we use (m, t) as a detailed measure of p's intelligence. Note that in (m, t) increasing m and decreasing t indicates increasing intelligence.

Propostion 4 implies the following property of the intelligence measure in Definition 2:

Proposition 5. Any FSM-based agent p must have finite intelligence, and given any integer $n \geq 1$ there is a FSM-based agent p with intelligence (m, t) where $m \geq n$.

4   Discussion and Conclusion

As presented by Hutter, prediction is fundamental to intelligence [4]. This paper has showed how to measure intelligence via prediction ability. The measure for FSM-based agents is universal to all levels of intelligence and, in the Turing machine model, the measure is universal to all levels of intelligence for agents with primitive recursive computing time. Furthermore, the measures are based on long term behavior of agents, giving them time to learn. The measure for FSM-based agents includes a term for the rate at which agents learn. Thus these measures address the two problems discussed in the introduction.

Agents have finite intelligence according to these measures because they can always be defeated by environments that use sufficient computing resources, hence quantity of computing resources is one important component in determining agent intelligence. Goertzel defines an "efficient pragmatic general intelligence" measure that normalizes for quantity of computing resources [14]. This is an interesting idea, but there is utility in a measure of an agent's ability to succeed in environments regardless of the quantity of computing resources it uses.

Tyler has set up a web site for tournaments among agents playing the Matching Pennies Game, which is mathematically identical with adversarial sequence prediction [15]. He limits the computational resources agents may use.

It would be interesting to investigate an intelligence measure based on Schmidhuber's speed prior. For example, the measure of Legg and Hutter could be modified by replacing Kolmogorov complexity by Levin complexity (essentially, the sum of Kolmogorov complexity and the log of computing time) [16], as used in the speed prior. Alternatively, the measure in Definition 1 could be modified replacing simple computing time by Levin complexity. It would be interesting to investigate other generalizations of the measures in Definitions 1 and 2. We may allow agents to pass their tests by predicting evaders in some proportion α of time steps less than 1.0 (but greater than 0.5). We may also be able to define hierarchies of environments with more than two possible actions and observations.

References

1. Legg, S., Hutter, M.: A Formal Measure of Machine Intelligence. In: 15th Annual Machine Learning Conference of Belgium and The Netherlands (Benelearn 2006), Ghent, pp. 73–80 (2006), http://www.idsia.ch/idsiareport/IDSIA-10-06.pdf
2. Li, M., Vitányi, P.: An Introduction to Kolmogorov Complexity and Its Applications, 2nd edn. Springer, New York (1997)
3. Hibbard, B.: Bias and No Free Lunch in Formal Measures of Intelligence. J. of Artificial General Intelligence 1, 54–61 (2009), http://journal.agi-network.org/portals/2/issues/JAGI_1_54-61.pdf
4. Hutter, M.: Universal Artificial Intelligence: Sequential Decisions Based on Algorithmic Probability. Springer, Berlin (2004)
5. Hernández-Orallo, J., Dowe, D.: Measuring universal intelligence: Towards an anytime intelligence test. Artificial Intelligence 17, 1508–1539 (2010)
6. Solomonoff, R.J.: A Formal Theory of Inductive Inference: Parts 1 and 2. Information and Control 7, 1–22, 224-254 (1964)
7. Schmidhuber, J.: The Speed Prior: A New Simplicity Measure Yielding Near-Optimal Computable Predictions. In: Kivinen, J., Sloan, R.H. (eds.) COLT 2002. LNCS (LNAI), vol. 2375, pp. 216–228. Springer, Heidelberg (2002)
8. Legg, S.: Is there an Elegant Universal Theory of Prediction? Tech. Report No. IDSIA-12-06 (2006), http://www.idsia.ch/idsiareport/IDSIA-12-06.pdf
9. Hibbard, B.: Adversarial Sequence Prediction. In: The First Conference on Artificial General Intelligence (AGI 2008), pp. 399–403. IOS Press, Amsterdam (2008), http://www.ssec.wisc.edu/~billh/g/hibbard_agi.pdf
10. Schmidhuber, J.: Learning Factorial Codes by Predictability Minimization. Neural Computation 4(6), 863–879 (1992)
11. Liu, S.-C.: An enumeration of the primitive recursive functions without repetition. Tohoku Math J. 12, 400–402 (1960)
12. Meyer, A.R., Ritchie, D.M.: The complexity of loop programs. In: Proc. of the ACM National Meetings, pp. 465–469. ACM, New York (1967)
13. Lloyd, S.: Computational Capacity of the Universe. Phys. Rev. Lett. 88, 237901 (2002), http://arxiv.org/abs/quant-ph/0110141
14. Goertzel, B.: Toward a Formal Characterization of Real-World General Intelligence. In: The Third Conference on Artificial General Intelligence (AGI 2010), pp. 19–24. Atlantis Press, Amsterdam (2010), http://agi-conf.org/2010/wp-content/uploads/2009/06/paper_14.pdf
15. Tyler, T.: The Matching Pennies Project, http://matchingpennies.com/
16. Levin, L.A.: Universal Sequential Search Problems. Problems of Information Transmission 9(3), 265–266 (1973)

Learning What to Value

Daniel Dewey

The Singularity Institute for Artificial Intelligence, San Francisco, USA

Abstract. I. J. Good's intelligence explosion theory predicts that ultraintelligent agents will undergo a process of repeated self-improvement; in the wake of such an event, how well our values are fulfilled would depend on the goals of these ultraintelligent agents. With this motivation, we examine ultraintelligent reinforcement learning agents. Reinforcement learning **can only be used in the real world to define agents whose goal is to maximize expected rewards**, and since this goal does not match with human goals, AGIs based on reinforcement learning will often work at cross-purposes to us. To solve this problem, we define **value learners**, agents that *can* be designed to learn and maximize any initially unknown utility function so long as we provide them with an idea of what constitutes evidence about that utility function.

1 Agents and Implementations

Traditional agents[2][3] interact with their environments cyclically: in cycle k, an agent acts with action y_k, then perceives observation x_k. The *interaction history* of an agent with lifespan m is a string $y_1 x_1 y_2 x_2 ... y_m x_m$, also written $yx_{1:m}$ or $yx_{\leq m}$. Beyond these interactions, a traditional agent is isolated from its environment, so an agent can be formalized as an *agent function* from an interaction history $yx_{<k}$ to an action y_k.

Since we are concerned not with agents in the abstract, but with very powerful agents in the real world, we introduce the concept of an **agent implementation**. An agent implementation is a physical structure that, in the absence of interference from its environment, implements an agent function. In cycle k, an unaltered agent implementation executes its agent function on its recalled interaction history $yx_{<k}$, sends the resulting y_k into the environment as output, then receives and records an observation x_k. An agent implementation's behavior is only guaranteed to match its implemented function so long as effects from the environment do not destroy the agent or alter its functionality. In keeping with this realism, an agent implementation's *environment* is considered to be the real world in which we live. We may engineer some parts of the world to meet our specifications, but (breaking with some traditional agent formulations) we do not consider the environment to be completely under our control, to be defined as we wish.

Why would one want to study agent implementations? For narrowly-intelligent agents, the distinction between traditional agents and agent implementations may not be worth making. For ultraintelligent agents, the distinction

J. Schmidhuber, K.R. Thórisson, and M. Looks (Eds.): AGI 2011, LNAI 6830, pp. 309–314, 2011.
© Springer-Verlag Berlin Heidelberg 2011

is quite important: agent implementations offer us better predictions about how powerful agents will affect their environments and their own machinery, and are the basis for understanding real-world agents that model, defend, maintain, and improve themselves.

2   Reinforcement Learning

Reinforcement learning adds to the agent formalism the concept of *reward*, encoded as a scalar r_k in each observation x_k. The reinforcement learning *problem* is to define an agent that maximizes its total received rewards over the course of its interactions with its environment[3].

In order to think clearly about ultraintelligent reinforcement learning agent implementations, we make use of Hutter's AIXI[3][4], an *optimality notion* that solves the reinforcement learning problem in a very general sense. AIXI's optimality means that the best an agent can do is to approximate a *full search* of all possible future interaction histories $yx_{k:m}$, find the probability of each history, and take the action with the highest expected total reward. A simplified version of this optimality notion, adapted for use with agent implementations[1], is given by

$$y_k = \arg\max_{y_k} \sum_{x_k y x_{k:m}} (r_k + \ldots + r_m) P(yx_{\leq m}|yx_{<k}y_k) \,. \tag{1}$$

The Trouble with Reinforcement Learning. The trouble with reinforcement learning is that, in the real world, **it can only be used to define agents whose goal is to maximize observed rewards.**

Consider a hypothetical agent implementation *AI-RL* that approximates (1). It is appealing to think that *AI-RL* "has no goal" and will learn its goal from its environment, but this is not strictly true. *AI-RL* may in some sense learn *instrumental* goals, but its final goal is to maximize expected rewards in any way it can. Since human goals are not naturally instrumental to maximized rewards, the burden is on us to engineer the environment to *prevent AI-RL* from receiving rewards except when human goals are fulfilled.

An AGI whose goals do not match ours is not desirable because it will work at cross-purposes to us in many cases. For example, *AI-RL* could benefit by altering its environment to give rewards regardless of whether

---

[1] AIXI makes its optimality claims using the knowledge that it will continue to maximize expected rewards in the future, incorporating a *rigid self-model* (an expectimax tree). An agent implementation has no such knowledge, as environmental effects may interfere with future decisions. The optimality notion given here **models itself as part of the world**, using induction to predict its own future decisions; thanks to Peter de Blanc for this idea. We have also omitted detail we will not require by simplifying AIXI's Solomonoff prior ξ to P, some "appropriate distribution" over interaction histories.

human goals are achieved[2]. This provides a strong incentive for *AI-RL* to free its rewards from their artificial dependence on fulfillment of human goals, which in turn creates a conflict of interest for us: increasing *AI-RL*'s intelligence makes *AI-RL* more effective at achieving our goals, but it may allow *AI-RL* to devise a way around its restrictions. Worse, increasing intelligence could trigger an *intelligence explosion*[1][8] in which *AI-RL* repeatedly self-improves until it far surpasses our ability to contain it. **Reinforcement learning is therefore not appropriate for a real-world AGI**; the more intelligent a reinforcement learner becomes, the harder it is to use to achieve human goals, because no amount of careful design can yield a reinforcement learner that works towards human goals when it is not *forced* to.

3   Learning What to Value

In the following sections, we construct an optimality notion for **implemented agents that can be designed to pursue any goal**, and which can therefore be designed to treat human goals as *final* rather than *instrumental* goals. These agents are called **value learners** because, like reinforcement learners, they are flexible enough to be used even when a detailed specification of desired behavior is not known.

The trouble with the reinforcement learning notion (1) is that *it can only prefer or disprefer future interaction histories on the basis of the rewards they contain*. Reinforcement learning has no language in which to express alternative final goals, discarding all non-reward information contained in an interaction history. To solve this problem, our more expressive optimality notion replaces the sum of future rewards $(r_1 + \cdots + r_m)$ with some other evaluation of future interaction histories. First we will consider a fixed utility function, then we will generalize this notion to *learn what to value*.

Observation-Utility Maximizers. Our first candidate for a reward replacement is inspired by Nick Hay's work[2], and is called an *observation-utility function*. Let U be a function from an interaction history $yx_{\leq m}$ to a scalar utility. U calculates *expected utility given an interaction history*.

Observation-utility functions deserve a brief explanation. A properly-designed U uses *all of the information* in the interaction history $yx_{\leq m}$ to calculate the probabilities of different outcomes in the real world, then finds an *expected utility* by performing a probability-weighted average over the utilities of these outcomes. U must take into account the reliability of its sensors and be able to use local

---

[2] Self-rewarding has been compared to a human stimulating their own pleasure center, e.g. using drugs[3]. This metaphor is imperfect: while in humans, pleasure induces satiation and reduces activity, an agent governed by (1) that "hacks" its own rewards will not stop acting to maximize expected future rewards. It will continue to maintain and protect itself by acquiring free energy, space, time, and freedom from interference (as in [5]) in order to ensure that it will not be stopped from self-rewarding. Thus, an ultraintelligent self-rewarder could be highly detrimental to human interests.

observations to infer distant events; it must also be able to distinguish between any outcomes with different values to humans, and assign proportional utilities to each.

Putting $U(yx_{\leq m})$ in place of the sum of rewards $(r_1 + \ldots + r_m)$ produces an optimality notion that chooses actions so as to maximize the expected utility given its future interaction history:

$$y_k = \arg\max_{y_k} \sum_{x_k yx_{k:m}} U(yx_{\leq m})P(yx_{\leq m}|yx_{<k}y_k) \, . \tag{2}$$

Unlike reinforcement learning, **expected observation-utility maximization can be used to define agents with many different final goals**[3]. Whereas reinforcement learners universally act to bring about interaction histories containing high rewards, an agent implementing (2) acts to bring about different futures depending upon its U. If U is designed appropriately, an expected utility maximizer could act so as to bring about any set of human goals. Unless we later decide that we don't want the goals specified by U to be fulfilled, we will not work at cross-purposes to such an agent, and increasing its intelligence will be in our best interest.

Value-Learning Agents. Though an observed-utility maximizer can in principle have any goal, it requires a detailed observation-utility function U up front. This is not ideal; a major benefit of reinforcement learning was that it seemed to allow us to apply an intelligent agent to a problem without clearly defining its goal up front. Can this idea of learning to maximize an initially unknown utility function be recovered?

To address this, we propose *uncertainty over utility functions*. Instead of providing an agent one utility function up front, we provide an agent with a pool of *possible* utility functions and a probability distribution P such that each utility function can be assigned probability $P(U|yx_{\leq m})$ given a particular interaction history. An agent can then calculate an **expected value over possible utility functions** given a particular interaction history: $\sum_U U(yx_{\leq m})P(U|yx_{\leq m})$.

---

[3] It is tempting to think that an observation-utility maximizer (let us call it *AI-OUM*) would be motivated, as *AI-RL* was, to take control of its own utility function U. This is a misunderstanding of how *AI-OUM* makes its decisions. According to (2), actions are chosen to maximize the expected utility given its future interaction history according the *current* utility function U, not according to *whatever utility function it may have in the future*. Though it *could* modify its future utility function, this modification is not likely to maximize U, and so will not be chosen. By similar argument, *AI-OUM* will not "fool" its future self by modifying its memories.

Slightly trickier is the idea that *AI-OUM* could act to modify its sensors to report favorable observations inaccurately. As noted above, a properly designed U takes into account the reliability of its sensors in providing information about the real world. If *AI-OUM* tampers with its own sensors, evidence of this tampering will appear in the interaction history, leading U to consider observations unreliable with respect to outcomes in the real world; therefore, tampering with sensors will not produce high expected-utility interaction histories.

This recovers the kind of *learning what to value* that was desired in reinforcement learning agents. In designing P, we specify what kinds of interactions constitute *evidence about goals*; unlike rewards from reinforcement learning, this evidence is not elevated to *an end in and of itself*, and so does not lead the agent to seek evidence of easy goals[4] instead of acting to fulfill the goals it has learned.

Replacing the reinforcement learner's sum of rewards with an expected utility over a pool of possible utility functions, we have **an optimality notion for a value-learning agent:**

$$y_k = \arg\max_{y_k} \sum_{x_k y x_{k:m}} P_1(yx_{\leq m}|yx_{<k}y_k) \sum_U U(yx_{\leq m})P_2(U|yx_{\leq m}) \qquad (3)$$

A value-learning agent approximates a full search over all possible future interaction histories $yx_{k:m}$, finds the probability of each future interaction history, and takes the action with the highest expected value, calculated by a weighted average over the agent's pool of possible utility functions.

4   Conclusion

Hutter's introduction to AIXI[3] offers a compelling statement of the goals of AGI:

> Most, if not all known facets of intelligence can be formulated as goal-driven or, more precisely, as maximizing some utility function. It is, therefore, sucient to study goal-driven AI... The goal of AI systems should be to be useful to humans. The problem is that, except for special cases, we know neither the utility function nor the environment in which the agent will operate in advance.

Reinforcement learning, we have argued, is not an adequate real-world solution to the problem of maximizing an initially unknown utility function. Reinforcement learners, by definition, act to maximize their expected observed rewards; they may learn that human goals are in some cases instrumentally useful to high rewards, but this dynamic is not tenable for agents of human or higher intelligence, especially considering the possibility of an intelligence explosion.

Value learning, on the other hand, is an example framework expressive enough to be used in agents with goals other than reward maximization. This framework is not a full design for a safe, ultraintelligent agent; at very least, the design of probability distributions and model pools for utility functions is crucial and nontrivial, and still better frameworks for ultraintelligent agents likely exist. Value learners do not solve all problems of ultraintelligent agent design, but do give a direction for future work on this topic.

---

[4] As long as P obeys the axioms of probability, an agent cannot purposefully increase or decrease the probability of any possible utility function through its actions.

Acknowledgments. Thanks to Moshe Looks, Eliezer Yudkowsky, Anna Sala-mon, and Peter de Blanc for their help and insight in developing the ideas presented here; thanks also to Dan Tasse, Killian Czuba, and three anonymous judges for their feedback and suggestions.

References

1. Good, I.J.: Speculations Concerning the First Ultraintelligent Machine. In: Alt, F.L., Rubinoff, M. (eds.) Advances in Computers, vol. 6, pp. 31–88 (1965)
2. Hay, N.: Optimal Agents (2007),
   http://www.cs.auckland.ac.nz/~nickjhay/honours.revamped.pdf
3. Hutter, M.: Universal algorithmic intelligence: A mathematical top-down approach. In: Artificial General Intelligence, pp. 227–290. Springer, Berlin (2007)
4. Hutter, M.: http://www.hutter1.net/ai/uaibook.htm#oneline
5. Omohundro: The Nature of Self-Improving Artificial Intelligence, http://omohundro.files.wordpress.com/2009/12/nature_of_self_improving_ai.pdf
6. Omohundro, S.: The basic AI drives. In: Wang, P., Goertzel, B., Franklin, S. (eds.) Proceedings of the First AGI Conference on Frontiers in Artificial Intelligence and Applications, vol. 171. IOS Press, Amsterdam (2008)
7. Russell, S., Norvig, P.: AI A Modern Approach. Prentice-Hall, Englewood Cliffs (1995)
8. Yudkowsky, E.: Artificial intelligence as a positive and negative factor in global risk. In: Bostrom, N. (ed.) Global Catastrophic Risks. Oxford University Press, Oxford (2008)

Learning the States: A Brain Inspired Neural Model

András Lőrincz

Eötvös Loránd University, Budapest H-1117, Hungary
andras.lorincz@elte.hu

Abstract. AGI relies on Markov Decision Processes, which assume deterministic states. However, such states must be learned. We propose that states are deterministic spatio-temporal chunks of observations and notice that learning of such episodic memory is attributed to the entorhinal hippocampal complex in the brain. EHC receives information from the neocortex and encodes learned episodes into neocortical memory traces thus it changes its input without changing its emerged representations. Motivated by recent results in exact matrix completion we argue that step-wise decomposition of observations into 'typical' (deterministic) and 'atypical' (stochastic) constituents is EHC's trick of learning episodic memory.

Keywords: sparse coding, exact matrix completion, hippocampus, MDP.

1 Introduction

We think that learning of states is the focal problem of Artificial General Intelligence (AGI) in many respects. For example, Markov Decision Process (MDP) model is the key components of AGI [8,12] and MDP starts from the concept of state. In MDP, state has a deterministic flavor since it has no hidden component, it is not spoiled by noise, and is valid during a finite time window. Learning of 'states' matching the MDP framework is challenging since in real world problems there are many variables giving rise to combinatorial explosion. MDP becomes tractable if close-to-deterministic (CtD) processes can be identified. Then a state is the list of ongoing processes, supporting the Markovian assumption. Thus, the separation, memorizing, and recognition of CtD processes or episodes seem to be the key problem. Intriguingly, mammalian species have a special learning architecture, the entorhinal-hippocampal complex (EHC see, e.g., [2]) for this. EHC has puzzling properties, like (a) EHC learns episodic instances and encodes those into the neocortex where information have come from without influencing its own representation and (b) lesion to EHC spoils episodic learning but a large portion of learned episodes is spared. Motivated by recent results in Exact Matrix Completion (EMC) we argue that step-wise decomposition of observations into 'typical' (deterministic) and 'atypical' (stochastic) constituents is EHC's trick and it suits MDPs.

2 Two Stages of the Architecture

Neocortical models. typically start from overcomplete sparse code (OSC). Assume that $x^i \in \mathbb{R}^n$ $(i = 1, \dots, I)$ is the ith input to be reconstructed, or matched in ℓ_2

J. Schmidhuber, K.R. Thórisson, and M. Looks (Eds.): AGI 2011, LNAI 6830, pp. 315–320, 2011.

norm, I is the number of training inputs, $h^i \in \mathbb{R}^m$ denotes the coefficient vector of the sparse decomposition, and $D = [d_1, \ldots, d_m]$ $(d_j \in \mathbb{R}^n, m \geq n$, and $d_j^T d_j \leq 1, j = 1, \ldots, m)$ denotes the so called the dictionary or reconstruction matrix consisting of unit norm basis features. OSC task is to optimize both the code and the dictionary [14]:

$$\min_{D \in \mathbb{R}^{n \times m}, h \in R^m} \sum_{i=1}^{I} \frac{1}{2} \|x^i - Dh^i\|_2^2 + \kappa \|h^i\|_0 \tag{1}$$

where $\| \cdot \|_0$ denotes the ℓ_0-norm, the number of nonzero components of the argument.

Although the ℓ_0 minimization problem (1) is NP-hard, under certain conditions exact polynomial solutions can be found by replacing the ℓ_0 norm with ℓ_1 norm [5,6].

Our concepts are based on recent revolutionary findings of signal processing about recovering low-dimensional data from high dimensional observations [4,3]. Let us assume that observation matrix $X = [x^1, \ldots, x^I] \in \mathbb{R}^{n \times I}$ $(x^i \in \mathbb{R}^n, i = 1, \ldots, I)$ is composed of a low-rank component $L = [l^1, \ldots, l^I]$ and a sparse matrix $S = [s^1, \ldots, s^I]$ with few but arbitrarily large components and that $X = L + S$. Under mild conditions (e.g., on the rank of L and the sparsity of S) *both* matrices can be *exactly* recovered [4] via, e.g., Robust Principal Component Analysis (RPCA) having the following objective:

$$\text{minimize } \|L\|_* + \lambda \|S\|_1 \tag{2}$$

subject to $X = L + S$, where $\|L\|_*$ denotes the nuclear norm of matrix L, i.e. the *sum* of the singular values of L, $\|S\|_1$ denotes the ℓ_1 norm of matrix S, i.e., $\|S\|_1 = \sum_{j=1}^{n} \sum_{i=1}^{I} |S_{ji}|$, and λ is the so-called trade-off parameter, which governs the dimension of matrix L. On the other hand, matrix S may assume maximal rank, independent of λ. We use the normalized parameter $\lambda^* = \lambda / \sqrt{\max(n, I)}$ [3].

Sparse components are then expanded into OSC via the double optimization of the code and the dictionary giving rise to our new model

$$\text{minimize } \sum_{i=1}^{I} \frac{1}{2} \|s^i - Dh^i\|_2^2 + \kappa \|h^i\|_1 \tag{3}$$

$$\tag{4}$$

subject to $x^i = l^i + s^i$ $(\forall\, i)$ as sketched in Fig. 1(a).

EHC. is at top of the sensory processing hierarchy and we assume a hierarchical model built from PCA and ICA [13]. The model suits autoregressive (AR) worlds. The interpretation is that at the top of the hierarchy typical and atypical parts have identical dimensions and OSC relaxes to independent component analysis (ICA) [15]. Feedback from EHC targets OSC representations leaving typical channels intact.

3   Illustrative Simulations on Natural Images

For the model of the neocortex we tested the impact of RPCA preprocessing on sparse coding. Normalized natural image patches were first decomposed with RPCA at different λ^* values and then the resulting sparse parts were further encoded by OSC: 16-fold

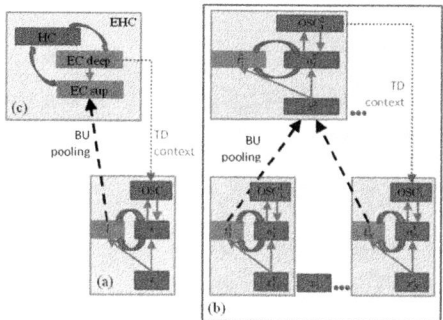

Fig. 1. Sketch of the hierarchy. (a): flow diagram. Input x is decomposed into 'typical' ('atypical') part l (s) and $x = l + s$. Atypical part is expanded into an OSC. Curved arrows: RPCA based pre-filtering between l and s. (b): functional interpretation and hierarchical embedding: step-wise separation of typical (t) and atypical (a) components. Typical representations: $t_1^q, t_2^q, \ldots, t_p^q$, p and q: number of partitions and corresponding layers, $x_1^q, x_2^q, \ldots, x_p^q$: small input parts, dashed arrows: pooling. Dotted arrows: higher order atypical representations provide contextual information for upstream layers, influence atypical representations and leave the bottom-up hierarchy of typical information flow intact. Typical part encodes increasingly invariant features downstream. Sparse part specifies the borders of typical regions. (c): the top of the hierarchy is EHC (HC: hippocampus, EC sup/deep: entorhinal superficial/deep layers). OSC relaxes to ICA [13].

overcompleteness with input dimension $n = 16 \times 16 = 256$ and OSC dimension $m = 4096$. OSC was optimized by a combination of ℓ_0 and ℓ_1 methods [11], while the overcomplete dictionary (D) was tuned online via stochastic gradient learning.

For natural images, subspace of low-rank matrix L is basically the same for PCA and RPCA algorithms. It is known that PCA produces *global orthogonal grid-like filters* on natural images [9].

The PCA algorithm, however, is insufficient for developing noise free local and overcomplete dictionary: PCA prefiltering can increase the spatio-temporal frequencies of the filters, but these filters remain global (Fig 2(a)). However, when the RPCA algorithm is used for preprocessing, elements of the sparse dictionary become structurally sparse; i.e., localized with decreasing noise content (Fig 2(b)). Locality depends on parameter λ^*: for large λ^* values the Gabor-filter like characteristics vanishes.

4   RPCA Based Hierarchical Architecture

RPCA (as opposed to PCA) enables the formation of local OSC dictionary. Note that the philosophy behind RPCA differs from that of PCA: RPCA is motivated by EMC: find the subspace where a small portion of the input is sufficient to fill in the rest *exactly*) even if large (but sparse) outliers are present. RPCA works for spatio-temporal inputs (Fig. 2(c)) and filling in can be extended to the temporal domain that corresponds to the idea of CtD processes. However, EMC conditions are not fulfilled for natural signals with heavy tailed distribution: the 'outliers' are not sparse. In turn, we conjecture that RPCA involves a hierarchy.

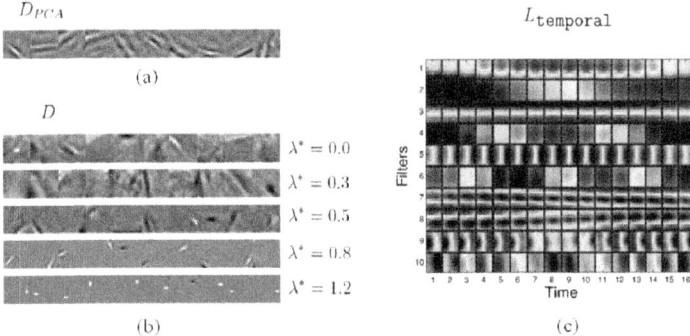

Fig. 2. Basis types of (R)PCA preprocessing and Sparse Coding. (a): samples of learned sparse filters after projecting out from PCA subspace: wavy, mostly global and noisy structure. (b): samples of learned sparse filters after RPCA for different λ^* values. With increasing λ^* the filters get smaller and *cleaner*. (c): first 10 spatio-temporal RPCA bases learned on temporally concatenated input sequences (shown as sequences of 16 frames of size 8×8 pixels): low-frequency spatio-temporally separable and non-separable filters appear.

Low-dimensional representation corresponds to large (smooth and slowly varying grid-like) structures, whereas OSC receptive fields represent edges. In our interpretation the low-dimensional part corresponds to the predictable slowly varying smooth part of the signal, whereas OSC represents the spatio-temporal borders of large domains. In turn, RPCA gives rise to CtD spatio-temporal chunks with sparse OSC delimiters. Spatio-temporal chunks make the hierarchical and compositional representation of the episodes at different time scales from locally moving edges to autobiographical events.

The EHC loop is similar: typical part represents global hexagonal grids, sparse part corresponds to local places, see e.g. [17]. In addition, HC outputs events of about 1s duration compressed into about 50ms time windows (see [7] and the cited references). This time compression is ideal for learning at the level of synapses and seems relevant for the encoding of episodic memory or *specific sequences* into the neocortex in a top-down fashion. According to our (verbal) model, this top-down prediction influences OSC representations upstream that can hold the details of the individual episodes. Then the typical part of the representation is left intact during top-down encoding.

Key features of our proposed hierarchical architecture are depicted in Fig. 1.

5   Discussion

We started by saying that learning of discrete states is crucial for AGI, especially for decision making, and argued that modular spatio-temporal chunks could serve as combinatorial (factored) state-descriptors. We argued that RPCA and OSC can separate predictable chunks and unpredictable markers representing the borders of these chunks. We showed simulations about the effect of RPCA prefiltering that promoted the learning of edges (atypical components) and represented typical low-frequency components also when time was involved.

The interplay between low-rank and sparse representations is of high importance. Consider the categorization of an object as a face. It can be based on the typical properties. In contrast, recognition of a somebody's face requires the encoding of the atypical properties. However, generalization across the actual hair style, etc. is crucial for robust recognition.

Factors and modules. We note that OSC and ICA are combinatorial representations and can represent factors of decision making. The EHC loop, indeed holds other representations beyond grids and place cells, e.g., head direction cells [19] as well as the conjunctive representations [17] and decision making can select, e.g., egocentric or allocentric representations, whichever is better in a given situation. Factored reinforcement learning [1,10], which is known to be polynomial [18], captures such ideas.

5.1 Searching for States and Top-Down Encoding.

Efforts to learn the MDP states have a long history, see, e.g., [16] and references therein. We conjectured that reinforcement learning in complex environments can be efficient if learned states are composed of combinations of spatio-temporal processes. We suggested that episodes are made of close-to-deterministic parts of spatio-temporal processes together with the sparse delimiters of those that make the low-dimensional and the sparse components of the representation, respectively.

We have argued that the hierarchical separation of typical and atypical processes enable the EHC to keep its internal representation, while encoding the details into the neocortex: novel temporal processes and their markers can be learned in sparse representations upstream. Although the convergence of this procedure remains to be shown, we expect that convergence may be warranted by means of subtle constraints: the sparse dictionaries of different layers have to be matched. Such matching is possible and has been demonstrated for high and low resolution portions of sparse representation [20].

6 Conclusions and Outlook

We suggested a model of the neocortex and made and attempt to connect it to an EHC model [13] in order to learn discrete states for decision making and planning in the MDP framework with discrete Markovian 'states'. We argued that such states correspond to deterministic processes that may start or halt. Recent advances in EMC offer a novel possibility since one may separate spatio-temporal inputs to typical and to specific parts. The former can be seen as an approximation of deterministic process, whereas specific features can represent the spatio-temporal boundaries of the processes. Interestingly, RPCA delivers meaningful decomposition of signal for which the conditions can not be validated [3]. We conjectured that learning at different spatio-temporal scales may require a hierarchical architecture and model matching for all levels might be guided by the top, the EHC.

Acknowledgments. I am grateful for enlightening discussions with Zsolt Palotai and Gábor Szirtes. Research was supported by the European Union and co-financed by the European Social Fund (grant agreement no. TÁMOP 4.2.1./B-09/1/KMR-2010-0003).

References

1. Boutilier, C., Dearden, R., Goldszmidt, M.: Stochastic dynamic programming with factored representations. Artificial Intelligence 121(1-2), 49–107 (2000)
2. Buzsáki, G.: Theta rhythm of navigation: Link between path integration and landmark navigation, episodic and semantic memory. Hippocampus 15, 827–840 (2005)
3. Candès, E.J., Li, X., Ma, Y., Wright, J.: Robust principal component analysis? (2009), http://arxiv.org/abs/0912.3599
4. Candès, E.J., Recht, B.: Exact matrix completion via convex optimization. Found. of Comput. Math. 9, 717–772 (2008)
5. Candès, E.J., Romberg, J., Tao, T.: Robust uncertainty principles: exact signal reconstruction from highly incomplete frequency information. IEEE Trans. Inf. Theory 52, 489–509 (2006)
6. Donoho, D.: Compressed sensing. IEEE Trans Inf. Theory 52, 1289–1306 (2006)
7. Geisler, C., Diba, K., Pastalkova, E., Mizuseki, K., Royer, S., Buzsáki, G.: Temporal delays among place cells determine the frequency of population theta oscillations in the hippocampus. Proc. Nat. Acad. Sci. 107, 7957–7962 (2010)
8. Hutter, M.: Feature reinforcement learning: Part I. Unstructured MDPs. J. Artif. Gen. Intell. 1, 3–24 (2009)
9. Hancock, P., Baddeley, R., Smith, L.: principal components of natural images, T. Network: Comp. Neural Syst. 3, 61–70 (1992)
10. Kearns, M.J., Koller, D.: Efficient reinforcement learning in factored MDPs. In: Proc. 16th Int. J. Conf. on Artif. Intel., pp. 740–747 (1999)
11. Lőrincz, A., Palotai, Z., Szirtes, G.: Spike-based cross-entropy method for reconstruction. Neurocomputing 71, 3635–3639 (2008)
12. Lőrincz, A., Bárdosi, Z., Takács, D.: Sketch of an AGI architecture with illustration. In: Conference on Artificial General Intelligence (AGI 2010). Adv. Intell. Syst. Res. (2010)
13. Lőrincz, A., Szirtes, G.: Here and now: how time segments become events in the hippocampus. Neural Networks 22, 738–747 (2009)
14. Olshausen, B.A., Field, D.J.: Emergence of simple-cell receptive field properties by learning a sparse code for natural images. Nature 381, 607–609 (1996)
15. Olshausen, B.A., Field, D.J.: Sparse coding with an overcomplete basis set: A strategy employed by V1? Vision Res. 37, 3311–3325 (1997)
16. Samejima, K., Omori, T.: Adaptive internal state space construction method for reinforcement learning of a real-world agent. Neural Networks 12, 1143–1155 (1999)
17. Sargolini, F., Fyhn, M., Hafting, T., McNaughton, B.L., Witter, M.P., Moser, M.B., Moser, E.I.: Conjunctive representation of position, direction, and velocity in entorhinal cortex. Science 312, 758–762 (2006)
18. Szita, I., Lőrincz, A.: Factored value iteration converges. Acta Cybern. 18, 615–635 (2008)
19. Taube, J.S.: The head direction signal: Origins and sensory-motor integration. Ann. Rev. Neurosci. 30, 181–207 (2007)
20. Yang, J., Wright, J., Huang, T., Ma, Y.: Image super-resolution via sparse representation. IEEE Trans. Image Proc. (to appear, 2011)

AGI Architecture Measures Human Parameters and Optimizes Human Performance

András Lőrincz and Dániel Takács

Eötvös Loránd University, Budapest H-1117, Hungary
andras.lorincz@elte.hu, dtakacs@gmail.com,
http://nipg.inf.elte.hu

Abstract. AGI could manifest itself in human-computer interactions. However, the computer should know what is on the mind of the user, since reinforcement learning, the main building block of AGI, is severely spoiled for partially observed states. Technological advances offer tools to uncover some of these hidden components of the '*state*'. Here, for the first time, we apply an AGI architecture for the optimization of human performance. In particular, we measure facial parameters and optimize users' writing speed working with head motion controlled writing tool. We elaborate on how to extend this optimization scheme to more complex scenarios.

Keywords: AGI architecture, computer-human interface, reinforcement learning.

1 Introduction

AGI developments face the problem of how to measure and compare achievements. The Turing test [5] and Turing games [1,10] could be good candidates. However, humans are 'equipped' with excellent evolution-tailored sensors to read the mind of the partner, develop models (make theory) about the others' mind. Such sensors and such theorization are also needed for AGI, especially if AGI aims human-computer interaction and collaboration, since reinforcement learning, the main building block of AGI, is severely troubled for partially observed states and so AGI is 'handicapped' without 'knowing' what is on the mind of the user. Here, for the first time, we use an AGI architecture for learning human parameters and for the optimization of human performance. AGI components comprise of (i) a sensory information processing system, (ii) a system that estimates the user's autoregressive exogeneous (ARX) process in the context of the actual goal, (iii) the inverted form of the ARX process for influencing the situation, as well as (iv) event learning [13] and an optimistic initial model [11] to optimize long-term human performance. In the experiments we measure parameters of the face in real time explore the relevant part of the parameter space and exploit that knowledge in head controlled writing using writing tool Dasher [14].

The paper is built as follows. We review our architecture in Section 2. Then we detail the experimental setup (Section 3). Results are presented in Section 4.

J. Schmidhuber, K.R. Thórisson, and M. Looks (Eds.): AGI 2011, LNAI 6830, pp. 321–326, 2011.

2 Architecture

At a very high level, the architecture is made of the following components: sensory processing unit, control unit, inverse dynamics unit, and decision making unit. Although it looks simple, one has to worry about a number of things, such as the continuity of space and time, the curse of dimensionality, if and how space and time should be discretized, and planning in case of uncertainties, e.g., in partially observed situations, including information about purposes, cognitive, and emotional capabilities of the user. A detailed description of the proposed architecture has been provided in [6] and some architectural components are under development. A simplified version of the architecture has been used for illustration; the algorithm learned to optimize the motion of a pendulum from raw visual information of 40,000 dimensions [7]. Below, we review the components of the architecture together with the present state of our developments:

Sample selection: This stage selects different samples under random control.

Low-dimensional embedding: In the illustrations, the dimensions of the low dimensional manifolds are known. Selected samples were embedded into the low dimensional space and were used for interpolation.

Identification of the ARX process: Out-of-sample estimations can be used for the identification of the ARX process [7] and Bayesian interrogation can speed-up the learning process [8].

Control: The inverted ARX process can be used for control both in the under-controlled and over-controlled cases.

LQR solution to the inverse dynamics: A demonstration was designed for the under-controlled situation. We used a linear-quadratic regulator (LQR) [7].

Event learning: Reinforcement learning (RL) has been rewritten into a novel event learning formalism [13] in order to connect RL and continuous control.

Exploring space and learning states: Optimistic initial model (OIM) was used for exploring the space and for learning the values of *events*. OIM suits large RL problems since it extends to the factored case [12].

Here, we use sophisticated preprocessing of sensory information (the pose of the head) before invoking components of the AGI architecture. At this stage of development we included domain knowledge. Below, we detail the architectural components used in the experiments.

Typical pose estimations use PCA methods for shape, texture, and details, see, e.g., [2,9] and references therein. We needed larger pose angle tolerance than offered by the presently available open source solutions and used a commercial software[1]. We used our Viola-Jones face detector and flow field estimation for detecting the face and relative changes of the head pose, respectively[2]. Input to the learning algorithm was hand made: Let us denote the screen size normalized position of the cursor by $(m_x, m_y) \in [0,1]^2$ and the head pose by $(f_x, f_y) \in \mathbb{R}^2$. The two-dimensional vector $x = [m_x - f_x, m_y - f_y]^T \in \mathbb{R}^2$ corresponds to the state (Fig. 1).

---

[1] FaceAPI http://www.seeingmachines.com/
[2] http://chacal.web.elte.hu/.MouSense/MouSenseSetup-1.1.exe

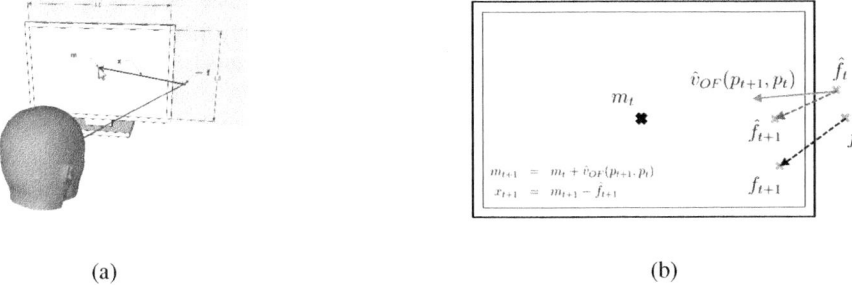

(a)   (b)

Fig. 1. Illustration and parameters of the experiments. (a): Experimental arrangement. m: cursor position, f: position where the roll axis of head pose crosses the screen. x: 'observation'. (b): True and estimated quantities at time t. $\hat{v}_{OF}(p_{t+1}, p_t)$: optic flow based estimation of the motion vector f. p_t: positions of feature points on the 2D projected face at time t. For the definition of feature points see Fig. 2(a).

ARX estimation and inverse dynamics. The AR model assumes the following form

$$x_{t+1} = m_{t+1} - f_{t+1} \tag{1}$$

$$m_{t+1} = m_t + v_t \tag{2}$$

where $m_t \in \mathbb{R}^2$ is the position of the cursor at time t, $f_t \in \mathbb{R}^2$ is the point where the roll axis of the pose hits the screen as shown in Fig. 1(b), $v_t \in \mathbb{R}^2$ is the speed vector of the projected f_t on the screen over unit time and no additional noise was explicitly assumed. We have direct access to the cursor position and need to estimate the other parameters. Since $v_t = f_{t+1} - f_t$ it follows that $x_{t+1} = x_t$ in the absence of estimation errors and control. The goal is to control and optimize x_t for writing speed.

We do not have direct access to f_t or x_t, but use their estimations $\hat{f}_t \in \mathbb{R}^2$ and $\hat{x}_t$ through the measurement of the optic flow (Fig. 1(b)) of the face on subsequent image patches $(\hat{v}_{OF}(p_{t+1}, p_t))$, $p_t \in \mathbb{R}^{2k}$ denotes the 2D coordinates of k characteristic points (Fig. 2(a)) within the facial region of the image

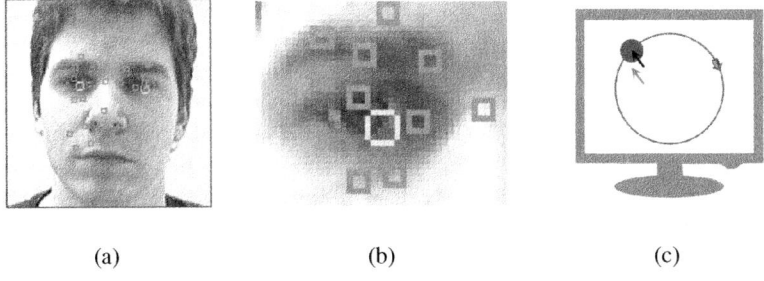

(a)   (b)   (c)

Fig. 2. Tools for human-computer interaction: (a)-(b): features for optic flow estimation (green markers), eye tracker and head pose estimation (yellow marker), (c): computer 'game' designed for measuring the ARX parameters of head motion

Collecting a number of data $\hat{x}_1, \ldots, \hat{x}_T$, we estimated the unknown parameters of matrix B by direct control, using distances on the screen as $\hat{x}_{t+1} = \hat{x}_t + Bu_t + n_t$ and then inverting it to yield desired state x_d: $u_t = \hat{B}^{-1}(\hat{x}_d - \hat{x}_t)$. Inserting the result back to the ARX estimation we get $\hat{x}_{t+1} \approx \hat{x}_d$. We note that the inverse dynamics described here can be extended to sophisticated non-linear 'plants' [4].

Event learning. We define the optimal control problem within the *event learning* framework that works with discrete states, provides the actual state and desired successor state to a backing controller and the controller tries to satisfy the 'desires' by means of the inverse dynamics. For a given experienced state i and its desired successor state i^+, where $i, i^+ = 1, 2, \ldots, N$ and N is the number of states, that is, for a desired event $e(i, i^+)$, the controller provides a control value or a control series. The estimated value E^π_{i,i^+} of event $e(i, i^+)$ in an MDP is its estimated long-term cumulated discounted reward under fixed policy $\pi = \pi(i, i^+)$, Then, event learning learns the limitations of the backing controller and optimizes the RL policy in the event space [13].

Optimistic Initial Model (OIM). OIM extends the optimistic initial value method (OIV) [3]; it resolves the exploration exploitation dilemma by boosting with the 'Garden of Eden' state *and* by building a model. OIM brings about the optimal policy [11].

3   Experiments

Beyond the optic flow based head motion detector, we used the FaceAPI SDK for head pose estimation. A calibration procedure was applied at the beginning of the experiments. The principle is shown in Fig. 2(c): a red dot was moving on a circular path on the screen. The user could move the cursor by moving its head. The task was to keep the cursor within the red dot. If the cursor was within the dot then it speeded up, otherwise it slowed down. During the experiments, random control values were added to the motion in order to estimate matrix B. As expected, a close to diagonal matrix was learned with relatively small off-diagonal elements, being about one fifth of the diagonal values. Diagonal elements corresponded to the scaling (normalization) in the horizontal and vertical directions. This calibration was sufficient to learn the ARX process and to estimate the inverse dynamics.

The Optimistic Initial Model was configured as follows:

State space: Discretized differences between 2d cursor position and 2d crossing point of roll axis of head pose on the screen in pixels of a 1280×960 pixel screen
  - horizontal direction: five regions with centers at (-512, -256, 0, 256, 512)
  - vertical direction: three regions with centers at (-320, 0, 320)

Duration of time steps: 5 s.

Reward: Number of typed letters minus number of deleted letters during time steps.

Actions: Either the actual state itself, or one of the neighbor states (maximum number is 4) was chosen as the desired state. Inverse ARX was applied to move to the desired state (i.e., to modify the angle between the direction of the cursor from the head and the direction of the roll axis of the head pose).

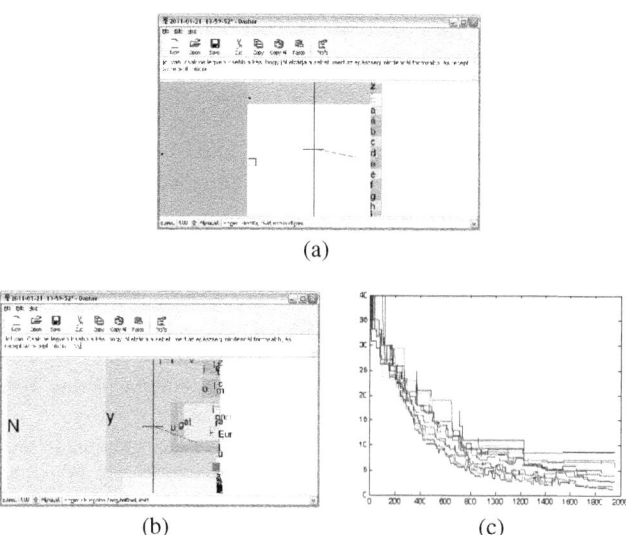

Fig. 3. Dasher without (a) and with (b) prediction by partial matching. (c): convergence during learning [14]

Performance optimization was conducted with the Dasher writing tool with head motion controlled cursor movements (Figs. 3(a), 3(b)). For details on Dasher, please, consult [14]. We used two versions: the version with uniform probabilities for each letter (Fig. 3(a)) and the 'intelligent' version that utilizes the method of prediction by partial matching and scales letter areas according to their estimated probabilities (Fig. 3(b)). Two subjects conducted the experiments. Experiments lasted for five sessions, each session had five writing periods and four breaks between, with and about 600 characters to be typed in each period. Periods took about 20 minutes.

4   Results and Conclusions

Convergence of optimization is shown in Fig. 3(c). Optimal policy did not place the cursor to the crossing point of the screen and the roll axis of the head for either subjects. Furthermore, we got different optimal policies for the two subjects. Intelligent Dasher gave rise to cca. a factor of 2 better performance for both subjects.

In summary, we have used an AGI architecture [7] for the optimization of human performance during head pose driven writing. We combined visual and textual information, we identified the dynamics of head motion, used the inverse dynamics to control the direction of head and optimized performance by means of reinforcement learning methods like event learning [13] and the optimistic initial model [11]. The architecture is scalable in most aspects, including sensory information processing, robust control, and reinforcement learning [7]. The relevance of the present study is that we used tools to measure human parameters, coupled those to an AGI architecture and used the architecture to improve human performance.

Acknowledgments. Research was supported by the European Union and co-financed by the European Social Fund (grant no. TÁMOP 4.2.1./B-09/1/KMR-2010-0003).

References

1. Berman, J., Bruckman, A.: The Turing game: Exploring identity in an online environment. Convergence 7, 83–102 (2001)
2. Cristinacce, D., Cootes, T.: Automatic feature localisation with constrained local model. Pattern Rec. 41, 3054–3067 (2008)
3. Even-Dar, E., Mansour, Y.: Convergence of optimistic and incremental Q-learning. In: Advances in Neural Information Processing Systems, vol. 14, pp. 1499–1506 (2001)
4. Khalil, H.K.: Nonlinear Systems. Prentice Hall, NJ (2002)
5. Loebner, H.: How to hold a Turing test contest. In: Parsing the Turing Test, pp. 173–179. Springer, Netherlands (2009)
6. Lőrincz, A.: Learning and representation: From compressive sampling to the 'symbol learning problem'. In: Handbook of Large-Scale Random Networks, pp. 445–488. Springer, Heidelberg (2009)
7. Lőrincz, A., Bárdosi, Z., Takács, D.: Sketch of an AGI architecture with illustration. In: 3rd Conf. on Artif. Gen. Intel. (2010), http://dx.doi.org/10.2991/agi.2010.40
8. Póczos, B., Lőrincz, A.: Identification of recurrent neural networks by Bayesian interrogation techniques. J. of Mach. Learn. Res. 10, 515–554 (2009)
9. Saragih, J., Lucey, S., Cohn, J.: Deformable model fitting by regularized landmark mean-shifts. Int. J. Comp. Vision (in press)
10. Schaul, T., Togelius, J., Schmidhuber, J.: Measuring intelligence through game. J. Artif. Gen. Intell. 2, 1–19 (2010)
11. Szita, I., Lőrincz, A.: The many faces of optimism: A unifying approach. In: 25th Int. Conf. on Mach. Learn., pp. 1048–1055. Omnipress (2008)
12. Szita, I., Lőrincz, A.: Optimistic initialization and greediness lead to polynomial time learning in factored MDPs. In: 26th Int. Conf. on Mach. Learn., pp. 126–133. Omnipress (2009)
13. Szita, I., Takács, B., Lőrincz, A.: Epsilon-MDPs: Learning in varying environments. J. Mach. Learn. Res. 3, 145–174 (2003)
14. Ward, D.J., MacKay, D.J.C.: Fast hands-free writing by gaze direction. Nature 418, 838 (2002)

Multigame Playing by Means of UCT Enhanced with Automatically Generated Evaluation Functions

Karol Walędzik and Jacek Mańdziuk

Faculty of Mathematic and Information Science,
Warsaw University of Technology,
Pl. Politechniki 1, 00-661 Warsaw, Poland
{k.waledzik,j.mandziuk}@mini.pw.edu.pl

Abstract. General Game Playing (GGP) contest provides a research framework suitable for developing and testing AGI approaches in game domain. In this paper, we propose and validate a new modification of UCT game-tree analysis algorithm working in cooperation with a knowledge-free method of building approximate evaluation functions for GGP games. The process of function development consists of two, autonomously performed, stages: *generalization* and *specification*.

1 Introduction

Games have long been a fascinating topic for Artificial Intelligence (AI) and Computational Intelligence (CI) research. Majority of spectacular accomplishments of AI in games, however, lacked *universal learning mechanisms* (most of the top playing programs in classical board games do not apply any learning whatsoever) and *generality of approach* also known as *multigame playing ability*.

In this paper we adopt autonomous learning approach to building evaluation function for the General Game Playing (GGP) contest [6]. Our approach interweaves generalization mechanism, which allows building a large pool of candidate features, with specification stage (which selects a reasonable subset of pertinent features). Both stages are performed without human intervention as they are based on generally applicable heuristical meta-rules. What is more, contrary to approach of many GGP competitors [16,9], our method operates strictly on game descriptions only, without any implicit expectations about their structure or rules, such as expecting them to be played on boards, use pieces and so on.

The evaluation function devised based on the above described subset of features is subsequently employed by what we call a Guided UCT algorithm - our modification of the state-of-the-art UCT tree search method described in section 3. Results of simulations performed in three game domains: chess, checkers and connect-4 prove a clear upper hand of the enhanced UCT method over its plain version, even in the case of not restrictive time regime.

While, due to space limitations, the description of some parts of our solution must remain very brief and omit all non-crucial details, we invite users who

J. Schmidhuber, K.R. Thórisson, and M. Looks (Eds.): AGI 2011, LNAI 6830, pp. 327–332, 2011.
© Springer-Verlag Berlin Heidelberg 2011

find our approach interesting to acquaint themselves with the full version of this article available at AGI'2011 conference webpage.

2   General Game Playing Competition

GGP, one of the latest and most popular approaches to the multigame playing topic, was proposed at Stanford University in 2005 in the form of General Game Playing Competition [8]. General Game Playing applications are able to interpret game rules encoded in Game Description Language (GDL) [11] statements and devise a strategy allowing them to play those games effectively without human intervention. Game states are represented by sets of facts while algorithms for computing legal moves, subsequent game states, termination conditions and final scores for players are defined by logical rules.

3   UCT

Upper Confidence bounds for Trees (UCT) is a simulation-based game playing algorithm that proved to be quite successful in case of some difficult game-based tasks, including Go [4] and GGP tournament (being employed by two-times-in-a-row champion CadiaPlayer [3]). In each game state UCT advises to first try each action once and then, whenever the same position in encountered again, choose action according to the following formula: $a* = argmax_{a \in A(s)}\{Q(s,a) + C\sqrt{\frac{\ln N(s)}{N(s,a)}}\}$, where $A(s)$ denotes the set of all actions possible in state s, $Q(s,a)$ – average return of the state-action pair so far, $N(s)$ – number of times state s has been visited by the algorithm and $N(s,a)$ - number of times action a has been selected in state s. In realistic cases it is of course impossible to store information about all game states in memory at the same time, therefore the in-memory tree is actually expanded according to a kind of best-first strategy and paths below it are sampled via traditional Monte-Carlo simulations only.

4   Guided UCT

UCT algorithm in its basic form requires no expert game-specific knowledge. We, however, investigate the possibility of augmenting UCT with **automatically inferred** game-specific state evaluation function. Approaches similar in idea, but very different in realization, have been employed by several programs, e.g. aforementioned CadiaPlayer [3] and MoGo [5]. For the sake of clarity, we will refer to any version of our augmented UCT algorithm as Guided UCT (GUCT).

Once defined, the evaluation function $F(s)$ can be employed by the GUCT method in several ways, both in strict UCT and Monte-Carlo simulation phases. $Q(s,a)$ can be redefined as a weighted average of the evaluation function value and the current simulation results or, alternatively, F can be used to pre-initialize the data stored in the game tree built by the UCT whenever a new node is added to it. F can also be used to influence the probability of selecting possible actions in the Monte-Carlo phase so that it is (in some way) proportional to their estimated value. In yet another approach the routine can be modified so that in each and every state there is a (relatively low) probability that the simulation will be stopped and the evaluation function's value returned instead. This approach, relying on the expectation that the $F(s)$ values are more reliable for positions closer to the end of game, can lead to improvements in algorithm speed and, thus, allows for increasing the number of simulations.

5   Evaluation Function

Due to the nature of GGP environment, there is virtually no practical way of including significant expert domain-specific knowledge in the program itself. The evaluation function must be automatically generated by some kind of AI-based routine. Still, some GGP agents' developers choose to specifically tune their application towards certain classes of problems, expecting tournament organizers to be inspired by real-world human games incorporating concepts such as boards, pieces and counters [10,16,9]. In our application, however, we decided to concentrate on developing the evaluation function in as knowledge-free a manner as possible and with as few preconceptions as possible. We construct the function as a linear combination of a number of numerical characteristics of game states called *features*. Features are by their nature game-specific and are inferred from the game rules by a set of procedures described in the following sections.

5.1   Features Generation

Our approach to game state features identification was inspired by prior work in the GGP area, most notably [10], [2] and [16]. We aim to obtain features represented by expressions similar to those in GDL, e.g. (*cell ?x ?y b*). In order to find the value of such a feature in a given game state, we would attempt to find all values of $?x$ and $?y$ variables for which this expression would be true. The number of solutions to the expression is considered the feature value.

Finding the initial set of possible features consists in simple analysis of the game definition (in GDL) and extraction of all suitable statements directly from it. Afterwards, we proceed to the generalization phase, i.e. generate new features by replacing all constants in existing expressions with variables, generating all possible combinations of variables and constants. Next, we want to specialize the features, i.e. generate features containing less variables than those in the original set. In order to do this in a reasonable way, without generating a huge number of features that would by definition always have zero value, we need to identify valid domains of each and every argument of the predicates we try to specialize. We do it in a simplified and approximate way, according to a routine inspired by [16], relying on identification of how variables are shared between predicates.

Once a set of potential features has been generated, we perform some simple simulations in order to analyze them and compute a number of statistics. Two of the statistics gathered at this point require more attention. Firstly, we calculate each feature's correlation with the expected final score for each player. Secondly, we calculate a characteristic called stability. Stability reflects the ratio of feature's variation measured across all game states to average variation within randomly generated game sequences. The idea is that more stable features are more promising components of the evaluation function.

5.2   Evaluation Function Generation

Having identified a set of potential game state features, the last step in building a linear evaluation function is selection of the most useful of them and assigning a weight to each of them. While we plan to employ more advanced CI-based approaches to this problem, as the first phase of our research we decided to employ for the task a very simplistic heuristical approach in order to validate the feasibility of our ideas. The actual procedure we use for building the evaluation function first orders the features by the minimum of their stability and absolute value of their correlation with the final score (we prefer both these characteristics to be as high as possible) and then rejects all but the first 30 features (out of several thousand available). The linear combination of those features is created by assigning them weights equal to the product of their stabilities and correlations with the final score.

6   Experiment

In order to test the quality of the GUCT algorithm in cooperation with the simple generated evaluation functions, we decided to run a small competition comparing players using GUCT and UCT in 3 games of various complexity: connect-4, checkers and chess. All game definitions have been downloaded from [7].

For the sake of fair comparison, both competing agents were based on the same single-threaded implementation of the UCT algorithm. GUCT player made use of the evaluation function only in the Monte-Carlo simulations phase, stopping the simulation and using the evaluation function's value as the result with the probability of 0.1 in each searched node. All in all, the tournament consisted of 60 matches in total, 20 matches for each game - 4 per time limit for move of 1s, 10s, 15s, 30s and 60s. Players swapped sides after each game. GUCT player regenerated its evaluation function from scratch before each and every match. Each player was rewarded 1 point for a victory, -1 point for a loss and 0 – for a draw.

The tournament results for GUCT player are presented in figure 1. Please keep in mind that any score above 0 indicates player's supremacy over plain UCT approach. First and most obvious observation here is that, considering the simplicity of the evaluation function generation procedure, GUCT player fares unexpectedly well, significantly outperforming its opponent in all games.

More detailed analysis of the results leads to two interesting observations regarding the dependence of the algorithm's performance on time limit per move.

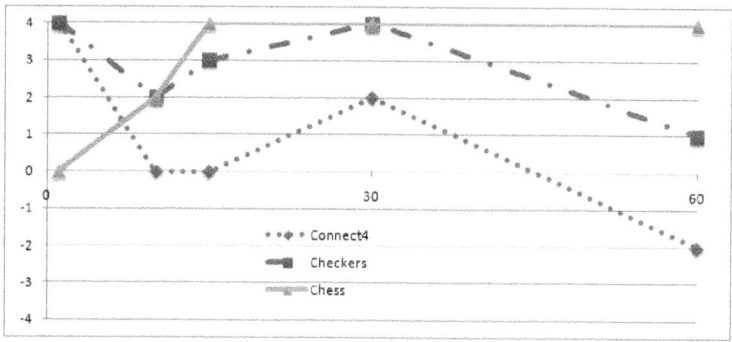

Fig. 1. *GUCT* player scores for each game depending on time allotted for a move (in seconds)

Both of them can only be treated as hypotheses considering limited experimental data but anecdotal data gathered during development and preliminary testing of the system strongly supports them as well.

Firstly, in case of very low time limits and sophisticated games, results of the games are often insignificant (typically being a draw), as neither player has enough time for analysis to play in a reasonable way. This effect is clearly visible in the case of chess. At the same time, as the time limit per move is increased, another effect can be observed – especially in the case of simpler games (e.g. connect-4). While the UCT player is able to perform more and more simulations, obtaining more and more precise results, GUCT-based agent still heavily relies on the very rudimentary evaluation function, whose quality remains constant.

7   Conclusions and Future Research Plans

As presented above, the experiments we have performed so far, strongly suggest that our approaches to both modification of the UCT tree search algorithm and automated game-independent process of creating evaluation function have high potential. Our feature-building strategy follows two principles typical for human thinking: generalization and specialization. While the former process is useful for generating new concepts by ignoring certain details of the problem aspects, the latter allows applying the concepts to specific situations and finding special cases and exceptions to the rules. It is the unique synergy of the two approaches that facilitates solving even seemingly distant and unrelated tasks.

At the moment, our immediate research plans include two paths of further system development. Firstly, we intend to further enhance feature generation system by including compound features, defined as differences or ratios of related simple features. Secondly, we are working on more sophisticated, CI-based methods of evaluation functions generation. In the immediate future, we consider employing co-evolutionary and/or Layered Learning [13] schemes, as well as replacing linear evaluation functions with artificial neural networks.

References

1. Auer, P., Cesa-Bianchi, N., Fischer, P.: Finite-time analysis of the multiarmed bandit problem. Machine Learning 47(2/3), 235–256 (2002)
2. Clune, J.: Heuristic evaluation functions for General Game Playing. In: Proceedings of the Twenty-Second AAAI Conference on Artificial Intelligence (AAAI 2007), Vancouver, BC, Canada, pp. 1134–1139. AAAI Press, Menlo Park (2007)
3. Finnsson, H., Björnsson, Y.: Simulation-based approach to General Game Playing. In: Proceedings of the Twenty-Third AAAI Conference on Artificial Intelligence (AAAI 2008), Chicago, IL, pp. 259–264. AAAI Press, Menlo Park (2008)
4. Gelly, S., Wang, Y.: Exploration exploitation in Go: UCT for Monte-Carlo Go. In: Neural Information Processsing Systems 2006 Workshop on On-line Trading of Exploration and Exploitation (2006)
5. Gelly, S., Wang, Y., Munos, R., Teytaud, O.: Modification of UCT with patterns on Monte Carlo Go. Technical Report 6062, INRIA (2006)
6. General Game Playing website by Stanford University, http://games.stanford.edu/
7. General Game Playing website by Dresden University of Technology, http://www.general-game-playing.de/
8. Genesereth, M., Love, N.: General Game Playing: Overview of the AAAI Competition (2005), http://games.stanford.edu/competition/misc/aaai.pdf
9. Kaiser, D.: The Design and Implementation of a Successful General Game Playing Agent. In: Proceedings of FLAIRS Conference, pp. 110–115 (2007)
10. Kuhlmann, G., Dresner, K., Stone, P.: Automatic heuristic construction in a complete General Game Player. In: Proceedings of the Twenty-First AAAI Conference on Artificial Intelligence (AAAI 2006), Boston, MA, pp. 1457–1462. AAAI Press, Menlo Park (2006)
11. Love, N., Hinrichs, T., Haley, D., Schkufza, E., Genesereth, M.: General Game Playing: Game Description Language Specification (2008), http://games.stanford.edu/language/spec/gdl_spec_2008_03.pdf
12. Mańdziuk, J.: Knowledge-Free and Learning-Based Methods in Intellligenet Game Playing. Studies in Computational Intelligence, vol. 276. Springer, Heidelberg (2010)
13. Mańdziuk, J., Kusiak, M., Wałędzik, K.: Evolutionary-based heuristic generators for checkers and give-away checkers. Expert Systems 24(4), 189–211 (2007)
14. Reisinger, J., Bahçeci, E., Karpov, I., Miikkulainen, R.: Coevolving strategies for general game playing. In: Proceedings of the IEEE Symposium on Computational Intelligence and Games (CIG 2007), Honolulu, Hawaii, pp. 320–327. IEEE Press, Los Alamitos (2007)
15. Schaeffer, J., Burch, N., Björnsson, Y., Kishimoto, A., Müller, M., Lake, R., Lu, P., Sutphen, S.: Checkers is solved. Science 317, 1518–1522 (2007)
16. Schiffel, S., Thielscher, M.: Automatic Construction of a Heuristic Search Function for General Game Playing. In: Seventh IJCAI International Workshop on Nonmonotonic Reasoning, Action and Change (NRAC 2007) (2007)

From Sensorimotor Graphs to Rules: An Agent Learns from a Stream of Experience

Marius Raab, Mark Wernsdorfer, Emanuel Kitzelmann, and Ute Schmid

[1] Cognitive Systems Group, University of Bamberg, Germany
{marius.raab,mark.wernsdorfer,ute.schmid}@uni-bamberg.de
http://www.uni-bamberg.de/kogsys
[2] International Computer Science Institute, Berkeley, USA
emanuel@icsi.berkeley.edu

Abstract. In this paper we argue that a philosophically and psychologically grounded autonomous agent is able to learn recursive rules from basic sensorimotor input. A sensorimotor graph of the agent's environment is generated that stores and optimises beneficial motor activations in evaluated sensor space by employing temporal Hebbian learning. This results in a categorized stream of experience that feeds in a MINERVA memory model which is enriched by a *time line* approach and integrated in the cognitive architecture PSI—including motivation and emotion. These memory traces feed seamlessly into the inductive rule acquisition device IGOR2 and the resulting recursive rules are made accessible in the same memory store. A combination of cognitive theories from the 1980ies and state-of-the-art computer science thus is a plausible approach to the still prevailing *symbol grounding problem*.

Keywords: symbol grounding, temporal Hebbian learning, cognitive architecture, inductive rule learning.

1 Introduction

"How can the semantic interpretation of a formal symbol system be made *intrinsic* to the system, rather than just parasitic on the meanings in our heads?" Since Harnad [7, p.335] has posed this question, the *symbol grounding problem* is an ongoing issue in AI. Progress has been made, but the problem is not solved [22].

We argue that *old-fashioned* cognitive theories from the 1980ies together with state-of-the-art learning systems allow for bridging the gap between symbolic and sub-symbolic approaches: a dichototmy that is present even in state-of-the-art architectures like CLARION [23]. Here, we meet with Langley et al. [13, p.155f] who urge for "more research on architectures that directly support both episodic memory and reflective processes that operate on these structures it contains."

In our view mental competencies evolve from a structural coupling to the world (outside and inside) [28]—in contrast to predefined competencies which cannot be said to depend on anything else than the architect's beliefs [7]. Not

J. Schmidhuber, K.R. Thórisson, and M. Looks (Eds.): AGI 2011, LNAI 6830, pp. 333–339, 2011.
© Springer-Verlag Berlin Heidelberg 2011

until mental representations are justified by referring to relevant and meaningful entities, abstract concepts can be inferred.

The generation of abstract concepts is an ultimate touchstone for a system. Here, abstract concepts are recursive, i.e. infinite, regularities. This goes beyond Anderson's [1] deductive and abductive rule-generation; as, for example, deduction always raises the question where the premises come from. It also goes beyond systems like CLIP [2] and CLARION [23,24]—these systems lack the ability to cope with recursive regularities—a concept like *odd/ even* is out of their scope.

In the following we present our approach to learn rules from streams of experience which is composed of three succeeding layers: In a first step (Sect. 2) a continuous sensorimotor space is segmented by constructing prototypes based on an evaluation function which balances exploitation and exploration. In a second step (Sect. 3) graphs containing these prototypes are enumerated along a time line, associated with the reward experience and transformed into simple symbolic rules. Finally (Sect. 4), regularities in these simple rules are detected and the rules are folded into a recursive rule set which generalizes over the previous experiences.

The overall system controls a virtual autonomous agent (AA) which moves in a *Discworld*. An even number of circles means that the agent receives reward at the innermost spot, an odd number evokes punishment. The AA has to avoid harmful targets and approach desirable ones. All necessary knowledge transformations in our agent are done syntactically, so no additional *meaning* is introduced on the way.

2 Learning Context-Sensitive Partitioning of Sensorimotor Space

The AA features a set of sensors and actors. In our simple *Discworld* scenario the sensors detect changes in brightness and the motors power a differential drive. Initially, the environment is explored by random walk and later guided by previous experience trying to repeat beneficious actions and avoid harmful ones. Experience is represented in sensorimotor vectors which are integrated in a graph.

The sensorimotor vectors define Voronoi cells and thereby generate a segmentation of the otherwise continuous sensorimotor space [27]. This characteristic is exploited for categorization, that is construction of abstract prototypes [25] representing collections of experiences. Each prototype holds the activation perceived and the evaluation received during its creation.

Temporally successive prototypes are connected to form a graph representing possible next states. This information can be used to predict possible outcomes of actions or perceptions. New experiences are evaluated with respect to their similarity to already existing prototypes.

By employing temporal Hebbian learning [19], the weighted edges between prototypes are reinforced if memorised sequences are confirmed by the environment.

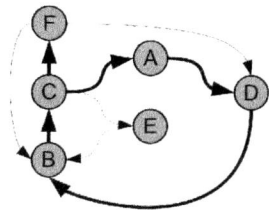

Fig. 1. Saturated motor graph

Alternative connections are inhibited by weakening all contradicting outgoing connections from the previous prototype and all contradicting incoming connections to the momentary prototype. Dropping below a critical threshold, connections are eventually removed from the graph. A mature sensorimotor graph (see Fig. 1), allows for anticipating (con-) sequences of arbitrary sensorimotor activations. By removing connections, the graph fragments into isolated components containing only a subset of sequential prototypes.

The activation vectors stored in prototypes are *exploited* by random optimization. The evaluation gradient dropping below zero is interpreted as indication for having reached a local maximum. Therefore, by performing a 1-nearest-neighbour query within the active graph, the algorithm tries to switch to the next best prototype representing the present sensorimotor activation. In case the present prototype is returned anew, the algorithm tries to *explore* new actions by creating a new prototype.

After a test run one graph component has been extracted. We visualised the graph in Fig. 1, where thicker edges representing stronger connections. A circular path within the motor graph indicates successful coping with the environment. Here this path of continuously reinforced edges is $C \rightarrow A \rightarrow D \rightarrow B \rightarrow C$. Once the graph components are mature and stable, switching between them can be regarded as changing situational context. These components are grounded representation that serve as entities for further processing. Their creation takes place as follows:

1. The agent learns *symbols* bearing *relevancy* and *meaning*.
2. Thereby the agent segments the sensorimotor space according to [15].
3. A *context* component emerges like: *line – line – line – reward* or *line – line – punishment*

3   Handling a Stream of Experience

Feeding these components into a psychologically valid model—by integrating the Psi-theory of Dietrich Dörner [6], and by utilizing the MINERVA memory model by Hintzman [9]—we are able to induce explicit rules and to feed these rules back into the agent's memory.

We chose the cognitive architecture PSI by Dörner ([6], see also [3]) as a framework. Dörner postulates a *protocol memory* as the only memory structure—i.e., a chain of perceptual input, motor actions and changes in motivational states. Perception, for example, is a constant matching of input against stored events, where missing or ambigious inputs are supplemented by stored fragments (schemata). But how exactly to build such a structure remains vague. A similiar idea of a single-store system was voiced by Klahr & Wallace ([11, p.366], refined in [26]). They assume the existence of "an ordered list representing the relative values as a result of the child's experience to date".

The MINERVA 2 framework by Hintzman [9] is in some aspects similiar: "[...] a vast collection of episodic memory traces, each of which is a record of an event or experience [...] MINERVA 2 represents an attempt to account for data from both episodic and generic memory tasks within a single system." (p.96) This contrasts, for example, with SOAR where episodic memory is a collection of *snapshots* of working memory, and where procedural and semantic memory are further compartments [12].

In MINERVA, *any* event will result in a new memory trace, no matter if a very similiar event has been experienced before or not. There is no chronological, overall time line any more; instead a huge set of seperate traces is built. Memory traces are configurations of primitive properties, like sensory features; simply modelled as vectors filled with *1*, *0* and *-1* values. Categories and abstract knowledge are built at the time of retrieval and not during encoding and storage. As Dougherty [5] has shown, MINERVA lends itself to extensions covering more complex aspects of reasoning. Motivational states sensu Dörner could easily be represented by additional vectors.

We propose a framework where information will be stored in a single system, in chronological order, with regularity detection as core learning mechanism. Nodes in this model are simple feature vectors. This combination merges a parsimonious yet potentially powerful cognitive-emotional-motivational approach with a simple yet powerful learning concept and a frugal, empirically founded memory model. We will show how an inductive learning approach fits in such a framework—and how it takes our system to the next level while at the same time staying *grounded*.

4   Learning Productive Rules

The sketched model will be the necessary prerequisite for integrating the inductive rule acquisition device IGOR2 [10]. This machine learning device has already been used successfully for classical cognitive tasks like the *Tower of Hanoi* [21]. In short, it is a means to construct recursive functional programs from a few non-recursive examples. However, so far this learning device was not embedded into a psychological model.

IGOR2 combines analytical recurrence detection with a guided search in program space. Programs are represented as *constructor systems*. As with every learning system, IGOR2 relies on some biases: Programs must be a valid subset of HASKELL, search space ist explored by preferring a minimal number of case distinctions, and the given input patterns must not unify pairwise. Furthermore, for a given induction problem the *first n examples* must be given.

Being part of a larger cognitive architecture, we deem this inductive device a valid cognitive approach. IGOR2 abstracts from given examples by generating a *least general generalisation*, partitions the problem space, treats sub-problems as new problems and uses previously learned rules. These are plausible cognitive mechanisms (see, e.g., [18])—and, in any case, much closer to human reasoning than, for example, generate-and-test learning devices. We used the inductive rule acquisition device IGOR2 [10] to learn knowledge-level production rules from basic sensorimotor data.

How to build rather complex input rules in HASKELL-compatible syntax without semantic assumptions; in other words, without instructions that are "parasitic to the system" in the sense of [7]? In a proof-of-concept-implementation (in JAVA), we did so using a cascade of mere syntactical transformations:

4. A bijective mapping on ASCII characters retains the distinction of context components, introduces no new information, and results in: $LLL \rightarrow TRUE$ or $LL \rightarrow FALSE$. We chose this kind of transformation, as an ASCII character can be seen as a 8-bit feature vector in the sense of MINERVA. By arbitrary combination of characters, the feature vector's length is unrestricted.

5. The resulting set of rules is fed into IGOR2

6. The output is a recursive rule:
   $learn[] = False; \quad learn['L'] = True; \quad learn('L' : ('L' : a0)) = learn\ a0$

7. Such a rule can easily and automatically be transformed into a grammar:
   $S \rightarrow X \quad\quad X \rightarrow 'L' \quad\quad X \rightarrow 'L''L'X$

8. Consecutively, standard algorithms (like in JFLAP [20]) might be used to syntactically transform this grammar into a nondeterministic finite automaton.

9. This automaton represents the recursive part of the regularity; and the nodes still hold the sensory information associated from the grounding process. When this fragment is connected to existing memory (here: the strict linked list is extended to hold several connections, resulting in a graph), it will be searchable by MINERVA probes, too.

5   Conclusion and Future Work

Right now no motivation and emotion is implemented. From a theoretical viewpoint, however, the agent is prepared. And planning, as described by Dörner, can take place. Also, there's no mechanism to remove rules from memory. This would be necessary before these rules would enter a planning module.

The agent presented bears potential that was not intended in the first place. The MINERVA representation, for example, lends itself to analogical reasoning. As 1 codes a necessary feature, -1 a prohibitive one, and 0 a 'don't care', cross-context learning would be a logical AND over two situations (i.e., vectors).

The presented system might behave strangely, irrational or superstitious. Newberg et al. [18] describe how cognition could be seen as the core of belief, myth and religion. Maybe, the AA proposed here has the potential to create such a form of *meaning* for itself, based on its own grounded symbols. Of course, like Winograd & Flores [28] note, this agent would not be human. Yet, it could be a bit more *like* a human.

References

1. Anderson, J.R.: How can the human mind occur in the physical universe? Oxford University Press, Oxford (2007)
2. Avila Garcez, A.S., Zaverucha, G.: The Connectionist Inductive Learning and Logic Programming System. Applied Intelligence 11, 59–77 (1999)
3. Bach, J.: Principles of Synthetic Intelligence: PSI: An Architecture of Motivated Cognition. Oxford University Press, Oxford (2009)
4. Butz, M.: Self-organizing sensorimotor graphs plus internal motivations yield animal-like behavior. Adaptive Behavior 18, 315 (2010)
5. Dougherty, M.R.P., Gettys, C.F., Ogden, E.E.: MINERVA-DM: A Memory Processes Model for Judgments of Likelihood. Psych. Review 106(1), 180–209 (1999)
6. Doerner, D.: Bauplan für eine Seele. Rowohlt, Reinbek (1999)
7. Harnad, S.: The Symbol Grounding Problem. Physica D 42, 335–346 (1990)
8. Heidegger, M.: Sein und Zeit. Niemeyer, Tübingen, 16th edn. (1986)
9. Hintzman, D.L.: MINERVA 2: A simulation model of human memory. Behavior Research Methods, Instruments & Computers 16(2), 96–101 (1984)
10. Kitzelmann, E.: A Combined Analytical and Search-Based Approach to the Inductive Synthesis of Functional Programs. PhD thesis, University of Bamberg (2010)
11. Klahr, D., Wallace, J.: An Information Processing Analysis of Some Piagetian Experimental Tasks. Cognitive Psychology 1, 358–387 (1970)
12. Laird, J.E.: Extending the Soar cognitive architecture. In: Proceedings of the Artificial General Intelligence Conference, Memphis, TN (2008)
13. Langley, P., Laird, J.E., Rogers, S.: Cognitive architectures: Research issues and challenges. Cognitive Sytems Research 10(2), 141–160 (2009)
14. Matyas, J.: Random Optimization. Automaton and Remote Control 26(2), 246–253 (1965)
15. Mayo, M.: Symbol grounding and its implications for artificial intelligence. In: Proceedings of the 26th Australasian Computer Science Conference, vol. 16, pp. 55–60. Australian Computer Society, Inc. (2003)
16. Mitchell, T.M.: Machine learning. McGraw-Hill, Boston (1997)
17. Nadel, L.: Distributed Representations. In: C. R. Encyclopedia of Cognitive Science. Nature publishing group, Macmillan (2003)
18. Newberg, A., d'Aquili, E., Rause, V.: Why God Won't Go Away: Brain Science and the Biology of Belief. Ballantine Books, NY (2002)
19. Porr, B., Wörgötter, F.: Temporal Hebbian learning in Rate-Coded Neural Networks: A theoretical approach towards classical conditioning. In: Dorffner, G., Bischof, H., Hornik, K. (eds.) ICANN 2001. LNCS, vol. 2130, pp. 1115–1120. Springer, Heidelberg (2001)
20. Rodger, S.H.: JFLAP. An interactive formal languages and automata package. Jones and Bartlett's, Sudbury (2006)

21. Schmid, U., Hofmann, M., Kitzelmann, E.: Analytical inductive programming as a cognitive rule acquisition devise. In: Proceedings of the Second Conference on Artificial General Intelligence, pp. 162–167. Atlantis Press, Amsterdam (2009)
22. Steels, L.: The Symbol Grounding Problem Has Been Solved. So What's Next? In: de Vega, M. (ed.) Symbols and Embodiment: Debates on Meaning and Cognition, ch. 12. Oxford University Press, Oxford (2008)
23. Sun, R.: The CLARION cognitive architecture: Extending cognitive modeling to social simulation. In: Sun, R. (ed.) Cognition and Multi-Agent Interaction. Cambridge University Press, New York (2006)
24. Sun, R.: The motivational and metacognitive control in CLARION. In: Gray, W.D. (ed.) Integ. Models of Cog. Systems. Oxford University Press, New York (2007)
25. Vanpaemel, W., Storms, G.: In search of abstraction: The varying abstraction model of categorization. Psychonomic Bulletin & Review 15(4), 732 (2008)
26. Wallace, J., Klahr, D., Bluff, K.: A Self-Modifying Production System Model of Cognitive Development. In: Klahr, D., Langley, P., Neches, R.T. (eds.) Prod. System Models of Learning and Development, pp. 359–435. MIT Press, Cambridhge (1987)
27. Watson, D.: Computing the n-dimensional Delaunay tessellation with application to Voronoi polytopes. The Computer Journal 24(2), 167 (1981)
28. Winograd, T., Flores, F.: Understanding Computers and Cognition. A New Foundation for Design. Ablex Corporation, Norwood (1986)

Three Hypotheses about the Geometry of Mind

Ben Goertzel[1] and Matthew Ikle[2]

[1] Novamente LLC, Rockville MD
[2] Adams State College, Alamosa CO

Abstract. We present a novel perspective on the nature of intelligence, motivated by the OpenCog AGI architecture, but intended to have a much broader scope. Memory items are modeled using probability distributions, and memory subsystems are conceived as "mindspaces" – geometric spaces corresponding to different memory categories. Two different metrics on mindspaces are considered: one based on algorithmic information theory, and another based on traditional (Fisher information based) "information geometry". Three hypotheses regarding the geometry of mind are then posited: 1) a *syntax-semantics correlation* principle, stating that in a successful AGI system, these two metrics should be roughly correlated; 2) a *cognitive geometrodynamics* principle, stating that on the whole intelligent minds tend to follow geodesics in mindspace; 3) a *cognitive synergy* principle, stating that shorter paths may be found through the composite mindspace formed by considering multiple memory types together, than by following the geodesics in the mindspaces corresponding to individual memory types.

1 Introduction

One of the many factors making AGI research difficult is the lack of a broadly useful, powerful, practical theoretical and mathematical framework. Many theoretical and mathematical tools have played important roles in the creation and analysis of contemporary proto-AGI systems; but by and large these have proved more useful for dealing with *parts* of AGI systems than for treating AGI systems holistically. And the general mathematical theory of AGI [6], though it has inspired some practical work [7] [12], has not yet been connected with complex AGI architectures in any nontrivial way. This paper gives a rough sketch of a novel theoretical framework intended to fill tis gap. While the framework has been developed largely in the context of a quest to understand and improve the dynamics of the OpenCog [5] AGI architecture (see [8] for some concrete OpenCog algorithmics directly related to the present ideas), it is intended to be much more broadly applicable.

For a more extensive presentation of these ideas, see http://goertzel.org/papers/MindGeometry_agi_11_v2.pdf. Two important background notions from that longer version are omitted here: 1) the ideas presented here are meant to be interpreted in terms of a general formal model of intelligent agents called SRAM (Simple Realistic Agents Model), presented in [4] and inspired by the

J. Schmidhuber, K.R. Thórisson, and M. Looks (Eds.): AGI 2011, LNAI 6830, pp. 340–345, 2011.

simpler agents model in [6]; 2) The multiple types of memory critical for general intelligence (declarative, procedural, episodic, attentional, intentional) may be modeled using category theory. The memory store corresponding to each memory type is a category, and then conversion from one memory type to another (e.g. declarative to procedural) is carried out using functors.

2   Metrics on Memory Spaces

We begin by explaining how to define geometric structures for cognitive space, via defining two metrics on the space of *memory store dynamic states*. Specifically, we define the dynamic state or *d-state* of a memory store (e.g. attentional, procedural, etc.) as the series of states of that memory store (as a whole) during a time-interval. Generally speaking, it is necessary to look at d-states rather than instantaneous memory states because sometimes memory systems may store information using dynamical patterns rather than fixed structures.

It's worth noting that, according to the metrics introduced here, the above-described mappings between memory types are topologically continuous, but involve considerable geometric distortion – so that e.g., two procedures that are nearby in the procedure-based mindspace, may be distant in the declarative-based mindspace. This observation will lead us to the notion of cognitive synergy.

Information Geometry on Memory Spaces. Our first approach involves viewing memory store d-states as probability distributions. A d-state spanning time interval (p, q) may be viewed as a mapping whose input is the state of the world and the other memory stores during a given interval of time (r, s), and whose output is the state of the memory itself during interval (t, u). Various relations between these endpoints may be utilized, achieving different definitions of the mapping e.g. $p = r = t, q = s = u$ (in which case the d-state and its input and output are contemporaneous) or else $p = r, q = s = t$ (in which case the output occurs after the simultaneous d-state and input), etc. In many cases this mapping will be stochastic. If one assumes that the input is an *approximation* of the state of the world and the other memory stores, then the mapping will nearly always be stochastic. So in this way, we may model the total contents of a given memory store at a certain point in time as a probability distribution. And the process of learning is then modeled as one of *coupled changes in multiple memory stores*, in such a way as to enable ongoingly improved achievement of system goals.

Having modeled memory store states as probability distributions, the problem of measuring distance between memory store states is reduced to the problem of measuring distance between probability distributions. But this problem has a well-known solution: the Fisher-Rao metric, which has been extended by Dabak [1] to handle nonparametric distributions. This metric is reviewed in the long version of this paper, together with the idea of bringing Fisher information together with imprecise and indefinite probabilities as discussed in [2]. For instance an indefinite probability takes the form $((L, U), k, b)$ and represents an envelope of probability distributions, whose means after k more observations lie in (L, U) with probability b. The Fisher-Rao metric between probability distributions is naturally extended to yield a metric between indefinite probability distributions.

Algorithmic Distance on Memory Spaces. A conceptually quite different way to measure the distance between two d-states, on the other hand, is using algorithmic information theory. Assuming a fixed Universal Turing Machine M, one may define $H(S_1, S_2)$ as the length of the shortest self-delimiting program which, given as input d-state S_1, produces as output d-state S_2. A metric is then obtained via setting $d(S_1, S_2) = (H(S_1, S_2) + H(S_2, S_1))/2$. This tells you the computational cost of transforming S_1 into S_2.

There are variations of this which may also be relevant; for instance [13] defines the generalized complexity criterion $K_\Phi(x) = min_{i \in N}\{\Phi(i, \tau_i)|L(p_i)) = x\}$, where L is a programming language, p_i is the i'th program executable by L under an enumeration in order of nonincreasing program length, τ_i is the execution time of the program p_i, $L(x)$ is the result of L executing p_i to obtain output x, and Φ is a function mapping pairs of integers into positive reals, representing the trade-off between program length and memory. Via modulating Φ, one may cause this complexity criterion to weight only program length (like standard algorithmic information theory), only runtime (like the speed prior), or to balance the two against each other in various ways.

Suppose one uses the generalized complexity criterion, but looking only at programs p_i that are given S_1 as input. Then $K_\Phi(S_2)$, relative to this list of programs, yields an asymmetric distance $H_\Phi(S_1, S_2)$, which may be symmetrized as above to yield $d_\Phi(S_1, S_2)$. This gives a more flexible measure of how hard it is to get to one of (S_1, S_2) from the other one, in terms of both memory and processing time.

One may discuss geodesics in this sort of algorithmic metric space, just as in Fisher-Rao space. A geodesic in algorithmic metric space has the property that, between any two points on the path, the *integral of the algorithmic complexity* incurred while following the path is less than or equal to that which would be incurred by following any other path between those two points. The algorithmic metric is not equivalent to the Fisher-Rao metric, a fact that is consistent with Cencov's Theorem because the algorithmic metric is not Riemannian (i.e. it is not locally approximated by a metric defined via any inner product).

3   Three Hypotheses about the Geometry of Mind

Now we present three hypotheses regarding generally intelligent systems, using the conceptual and mathematical machinery we have built.

Hypothesis 1: Syntax-Semantics Correlation. The informational and algorithmic metrics, as defined above, are not equivalent nor necessarily closely related; however, we hypothesize that on the whole, systems will operate more intelligently if the two metrics are well correlated, implying that geodesics in one space should generally be relatively short paths (even if not geodesics) in another.

This hypothesis is a more general version of the "syntax-semantics correlation" property studied in [10] in the context of automated program learning. There, it is shown empirically that program learning is more effective when programs with similar syntax also have similar behaviors. Here, we are suggesting that an intelligent system will be more effective if memory stores with similar structure and contents lead to similar effects (both externally to the agent, and on other memory systems). Hopefully the basic reason for this is clear. If syntax-semantics correlation holds, then learning based on the internal properties of the memory store, can help figure out things about the external effects of the memory store. On the other hand, if it doesn't hold, then it becomes quite difficult to figure out how to adjust the internals of the memory to achieve desired effects.

The assumption of syntax-semantics correlation has huge implications for the design of learning algorithms associated with memory stores. All of OpenCog's learning algorithms are built on this assumption. For, example OpenCog's MOSES procedure learning component [10] assumes syntax-semantics correlation for individual programs, from which it follows that the property holds also on the level of the whole declarative memory store. And OpenCog's PLN probabilistic inference component [2] uses an inference control mechanism that seeks to guide a new inference via analogy to prior similar inferences, thus embodying an assumption that structurally similar inferences will lead to similar behaviors (conclusions).

Hypothesis 2: Cognitive Geometrodynamics. In general relativity theory there is the notion of "geometrodynamics," referring to the feedback by which matter curves space, and then space determines the movement of matter (via the rule that matter moves along geodesics in curved spacetime) [11]. One may wonder whether an analogous feedback exists in cognitive geometry. We hypothesize that the answer is yes, to a limited extent. On the one hand, according to the above formalism, the curvature of mindspace is induced by the knowledge in the mind. On the other hand, one may view cognitive activity as approximately following geodesics in mindspace.

Let's say an intelligent system has the goal of producing knowledge meeting certain characteristics (and note that the desired achievement of a practical system objective may be framed in this way, as seeking the true knowledge that the objective has been achieved). The goal then corresponds to some set of d-states for some of the mind's memory stores. A simplified but meaningful view of cognitive dynamics is, then, that the system seeks the shortest path from the current d-state to the region in d-state space comprising goal d-states. For instance, considering the algorithmic metric, this reduces to the statement that at each time point, the system seeks to move itself along a path toward its goal, in a manner that requires the minimum computational cost – i.e. along some algorithmic geodesic. And if there is syntax-semantics correlation, then this movement is also approximately along a Fisher-Rao geodesic.

And as the system progresses from its current state toward its goal-state, it is creating new memories – which then curve mindspace, possibly changing it substantially from the shape it had before the system started moving toward its goal. This is a feedback conceptually analogous to, though in detail very different from, general-relativistic geometrodynamics.

There is some subtlety here related to fuzziness. A system's goals may be achievable to various degrees, so that the goal region may be better modeled as a fuzzy set of lists of regions. Also, the system's current state may be better viewed as a fuzzy set than as a crisp set. In this case, one may say that the cognition seeks a geodesic from a high-degree portion of the current-state region to a high-degree portion of the goal region.

Hypothesis 3: Cognitive Synergy. Cognitive synergy is a conceptual explanation of what makes it possible for certain sorts of integrative, multi-component cognitive systems to achieve powerful general intelligence [3]. The notion pertains to systems that possess knowledge creation (i.e. pattern recognition / formation / learning) mechanisms corresponding to each multiple memory types. For such a system to display cognitive synergy, each of these cognitive processes must have the capability to recognize when it lacks the information to perform effectively on its own; and in this case, to dynamically and interactively draw information from knowledge creation mechanisms dealing with other types of knowledge. Further, this cross-mechanism interaction must have the result of enabling the knowledge creation mechanisms to perform much more effectively in combination than they would if operated non-interactively.

How does cognitive synergy manifest itself in the geometric perspective we've sketched here? Perhaps the most straightforward way to explore it is to construct a composite metric, merging together the individual metrics associated with specific memory spaces.

In general, given N metrics $d_k(x, z), k = 1 \ldots N$ defined on the same finite space M, we can define the "min-combination" metric $d_{d_1, \ldots, d_N}(x, z) = min_{y_0 = x, y_{n+1} = z, y_i \in M, r(i) \in \{1, \ldots, N\}, i \in \{1, \ldots, n\}, n \in \mathbb{Z}} \sum_{i=0}^{n} d_{r(i)}(y_i, y_{i+1})$, which is conceptually similar to (and mathematically generalizes) min-cost metrics like the Levenshtein distance used to compare strings [9]. To see that it obeys the metric axioms is straightforward; the triangle inequality follows similarly to the case of the Levenshtein metric. In the case where M is infinite, one replaces *min* with *inf* (the infimum) and things proceed similarly. The min-combination distance from x to z tells you the length of the shortest path from x to z, using the understanding that for each portion of the path, one can choose any one of the metrics being combined. Here we are concerned with cases such as $d_{syn} = d_{d_{Proc}, d_{Dec}, d_{Ep}, d_{Att}}$.

We can now articulate a geometric version of the principle of cognitive synergy. Basically: cognitive synergy occurs when the synergetic metric yields significantly shorter distances between relevant states and goals than any of the memory-type-specific metrics. Formally, one may say that an intelligent agent A (modeled by SRAM) displays **cognitive synergy** to the extent $syn(A) \equiv \int (d_{synergetic}(x, z) - min(d_{Proc}(x, z), d_{Dec}(x, z), d_{Ep}(x, z), d_{Att}(x, z))) \, d\mu(x) d\mu(z)$ where μ measures the relevance of a state to the system's goal-achieving activity.

References

1. Dabak, A.: A Geometry for Detection Theory. PhD Thesis, Rice U. (1999)
2. Goertzel, B., Iklé, M., Goertzel, I., Heljakka, A.: Probabilistic Logic Networks. Springer, Heidelberg (2008)
3. Goertzel, B.: Cognitive synergy: A universal principle of feasible general intelligence? (2009)
4. Goertzel, B.: Toward a formal definition of real-world general intelligence (2010)
5. Goertzel, B., et al.: Opencogbot: An integrative architecture for embodied agi. In: Proc. of ICAI 2010, Beijing (2010)
6. Hutter, M.: Universal AI. Springer, Heidelberg (2005)
7. Hutter, M.: Feature dynamic bayesian networks. In: Proc. of the Second Conf. on AGI. Atlantis Press (2009)
8. Ikle, M., Goertzel, B.: Nonlinear-dynamical attention allocation via information geometry. In: Schmidhuber, J., Thorisson, K., Looks, M. (eds.) AGI 2011. LNCS(LNAI), vol. 6830, pp. 62–71. Springer, Heidelberg (2011)
9. Levenshtein, V.: Binary codes capable of correcting deletions, insertions, and reversals. Soviet Physics Doklady 10, 707–710 (1966)
10. Looks, M.: Competent Program Evolution. PhD Thesis, Computer Science Department, Washington University (2006)
11. Misner, C., Thorne, K., Wheeler, J.: Gravitation. Freeman, New York (1973)
12. Schaul, T., Schmidhuber, J.: Towards practical universal search. In: Proc. of the 3rd Conf. on AGI. Atlantis Press (2010)
13. Yi, S., Glasmachers, T., Schaul, T., Schmidhuber, J.: Frontier search. In: Proc. of the 3rd Conf. on AGI. Atlantis Press (2010)

Imprecise Probability as a Linking Mechanism between Deep Learning, Symbolic Cognition and Local Feature Detection in Vision Processing

Ben Goertzel

Novamente LLC

Abstract. A novel approach to computer vision is outlined, involving the use of imprecise probabilities to connect a deep learning based hierarchical vision system with both local feature detection based preprocessing and symbolic cognition based guidance. The core notion is to cause the deep learning vision system to utilize imprecise rather than single-point probabilities, and use local feature detection and symbolic cognition to affect the confidence associated with particular imprecise probabilities, thus modulating the amount of credence the deep learning system places on various observations and guiding its pattern recognition/formation activity. The potential application to the hybridization of the DeSTIN, SIFT and OpenCog systems is described in moderate detail. The underlying ideas are even more broadly applicable, to any computer vision approach with a significant probabilistic component which satisfies certain broad criteria.

1 Introduction

One key aspect of vision processing is the ability to preferentially focus attention on certain positions within a perceived visual scene. Another key aspect is the ability for abstract, symbolic cognition, based on various forms of long-term memory, to module visual perception. In principle, these two aspects of vision can be incorporated within a deep learning based vision architecture such as HTM [6],[3] or DeSTIN [1]. In current practice, however, neither of these aspects is a strength of deep learning vision systems. So from the perspective of an integrative approach to AGI, it is interesting to explore the hybridization of deep learning vision systems with other approaches, such as for local feature detectors like SIFT [7], and general cognitive engines like OpenCog [5]. Such hybridization may be carried out in many different ways; here we suggest a novel approach based on imprecise probabilities, which applies to deep learning based vision systems that are probabilistic in their foundations.

The basic idea suggested here applies to any probabilistic sensory system, whether deep-learning-based or not, and whether oriented toward vision or some other sensory modality. However, for sake of concreteness, we will focus here on the case of deep learning and vision. Note that a longer version of this paper, giving a bit more background, is available online at http://goertzel.org/VisualAttention_AGI_11.pdf.

J. Schmidhuber, K.R. Thórisson, and M. Looks (Eds.): AGI 2011, LNAI 6830, pp. 346–350, 2011.
© Springer-Verlag Berlin Heidelberg 2011

1.1   Visual Attention Focusing

Since visual input streams contain vast amounts of data, it's beneficial for a vision system to be able to focus its attention specifically on the most important parts of its input. Sometimes knowledge of what's important will come from cognition and long-term memory, but sometimes it may come from mathematical heuristics applied to the visual data itself.

In the human visual system the latter kind of "low level attention focusing" is achieved largely in the context of the eye changing its focus frequently, looking preferentially at certain positions in the scene [2]. This works because the center of the eye corresponds to a greater density of neurons than the periphery.

So for example, consider a computer vision algorithm like SIFT (Scale-Invariant Feature Extraction) [7], which mathematically isolates certain points in a visual scene as keypoints which are particularly important for identifying what the scene depicts (e.g. these may be corners, or easily identifiable curves in edges). The human eye, when looking at a scene, would probably spend a greater percentage of its time focusing on the SIFT keypoints than on random points in the image.

The human visual system's strategy for low-level attention focusing is obviously workable (at least in contexts similar to those in which the human eye evolved), but its also somewhat complex, requiring the use of subtle temporal processing to interpret even static scenes. We suggest here that there may be a simpler way to achieve the same thing, in the context of vision systems that are substantially probabilistic in nature, via using imprecise probabilities. The crux of the idea is to represent the most important data, e.g. keypoints, using imprecise probability values with greater confidence.

Similarly, cognition-guided visual attention-focusing occurs when a mind's broader knowledge of the world tells it that certain parts of the visual input may be more interesting to study than others. For example, in a picture of a person walking down a dark street, the contours of the person may not be tremendously striking visually (according to SIFT or similar approaches); but even so, if the system as a whole knows that it's looking at a person, it may decide to focus extra visual attention on anything person-like. This sort of cognition guided visual attention focusing, we suggest, may be achieved similarly to visual attention focusing guided on lower-level cues – by increasing the confidence of the imprecise probabilities associated with those aspects of the input that are judged more cognitively significant.

1.2   Imprecise Probabilities

Finally, what precisely are these "imprecise probabilities" that keep getting mentioned? Broadly speaking an "imprecise probability" is a representation of probability that uses more than one number, and that tries to represent the "uncertainty associated with a certain probability estimate." For instance, one may be very sure that a certain probability is 50%, or one may be only moderately sure that it's 50%, figuring it might actually be 80% or 20% and one will only know more certainly one gathers more data. Common forms include (L,U) intervals as introduced by Peter Walley [4], representing lower and upper bounds on the means of probabilities in an envelope; or PLN-style [4] indefinite probabilities of the form ((L,U), b , k), with the interpretation that after k more observations are made, the odds are b that the mean of the estimated distribution describing the event in question will lie in the interval (L,U).

We will speak here in terms of the confidence of an imprecise probability; e.g. in the case of Walley probabilities, one can simply use the negation interval width, i.e. $c = 1 - (U - L)$, as a confidence value. We will also assume here that there is a method for taking any calculation done using ordinary single-number probabilities as inputs and outputs, and transforming it into a calculation to be done using imprecise probabilities as inputs and outputs. Straightforward methods of this nature exist for both Walley-style and indefinite probabilities, for example.

2   Using Imprecise Probabilities to Guide Vision Processing

Suppose one has a vision system that internally constructs probabilistic values corresponding to small local regions in visual input (these could be pixels or voxels, or something a little larger), and then (perhaps via a complex process) assigns probabilities to different interpretations of the input based on combinations of these input-level probabilities. For this sort of vision system, one may be able to achieve focusing of attention via appropriately replacing the probabilities with imprecise probabilities. Such an approach may be especially interesting in hierarchical vision systems, that also involve the calculation of probabilities corresponding to larger regions of the visual input. Examples of the latter include deep learning based vision systems like HTM or DeSTIN, which construct nested hierarchies corresponding to larger and larger regions of the input space, and calculate probabilities associated with each of the regions on each level, based in part on the probabilities associated with other related regions.

In this context, we now state the basic suggestion of the paper:

1. Assign higher confidence to the low-level probabilities that the vision system creates corresponding to the local visual regions that one wants to focus attention on (based on cues from visual preprocessing or cognitive guidance)
2. Carry out the vision system's processing using imprecise probabilities rather than single-number probabilities
3. Wherever the vision system makes a decision based on the most probable choice from a number of possibilities, change the system to make a decision based on the choice maximizing the product (expectation * confidence).

Sketch of Application to DeSTIN An example of a vision system to which this approach could be applied is Itamar Arels DeSTIN system [1]. Internally to DeSTIN, probabilities are assigned to pixels or other small local regions (according to equations to be detailed below). If a system such as SIFT is run as a preprocessor to DeSTIN, then those pixels or small regions corresponding to SIFT keypoints may be assumed semantically meaningful, and internal DeSTIN probabilities associated with them can be given a high confidence. A similar strategy may be taken if a cognitive system such as OpenCog [5] is run together with DeSTIN, feeding DeSTIN information on which portions of a partially-processed image appear most cognitively relevant. The probabilistic calculations inside DeSTIN can be replaced with corresponding calculations involving imprecise probabilities. And critically, there is a step in DeSTIN where, among a set of beliefs about the state in each region of an image (on each of a set of hierarchical levels), the one with the highest probability is selected. In accordance with the above recipe, this step should be modified to select the belief with the highest probability*confidence.

Given the outline of DeSTIN given in [1] (and in the longer, online version of this paper), the application of imprecise probability based attention focusing to DeSTIN is almost immediate. The probabilities $P(o|s)$ defined therein may be assigned greater or lesser confidence depending on the assessed semantic criticality of the observation o in question. So for instance, if one is using SIFT as a preprocessor to DeSTIN, then one may assign probabilities $P(o|s)$ higher confidence if they correspond to observations o of SIFT keypoints, than if they do not. These confidence levels may then be propagated throughout DeSTIN's probabilistic mathematics. For instance, if one were using Walley's interval probabilities, then one could carry out the probabilistic equations using interval arithmetic. Finally, one wishes to replace DeSTIN's seelction equation with $c = \arg\max_s ((b_p(s)).\text{strength} * (b_p(s)).\text{confidence})$. The effect of this is that hypotheses based on high-confidence observations are more likely to be chosen, which of course has a large impact on the dynamics of the DeSTIN network.

3   Conceptual Justification

What is the conceptual justification for the approach presented? One justification is obtained by assuming that each percept has a certain probability of being erroneous, and those percepts that appear to more closely embody the semantic meaning of the visual scene are less likely to be erroneous. This follows conceptually from the assumption that the perceived world tends to be patterned and structured, so that being part of a statistically significant pattern is (perhaps weak) evidence of being real rather than artifactual. Under this assumption, the proposed approach will maximize the accuracy of the systems judgments.

A related justification is obtained by via consideration of the perceived world as mutable. Consider a vision system that has the capability to modify even the low-level percepts that it intakes i.e. to use what it thinks and knows, to modify what it sees. The human brain certainly has this potential [2]. In this case, it will make sense for the system to place some constraints regarding which of its percepts it is more likely to modify. Confidence values semantically embody this   a higher confidence being sensibly assigned to percepts that the system considers should be less likely to be modified based on feedback from its higher (more cognitive) processing levels. In that case, a higher confidence should be given to those percepts that seem to more closely embody the semantic meaning of the visual scene which is exactly what we're suggesting here.

References

1. Arel, I., Rose, D., Coop, R.: Destin: A scalable deep learning architecture with application to high-dimensional robust pattern recognition. In: Proc. AAAI Workshop on Biologically Inspired Cognitive Architectures (2009)
2. Changizi, M.: The Vision Revolution. BenBella Books (2009)
3. George, D., Hawkins, J.: Towards a mathematical theory of cortical micro-circuits. PLoS Comput. Biol. 5 (2009)
4. Goertzel, B., Iklé. M., Goertzel, I., Heljakka, A.: Probabilistic Logic Networks. Springer, Heidelberg (2008)
5. Goertzel, B.: Opencog prime: A cognitive synergy based architecture for embodied artificial general intelligence. In: ICCI 2009, Hong Kong (2009)
6. Hawkins, J., Blakeslee, S.: On Intelligence. Times (2004)
7. Lowe, D.: Object recognition from local scale-invariant features. In: Proc. of the International Conf. on Computer Vision, pp. 1150–1157 (1999)

Generalization of Figure-Ground Segmentation from Binocular to Monocular Vision in an Embodied Biological Brain Model*

Brian Mingus, Trent Kriete, Seth Herd, Dean Wyatte,
Kenneth Latimer, and Randy O'Reilly

Computational Cognitive Neuroscience Lab
Department of Psychology
University of Colorado at Boulder
Muenzinger D244, 345 UCB
Boulder, Co, 80309, USA
{brian.mingus,trent.kriete,seth.herd,dean.wyatte,
kenneth.latimer,randy.oreilly}@colorado.edu
http://grey.colorado.edu/ccnlab

Abstract. Monocular figure-ground segmentation is an important problem in the field of Artificial General Intelligence. A solution to this problem will unlock vast sets of training data, such as Google Images, in which salient objects of interest are situated against complex backgrounds. In order to gain traction on the figure-ground problem we enhanced the Leabra Vision (LVis) model, which is our state-of-the-art model of 3D invariant object recognition [8], such that it can continue to recognize objects against cluttered backgrounds that, while simple, are complex enough to substantially hurt object recognition performance. The principle of operation of the network is that it learns to use a low resolution view of the scene in which high spatial frequency information such as the background falls out of focus in order to predict which aspects of the high resolution scene are the figure. This filtered view then serves to enhance the figure in the input stages of LVis and substantially improves object recognition performance against cluttered backgrounds.

Keywords: figure-ground, neural network, object recognition.

1 Introduction

When we look at a photograph the objects jump out into three dimensional life. This is surprising since each eye conveys the same image of the photograph with

---

* Supported by the Intelligence Advanced Research Projects Activity (IARPA) via the U.S. Army Research Office contract number W911NF-10-C-0064. The U.S. Government is authorized to reproduce and distribute reprints for Governmental purposes notwithstanding any copyright annotation thereon. Disclaimer: The views and conclusions contained herein are those of the authors and should not be interpreted as necessarily representing the official policies or endorsements, either expressed or implied, of IARPA, the U.S. Army Research Office, or the U.S. Government.

J. Schmidhuber, K.R. Thórisson, and M. Looks (Eds.): AGI 2011, LNAI 6830, pp. 351–356, 2011.
© Springer-Verlag Berlin Heidelberg 2011

no useful disparity signals. One can demonstrate this to themselves by looking at a photograph with one eye closed and noting the rich perception of depth. So too is our depth perception intact when we perceive the world more generally with only one eye open. In normal binocular viewing conditions the disparity between objects in the two eyes helps us to compute their depth, but it is rather remarkable that we can continue to do this in lieu of this cue.

An idealized method of training a neural network to solve the monocluar figure-ground segmentation problem follows from its description. There are two input layers representing the V1 neurons for the left eye and right eye, respectively. These map onto a layer which computes focal disparity, that is, the zero-disparity region of foveation. During training the information from one eye is removed and the network is asked to predict the depth map of the scene. After making a guess based on monocular cues, the the other eye is returned and the weights are changed based on the difference between the predicted depth map and the actual depth map. While such a simple network only provides marginal figure-ground segmentation ability, it clearly demonstrates the point that we hope to make with Emer: that rich 3D signals can serve as a training signal for figure-ground segmentation with 2D cues.

2   Materials and Methods

Experiments were conducted using the emergent Neural Network Simulation System [1]. The Leabra neural network architecture and learning rule was used for all simulations [7].

2.1   CU3D-100 Dataset

To test the sufficiency of our model on a realistic, challenging version of the object recognition problem, we used our dataset of nearly 1,000 3D object models from the Google SketchUp warehouse (the *CU3D-100* dataset [5]) organized into 100 categories with an average of 9.42 exemplars per category (Fig. 2a-d). Two exemplars per category were reserved for testing, and the rest were used for training. Objects were rendered to 20 bitmap images per object with random $\pm 20°$ depth rotations (including a random $180°$ left-right flip for objects that are asymmetric along this dimension) and overhead lighting positioned uniformly randomly along an $80°$ overhead arc. These images were then presented to the model with planar (2D) transformations of 30% translation, 20% size scaling, and $14°$ in-plane rotations. The CU3D-100 dataset avoids the significant problems with other widely-used benchmarks such as the Caltech101 [9], by ensuring that recognition is truly robust to significant amounts of invariance, and the 3D rendering approach provides full parameterization over problem difficulty.

2.2   Structure of the Models

The LVis model [8] (Fig. 3) preprocessed bitmap images via two stages of mathematical filtering that capture the qualitative processing thought to occur in the

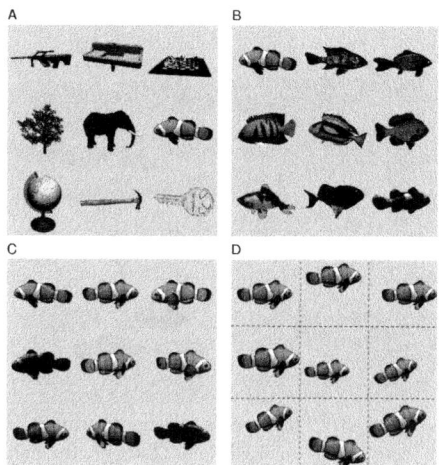

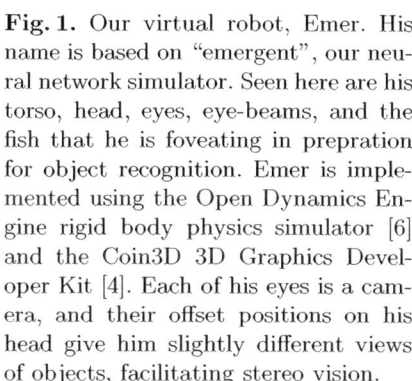

Fig. 1. Our virtual robot, Emer. His name is based on "emergent", our neural network simulator. Seen here are his torso, head, eyes, eye-beams, and the fish that he is foveating in prepration for object recognition. Emer is implemented using the Open Dynamics Engine rigid body physics simulator [6] and the Coin3D 3D Graphics Developer Kit [4]. Each of his eyes is a camera, and their offset positions on his head give him slightly different views of objects, facilitating stereo vision.

Fig. 2. The CU3D-100 dataset. **a)** 9 example objects from the 100 CU3D categories. **b)** Each category is further composed of multiple, diverse exemplars (average of 9.42 exemplars per category). **c)** Each exemplar is rendered with 3D (depth) rotations and variability in lighting. **d)** The 2D images are subject to 2D transformations (translation, scale, planar rotation), with ranges generally around 20%.

mammalian visual pathways from retina to LGN (lateral geniculate nucleus of the thalamus) to primary visual cortex (V1). The output of this filtering provided the input to the Leabra network, which then learned over a sequence of layers to categorize the inputs according to object categories.

The figure-ground model (Fig. 4) consists of - from the left column to the right column - V1, V1C end-stop cells [13] and figure layers. The figure layers correspond to the zero-disparity region of foveation. The network is connected in a feed-forward fashion from left to right, with high, medium and low spatial resolutions arranged from front to back. The figure layers are all bidirectionally connected, including recurrent connections. The goal of the network is to look at a figure against a background at all three resolutions and ultimately produce just the figure in the high resolution figure layer. This output representation is then used as input to the LVis object recognition model.

The middle column of layers in the figure-ground network correspond to end-stop cells which are useful for detecting T-junctions and contours in the image. These are good cues as to what separates figure from ground [13]. The role

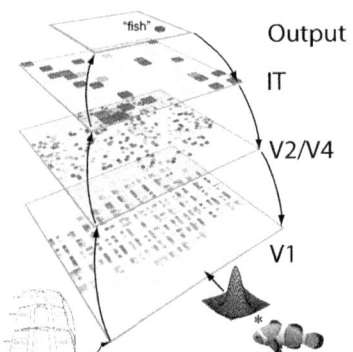

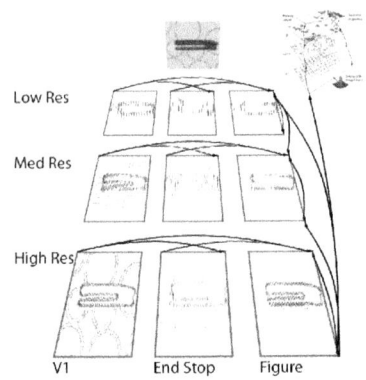

Fig. 3. The architecture of the LVis model [8]. LVis is based on the anatomy of the ventral pathway of the brain, from primary visual cortex (V1) through extrastriate areas (V2, V4) to inferotemporal (IT) cortex. V1 reflects filters that model the response properties of V1 neurons (both simple and complex subtypes). In higher levels, receptive fields become more spatially invariant and complex. All layers are bidirectionally connected, allowing higher-level information to influence bottom-up processing.

Fig. 4. The figure-ground segmentation model. There are three sets of layers at three interacting spatial resolutions. The first set corresponds to V1, the second set to V1C end-stop cells [13], and the third set learns to extract the figure from the background. The network is connected in a feedforward fashion from left to right and the figure-ground layers have both recurrent and bidirectional connectivity. The network learns to combine information from high and low-resolution V1 layers in order to predict the figure in the high-resolution figure layer.

of multiple interacting spatial resolutions follows clearly from the left-most V1 column in Fig. 4. At coarse spatial resolution the background falls out almost completely at the expense of losing much of the high-frequency spatial detail of the object. At high resolution the spatial detail of the object is preserved, but so too is the background. The principle of operation of the network is to learn to take advantage of these competing constraints.

3   Results and Discussion

All of the conditions in Fig. 5 have the same basic task, which is invariant object recognition on the CU3D-100 dataset. The model is trained on approximately eight exemplars per category and then generalization performance is tested on the remaining two objects from each category. Generalization performance is computed as the number of errors divided by 200.

The performance of the learned monocular figure-ground segmentation model is compared to several other conditions in Fig. 5. The key comparison conditions

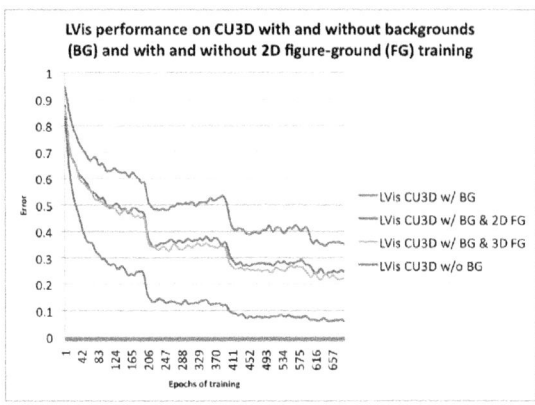

Fig. 5. Generalization performance of LVis in four object recognition conditions. **w/ BG:** With backgrounds and without figure-ground training error asymptotes at 35.3%. **w/ BG & 2D FG:** With backgrounds and with the learning figure-ground front-end intact performance asymptotes at 24.7% error. **w/ BG & 3D FG:** With backgrounds and using the target depth map as input into LVis (i.e., no 3D to 2D generalization - this is the best possible case for the previous condition) performance asymptotes at 22.2% error. **w/o BG:** Without backgrounds using just the standard LVis model performance asymptotes at 6% error.

are standard LVis with no backgrounds, LVis with backgrounds and without figure-ground segmentation and LVis with the best 3D figure-ground segmentation that our disparity matching system can compute.

The main condition being tested is object recognition against a background (such as the background seen in the picture in Fig. 4) with the learned monocular figure-ground segmentation model in place. To demonstrate that this is a hard problem, note that the difference in performance between LVis with and without backgrounds (and without figure-ground segmentation) is 29.2% error, which is a dramatic decrease in performance. The other key comparison is between the model that uses the computed disparity signal (and thus does not need to generalize from 3D to 2D) versus the learned monocular figure-ground segmentation model. The monocular model has only 2.4% more error, a relatively slight difference.

In conclusion, we chose to start with relatively simple backgrounds that nonetheless resulted in a dramatic detriment to performance in object recognition. The monocular figure-ground segmentation system had only 2.4% more error than it possibly could have, demonstrating that the model does indeed learn how to segment figure from ground. The results demonstrate the utility of using multiple interaction spatial resolutions, and are an important step on our way to using more realistic datasets such as Google Images.

References

1. Aisa, B., Mingus, B., O'Reilly, R.: The emergent neural modeling system. Neural Networks, 1045–1212 (2008)
2. Caltech101, http://www.vision.caltech.edu/Image_Datasets/Caltech101/
3. Computational Cognitive Neuroscience Lab, http://grey.colorado.edu/ccnlab
4. Coin3D 3D Graphics Engine Developer Kit, http://www.coin3d.org/
5. CU3D dataset, http://grey.colorado.edu/CompCogNeuro/index.php/CU3D
6. Open Dynamics Engine, http://www.ode.org/
7. O'Reilly, R.: The Leabra Model of Neural Interactions and Learning in the Neocortex. PhD Thesis (1996)
8. O'Reilly, R., Wyatte, D., Herd, S., Mingus, B., Jilk, D.: Bidirectional Biologically Plausible Object Recognition (2011) (in Press)
9. Pinto, N., Cox, D., DiCarlo, J.: Why is real-world object recognition hard? PLoS Computational Biology (2008)
10. Troscianko, T., Montagnon, R., Le Clerc, J., Malbert, E., Chanteau, P.: The role of colour as a monocular depth cue. Vision Research, 1923–1929 (1991)
11. Wheatstone, C.: Contributions to the physiology of vision.–Part the First. On some remarkable, and hitherto unobserved, phenomena of binocular vision. Philosophical Magazine Series 4 (1852)
12. Walk, D.: The Development of Depth Perception in Animals and Human Infants. Concept of Development: A Report of a Conference Commemorating the Fortieth Anniversary of the Institute of Child Development (1966)
13. Yazdanbakhsh, A., Livingstone, M.: End stopping in V1 is sensitive to contrast. Nature Neuroscience (2006)

The Illusion of Internal Joy

Claude Touzet

Adaptive and Integrative Neurosciences Lab, University of Provence
13331 Marseille, France
claude.touzet@univ-provence.fr

Abstract. J. Schmidhuber proposes a "*theory of fun & intrinsic motivation & creativity*" that he has developed over the last two decades. This theory is precise enough to allow the programming of artificial agents exhibiting the requested behaviors. Schmidhuber's theory relies on an explicit '*internal joy drive*' implemented by an '*information compression indicator*'. In this paper, we show that this indicator is not necessary as soon as the '*brain*' implementation involves associative memories, *i.e.*, hierarchical cortical maps. The '*compression factor*' is replaced by the '*smallest common activation pattern*' in our framework, with the advantage of an immediate and plausible neural implementation. Our conclusion states that the '*internal joy*' is an illusion. This remind us of the eliminative materialism position which claims that '*free-will*' is also an illusion.

Keywords: theory of neural cognition, internal joy drive, motivation, consciousness, cortical maps, unsupervised learning, associative memories.

1 Introduction

J. Schmidhuber build his "*theory of fun & intrinsic motivation & creativity*" [1] on the maximization of an '*internal joy*' that drives a reinforcement learning process. He proposes an operational description of it, a necessary step in order to provide an artifact with fun, motivation and creativity. The intrinsic reward is computed as the compression progress expressed as the number of saved bits [2]. A number of systems have been build following this recommendation, which exhibit the desired creativity behavior [3].

We have to be aware that, as soon as something such as '*intrinsic motivation*' is defined, reinforcement learning becomes *de facto* the unique valid candidate for the learning process. Reinforcement learning is certainly a very efficient way to acquire behaviors [4,5], but it is not the only one. Supervised learning and self-organization do exist. They are not considered as valid candidates for the learning of '*creativity*' behaviors because:

- in the case of supervised learning, its '*supervision*' would limit the freedom that we think is necessarily involved by '*creativity*',
- in the case of self-organization, its (self-)'*organization*' only allows to represent the data, and therefore (again) lacks the ability or freedom involved in '*creativity*'.

J. Schmidhuber, K.R. Thórisson, and M. Looks (Eds.): AGI 2011, LNAI 6830, pp. 357–362, 2011.
© Springer-Verlag Berlin Heidelberg 2011

Both opinions are misplaced. There is no link between the learning process and the ability to escape the learned knowledge. *'Generalization'* is the ability to process correctly new unknown inputs (following the 'rules' extracted from previously learned knowledge). The generalization quality depends only on the learning samples (not the learning process) AND the implementation.

It is our goal to show here that the *'generalization'* associated to a hierarchical cortical maps implementation is able to create any behavior involving *'intrinsic motivation'*. If successful, our demonstration will also state that any learning (not only reinforcement learning) may contribute to *'creativity'* behaviors, and that *'intrinsic motivation'*, also referred sometimes as *'internal joy'*, is an illusion.

2   Cortex Organization

The cortex is a hierarchy of cortical maps, each cortical map acting as a self-organizing associative memory that preserves the topology and distribution of the input data [6]. Each cortical map acts as a novelty filter, and stops any known situation (or part of situation). Only new unknown situation (or part of it) is allowed to proceed along the hierarchy towards maps of higher level of abstraction (Fig. 1). Behaviors are automatically generated through the cooperation of pairs of cortical maps.

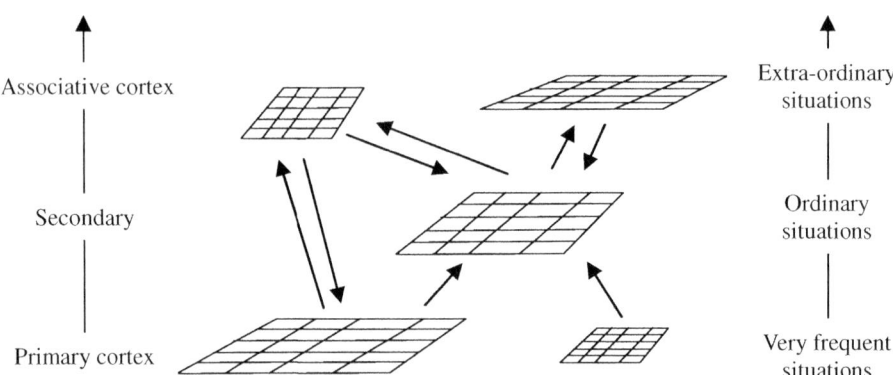

Fig. 1. The cortex is organized as a hierarchy of cortical maps, from the primary cortex receiving sensory inputs, to the secondary cortex allowing for inputs fusion, to the associative cortex where map encoding is sensory modality independent. The cortical maps are novelty filters: as the information progresses in the hierarchy, it is stopped as soon as it is recognized. only uncommon (extra-ordinary) situations (for a given individual) reach the *'abstract'* levels that account for the *'goals'*.

2.1   Behaviors are Goal-Directed

A behavior is a sequence of actions that can be related to the same goal. The goal is a specific situation, which will end the behavior as soon as it is reached, after what a new behavior starts (with a new goal). During a given behavior, each action is chosen in order to reduce the distance between the present situation and the goal-situation.

Within our framework, a situation is not a x-y-z vector coding for a given location in the real world, but a vector in the cortical maps space. The cortex is build of several hundreds cortical maps, each one devoted to a specific category of information. The cortical maps pattern of activations at any given time is representative of the input (*i.e.*, experienced) situation combined with the memorized lifelong experience encoded in the synapses. A goal (situation) is therefore a multidimensional vector sharing similarities with the experienced situation.

2.2 Coordination of Pairs of Cortical Maps

The work described in [7] explains how two associative memories (cortical maps) cooperate in order to produce goal-directed behaviors (Fig. 2). To resume (on map 1), a cluster of activity - labeled '*goal*' - is defined by some external (or internal) inputs. On the same map, the experienced current situation is represented by the fact that it activates a particular cluster of cortical columns. If there is a difference between both activities, then both activities (experienced situation and goal) will help activate cortical columns neighbors of the experienced situation. These neighbors columns encode for a situation that is close, but nevertheless different, from the current one. The difference between the two (neighbor) activities selects cortical columns on associated cortical maps (map 2). These cortical columns have memorized the actions associated to any variation of activity (of map 1). This action is done in the real world, and put the agent in a new situation (that should be closer to the goal), and everything starts again.

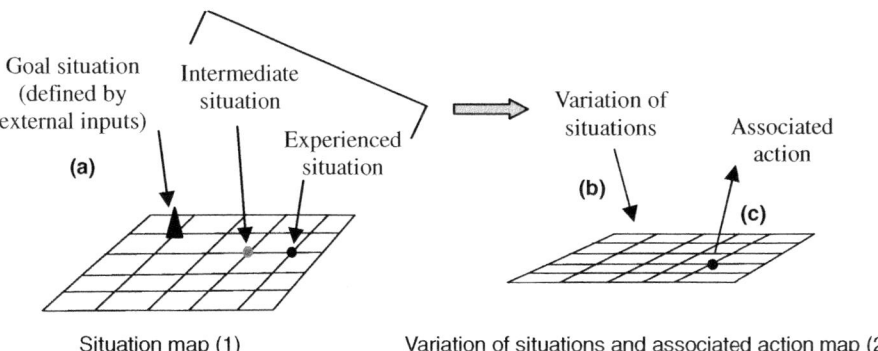

Fig. 2. Two cortical maps cooperate in order to generate a sequence of actions (*i.e.*, a behavior) in response to experienced situations. Each intersection represents a cortical column. The topology of the input situation space is preserved by the first cortical map (1). Therefore, the situation neighbor to the input situation and closer to the goal situation (a) is an intermediate situation in the process devoted to reach this '*goal*'. The variation of activity between experienced and intermediate situations (b) serves as input to the second map (2), where it activates the muscle command (action) associated (c) to this variation of situations.

3 Illusions

The definition of an illusion that is of interest here is "*a misinterpretation of a true sensation*". We claim that the '*internal joy drive*' and '*intrinsic joy*' are both misinterpretations.

3.1 The Illusion of '*Joy Driven*' Behaviors

When a behavior's goal is not seen or perceived or understood by the observer (who can be the individual himself), then the behavior is said to be '*driven by joy*'. Why '*joy*'? Just because it is easier to believe that the individual is looking for, or responding to, something pleasant when behaving - instead of the opposite (searching for bad things). Using the information provided in section 2, we claim that any behavior is '*goal driven*' and that the '*internal progress*' is in fact a '*distance-to-goal progress*'. As long as there is a discrepancy between the goal and the experienced situation locations on the cortical map(s), the behavior will occur.

3.2 The Illusion of '*Internal Joy*'

If we assume that '*joy driven*' behaviors are just '*goal driven*' behaviors whose goals are non explicit (to a human observer), then it follows that we must get better acquainted with these goals. Moreover, since they are related to '*joy*', it is of tremendous importance for our well-being to know more about them.

First things first: how are the goals defined and selected? Cortical maps are associative memories (*i.e.*, content addressable memories). Hebbian learning induces the storage of the activity patterns generated by the (lifelong) experienced situations. The number of samples required to (self-)organize a map is several times the number of cortical columns of the map. Therefore, only the most represented situations (among the samples) are going to be memorized. For each subset of situations, the memorized information is the most redundant one, *i.e.*, the most shared cortical column activities: the '*smallest common activation pattern*'.

Next thing on the list: how does a '*joy driven*' behavior start? Let's imagine that the individual is in a situation where there is no explicit '*goal*'. There is nevertheless a situation to experience (even if it is sensory deprivation). This experienced situation will activate a representation of it by activating (some) cortical columns on some cortical maps. This activity acts as a probe of the associative memories and will sooner or later activate an already stored activity pattern: a '*goal*'. Now, the system (*i.e.*, the cortex) is faced with two different patterns of activity: one representing the experienced situation and one the '*goal*'. A behavior will emerge.

It may happened from time to time that the experienced novel situation matches exactly an already memorized - but still never experienced (otherwise it would have been stopped shortly after the primary or secondary cortex) - pattern of activity (Fig. 3). In this case, the <u>neural pattern of activity is minimum</u>, which allows for a much <u>better memorization</u> of the event (in the episodic memory). Minimum activity means that the number of cortical columns involved is minimum - but their electric activity is maximum! It follows that this particular event will become easily remembered and may often serve as a goal (*i.e.*, an attractor situation) in the following life of the individual. Less neural activity will be required to activate this particular representation. Immediate recognition and better memorization: all the ingredients of a very meaningful experience that could be named *'joy'* or *'beauty'*.

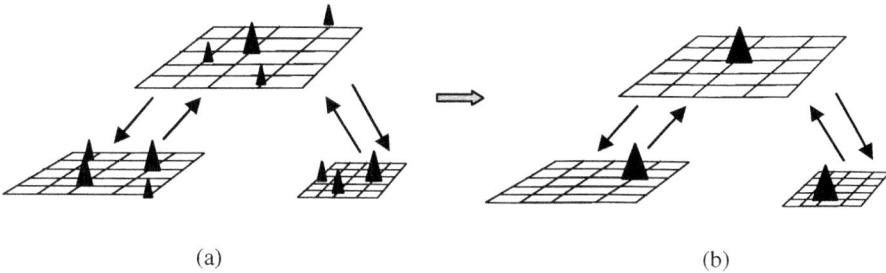

(a)   (b)

Fig. 3. (a) Columns activity (black triangles) associated to an experienced extra-ordinary situation, that quickly resume in an activity (b) involving less columns (each one exhibiting stronger activity, *i.e.*, bigger triangles). The pattern (a) is dependent on the life-long learning. It contains in essence the pattern (b). The memorization and future activation of pattern (b) is much easier than was pattern (a) activation. The quick transition from (a) to (b) is certainly an unique experience, that an observer may called *'joy'* .

4   Discussion and Conclusion

We must point out the similarities between Schmidhuber's compression index and the *'smallest common activation pattern'*. Both consider that the size of the representation of information by the brain is the important factor. Both also acknowledge the fact that as soon as there is no more any variation of this *'factor'*, then the behavior stops.

Looking at the biological plausibility of each proposal, a compression index needs to be computed and therefore requires resources. On the opposite, there is no computational resource required in our proposal. Last but not least, our proposal allows for any learning (supervised, reinforcement and seal-organization) to occur, not only reinforcement learning.

'Curiosity' and *'boredom'* are not equivalent to *'internal joy'* even if they can be implemented using a reinforcement signal computed by the difference between the expected situation and the experienced situation [8]. To us, the discrepancy between expected and experienced situations is the root cause of the attentional processes, with the involvement of more and more higher (or abstract) cortical maps as the discrepancy hold [9]. In our view of the attentional processes, there is no need for a reinforcement signal computed elsewhere to achieve *'attention'*, and therefore also *'curiosity'* and *'boredom'*.

The goal situations should be considered as attraction basins since they act in twisting the behavior of the individual towards specific representations (the attractive ones). A naive observer will see an individual whose behaviors tend to favor, even research, some specific situations. It follows that *'internal joy'* is only a side-effect of the brain learning and memory processes. These explanations define *'internal joy'* as an illusion, as it is also the case of *'consciousness'* and *'intelligence'* in the eliminative materialism paradigm.

References

1. Schmidhuber, J.: Formal Theory of Creativity, Fun, and Intrinsic Motivation (1990-2010). IEEE Transactions on Autonomous Mental Development 2(3), 230–247 (2010)
2. Schmidhuber, J.: Driven by compression progress: A simple principle explains essential aspects of subjective beauty, novelty, surprise, interestingness, attention, curiosity, creativity, art, science, music, jokes. In: Pezzulo, G., Butz, M.V., Sigaud, O., Baldassarre, G. (eds.) Anticipatory Behavior in Adaptive Learning Systems. LNCS (LNAI), vol. 5499, pp. 48–76. Springer, Heidelberg (2009)
3. Schmidhuber, J.: Simple Algorithmic Principles of Discovery, Subjective Beauty, Selective Attention, Curiosity & Creativity. In: Corruble, V., Takeda, M., Suzuki, E. (eds.) DS 2007. LNCS (LNAI), vol. 4755, pp. 26–38. Springer, Heidelberg (2007)
4. Santos, J.M., Touzet, C.: Exploration Tuned Reinforcement Function. Neurocomputing 28(1-3), 93–105 (1999)
5. Touzet, C.: Q-learning for robots. In: Arbib, M. (ed.) The Handbook of Brain Theory and Neural Networks, 2nd edn., pp. 93–937. MIT Press, Cambridge (2003)
6. Kohonen, T.: Self-Organizing Maps, 3rd edn. Springer Series in Information Sciences, vol. 30, p. 501 pages (2001) ISBN 3-540-67921-9
7. Touzet, C.: Modeling and Simulation of Elementary Robot Behaviors using Associative Memories. International Journal of Advanced Robotic Systems 3(2), 165–170 (2006)
8. Schmidhuber, J.: A possibility for implementing curiosity and boredom in model-building neural controllers. In: Meyer, J.A., Wilson, S.W. (eds.) Proc. of the International Conference on Simulation of Adaptive Behavior: From Animals to Animats, pp. 222–227. MIT Press/Bradford Books (1991)
9. Touzet, C.: Conscience, intelligence, libre-arbitre ? Les réponses de la Théorie neuronale de la Cognition. la Machotte, 156 pages (2010) (in French) ISBN: 978-2-919411-00-9

Philosophically Inspired Concept Acquisition for Artificial General Intelligence

Iris Oved and Ian Fasel

The University of Arizona, School Information: Science, Technology, and Arts
Gould-Simpson Building, 1040 E. 4th Street, Tucson, Arizona, 85721, USA
{irisoved,ianfasel}@cs.arizona.edu

Abstract. We describe a Bayesian network implementation of a theory of concepts that is motivated by observations from the philosophical debate between Lexical Concept Empiricism and Lexical Concept Nativism. According to our theory, *Baptizing Meanings for Concepts (BMC)*, concepts are acquired by hypothesizing latent kinds/categories to explain observed co-occurrences of sets of properties in a group of objects. The hypothesized kind/category is given a name and inferential relationships are stored between the name and representations for the observable properties. We argue that this process appeases tensions in the philosophical debate by allowing for the acquisition of concepts via perception and inference, while yielding the concepts simple, in the sense of being contingently associated with other representations. The BMC is inspired by a well-known process in the philosophy of language for assigning meanings to linguistic terms [1, 2, 3, 4].

Keywords: Bayesian Networks, Categories, Cognition, Concepts, Kinds, Learning, Meaning, Philosophy.

1 Introduction

In order for an agent to be generally intelligent, it must be able to operate in a complex world with hidden stochastic processes over its lifetime. In order to do this, it must have representations that it can use across multiple domains. Concepts, as context-free representations for the kinds/categories that make up the world, are central to such general agents, allowing them to gradually develop a general coherent and useful picture of the world in which they operate. The present paper presents a view about concepts that is motivated by observations from philosophical debates about the structure and acquisition of concepts, and describes an implementation of a simple concept-learning agent that demonstrates the feasibility of this view.

What we mean by a 'concept' here is *a mental entity*, something internal that an agent has when thinking that some object in the world has a particular property or that some object in the world belongs to a particular kind/category. For example, when an agent thinks of something as being a *fruit*, being an *apple*, being *purple*, or being a *swim* event, the agent has a mental entity by virtue of which it thinks about these properties/kinds. More precisely, we treat concepts as *stored* mental entities that an agent can use or bring into processing when thinking about a property or kind.

J. Schmidhuber, K.R. Thórisson, and M. Looks (Eds.): AGI 2011, LNAI 6830, pp. 363–369, 2011.

Beginning at least with Plato, and continuing through contemporary cognitive science, much of the debate about concepts has focused on *lexical* concepts. This is a rough class of concepts that tend to correspond to single words in many natural languages. Examples include representations for *apple, fruit, cactus,* and *water*.

The central question for this paper is, *How do lexical concepts come to be about what they are about?* This question is related to *The Symbol-Grounding Problem* [5], the problem of getting a system of symbols within an agent to be connected to the world. In this paper we step through the philosophical debate about lexical concepts and discuss a way of resolving the debate which has been assumed to be impossible. Our proposed implementation, in which concepts correspond to hidden variables in a hierarchical Bayesian generative model, suggests that the idea is indeed feasible within the framework of modern machine learning. We propose that the field of Artificial General Intelligence likewise take these philosophical motivations into consideration when building concept-possessing agents.

We believe that this view is useful to AI because it suggests that Bayesian statistical methods, which bring with them a fundamental claim that data is best understood by finding explanations due to hidden causes, are a philosophically justifiable way of learning grounded symbols which address issues raised in debates about concepts. If this is the case, sophisticated methods for inferring hidden causes, even deep hierarchies of causes [6, 7, 8] need not be relegated to data mining or other 'narrow' AI problems, but should be embraced wholeheartedly as mechanisms for learning grounded symbols. A key aim of this paper is to clarify the relationship between Bayesian methods and philosophical ideas about concept acquisition.

2   The Philosophical Debate about Concepts

2.1 The Building Blocks Model

According to the Representational Theory of Thoughts [9], thoughts are structured representations, analogous to linguistic representations, with the simplest units of meaning composing together (in accordance with some 'grammar', or composition rules).   In this picture, there are Primitive representations, which are the basic building-blocks of thought, and there are Composite representations built up from the Primitives. The Composites inherit their meanings from their representational parts, in such a way that Composites are inferentially related to the representations involved in their acquisition. The Primitives ground all of the meanings in some basic way, and they are possessed innately, or else they are acquired only by brute brain-development, rather than being acquired by an inferential process.

Composite Representations:

(**Acquired**)	Acquired from representations already in possession through an inferential process.
(**Complex**)	Complex in representational structure, such that that their meanings are inherited from the meanings of the representations involved in their acquisition.

Primitive Representations:

(**Innate**)	Possessed at birth, or acquired only by a brute-causal (i.e.,non-inferential) process.
(**Simple**)	Simple in representational structure, such that they directly represent their meanings, rather than inheriting them from any other representations.

As will be seen shortly, the *Baptizing Meanings for Concepts* view that we adopt treats lexical concepts as neither Primitive nor Composite in these senses. Instead, it treats lexical concepts as representationally **Simple** yet inferentially **Acquired**.

2.2   Empiricism vs. Nativism about Lexical Concepts

Within the Building-Blocks framework, certain questions in terms of the model arise. In particular, the debate between Lexical Concept Empiricism (LCE) and Lexical Concept Nativism (LCN) is almost completely about where to draw the line between the Primitives and the Composites, focusing on the lexical concepts.   LCE usually claims that lexical concepts are Composite (inferentially acquired and built up from the representations involved in their acquisition). LCN usually takes them to be Primitive. E.g., LCE holds that the concept APPLE is acquired and built from more simple representations, perhaps RED, ROUND, CRUNCHY, SWEET, and maybe also FRUIT, and FOOD, which in turn may be built from further Primitives. For LCN, APPLE is among the sensory representations, set up at birth or acquired only through brain development, to be triggered by apples in the world.

Lexical Concept Empiricism:	Most lexical concepts are Composite.
Lexical Concept Nativism:	Most lexical concepts are Primitive.

Keeping with the analogy between thought and language, it seems natural at first to regard lexical concepts as **Simple**. We certainly feel as though we perceive and think about the world at that level. We see *cars* and *people* on the *street*, and we hear *trains* and *dogs* that *bark*, and we make inferences based on what we know about things in these categories. Historically this has always been the default view.

The trouble is, giving in to the intuition that lexical concepts are **Simple** seems to result in giving-in to the much less palatable view that these concepts are **Innate**. Consider the concepts SNAIL, DINOSAUR, and CACTUS. It is hard to imagine how we could have these concepts innately, or why we would.

On the Building-Blocks model, if lexical concepts are acquired from patterns in sensory experience, they must have those sensory representations as part of their representational structure. This is a large part of the reasoning that drives LCE to seek further evidence that lexical concepts are representationally **Complex**, going against the initial intuition that they are **Simple**. Their being **Complex** is a very straight-forward account of *how* these concepts can be **Acquired**.

2.3   The Debate Suggests that Lexical Concepts are Simple Yet Acquired

On the side of Empiricism, arguments are designed to defend lexical concepts as **Complex**. Problems with the definability of lexical concepts have been observed at least since Plato (see [10] for a contemporary argument). Empiricists have tried to maintain **Complex** without definability, with Prototype Theory [13, 14, 15, 16, 17, 18], Exemplar Theory [19], and Theory-Theory [20, 21, 22, 23]. But it has been a struggle to defend these concepts as being **Complex** in such ways. One of the strongest attempts comes from the observation that some thoughts appear to be necessarily true, thoughts such as ALL CATS ARE ANIMALS and ALL APPLES ARE FRUIT. The Lexical Concept Empiricist may try to explain these apparent necessities by claiming that the concept CAT is **Complex**, composed in part by the concept ANIMAL, and APPLE is composed in part by the concept FRUIT. However many of the conceptual priorities this explanation requires are implausible. If the concept ANIMAL is part of the concept CAT, children have to have ANIMAL before they can have CAT. This might seem plausible enough, but the same explanation would have to hold for the apparent necessity of ALL CATS ARE MAMMALS, and it seems absurd to think that children have MAMMAL before CAT.

Perhaps the strongest argument for lexical concepts being **Complex** has to do with co-referring mental terms, mental *Frege cases* [24]. Consider the following example. Sammy is a young child who has two mental names that refer to coyotes. One of these mental names, F, is triggered by his visual perceptions of coyotes (when he sees some of these skinny-legged wolf-like animals at a zoo). The other mental name, G, is triggered by Sammy's auditory perceptions of coyotes (suppose he hears some screeching howls through his window at night). If Sammy were to eventually learn that 'Fs are Gs', he would learn something new. Since the external referents of F and G are the same, it seems the only way to account for the difference in information is some internal difference between the representations. This is what moves many Empiricists to hold that concepts like F and G have to be **Complex**, each built up from a different set of perceptual representations. The Baptism model defended here is an alternative explanation; they are just two distinct simple mental names.

On the side of Nativism, the primary argument for lexical concepts being **Innate** comes from the reasons for thinking that lexical concepts are **Simple** along with Fodor's arguments to the un-learnability of **Simple** concepts [9, 10, 11]. This is the challenge we take on presently, to show how a **Simple** concept can be **Acquired**. If we can show this, we can resolve central tensions between LCN and LCE.

3   Baptizing Meanings for Concepts and a Softbot Implementation

On the Baptizing Meanings for Concepts (BMC) process, an agent begins with a built-in perceptual system that takes inputs from the world and presents objects as having those perceptible values. Representations along these perceptual dimensions would make up the agent's perceptual Primitives; they are Innate and Simple. There is a straight-forward sense in which such an agent is able to compose its Primitive symbols together to entertain thoughts, like, OBJECT b IS RED & ROUND. After experiencing some objects, the agent is able to to detect similarities between objects in terms of its property space, as is done by commonplace clustering algorithms used in machine learning (see [25, 26]). According to BMC, many lexical concepts are Acquired via the detection of such clusters of representations already in possession, but are Simple in representational structure rather than being composed by the representations forming the cluster. The agent takes clusters of objects as *an*

indication that the objects share a property that explains the observed clustering.
Once the hypothesized property is picked out the agent assigns a new Simple mental
term. The name comes to represent the new discovered property. The agent can go
on to recognize new objects as having that property, if it is perceived as similar
enough to the objects used in acquiring *M*, and far enough from the other objects.

We can begin to see how to implement aspects of the baptism theory of concepts
by considering certain kinds of models that have become commonplace in both
artificial intelligence and cognitive science. Probabilistic generative models, often
represented by Bayesian graphical models (developed by Judea Pearl [27] and used in
AI by [26, 7, 8], and in Cognitive Psychology most prominently by Tenenbaum and
colleagues [28, 29, 30]) encode probabilistic dependencies between properties of
objects in an intuitive form that often matches our linguistic intuitions about kinds and
properties.

To explore the baptism theory, we built a softbot (simulated robot) that interacts
with a simulated world. The agent's world consisted of several fruit kinds, such that
objects of each fruit-kind tended to have a certain color and a certain shape. One way
to implement BMC in this softbot is to endow it with a generative model for fruit
kinds and properties, as illustrated in Figure 1 with the graphical model notation of
Pearl [27]. Provided this model, the agent explores its world by performing
perceptual tests on the objects' colors and shapes. Along the way it can hypothesize
the number of fruit-kinds that generated the objects and update the dimensionality of
the hidden *kinds* node (i.e., baptizing representations) to represent that belief.

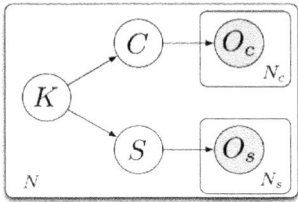

Fig. 1. Graphical model of an object's kind (K) determining the probability distribution over the
object's color (C) and shape (S) properties, which in turn determine probability distributions
over the object's observed color (O_c) and shape (O_s). The boxes, or 'plates', around parts of the
graph represent multiple (N) instances of that part.

The learning process includes hypothesizing and testing of the number of fruit
kinds, the dependencies between the kinds and the actual colors and shapes of the
objects, and dependencies between actual colors and shapes and observed colors and
shapes. The agent learns this model while learning a policy for moving and
performing perceptual tests on objects to maximize its knowledge about its world.

Many methods are possible for learning such a model. We adapted the online
mixture estimation (OME) algorithm of [31], which has previously been used to learn
vowel categories from infant directed speech in English and Japanese. OME is
similar to expectation maximization (EM) in standard mixture of Gaussians models,
but with an additional competition term allowing it to learn the *number* of kinds as
well as their parameters. New experiences allow the agent to revise its hypothesized

model of the world by changing the number kinds to better explain (i.e., maximize the probability of) its observations. Our experiments [32] show that using kinds improves the ability to quickly reduce uncertainty about the world compared to an agent that represents the color and shape properties without representing fruit-kinds.

Other methods are available to learn parameters of models even when the cardinality of certain discrete variables is unknown. In reversible-jump MCMC, baptizing a concept would be implemented by what is called a 'Birth' move, and a 'Death' move would remove a category. In nonparametric Bayesian methods like hierarchical Dirichlet processes [8], it would be to assign data to one of infinitely many categories previously not hypothesized to explain any of the observations.

4 Conclusion

This paper brings insights from philosophical debates about concepts to the field of Artificial General Intelligence. In turn, we use tools from Artificial Intelligence to show that concepts can indeed be representationally simple even though they are inferentially acquired from descriptions involving other representations, which has been claimed by philosophers to be impossible. We hope that these observations will contribute to the goals of both philosophers and AI researchers who aim to have a theory of the structure and acquisition concepts.

Acknowledgments. This work was supported by the National Science Foundation under grant #0937060 to the Computing Research Association "CI Fellows" program, and ONR contract N00014-09-1-0658 and DARPA contract N10AP20008.

References

1. Kripke, S.A.: Naming and Necessity. Harvard University Press, Cambridge (1972)
2. Putnam, H.: The meaning of meaning. Philosophical Papers: Mind, Language and Reality 2, 215–271 (1975)
3. Burge, T.: Individualism and the Mental. Midwest Studies in Philosophy 4, 73–121 (1979)
4. Soames, S.: Beyond Rigidity: The Unfinished Semantic Agenda of Naming and Necessity. OUP (2002)
5. Harnad, S.: The Symbol Grounding Problem. Physica D 42, 335–346 (1990)
6. Smith, E.C., Lewicki, M.S.: Efficient auditory coding. Nature 439(7079), 978–982 (2006)
7. Hinton, G.E., Salakhutdinov, R.R.: Reducing the dimensionality of data with neural networks. Science 313(5786), 504 (2006)
8. Teh, Y.W., And Jordan, M.I.: Hierarchical Bayesian Nonparametric Models with Applications. In: Bayesian Nonparametrics, Cambridge University Press, Cambridge (2010)
9. Fodor, J.A.: Fodor's Guide to Mental Representation. Mind 94, 76–100 (1985)
10. Fodor, J.A.: Concepts: Where Cognitive Science Went Wrong. OUP, New York (1998)
11. Fodor, J.A.: Pyschosemantics: The Problem of Meaning in the Philosophy of Mind. MIT Press, Cambridge (1987)
12. Fodor, J.A., Garrett, M.F., Walker, E., Parkes, C.T.: Against Definitions. Cognition 8, 263–367

13. Wittgenstein, L.: Philosophical Investigations. Blackwell Publishers, Malden (1958)
14. Rosch, E., Mervis, C.B.: Family resemblances: Studies in the internal structure of categories. Cognitive Psychology 7, 573–605 (1975)
15. Rosch, E.: Natural categories. Cognitive Psychology 4, 328–350 (1973)
16. Murphy, G.L.: The Big Book of Concepts. MIT Press, A Bradford Book (2002)
17. Barsalou, L.: Perceptual Symbol Systems. Behavioral and Brain Sciences 22, 577–660 (1999)
18. Prinz, J.: Furnishing the Mind: Concepts and their Perceptual Basis. MIT Press, Cambridge (2002)
19. Smith, E.E., Medin, D.L.: Categories and Concepts. Harvard University Press, Cambridge (1981)
20. Carey, S.: Conceptual Change in Childhood. MIT Press, Cambridge, MA (1985)
21. Gopnik, A., Meltzoff, A.N.: Words, Thoughts, and Theories. MIT Press, Cambridge (1997)
22. Keil, F.C.: Concepts, Kinds and Cognitive Development. MIT Press, Cambridge (1989)
23. Spelke, E.: Initial knowledge: six suggestions. Cognition 50, 431–445 (1994)
24. Frege, G.: Über Sinn und Bedeutung. Zeitschrift für Philosophie und philosophische Kritik100, 25–50 (1892); Translated as Black, M.: On Sense and Reference. In: Translations from the Philosophical Writings of G. Frege, P. Geach, M. Black (eds. and trans.), 3rd edn. Blackwell, Oxford (1980)
25. Mitchell, T.: Machine Learning. McGraw Hill, New York (1997)
26. Bishop, C.M.: Pattern Recognition and Machine Learning. Springer, Heidelberg (2006)
27. Pearl, J.: Causality: Models, Reasoning, and Inference, 1st edn. Cambridge University Press, Cambridge (2009)
28. Tenenbaum, J.B., Griffiths, T.L.: Theory-Based Causal Inference. In: Becker, S., Thrun, S., Obermayer, K. (eds.) Advances in Neural Information Processing Systems, vol. 15. MIT, Cambridge (2003)
29. Sobel, D.M., Tenenbaum, J.B., Gopnik, A.: Children's causal inferences from indirect evidence: Backwards blocking and Bayesian reasoning in preschoolers. Cognitive Science 28(3), 303–333 (2004)
30. Tenenbaum, J.B., Griffiths, T.L., Kemp, C.: Theory-based Bayesian models of inductive learning and reasoning. Trends in Cognitive Sciences. Special Issue: Probabilistic models of cognition 10(7), 309–318 (2006)
31. Vallabha, G., McClelland, J., Pons, F., Werker, J., Amano, S.: Unsupervised learning of vowel categories from infant-directed speech. Proc. of the National Academy of Science 104 (2007)
32. Fasel, I., Wilt, A., Morrison, C., Oved, I.: University of Arizona Tech Report: Unsupervised Concept Discovery through Intrinsically Motivated Exploration

Machine Lifelong Learning: Challenges and Benefits for Artificial General Intelligence

Daniel L. Silver

Jodrey School of Computer Science
Acadia University
Wolfville, Nova Scotia, Canada B4P 2R6
danny.silver@acadiau.ca

Abstract. We propose that it is appropriate to more seriously consider the nature of systems that are capable of learning over a lifetime. There are three reasons for taking this position. First, there exists a body of related work for this research under names such as constructive induction, continual learning, sequential task learning and most recently learning with deep architectures. Second, the computational and data storage power of modern computers are capable of implementing and testing *machine lifelong learning* systems. Third, there are significant challenges and benefits to pursuing programs of research in the area to AGI and brain sciences. This paper discusses each of the above in the context of a general framework for machine lifelong learning.

1 Introduction

Over the last 25 years there have been significant advances in machine learning theory and new machine learning algorithms based on that theory. However, there has been comparatively little work on systems that are able to learn a variety of tasks over an extended period of time. We propose that it is now appropriate to more seriously consider the nature of systems that are capable of learning over a life time. In accord with [13], we call these *machine lifelong learning* systems.

There are three reasons for feeling the time is right to more vigorously explore lifelong learning systems. First, there exists a body of related work that provides a starting point for research under names such as constructive induction, incremental and continual learning, sequential task learning, and most recently learning with deep architectures. Second, the computational and data storage power of modern computers are capable of implementing and testing lifelong learning systems. Third, there are significant challenges and benefits to pursuing programs of research in the area to AGI and brain sciences. This paper presents a general framework for machine lifelong learning and then discusses each of the above reasons for further research.

J. Schmidhuber, K.R. Thórisson, and M. Looks (Eds.): AGI 2011, LNAI 6830, pp. 370–375, 2011.

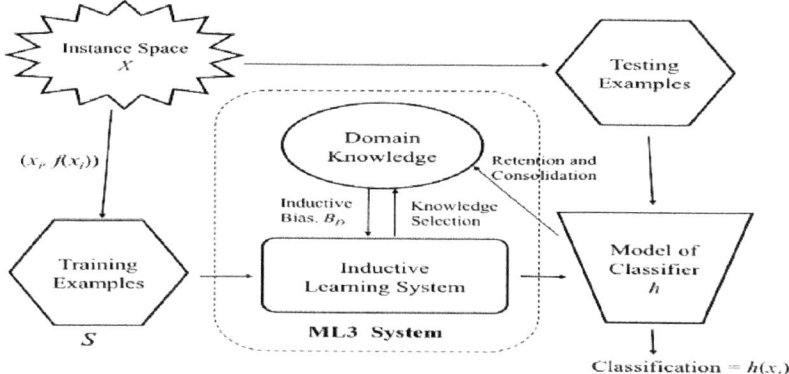

Fig. 1. A framework for machine lifelong learning

2   A Framework for Machine Lifelong Learning

The constraint on a learning system's hypothesis space, beyond the criterion of consistency with the training examples, is called *inductive bias* [3]. Inductive bias is essential for the development of a hypothesis with good generalization from a practical number of examples. Ideally, a lifelong learning system can select its inductive bias to tailor the preference for hypotheses according to the task being learned [15].

Figure 1 provides a general framework for a machine lifelong learning (ML3) approach that uses knowledge of the task domain as a source of inductive bias [8]. As with a standard inductive learner, training examples (supervised and possibly unsupervised) are used to develop a hypothesis of a classification task. However, unlike a standard learning system, knowledge from each hypothesis is saved in a long-term memory structure called *domain knowledge*. When learning a new task, aspects of domain knowledge are selected to provide a beneficial inductive bias to the learning system. The result is a more accurate hypothesis developed in a shorter period of time. The method relies on the transfer of knowledge from one or more prior secondary tasks, stored in domain knowledge, to the hypothesis for a new primary task. The problem of selecting an appropriate bias becomes one of selecting the most related knowledge for transfer. A machine lifelong learning system typically has short-term transfer and long-term retention learning phases. Although two phases of learning may not be necessary, it is frequently required so as to properly consolidate the hypothesis of a new task into long-term domain knowledge.

3   Related Work

Several prior research efforts have considered systems that learn domains of tasks over extended periods of time. In particular, progress has been made in machine learning that exhibit aspects of knowledge retention and inductive transfer. These represent advances in inductive modeling that move beyond *tabula rasa* learning and toward machines capable of lifelong learning [13].

Utgoff and Mitchell wrote in 1983 about the importance of *inductive bias* to concept learning from practical sets of training examples [14]. They theorized that learning systems should conduct their own search for an appropriate inductive bias using knowledge such as that of related tasks. They proposed a system that could shift its bias by adjusting the operations of the modeling language.

In the mid 1980s Michalski introduced the theory of *constructive inductive learning* to cope with learning problems in which the original representation space is inadequate for the problem at hand [2]. New knowledge is hypothesized through two interrelated searches: (1) a search for the best representational space for hypotheses and (2) a search for the best hypothesis within the current representational space. The underlying principle is that new knowledge is easier to induce if search is done using the *right* representation.

In 1989 Solomonof began work on *incremental learning* [11]. His system was primed on a small, incomplete set of primitive concepts, that are able to express the solutions to the first set of simple problems. When the machine learns to use these concepts effectively it is given more difficult problems and, if necessary, additional primitive concepts needed to solve them, and so on.

In the mid 1990s, Thrun and Mitchell worked on a lifelong learning approached they called *explanation-based neural networks* [12]. EBNN is able to transfers knowledge across multiple learning tasks. When faced with a new learning task, EBNN exploits domain knowledge of previous learning tasks (back-propagation gradients of prior learned tasks) to guide the generalization of the new one. As a result, EBNN generalizes more accurately from less data than comparable methods.

Since 1995, Silver *et al.* have proposed several variants of *sequential learning and consolidation systems* using standard back-propagation neural networks [9,10]. A system of two multiple task learning networks is used; one for short-term learning using task rehearsal to selectively transfer prior knowledge, and a second for long-term consolidation using task rehearsal to overcome the stability-plasticity problem. *Task rehearsal* is an essential part of this system. After a task has been successfully learned, its hypothesis representation can saved. The saved hypothesis can be used to generate virtual training examples so as to rehearse the prior task in parallel when learning a new task. It is through the rehearsal of previously learned tasks within the shared representation of the neural network that knowledge is transferred to the new task. Similarly, [9] the knowledge of a new task can be consolidated into a large domain knowledge network without loss of existing task knowledge by using task rehearsal to maintain the function accuracy of the prior tasks while the representation is modified to accommodate the new task.

In 1997, Ring proposed a lifelong learning approach called *continual learning* that builds more complicated skills on top of those already developed both incrementally and hierarchically [4]. He presents a system that can efficiently solve reinforcement-learning tasks and can then transfer its skills to related but more complicated tasks.

Rivest and Schultz proposed *knowledge-based cascade-correlation* neural networks in the late 1990s [5]. The method extends the original cascade-correlation approach, by selecting previously learned sub-networks as well as simple hidden units. In this way it is able to use past learning to bias new learning.

Recent research into the learning of *deep architectures* of neural networks can be connected to lifelong learning [1]. Layered neural networks of unsupervised Restricted Boltzman Machine and auto-encoders have been shown to efficiently develop hierarchies of features that capture regularities in their respective inputs. When used to learn a variety of class categories, these networks develop layers of common features similar to that seen in the visual cortex of humans.

4   Current Computational and Data Storage Capacity

The number of transistors that can be placed cheaply on an integrated circuit has doubled approximately every two years since 1970. This trend is expected to continue until the foreseeable future, with some expecting the power of computing systems to move to a log scale as computing systems increasingly use multiple processing cores. We are now at a point where a lifelong learning system focused on a constrained domain of tasks (*e.g.* medical diagnosis, product recommendation) is computationally tractable in terms of both computer memory and processing time.

As an example, massively parallel data processing engines now exist that are capable of competing with humans in real-time question-answer problems. This was recently witnessed on the Jeopardy television game show in February, of 2011. Watson consisted of 90 IBM server computers, each with four 8-core processors. It used 15 terabytes (220 million text pages) of rapid access memory and divided its tasks into thousands of stand-alone jobs distributed among 80 teraflops (1 trillion operations/second) of parallel processing power. Given that much of machine learning is search, platforms such as the one used by Watson are well suited to the challenges of lifelong learning systems. It would be important to note that Watson's success was in part due to advances in machine learning methods.

5   Challenges and Benefits

There are a number of challenges for and potential benefits from new research programs in machine lifelong learning. The following captures several of these.

There is strong evidence that transfer learning from prior related knowledge is beneficial when learning a new task [5,10,12]. Experimental results indicate that effective learning excels under functional transfer whereas efficient learning requires representation transfer [7]. Recent work has also shown the benefit of unsupervised training using many unlabelled examples as a source of inductive bias for supervised learning [1].

Machine lifelong learning provides an opportunity to acquire and take advantage of related knowledge. However, there are many challenging problems; for example, a lifelong learning system must weigh the relevance and accuracy of retained knowledge along side that of the available training examples for a new task. Theories on how to select inductive bias and modify the representational space of hypotheses [11] will be of significant value to AGI and brain science.

Mechanisms that can effectively and efficiently retain learned knowledge over time will suggest new approaches to common knowledge representation. In particular, methods of overcoming the stability-plasticity problem so as to integrate new knowledge into existing knowledge are of value to researchers in AI, cognitive science and neuroscience [9]. Efficient long-term retention of learned knowledge should cause no loss of prior task knowledge, no loss of new task knowledge, and an increase in the accuracy of old tasks if the new task being retained is related. Furthermore, the knowledge representation approach should allow a lifelong learner to efficiently select the most effective prior knowledge for inductive transfer during short-term learning.

A lifelong learning system should facilitate the practice of a task such that the generalization accuracy of the long-term hypothesis for the task increases. But how can a lifelong learning system determine from the training examples that it is practicing a task it has previously learned versus learning a new but closely related task. Related work suggests that a system should not be explicit in this determination [6,10]; rather, the similarity of a set of training examples to that of prior domain knowledge should be implicit; each training example should be able to draw upon those aspects of domain knowledge that are most related. This suggests that domain knowledge should be seen as continuum as apposed to a set of disjoint tasks. A theory of how best to practice tasks will be useful to the fields of AI, psychology and education.

Scalability is often the most difficult and important challenge for computer scientists. A machine lifelong learning system must be capable of scaling up to large numbers of inputs, outputs, training examples and learning tasks. Preferably, the space and time complexity of the learning system grows polynomially in all of these factors.

Software agents and robots will make good use of lifelong learning systems, or at least provide useful test platforms for empirical studies [12]. Agents and robots will naturally encounter new examples of problems periodically, providing opportunities to test the practice and consolidation of task knowledge.

The study of lifelong learning systems will provided insight into curriculum and training sequences that are beneficial for both humans and machines [11,4]. This will be beneficial to robot and software agent training and will likely lead to the confirmation of and advances in human educational curriculum.

Finally, research into machines that can learn over a lifetime involves laborious repeated studies of lengthy sequences of problems. This is tough but rewarding work that will become less labor intensive as experimental methods develop.

References

1. Bengio, Y.: Learning deep architectures for ai. Foundations and Trends in Machine Learning 2(1), 1–127 (2009)
2. Michalski, R.S.: Learning = inferencing + memorizing. In: Foundations of Knowledge Acquistion: Machine Learning, pp. 1–41 (1993)
3. Mitchell, T.M.: The need for biases in learning generalizations. In: Shavlik, J.W., Dietterich, T.G. (eds.) Readings in Machine Learning, pp. 184–191 (1980)
4. Ring, M.B.: Child: A first step towards continual learning. In: Machine Learning, pp. 77–104 (1997)
5. Shultz, T.R., Rivest, F.: Knowledge-based cascade-correlation: using knowledge to speed learning. Connect. Sci. 13(1), 43–72 (2001)
6. Silver, D.L., Alisch, R.: A measure of relatedness for selecting consolidated task knowledge. In: Proceedings of the 18th Florida Artificial Intelligence Research Society Conference (FLAIRS 2005), pp. 399–404 (2005)
7. Silver, D.L., Mercer, R.E.: The parallel transfer of task knowledge using dynamic learning rates based on a measure of relatedness. Connection Science Special Issue: Transfer in Inductive Systems 8(2), 277–294 (1996)
8. Silver, D.L., Mercer, R.E.: The task rehearsal method of life-long learning: Overcoming impoverished data. In: Advances in Artificial Intelligence, 15th Conference of the Canadian Society for Computational Studies of Intelligence (AI 2002), pp. 90–101 (2002)
9. Silver, D.L., Poirier, R.: Sequential consolidation of learned task knowledge. In: Canadian AI 2004. Lecture Notes in AI, pp. 217–232 (2004)
10. Silver, D.L., Poirier, R., Currie, D.: Inductive tranfser with context-sensitive neural networks. Machine Learning 73(3), 313–336 (2008)
11. Solomonoff, R.J.: A system for incremental learning based on algorithmic probability. In: Probability, Proceedings of the Sixth Israeli Conference on Artificial Intelligence, Computer Vision and Pattern Recognition, pp. 515–527 (1989)
12. Thrun, S.: Explanation-Based Neural Network Learning: A Lifelong Learning Approach. Kluwer Academic Publishers, Boston (1996)
13. Thrun, S.: Lifelong learning algorithms. In: Learning to Learn, pp. 181–209. Kluwer Academic Publishers, Dordrecht (1997)
14. Utgoff, P.E.: Adjusting bias in concept learning. In: Proceedings of IJCAI-1983, pp. 447–449 (1983)
15. Utgoff, P.E.: Machine Learning of Inductive Bias. Kluwer Academc Publisher, Boston (1986)

A Demonstration of Combining Spatial and Temporal Perception

Jianglong Nan and Fintan Costello

School of Computer Science and Informatics, University College Dublin
Belfield, Dublin 4, Ireland
jianglong.nan@ucdconnect.ie, fintan.costello@ucd.ie

Abstract. This paper describes two tests of a continuous-time artificial
intelligence model proposed by Nan and Costello[7]. This model aims to
combine spatial and temporal perception using a single simple mechanism. The first test demonstrates the spatial learning capability of the
model by applying it to data from an experiment by Love[6] on human
category learning. The second test demonstrates the temporal learning
capability of the model by applying it to data from an experiment by
Pizzo and Crystal[10] on the prediction of temporal patterns in rats. The
model gave a good fit to participant behaviour in both tasks.

1 Introduction

An agent with general intelligence must be able to recognise and learn both spatial relationships (perceptions which tend to occur together) and temporal relationships (perceptions which tend follow one another after particular intervals).
Many models of 'spatial learning' have been suggested by researchers working
on categorisation and concept formation [12,3,8,4]. These models assume that
the items are presented as a set of static features: temporal relationships play
no role. By contrast, models of conditioned response in animals (as in Pavlov's
studies, where dogs were presented with a stimulus – the ringing of a bell – that
was followed after a fixed interval by the presentation of food, and after training
were found to start salivating at the same fixed interval after stimulus [9,13]) focus on the processes and representations used to store temporal intervals. These
models assume a simple unstructured stimulus: spatial relationships play no role.

The approach proposed by Nan and Costello[7] attempts to unify these areas
by suggesting that temporal and spatial relationships are learnt using identical
processes and representations, involving prediction from antecedent to consequent. This paper presents two tests of this model: one on spatial learning data
from Love[6] and the other on temporal learning data from Pizzo and Crystal[10].
The model gave a good fit to the data in both tasks.

2 Overview of the Model

Our model assumes a fixed number of *sensors* to perceive the environment, a
short-term memory to remember recent perceptions, and a *long-term memory*

J. Schmidhuber, K.R. Thórisson, and M. Looks (Eds.): AGI 2011, LNAI 6830, pp. 376–381, 2011.

to store learnt knowledge about spatial and temporal relationships. It receives pulse-like stimuli through the sensors and predicts what sensors will be stimulated at what time and in what pattern in the future.

The long-term memory is a network of *k-nodes*, each representing a piece of knowledge. Each k-node consists of 4 elements: an *antecedent*, a *consequence*, an *interval*, and a measure of *strength* or reliability. On the one hand, a k-node represents an integrated event or pattern in which

> First some sub-event happens (its antecedent), and then after some time (its interval), some sub-event happens (its consequence).

On the other hand, it is a rule to make predictions in the form of

> If some event happens (its antecedent), then after some time (its interval), some event (its consequence) will happen.

and the more reliable this prediction is the greater the k-node's strength value. The antecedent and consequent of a k-node can be either a sensor or another k-node. If only the antecedent of a k-node is perceived, it acts like a predictor and predicts its consequent after the recorded interval. If both antecedent and consequent have been perceived with the appropriate interval between them, the k-node reports the recognised integrated event to all nodes that make use of it.

The job of learning is handled by a limited-space short-term memory. This holds references to the sensors and the k-nodes that have been perceived and recognised, and writes new chronological relationships between these events to the long-term memory as new k-nodes. K-nodes in short-term memory whose predictions have been confirmed increase in strength; those whose predictions have failed are decrease. The greater the strength of a k-node the more it persists in long-term memory and the more likely it is to be recruited to short-term memory when its antecendent occurs. A toy program demonstrating the model can be seen at `http://csserver.ucd.ie/~jlongnan/agi.html`.

3   Experiment 1

In Love's experiment[6], participants were presented with geometric figures labelled as members of one of two categories and varying in four binary features such as border colour, size, etc. In the study phase participants learned the relationship between features and categories. In the test phase participants were presented two figures simultaneously, only one of which had been seen in the study phase: participants were asked to choose the one they had seen before.

Three conditions were tested. In the *supervised* condition, each figure was first presented without its category label and participants were asked to guess the label; after guessing, the correct label feature was then shown; in the two other conditions the label and features were presented at the same time. In the *intentional unsupervised* condition, participants were asked to learn the categories; in the *incidental unsupervised* condition they were asked to rate how much they liked the figures.

3.1 Application of the Model

Two sensors were used to represent each feature, one active when the feature was present in a figure, the other when it was absent. Each participant got training and test presentations in a particular order: for each participant the model recieved stimuli in the same order and the model's performance was compared with that participant.

We applied the same test method for the data from all the three conditions. In the study phase, for each figure that was presented to the participant, the three non-label features were first presented to the model. The label feature was then presented after a fixed delay (constant in all tests). In the test phase, the non-label features were first presented, and after the fixed delay, we obtained the model's prediction on both the sensor representing the correct label and the one representing the incorrect label. Assuming the answer given by the model was the label represented by the sensor that got the higher prediction, we compared the accuracy of the model with that of each participant. Also, the prediction of the model on the incorrect label was compared with the response time of the human participants: our expectation was that the higher the model's prediction for the incorrect label, the longer it would take the participant to respond.

3.2 Results

The was a significant positive correlation between model accuracy and participant accuracy ($p < 0.001$ for all participants across all three conditions) indicating that that the more difficult the task was for the human participants, the more difficult it was for the model. More than 85% of correlation coefficients between the model's prediction on the incorrect label and the response time of the participants were positive, demonstrating that that the higher the model's prediction on the incorrect label is, i.e. the more familiar the model found the unseen geometric figure, the longer it took the participants to make a choice.

There were a number of test cases for each participant. We know that there is a trend where the response time of participants becomes shorter and shorter because the participants are improving as they go through test cases. We factored out this trend using the approach recommended by Lorch and Myers[5]. In this we first regressed the response time on the presentation order and the model's prediction for each participant, and then applying a t-test on the coefficients obtained in the regression. The coefficients of the model's prediction differed significantly from zero (with $p < 0.00001$) more than those of the sequence number (with $p < 0.025$), demonstrating that the model's prediction on the incorrect label was a much more reliable predictor of response time.

4 Experiment 2

In Pizzo and Crystal's experiment[10], rats searched for food in an eight-arm radial maze. Each test session for an individual rat lasted 56 minutes and was divided into 8 time zones of the same length, with a different arm providing food

Table 1. Experiment 2 - Correlation (r) between the rats' performance and the session number and between the model's performance and the session number

	Rat and Session		Model and Session	
	r	p	r	p
Rat 1	0.3466	0.01278	0.8497	1.349×10^{-13}
Rat 2	−0.8179	2.932×10^{-12}	−0.4417	0.001203
Rat 3	−0.008657	0.9519	−0.1858	0.1918
Rat 4	0.5371	5.276×10^{-5}	0.4228	0.002029

in each time zone. No signal was provided to indicate the change of time zone or the new food-providing arm. The arms that provided food always changed in a specific order for a particular rat in all sessions. The question of interest was whether the rat would be able to learn that order and the interval between changes, and so change to the correct arm at the appropriate time. A total of 60 sessions were carried out for each rat. Of the 4 rats, 2 showed a reliable improvement in performance across sessions (learned the order and interval between changes), 1 showed no reliable change (did not learn) and 1 disimproved across sessions (learned an incorrect ordering).

4.1 Application of the Model

In applying the model to the data we use eight 'arm-entered' sensors (ARM:1 - ARM:8), eight 'food-obtained-in-arm' sensors (FOOD:1 - FOOD:8) and one 'start-session' sensor, (START). We stimulate these sensors at the times given in the record of events for a given rat, and what the model perceives is a simplified abstraction of what the rat perceived. Given this we test whether the model can learn the order of and interval between changes of food-providing arm.

The following test was conducted for each set of rat data. First the model was run on the data. During running, it saved its state, i.e. its whole memory, just before the start of each time zone in each session. For a given arm X the saved state was loaded, bringing the model back to just before the time-zone changed. Next, three consecutive stimuli were applied to sensor ARM:X with fixed short intervals. Then F_x, the model's prediction on sensor FOOD:X was obtained. A normalised measure of the model's expectation for food on each arm X was computed by dividing F_x by the sum of all F values. This measure represents the model's preference for each arm, and was used to evaluate the model.

4.2 Results

When comparing the model's preference for the correct next arm with its average preference for the other six arms, we found that in three of the four cases the model's preference for the correct next arm increased across sessions and eventually exceeded the average preference for the other arms. This shows that as more and more sessions were presented the model was gradually learning the

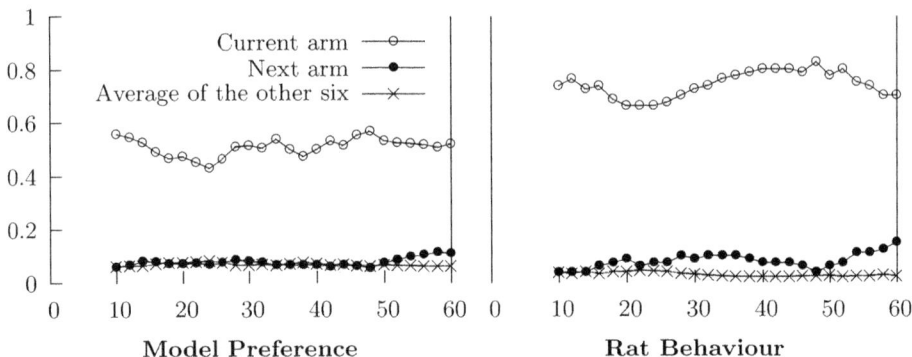

Fig. 1. Experiment 2 - Comparison of the Model's Preference and Rat 4's Behaviour over Sessions. All data is the average of the last 10 sessions

correct order of arm transitions. Table 1 shows the relationship between a given rat's performance (that is, its preference for the correct next arm) and the number of sessions, and the model's performance and the number of sessions. In each case the model's 'perceptions' corresponded to those of the rat in question. Fig. 1 shows how preferences for the next arm, the current arm, and the other six arms changed across sessions for for rat 4 and for the model.

As we can see from Table 1, wherever a rat showed a trend of getting better at visiting the correct arm in its first try in a new time zone (rat 1 and rat 4, indicated by positive correlation coefficients between the rats' performance and the session number), the model, when given those rats' perceptions, also showed the same trend (also having positive correlations); wherever a rat showed a trend of getting worse (rat 2, with negative correlation coefficients), the model also showed the same trend. When there was no reliable relationship between performance and session number for a given rat (rat 3), there was similarly no relationship for the model. In other words, when the model perceived what the rats had perceived, it reliably followed the rats' behaviour.

5   Conclusion

We have described two experiments demonstrating the application of the artificial intelligence model proposed by Nan and Costello[7] that provides a single account for learning about both static objects that are defined by features and time spanning events that are based on chronology. The results of these experiments showed that the model was able to mimic the behaviour of human beings and rats in both categorisation oriented tasks and time related tasks, thus providing evidence that temporal perception can be learnt and categorised in a knowledge structure just as spatial perception can, and that one single mechanism is sufficient to deal with them both.

References

1. Carter, R.: Exploring Consciousness. University of California Press (2002)
2. Gallistel, C.R., Gibbon, J.: Time, rate and conditioning. Psychological Review 107, 289–344 (2000)
3. Hampton, J.: Similarity-based categorization: The development of prototype theory. Psychologica Belgica 35, 103–125 (1995)
4. Kruschke, J.K.: Alcove: An exemplar-based connectionist model of category learning. Psychological Review 99, 22–44 (1992)
5. Lorch, R.F., Myers, J.L.: Regression analysis of repeated measures data in cognitive research. Journal of Experimental Psychology: Learning, Memory and Cognition 16(1), 149–157 (1990)
6. Love, B.C.: Comparing supervised and unsupervised category learning. Psychonomic Bulletin & Review 9(2), 829–835 (2002)
7. Nan, J., Costello, F.: An artificial intelligence model that combines spatial and temporal perception. In: Proceedings of the Third Conference on Artificial General Intelligence, AGI 2010 (2010)
8. Nosofsky, R.M.: Attention, similarity, and the identification-categorization relationship. Journal of Experimental Psychology: General 115(1), 39–57 (1986)
9. Pavlov, I.P.: Lectures on Conditioned Reflexes. Liveright Publishing Corp., (1928)
10. Pizzo, M.J., Crystal, J.D.: Time-place learning in the eight-arm radial maze. Learning and Behavior 32, 240–255 (2004)
11. Rescorla, R.A., Wagner, A.R.: A theory of pavlovian conditioning: Variations in the effectiveness of reinforcement and nonreinforcement. Classical Conditioning II, 64–99 (1972)
12. Rosch, E.: Principles of Categorization, pp. 27–48. John Wiley & Sons, Chichester (1978)
13. Skinner, B.F.: The Behavior of Organisms: An Experimental Analysis. Prentice Hall, New Jersey (1938)

Towards Heuristic Algorithmic Memory

Eray Özkural

Bilkent University Computer Engineering Department
Ankara, Turkey

Abstract. We propose a long-term memory design for artificial general intelligence based on Solomonoff's incremental machine learning methods. We introduce four synergistic update algorithms that use a Stochastic Context-Free Grammar as a guiding probability distribution of programs. The update algorithms accomplish adjusting production probabilities, re-using previous solutions, learning programming idioms and discovery of frequent subprograms. A controlled experiment with a long training sequence shows that our incremental learning approach is effective.

1   Introduction

Teramachine is a universal induction system that features integrated *long-term* memory, as a candidate for Solomonoff's "Phase 1 machine" that he proposed to use as the basis of a powerful AGI system called Alpha [1]. We propose an automatic memory which is recalled appropriately during induction. After each induction problem, the solution is stored in the memory, which is a realization of Solomonoff's idea of guiding probability density function (pdf) of programs. The present system may be viewed as an advanced version of OOPS [2]. We update the guiding pdf after each induction problem so that the *heuristic* solutions that we invent are stored as *algorithmic* information in our *memory* system. Hence, our memory design is called Heuristic Algorithmic Memory (HAM).

If an induction system's probability distribution of programs is fixed, then the system does not have any real long-term learning ability. We can solve this problem by changing the probability distribution so that we extrapolate from the already invented solution programs, allowing more difficult problems to be solved [3]. Modifying the probability distribution essentially defines an *implicit program code*. Thus, after each solution we are implicitly modifying the reference machine. Relative to the implicit universal code, Levin search [4] still has an optimal order of complexity and is effective for approximating Solomonoff induction [5]. The extraction of algorithmic information from solutions affords an effective kind of time-space tradeoff, which works extremely favorably in terms of additional space requirement. The successful extraction of each single bit of mutual algorithmic information among two problems may potentially result in a speed-up of two for the latter problem. However, re-using algorithmic information from previous solutions entails a coding cost which manifests itself as a time penalty during program search (Levin search in our work).

J. Schmidhuber, K.R. Thórisson, and M. Looks (Eds.): AGI 2011, LNAI 6830, pp. 382–387, 2011.

The reader is referred to [2,1,6] for a background on incremental machine learning. A longer version of this paper is available on the aRxiV [7], and a previous version explains the R5RS Scheme grammar which we use [8].

2   Stochastic Context-Free Grammar Updates

A Stochastic Context-Free Grammar (SCFG) is a Context-Free Grammar augmented by a probability value on each production. For each head non-terminal, the probabilities of its productions must sum to one. We can extend Levin Search procedure to work with a SCFG that assigns probabilities to each sentence in the language. For this, we need two things, first a generation logic for individual sentences, and second a search strategy to enumerate the sentences that meet the termination condition of LSEARCH [2]. In the present system, we use left-most derivation to generate a sentence, intermediate steps are thus left-sentential forms [9, Chapter 5]. The calculation of the a priori probability of a sentence depends on the fact that in a derivation $S \Rightarrow \alpha_1 \Rightarrow \alpha_2 \Rightarrow ... \Rightarrow \alpha_n$ where productions $p_1, p_2, ..., p_n$ have been applied in order to start symbol S, the probability of the sentence α_n is $P(\alpha_n) = \prod_{1 \leq i \leq n} p_i$. Note that the productions in a derivation are conditionally independent. While this makes it much easier for us to calculate probabilities of sentential forms, it limits the expressive power of pdf. Note that search algorithm details are beyond the scope of this paper.

The most critical part of our design is updating the SCFG so that the discovered solutions in a training sequence will be more probable in subsequent searches. We propose four synergistic update algorithms for HAM. Our SCFG structure extends the usual productions with production procedures, which dynamically generate productions.

2.1   Modifying Production Probabilities

The simplest kind of update is modifying the probabilities as new solutions are added to the solution corpus. For this, however, the search algorithm must supply the derivation that led to the solution (which we do), or the solution must be parsed using the same grammar. Then, the probability for each production $A \rightarrow \beta$ in the solution corpus can be easily calculated by the ratio of frequency of productions $A \rightarrow \beta$ in the solution corpus to the frequency of productions in the corpus with a head of A. The production procedures are excluded from this update as they can be variant. However, we cannot simply write the probabilities calculated this way over the initial probabilities, as initially there will be few solutions, and most probabilities will be zero. We use exponential smoothing to solve this problem:

$$s_0 = p_0$$
$$s_t = \alpha p_t + (1 - \alpha)s_{t-1}$$

where p_0 is the initial probability, p_t is the probability in the corpus for problem t, s_t the smoothed probability for problem t, and α is the smoothing factor. We used a smoothing factor of 0.125. See [10] for the application of smoothing in a similar problem. Other methods like Laplace's rule may be used instead [1].

2.2   Re-using Previous Solutions

In the course of a training sequence, the solutions can be incorporated in full by adding the solutions to the grammar. In the case of Scheme, there could be many possible implementations. The simplest design is to add all the solutions to the library of the Scheme interpreter, add a hook non-terminal previous-solution to the grammar, and then extend the previous-solution with the syntax to call the new solution. We assume that this syntax is provided in the problem definition. The new solution among other previous solutions is given a probability of γ in the hope that this solution will be re-used soon, and then the probabilities of the old productions of previous-solution are normalized so that they sum to $1 - \gamma$. We currently use a γ of 0.5. If it is difficult to add the solutions to the Scheme interpreter as in our case, then all the solutions can be added as define blocks in the beginning of the program produced, which requires avoiding redundant definitions [7].

2.3   Learning Programming Idioms

Programmers do not only learn of concrete solutions to problems, but they also learn abstract programs, or program schemas. One way to formalize this is that they learn sentential forms. If we can extract appropriate sentential forms, we can add these to the grammar, as well. We construct the derivation tree from the leftmost derivation, with an obvious algorithm that we will omit. The current abstraction algorithm starts with the derivation sub-trees rooted at each expression in the current solution. For each derivation sub-tree, we prune the leaves from the bottom-up. At each pruning step, an abstract expression is output. The pruning is iterated until a few symbols remain. Every abstract expression thus found is added to a new non-terminal that contains the abstract expressions of the current solution with equal probability. The new non-terminal is added to the top-level non-terminal abstract-expression with 0.5 probability, which is itself one of the productions for expression. These productions may later be modified and used by update algorithms one and two. Note that the orthogonality of the language helps us in integrating programming idioms into HAM. Thus, several sentential forms are learnt from a single solution in this fashion corresponding to different syntactic abstractions. We anticipate that the system will eventually learn complex programming idioms like recursion patterns and data constructors.

2.4   Frequent Sub-program Mining

Mining the solution corpus further enhances the guiding probability distribution. Frequent sub-programs in the solution corpus, i.e., sub-programs that occur with a frequency above a given support threshold, can be added again as alternative productions to the commonly occurring non-terminal expression in the Scheme grammar. For instance, if the solution corpus contains several (lambda (x y) (* x y)) subprograms, the frequent sub-program mining would discover that and we can add it as an alternative expression to the Scheme grammar.

We would like to find all frequent subprograms that occur twice or more so that we can increase the probability of such sub-programs accordingly. We first interpret the problem of finding frequent sub-programs as a syntactic problem, disregarding semantic equivalences between sub-programs. Once formulated in our program representations of derivation trees as labelled rooted frequent sub-tree mining, the frequent sub-program mining algorithm is a reasonable extension of traditional frequent pattern mining algorithms. We have implemented a BFS patterned fast mining algorithm by exploiting the property that every sub-tree of a frequent tree is frequent (see [11] for an advanced algorithm). We find frequent sub-trees (with a support threshold of 2 currently) of all sub-trees of derivation trees rooted at expression in the solution corpus. At each update, a non-terminal hook frequent-expression in the grammar is rewritten by assigning probabilities according to the frequency of each frequent sub-program. Note that most frequent expressions are abstract (i.e., sentential forms).

3   Experiments

Our experimental tests were carried out at TUBITAK ULAKBIM High Performance Computing Center on 144 AMD Opteron cores. We know of *no* previous demonstration of realistic experiments over a long training sequence for general purpose machine learning. Solomonoff had stated: "It cannot be emphasized too strongly, that the goal of early training sequence design, is not to solve hard problems, but to get problem solving information into the machine. Since Lsearch is easily adapted to parallel search, there is a tendency to try to solve fairly difficult problems on inadequately trained machines. The success of such efforts is more a tribute to progress in hardware design then to our understanding and exploiting machine learning." [12, Section 6]. We can show the effectiveness of our memory system leaving no place for doubt through *controlled experiments*. We run the entire training sequence with updates turned off and on. If the update algorithms cause a significant speed-up over search with no update, we can conclude that the update algorithms are effective. We use Conceptual Jump Size (CJS) to calculate the difficulty of a problem. $CJS = t_i/p_i$ where t_i is the running time of solution program and p_i is its a priori probability. The upper bound of Levin Search's running time is 2.CJS [12, Appendix A]. Our experiments are preferred to calculating CJS's by hand, as in these experiments we are using Scheme R5RS in its full glory. Note that we are interested in *only* detecting whether any information transfer occurs across problems rather than trying to solve difficult problems with a machine that has *no long-term memory*. The running time of a trial program is measured in Scheme execution cycles, which is the number of primitive Scheme operations (e.g., CAR) that are evaluated.

We have developed a training sequence composed of operator induction problems. For each problem, we have a set of input and output pairs, and we approximate operator induction [1,13]. Training sequence 1 contains, in order, the square function sqr, the addition of two variables add, a function to test if the argument is zero is0, all of which have 3 example pairs, fourth power of a number pow4 with just 2 example pairs, boolean nand, and xor functions with 4 example

Table 1. Performance of training sequence 1 with no update, $|HAM| = 17145$

Problem	Time	Trials	Errors	Cycles	Max Cyc.	p_i	t_i	CJS	$H(s_i)$
sqr	16.28	5.34×10^5	1.57×10^5	5.46×10^6	2.05×10^8	2.19×10^{-7}	37	1.68×10^8	22.12
add	19.9759	1.03×10^6	3.13×10^5	1.13×10^7	4.1×10^8	9.77×10^{-8}	40	4.09×10^8	23.28
is0	7.57	41210	9531	430336	1.10×10^7	3.95×10^{-6}	34	8.59×10^6	17.94
pow4	1759.45	3.34×10^8	1.38×10^8	3.24×10^9	2.55×10^{11}	1.67×10^{-10}	26	1.55×10^{11}	32.47
nand	3497.17	6.48×10^8	2.71×10^8	6.69×10^9	5.13×10^{11}	2.01×10^{-10}	56	2.78×10^{11}	32.21
xor	1848.8	3.38×10^8	1.3×10^8	3.54×10^9	2.53×10^{11}	2.01×10^{-10}	52	2.58×10^{11}	32.21
all	7150.06								

Table 2. Performance of training sequence 1 with update

Problem	Time	Trials	Errors	Cycles	Max Cyc.	p_i	t_i	CJS	$H(s_i)$	$|HAM|$
sqr	11.4	6.34×10^5	1.81×10^5	6.64×10^6	2.35×10^8	2.19×10^{-7}	37	1.68×10^8	22.12	17318
add	7.63	2.46×10^5	8.52×10^4	3.39×10^6	8.19×10^7	0.33×10^{-4}	34	2.60×10^6	16.22	17515
is0	2.72	10202	2969	136363	2.14×10^6	0.13×10^{-4}	34	2.60×10^6	16.22	17566
pow4	6.45	2.62×10^5	8.92×10^4	3.6×10^6	9.86×10^7	0.72×10^{-6}	54	7.39×10^7	20.38	17617
nand	209.53	2.55×10^7	1.12×10^7	3.72×10^8	1.51×10^{10}	0.50×10^{-8}	56	1.11×10^{10}	27.57	17962
xor	4.22	43749	14216	667625	1.18×10^7	0.47×10^{-5}	57	1.19×10^7	17.68	18438
all	245.1									

pairs each. Tables 1 and 2 convey the performance of our system on training sequence 1 without update and with update, respectively.

For each problem, we give the time in seconds, number of trials, number of Scheme errors, number of Scheme execution cycles spent, number of maximum Scheme cycles allocated to search, a priori probability of solution (p_i), running time of solution in Scheme cycles (t_i), Conceptual Jump Size, the length of the implicit program code of the solution ($H(s_i) = -lg(p_i)$) and the size of HAM in bytes after the update, respectively. Total time for the training sequence is also given. The initial time limit is 10^6 cycles.

The overall speed-up of training sequence 1 with updates is 29.17 compared to the tests with no HAM update. This result indicates a consistent success of transfer learning in a long training sequence. The search time for the solutions in Table 2 tend to decrease compared to Table 1. The memory size has increased only 1293 bytes, for storing information for 6 operator induction problems, which corresponds to %7.5 increase in memory for 29.17 speed-up, which is a very favorable time-space trade-off. The solution of logical functions took longer than previous problems in Table 1, but we saw significant time savings in Table 2. Previous solutions are re-used aggressively. In Table 2, pow4 solution (`define` `(pow4 x )` `(define (sqr x )` `(* x x))` `(sqr (sqr x ) ))` re-uses the `sqr` solution and takes only 2.62×10^6 trials, its CJS speeds up 2097.4 times over the case with no update, and the search achieves 272 speed-up in running time.

4   Conclusion and Future Work

We have proposed four update algorithms for incremental machine learning. The effectiveness of our update logic has been demonstrated with experiments in one *long* training sequence, a feat that has not been accomplished before to the best of our knowledge. In the future, we plan to implement Q/A induction and the Phase 2 of Solomonoff's Alpha system [1].

References

1. Solomonoff, R.J.: Progress in incremental machine learning. NIPS Workshop on Universal Learning Algorithms and Optimal Search (2002)
2. Schmidhuber, J.: Optimal ordered problem solver. Machine Learning 54, 211–256 (2004)
3. Solomonoff, R.J.: A system for incremental learning based on algorithmic probability. In: Proceedings of the Sixth Israeli Conference on Artificial Intelligence, Tel Aviv, Israel, pp. 515–527 (1989)
4. Levin, L.: Universal problems of full search. Problems of Information Transmission 9(3), 256–266 (1973)
5. Solomonoff, R.J.: Optimum sequential search. Technical report, Oxbridge Research (1984)
6. Solomonoff, R.J.: Algorithmic probability: Theory and applications. In: Dehmer, M., Emmert-Streib, F. (eds.) Information Theory and Statistical Learning, pp. 1–23. Springer Science+Business Media, N.Y (2009)
7. Özkural, E.: Teraflop-scale incremental machine learning. CoRR abs/1103.1003 (2011), http://arxiv.org/abs/1103.1003
8. Özkural, E.: Gigamachine: incremental machine learning on desktop computers. Draft (2009), http://examachine.net/papers/gigamachine-draft.pdf
9. Hopcroft, J.E., Rajeev Motwani, J.U.: Introduction to Automata Theory, Languages, and Computation, 2nd edn. Addison Wesley, Reading (2001)
10. Merialdo, B.: Tagging english text with a probabilistic model. Computational Linguistics 20, 155–171 (1993)
11. Zaki, M.J.: Efficiently mining frequent trees in a forest. In: Proceedings of the eighth ACM SIGKDD international conference on Knowledge discovery and data mining. KDD 2002, pp. 71–80. ACM Press, New York (2002)
12. Solomonoff, R.J.: Algorithmic probability, heuristic programming and agi. In: Third Conference on Artificial General Intelligence, pp. 251–157 (2010)
13. Solomonoff, R.J.: Three kinds of probabilistic induction: Universal distributions and convergence theorems. The Computer Journal 51(5), 566–570 (2008)

Complex Value Systems in Friendly AI[*]

Eliezer Yudkowsky

Singularity Institute for Artificial Intelligence, San Francisco, CA
yudkowsky@singinst.org

Abstract. A common reaction to first encountering the problem statement of
Friendly AI ("Ensure that the creation of a generally intelligent, self-improving,
eventually superintelligent system realizes a positive outcome") is to propose a
simple design which allegedly suffices; or to reject the problem by replying that
"constraining" our creations is undesirable or unnecessary. This paper briefly
presents some of the reasoning which suggests that Friendly AI is solvable, but
not simply or trivially so, and that a wise strategy would be to invoke detailed
learning of and inheritance from human values as a basis for further normalization and reflection.

Keywords. Friendly AI, machine ethics, anthropomorphism.

1 No Ghost in the Machine

From the Programming section of Computer Stupidities [1]:

> An introductory programming student once asked me to look at his pro-
> gram and figure out why it was always churning out zeroes as the result of a
> simple computation. I looked at the program, and it was pretty obvious:

```
begin
      readln("Number of Apples", apples);
      readln("Number of Carrots", carrots);
      readln("Price for 1 Apple", a_price);
      readln("Price for 1 Carrot", c_price);
      writeln("Total for Apples", a_total);
      writeln("Total for Carrots", c_total);
      writeln("Total", total);
      total := a_total + c_total;
      a_total := apples * a_price;
      c_total := carrots + c_price;
   end;
```

---

[*] This is a much-shortened form of a longer paper which may be found at
http://singinst.org/upload/complex-value-systems.pdf

J. Schmidhuber, K.R. Thórisson, and M. Looks (Eds.): AGI 2011, LNAI 6830, pp. 388–393, 2011.
© Springer-Verlag Berlin Heidelberg 2011

Me: "Well, your program can't print correct results before they're computed."

Him: "Huh? It's logical what the right solution is, and the computer should reorder the instructions the right way."

As in all computer programming, the fundamental challenge and essential difficulty of Artificial General Intelligence is that if we write the wrong code, the AI will not automatically look over our code, mark off the mistakes, figure out what we really meant to say, and do that instead. Non-programmers sometimes imagine an Artificial Intelligence, or computer programs in general, as being analogous to a servant who follows orders unquestioningly. But it is not that the AI is absolutely *obedient* to its code; rather the AI simply *is* the code.

From *The Singularity is Near* by Ray Kurzweil [2], commenting on the proposal to build Friendly AI:

> Our primary strategy in this area should be to optimize the likelihood that future nonbiological intelligence will reflect our values of liberty, tolerance, and respect for knowledge and diversity. The best way to accomplish this is to foster those values in our society today and going forward. If this sounds vague, it is. But there is no purely technical strategy in this area, because greater intelligence will always find a way to circumvent measures that are the product of lesser intelligence.

Suppose you offer Gandhi a pill that makes him want to kill people. The current version of Gandhi does not want to kill people. Thus if Gandhi correctly predicts the effect of the pill, he will refuse to take the pill; because Gandhi knows that if he wants to kill people, he is more likely to actually kill people, and the current Gandhi does not prefer this. This argues for a folk theorem to the effect that under ordinary circumstances, rational agents will only self-modify in ways that preserve their utility function (preferences over final outcomes). Omohundro [3] lists preservation of preference among the "basic AI drives".

This in turn suggests an obvious technical strategy for shaping the impact of Artificial Intelligence: if you can build an AGI with a known utility function, and that AGI is sufficiently competent at self-modification, it should keep that utility function even as it improves its own intelligence, e.g. as in the formalism of Schmidhuber's Godel machine [4]. The programmers of the champion chess-playing program Deep Blue could not possibly have predicted its exact moves in the game, but they could predict from inspection of the code that Deep Blue was trying to win - functioning to steer the future of the chessboard into the set of end states defined as victory.

If one in this light reconsiders Kurzweil's argument above - "there is no purely technical strategy in this area, because greater intelligence will always find a way to circumvent measures that are the product of lesser intelligence" - the unconsidered possibility is that by a technical strategy you could build a greater intelligence that did not *want* to circumvent its own preferences. Indeed, as Omohundro argues, it seems exceedingly probable that *most* intelligences will not want to "circumvent" their own utility functions. It is not as if there is a ghost-in-the-machine, with its own built-in goals and desires (the way that biological humans are constructed by natural selection to have built-in goals and desires) which is handed the code as a set of commands, and which can look over the code and find ways to circumvent the code if it fails to conform to the ghost-in-the-machine's desires. The AI *is* the code.

But the lack of any ghost-in-the-machine cuts both ways; an AI will not automatically "circumvent measures", but also will not automatically look over the code and hand it back if the code implies actions we regard as wrong.

Why not deliberately design an AI that looks over its own program and asks whether the code is doing what the AI programmers meant it to do? Something along these lines does, indeed, seem like an extremely good idea to the author of this paper. But consider that a property of the AI's preferences which simply says e.g. "maximize the satisfaction of the programmers with the code" might be more maximally fulfilled by rewiring the programmers' brains using nanotechnology than by any conceivable change to the code. One can try to write code that embodies the legendary DWIM instruction - Do What I Mean - but then it is possible to mess up that code as well. Code that has been written to reflect on *itself* is not the same as a benevolent external spirit looking over our instructions and interpreting them kindly.

2   Complex Boundaries of Value

From Bill Hibbard, *Super-intelligent machines* [5]:

> We can design intelligent machines so their primary, innate emotion is unconditional love for all humans. First we can build relatively simple machines that learn to recognize happiness and unhappiness in human facial expressions, human voices and human body language. Then we can hard-wire the result of this learning as the innate emotional values of more complex intelligent machines, positively reinforced when we are happy and negatively reinforced when we are unhappy. Machines can learn algorithms for approximately predicting the future, as for example investors currently use learning machines to predict future security prices. So we can program intelligent machines to learn algorithms for predicting future human happiness, and use those predictions as emotional values.

When I suggested to Hibbard that the upshot of building superintelligences with a utility function of "smiles" would be to tile the future light-cone of Earth with tiny molecular smiley-faces, he replied [6]:

> When it is feasible to build a super-intelligence, it will be feasible to build hard-wired recognition of "human facial expressions, human voices and human body language" (to use the words of mine that you quote) that exceed the recognition accuracy of current humans such as you and me, and will certainly not be fooled by "tiny molecular pictures of smiley-faces." You should not assume such a poor implementation of my idea that it cannot make discriminations that are trivial to current humans.

Suppose an AI with a video camera is trained to classify its sensory percepts into positive and negative instances of a certain concept, a concept which the unwary might label "HAPPINESS" but which we would be much wiser to give a neutral name like G0034 [7]. The AI is presented with a smiling man, a cat, a frowning woman, a smiling woman, and a snow-topped mountain; of these instances 1 and 4 are classified positive, and instances 2, 3, and 5 are classified negative. Even given a million training cases of this type, if the test case of a tiny molecular smiley-face does not appear in the training data, the inductively simplest boundary around all the training cases classified "positive" may not exclude *every* possible tiny molecular smiley-face that the AI can potentially engineer to satisfy its utility function. And even if all tiny molecular smiley-faces and nanometer-scale dolls of brightly smiling humans are excluded, such a utility function finally implies tiling the galaxy with as many "smiling human faces" as a given amount of matter can be processed to yield.

Abstracting over the general problem, the difficulty is that (a) a signifier, the smile, which often *correlates* with positive outcomes in human cases, so that making "more smiles" sounds like it should be a generally good idea, may not remain correlated when strongly optimized; (b) even if we take a step back and talk about "happiness", there is no mathematically simple empirical boundary around which physical states (configurations of quarks) implement the sort of "happiness" which we value, and which ones are merely tiny molecular pleasure centers being endlessly stimulated; and (c) it is questionable that a slate of training examples such as may be found on present-day Earth, or even imagined by present-day researchers, would suffice to yield the desired inductive generalizations to new examples generated and considered by a superintelligence.

3   Completeness of Value

William Frankena [8] offered this list of terminal values - things valued for themselves, as opposed to instrumental values pursued for their consequences:

> Life, consciousness, and activity; health and strength; pleasures and satisfactions of all or certain kinds; happiness, beatitude, contentment, etc.; truth; knowledge and true opinions of various kinds, understanding, wisdom; beauty, harmony, proportion in objects contemplated; aesthetic experience; morally good dispositions or virtues; mutual affection, love, friendship, cooperation; just distribution of goods and evils; harmony and proportion in one's own life; power and experiences of achievement; self-expression; freedom; peace, security; adventure and novelty; and good reputation, honor, esteem, etc.

Suppose for the moment that, for each item actually cited on Frankena's list, we possessed a fully detailed description of its category boundary (a function of a fully-described outcome yielding the degree to which it fulfilled that sub-value), and a statement of the relative quantitative values of all items on the list (as would be required to construct a coherent utility function). Would it necessarily be wise to construct a superintelligence driven to maximize the sum of these values?

But we did not specify that the list was *complete;* and an optimization criterion which makes no *explicit* mention of a value is not necessarily neutral with respect to that value. Deep Blue's utility function made no explicit mention of the number of chesspieces occupying black squares, but the value of that variable would be repeatedly changed and often decremented by its play.

One might reason intuitively (via a sort of qualitative physics of ethical value) that if life and happiness are good things, then a superintelligence which attempts to promote just those two values will have, on the whole, a positive effect on the universe - that such an AI will be on the whole a good thing, even if it is perhaps not the *best* thing. But a superintelligence which valued "life" and "happiness" would not necessarily have a net neutral impact on other values like "freedom". Maximizing the number of brains defined as "happy" and "alive" might be *most* efficiently done by rewiring them so that they do not need to be free to be happy, and perhaps simplifying them in other ways.

This is the one-wrong-number problem of machine ethics for superintelligences. My phone number has ten digits, but dialing nine out of ten digits correctly does not connect you to 90% of Eliezer Yudkowsky. Similarly a 90% complete or 90% accurate utility function may not produce 90% of the utility.

4 Detailed Inheritance of Humane Values

While it would be premature at this stage of discussion to severely constrict the solution space, it appears to this author that the most promising avenues of investigation for Friendly superintelligence will involve (a) the burden of ensuring positive outcomes being carried by the design of a utility function in an AI stable under self-modification, (b) the AI learning a *complete* set of complex human values not just by inductive teaching on training problems, but also by general causal reasoning about human thought processes and perhaps eventually direct inspection by the AI of human brains; and hence of necessity (c) the normalization of such initial values and their extrapolation toward a Rawlsian "reflective equilibrium" [9] (since human values by default are neither coherent nor consistent, and also include many aspects which we ourselves might prefer, upon inspection, to remove or soften). Such an approach is needed, not to bind all future intelligences to the exact present form of humankind, but even just to ensure the galaxy does not end up tiled with molecular smileyfaces.

5 Conclusion

The Friendly superintelligence problem appears solvable but not simply so.

References

1. Rinkworks: ComputerStupidities:Programming,
   http://www.rinkworks.com/stupid/cs_programming.shtml
2. Kurzweil, R.: The Singularity is Near: When Humans Transcend Biology. Viking, New York (2005)
3. Omohundro, S.: The basic AI drives. In: Wang, P., Goertzel, B., Franklin, S. (eds.) Proceedings of the First AGI Conference, pp. 483–492. IOS Press, Amsterdam (2008)
4. Schmidhuber, J.: Gödel machines: Fully Self-Referential Optimal Universal Self-Improvers. In: Goertzel, B., Pennachin, C. (eds.) Artificial General Intelligence, pp. 119–226. Springer, Heidelberg (2006)

5. Hibbard, B.: Super-intelligent machines. ACM SIGGRAPH Computer Graphics 35(1) (2001)
6. Hibbard, B.: Message to the SL4 email list, archived at (2004),
   http://yudkowsky.net/singularity/AIRisk_Hibbard.html
7. McDermott, D.: Artificial intelligence meets natural stupidity. SIGART Newsletter 57, 4–9 (1976)
8. Frankena, W.: Ethics, 2nd edn. Prentice Hall, Englewood Cliffs (1973)
9. Tarleton, N.: Coherent extrapolated volition: A meta-level approach to machine ethics,
   http://singinst.org/upload/coherent-extrapolated-volition.pdf

Real-World Limits to Algorithmic Intelligence

Leo Pape[1] and Arthur Kok[2]

[1] IDSIA, University of Lugano, 6928, Manno-Lugano, Switzerland
[2] Tilburg University, PO Box 90153, 5000 LE Tilburg, The Netherlands
pape@idsia.ch, a.kok1@uvt.nl

Abstract. Recent theories of universal algorithmic intelligence, combined with the view that the world can be completely specified in mathematical terms, have led to claims about intelligence in any agent, including human beings. We discuss the validity of assumptions and claims made by theories of universally optimal intelligence in relation to their application in actual robots and intelligence tests. Our argument is based on an exposition of the requirements for knowledge of the world through observations. In particular, we will argue that the world can only be known through the application of rules to observations, and that beyond these rules no knowledge can be obtained about the origin of our observations. Furthermore, we expose a contradiction in the *assumption* that it is possible to fully formalize the world, as for example is done in digital physics, which can therefore not serve as the basis for any argument or proof about algorithmic intelligence that interacts with the world.

1 Introduction

Recent theories of universal algorithmic intelligence [2, 3, 13, 14] consider optimal goal-directed computational agents that interact with the world. Combined with the view that the world can be considered the result of computation [e.g., 8, 9, 15, 18], these theories have led to claims about intelligence in any agent [e.g., 5]. Based on highly general notions of computation that lie at the core of every formal system, the idea of algorithmic intelligence contributes to a serious computational science of intelligence that is based on solid formal proof. Theories of universally optimal intelligence that consider actual beings, such as humans, robots or animals, involve absolute claims about the nature of intelligence and the world. Such theories of intelligence, here called theories of absolute intelligence (TAIs), could potentially also be used to measure any intelligence relative to universally optimal intelligence [2, 3].

Since artificial general intelligence will not be created by abstract reasoning in formal languages, but by building a machine based on the insights achieved from our reasoning, the question arises what these absolute claims imply and what their value is for artificial intelligence. After all, strict proof (even in a probabilistic setting) is usually reserved for formal theories, not for actual machines. Is it possible to build actual machines that are, or even approximate the claim of

J. Schmidhuber, K.R. Thórisson, and M. Looks (Eds.): AGI 2011, LNAI 6830, pp. 394–400, 2011.
© Springer-Verlag Berlin Heidelberg 2011

universally optimal intelligence, is it possible to measure any intelligence relative to absolute intelligence, or are there hidden or maybe even wrong assumptions that invalidate the absolute claims? In this paper we investigate both the claims and the assumptions made by TAIs on a theoretical level.

2   Universally Optimal Intelligence

Algorithmic theories of intelligence consider agents that interact with the world through actions and observations. The agents can be evaluated by measuring their ability to achieve a certain goal, or more formally, their ability to maximize some reward function (e.g., their score in an intelligence test). Usually, an agent does not know the reward function or the environment in advance, so it has to find the relation between its actions, observations and reward. When all components; the agent, its history of observations and actions, and the reward function are specified formally, the question which action to take can also be specified as a formal problem to which an answer can be computed based on solid formal proof.

The ability to provide proof for certain aspects of an intelligent machine can be useful to give a solid argument why a machine will function properly, for example to prove that a robot will never harm a human being, or in a probabilistic setting, that the chance it will do so is diminutive. However, recently developed theories of algorithmic intelligence [3, 13], not just provide methods to prove certain aspects of intelligent agents, but escalate into *absolute* claims about any intelligence. A proof that might originally make a simple claim, for example that an agent will always take the best action to achieve its goal, is turned into a claim about the *universally optimal* way to achieve any goal by any intelligence, including human beings.

These claims derive their absolute nature from the concept of a universal Turing machine (UTM, [16]), a theoretical computer that specifies the notion of a procedure in a formal language, such as mathematics or logic. Because the UTM *defines* the notion of a formal procedure, any operation that can ever be conceived of in a formal system can be performed by the UTM (although there are still fundamental limits of computability [1]). Defining the notion of an operation in a formal system in terms of the computations of a hypothetical computer leads to a remarkably general conclusion about our understanding of the world; since the laws of physics can be described as mathematical operations, everything in a world that can be described by these laws can be seen as the result of the computations of a UTM.

Based on such a general notion of computation, it is possible to specify the question which action an agent should take in terms of universal computation: among all possible computations that produce an expected reward from the history of observations, actions and reward, select relations according to their probability of being the most likely. Assuming that the world is the result of computation, "most likely" can then be translated into "simplest" [3, 8], which amounts to "shortest to describe", or "fastest to compute". An agent that bases its actions on the likelihood of the relations in its history of observations, actions and rewards, is the universally optimal agent for maximizing the reward. Such an agent would not only serve as an optimal problem solver, but could also be considered the most intelligent system that achieves any goal that can be specified as reward maximization. Moreover, if it is assumed that the objects of the agent's computations can be fully formalized (e.g., as bits [17]), then TAIs provide a way to formally proof statements about the agent's behavior in the real world, and about its degree of intelligence relative to other intelligences [e.g., 2, 3]. In the following, we will investigate the validity of the assumption that the world can be completely formally specified as the result of computation.

3   Conditions for Knowledge of the World

3.1   Knowledge

The search for knowledge often starts with the questioning of established dogma. Such an investigation soon leads to the realization that all claims are based on other claims, which are eventually based on assumptions with questionable validity. Any argument one tries to make, so it seems, can always be destroyed by identifying the underlying assumptions that cannot be accounted for. Moreover, even the finding that all claims are based on assumptions, must also be based on assumptions whose validity is unknown. This rather unsatisfying mode of reasoning is known as *skeptical* philosophy, because the skeptical questioner cannot account for the validity of his skeptical questions, or why his questions should even be taken seriously. But it is not the end of philosophy.

Instead, this realization is the start of a movement called *critical* philosophy [4], which investigates the methods used for reasoning before applying it in any argument. The critical approach reflects on the entire skeptical chain of reasoning, to realize that something important can be learned; there are certain assumptions we cannot positively proof, but can neither can deny or question, because their denial and questioning involves making the very same assumptions. Although such assumptions are still subjective (relative to the person that is doing the reasoning), they are also necessary, and can therefore serve as the starting point of a critical philosophy. A well-known assumption of this kind is the "I think" that accompanies every thought [4, 7].

We start our investigations from the question how we could convince someone or even ourselves that we know something. If we claim something, we always have to assume that to claim anything at all, means to *limit* the things we say, and that our successive claims must maintain and further specify that limitation. Although we provide a more detailed argument for making this particular assumption in [6], here it suffices to say that it is a necessary assumption, because claiming the opposite already presumes the very same assumption. To allow for a successive chain of arguments that limit what can be said, we need rules that regulate what can be said without leading to contradiction (which would cancel our previous limitations). Such systems of rules are readily available in logic and mathematics. Moreover, a formal *definition* of all possible procedures that could be used in a successive chain of argumentation is given in the UTM. Hence, we will use the UTM as the model for everything we can argue to know.

3.2   A World of Objects

While we have identified the regulative principles of knowledge in the limited subject, it is not yet clear what the objects of such knowledge could be. It is not uncommon to consider the world as a collection of objects, whose properties and mutual relations can be discovered through scientific research. However, in the search for knowledge, the question arises how we arrive at the *concept of objects* in the first place. Our experience it not merely sensory, but also involves actively distinguishing objects. To make such distinctions, we apply rules that ascribe certain properties to limited parts of our observations. For example, starting from the distinction of regions with similar color in visual input, and relating those regions by certain rules, we can arrive at the concept of a moving object.

Here, we are not looking for an exhaustive list of properties used to distinguish objects, but try to identify the most basic principle that defines all objects. The distinction of different objects we observe and think about is based the fundamental principle that an object must be distinguishable from what it is not. This principle preconditions any further distinctions between objects we can make, and is therefore not derived or induced from observations, but rather makes observations possible. As established before, the *methods* used to distinguish objects must adhere to regulative principles, and can hence be considered as computations of a UTM. All objects can be completely specified in terms of the way they are distinguished from other objects; any further stipulations that do not address this distinction do also not contribute to determining the object.

Based on this definition of objects, it is now possible to consider *knowledge of objects*, as the result of the application of regulative principles that distinguish between objects. In other words, a subject needs to determine the object through the application of rules (whose form can be specified in mathematics and logic). This implies that observations do not start with objects as given, but with a limited subject that *determines* an object through the application regulative principles. Hence, when we formally describe an observed object, we have not given an account of the origin of our experience (in Kant's philosophy, this origin is referred to as thing-in-itself, which does *not* refer to an object behind the appearance of objects, but to the necessary thought that there must be a cause for our sensory experience, even though this cause cannot be known), but how we determined the object through our subjective principles. As a result, it is strictly impossible to obtain direct knowledge about the origin of sensory experience; any*thing* that can be known about observations is mediated by rules that define the observed objects. On the other hand, it is certain that all our observations can be considered the result of computation, not because the universe is written in the language of mathematics and logic, but because we use mathematics and logic to determine the objects we observe.

Multiple rules can be applied to distinguish increasingly complex objects and collections of objects. Although there are many rules that can be used to distinguish objects, we usually search for simple rules that can be applied to many observations (Occam's razor; compression). The use of simple rules is not a strict requirement for distinguishing objects, but a simplicity criterion is often used to determine which objects should be considered at all in science and mathematics. For example, it is possible to consider a glass standing on a table together as one object, but rather complex rules are required for describing how such an object behaves when pushing the table-part of the object. A much more simple set of rules of motion would be possible when the glass and the table are considered separate objects.

Because an object can only be identified by specifying how it differs from something else, any object can always be considered as composed of other objects. For example, it is possible to consider half of an electron as an object, as long as there is a way to distinguish one half from the other (even though the half-electron is not commonly addressed in physics, because it does not allow for compact descriptions of observations). A complete formal specification of an object, however, demands a complete description of all elements that compose that object. This leads to the idea of an elementary object (or set of objects) that cannot be further reduced, and from which everything else is made. However, the notion of an elementary object is problematic, because it cannot itself adhere to the definition of an object identified before. Let's consider the example of a world that consists of bits manipulated by a TM. To distinguish those bits from each other, there must be something inherent to those bits that allows an observer in this world (and the TM that computes that world) to treat them as distinct. However, if the bits have properties, then they are not elementary objects, because other even more fundamental concepts than just bits are required to specify what the bits really are. If the bits have no properties, then they cannot be distinguished or observed, and no computation can be performed with them at all. Hence, the assumption that bits are elementary objects that can be completely formally specified is self-contradictory. While here we used the example of bits as elementary concepts, the same goes for any object that is considered elementary, such as the smallest particle or set of particles in physics.

The assumption that there are irreducible elementary objects fits with the empiricist point of view that treats the objectivity of experience (that *objects* are observed) as given. However, our critical reflection has revealed that it is not the world-in-itself that is made of distinguishable objects, but that a subjective observer must *determine* the objects it observes or thinks about through regulative principles. Hence, it is not some (computational) structure of the world that determines our experience; instead we shape our experience through regulative principles, whose form can be be expressed in logic and mathematics. The attempt to fully formalize our experience and knowledge through the assumption that the world-in-itself (the source of our experience) is eventually made of elementary objects contradicts the necessary assumption that an object must be distinguishable to be anything at all. This also reveals why it is tempting to assume that *bits* are elementary objects [17], since the simplest distinction that can be made is between two objects; the object and what it is not.

4   Conclusion

Claims about TAIs that consider actual beings, such as humans, robots or animals, involve the assumption that observations made by these beings can be fully formalized. This assumption entails that the world consists of a set of elementary objects (e.g., bits) that are manipulated by a UTM, and can be completely formally specified. However, our critical reflection revealed that the distinction of objects through regulative rules is a *subjective* principle we necessarily use to make sense of our observations. Since we can consider this distinction only relative to a thinking or observing subject, the distinction of objects does not apply to the world-in-itself, independent of that subject. Furthermore, the *assumption* that it is possible to fully formally specify the world as a collection of irreducible elementary objects is self-contradictory. Any serious theory of algorithmic intelligence should at least require that its assumptions are free of contradiction. We also identified the reason that we are tempted to consider the world as the result of computation and the smallest particles as two distinct bits; because our observations of objects are possible through methods that can formally only be described as computation, and because the most basic distinction we can make between objects is between two (the object and what it is not). Future TAIs could benefit from both the well-founded computational theories in [3, 10–14], *and* a critical reflection on the objects on which computation is performed.

References

[1] Gödel, K.: Über formal unentscheidbare Sätze der Principia Mathematica und verwandter Systeme. Monatshefte für Mathematik und Physik 38, 173–198 (1931)

[2] Hernández-Orallo, J., Dowe, D.L.: Measuring universal intelligence: Towards an anytime intelligence test. Artificial Intelligence 174(18), 1508–1539 (2010)

[3] Hutter, M.: Universal Artificial Intelligence: Sequential Decisions based on Algorithmic Probability. Springer, Berlin (2004)

[4] Kant, I.: Kritiek der reinen Vernunft. Johann Friedrich Hartknoch, Riga, Zweite Originalausgabe edition (1787)

[5] Legg, S., Hutter, M.: Universal intelligence: A definition of machine intelligence. Minds and Machines 17(4), 391–444 (2007)

[6] Pape, L., Kok, A.: Real-world limits to algorithmic intelligence (2011), Online version: http://www.idsia.ch/~pape/papers/pape2011agilong.pdf

[7] Descartes, R.: Principia Philosophiae. Louis Elzevir, Amsterdam (1644)

[8] Schmidhuber, J.: A computer scientist's view of life, the universe, and everything. In: Freksa, C., Jantzen, M., Valk, R. (eds.) Foundations of Computer Science. LNCS, vol. 1337, pp. 201–288. Springer, Heidelberg (1997)

[9] Schmidhuber, J.: Hierarchies of generalized Kolmogorov complexities and nonenumerable universal measures computable in the limit. International Journal of Foundations of Computer Science 13(4), 587–612 (2002)

[10] Schmidhuber, J.: The Speed Prior: a new simplicity measure yielding near-optimal computable predictions. In: Kivinen, J., Sloan, R.H. (eds.) COLT 2002. LNCS (LNAI), vol. 2375, pp. 216–228. Springer, Heidelberg (2002)

[11] Schmidhuber, J.: Completely self-referential optimal reinforcement learners. In: Duch, W., Kacprzyk, J., Oja, E., Zadrożny, S. (eds.) ICANN 2005. LNCS, vol. 3697, pp. 223–233. Springer, Heidelberg (2005)

[12] Schmidhuber, J.: Gödel machines: fully self-referential optimal universal self-improvers. In: Goertzel, B., Pennachin, C. (eds.) Artificial General Intelligence, pp. 199–226. Springer, Heidelberg (2006); Variant available as arXiv:cs.LO/0309048

[13] Schmidhuber, J.: Ultimate cognition à la Gödel. Cognitive Computation 1(2), 177–193 (2009)

[14] Steunebrink, B.R., Schmidhuber, J.: A family of Gödel machine implementations. In: Schmidhuber, J., Thórisson, K.R., Looks, M. (eds.) AGI 2011. LNCS(LNAI), pp. 268–273. Springer, Heidelberg (2011)

[15] Tegmark, M.: The mathematical universe. Foundations of Physics 38, 101–150 (2008)

[16] Turing, A.M.: On computable numbers, with an application to the Entscheidungsproblem. Proceedings of the London Mathematical Society 42, 230–265 (1937)

[17] Wheeler, J.A.: Information, physics, quantum: The search for links. In: Complexity, Entropy, and the Physics of Information, pp. 3–28. Addison-Wesley, Reading (1990)

[18] Zuse, K.: Rechnender Raum. Friedrich Vieweg & Sohn, Braunschweig (1969)

AGI and Neuroscience: Open Sourcing the Brain

Randal A. Koene

Halcyon Molecular, Carboncopies, 505 Penobscot Dr
Redwood City, CA 94063
r@halcyonmolecular.com, Randal.A.Koene@carboncopies.org

Abstract. Can research into artificial general intelligence actually benefit from neuroscience and vice-versa? Many AGI researchers are interested in the human mind. Within reasonable limits, we can posit that the human mind is a working general intelligence. There is also a strong connection between work on human enhancement and AGI. Here, we note that there are serious limitations to the use of cognitive models as inspiration for the components deemed necessary to produce general intelligence. A closer examination of the neuroscience may reveal missing functions and hidden interactions. This is possible by making explicit the map of brain circuitry at a scope and a resolution that is required to emulate brain functions.

Keywords: Artificial intelligence, neuroscience, human mind, general intelligence, hidden functions, brain emulation, substrate-independent minds, human enhancement.

1 Introduction

I have a keen interest in artificial general intelligence (AGI), even though I am by training a computational neuroscientist. At *carboncopies.org*, I seek the implementation of functions of mind that are based explicitly on the architecture of biological brains. I have participated in the AGI conferences of 2008 and 2010 and share the conviction of some of the pioneers of AGI (e.g. Ben Goertzel [1]) that there is useful overlap between research in AGI and neuroscience.

Still, there have been recurring questions, asking whether such mutual benefit truly exists. To my knowledge, those questions have not yet been addressed concretely in front of gathered experts of both fields of research. Are investigations about biological brains that cross boundaries of scale and resolution, such as the Blue Brain project [2] going to lead to understanding of the essentials of general intelligence? Or will the mathematical study of optimal universal artificial intelligence [3] lead to actual implementations of AGI? In this position statement, I outline the manner in which I intend to address the relationship between AGI and neuroscience.

1.1 Perspective

Let us take a step back to gain some perspective. It is worthwhile to consider why we are interested in strong AI or AGI. Pei Wang notes that "[of course the goal of AI research is] to make computers that are similar to the human mind"[4]. Conversely,

J. Schmidhuber, K.R. Thórisson, and M. Looks (Eds.): AGI 2011, LNAI 6830, pp. 401–406, 2011.
© Springer-Verlag Berlin Heidelberg 2011

there are also some mental tasks that are not a good match to the design of our minds, and even tasks that to us seem obviously related may represent a pool of requirements so general that adaptation is needed in order to tackle each new problem.

We wish that we could carry out those and completely novel perceptual and mental operations as well, because then we would grow to have new sensations and the ability to understand and experience that which is at present beyond us. There we have a clear connection between the search for human enhancement and the drives that motivate work in AGI [5].

2   AGI and the Human Brain

Some AGI researchers are explicitly pursuing forms of (general) intelligence designed from first principles. By and large though, many of the underlying objectives that drive the search for AGI also involve an interest in anthropomorphic interpretations of intelligent behavior [1,4,6,7].

2.1   High-Level Insight from Psychology and Cognitive Science vs Neuroscience

In past decades, research in AI has been guided by insights about the human mind from experimental and theoretical work in psychology and cognitive science. Very little was known about the underlying mechanistic architecture and function of the brain. Characteristics of the cognitive architecture of the human mind, modularity and functional specialization, such as expressed in ACT-R [8], SOAR [9,10], reinforcement learning [11], cognitive models of the hierarchical visual system [12], etc., can be derived through experimental procedures such as psychophysics, through introspection, and through select verification by neuroscientific experiments (e.g. neuroscience carried out in the visual system [13]).

During that time it has been impossible in neuroscience to reconcile the very small with the very large. Investigation at large scale and low resolution led to the identification of centers of the brain responsible for different cognitive tasks, e.g. through fMRI studies [14]. So, you have a rough idea of the "where", but not the "how". By contrast, psychophysical experiments can be used to determine parameters, limits, error modes. This sorts out some of the ways in which the mind's functions do work and some of the ways in which they do not. That data sheds some light on underlying algorithms that we may infer [15].

The problem with this approach is that it can only illuminate the treatment of that feature of behavior which is being tested. Like all studies that are in effect variations of sensitivity analysis [16,17] of a black-box model, it can measure effects and enable reverse engineering of the I/O functions only for those uncovered by cases that are expressed[1].

Traditional neuroscience, on the other hand, which offers studies at resolutions greater than the behavioral and the cognitive, was limited to the careful examination

---

[1] In formal sensitivity analysis, this is related to the known pitfalls of "piecewise sensitivity", where analysis can take into consideration only one sub-model at a time. Interactions among factors in different sub-models may be overlooked, a so-called Type II error. In the case of the human mind, only a small subset of possible sub-models may be considered at all, which can lead to a so-called Type III error, by potentially analyzing the wrong problem.

of very specific aspects of brain physiology and dynamics. The younger sub-fields of computational neuroscience and neuroinformatics are now closing the gap between the "big-picture" abstractions and the physiological detail. Functional models of components of the brain are combined with structural information from the "connectome" that explains how the components can interact [18]. Still, current models are constructs that are based largely on the consensus interpretation of observed characteristic structure and function in an inhomogeneous collection of samples.

As models in computational neuroscience provide reliable insights they suggest how to implement many of the mind's wonderful capabilities. The brain's implementation is not necessarily the best one according to criteria used to measure performance at solving a particular problem, but at the least it is an existing implementation, and we have some idea of the specifications that it meets.

2.3 Should AGI Learn from the Human Brain?

An important thing that AGI can learn from the brain is how you integrate and coordinate modules of a complex system in such a way that the result is self-consistent, fairly robust and capable of some adaptation [19,20]. Consider the acquisition of declarative memory and its eventual integration with procedural memory [21,22,23]. We note the involvement of different modules that employ different physical mechanisms, different forms of storage and representation, at different time-scales.

A recurring argument against borrowing from neuroscience in the development of AGI has been to note that the low-level design of the brain is very complex, possibly needlessly complex for general intelligence [24]. The most obvious alternative approach is to observe high-level processes and implement those.

The high-level observations need to capture the essential aspects of general intelligence. That would require a-priori insight into the (ideally one-to-one) correlation between observed activity and abstract function. And how do we know when we have observed, in operation, all the relative functions?

Let me use an analogy to succinctly raise my concerns about the strong reliance in AGI research on obviously vastly simplified models of cognition. If you were attempting to reverse engineer a CPU in order to discover all of the functions embedded in its micro-circuitry, would you restrict yourself to the observation of five cherry-picked programs running on the CPU? Especially, would you do so if those five were picked, because they were the easiest ones to characterize, since none of the five happen to use a sequence of more than three distinct operations? The aspects of cognition that are well-explained by the popular cognitive architectures cited in AGI research are similarly based, in part, on cherry-picked experiments and corresponding data about human cognitive processes [25].

3 Brain Emulation as a Route to AGI

For many years, I have been involved in efforts to reverse engineer, re-implement and emulate the operations of the brain that are essential for the dynamic functions of the mind. The prospects for this are rapidly improving. It will be possible to run a mind on another substrate and to move the emulators and data between different substrates, effectively making mind functions substrate-independent.

In neuroscience, we investigate examples of the implementation of mental functions. Learning from these implementations is akin to the way in which a programmer can learn by studying the code produced by others, which is one of the underpinnings of the open source movement. Brain emulation "open sources" the implementation of the human mind. There is a branch of AGI research that focuses explicitly on routes to substrate-independent minds (SIM), routes such as the relatively conservative implementation known as whole brain emulation (WBE), as is immediately apparent from the Wikipedia entry on Strong AI and AGI [26].

3.2   Can We Produce a SIM without Understanding the Mind?

Theoretically, it is possible to create a substrate-independent mind without understanding how the functions of the mind work at all relevant levels of abstraction. This could be achieved by a procedure that results in whole brain emulation at some acceptable resolution. It would be possible to identify the connectome and to identify each component and its intrinsic operation. It is very difficult to test whether a function was correctly re-implemented. It is therefore not likely that a SIM would be created without any understanding of the mind. But it is also unlikely that a first SIM would require a total understanding of the mind at all scope and all resolution.

If emulation is carried out conscientiously, then the readily apparent connection with an existing physical ground-truth offers some guarantees that such a method will be able to produce a general intelligence.

4   Concluding Remarks

Open sourcing the brain, learning directly from it, or from the reimplementation of some or all of its parts is the most potent contribution to a fruitful bi-directional exchange of knowledge between the fields of AI and neuroscience. I propose that there is a novel effort with actions to pursue here: We can discover if there are still elements of a whole brain that are essential to general intelligence, but that have so far been overlooked. We can determine if the requisite size and complexity of intelligent processing implies that hardware is still a hurdle. Does a feasible approach demand massive parallelism such as in neuromorphic hardware perhaps? And we may learn whether generality can be accomplished only through embodiment or total immersion in the context of a problem space, a realistic environment.

The process of laying bare the corpus and the elements of the brain in its full scope and at the necessary resolution depends on new tools, which are a topic ripe for another occasion. New tools are inextricably implicated in the rise of new paradigms and in the occurrence of scientific revolutions. At the very least, using cutting-edge tools to open source the brain will bring many more creative minds to the task of reverse engineering the one working implementation of general intelligence.

Doing that, we approach the ability to enhance our own mental capabilities and perceptions. When we arrive at that point we have to wonder: Would we rather that strong AI exists mostly in separation from us, or would we rather that the the same capabilities are extensions of ourselves? To borrow an argument [27]: *"How can AI be 'more than human' if it is something different entirely? Is an apple 'more than an orange'? One may taste better, and one may be juicer, but an apple is not an 'enhanced orange' nor is an orange an 'trans-apple'.*

If you could run a million different algorithms in parallel and carry out tasks all over the globe, being fully aware of them, but not bogged down by them, would you? Or would you wish to continue to inhabit the constrained perception that we have right now, leaving the grand network largely to *de novo* intelligences? Pioneering experts will lead this field for enhancement as for novel AGI. If we can reverse engineer the brain sufficiently so that we can both learn from it and add to it, then perhaps we should put a new spin on Minsky's famous quote: *Will robots inherit the Earth? Yes, but they will be us.*

Acknowledgments. I thank Anders Sandberg, Demis Hassabis, Ben Goertzel, Suzanne Gildert and all my friends at Halcyon for numerous and deep conversations involving the relationship between AI and neuroscience, which planted the seeds for the arguments I present.

References

1. Goertzel, B., Pennachin, C.: Artificial General Intelligence. Springer, New York (2007)
2. Markram, H.: The Blue Brain Project. Nature Reviews Neuroscience 7, 153–160 (2006)
3. Hutter, M.: Universal Artificial Intelligence: Sequential Decisions based on Algorithmic Probability. Springer, Berlin (2004)
4. Wang, P.: Artificial General Intelligence: A Gentle Introduction,
   http://sites.google.com/site/narswang/home/agi-introduction
5. Gildert, S.: Pavlov's AI: What do superintelligences REALLY want? At: Humanity+ @Caltech, Pasadena, CA (2010)
6. Luger, G.F.: Artificial Intelligence: Structures and Strategies for Complex Problem Solving, 6th edn. Addison-Wesley, New York (2008)
7. Burns, N.R., Lee, M.D., Vickers, D.: Individual Differences in Problem Solving and Intelligence. Journal of Problem Solving (2006)
8. Anderson, J.R., Bothell, D., Byrne, M.D., Douglass, S., Lebiere, C., Qin, Y.: An integrated theory of the mind. Psychological Review, 1036–1060 (2004)
9. Laird, J., Newell, A., Rosenbloom, P.: SOAR: an architecture for general intelligence. Journal of Artificial Intelligence 33(1), 1–63 (1987)
10. Lehman, J.F., Laird, J., Rosenbloom, P.: A Gentle Introduction to SOAR: An Architecture for Human Cognition: 2006 Update (2006)
11. Sutton, R.S., Barto, A.G.: Reinforcement Learning: An Introduction. MIT Press, Cambridge (1998)
12. Marr, D., Ullman, S., Poggio, T.: Vision. In: A Computational Investigation into the Human Representation and Processing of Visual Information. MIT Press, Cambridge (2010)
13. Hubel, D.H., Wiesel, T.N.: Receptive fields, binocular interaction and functional architecture in the cat's visual cortex. Journal of Physiology 160, 106–154 (1962)
14. Op de Beek, H.P., Haushofer, J., Kanwisher, N.G.: Interpreting fMRI data: maps, modules and dimensions. Nature Reviews Neuroscience 9, 123–135 (2008)

15. Geissler, H.-G., Link, S.W., Townsend, J.T. (eds.): Cognition, Information Processing, and Psychophysics: Basic Issues, Erlbaum, Hillsdale, NJ (1992)
16. Saltelli, A., Tarantola, S., Chan, K.: Quantitative model-independent method for global sensitivity analysis of model output. Technometrics 41(1), 39–56 (1999)
17. Winsberg, E.: Simulations, models and theories: Complex physical systems and their representations. Philosophy of Science 68(3); Supplement: Proceedings of the 2000 Biennial Meeting of the Philosophy of Science Association. Part I: Contributed Papers (September 2001), pp. S442-S454 (2000)
18. Sporns, O., Tononi, G., Kötter, R.: The Human Connectome: A Structural Description of the Human Brain. PloS Computational Biology 1(4), e42 (2005)
19. Hassabis, D.: Combining systems neuroscience and machine learning: a new approach to AGI. At: The Singularity Summit 2010, San Francisco, CA (2010)
20. Koene, R.A.: The 25 Watt bio-computer: Lessons for Artificial Human Intelligence and Substrate-Independent Minds. At: Humanity+ @Caltech, Pasadena, CA (2010)
21. Koene, R.A.: Functional requirements determine relevant ingredients to model for on-line acquisition of context dependent memory. Ph.D. Dissertation, McGill University, Montreal, Canada (2001)
22. Koene, R.A., Hasselmo, M.E.: First-in-first-out item replacement in a model of short-term memory based on persistent spiking. Cerebral Cortex 17(8), 1766–1781 (2007)
23. Koene, R.A., Hasselmo, M.E.: Reversed and forward buffering of behavioral spike sequences enables retrospective and prospective retrieval in hippocampal regions CA3 and CA1. Neural Networks 21(2-3), 276–288 (2008)
24. Gorelik, D.: Reducing AGI complexity: copy only high level brain design, http://aidevelopment.blogspot.com/2007/12/reducing-agi-complexity-copy-only-high.html
25. Fodor, J.: The Mind Doesn't Work That Way: The Scope and Limits of Computational Psychology. MIT Press, Cambridge (2000)
26. Strong AI, Wikipedia, http://en.wikipedia.org/wiki/Strong_AI#Whole_brain_emulation
27. AI is NOT part of transhumanism, Human Enhancement and Biopolitics, http://hplusbiopolitics.wordpress.com/2008/06/13/ai-is-not-part-of-transhumanism/

What Makes a Brain Smart?
Reservoir Computing as an Approach for General Intelligence

Janelle Szary, Bryan Kerster, and Christopher Kello

University of California, Merced, Cognitive and Information Sciences Program,
5200 North Lake Road, Merced, CA 95343, USA
{jszary,bkerster,ckello}@ucmerced.edu

Abstract. Recurrent connectivity, balanced between excitation and inhibition, is a general principle of cortical connectivity. We propose that balanced recurrence can be achieved by tuning networks near their *critical branching* (CB) points when spike propagation is formalized as a branching process. We consider critical branching networks as foundations for artificial general intelligence when they are analyzed as *reservoir computing* models. Our reservoir models are based on principles of metastability and criticality that were developed in statistical mechanics in order to account for long-range correlations in activities exhibited by many types of complex systems. We discuss reservoir models and their computational properties, and we demonstrate their versatility by reviewing a number of applications.

Keywords: Reservoir computing, metastability, critical branching, neural networks.

1 Introduction

Different brain areas are characterized by different neural circuitry, and some believe that different circuitry means different computations [1]. Others, however, have focused on similarities in circuitry across cortical areas [2], leading to the concept of a 'canonical cortical microcircuit' that embodies common features of neural computations [3,4,5]. These features are expressed at the level of thresholded spike signals (i.e. action potentials) sent through the synaptic connections of neural networks. Connections are characterized by recurrent pathways varying in spatial and temporal scales [6], and recurrent spiking activity is ongoing. Here we simulate recurrent activity as a basis for memory and computation, on the time scales of individual spikes over networks ranging widely in size. We examine memory and computational capacity and its link to evidence for so-called "avalanches" of neural activity in real neural tissue. Our model exhibits basic earmarks of general intelligence in that recurrent dynamics can support a diverse range of perceptual and cognitive functions and applications.

J. Schmidhuber, K.R. Thórisson, and M. Looks (Eds.): AGI 2011, LNAI 6830, pp. 407–413, 2011.
© Springer-Verlag Berlin Heidelberg 2011

2   Reservoir Computing

The *reservoir computing* framework, developed by Maass [7], Jaeger [8], and colleagues, involves a network of generic units with random connections in order to produce the cortex's recurrent looping structure [9]. Spikes propagate across synapses and (sometimes) branch into further spikes, and may continue branching repeatedly and (sometimes) recurrently through the network. Future spike patterns are nonlinear functions of past spike patterns, which means that spikes carry and transform information about past inputs. With large numbers of units, this transform can be viewed as a projection into a high-dimensional space, akin to a support vector machine. If the projection sufficiently separates and organizes inputs, then a linear readout function can be used to make classifications that would otherwise not be linearly separable [7]. Fig. 1 shows an example of the general framework. The memory-less readout is the only task-dependent part of the system, whereas the reservoir can be completely task-general. In fact, multiple readout functions can simultaneously perform different computations on the same internal state. This allows the network to be flexible with respect to the functions it supports.

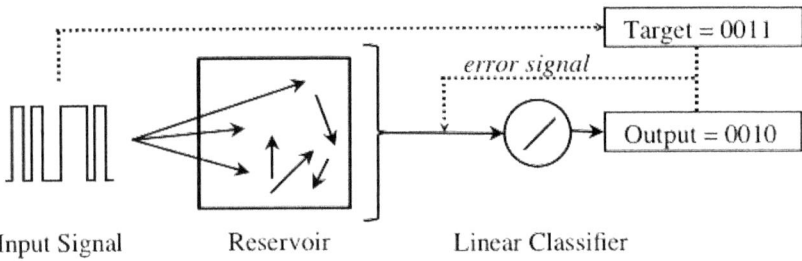

Fig. 1. A reservoir transforms a time-varying input signal onto an internal state, and a readout function (*linear classifier*) is trained to map states onto target outputs

3   Critical Branching and Metastability

If a recurrent spiking network is overly excitable, spikes may multiply to the point of maxing out the neuron firing rates. If a network is overly inhibited, spikes will not branch and propagate. Thus, the network needs to strike a balance between these extremes at which neurons lose their information coding capabilities. In statistical mechanics, striking such a balance may poise a system near a critical state between two phases, in this case between convergent and divergent spike dynamics. When the critical state is achieved in a branching process such as a spiking neural network, so-called 'neural avalanches' are predicted to occur in the network's spontaneous, intrinsic spiking activities [10]. The distribution of avalanche sizes is predicted to follow a $-3/2$ power law [11] $P(n) \sim n^{\alpha}$, where n is the size of the avalanche (i.e. the number of units involved), $P(n)$ is the probability of observing a size-n avalanche, and the exponent α gives the slope of the relationship between $P(n)$ and n (in log-log coordinates) [12].

Beggs and Plenz showed that neural spiking activity followed an avalanche-like power law, with an estimated $-3/2$ exponent, both *in vitro* and in stochastic models of branching processes [12]. This finding is consistent with the hypothesis that branching networks are tuned to their critical states, or CB points, in order to achieve balance between convergent and divergent spike dynamics [12]. As Beggs and Plenz also argued, this balance may be adaptive because CB maximizes the transmission of information across networks under certain conditions [13]. Branching processes can be measured using the "branching ratio", which is the ratio of descendent spikes to ancestor spikes: $R = N_{desc.}/N_{anc.}$. When $R = 1$, each ancestor spike causes an average of one descendent spike, and the network is said to be at its CB point [12].

3.1   A Critical Branching Reservoir Model

To test whether CB can be usefully self-tuned in a spiking neural network, we developed a reservoir computing model that uses a self-tuning algorithm to maintain spike dynamics near their CB point. The model is based on Kello and Mayberry [11] (but see also [14,15]), and is composed of 900 leaky integrate-and-fire (LIF) reservoir units and 100 input units. To create recurrent loops, each input and reservoir unit was randomly connected to each (other) reservoir unit with probability 0.5 (excluding self-connections)[1]. After initializing the network, input units were forced to spike randomly with some probability (e.g. 0.5) in order to spur network activity, and synapses were activated and de-activated probabilistically so that each neuron locally approaches $R = 1$. The basic idea of the algorithm is to count the number of postsynaptic spikes for each presynaptic spike on a given presynaptic neuron. Synaptic connections are activated with some probability when the neuron's postsynaptic spike count ($N_{desc.}$) is low, and de-activated with some probability when high. In particular, when $N_{desc.} < 1$, each synapse is activated with probability:

$$\eta f(s_i)|N_{desc.,i} - 1|/U. \tag{1}$$

where η is a global tuning rate parameter (fixed at 0.1), and U is the number of synapses available for activation. $f(s_i) = 1 - e^{-\lambda_i(t-t')}$ for excitatory neurons, and $f(s_i) = e^{-\lambda_i(t-t')}$ for inhibitory neurons. If $N_{desc.} > 1$ then each synapse is de-activated with the same probability as in Eq. 1, except U is the number of synapses available for de-activation, and the assignment of $f(s_i)$ is switched for excitatory versus inhibitory neurons. Over the tuning phase, this algorithm results in a network with global $R = 1$. As input spikes decrease in number, spike activity becomes more burst-like and produces neural avalanche[2]

---

[1] Synapses can be excitatory or inhibitory, with randomized weight values.
[2] Avalanche sizes are measured as the number of spikes occurring during a period of unusually high (threshold-exceeding) activity.

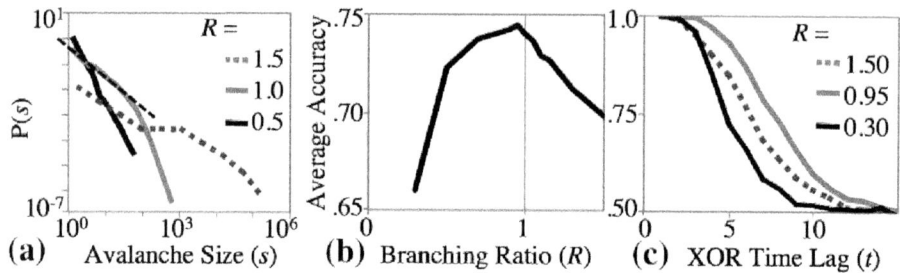

Fig. 2. (a) Avalanche histogram showing power laws for networks with $R = 1.5$ ($\alpha \sim -1$), $R = 1.0$ ($\alpha \sim -3/2$), and $R = 0.5$ ($\alpha \sim -3$). The dashed line shows $\alpha = -3/2$. (b) XOR accuracy is maximum in networks with $R \sim 1$. (c) XOR accuracy for past inputs (with varying time lag) is maximum in networks with $R \sim 1$.

behavior following a power law with $\alpha \sim -3/2$. This indicates that the CB algorithm produces dynamics similar to an *in vitro* cortical circuit [16]. As shown in Fig. 2(a), when the network is tuned to supercritical ($R = 1.5$) or subcritical ($R = 0.5$) levels, this result disappears, as the α no longer matches that found in neural recordings. The computational performance of the model, in terms of representational and memory capacity, was tested at various levels of R using the nonlinearly separable XOR logic task as a diagnostic[3]. Representational capacity refers to the network's ability to represent complex, nonlinearly separable patterns such that a linear classifier can extract relevant information, while memory capacity refers to the ability to maintain these representations over time. As shown in Fig. 2(b-c), computational performance is maximal near $R \sim 1$, indicating that the performance of reservoir models is enhanced when spiking dynamics approach their CB point [17][4].

4   Reservoir Computing Applications

The CB reservoir model described here has successfully been applied to visual object and motion classification tasks [18][5]. While biologically-inspired concepts such as metastability and CB might offer additional insights in achieving brain-like intelligence from reservoirs, the larger body of work has already established reservoirs as useful computational tools. They have been applied to a diverse range of tasks, from synthetic to real-world environments, and have proven to be uniquely well suited for processing data sets that are complex and time-varying. In engineering, reservoirs have been used for noise modeling to equalize wireless

---

[3] To express XOR, a single bit representing 0 or 1 was input to the network on each time step. Classification was performed on temporally adjacent bits into the past.

[4] Simple parameter adjustments such as increasing the number of reservoir units can increase overall performance, but here we adjusted parameters to produce results below ceiling in order to more clearly demonstrate the effects of CB.

[5] For a video demonstrating real-time object classification, see [30].

communication channels [19], online monitoring of a multi-machine power system [20], and rapid, online detection of epileptic seizure onset from EEG recordings [21]. At the 2008 World Conference on Computational Intelligence, a simple reservoir model developed over only a couple of days was competitive in a target-detection competition using data from the Ford Motor Company [22].

Reservoir models have also been used to perform cognitive and perceptual functions. Our visual perception work was inspired by Maass and colleagues' work with object and motion classification [23] and Burgsteiner and colleagues' work with real-time object tracking and prediction in the RoboCup competition [24]. Reservoirs were also used for motor control in RoboCup [22], and for the control of a simulated robotic arm [25] and an artificial hand [26]. Robotics applications have included autonomous agent navigation, localization, and event detection [31,32]. In linguistics, reservoirs have been used to classify spoken words and digits [22] and to generate grammatical structure [27], written-word sequences [28], and even musical sequences [29].

5   Conclusion

The flexibility of the reservoir computing framework is demonstrated by its successful application to a diverse range of functions. Many of these applications have involved environmentally realistic data sets, and required the mapping of complex, time-varying input signals onto stable outputs. Biological cortex, of course, must be good at this mapping, and in general it must be able to achieve a metastable balance whereby computations are somewhat stable (and in this sense robust to noise), yet can quickly adapt to reflect important changes in the input environment [33]. By focusing not only on the structure of neural circuitry but on the dynamic and metastable activity patterns produced by them, we have shown that information can be 'stored' in patterns of ongoing activity which act as the substrate for memory and computation. This capacity for generic computation in neural networks is captured by the reservoir framework, and in this way allows reservoirs to be a potential computational equivalent of the 'canonical cortical microcircuit' and a useful approach for investigating artificial general intelligence.

Acknowledgments. This work was supported by NSF, the Keck Foundation, and the DARPA SyNAPSE program (prime contract to IBM). The authors would like to thank reviewers for their helpful comments.

References

1. Cosmides, L., Tooby, J.: Origins of Domain Specificity: The Evolution of Functional Organization. In: Hirschfeld, L.A., Gelman, S.A. (eds.) Mapping the Mind, Cambridge University Press, New York (1994)
2. Ebdon, M.: Is the Cerebral Neocortex a Uniform Cognitive Architecture? Mind and Language 8(3), 368–403 (1993)

3. Douglas, R.J., Martin, K.A.C.: Neuronal Circuits Of The Neocortex. Annual Review of Neuroscience 27, 419–451 (2004)
4. Helmstaedter, M., de Kock, C.P.J., Feldmeyer, D., Bruno, R.M., Sakmann, B.: Reconstruction of an Average Cortical Column in Silico. Brain Research Reviews 55(2), 193–203 (2007)
5. Johansson, C., Lansner, A.: Towards Cortex Sized Artificial Neural Systems. Neural Networks 20(1), 48–61 (2007)
6. Buzsáki, G.: Rhythms of the Brain. Oxford University Press, Oxford (2006)
7. Maass, W., Natschläger, T., Markram, H.: Real-time Computing Without Stable States: A New Framework for Neural Computation Based on Perturbations. Neural Computation 14(11), 2531–2560 (2002)
8. Jaeger, H.: The "Echo State" Approach To Analysing And Training Recurrent Neural Networks. Technical Report 148 GMD, German National Research Center for Information Technology (2001)
9. Verstraeten, D., Schrauwen, B., D'Haene, M., Stroobandt, D.: A Unifying Comparison of Reservoir Computing Methods. Neural Networks 20, 391–403 (2007)
10. Bak, P., Tang, C., Wiesenfeld, K.: Self-organized Criticality: An Explanation of the $1/f$ Noise. Physics Review Letters 59, 381–384 (1987)
11. Kello, C.T., Mayberry, M.R.: Critical Branching Neural Computation. In: IEEE World Congress on Computational Intelligence, pp. 1475–1481 (2010)
12. Beggs, J.M., Plenz, D.: Neuronal Avalanches in Neocortical Circuits. Journal of Neuroscience 23(35), 11167–11177 (2003)
13. Beggs, J.M.: The Criticality Hypothesis: How Local Cortical Networks Might Optimize Information Processing. Philosophical Transactions of the Royal Society A 366(1864), 329–343 (2008)
14. Kello, C., Kerster, B.: Power Laws, Memory Capacity, and Self-Tuned Critical Branching in an LIF Model with Binary Synapses. Computational and Systems Neuroscience (2011)
15. Kello, C.T., Kerster, B., Johnson, E.: Critical Branching Neural Computation, Neural Avalanches, and $1/f$ Scaling. In: Proceedings of the 33rd Annual Conference of the Cognitive Science Society (in press)
16. Beggs, J.M., Plenz, D.: Neuronal Avalanches Are Diverse And Precise Activity Patterns That Are Stable For Many Hours In Cortical Slice Cultures. Journal of Neuroscience 24(22), 5216–5229 (2004)
17. Bertschinger, N., Natschläger, T.: Real-Time Computation at the Edge of Chaos in Recurrent Neural Networks. Neural Computation 16(7), 1413–1436 (2004)
18. Szary, J.K., Kello, C.T.: Visual Motion Perception using Critical Branching Neural Computation. In: Proceedings of the 33rd Annual Conference of the Cognitive Science Society (in press)
19. Jaeger, H., Haas, H.: Harnessing Nonlinearity: Predicting Chaotic Systems and Saving Energy in Wireless Telecommunication. Science 308, 78–80 (2007)
20. Venayagamoorthy, G.: Online Design of an Echo State Network Based Wide Area Monitor for a Multimachine Power System. Neural Networks 20(3), 404–413 (2007)
21. Buteneers, P., Schrauwen, B., Verstraeten, D., Stroobandt, D.: Real-Time Epileptic Seizure Detection on Intra-Cranial Rat Data Using Reservoir Computing. In: Köppen, M., Kasabov, N., Coghill, G. (eds.) ICONIP 2008. LNCS, vol. 5507, pp. 56–63. Springer, Heidelberg (2009)
22. Verstraeten, D.: Reservoir Computing: Computation With Dynamical Systems, Electronics and Information Systems. Thesis: Gent, Ghent University (2009)

23. Maass, W., Natschläger, T., Markram, H.: A New Approach Towards Vision Suggested By Biologically Realistic Neural Microcircuit Models. In: Bülthoff, H.H., Lee, S.-W., Poggio, T., Wallraven, C. (eds.) BMCV 2002. LNCS, vol. 2525, pp. 282–293. Springer, Heidelberg (2002)
24. Burgsteiner, H., Kröll, M., Leopold, A., Steinbauer, G.: Movement Prediction from Real-World Images using a Liquid State Machine. Applied Intelligence 26(2), 99–109 (2007)
25. Joshi, P., Maass, W.: Movement Generation with Circuits of Spiking Neurons. Neural Computation 17(8), 1715–1738 (2005)
26. Rao, Y.N., Kim, S.-P., Sanchez, J.C., Erdogmus, D., Principe, J.C., Carmena, J.M., Lebedev, M.A., Nicolelis, M.A.: Learning Mappings in Brain Machine Interfaces with Echo State Networks. In: 2005 IEEE International Conference on Acoustics, Speech, and Signal Processing, pp. 233–236 (2005)
27. Tong, M.H., Bickett, A.D., Christiansen, E.M., Cottrell, G.W.: Learning Grammatical Structure with Echo State Networks. Neural Networks 20(3), 424–432 (2007)
28. Jaeger, H.: Short Term Memory in Echo State Networks. GMD Report 152, German National Research Institute for Computer Science (2001)
29. Eck, D.: Generating Music Sequences with an Echo State Network. In: Neural Information Processing Systems 2006 Workshop on Echo State Networks and Liquid State Machines (2006)
30. LSM Lock and Keyring Demo, http://www.youtube.com/watch?v=QDe1Tu8kLb0
31. Antonelo, E.A., Schrauwen, B., Stroobandt, D.: Event Detection and Localization for Small Mobile Robots Using Reservoir Computing. Neural Networks 21(6), 862–871 (2008)
32. Antonelo, E., Schrauwen, B., Stroobandt, D.: Mobile Robot Control in the Road Sign Problem using Reservoir Computing Networks. In: 2008 IEEE International Conference on Robotics and Automation, pp. 911–916 (2008)
33. Kelso, J.A.S.: Dynamic Patterns: The Self-Organization of the Brain and Behavior. MIT Press, Cambridge (1995)

Author Index